PROBLEMS

An Introductory Book

By

MORRIS WEITZ

The Ohio State University

PROBLEMS IN AESTHETICS

IN AESTHETICS

of Readings

The Macmillan Company · New York

First Printing

Library of Congress catalog card number: 59-5012

The Macmillan Company, New York
Brett-Macmillan Ltd., Galt, Ontario

Printed in the United States of America

Preface

This anthology has been assembled in the conviction that beginning students in aesthetics should have available, in the same volume, some of the excellent aesthetic analyses by philosophers and others written before the twentieth century as well as those written in our own time. Thus, I have tried to present the best discussions of the main problems of aesthetics regardless of their dates of composition.

I have also tried to give to aesthetics some of the philosophical dignity it deserves. In an anthology this means, at the least, to set forth aesthetics as a series of interrelated but clearly stateable problems which can be discussed with the same rigor and intelligibility as other, similarly difficult problems in philosophy. Accordingly, I have organized the readings around certain sets of basic problems that still seem worth debating and attempting to solve. Of course it has not been possible to represent all the problems of aesthetics or even, more regrettably, to include all the best available readings on the issues selected. I have, therefore, concentrated on basic problems and some of their ablest discussants. Each selection deals precisely with the specific problem at hand. The selections are well wrought; they advance the philosophical discussion even, I hope, to the extent that no one can study them and come away with the feeling that aesthetics, as sometimes supposed, is dreary. If I am right, this collection of readings should help to quash the charge that aesthetics is less exciting than some other fields of intellectual inquiry. To be sure, there are dull essays in aesthetics, as there are everywhere, but I have some confidence that the reader will look in vain for them here.

The book is divided into six parts. They present one kind of logical and pedagogical unity, namely, a progression from certain basic general problems of aesthetics to more specific ones. But individual instructors vary in their interests, and there is no reason why one cannot begin where he likes, say, with Part three—on the arts—and work back to the first one, or even with Part four—on tragedy—which, for some students and teachers, may be the most propitious introduction to aesthetics.

I have provided introductions to the six parts and shorter ones to the separate sections of Parts two and three. In these, I have not tried to solve any problem, but only to state each one as clearly as I could and to relate it to the relevant readings. All the introductions have been kept brief, in the awareness that each instructor has his own contextual ways of putting a problem.

Each part—each section of the second and third parts—concludes with a selected bibliography. In each case, there is a minimum list. Enterprising students can make their own way from these lists. I have noted inexpensive paperback editions of suggested readings available at the time of writing.

Finally, I wish to express my gratitude to a number of my colleagues: Henry David Aiken, of Harvard University; Charles L. Stevenson, of the University of Michigan; Raymond Hoekstra, of Wayne University; Philip Nochlin, of Vassar College—all of whom got me from an extremely tentative outline to the permanent one filled out here (although they are not responsible for the latter); and especially to my Ohio State University colleagues, Roy Harvey Pearce and Franklin Ludden, who led me out of all sorts of alleys and more than once put me back on the broad highway. I wish also to add a note of thanks to Mrs. Jacqueline Sisson, the Art Librarian at O.S.U., for her numerous aids; to Mrs. Mary Anne Herman, who helped with the typing chores; and, to Mr. J. G. Case and other members of the College Department of The Macmillan Company for their invaluable and ever-courteous help.

Contents

III. The Arts

Contents   ix

IV. Tragedy and the Problem of Genres

V. The Problem of Response to Art

VI. Criticism

I

What Is Art?

Introduction

The question, "what is art?," is as old as the history of aesthetics. It is, of course, true that before the arts of poetry, music, painting, and sculpture were brought under the category of "Fine Arts," in the eighteenth century, the problem was traditionally specified as, "what is the nature of poetry, music, sculpture, or painting?" But essentially the problem has remained the same: to state the defining properties of art. From Plato to the present day, philosophers, critics, and artists have tried to answer this question. It is the very model of a philosophical problem: What do, for example, the works of art, *Oedipus Rex*, the Parthenon, the *Iliad*, Chartres Cathedral and, to come up to date, Picasso's "Guernica," have in common?

The word, *art*, is ambiguous; consequently, philosophers have not always meant by the question, "what is art?," what do works of art have in common? Indeed, philosophers seem to be divided on the meaning of the question. Some have concentrated on art as the making of works of art, and have tried to characterize and distinguish from other activities this process of creation. Others have dealt with the product itself. Now, in order to avoid this fundamental ambiguity of "art" as "process-product," we shall refer to the former (process) as *artistic creation* and to the latter (product) as *art* or *work of art*. Thus, throughout the editorial materials of this anthology, "art" will be used in its sense of "work of art," the *product* of artistic creation.

In this part we shall concern ourselves with the problem of what a work of art, that is, a poem, a play, a statue, a musical composition, is in the sense of its defining properties. All the great traditional aesthetic theories incorporate within them an answer to this basic question as to what property or collection of properties a work of art has by virtue of which it is a work of art and not something else. Each of the selections converges upon this problem of the nature of art.

First in our selections comes Plato, followed by Aristotle and Plotinus. All three offer metaphysical theories, placing art in the general context of their world views. All three are deeply concerned with art as imitation. For Plato, there is the truly real, the Forms—"The Ideal Bed" of the *Republic*—and there are earthly beds, less real and, finally, images and paintings of beds, less real than the earthly beds of which they are but shadows or appearances. Earthly beds are more or less imitations of "The Ideal Bed." Painted beds are imitations of these earthly imitations, hence are two removes from Reality. The painting (or the work of art) is mere appearance in relation to reality, and consequently is to be repudiated. Aristotle also places art in the genus of imitation and goes on to distinguish each art in terms of its medium, object, and manner of imitation; and because art as imitation, like natural objects in general, embodies universals or Forms, it is not, to Aristotle, metaphysically suspect, but a revelation of reality. For Plotinus also, works of art are imitations, as indeed is everything else in so far as everything derives from and returns to the One or the Forms. Art is one aspect of the manifestations of the truly Real, which is also the truly Beautiful. It is the embodiment of the One in the materials of this world, engendered by the activity of the artist's soul. Indeed, art is more real than the natural object it may represent because of this participation in it of the artist's soul. One need only remember the impact of this view of art on Michelangelo's work, especially his sculpture, to recognize the importance of Plotinus in the history of aesthetics. (See the bibliographical reference to Panofsky's essay on Michelangelo at the end of this part of readings.) For Plotinus, then, art is an imitation of reality and is praiseworthy on that account.

Reynolds also is primarily concerned with imitation but, because in his time (the eighteenth century) it had become almost synonymous with mere copying, he rejects the doctrine that art is imitation. His *Discourses on Art*, embodying all the aesthetic tendencies of the late eighteenth century, is a mixture of classical and romantic principles: adherence to the depiction of an ideal in nature instead of representation of detail; the importance of imagination over imitation; and the need for good taste and sensibility. These add up to Reynold's view that art is essentially an enlargement rather than an imitation of nature, being somewhat in the same relation to it, he says, as civilization is to the original state of man.

The modern period is represented by selections from Roger Fry, DeWitt Parker, Jacques Maritain, and Benedetto Croce, all of whom break with the tradition that works of art are imitations of anything and stress other defining features of art in their attempt to answer the question, "what do works of art have in common by virtue of which they are works of art?" For Fry, works of art are essentially created plastic forms, a doctrine he illustrates in his essay especially in relation to painting. Parker makes the fundamental point that any work of art has a set of three defining properties, which he specifies as the expression of wishes in a linguistic medium, organized by principles of form. Maritain singles out as the important factor of works of art their status as artifact, that is, that they are objects made by man through his application of the practical intellect. Croce, in opposition to Parker, Fry, and Maritain, maintains that the work of art is identical with the activity of making it in his simple definition that art is intuiton.

The final selection is a relatively short but excellent history of our problem. Yet, even so, embedded in Ernst Cassirer's essay is his own original suggestion, developed more fully by his successor, Susanne Langer, in her recent writings, that art is essentially symbolic form.

Plato

ART AS APPEARANCE*

Of the many excellences which I perceive in the order of our State, there is none which upon reflection pleases me better than the rule about poetry.

To what do you refer?

To the rejection of imitative poetry, which certainly ought not to be received; as I see far more clearly now that the parts of the soul have been distinguished.

What do you mean?

Speaking in confidence, for I should not like to have my words repeated to the tragedians and the rest of the imitative tribe—but I do not mind saying to you, that all poetical imitations are ruinous to the understanding of the hearers, and that the knowledge of their true nature is the only antidote to them.

Explain the purport of your remark.

* From Plato's *The Republic*, trans., Benjamin Jowett, in *The Dialogues of Plato* (3rd. ed., London: Oxford University Press, 1892), Book X, pp. 595a-608b.

Plato (428/7 – 348/7 B.C.), famous Greek philosopher, wrote *The Republic* in about 373 B.C. His other dialogues, *Ion* and *Phaedrus,* also discuss aesthetic problems.

Well, I will tell you, although I have always from my earliest youth had an awe and love of Homer, which even now makes the words falter on my lips, for he is the great captain and teacher of the whole of that charming tragic company; but a man is not to be reverenced more than the truth, and therefore I will speak out.

Very good, he said.

Listen to me then, or rather, answer me.

Put your question.

Can you tell me what imitation is? for I really do not know.

A likely thing, then, that I should know.

Why not? for the duller eye may often see a thing sooner than the keener.

Very true, he said; but in your presence, even if I had any faint notion, I could not muster courage to utter it. Will you enquire yourself?

Well, then, shall we begin the enquiry in our usual manner: Whenever a number of individuals have a common name, we assume them to have also a corresponding idea or form. Do you understand me?

I do.

Let us take any common instance; there are beds and tables in the world—plenty of them, are there not?

Yes.

But there are only two ideas or forms of them—one the idea of a bed, the other of a table.

True.

And the maker of either of them makes a bed or he makes a table for our use, in accordance with the idea—that is our way of speaking in this and similar instances—but no artificer makes the ideas themselves: how could he?

Impossible.

And there is another artist,—I should like to know what you would say of him.

Who is he?

One who is the maker of all the works of all other workmen.

What an extraordinary man!

Wait a little, and there will be more reason for your saying so. For this is he who is able to make not only vessels of every kind, but plants and animals, himself and all other things—the earth and heaven, and the things which are in heaven or under the earth; he makes the gods also.

He must be a wizard and no mistake.

Oh! you are incredulous, are you? Do you mean that there is no such maker or creator, or that in one sense there might be a maker of all these things but in another not? Do you see that there is a way in which you could make them all yourself?

What way?

An easy way enough; or rather, there are many ways in which the feat might be quickly and easily accomplished, none quicker than that of turning a mirror round and round—you would soon enough make the sun and the heavens, and the earth and yourself, and other animals and plants, and all the other things of which we were just now speaking, in the mirror.

Yes, he said; but they would be appearances only.

Very good, I said, you are coming to the point now. And the painter too is, as I conceive, just such another—a creator of appearances, is he not?

Of course.

But then I suppose you will say that what he creates is untrue. And yet there is a sense in which the painter also creates a bed?

Yes, he said, but not a real bed.

And what of the maker of the bed? Were you not saying that he too makes, not the idea which, according to our view, is the essence of the bed, but only a particular bed?

Yes, I did.

Then if he does not make that which exists he cannot make true existence, but only some semblance of existence; and if any one were to say that the work of the maker of the bed, or of any other workman, has real existence, he could hardly be supposed to be speaking the truth.

At any rate, he replied, philosophers would say that he was not speaking the truth.

No wonder, then, that his work too is an indistinct expression of truth.

No wonder.

Suppose now that by the light of the examples just offered we enquire who this imitator is?

If you please.

Well then, here are three beds: one existing in nature, which is made by God, as I think that we may say—for no one else can be the maker?

No.

There is another which is the work of the carpenter?

Yes.

And the work of the painter is a third?

Yes.

Beds, then, are of three kinds, and there are three artists who super-intend them: God, the maker of the bed, and the painter?

Yes, there are three of them.

God, whether from choice or from necessity, made one bed in nature and one only; two or more such ideal beds neither ever have been nor ever will be made by God.

Why is that?

Because even if He had made but two, a third would still appear behind them which both of them would have for their idea, and that would be the ideal bed and not the two others.

Very true, he said.

God knew this, and He desired to be the real maker of a real bed, not a particular maker of a particular bed, and therefore He created a bed which is essentially and by nature one only.

So we believe.

Shall we, then, speak of Him as the natural author or maker of the bed?

Yes, he replied; inasmuch as by the natural process of creation He is the author of this and of all other things.

And what shall we say of the carpenter—is not he also the maker of the bed?

Yes.

But would you call the painter a creator and maker?

Certainly not.

Yet if he is not the maker, what is he in relation to the bed?

I think, he said, that we may fairly designate him as the imitator of that which the others make.

Good, I said; then you call him who is third in the descent from nature an imitator?

Certainly, he said.

And the tragic poet is an imitator, and therefore, like all other imi-tators, he is thrice removed from the king and from the truth?

That appears to be so.

Then about the imitator we are agreed. And what about the painter?—I would like to know whether he may be thought to imitate that which originally exists in nature, or only the creations of artists?

The latter.

As they are or as they appear? You have still to determine this.

What do you mean?

I mean, that you may look at a bed from different points of view, obliquely or directly or from any other point of view, and the bed will appear different, but there is no difference in reality. And the same of all things.

Yes, he said, the difference is only apparent.

Now let me ask you another question: Which is the art of painting designed to be—an imitation of things as they are, or as they appear—of appearance or of reality?

Of appearance.

Then the imitator, I said, is a long way off the truth, and can do all things because he lightly touches on a small part of them, and that part an image. For example: A painter will paint a cobbler, carpenter, or any other artist, though he knows nothing of their arts; and, if he is a good artist, he may deceive children or simple persons, when he shows them his picture of a carpenter from a distance, and they will fancy that they are looking at a real carpenter.

Certainly.

And whenever any one informs us that he has found a man who knows all the arts, and all things else that anybody knows, and every single thing with a higher degree of accuracy than any other man—whoever tells us this, I think that we can only imagine him to be a simple creature who is likely to have been deceived by some wizard or actor whom he met, and whom he thought all-knowing, because he himself was unable to analyze the nature of knowledge and ignorance and imitation.

Most true.

And so, when we hear persons saying that the tragedians, and Homer, who is at their head, know all the arts and all things human, virtue as well as vice, and divine things too, for that the good poet cannot compose well unless he knows his subject, and that he who has not this knowledge can never be a poet, we ought to consider whether here also there may not be a similar illusion. Perhaps they may have come across imitators and been deceived by them; they may not have remembered when they saw their works that these were but imitations thrice removed from the truth, and could easily be made without any knowledge of the truth, because they are appearances only and not realities? Or, after all, they may be in the right, and poets do really know the things about which they seem to the many to speak so well?

The question, he said, should by all means be considered.

Now do you suppose that if a person were able to make the original as well as the image, he would seriously devote himself to the image-making branch? Would he allow imitation to be the ruling principle of his life, as if he had nothing higher in him?

I should say not.

The real artist, who knew what he was imitating, would be interested in realities and not in imitations; and would desire to leave as memorials of himself works many and fair; and, instead of being the author of encomiums, he would prefer to be the theme of them.

Yes, he said, that would be to him a source of much greater honour and profit.

Then, I said, we must put a question to Homer; not about medicine, or any of the arts to which his poems only incidentally refer: we are not going to ask him, or any other poet, whether he has cured patients like Asclepius, or left behind him a school of medicine such as the Asclepiads were, or whether he only talks about medicine and other arts at second hand; but we have a right to know respecting military tactics, politics, education, which are the chiefest and noblest subjects of his poems, and we may fairly ask him about them. "Friend Homer," then we say to him, "if you are only in the second remove from truth in what you say of virtue, and not in the third—not an image maker or imitator—and if you are able to discern what pursuits make men better or worse in private or public life, tell us what State was ever better governed by your help? The good order of Lacedaemon is due to Lycurgus, and many other cities great and small have been similarly benefited by others; but who says that you have been a good legislator to them and have done them any good? Italy and Sicily boast of Charondas, and there is Solon who is renowned among us; but what city has anything to say about you?" Is there any city which he might name?"

I think not, said Glaucon; not even the Homerids themselves pretend that he was a legislator.

Well, but is there any war on record which was carried on successfully by him, or aided by his counsels, when he was alive?

There is not.

Or is there any invention of his, applicable to the arts or to human life, such as Thales the Milesian or Anarcharsis the Scythian, and other ingenious men have conceived, which is attributed to him?

There is absolutely nothing of the kind.

But, if Homer never did any public service, was he privately a guide or teacher of any? Had he in his lifetime friends who loved to associate with him, and who handed down to posterity an Homeric way of life, such as was established by Pythagoras who was so greatly beloved for his wisdom, and whose followers are to this day quite celebrated for the order which was named after him?

Nothing of the kind is recorded of him. For surely, Socrates, Creophylus, the companion of Homer, that child of flesh, whose name always makes us laugh, might be more justly ridiculed for his stupidity, if, as is said, Homer was greatly neglected by him and others in his own day when he was alive?

Yes, I replied, that is the tradition. But can you imagine, Glaucon, that if Homer had really been able to educate and improve mankind—if he had possessed knowledge and not been a mere imitator—can you imagine, I say, that he would not have had many followers, and been honoured and loved by them? Protagoras of Abdera, and Prodicus of Ceos, and a host of others, have only to whisper to their contemporaries: "You will never be able to manage either your own house or your own State until you appoint us to be your ministers of education"—and this ingenious device of theirs has such an effect in making men love them that their companions all but carry them about on their shoulders. And is it conceivable that the contemporaries of Homer, or again of Hesiod, would have allowed either of them to go about as rhapsodists, if they had really been able to make mankind virtuous? Would they not have been as unwilling to part with them as with gold, and have compelled them to stay at home with them? Or, if the master would not stay, then the disciples would have followed him about everywhere, until they had got education enough?

Yes, Socrates, that, I think, is quite true.

Then must we not infer that all these poetical individuals, beginning with Homer, are only imitators; they copy images of virtue and the like, but the truth they never reach? The poet is like a painter who, as we have already observed, will make a likeness of a cobbler though he understands nothing of cobbling; and his picture is good enough for those who know no more than he does, and judge only by colours and figures.

Quite so.

In like manner the poet with his words and phrases[1] may be said to lay on the colours of the several arts, himself understanding their nature only enough to imitate them; and other people, who are as ignorant as he is, and judge only from his words, imagine that if he speaks of cobbling, or of military tactics, or of anything else, in metre and harmony and rhythm, he speaks very well—such is the sweet influence which melody and rhythm by nature have. And I think that you must have observed again and again what a poor appearance the tales of poets make when stripped of the colours which music puts upon them, and recited in simple prose.

Yes, he said.

They are like faces which were never really beautiful, but only blooming; and now the bloom of youth has passed away from them?

[1] Or, "with his nouns and verbs."

Exactly.

Here is another point: The imitator or maker of the image knows nothing of true existence; he knows appearances only. Am I not right?

Yes.

Then let us have a clear understanding, and not be satisfied with half an explanation.

Proceed.

Of the painter we say that he will paint reins, and he will paint a bit?

Yes.

And the worker in leather and brass will make them?

Certainly.

But does the painter know the right form of the bit and reins? Nay, hardly even the workers in brass and leather who make them; only the horseman who knows how to use them—he knows their right form.

Most true.

And may we not say the same of all things?

What?

That there are three arts which are concerned with all things: one which uses, another which makes, a third which imitates them?

Yes.

And the excellence or beauty or truth of every structure, animate or inanimate, and of every action of man, is relative to the use for which nature or the artist has intended them.

True.

Then the user of them must have the greatest experience of them, and he must indicate to the maker the good or bad qualities which develop themselves in use; for example, the flute-player will tell the flute-maker which of his flutes is satisfactory to the performer; he will tell him how he ought to make them, and the other will attend to his instructions?

Of course.

The one knows and therefore speaks with authority about the goodness and badness of flutes, while the other, confiding in him, will do what he is told by him?

True.

The instrument is the same, but about the excellence or badness of it the maker will only attain to a correct belief; and this he will gain from him who knows, by talking to him and being compelled to hear what he has to say, whereas the user will have knowledge?

True.

But will the imitator have either? Will he know from use whether or no his drawing is correct or beautiful? Or will he have right opinion from being compelled to associate with another who knows and gives him instructions about what he should draw?

Neither.

Then he will no more have true opinion than he will have knowledge about the goodness or badness of his imitations?

I suppose not.

The imitative artist will be in a brilliant state of intelligence about his own creations?

Nay, very much the reverse.

And still he will go on imitating without knowing what makes a thing good or bad, and may be expected therefore to imitate only that which appears to be good to the ignorant multitude?

Just so.

Thus far then we are pretty well agreed that the imitator has no knowledge worth mentioning of what he imitates. Imitation is only a kind of play or sport, and the tragic poets, whether they write in Iambic or in Heroic verse, are imitators in the highest degree?

Very true.

And now tell me, I conjure you, has not imitation been shown by us to be concerned with that which is thrice removed from the truth?

Certainly.

And what is the faculty in man to which imitation is addressed?

What do you mean?

I will explain: The body which is large when seen near, appears small when seen at a distance?

True.

And the same object appears straight when looked at out of the water, and crooked when in the water; and the concave becomes convex, owing to the illusion about colours to which the sight is liable. Thus every sort of confusion is revealed within us; and this is that weakness of the human mind on which the art of conjuring and of deceiving by light and shadow and other ingenious devices imposes, having an effect upon us like magic.

True.

And the arts of measuring and numbering and weighing come to the rescue of the human understanding—there is the beauty of them—and the apparent greater or less, or more or heavier, no longer have the mastery over us, but give way before calculation and measure and weight?

Most true.

And this, surely, must be the work of the calculating and rational principle in the soul?

To be sure.

And when this principle measures and certifies that some things are equal, or that some are greater or less than others, there occurs an apparent contradiction?

True.

But were we not saying that such a contradiction is impossible—the same faculty cannot have contrary opinions at the same time about the same thing?

Very true.

Then that part of the soul which has an opinion contrary to measure is not the same with that which has an opinion in accordance with measure?

True.

And the better part of the soul is likely to be that which trusts to measure and calculation?

Certainly.

And that which is opposed to them is one of the inferior principles of the soul?

No doubt.

This was the conclusion at which I was seeking to arrive when I said that painting or drawing, and imitation in general, when doing their own proper work, are far removed from truth, and the companions and friends and associates of a principle within us which is equally removed from reason, and that they have no true or healthy aim.

Exactly.

The imitative art is an inferior who marries an inferior, and has inferior offspring.

Very true.

And is this confined to the sight only, or does it extend to the hearing also, relating in fact to what we term poetry?

Probably the same would be true of poetry.

Do not rely, I said, on a probability derived from the analogy of painting; but let us examine further and see whether the faculty with which poetical imitation is concerned is good or bad.

By all means.

We may state the question thus:—Imitation imitates the actions of men, whether voluntary or involuntary, on which, as they imagine, a good or bad result has ensued, and they rejoice or sorrow accordingly. Is there anything more?

No, there is nothing else.

But in all this variety of circumstances is the man at unity with himself—or rather, as in the instance of sight there was confusion and opposition in his opinions about the same things, so here also is there not strife and inconsistency in his life? Though I need hardly raise the question again, for I remember that all this has been already admitted; and the soul has been acknowledged by us to be full of these and ten thousand similar oppositions occurring at the same moment?

And we were right, he said.

Yes, I said, thus far we were right; but there was an omission which must now be supplied.

What was the omission?

Were we not saying that a good man, who has the misfortune to lose his son or anything else which is most dear to him, will bear the loss with more equanimity than another?

Yes.

But will he have no sorrow, or shall we say that although he cannot help sorrowing, he will moderate his sorrow?

The latter, he said, is the truer statement.

Tell me: will he be more likely to struggle and hold out against his sorrow when he is seen by his equals, or when he is alone?

It will make a great difference whether he is seen or not.

When he is by himself he will not mind saying or doing many things which he would be ashamed of any one hearing or seeing him do?

True.

There is a principle of law and reason in him which bids him resist, as well as a feeling of his misfortune which is forcing him to indulge his sorrow?

True.

But when a man is drawn in two opposite directions, to and from the same object, this, as we affirm, necessarily implies two distinct principles in him?

Certainly.

One of them is ready to follow the guidance of the law?

How do you mean?

The law would say that to be patient under suffering is best, and that we should not give way to impatience, as there is no knowing whether such things are good or evil; and nothing is gained by impatience; also, because no human thing is of serious importance, and grief stands in the way of that which at the moment is most required.

What is most required? he asked.

That we should take counsel about what has happened, and when the dice have been thrown order our affairs in the way which reason deems best; not, like children who have had a fall, keeping hold of the part struck and wasting time in setting up a howl, but always accustoming the soul forthwith to apply a remedy, raising up that which is sickly and fallen, banishing the cry of sorrow by the healing art.

Yes, he said, that is the true way of meeting the attacks of fortune.

Yes, I said; and the higher principle is ready to follow this suggestion of reason?

Clearly.

And the other principle, which inclines us to recollection of our troubles and to lamentation, and can never have enough of them, we may call irrational, useless, and cowardly?

Indeed, we may.

And does not the latter—I mean the rebellious principle—furnish a great variety of materials for imitation? Whereas the wise and calm temperament, being always nearly equable, is not easy to imitate or to appreciate when imitated, especially at a public festival when a promiscuous crowd is assembled in a theatre. For the feeling represented is one to which they are strangers.

Certainly.

Then the imitative poet who aims at being popular is not by nature made, nor is his art intended, to please or to affect the rational principle in the soul; but he will prefer the passionate and fitful temper, which is easily imitated?

Clearly.

And now we may fairly take him and place him by the side of the painter, for he is like him in two ways: first, inasmuch as his creations have an inferior degree of truth—in this, I say, he is like him; and he is also like him in being concerned with an inferior part of the soul; and therefore we shall be right in refusing to admit him into a well-ordered State, because he awakens and nourishes and strengthens the feelings and impairs the reason. As in a city when the evil are permitted to have authority and the good are put out of the way, so in the soul of man, as we maintain, the imitative poet implants an evil constitution, for he indulges the irrational nature which has no discernment of greater and less, but thinks the same thing at one time great and at another small—he is a manufacturer of images and is very far removed from the truth.

Exactly.

But we have not yet brought forward the heaviest count in our accusation:—the power which poetry has of harming even the good (and there are very few who are not harmed), is surely an awful thing?

Yes, certainly, if the effect is what you say.

Hear and judge: The best of us, as I conceive, when we listen to a passage of Homer, or one of the tragedians, in which he represents some pitiful hero who is drawling out his sorrows in a long oration, of weeping, and smiting his breast—the best of us, you know, delight in giving way to sympathy, and are in raptures at the excellence of the poet who stirs our feelings most.

Yes, of course I know.

But when any sorrow of our own happens to us, then you may observe that we pride ourselves on the opposite quality—we would fain be quiet and patient; this is the manly part, and the other which delighted us in the recitation is now deemed to be the part of a woman.

Very true, he said.

Now can we be right in praising and admiring another who is doing that which any one of us would abominate and be ashamed of in his own person?

No, he said, that is certainly not reasonable.

Nay, I said, quite reasonable from one point of view.

What point of view?

If you consider, I said, that when in misfortune we feel a natural hunger and desire to relieve our sorrow by weeping and lamentation, and that this feeling which is kept under control in our own calamities is satisfied and delighted by the poets;—the better nature in each of us, not having been sufficiently trained by reason or habit, allows the sympathetic element to break loose because the sorrow is another's; and the spectator fancies that there can be no disgrace to himself in praising and pitying any one who comes telling him what a good man he is, and making a fuss about his troubles; he thinks that the pleasure is a gain, and why should he be supercilious and lose this and the poem too? Few persons ever reflect, as I should imagine, that from the evil of other men something of evil is communicated to themselves. And so the feeling of sorrow which has gathered strength at the sight of the misfortunes of others is with difficulty repressed in our own.

How very true!

And does not the same hold also of the ridiculous? There are jests which you would be ashamed to make yourself, and yet on the comic stage, or indeed in private, when you hear them, you are greatly amused by them, and are not at all disgusted at their unseemliness;—the case of pity is repeated;— there is a principle in human nature which is disposed to raise a laugh, and this which you once restrained by reason, because you were afraid of being thought a buffoon, is now let out again; and having stimulated the risible faculty at the theatre, you are betrayed unconsciously to yourself into playing the comic poet at home.

Quite true, he said.

And the same may be said of lust and anger and all the other affections, of desire and pain and pleasure, which are held to be inseparable from every action—in all of them poetry feeds and waters the passions instead of drying them up; she lets them rule, although they ought to be controlled, if mankind are ever to increase in happiness and virtue.

I cannot deny it.

Therefore, Glaucon, I said, whenever you meet with any of the eulogists of Homer declaring that he has been the educator of Hellas, and that he is profitable for education and for the ordering of human things, and that you should take him up again and again and get to know him and regulate your whole life according to him, we may love and honour those who say these things—they are excellent people, as far as their lights extend; and we are ready to acknowledge that Homer is the greatest of poets and first of tragedy writers; but we must remain firm in our conviction that hymns to the gods and praises of famous men are the only poetry which ought to be admitted into our State. For if you go beyond this and allow the honeyed muse to enter, either in epic or lyric verse, not law and the reason of mankind, which by common consent have ever been deemed best, but pleasure and pain will be the rulers in our State.

That is most true, he said.

And now since we have reverted to the subject of poetry, let this our defence serve to show the reasonableness of our former judgment in sending away out of our State an art having the tendencies which we have described; for reason constrained us. But that she may not impute to us any harshness or want of politeness, let us tell her that there is an ancient quarrel between philosophy and poetry; of which there are many proofs, such as the saying of "the yelping hound howling at her lord," or of one "mighty in the vain talk of fools," and "the mob of sages circumventing Zeus," and the "subtle thinkers who are beggars after all"; and there are innumerable other signs of ancient enmity between them. Notwithstanding this, let us assure our sweet friend and the sister arts of imitation that if she will only prove her title to exist in a well-ordered State we shall be delighted to receive her— we are very conscious of her charms; but we may not on that account betray the truth. I dare say, Glaucon, that you are as much charmed by her as I am, especially when she appears in Homer?

Yes, indeed, I am greatly charmed.

Shall I propose, then, that she be allowed to return from exile, but upon this condition only—that she make a defence of herself in lyrical or some other metre?

Certainly.

And we may further grant to those of her defenders who are lovers of poetry and yet not poets the permission to speak in prose on her behalf: let them show not only that she is pleasant but also useful to States and to human life, and we will listen in a kindly spirit; for if this can be proved we shall surely be the gainers—I mean, if there is a use in poetry as well as a delight?

Certainly, he said, we shall be the gainers.

If her defence fails, then, my dear friend, like other persons who are enamoured of something, but put a restraint upon themselves when they think their desires are opposed to their interests, so too must we after the manner of lovers give her up, though not without a struggle. We too are inspired by that love of poetry which the education of noble States has implanted in us, and therefore we would have her appear at her best and truest; but so long as she is unable to make good her defence, this argument of ours shall be a charm to us, which we will repeat to ourselves while we listen to her strains; that we may not fall away into the childish love of her which captivates the many. At all events we are well aware that poetry being such as we have described is not to be regarded seriously as attaining to the truth; and he who listens to her, fearing for the safety of the city which is within him, should be on his guard against her seductions and make our words his law.

Yes, he said, I quite agree with you.

Yes, I said, my dear Glaucon, for great is the issue at stake, greater than appears, whether a man is to be good or bad. And what will any one be profited if under the influence of honour or money or power, aye, or under the excitement of poetry, he neglect justice and virtue?

Yes, he said; I have been convinced by the argument, as I believe that any one else would have been.

Aristotle

ART AS IMITATION*

I propose to treat of Poetry in itself and of its various kinds, noting the essential quality of each; to inquire into the structure of the plot as requisite to a good poem; into the number and nature of the parts of which a poem is composed; and similarly into whatever else falls within the same inquiry. Following, then, the order of nature, let us begin with the principles which come first.

2. Epic poetry and Tragedy, Comedy also and Dithyrambic poetry, and the music of the flute and of the lyre in most of their forms, are all in their general conception modes of imitation. 3. They differ, however, from one another in three respects,—the medium, the objects, the manner or mode of imitation, being in each case distinct.

4. For as there are persons who, by conscious art or mere habit, imitate and represent various objects through the medium of colour and form, or again by the voice; so in the arts above mentioned, taken as a whole, the imitation is produced by rhythm, language, or "harmony," either singly or combined.

Thus in the music of the flute and of the lyre, "harmony" and rhythm alone are employed; also in other arts, such as that of the shepherd's pipe, which are essentially similar to these. 5. In dancing, rhythm alone is used without "harmony"; for even dancing imitates character, emotion, and action, by rhythmical movement.

6. There is another art which imitates by means of language alone, and that either in prose or verse—which verse, again, may either combine different metres or consist of but one kind—but this has hitherto been without a name. 7. For there is no common term we could apply to the mimes of Sophron and Xenarchus and the Socratic dialogues on the one hand; and, on the other, to poetic imitations in iambic, elegiac, or any similar metre. People do, indeed, add the word "maker" or "poet" to the name of the metre, and speak of elegiac poets, or epic (that is, hexameter) poets, as if it were not the imitation that makes the poet, but the verse that entitles them all indiscriminately to the name. 8. Even when a treatise on medicine or

* From Aristotle's *Poetics,* trans., S. H. Butcher (London: The Macmillan Company, Ltd., 1911), Chs. 1-5. Copyright, 1911, by The Macmillan Company, Ltd. Reprinted by permission.

Aristotle (385/4 – 322 B.C.) wrote the *Poetics* about 330 B.C. It is probably the most influential work ever written in aesthetics.

natural science is brought out in verse, the name of poet is by custom given to the author; and yet Homer and Empedocles have nothing in common but the metre, so that it would be right to call the one poet, the other physicist rather than poet. 9. On the same principle, even if a writer in his poetic imitation were to combine all metres, as Chaeremon did in his Centaur, which is a medley composed of metres of all kinds, we should bring him too under the general term poet. So much then for these distinctions.

10. There are, again, some arts which employ all the means above mentioned,—namely, rhythm, tune and metre. Such are Dithyrambic and Nomic poetry, and also Tragedy and Comedy; but between them the difference is, that in the first two cases these means are all employed in combination, in the latter, now one means is employed, now another.

Such, then, are the differences of the arts with respect to the medium of imitation.

II

Since the objects of imitation are men in action, and these men must be either of a higher or a lower type (for moral character mainly answers to these divisions, goodness and badness being the distinguishing marks of moral differences), it follows that we must represent men either as better than in real life, or as worse, or as they are. It is the same in painting. Polygnotus depicted men as nobler than they are, Pauson as less noble, Dionysius drew them true to life.

2. Now it is evident that each of the modes of imitation above mentioned will exhibit these differences, and become a distinct kind in imitating objects that are thus distinct. 3. Such diversities may be found even in dancing, flute-playing, and lyre-playing. So again in language, whether prose or verse unaccompanied by music. Homer, for example, makes men better than they are; Cleophon as they are; Hegemon the Thasian, the inventor of parodies, and Nicochares, the author of the Deiliad, worse than they are. 4. The same thing holds good of Dithyrambs and Nomes; here too one may portray different types, as Timotheus and Philoxenus differed in representing their Cyclopes. The same distinction marks off Tragedy from Comedy; for Comedy aims at representing men as worse, Tragedy as better than in actual life.

III

There is still a third difference—the manner in which each of these objects may be imitated. For the medium being the same, and the objects the same, the poet may imitate by narration—in which case he can either take another personality as Homer does, or speak in his own person, unchanged—or he may present all his characters as living and moving before us.

2. These, then, as we said at the beginning, are the three differences which distinguish artistic imitation—the medium, the objects and the manner. So that from one point of view, Sophocles is an imitator of the same kind as Homer—for both imitate higher types of character; from another point of view, of the same kind as Aristophanes—for both imitate persons acting and doing. 3. Hence, some say, the name of "drama" is given to such poems, as representing action. For the same reason the Dorians claim the invention both of Tragedy and Comedy. The claim to Comedy is put forward by the Megarians,—not only by those of Greece proper, who allege that it originated under their democracy, but also by the Megarians of Sicily, for the poet Epicharmus, who is much earlier than Chionides and Magnes, belonged to that country. Tragedy too is claimed by certain Dorians of the Peloponnese. In each case they appeal to the evidence of language. Villages, they say, are by them called χῶμαι, by the Athenians δῆμοι: and they assume that Comedians were so named not from χωμάζειν, "to revel," but because they wandered from village to village (χατὰ χώμας), being excluded contemptuously from the city. They add also that the Dorian word for "doing" is δρᾶν, and the Athenian, πράττειν.

4. This may suffiice as to the number and nature of the various modes of imitation.

IV

Poetry in general seems to have sprung from two causes, each of them lying deep in our nature. 2. First, the instinct of imitation is implanted in man from childhood, one difference between him and other animals being that he is the most imitative of living creatures; and through imitation he learns his earliest lessons; and no less universal is the pleasure felt in things imitated. 3. We have evidence of this in the facts of experience. Objects which in themselves we view with pain, we delight to contemplate when reproduced with minute fidelity: such as the forms of the most ignoble animals and of dead bodies. 4. The cause of this again is, that to learn gives the liveliest pleasure, not only to philosophers but to men in general; whose capacity, however, of learning is more limited. 5. Thus the reason why men enjoy seeing a likeness is, that in contemplating it they find themselves learning or inferring, and saying perhaps. "Ah, that is he." For if you happen not to have seen the original, the pleasure will be due not to the imitation as such, but to the execution, the colouring, or some such other cause.

6. Imitation, then, is one instinct of our nature. Next, there is the instinct for "harmony" and rhythm, metres being manifestly sections of rhythm. Persons, therefore, starting with this natural gift developed by degrees their special aptitudes, till their rude improvisations gave birth to Poetry.

7. Poetry now diverged in two directions, according to the individual character of the writers. The graver spirits imitated noble actions, and the actions of good men. The more trivial sort imitated the actions of meaner persons, at first composing satires, as the former did hymns to the gods and the praises of famous men. 8. A poem of the satirical kind cannot indeed be put down to any author earlier than Homer; though many such writers probably there were. But from Homer onward, instances can be cited,— his own Margites, for example, and other similar compositions. The appropriate metre was also here introduced; hence the measure is still called the iambic or lampooning measure, being that in which people lampooned one another. 9. Thus the older poets were distinguished as writers of heroic or of lampooning verse.

As, in the serious style, Homer is pre-eminent among poets, for he alone combined dramatic form with excellence of imitation, so he too first laid down the main lines of Comedy, by dramatizing the ludicrous instead of writing personal satire. His Margites bears the same relation to Comedy that the Iliad and Odyssey do to Tragedy. 10. But when Tragedy and Comedy came to light, the two classes of poets still followed their natural bent: the lampooners became writers of Comedy, and the Epic poets were succeeded by Tragedians, since the drama was a larger and higher form of art.

11. Whether Tragedy has as yet perfected its proper types or not; and whether it is to be judged in itself, or in relation also to the audience,— this raises another question. 12. Be that as it may, Tragedy—as also Comedy —was at first mere improvisation. The one originated with the leaders of the Dithyramb, the other with those of the phallic songs, which are still in use in many of our cities. Tragedy advanced by slow degrees; each new element that showed itself was in turn developed. Having passed through many changes, it found its natural form, and there it stopped.

13. Aeschylus first introduced a second actor; he diminished the importance of the Chorus, and assigned the leading part to the dialogue. Sophocles raised the number of actors to three, and added scene-painting. 14. Moreover, it was not till late that the short plot was discarded for one of greater compass, and the grotesque diction of the earlier satyric form for the

stately manner of Tragedy. The iambic measure then replaced the trochaic tetrameter, which was originally employed when the poetry was of the satyric order, and had greater affinities with dancing. Once dialogue had come in, Nature herself discovered the appropriate measure. For the iambic is, of all measures, the most colloquial: we see it in the fact that conversational speech runs into iambic form more frequently than into any other kind of verse; rarely into hexameters, and only when we drop the colloquial intonation. 15. The additions to the number of "episodes" or acts, and the other improvements of which tradition tells, must be taken as already described; for to discuss them in detail would, doubtless, be a large undertaking.

V

Comedy is, as we have said, an imitation of characters of a lower type—not, however, in the full sense of the word bad, the Ludicrous being merely a subdivision of the ugly. It consists in some defect or ugliness which is not painful or destructive. To take an obvious example, the comic mask is ugly and distorted, but does not imply pain.

2. The successive changes through which Tragedy passed, and the authors of these changes, are well known, whereas Comedy has had no history, because it was not at first treated seriously. It was late before the Archon granted a comic chorus to a poet; the performers were till then voluntary. Comedy had already taken definite shape when comic poets, distinctively so called, are heard of. 3. Who introduced masks, or prologues, or increased the number of actors—these and other similar details remain unknown. As for the plot, it came originally from Sicily; but of Athenian writers Crates was the first who, abandoning the "iambic" or lampooning form, generalized his themes and plots.

4. Epic poetry agrees with Tragedy in so far as it is an imitation in verse of characters of a higher type. They differ, in that Epic poetry admits but one kind of metre, and is narrative in form. They differ, again, in their length: for Tragedy endeavours, as far as possible, to confine itself to a single revolution of the sun, or but slightly to exceed this limit; whereas the Epic action has no limits of time. This, then, is a second point of difference; though at first the same freedom was admitted in Tragedy as in Epic poetry.

5. Of their constituent parts some are common to both, some peculiar to Tragedy. Whoever, therefore, knows what is good or bad Tragedy, knows also about Epic poetry: for all the elements of an Epic poem are found in Tragedy, but the elements of a Tragedy are not all found in the Epic poem.

Plotinus

ART AS BEAUTY*

BEAUTY

1.

Beauty addresses itself chiefly to sight; but there is a beauty for the hearing too, as in certain combinations of words and in all kinds of music, for melodies and cadences are beautiful; and minds that lift themselves above the realm of sense to a higher order are aware of beauty in the conduct of life, in actions, in character, in the pursuits of the intellect; and there is the beauty of the virtues. What loftier beauty there may be, yet, our argument will bring to light.

What, then, is it that gives comeliness to material forms and draws the ear to the sweetness perceived in sounds, and what is the secret of the beauty there is in all that derives from Soul?

Is there some One Principle from which all take their grace, or is there a beauty peculiar to the embodied and another for the bodiless? Finally, one or many, what would such a Principle be?

Consider that some things, material shapes for instance, are gracious not by anything inherent but by something communicated, while others are lovely of themselves, as, for example, Virtue.

The same bodies appear sometimes beautiful, sometimes not; so that there is a good deal between being body and being beautiful.

What, then, is this something that shows itself in certain material forms? This is the natural beginning of our enquiry.

What is it that attracts the eyes of those to whom a beautiful object is presented, and calls them, lures them, towards it, and fills them with joy at the sight? It we possess ourselves of this, we have at once a standpoint for the wider survey.

* From Plotinus' *The Enneads*, trans., Stephen MacKenna (London: Faber & Faber Ltd., 1930) I, 6, 1-9; V, 8, 1, 5. Copyright, 1917, 1930, Philip Lee Warner, Publisher to the Medici Society, Ltd. Reprinted by permission of Faber & Faber, Ltd., and Pantheon Books, Inc.

Plotinus (204-269), the founder of the Roman School of Neo-Platonism, produced an original synthesis of Plato's philosophy, stressing the notion of emanation from the One to everything else, including art and beauty. His works were arranged by his disciple and biographer, Porphyry, into sets of nine essays each, hence, the term, *Enneads*. His influence on artistic creation, especially on that of Michelangelo, has been profound.

Almost everyone declares that the symmetry of parts towards each other and towards a whole, with, besides, a certain charm of colour, constitutes the beauty recognised by the eye, that in visible things, as indeed in all else, universally, the beautiful thing is essentially symmetrical, patterned.

But think what this means.

Only a compound can be beautiful, never anything devoid of parts; and only a whole; the several parts will have beauty, not in themselves, but only as working together to give a comely total. Yet beauty in an aggregate demands beauty in details; it cannot be constructed out of ugliness; its law must run throughout.

All the loveliness of colour and even the light of the sun, being devoid of parts and so not beautiful by symmetry, must be ruled out of the realm of beauty. And how comes gold to be a beautiful thing? And lightning by night, and the stars, why are these so fair?

In sounds also the simple must be proscribed, though often in a whole noble composition each several tone is delicious in itself.

Again since the one face, constant in symmetry, appears sometimes fair and sometimes not, can we doubt that beauty is something more than symmetry, that symmetry itself owes its beauty to a remoter principle?

Turn to what is attractive in methods of life or in the expression of thought; are we to call in symmetry here? What symmetry is to be found in noble conduct, or excellent laws, in any form of mental pursuit?

What symmetry can there be in points of abstract thought?

The symmetry of being accordant with each other? But there may be accordance or entire identity where there is nothing but ugliness: the proposition that honesty is merely a generous artlessness chimes in the most perfect harmony with the proposition that morality means weakness of will; the accordance is complete.

Then again, all the virtues are a beauty of the soul, a beauty authentic beyond any of these others; but how does symmetry enter here? The soul, it is true, is not a simple unity, but still its virtue cannot have the symmetry of size or of number: what standard of measurement could preside over the compromise or the coalescence of the soul's faculties or purposes?

Finally, how by this theory would there be beauty in the Intellectual-Principle, essentially the solitary?

2.

Let us, then, go back to the source, and indicate at once the Principle that bestows beauty on material things.

Undoubtedly this Principle exists; it is something that is perceived at the first glance, something which the soul names as from an ancient knowledge and, recognizing, welcomes it, enters into unison with it.

But let the soul fall in with the Ugly and at once it shrinks within itself, denies the thing, turns away from it, not accordant, resenting it.

Our interpretation is that the soul—by the very truth of its nature by its affiliation to the noblest Existents in the hierarchy of Being—when it sees anything of that kin, or any trace of that kinship, thrills with an immediate delight, takes its own to itself, and thus stirs anew to the sense of its nature and of all its affinity.

But, is there any such likeness between the loveliness of this world and the splendours in the Supreme? Such a likeness in the particulars would make the two orders alike: but what is there in common between beauty here and beauty There?

We hold that all the loveliness of this world comes by communion in Ideal-Form.

All shapelessness whose kind admits of pattern and form, as long as it remains outside of Reason and Idea, is ugly by that very isolation from the Divine-Thought. And this is the Absolute Ugly: an ugly thing is something that has not been entirely mastered by pattern, that is by Reason, the Matter not yielding at all points and in all respects to Ideal-Form.

But where the Ideal-Form has entered, it has grouped and co-ordinated what from a diversity of parts was to become a unity: it has rallied confusion into co-operation: it has made the sum one harmonious coherence: for the Idea is a unity and what it moulds must come to unity as far as multiplicity may.

And on what has thus been compacted to unity, Beauty enthrones itself, giving itself to the parts as to the sum: when it lights on some natural unity, a thing of like parts, then it gives itself to that whole. Thus, for an illustration, there is the beauty, conferred by craftsmanship, of all a house with all its parts, and the beauty which some natural quality may give to a single stone.

This, then, is how the material thing becomes beautiful—by communicating in the thought that flows from the Divine.

3.

And the soul includes a faculty peculiarly addressed to Beauty—one incomparably sure in the appreciation of its own, never in doubt whenever any lovely thing presents itself for judgement.

Or perhaps the soul itself acts immediately, affirming the Beautiful where it finds something accordant with the Ideal-Form within itself, using this Idea as a canon of accuracy in its decision.

But what accordance is there between the material and that which antedates all Matter?

On what principle does the architect, when he finds the house standing before him correspondent with his inner ideal of a house, pronounce it beautiful? Is it not that the house before him, the stones apart, is the inner idea stamped upon the mass of exterior matter, the indivisible exhibited in diversity?

So with the perceptive faculty: discerning in certain objects the Ideal-Form which has bound and controlled shapeless matter, opposed in nature to Idea, seeing further stamped upon the common shapes some shape excellent above the common, it gathers into unity what still remains fragmentary, catches it up and carries it within, no longer a thing of parts, and presents it to the Ideal-Principle as something concordant and congenial, a natural friend: the joy here is like that of a good man who discerns in a youth the early signs of a virtue consonant with the achieved perfection within his own soul.

The beauty of colour is also the outcome of a unification: it derives from shape, from the conquest of the darkness inherent in Matter by the pouring-in of light, the unembodied, which is a Rational-Principle and an Ideal-Form.

Hence it is that Fire itself is splendid beyond all material bodies, holding the rank of Ideal-Principle to the other elements, making ever upwards, the subtlest and sprightliest of all bodies, as very near to the unembodied; itself alone admitting no other, all the others penetrated by it: for they take warmth but this is never cold; it has colour primally; they receive the Form of colour from it: hence the splendour of its light, the splendour that belongs to the Idea. And all that has resisted and is but uncertainly held by its light remains outside of beauty, as not having absorbed the plenitude of the Form of colour.

And harmonies unheard in sound create the harmonies we hear and wake the soul to the consciousness of beauty, showing it the one essence in another kind: for the measures of our sensible music are not arbitrary but are determined by the Principle whose labour is to dominate Matter and bring pattern into being.

Thus far of the beauties of the realm of sense, images and shadow-pictures, fugitives that have entered into Matter—to adorn, and to ravish, where they are seen.

4.

But there are earlier and loftier beauties than these. In the sense-bound life we are no longer granted to know them, but the soul, taking no help from the organs, sees and proclaims them. To the vision of these we must mount, leaving sense to its own low place.

As it is not for those to speak of the graceful forms of the material world who have never seen them or known their grace—men born blind, let us suppose—in the same way those must be silent upon the beauty of noble conduct and of learning and all that order who have never cared for such things, nor may those tell of the splendour of virtue who have never known the face of Justice and of Moral-Wisdom beautiful beyond the beauty of Evening and of Dawn.

Such vision is for those only who see with the Soul's sight—and at the vision, they will rejoice, and awe will fall upon them and a trouble deeper than all the rest could ever stir, for now they are moving in the realm of Truth.

This is the spirit that Beauty must ever induce, wonderment and a delicious trouble, longing and love and a trembling that is all delight. For the unseen all this may be felt as for the seen; and this the Souls feel for it, every soul in some degree, but those the more deeply that are the more truly apt to this higher love—just as all take delight in the beauty of the body but all are not stung as sharply, and those only that feel the keener wound are known as Lovers.

5.

These Lovers, then, lovers of the beauty outside of sense, must be made to declare themselves.

What do you feel in presence of the grace you discern in actions, in manners, in sound morality, in all the works and fruits of virtue, in the beauty of souls? When you see that you yourselves are beautiful within, what do you feel? What is this Dionysiac exultation that thrills through your being, this straining upwards of all your Soul, this longing to break away from the body and live sunken within the veritable self?

These are no other than the emotions of Souls under the spell of love.

But what is it that awakens all this passion? No shape, no colour, no grandeur of mass: all is for a Soul, something whose beauty rests upon no colour, for the moral wisdom the Soul enshrines and all the other hueless splendour of the virtues. It is that you find in yourself, or admire in another, loftiness of spirit; righteousness of life; disciplined purity; courage of the majestic face; gravity; modesty that goes fearless and tranquil and passionless; and, shining down upon all, the light of godlike Intellection.

All these noble qualities are to be reverenced and loved, no doubt, but what entitles them to be called beautiful?

They exist: they manifest themselves to us: anyone that sees them must admit that they have reality of Being; and is not Real-Being, really beautiful?

But we have not yet shown by what property in them they have wrought the Soul to loveliness: what is this grace, this splendour as of Light, resting upon all the virtues?

Let us take the contrary, the ugliness of the Soul, and set that against its beauty: to understand, at once, what this ugliness is and how it comes to appear in the Soul will certainly open our way before us.

Let us then suppose an ugly Soul, dissolute, unrighteous: teeming with all the lusts; torn by internal discord; beset by the fears of its cowardice and the envies of its pettiness; thinking, in the little thought it has, only of the perishable and the base; perverse in all its impulses; the friend of unclean pleasures; living the life of abandonment to bodily sensation and delighting in its deformity.

What must we think but that all this shame is something that has gathered about the Soul, some foreign bane outraging it, soiling it, so that, encumbered with all manner of turpitude, it has no longer a clean activity or a clean sensation, but commands only a life smouldering dully under the crust of evil; that, sunk in manifold death, it no longer sees what a Soul should see, may no longer rest in its own being, dragged ever as it is towards the outer, the lower, the dark?

An unclean thing, I dare to say; flickering hither and thither at the call of objects of sense, deeply infected with the taint of body, occupied always in Matter, and absorbing Matter into itself; in its commerce with the Ignoble it has trafficked away for an alien nature its own essential Idea.

If a man has been immersed in filth or daubed with mud his native comeliness disappears and all that is seen is the foul stuff besmearing him: his ugly condition is due to alien matter that has encrusted him, and if he is to win back his grace it must be his business to scour and purify himself and make himself what he was.

So, we may justly say, a Soul becomes ugly—by something foisted upon it, by sinking itself into the alien, by a fall, a descent into body, into Matter. The dishonour of the Soul is in its ceasing to be clean and apart. Gold is degraded when it is mixed with earthy particles; if these be worked out, the gold is left and is beautiful, isolated from all that is foreign, gold with gold alone. And so the Soul; let it be but cleared of the desires that come by its too intimate converse with the body, emancipated from all the passions, purged of all that embodiment has thrust upon it, withdrawn, a solitary, to itself again—in that moment the ugliness that came only from the alien is stripped away.

6.

For, as the ancient teaching was, moral-discipline and courage and every virtue, not even excepting Wisdom itself, all is purification.

Hence the Mysteries with good reason adumbrate the immersion of the unpurified in filth, even in the Nether-World, since the unclean loves filth for its very filthiness, and swine foul of body find their joy in foulness.

What else is Sophrosyny, rightly so-called, but to take no part in the pleasures of the body, to break away from them as unclean and unworthy of the clean? So too, Courage is but being fearless of the death which is but the parting of the Soul from the body, an event which no one can dread whose delight is to be his unmingled self. And Magnanimity is but disregard for the lure of things here. And Wisdom is but the Act of the Intellectual-Principle withdrawn from the lower places and leading the Soul to the Above.

The Soul thus cleansed is all Idea and Reason, wholly free of body, intellective, entirely of that divine order from which the wellspring of Beauty rises and all the race of Beauty.

Hence the Soul heightened to the Intellectual-Principle is beautiful to all its power. For Intellection and all that proceeds from Intellection are the Soul's beauty, a graciousness native to it and not foreign, for only with these is it truly Soul. And it is just to say that in the Soul's becoming a good and beautiful thing is its becoming like to God, for from the Divine comes all the Beauty and all the Good in beings.

We may even say that Beauty *is* the Authentic-Existents and Ugliness is the Principle contrary to Existence: and the Ugly is also the primal evil; therefore its contrary is at once good and beautiful, or is Good and Beauty: and hence the one method will discover to us the Beauty-Good and the Ugliness-Evil.

And Beauty, this Beauty which is also The Good, must be posed as The First: directly deriving from this First is the Intellectual-Principle which is pre-eminently the manifestation of Beauty; through the Intellectual-Principle Soul is beautiful. The beauty in things of a lower order—actions and pursuits for instance—comes by operation of the shaping Soul which is also the author of the beauty found in the world of sense. For the Soul, a divine thing, a fragment as it were of the Primal Beauty, makes beautiful to the fulness of their capacity all things whatsoever that it grasps and moulds.

7.

Therefore we must ascend again towards the Good, the desired of every Soul. Anyone that has seen This, knows what I intend when I say that it is beautiful. Even the desire of it is to be desired as a Good. To attain it is for those that will take the upward path, who will set all their forces towards it, who will divest themselves of all that we have put on in our descent:—so, to those that approach the Holy Celebrations of the Mysteries, there are appointed purifications and the laying aside of the garments worn before, and the entry in nakedness—until, passing, on the upward way, all that is other than the God, each in the solitude of himself shall behold that solitary-dwelling Existence, the Apart, the Unmingled, the Pure, that from Which all things depend, for Which all look and live and act and know, the Source of Life and of Intellection and of Being.

And one that shall know this vision—with what passion of love shall he not be seized, with what pang of desire, what longing to be molten into one with This, what wondering delight! If he that has never seen this Being must hunger for It as for all his welfare, he that has known must love and reverence It as the very Beauty; he will be flooded with awe and gladness, stricken by a salutary terror; he loves with a veritable love, with sharp desire; all other loves than this he must despise, and disdain all that once seemed fair.

This, indeed, is the mood even of those who, having witnessed the manifestation of Gods or Supernals, can never again feel the old delight in the comeliness of material forms: what then are we to think of one that contemplates Absolute Beauty in Its essential integrity, no accumulation of flesh and matter, no dweller on earth or in the heavens—so perfect Its purity—far above all such things in that they are non-essential, composite, not primal but descending from This?

Beholding this Being—the Choragos of all Existence, the Self-Intent that ever gives forth and never takes—resting, rapt, in the vision and possession of so lofty a loveliness, growing to Its likeness, what Beauty can the soul yet lack? For This, the Beauty supreme, the absolute, and the primal, fashions Its lovers to Beauty and makes them also worthy of love.

And for This, the sternest and the uttermost combat is set before the

Souls; all our labour is for This, lest we be left without part in this noblest vision, which to attain is to be blessed in the blissful sight, which to fail of is to fail utterly.

For not he that has failed of the joy that is in colour or in visible forms, not he that has failed of power or of honours or of kingdom has failed, but only he that has failed of only This, for Whose winning he should renounce kingdoms and command over earth and ocean and sky, if only, spurning the world of sense from beneath his feet, and straining to This, he may see.

8.

But what must we do? How lies the path? How come to vision of the inaccessible Beauty, dwelling as if in consecrated precincts, apart from the common ways where all may see, even the profane?

He that has the strength, let him arise and withdraw into himself, foregoing all that is known by the eyes, turning away for ever from the material beauty that once made his joy. When he perceives those shapes of grace that show in body, let him not pursue: he must know them for copies, vestiges, shadows, and hasten away towards That they tell of. For if anyone follow what is like a beautiful shape playing over water—is there not a myth telling in symbol of such a dupe, how he sank into the depths of the current and was swept away to nothingness? So too, one that is held by material beauty and will not break free shall be precipitated, not in body but in Soul, down to the dark depths loathed of the Intellective-Being, where, blind even in the Lower-World, he shall have commerce only with shadows, there as here.

"Let us flee then to the beloved Fatherland": this is the soundest counsel. But what is this flight? How are we to gain the open sea? For Odysseus is surely a parable to us when he commands the flight from the sorceries of Circe or Calypso—not content to linger for all the pleasure offered to his eyes and all the delight of sense filling his days.

The Fatherland to us is There whence we have come, and There is The Father.

What then is our course, what the manner of our flight? This is not a journey for the feet; the feet bring us only from land to land; nor need you think of coach or ship to carry you away; all this order of things you must set aside and refuse to see: you must close the eyes and call instead upon another vision which is to be waked within you, a vision, the birth-right of all, which few turn to use.

9.

And this inner vision, what is its operation?

Newly awakened it is all too feeble to bear the ultimate splendour. Therefore the Soul must be trained—to the habit of remarking, first, all noble pursuits, then the works of beauty produced not by the labour of the arts but by the virtue of men known for their goodness: lastly, you must search the souls of those that have shaped these beautiful forms.

But how are you to see into a virtuous soul and know its loveliness?

Withdraw into yourself and look. And if you do not find yourself beautiful yet, act as does the creator of a statue that is to be made beautiful: he cuts away here, he smoothes there, he makes this line lighter, this other purer, until a lovely face has grown upon his work. So do you also: cut away all that is excessive, straighten all that is crooked, bring light to all that is overcast, labour to make all one glow of beauty and never cease chiselling your statue, until there shall shine out on you from it the godlike splendour of virtue, until you shall see the perfect goodness surely established in the stainless shrine.

When you know that you have become this perfect work, when you are self-gathered in the purity of your being, nothing now remaining that can shatter that inner unity, nothing from without clinging to the authentic man, when you find yourself wholly true to your essential nature, wholly that only veritable Light which is not measured by space, not narrowed to any circumscribed form nor again diffused as a thing void of term, but ever unmeasurable as something greater than all measure and more than all quantity—when you perceive that you have grown to this, you are now become very vision: now call up all your confidence, strike forward yet a step—you need a guide no longer—strain, and see.

This is the only eye that sees the mighty Beauty. If the eye that adventures the vision be dimmed by vice, impure, or weak, and unable in its cowardly blenching to see the uttermost brightness, then it sees nothing even though another point to what lies plain to sight before it. To any vision must be brought an eye adapted to what is to be seen, and having some likeness to it. Never did eye see the sun unless it had first become sunlike, and never can the soul have vision of the First Beauty unless itself be beautiful.

Therefore, first let each become godlike and each beautiful who cares to see God and Beauty. So, mounting, the Soul will come first to the Intellectual-Principle and survey all the beautiful Ideas in the Supreme and will avow that this is Beauty, that the Ideas are Beauty. For by their efficacy comes all Beauty else, by the offspring and essence of the Intellectual-Being. What is beyond the Intellectual-Principle we affirm to be the nature of Good radiating Beauty before it. So that, treating the Intellectual-Kosmos as one, the first is the Beautiful: if we make distinction there, the Realm of Ideas constitutes the Beauty of the Intellectual Sphere; and The Good, which lies beyond, is the Fountain at once and Principle of Beauty: the Primal Good and the Primal Beauty have the one dwelling-place and, thus, always, Beauty's seat is There.

ON THE INTELLECTUAL BEAUTY

1.

It is a principle with us that one who has attained to the vision of the Intellectual Beauty and grasped the beauty of the Authentic Intellect will be able also to come to understand the Father and Transcendent of that Divine Being. It concerns us, then, to try to see and say, for ourselves and as far as such matters may be told, how the Beauty of the divine Intellect and of the Intellectual Kosmos may be revealed to contemplation.

Let us go to the realm of magnitudes:—Suppose two blocks of stone lying side by side: one is unpatterned, quite untouched by art; the other has been minutely wrought by the craftsman's hands into some statue of god or man, a Grace or a Muse, or if a human being, not a portrait but a creation in which the sculptor's art has concentrated all loveliness.

Now it must be seen that the stone thus brought under the artist's hand to the beauty of form is beautiful not as stone—for so the crude block would be as pleasant—but in virtue of the form or idea introduced by the art. This form is not in the material; it is in the designer before ever it enters the stone; and the artificer holds it not by his equipment of eyes and hands but by his participation in his art. The beauty, therefore, exists in a far higher state in the art; for it does not come over integrally into the work; that original beauty is not transferred; what comes over is a derivative and a minor: and even that shows itself upon the statue not integrally and with entire realization of intention but only in so far as it has subdued the resistance of the material.

Art, then, creating in the image of its own nature and content, and working by the Idea or Reason-Principle of the beautiful object it is to produce, must itself be beautiful in a far higher and purer degree since it is the seat and source of that beauty, indwelling in the art, which must naturally be more complete than any comeliness of the external. In the degree in which the beauty is diffused by entering into matter, it is so much the weaker than that concentrated in unity; everything that reaches outwards is the less for it, strength less strong, heat less hot, every power less potent, and so beauty less beautiful.

Then again every prime cause must be, within itself, more powerful than its effect can be: the musical does not derive from an unmusical source but from music; and so the art exhibited in the material work derives from an art yet higher.

Still the arts are not to be slighted on the ground that they create by imitation of natural objects; for, to begin with, these natural objects are themselves imitations; then, we must recognize that they give no bare reproduction of the thing seen but go back to the Ideas from which Nature itself derives, and, furthermore, that much of their work is all their own; they are holders of beauty and add where nature is lacking. Thus Pheidias wrought the Zeus upon no model among things of sense but by apprehending what form Zeus must take if he chose to become manifest to sight.

5.

All that comes to be, work of nature or of craft, some wisdom has made: everywhere a wisdom presides at a making.

No doubt the wisdom of the artist may be the guide of the work; it is sufficient explanation of the wisdom exhibited in the arts; but the artist himself goes back, after all, to that wisdom in Nature which is embodied in himself; and this is not a wisdom built up of theorems but one totality, not a wisdom consisting of manifold detail co-ordinated into a unity but rather a unity working out into detail.

Now, if we could think of this as the primal wisdom, we need look no further, since, at that, we have discovered a principle which is neither a derivative nor a "stranger in something strange to it." But if we are told that, while this Reason-Principle is in Nature, yet Nature itself is its source, we ask how Nature came to possess it; and, if Nature derived it from some other source, we ask what that other source may be; if, on the contrary, the principle is self-sprung, we need look no further: but if (as we assume) we are referred to the Intellectual-Principle we must make clear whether the Intellectual-Principle engendered the wisdom: if we learn that it did, we ask whence: if from itself, then inevitably, it is itself Wisdom.

The true Wisdom, then (found to be identical with the Intellectual-Principle) is Real Being; and Real Being is Wisdom; it is wisdom that gives value to Real Being; and Being is Real in virtue of its origin in wisdom. It follows that all forms of existence not possessing wisdom are, indeed, Beings in right of the wisdom which went to their forming, but, as not in themselves possessing it, are not Real Beings.

We cannot therefore think that the divine Beings of that sphere, or the other supremely blessed There, need look to our apparatus of science: all of that realm (the very Beings themselves), all is noble image, such images as we may conceive to lie within the soul of the wise—but There not as inscription but as authentic existence. The ancients had this in mind when they declared the Ideas to be Beings, Essentials.

Joshua Reynolds

DISCOURSE XIII*

Art not merely Imitation, but under the Direction of the Imagination. In what Manner Poetry, Painting, Acting, Gardening, and Architecture depart from Nature

GENTLEMEN,

To discover beauties, or to point out faults, in the works of celebrated masters, and to compare the conduct of one artist with another, is certainly no mean or inconsiderable part of criticism; but this is still no more than to know the art through the artist. This test of investigation must have two capital defects; it must be narrow, and it must be uncertain. To enlarge the boundaries of the art of painting, as well as to fix its principles, it will be necessary, that *that* art and *those* principles should be considered in their correspondence with the principles of the other arts which, like this, address themselves primarily and principally to the imagination. When those connected and kindred principles are brought together to be compared, another comparison will grow out of this; that is, the comparison of them all with those of human nature, from whence arts derive the materials upon which they are to produce their effects.

When this comparison of art with art, and of all arts with the nature of man, is once made with success, our guiding lines are as well ascertained and established, as they can be in matters of this description.

* From Joshua Reynolds' *Discourses on Art*, 1769-1790. *Discourse XIII* was delivered in 1786.

Sir Joshua Reynolds (1723-1792), famous portrait painter, intimate friend of Dr. Samuel Johnson, was the first president of the Royal Academy which office provided him the opportunity to deliver his *Discourses* as a summation of eighteenth century aesthetics.

This, as it is the highest style of criticism, is at the same time the soundest; for it refers to the eternal and immutable nature of things.

You are not to imagine that I mean to open to you at large, or to recommend to your research, the whole of this vast field of science. It is certainly much above my faculties to reach it; and though it may not be above yours to comprehend it fully, if it were fully and properly brought before you, yet perhaps the most perfect criticism requires habits of speculation and abstraction, not very consistent with the employment which ought to occupy and the habits of mind which ought to prevail in a practical artist. I only point out to you these things, that when you do criticize (as all who work on a plan will criticize more or less), your critcism may be built on the foundation of true principles; and that though you may not always travel a great way, the way that you do travel may be the right road.

I observe, as a fundamental ground, common to all the arts with which we have any concern in this discourse, that they address themselves only to two faculties of the mind, its imagination and its sensibility.

All theories which attempt to direct or to control the art, upon any principles falsely called rational, which we form to ourselves upon a supposition of what ought in reason to be the end or means of art, independent of the known first effect produced by objects on the imagination, must be false and delusive. For though it may appear bold to say it, the imagination is here the residence of truth. If the imagination be affected, the conclusion is fairly drawn; if it be not affected, the reasoning is erroneous, because the end is not obtained; the effect itself being the test, and the only test, of the truth and efficacy of the means.

There is in the commerce of life, as in art, a sagacity which is far from being contradictory to right reason, and is superior to any occasional exercise of that faculty; which supersedes it; and does not wait for the slow progress of deduction, but goes at once, by what appears a kind of intuition, to the conclusion. A man endowed with this faculty feels and acknowledges the truth, though it is not always in his power, perhaps, to give a reason for it; because he cannot recollect and bring before him all the materials that gave birth to his opinion; for very many and very intricate considerations may unite to form the principle, even of small and minute parts, involved in, or dependent on, a great system of things: though these in process of time are forgotten, the right impression still remains fixed in his mind.

This impression is the result of the accumulated experience of our whole life, and has been collected, we do not always know how, or when. But this mass of collective observation, however acquired, ought to prevail over that reason, which, however powerfully exerted on any particular occasion, will probably comprehend but a partial view of the subject; and our conduct in life as well as in the arts is, or ought to be, generally governed by this habitual reason: it is our happines that we are enabled to draw on such funds. If we were obliged to enter into a theoretical deliberation on every occasion, before we act, life would be at a stand, and art would be impracticable.

It appears to me, therefore, that our first thoughts, that is, the effect which anything produces on our minds, on its first appearance, is never to be forgotten; and it demands for that reason, because it is the first, to be laid up with care. If this be not done, the artist may happen to impose on himself by partial reasoning; by a cold consideration of those animated thoughts which proceed, not perhaps from caprice or rashness (as he may afterwards conceit), but from the fulness of his mind, enriched with the copious stores of all the various inventions which he had ever seen, or had ever passed in his mind. These ideas are infused into his design, without any conscious effort; but if he be not on his guard, he may reconsider and correct them, till the whole matter is reduced to a commonplace invention.

This is sometimes the effect of what I mean to caution you against; that is to say, an unfounded distrust of the imagination and feeling, in favor of narrow, partial, confined, argumentative theories; and of principles that seem to apply to the design in hand; without considering those general impressions on the fancy in which real principles of *sound reason*, and of much more weight and importance, are involved, and, as it were, lie hid, under the appearance of a sort of vulgar sentiment.

Reason, without doubt, must ultimately determine everything; at this minute it is required to inform us when that very reason is to give way to feeling.

Though I have often spoken of that mean conception of our art which confines it to mere imitation, I must add, that it may be narrowed to such a mere matter of experiment, as to exclude from it the application of science, which alone gives dignity and compass to any art. But to find proper foundations for science is neither to narrow nor to vulgarize it; and this is sufficiently exemplified in the success of experimental philosophy. It is the false system of reasoning, grounded on a partial view of things, against which I would most earnestly guard you. And I do it the rather, because those narrow theories, so coincident with the poorest and most miserable practice, and which are adopted to give it countenance, have not had their origin in the poorest minds, but in the mistakes, or possibly in the mistaken interpretations, of great and commanding authorities. We are not therefore in this case misled by feeling, but by false speculation.

When such a man as Plato speaks of painting as only an imitative art, and that our pleasure proceeds from observing and acknowledging the truth of the imitation, I think he misleads us by a partial theory. It is in this poor, partial, and so far false view of the art, that Cardinal Bembo has chosen to distinguish even Raffaelle himself, whom our enthusiasm honors with the name of Divine. The same sentiment is adopted by Pope in his epitaph on Sir Godfrey Kneller; and he turns the panegyric solely on imitation, as it is a sort of deception.

I shall not think my time misemployed, if by any means I may contribute to confirm your opinion of what ought to be the object of your pursuit; because, though the best critics must always have exploded this strange idea, yet I know that there is a disposition towards a perpetual recurrence to it, on account of its simplicity and superficial plausibility. For this reason I shall beg leave to lay before you a few thoughts on this subject; to throw out some hints that may lead your minds to an opinion (which I take to be the truth), that painting is not only to be considered as an imitation, operating by deception, but that it is, and ought to be, in many points of view, and strictly speaking, no imitation at all of external nature. Perhaps it ought to be as far removed from the vulgar idea of imitation, as the refined civilized state in which we live, is removed from a gross state of nature; and those who have not cultivated their imaginations, which the majority of mankind certainly have not, may be said, in regard to arts, to continue in this state of nature. Such men will always prefer imitation to that excellence which is addressed to another faculty that they do not possess; but these are not the persons to whom a painter is to look, any more than a judge of morals and manners ought to refer controverted points upon those subjects to the opinions of people taken from the banks of the Ohio, or from New Holland.

It is the lowest style only of arts, whether of painting, poetry, or music, that may be said, in the vulgar sense, to be naturally pleasing. The higher efforts of those arts, we know by experience, do not affect minds wholly uncultivated. This refined taste is the consequence of education and habit; we are born only with a capacity of entertaining this refinement, as we are born with a disposition to receive and obey all the rules and regulations of society; and so far it may be said to be natural to us, and no further.

What has been said, may show the artist how necessary it is, when he looks about him for the advice and criticism of his friends, to make some distinction of the character, taste, experience, and observation in this art of those from whom it is received. An ignorant uneducated man may, like Apelles's critic, be a competent judge of the truth of the representation of a sandal; or to go somewhat higher, like Molière's old woman, may decide upon what is nature, in regard to comic humor; but a critic in the higher style of art ought to possess the same refined taste, which directed the artist in his work.

To illustrate this principle by a comparison with other arts, I shall now produce some instances to show, that they, as well as our own art, renounce the narrow idea of nature, and the narrow theories derived from that mistaken principle, and apply to that reason only which informs us not what imitation is,—a natural representation of a given object,—but what it is natural for the imagination to be delighted with. And perhaps there is no better way of acquiring this knowledge, than by this kind of analogy: each art will corroborate and mutually reflect the truth on the other. Such a kind of juxtaposition may likewise have this use, that whilst the artist is amusing himself in the contemplation of other arts, he may habitually transfer the principles of those arts to that which he professes; which ought to be always present in his mind, and to which everything is to be referred.

So far is art from being derived from, or having any immediate intercourse with, particular nature as its model, that there are many arts that set out with a professed deviation from it.

This is certainly not so exactly true in regard to painting and sculpture. Our elements are laid in gross common nature,—an exact imitation of what is before us: but when we advance to the higher state, we consider this power of imitation, though first in the order of acquisition, as by no means the highest in the scale of perfection.

Poetry addresses itself to the same faculties and the same dispositions as painting, though by different means. The object of both is to accommodate itself to all the natural propensities and inclinations of the mind. The very existence of poetry depends on the license it assumes of deviating from actual nature, in order to gratify natural propensities by other means, which are found by experience full as capable of affording such gratification. It sets out with a language in the highest degree artificial, a construction of measured words, such as never is, nor ever was used by man. Let this measure be what it may, whether hexameter or any other metre used in Latin or Greek—or rhyme, or blank verse varied with pauses and accents, in modern languages,—they are all equally removed from nature, and equally a violation of common speech. When this artificial mode has been established as the vehicle of sentiment, there is another principle in the human mind, to which the work must be referred, which still renders it more artificial, carries it still further from common nature, and deviates only to render it more perfect. That principle is the sense of congruity, coherence, and consistency, which is a real existing principle in man; and it must be gratified. Therefore having once adopted a style and a measure not found in common discourse, it is required that the sentiments also should be in the same proportion elevated above common nature, from the necessity of there being an agreement of the parts among themselves, that one uniform whole may be produced.

To correspond therefore with this general system of deviation from nature, the manner in which poetry is offered to the ear, the tone in which it is recited, should be as far removed from the tone of conversation, as the words of which that poetry is composed. This naturally suggests the idea of modulating the voice by art, which I suppose may be considered as accomplished to the highest degree of excellence in the recitative of the Italian Opera; as we may conjecture it was in the chorus that attended the ancient drama. And though the most violent passions, the highest distress, even death itself, are expressed in singing or recitative, I would not admit as sound criticism the condemnation of such exhibitions on account of their being unnatural.

If it is natural for our senses, and our imaginations, to be delighted with singing, with instrumental music, with poetry, and with graceful action, taken separately (none of them being in the vulgar sense natural, even in that separate state); it is conformable to experience, and therefore agreeable to reason as connected with and referred to experience, that we should also be delighted with this union of music, poetry, and graceful action, joined to every circumstance of pomp and magnificence calculated to strike the senses of the spectator. Shall reason stand in the way, and tell us that we ought not to like what we know we do like, and prevent us from feeling the full effect of this complicated exertion of art? This is what I would understand by poets and painters being allowed to dare everything; for what can be more daring, than accomplishing the purpose and end of art, by a complication of means, none of which have their archetypes in actual nature?

So far therefore is servile imitation from being necessary, that whatever is familiar, or in any way reminds us of what we see and hear every day, perhaps does not belong to the higher provinces of art, either in poetry or painting. The mind is to be transported, as Shakespeare expresses it, *beyond the ignorant present* to ages past. Another and a higher order of beings is supposed; and to those beings everything which is introduced into the work must correspond. Of this conduct, under these circumstances, the Roman and Florentine schools afford sufficient examples. Their style by this means is raised and elevated above all others; and by the same means the compass of art itself is enlarged.

We often see grave and great subjects attempted by artists of another school; who, though excellent in the lower class of art, proceeding on the principles which regulate that class, and not recollecting, or not knowing, that they were to address themselves to another faculty of the mind, have become perfectly ridiculous.

The picture which I have at present in my thoughts is a sacrifice of Iphigenia, painted by Jan Steen, a painter of whom I have formerly had occasion to speak with the highest approbation; and even in this picture, the subject of which is by no means adapted to his genius, there is nature and expression; but it is such expression, and the countenances are so familiar, and consequently so vulgar, and the whole accompanied with such finery of silks and velvets, that one would be almost tempted to doubt, whether the artist did not purposely intend to burlesque his subject.

Instances of the same kind we frequently see in poetry. Parts of Hobbes's translation of Homer are remembered and repeated merely for the familiarity and meanness of their phraseology, so ill corresponding with the ideas which ought to have been expressed, and, as I conceive, with the style of the original.

We may proceed in the same manner through the comparatively inferior branches of art. There are in works of that class, the same distinction of a higher and a lower style; and they take their rank and degree in proportion as the artist departs more, or less, from common nature, and makes it an object of his attention to strike the imagination of the spectator by ways belonging specially to art,—unobserved and untaught out of the school of its practice.

If our judgments are to be directed by narrow, vulgar, untaught, or rather ill-taught reason, we must prefer a portrait by Denner or any other high finisher, to those of Titian or Vandyck; and a landscape of Vanderheyden to those of Titian or Rubens; for they are certainly more exact representations of nature.

If we suppose a view of nature represented with all the truth of the *camera obscura*, and the same scene represented by a great artist, how little and mean will the one appear in comparison of the other, where no superiority is supposed from the choice of the subject. The scene shall be the same, the difference only will be in the manner in which it is presented to the eye. With what additional superiority then will the same artist appear when he has the power of selecting his materials, as well as elevating his style? Like Nicolas Poussin, he transports us to the environs of ancient Rome, with all the objects which a literary education makes so precious and interesting to man: or, like Sebastian Bourdon, he leads us to the dark antiquity of the Pyramids of Egypt; or, like Claude Lorrain, he conducts us to the tranquility of arcadian scenes and fairyland.

Like the history-painter, a painter of landscapes in this style and with this conduct sends the imagination back into antiquity; and, like the poet, he makes the elements sympathize with his subject; whether the clouds roll in volumes, like those of Titian or Salvator Rosa, or, like those of Claude, are gilded with the setting sun; whether the mountains have sudden and bold projections, or are gently sloped; whether the branches of his trees shoot out abruptly in right angles from their trunks, or follow each other with only a gentle inclination. All these circumstances contribute to the general character of the work, whether it be of the elegant, or of the more sublime kind. If we add to this the powerful materials of lightness and darkness, over which the artist has complete dominion, to vary and dispose them as he pleases; to diminish, or increase them, as will best suit his purpose, and correspond to the general idea of his work; a landscape thus conducted, under the influence of a poetical mind, will have the same superiority over the more ordinary and common views, as Milton's *Allegro* and *Penseroso* have over a cold prosaic narration or description; and such a picture would make a more forcible impression on the mind than the real scenes, were they presented before us.

If we look abroad to other arts, we may observe the same distinction, the same division into two classes; each of them acting under the influence of two different principles, in which the one follows nature, the other varies it, and sometimes departs from it.

The theatre, which is said *to hold the mirror up to nature*, comprehends both those sides. The lower kind of comedy or farce, like the inferior style of painting, the more naturally it is represented, the better; but the higher appears to me to aim no more at imitation, so far as it belongs to anything like deception, or to expect that the spectators should think that the events there represented are really passing before them, than Raffaelle in his cartoons, or Poussin in his sacraments, expected it to be believed, even for a moment, that what they exhibited were real figures.

For want of this distinction, the world is filled with false criticism. Raffaelle is praised for naturalness and deception, which he certainly has not accomplished, and as certainly never intended; and our late great actor, Garrick, has been as ignorantly praised by his friend Fielding; who doubtless imagined he had hit upon an ingenious device, by introducing in one of his novels (otherwise a work of the highest merit) an ignorant man, mistaking Garrick's representation of a scene in Hamlet for reality. A very little reflection will convince us, that there is not one circumstance in the whole scene that is of the nature of deception. The merit and excellence of Shakespeare, and of Garrick, when they were engaged in such scenes, is of a different and much higher kind. But what adds to the falsity of this intended compliment is that the best stage-representation appears even more unnatural to a person of such a character, who is supposed never to have seen a play before, than it does to those who have had a habit of allowing for those necessary deviations from nature which the art requires.

In theatric representation, great allowances must always be made for the place in which the exhibition is represented; for the surrounding company, the lighted candles, the scenes visibly shifted in your sight, and the language of blank verse, so different from common English; which merely as English must appear surprising in the mouths of Hamlet, and all the court and natives of Denmark. These allowances are made; but their being made puts an end to all manner of deception: and further, we know that the more low, illiterate, and vulgar any person is, the less he will be disposed to make these allowances, and of course to be deceived by any imitation; the things in which the trespass against nature and common probability is made in favor of the theatre being quite within the sphere of such uninformed men.

Though I have no intention of entering into all the circumstances of unnaturalness in theatrical representations, I must observe, that even the expression of violent passion is not always the most excellent in proportion as it is the most natural; so great terror and such disagreeable sensations may be communicated to the audience, that the balance may be destroyed by which pleasure is preserved, and holds its predominance in the mind: violent distortion of action, harsh screamings of the voice, however great the occasion, or however natural on such occasion, are therefore not admissible in the theatric art. Many of these allowed deviations from nature arise from the necessity which there is, that everything should be raised and enlarged beyond its natural state; that the full effect may come home to the spectator, which otherwise would be lost in the comparatively extensive space of the theatre. Hence the deliberate and stately step, the studied grace of action, which seems to enlarge the dimensions of the actor, and alone to fill the stage. All this unnaturalness, though right and proper in its place, would appear affected and ridiculous in a private room; *quid enim deformius, quam scenam in vitam transferre?*[1]

And here I must observe, and I believe it may be considered as a general rule, that no art can be engrafted with success on another art. For though they all profess the same origin, and to proceed from the same stock,

---

[1] "For what [would be] more unbecoming than to transfer a scene from drama to actual life?"

yet each has its own peculiar modes both of imitating nature, and of deviating from it, each for the accomplishment of its own particular purpose. These deviations, more especially, will not bear transplantation to another soil.

If a painter should endeavor to copy the theatrical pomp and parade of dress and attitude, instead of that simplicity, which is not a greater beauty in life than it is in painting, we should condemn such pictures, as painted in the meanest style.

So also gardening, as far as gardening is an art, or entitled to that appellation, is a deviation from nature; for if the true taste consists, as many hold, in banishing every appearance of art, or any traces of the footsteps of man, it would then be no longer a garden. Even though we define it "Nature to advantage dress'd," and in some sense is such, and much more beautiful and commodious for the recreation of man; it is, however, when so dressed, no longer a subject for the pencil of a landscape-painter, as all landscape-painters know, who love to have recourse to nature herself, and to dress her according to the principles of their own art; which are far different from those of gardening, even when conducted according to the most approved principles; and such as a landscape-painter himself would adopt in the disposition of his own grounds, for his own private satisfaction.

I have brought together as many instances as appear necessary to make out the several points which I wished to suggest to your consideration in this discourse, that your own thoughts may lead you further in the use that may be made of the analogy of the arts, and of the restraint which a full understanding of the diversity of many of their principles ought to impose on the employment of that analogy.

The great end of all those arts is, to make an impression on the imagination and the feeling. The imitation of nature frequently does this. Sometimes it fails, and something else succeeds. I think therefore the true test of all the arts is not solely whether the production is a true copy of nature, but whether it answers the end of art, which is to produce a pleasing effect upon the mind.

It remains only to speak a few words of architecture, which does not come under the denomination of an imitative art. It applies itself, like music (and I believe we may add poetry), directly to the imagination, without the intervention of any kind of imitation.

There is in architecture, as in painting, an inferior branch of art, in which the imagination appears to have no concern. It does not, however, acquire the name of a polite and liberal art, from its usefulness, or administering to our wants or necessities, but from some higher principle: we are sure that in the hands of a man of genius it is capable of inspiring sentiment, and of filling the mind with great and sublime ideas.

It may be worth the attention of artists to consider what materials are in their hands, that may contribute to this end; and whether this art has it not in its power to address itself to the imagination with effect, by more ways than are generally employed by architects.

To pass over the effect produced by that general symmetry and proportion, by which the eye is delighted, as the ear is with music, architecture certainly possesses many principles in common with poetry and painting. Among those which may be reckoned as the first is that of affecting the imagination by means of association of ideas. Thus, for instance, as we have naturally a veneration for antiquity, whatever building brings to our remembrance ancient customs and manners, such as the castles of the barons of ancient chivalry, is sure to give this delight. Hence it is that *towers and battlements*[2] are so often selected by the painter and the poet, to make a part of the composition of their ideal landscape; and it is from hence in a great degree, that in the buildings of Vanbrugh, who was a poet as well as an architect, there is a greater display of imagination than we shall find perhaps in any other, and this is the ground of the effect we feel in many of his works, notwithstanding the faults with which many of them are justly charged. For this purpose, Vanbrugh appears to have had recourse to some of the principles of the Gothic architecture; which, though not so ancient as the Grecian, is more so to our imagination, with which the artist is more concerned than with absolute truth.

The barbaric splendor of those Asiatic buildings, which are now publishing by a member of this Academy, may possibly, in the same manner, furnish an architect, not with models to copy, but with hints of composition and general effect, which would not otherwise have occurred.

It is, I know, a delicate and hazardous thing (and as such I have already pointed it out), to carry the principles of one art to another, or even to reconcile in one object the various modes of the same art, when they proceed on different principles. The sound rules of the Grecian architecture are not to be lightly sacrificed. A deviation from them, or even an addition to them, is like a deviation or addition to, or from, the rules of other arts,— fit only for a great master, who is thoroughly conversant in the nature of man, as well as all combinations in his own art.

It may not be amiss for the architect to take advantage *sometimes* of that to which I am sure the painter ought always to have his eyes open, I

[2] Towers and battlements it sees
  Bosom'd high in tufted trees.—MILTON, "L'Allegro."

mean the use of accidents; to follow when they lead, and to improve them, rather than always to trust to a regular plan. It often happens that additions have been made to houses, at various times, for use or pleasure. As such buildings depart from regularity, they now and then acquire something of scenery by this accident, which I should think might not unsuccessfully be adopted by an architect, in an original plan, if it does not too much interfere with convenience. Variety and intricacy is a beauty and excellence in every other of the arts which address the imagination; and why not in architecture?

The forms and turnings of the streets of London, and other old towns, are produced by accident, without any original plan or design; but they are not always the less pleasant to the walker or spectator, on that account. On the contrary, if the city had been built on the regular plan of Sir Christopher Wren, the effect might have been, as we know it is in some new parts of the town, rather unpleasing; the uniformity might have produced weariness, and a slight degree of disgust.

I can pretend to no skill in the detail of architecture. I judge now of the art, merely as a painter. When I speak of Vanbrugh, I mean to speak of him in the language of our art. To speak then of Vanbrugh in the language of a painter, he had originality of invention, he understood light and shadow, and had great skill in composition. To support his principal object he produced his second and third groups or masses; he perfectly understood in his art what is the most difficult in ours, the conduct of the background, by which the design and invention is set off to the greatest advantage. What the background is in painting, in architecture is the real ground on which the building is erected; and no architect took greater care than he that his work should not appear crude and hard: that is, it did not abruptly start out of the ground without expectation or preparation.

This is a tribute which a painter owes to an architect who composed like a painter; and was defrauded of the due reward of his merit by the wits of his time, who did not understand the principles of composition in poetry better than he; and who knew little or nothing of what he understood perfectly, the general ruling principles of architecture and painting. His fate was that of the great Perrault; both were the objects of the petulant sarcasms of factious men of letters; and both have left some of the fairest ornaments which to this day decorate their several countries; the façade of the Louvre, Blenheim, and Castle Howard.

Upon the whole, it seems to me, that the object and intention of all the arts is to supply the natural imperfection of things, and often to gratify the mind by realizing and embodying what never existed but in the imagination.

It is allowed on all hands, that facts and events, however they may bind the historian, have no dominion over the poet or the painter. With us, history is made to bend and conform to this great idea of art. And why? Because these arts, in their highest province, are not addressed to the gross senses, but to the desires of the mind, to that spark of divinity which we have within, impatient of being circumscribed and pent up by the world which is about us. Just so much as our art has of this, just so much of dignity, I had almost said of divinity, it exhibits; and those of our artists who possessed this mark of distinction in the highest degree acquired from thence the glorious appellation of Divine.

Roger Fry

AN ESSAY IN AESTHETICS*

A certain painter, not without some reputation at the present day, once wrote a little book on the art he practices, in which he gave a definition of that art so succinct that I take it as a point of departure for this essay.

"The art of painting," says that eminent authority, "is the art of imitating solid objects upon a flat surface by means of pigments." It is delightfully simple, but prompts the question—Is that all? And, if so, what a deal of unnecessary fuss has been made about it. Now, it is useless to deny that our modern writer has some very respectable authorities behind him. Plato, indeed, gave a very similar account of the affair, and himself put the question—is it then worth while? And, being scrupulously and relentlessly logical, he decided that it was not worth while, and proceeded to turn the artists out of his ideal republic. For all that, the world has continued obstinately to consider that painting was worth while, and though, indeed, it has never quite made up its mind as to what, exactly, the graphic arts did for it, it has persisted in honoring and admiring its painters.

Can we arrive at any conclusions as to the nature of the graphic arts, which will at all explain our feelings about them, which will at least put them into some kind of relation with the other arts, and not leave us in the extreme perplexity, engendered by any theory of mere imitation? For, I suppose, it must be admitted that if imitation is the sole purpose of the

* From Roger Fry's *Vision and Design*. Copyright, 1920, by Chatto & Windus, Ltd. Reprinted by permission of Chatto & Windus, Ltd.

Roger Fry (1866-1934) was an English art critic, art historian, painter, and member of the famous Bloomsbury Group in London. He wrote extensively on art and some of its aesthetic problems.

graphic arts, it is surprising that the works of such arts are ever looked upon as more than curiosities, or ingenious toys, are ever taken seriously by grown-up people. Moreover, it will be surprising that they have no recognizable affinity with other arts, such as music or architecture, in which the imitation of actual objects is a negligible quantity.

To form such conclusions is the aim I have put before myself in this essay. Even if the results are not decisive, the inquiry may lead us to a view of the graphic arts that will not be altogether unfruitful.

I must begin with some elementary psychology, with a consideration of the nature of instincts. A great many objects in the world, when presented to our senses, put in motion a complex nervous machinery, which ends in some instinctive appropriate action. We see a wild bull in a field; quite without our conscious interference a nervous process goes on, which, unless we interfere forcibly, ends in the appropriate reaction of flight. The nervous mechanism which results in flight causes a certain state of consciousness, which we call the emotion of fear. The whole of animal life, and a great part of human life, is made up of these instinctive reactions to sensible objects, and their accompanying emotions. But man has the peculiar faculty of calling up again in his mind the echo of past experiences of this kind, of going over it again, "in imagination" as we say. He has, therefore, the possibility of a double life; one the actual life, the other the imaginative life. Between these two lives there is this great distinction, that in the actual life the processes of natural selection have brought it about that the instinctive reaction, such, for instance, as flight from danger, shall be the important part of the whole process, and it is towards this that the man bends his whole conscious endeavor. But in the imaginative life no such action is necessary, and, therefore, the whole consciousness may be focussed upon the perceptive and the emotional aspects of the experience. In this way we get, in the imaginative life, a different set of values, and a different kind of perception.

We can get a curious side glimpse of the nature of this imaginative life from the cinematograph. This resembles actual life in almost every respect, except that what the psychologists call the conative part of our reaction to sensations, that is to say, the appropriate resultant action is cut off. If, in a cinematograph, we see a runaway horse and cart, we do not have to think either of getting out of the way or heroically interposing ourselves. The result is that in the first place we *see* the event much more clearly; see a number of quite interesting but irrelevant things, which in real life could not struggle into our consciousness, bent, as it would be, entirely upon the problem of our appropriate reaction. I remember seeing in a cinematograph the arrival of a train at a foreign station and the people descending from the carriages; there was no platform, and to my intense surprise I saw several people turn right round after reaching the ground, as though to orientate themselves; an almost ridiculous performance, which I had never noticed in all the many hundred occasions on which such a scene had passed before my eyes in real life. The fact being that at a station one is never really a spectator of events, but an actor engaged in the drama of luggage or prospective seats, and one actually sees only so much as may help to the appropriate action.

In the second place, with regard to the visions of the cinematograph, one notices that whatever emotions are aroused by them, though they are likely to be weaker than those of ordinary life, are presented more clearly to the consciousness. If the scene presented be one of an accident, our pity and horror, though weak, since we know that no one is really hurt, are felt quite purely, since they cannot, as they would in life, pass at once into actions of assistance.

A somewhat similar effect to that of the cinematograph can be obtained by watching a mirror in which a street scene is reflected. If we look at the street itself we are almost sure to adjust ourselves in some way to its actual existence. We recognize an acquaintance, and wonder why he looks so dejected this morning, or become interested in a new fashion in hats—the moment we do that the spell is broken, we are reacting to life itself in however slight a degree, but, in the mirror, it is easier to abstract ourselves completely, and look upon the changing scene as a whole. It then, at once, takes on the visionary quality, and we become true spectators, not selecting what we will see, but seeing everything equally, and thereby we come to notice a number of appearances and relations of appearances, which would have escaped our notice before, owing to that perpetual economizing by selection of what impressions we will assimilate, which in life we perform by unconscious processes. The frame of the mirror, then, does to some extent turn the reflected scene from one that belongs to our actual life into one that belongs rather to the imaginative life. The frame of the mirror makes its surface into a very rudimentary work of art, since it helps us to attain to the artistic vision. For that is what, as you will already have guessed, I have been coming to all this time, namely that the work of art is intimately connected with the secondary imaginative life, which all men live to a greater or less extent.

That the graphic arts are the expression of the imaginative life rather than a copy of actual life might be guessed from observing children. Children, if left to themselves, never, I believe, copy what they see, never, as we say, "draw from nature," but express, with a delightful freedom and sincerity, the mental images which make up their own imaginative lives.

Art, then, is an expression and a stimulus of this imaginative life, which is separated from actual life by the absence of responsive action. Now this responsive action implies in actual life moral responsibility. In art we have no such moral responsibility—it presents a life freed from the binding necessities of our actual existence.

What then is the justification for this life of the imagination which all human beings live more or less fully? To the pure moralist, who accepts nothing but ethical values, in order to be justified, it must be shown not only *not* to hinder but actually to forward right action, otherwise it is not only useless but, since it absorbs our energies, positively harmful. To such a one two views are possible, one the Puritanical view at its narrowest, which regards the life of the imagination as no better or worse than a life of sensual pleasure, and therefore entirely reprehensible. The other view is to argue that the imaginative life does subserve morality. And this is inevitably the view taken by moralists like Ruskin, to whom the imaginative life is yet an absolute necessity. It is a view which leads to some very hard special pleading, even to a self-deception which is in itself morally undesirable.

But here comes in the question of religion, for religion is also an affair of the imaginative life, and, though it claims to have a direct effect upon conduct, I do not suppose that the religious person if he were wise would justify religion entirely by its effect on morality, since that, historically speaking, has not been by any means uniformly advantageous. He would probably say that the religious experience was one which corresponded to certain spiritual capacities of human nature, the exercise of which is in itself good and desirable apart from their effect upon actual life. And so, too, I think the artist might if he chose take a mystical attitude, and declare that the fullness and completeness of the imaginative life he leads may correspond to an existence more real and more important than any that we know of in mortal life.

And in saying that, his appeal would find a sympathetic echo in most minds, for most people would, I think, say that the pleasures derived from art were of an altogether different character and more fundamental than merely sensual pleasures, that they did exercise some faculties which are felt to belong to whatever part of us there may be which is not entirely ephemeral and material.

It might even be that from this point of view we should rather justify actual life by its relation to the imaginative, justify nature by its likeness to art. I mean this, that since the imaginative life comes in the course of time to represent more or less what mankind feels to be the completest expression of its own nature, the freest use of its innate capacities, the actual life may be explained and justified by its approximation here and there, however partially and inadequately, to that freer and fuller life.

Before leaving this question of the justification of art, let me put it in another way. The imaginative life of a people has very different levels at different times, and these levels do not always correspond with the general level of the morality of actual life. Thus in the thirteenth century we read of barbarity and cruelty which would shock even us; we may, I think, admit that our moral level, our general humanity is decidedly higher to-day, but the level of our imaginative life is incomparably lower; we are satisfied there with a grossness, a sheer barbarity and squalor which would have shocked the thirteenth century profoundly. Let us admit the moral gain gladly, but do we not also feel a loss; do we not feel that the average business man would be in every way a more admirable, more respectable being if his imaginative life were not so squalid and incoherent? And, if we admit any loss then, there is some function in human nature other than a purely ethical one, which is worthy of exercise.

Now the imaginative life has its own history both in the race and in the individual. In the individual life one of the first effects of freeing experience from the necessities of appropriate responsive action is to indulge recklessly the emotion of self-aggrandizement. The day-dreams of a child are filled with extravagant romances in which he is always the invincible hero. Music —which of all the arts supplies the strongest stimulus to the imaginative life, and at the same time has the least power of controlling its direction—music, at certain stages of people's lives, has the effect merely of arousing in an almost absurd degree this egoistic elation, and Tolstoy appears to believe that this is its only possible effect. But with the teaching of experience and the growth of character the imaginative life comes to respond to other instincts and to satisfy other desires, until, indeed, it reflects the highest aspirations and the deepest aversions of which human nature is capable.

In dreams and when under the influence of drugs the imaginative life passes out of our own control, and in such cases its experiences may be highly undesirable, but whenever it remains under our own control it must always be on the whole a desirable life. That is not to say that it is always pleasant, for it is pretty clear that mankind is so constituted as to desire much besides pleasure, and we shall meet among the great artists, the great exponents, that is, of the imaginative life, many to whom the merely pleasant is very rarely a part of what is desirable. But this desirability of the imaginative life does distinguish it very sharply from actual life, and is the direct result of that first fundamental difference, its freedom from necessary external conditions. Art, then, is, if I am right, the chief organ of the imaginative life; it is by art that it is stimulated and controlled within us, and, as we have seen, the imaginative life is distinguished by the greater clearness of its perception, and the greater purity and freedom of its emotion.

First with regard to the greater clearness of perception. The needs of our actual life are so imperative, that the sense of vision becomes highly specialized in their service. With an admirable economy we learn to see only so much as is needful for our purposes; but this is in fact very little, just enough to recognize and identify each object or person; that done, they go into an entry in our mental catalogue and are no more really seen. In actual life the normal person really only reads the labels as it were on the objects around him and troubles no further. Almost all the things which are useful in any way put on more or less this cap of invisibility. It is only when an object exists in our lives for no other purpose than to be seen that we really look at it, as for instance at a China ornament or a precious stone, and towards such even the most normal person adopts to some extent the artistic attitude of pure vision abstracted from necessity.

Now this specialization of vision goes so far that ordinary people have almost no idea of what things really look like, so that oddly enough the one standard that popular criticism applies to painting, namely, whether it is like nature or not, is one which most people are, by the whole tenor of their lives, prevented from applying properly. The only things they have ever really *looked* at being other pictures; the moment an artist who has looked at nature brings to them a clear report of something definitely seen by him, they are wildly indignant at its untruth to nature. This has happened so constantly in our own time that there is no need to prove it. One instance will suffice. Monet is an artist whose chief claim to recognition lies in the fact of his astonishing power of faithfully reproducing certain aspects of nature, but his really naïve innocence and sincerity were taken by the public to be the most audacious humbug, and it required the teaching of men like Bastien-Lepage, who cleverly compromised between the truth and an accepted convention of what things looked like, to bring the world gradually round to admitting truths which a single walk in the country with purely unbiassed vision would have established beyond doubt.

But though this clarified sense perception which we discover in the imaginative life is of great interest, and although it plays a larger part in the graphic arts than in any other, it might perhaps be doubted whether, interesting, curious, fascinating as it is, this aspect of the imaginative life would ever by itself make art of profound importance to mankind. But it is different, I think, with the emotional aspect. We have admitted that the emotions of the imaginative are generally weaker than those of actual life. The picture of a saint being slowly flayed alive, revolting as it is, will not produce the same physical sensations of sickening disgust that a modern man would feel if he could assist at the actual event; but they have a compensating clearness of presentment to the consciousness. The more poignant emotions of actual life have, I think, a kind of numbing effect analogous to the paralyzing influence of fear in some animals; but even if this experience be not generally admitted, all will admit that the need for responsive action hurries us along and prevents us from ever realizing fully what the emotion is that we feel, from co-ordinating it perfectly with other states. In short, the motives we actually experience are too close to us to enable us to feel them clearly. They are in a sense unintelligible. In the imaginative life, on the contrary, we can both feel the emotion and watch it. When we are really moved at the theatre we are always both on the stage and in the auditorium.

Yet another point about the emotions of the imaginative life—since they require no responsive action we can give them a new valuation. In real life we must to some extent cultivate those emotions which lead to useful action, and we are bound to appraise emotions according to the resultant action. So that, for instance, the feelings of rivalry and emulation do get an encouragement which perhaps they scarcely deserve, whereas certain feelings which appear to have a high intrinsic value get almost no stimulus in actual life. For instance, those feelings to which the name of the cosmic emotion has been somewhat unhappily given find almost no place in life, but, since they seem to belong to certain very deep springs of our nature, do become of great importance in the arts.

Morality, then, appreciates emotion by the standard of resultant action. Art appreciates emotion in and for itself.

This view of the essential importance in art of the expression of the emotions is the basis of Tolstoy's marvelously original and yet perverse and even exasperating book, "What is Art?" and I willingly confess, while disagreeing with almost all his results, how much I owe to him.

He gives an example of what he means by calling art the means of communicating emotions. He says, let us suppose a boy to have been pursued in the forest by a bear. If he returns to the village and merely states that he was pursued by a bear and escaped, that is ordinary language, the means of communicating facts or ideas; but if he describes his state first of heedlessness, then of sudden alarm and terror as the bear appears, and finally of relief when he gets away, and describes this so that his hearers share his emotions, then his description is a work of art.

Now in so far as the boy does this in order to urge the villagers to go out and kill the bear, though he may be using artistic methods, his speech is not a pure work of art; but if of a winter evening the boy relates his experience for the sake of the enjoyment of his adventure in retrospect, or better still, if he makes up the whole story for the sake of the imagined emotions, then his speech becomes a pure work of art. But Tolstoy takes the other view, and values the emotions aroused by art entirely for their reaction upon actual life, a view which he courageously maintains even when it leads him to condemn the whole of Michelangelo, Raphael and Titian, and most of Beethoven, not to mention nearly everything he himself has written, as bad or false art.

Such a view would, I think, give pause to any less heroic spirit. He would wonder whether mankind could have always been so radically wrong about a function that, whatever its value be, is almost universal. And in point of fact he will have to find some other word to denote what we now call art. Nor does Tolstoy's theory even carry him safely through his own book, since, in his examples of morally desirable and therefore good art, he has to admit that these are to be found, for the most part, among works of inferior quality. Here, then, is at once the tacit admission that another standard than morality is applicable. We must therefore give up the attempt to judge the work of art by its reaction on life, and consider it as an expression of emotions regarded as ends in themselves. And this brings us back to the idea we had already arrived at, of art as the expression of the imaginative life.

If, then, an object of any kind is created by man not for use, for its fitness to actual life, but as an object of art, an object subserving the imaginative life, what will its qualities be? It must in the first place be adapted to that disinterested intensity of contemplation, which we have found to be the effect of cutting off the responsive action. It must be suited to that heightened power of perception which we found to result therefrom.

And the first quality that we demand in our sensations will be order, without which our sensations will be troubled and perplexed, and the other quality will be variety, without which they will not be fully stimulated.

It may be objected that many things in nature, such as flowers, possess these two qualities of order and variety in a high degree, and these objects do undoubtedly stimulate and satisfy that clear disinterested contemplation which is characteristic of the æsthetic attitude. But in our reaction to a work of art there is something more—there is the consciousness of purpose, the consciousness of a peculiar relation of sympathy with the man who made this thing in order to arouse precisely the sensations we experience. And when we come to the higher works of art, where sensations are so arranged that they arouse in us deep emotions, this feeling of a special tie with the man who expressed them becomes very strong. We feel that he has expressed something which was latent in us all the time, but which we never realized, that he has revealed us to ourselves in revealing himself. And this recognition of purpose is, I believe, an essential part of the æsthetic judgment proper.

The perception of purposeful order and variety in an object gives us the feeling which we express by saying that it is beautiful, but when by means of sensations our emotions are aroused we demand purposeful order and variety in them also, and if this can only be brought about by the sacrifice of sensual beauty we willingly overlook its abence.

Thus, there is no excuse for a china pot being ugly, there is every reason why Rembrandt's and Degas' pictures should be, from the purely sensual point of view, supremely and magnificently ugly.

This, I think, will explain the apparent contradiction between two distinct uses of the word beauty, one for that which has sensuous charm, and one for the æsthetic approval of works of imaginative art where the objects presented to us are often of extreme ugliness. Beauty in the former sense belongs to works of art where only the perceptual aspect of the imaginative life is exercised, beauty in the second sense becomes as it were supersensual, and is concerned with the appropriateness and intensity of the emotions aroused. When these emotions are aroused in a way that satisfies fully the needs of the imaginative life we approve and delight in the sensations through which we enjoy that heightened experience because they possess purposeful order and variety in relation to those emotions.

One chief aspect of order in a work of art is unity; unity of some kind is necessary for our restful contemplation of the work of art as a whole, since if it lacks unity we cannot contemplate it in its entirety, but we shall pass outside it to other things necessary to complete its unity.

In a picture this unity is due to a balancing of the attractions of the eye about the central line of the picture. The result of this balance of attractions is that the eye rests willingly within the bounds of the picture. Dr. Denman Ross of Harvard University has made a most valuable study of the elementary considerations upon which this balance is based in his "Theory of Pure Design." He sums up his results in the formula that a composition is of value in proportion to the number of orderly connections which it displays.

Dr. Ross wisely restricts himself to the study of abstract and meaningless forms. The moment representation is introduced forms have an entirely new set of values. Thus a line which indicated the sudden bend of a head in a certain direction would have far more than its mere value as line in the composition because of the attraction which a marked gesture has for the eye. In almost all paintings this disturbance of the purely decorative values by reason of the representative effect takes place, and the problem becomes too complex for geometrical proof.

This merely decorative unity is, moreover, of very different degrees of intensity in different artists and in different periods. The necessity for a closely woven geometrical texture in the composition is much greater in heroic and monumental design than in genre pieces on a small scale.

It seems also probable that our appreciation of unity in pictorial design is of two kinds. We are so accustomed to consider only the unity which results from the balance of a number of attractions presented to the eye simultaneously in a framed picture that we forget the possibility of other pictorial forms.

In certain Chinese paintings the length is so great that we cannot take in the whole picture at once, nor are we intended to do so. Sometimes a landscape is painted upon a roll of silk so long that we can only look at it in successive segments. As we unroll it at one end and roll it up at the other we traverse wide stretches of country, tracing, perhaps, all the vicissitudes of a river from its source to the sea, and yet, when this is well done, we have received a very keen impression of pictorial unity.

Such a successive unity is of course familiar to us in literature and music, and it plays its part in the graphic arts. It depends upon the forms being presented to us in such a sequence that each successive element is felt to have a fundamental and harmonious relation with that which preceded it. I suggest that in looking at drawings our sense of pictorial unity is largely of this nature; we feel, if the drawing be a good one, that each modulation of the line as our eye passes along it gives order and variety to our sensations. Such a drawing may be almost entirely lacking in the geometrical balance which we are accustomed to demand in paintings, and yet have, in a remarkable degree, unity.

Let us now see how the artist passes from the stage of merely gratifying our demand for sensuous order and variety to that where he arouses our emotions. I will call the various methods by which this is effected the emotional elements of design.

The first element is that of the rhythm of the line with which the forms are delineated.

The drawn line is the record of a gesture, and that gesture is modified by the artist's feeling which is thus communicated to us directly.

The second element is mass. When an object is so represented that we recognize it as having inertia we feel its power of resisting movement, or communicating its own movement to other bodies, and our imaginative re-action to such an image is governed by our experience of mass in actual life.

The third element is space. The same-sized square on two pieces of paper can be made by very simple means to appear to represent either a cube two or three inches high, or a cube of hundreds of feet, and our re-action to it is proportionately changed.

The fourth element is that of light and shade. Our feelings towards the same object become totally different according as we see it strongly illumi-nated against a black background or dark against light.

A fifth element is that of color. That this has a direct emotional effect is evident from such words as gay, dull, melancholy in relation to color.

I would suggest the possibility of another element, though perhaps it is only a compound of mass and space: it is that of the inclination to the eye of a plane, whether it is impending over or leaning away from us.

Now it will be noticed that nearly all these emotional elements of design are connected with essential conditions of our physical existence: rhythm appeals to all the sensations which accompany muscular activity; mass to all the infinite adaptations to the force of gravity which we are forced to make; the spatial judgment is equally profound and universal in its application to life; our feeling about inclined planes is connected with our necessary judgments about the conformation of the earth itself; light again, is so necessary a condition of our existence that we become intensely sensitive to changes in its intensity. Color is the only one of our elements which is not of critical or universal importance to life, and its emotional effect is neither so deep nor so clearly determined as the others. It will be seen, then, that the graphic arts arouse emotions in us by playing upon what one may call the overtones of some of our primary physical needs. They have, indeed, this great advantage over poetry, that they can appeal more directly and immediately to the emotional accompaniments of our bare physical existence.

If we represent these various elements in simple diagrammatic terms, this effect upon the emotions is, it must be confessed, very weak. Rhythm of line, for instance, is incomparably weaker in its stimulus of the muscular sense than is rhythm addressed to the ear in music, and such diagrams can at best arouse only faint ghost-like echoes of emotions of differing qualities; but when these emotional elements are combined with the presentation of natural appearances, above all with the appearance of the human body, we find that this effect is indefinitely heightened.

When, for instance, we look at Michelangelo's "Jeremiah," and realize

the irresistible momentum his movements would have, we experience powerful sentiments of reverence and awe. Or when we look at Michelangelo's
"Tondo" in the Uffizi, and find a group of figures so arranged that the planes
have a sequence comparable in breadth and dignity to the mouldings of the
earth mounting by clearly-felt gradations to an overtopping summit, innumerable instinctive reactions are brought into play.[1]

At this point the adversary (as Leonardo da Vinci calls him) is likely
enough to retort, "You have abstracted from natural forms a number of so-
called emotional elements which you yourself admit are very weak when
stated with diagrammatic purity; you then put them back, with the help of
Michelangelo, into the natural forms whence they were derived, and at once
they have value, so that after all it appears that the natural forms contain
these emotional elements ready made up for us, and all that art need do is
to imitate Nature."

But, alas! Nature is heartlessly indifferent to the needs of the imaginative life; God causes His rain to fall upon the just and upon the unjust. The
sun neglects to provide the appropriate limelight effect even upon a triumphant Napoleon or a dying Cæsar.[2] Assuredly we have no guarantee that
in nature the emotional elements will be combined appropriately with the
demands of the imaginative life, and it is, I think, the great occupation of
the graphic arts to give us first of all order and variety in the sensuous plane,
and then so to arrange the sensuous presentment of objects that the emotional elements are elicited with an order and appropriateness altogether
beyond what Nature herself provides.

Let me sum up for a moment what I have said about the relation of art
to Nature, which is, perhaps, the greatest stumbling-block to the understanding of the graphic arts.

I have admitted that there is beauty in Nature, that is to say, that certain objects constantly do, and perhaps any object may, compel us to regard
it with that intense disinterested contemplation that belongs to the imaginative life, and which is impossible to the actual life of necessity and action;
but that in objects created to arouse the æsthetic feeling we have an added
consciousness of purpose on the part of the creator, that he made it on purpose not to be used but to be regarded and enjoyed; and that this feeling
is characteristic of the æsthetic judgment proper.

[1] Rodin is reported to have said, "A woman, a mountain, a horse—they are all the
same thing; they are made on the same principles." That is to say, their forms, when
viewed with the disinterested vision of the imaginative life, have similar emotional
elements.

[2] I do not forget that at the death of Tennyson the writer in the *Daily Telegraph*
averred that "level beams of the setting moon streamed in upon the face of the dying
bard"; but then, after all, in its way the *Daily Telegraph* is a work of art.

When the artist passes from pure sensations to emotions aroused by means of sensations, he uses natural forms which, in themselves, are calculated to move our emotions, and he presents these in such a manner that the forms themselves generate in us emotional states, based upon the fundamental necessities of our physical and physiological nature. The artist's attitude to natural form is, therefore, infinitely various according to the emotions he wishes to arouse. He may require for his purpose the most complete representation of a figure, he may be intensely realistic, provided that his presentment, in spite of its closeness to natural appearance, disengages clearly for us the appropriate emotional elements. Or he may give us the merest suggestion of natural forms, and rely almost entirely upon the force and intensity of the emotional elements involved in his presentment.

We may, then, dispense once for all with the idea of likeness to Nature, of correctness or incorrectness as a test, and consider only whether the emotional elements inherent in natural form are adequately discovered, unless, indeed, the emotional idea depends at any point upon likeness, or completeness of representation.

DeWitt H. Parker

THE NATURE OF ART*

The assumption underlying every philosophy of art is the existence of some common nature present in all the arts, despite their differences in form and content; something the same in painting and sculpture; in poetry and drama; in music and architecture. Every single work of art, it is admitted, has a unique flavor, a *je ne sais quoi* which makes it incomparable with every other work; nevertheless, there is some mark or set of marks which, if it applies to any work of art, applies to all works of art, and to nothing else— a common denominator, so to say, which constitutes the definition of art, and serves to separate, though not to isolate, the field of art from other fields of human culture. Consistent with this assumption is the experience that the study of one art throws light upon the study of the other arts—painting upon sculpture; music upon poetry and painting, and so on; expressed by

* From DeWitt H. Parker's "The Nature of Art" (*Revue Internationale de Philosophie*, Brussels, Belgium, Première année, No. 4, July 15, 1939), 684-702. Reprinted by permission of *Revue Internationale de Philosophie*.

DeWitt H. Parker (1885-1949) was professor of philosophy at the University of Michigan. He wrote many books, including two on aesthetics, *The Analysis of Art* and *The Principles of Aesthetics*.

the familiar habit of characterizing one art in terms of another art, as when we speak of architecture as frozen music; poetry as a picture; the poetry of architecture; the music of color and line; and the like.

The philosophy of art has however many things against it. The very possibility of a definition of art may be challenged, on at least two grounds. In the first place, it may be claimed that there is no significant nature common to all the arts which could serve as a basis for a definition. One may try to show that only confusion has resulted from the interpretation of one art in terms of another art; and to what a long history of fruitless controversy and darkening of counsel could one point as evidence with regard, for example, to Horace's famous phrase—*ut pictura poesis;* poetry like a picture. Each art, one might hold, since it makes use of a peculiar medium—color, tone, or what else—is subject to laws uniquely characteristic of it, and follows no others. Even such terms as "painting" are likely to be more misleading than useful; for water color is a different sort of thing from oil; and mural painting, from easel pictures; and there is all the difference in the world, say, between a Byzantine mosaic and a Renaissance nude. Or what have ceramics in common with music; a skyscraper with Michelangelo's *Day and Night?* And while there may be some convenience in using a term like literature to include both the novels of Sinclair Lewis and Baudelaire's *Fleurs du Mal,* let anyone beware of judging either by the standards of the other! It is equally convenient in the general delivery room of a postoffice to put all letters the names of whose addresses begin with B in one box, and those whose names begin with P in another box; but it does not follow that the owners of the letters in one box are more significantly like each other than they are like the owners of letters in the other box. Thus might one oppose a radical pluralism regarding the arts to the monism maintained by the philosophers.

The second ground for skepticism regarding the possibility of a definition of art is the difficulty of finding, not some nature common to all the arts, which was the first difficulty, but some criterion by means of which the sphere of art can be definitely separated from other human activities. It is interesting to recall that the Greeks never sharply distinguished the aesthetic arts from the other arts and crafts, using a single word, *techne,* for all; and that, for them, beauty and the good, which may be present in any experience, were identical. And until the beginning of the eighteenth century, expert opinion—barring certain prophetic exceptions—was against any absolute separation of art from other elements of culture, leaning in general to the view that beauty is a kind of truth, distinguishable from the truth of science or philosophy in no essential particular. When finally as a result of the reflexions of such men as Dubos, Vico, Kant, and Schiller there was promise of a genuine philosophy of art, the view that art has a unique nature and function came, not long after, in the middle of the last century, to be associated with the so-called theory of art for art's sake—a theory which, because it tended completely to isolate art from life, brought the whole philosophy of art into disrepute. Aside from its philosophic basis, the theory of art for art's sake was largely a reaction of sensitive minds against what seemed at the time to be the brutalities of industrialism and democracy. A vivid expression of this attitude is given by Th. Gauthier in the introduction to his poems: "My world is bounded by my window pane," he says, "I write poetry because I have nothing to do; and I have nothing to do in order that I may write poetry." In other words, art is a realm entirely separated from the interests of real life—a refuge for detached and gifted souls from sordid political and economic struggles.

It was thus the unhappy fate of the philosophy of art to become entangled with the point of view of the dwellers in the ivory tower. And it was inevitable that there should appear a counter-movement of ideas going to the opposite extreme, seeking not only to bring art back into connection with life, but to prove against the philosophers that art has no peculiar nature or function. The psychological motivation behind this attitude is interesting to notice; for it was the exact opposite of the motive that lay behind the theory of art for art's sake. For whereas that was expressive of a horrified retreat from life, this was expressive of an intense love of life, and a constant preoccupation with its larger social problems. While for the aesthetes the life of their own time was hateful; for the defenders of this counter point of view there was loveliness and fascination in all that was novel and characteristic of the present as compared with the past.[1] The railway carriage seemed to them an aesthetically more effective thing than the horse-drawn carriage; the steamboat than the sailboat; the factory than the shop; the open forum of democratic discussion than the stuffy cabinet of kings. Beauty, it was felt, is no privilege of art; but a pervasive property of our common experience. The doctrine of the aesthetes that art is a more perfect thing than life was reversed: in comparison with the zestful richness of life, art seemed a poor affair, winning for itself significance only through its connection with life itself.

In our own day we find the same two opposing attitudes towards art. The one is well represented by such a statement as this from *Art* by Clive Bell: ". . . to appreciate a work of art we need bring with us nothing from life, no knowledge of its ideas and affairs, no familiarity with its emotions."

[1] The best example is the work of J. M. Guyau.

To represent the counter point of view I would quote from a young writer
on aesthetics as follows: "Anything in the world which satisfies any desire
may be regarded as beautiful . . . anyone who uses intelligence and skill
to fiill a need is an artist; and every work of man which ministers to want
is a work of art."[2] And the same motive is at work as in the last century,
protesting against the effort to find some distinctive sphere for art and
beauty, namely, the wish to think well of life in its current form—to proclaim the beauty of its democratic texture and the glory of its mechanisms;
only instead of steamboats and steam engines we hear of motor cars and
airplanes. Or the motive may be associated with that of the reformer,
namely, the wish to transform life into a new and presumably better form,
that of socialism. This motive is well expressed by a distinguished veteran
in philosophic analysis, who has recently turned his attention from the
troubled ground of social theory to the quieter pastures of art, as follows:
"The hostility to association of fine art with normal processes of living is a
pathetic, even tragic commentary on life as it is ordinarily lived. Only because that life is usually so stunted, aborted, slack, or heavy laden, is the
idea entertained that there is some inherent antagonism between the process
of normal living, and creation and enjoyment of works of aesthetic art."[3]
Sometimes the doctrine that there is some feature distinctive of art as compared with an airplane, or some quality peculiar to beauty as compared
with ordinary satisfactory experience is deemed to be a superstition symptomatic of an aristocratic or bourgeois ideology that should long ago have
atrophied in the body-politic. And in this also history is repeating itself.

To find the motivation of a point of view is not to refute it; and no theory
is ever held for long by serious men, or recurs again and again in the history
of thought without some evidence in its favor. The student of aesthetic theories who watches the rhythmic reappearance of opposing ideas learns to look
for the facts covered by each, and to draw the moral that none was wrong,
but only inadequate. And while it is impossible to frame a satisfactory theory
by mere eclectic synthesis of opinions, it remains true that the aesthetician
who neglects the history of his subject runs the risk of proclaiming as new
ideas that are centuries old, or of overlooking some aspect of a subject-
matter so complex and subtle that no one mind is able to see around and
into all of it. There are two deductions from the study of ideas regarding
art that leap to the eyes with especial force. The first is the impossibility of
finding some simple formula that will serve as a definition of art. All the so
popular brief definitions of art—"significant form," "expression," "intuition,"

---

[2] Van Meter Ames, *Introduction to Beauty*, p. xi.
[3] John Dewey, *Art as Experience*.

"objectified pleasure"—are fallacious, either because, while true of art, they are also true of much that is not art, and hence fail to differentiate art from other things; or else because they neglect some essential aspect of art. Art is itself so complex a fact that a satisfactory definition of it must also be complex, that is to say, must involve many characteristics. As the mathematicians would say, the characteristics must be not only necessary but sufficient. They must penetrate deep enough into the roots of art to meet the challenge of the pluralists and show that there is, after all, a significant sameness in all the arts,—despite their differences in technique and media,— connecting the fine with the applied arts, so far as the latter are beautiful, and the realistic with the fanciful and the idyllic. The other deduction is that however sharply art is differentiated from life, its deep connection with life must be revealed in any definition. This is the enduring truth underlying all criticism of the ivory tower. With these lessons from history in mind, I shall now briefly explain how I think a good account of art may be framed.

I begin with a truism, that a work of art has value; or, in other words, that it is a source of satisfaction. For a work of art is not a given thing, like a star or a tree, but a thing made by man, and for his pleasure. And I wish further to premiss that all value, as satisfaction, arises through the appeasement of what in a general way may be called desire. Desire in the broad sense in which I am using that term is at once the motivation of all experience, its inward drive, and the source of its value. And the truth underlying the opposition to every type of theory of art for art's sake is the fact that the substance of the aesthetic experience is the same as the substance of all experience, a satisfaction that is the result of the appeasement of identical desires. Almost any desire that urges man on in life reappears in his art. There are no peculiar elementary aesthetic interests or emotions. What is different is the mode by which desire is appeased. For while, in ordinary experience, desire is occupied with real objects and is satisfied through a course of action leading to a goal that involves interaction with the real environment physical or social, in the case of art, desire is directed upon immanent or fictitious objects, and is appeased, not through a course of action leading to a distant goal, but in present, given experience. This mode of satisfying desire I call satisfaction in the imagination. Such a use of the term imagination has been criticized on the ground that aesthetic appreciation is not always concerned with images or fictions, but in the case of music, or the color and line patterns of a picture, with sensory material. But such criticism betrays ignorance of the long use of the term in exactly the sense in which I am employing it in the history of critical writing. For example, in the *Spectator* Addison writes of the Pleasures of the Imagination, in which he includes the pleasures of a country landscape. But while it is true that in the aesthetic experience, sensory material is as important as imaginal, it is also true that all material there has the status of the image; that is to say, it has the same freedom from reference to the physical world of action that is possessed by images, as in a dream.

I can explain what I mean by imagination through a comparison between the experience to be derived from a still life picture and the experience which is had from the set-up from which it is painted. Let us suppose that the set-up contains a cup. Then the sensory material of our experience in each case with regard to the item of the cup is much the same—there is color and there is shape. And whatever satisfaction so dear to the connoisseur may be gained from the shape as shape and the color as color, will also be much the same. Moreover, the interpretation of this sensory material is the same in both cases: it is interpreted through the idea or meaning, cup. But observe now the differences between the two experiences. For while the interests that center in the real cup, such as filling it and drinking out of it, may be satisfied by a series of actions and interactions with it, these same interests cannot be so satisfied with regard to the picture of the cup. Yet they can be satisfied in a way, but only by the idea or appearance of the cup, as if the cup were seen in a dream. We can still *imagine* ourselves touching it and filling it and drinking out of it: to us it may be *as if* we were actually doing all these things with it; and in so imagining we may provide a satisfaction of a sort to the same habits or interests that would be satisfied if we were actually to handle it and drink from it. If we could give to a dream of a cup all the sensuous fullness and vividness characteristic of perception, then the aesthetic satisfaction which we could get out of the dream would be the same as that which we get out of the still life picture. In both cases the satisfaction would be a satisfaction in a given sensuous shape and in the immediacy of an idea or meaning, rather than a satisfaction in a course of action upon a real thing which this shape and this meaning might suggest. And this is what Kant meant when he said that aesthetic satisfaction is disinterested—a satisfaction in mere representation of objects, independent of anything that we can get out of the existence of the objects.

In imagination, ideas or meanings are as important as sensuous shapes. The denial of this is the grand error of our contemporary aesthetes. I have already quoted from the famous passage of Clive Bell in which this denial is expressed. Let me cite the whole of it. "The representative element in a work of art may or may not be helpful; always it is irrelevant. For to appreciate a work of art, we need bring with us nothing from life, no knowledge of its ideas and affairs, no familiarity with its emotions."

But could we say of any poetry, of such lines as these for example,

> O western wind, when wilt thou blow
> That the small rain down can rain?
> Christ, that my love were in my arms
> And I in my bed again.

that to appreciate their beauty we need bring with us nothing from life, no knowledge of its ideas and affairs, no familiarity with its emotions? It is true, of course, that without beauty of sensuous form there is no poetry; but it is equally true that without ideas, poetry is nothing but a sweet trivial jingle. One may object that Clive Bell was writing of painting, not of poetry; but it is no less false to the whole tradition and intent of painting to claim that the representative element, which is the element of meaning, is irrelevant. Significant indeed was the movement of modern art away from conventional and literal representation; but there is a valid middle ground, which all important painters have occupied, between the extremes of prosaic copying, and no representation at all. Universally significant for painting is the presence of object-meanings derived from nature and human life: the figure, the landscape, even the inner life as revealed through the face; the precise way in which such meanings are conveyed is unimportant, varying all the way from the schematism of early Christian art to the realism of a Masaccio; but the meanings as meanings have as legitimate a place in the art as rhythm, mass, space, light, and shade, and color. No one can fairly compare an abstraction of Braque with a painting by Renoir and fail to appreciate the rich value that is added by meaning: the former offers to the imagination an elemental satisfaction through the factors enumerated (Roger Fry's list); the latter, all of this, and a world besides. Music is the only art that can satisfy the hunger of the imagination through sensuous shape alone.

The necessity for the inclusion of meaning in imagination is proved by the case of architecture. As in a poem, there is a union of the sensuous beauty of formal pattern with underlying meaning, so in architecture there is a union of formal with functional layers of beauty. To eliminate either is arbitrarily to distort the simple facts of both creation and appreciation. The same truth holds for every work of the industrial and applied arts. The sole alternative to the recognition of the part that functional ideas play in the beauty of these things is to exclude them from the house of art altogether; but to do so with regard to, say pottery and basketry, would be as arbitrary as to deny beauty to Chartres or La Miniatura.[4] The industrial arts have always proved to be stumbling blocks to aesthetic theory. Is it said that the field of art is mere appearance, unreality, illusion: well, what is more real than a building or a pot? Or is it said that beauty has nothing to do with

---

[4] Work by Frank Lloyd Wright.

utility: well, is it not obvious that fitness of form to function plays a part
in the beauty of pots, baskets, houses, and the like? The only way to solve
the difficulty is to recognize that the practical meaning, as a pure meaning,
does enter into the aesthetic experience of such things. It is of course true
that the aesthetic value of a building is not the same as its practical value:
one does not have to live in it or own it in order to appreciate its beauty.
Or one does not have to wear a shoe in order to know that it is beautiful;
"window shopping"—a good example of imaginative satisfaction—proves
that this is so. Not that wearing the shoe or living in the house is a hindrance
to appreciation; they may, on the contrary, be helps; but the value that
arises from use is not the same as the aesthetic value. The aesthetic value
is a transfer of the practical value to the plane of imagination. The beauty
of the shoe is in the way the shoe looks, not in the way it feels; but it must
look as if it would feel good. So the beauty of the house is not the living well
in it; but the way it looks as if one could live well in it. It is in the memory
or anticipation of its service—twin phases of imagination—that its beauty
resides. The use is in action; the beauty in the pure meaning. The recognition that the practical meaning, as a pure meaning, may enter into the
beauty of an object thus solves the paradox of the industrial arts, and reconciles the contention of those who insist on the connnection of art with life,
with the disinterestedness of beauty proclaimed by the aesthetes and the
philosophers.

Our first item in the definition of art is then the provision of satisfaction
in the imagination, imagination being defined in a rich sense, inclusive of
sensuous patterns and meanings, in the way indicated. But like other single-
idea definitions, this criterion while necessary is not sufficient; for it does not
serve to exclude from art things that we know do not belong there. It does
not exclude the dream at night, the day-dream, and many kinds of play.
The simplest of all examples of satisfaction through the imagination is perhaps the day-dream. If a politician seeking office by election allows himself
to day-dream the ceremony whereby he is proclaimed the winner, it is clear
that he is getting satisfaction, not by a real course of action that leads him
in fact to his goal, but through a purely fictitious occurrence which he con-
jures up in his own mind, for himself. But, be it noted, the motivating desire
is the same in both cases, as I have insisted; the difference lying in the
method by means of which desire is satisfied. In the case of the dream at
night—certainly when the dream is what we call a pleasant dream—there
is again satisfaction of desire, but obviously not by means of a course of
action leading to a goal—for the dreamer, fast asleep, acts not at all—but
by means of images created by the desire itself. The same formula of satisfac-

tion through the imagination holds for the phantasy play of the child. The
lonely child that creates for itself a dream-companion, and carries on an
animated conversation with it; the little girl playing, as we say, with a doll,
but actually with an imaginary baby, are both satisfying an interest or habit
through an ideal, substitute object; like the dreamer and the artist, they
are creating a world out of fancies to meet their desires. It is correct therefore to speak of art as a dream—a waking dream—in both there is the
same creativeness; the same absorption in immediacy; and yet it is clear that
mere dreaming is not art.

The second criterion that I would propose in order that we may come
closer to the distinctive nature of art, is that art is social. By this I mean,
first negatively, that the satisfactions of art do not depend upon factors
peculiar to an individual, but rather, positively, upon types of objects that
may be present in the experience of anyone. The satisfaction that is taken
in a keepsake—a lock of hair, a faded rose—illustrates a satisfaction that
depends upon the special "conditioning" of the individual; so likewise does
the satisfaction taken by the victor in a contest—impossible obviously for
the vanquished. It is equally impossible for me to share your satisfaction
in your dreams, because both the sources of satisfaction and the dream
images which are the objects of the satisfaction, are private. But in the case
of art, the satisfaction does not depend upon the peculiar circumstances and
conditioning of the individual, but upon patterns of sensa and meanings
that are potentially universal. You cannot dream the dream that I dream,
but you can see the same pattern of color or hear the same harmonies and
melodies that I hear; and you can understand the same meanings that I
understand, when we both read a poem or look at a picture. I do not mean
to deny, of course, the evident differences that exist among the experiences
of the same work of art in the case of different individuals. When I read

> Son of man
> You cannot say or guess, for you know only
> A heap of broken images, where the sun beats

the associations aroused by each key word in my mind and in yours will
differ; yet there will be a core of meaning that will be the same; and this
sameness will grow greater and approximate the meaning of the poet, as
we study the poem more carefully. Sometimes no definite meaning, but only
a mood will be communicated, as when we read Gertrude Stein's *Portrait of
Picasso*, a mood that the writer may mistake for the essence of the object—
but that does not matter.

But when I say that art is social I mean even more than this. I mean
not only that there are common factors in our enjoyment of it, but that our

enjoyment depends partly upon our knowing that this is so. We may enjoy
a work of art in loneliness, but afterwards we want to talk about it to our
friends, and make sure that they too enjoyed it. I would even venture to
assert that if some despot were to decree that no one should from this day
forth speak or write or in any other way communicate with his fellows
about books, pictures, plays, music, there would be an end to aesthetic creation and enjoyment. Art could not survive in a world of utter privacy and
silence. The communicability of the value of art is, as Kant insisted, an
essential fact about it. A work of art cannot be beautiful just for me, because
its beauty, that is to say, its value, depends upon the possibility of sharing it.

Not only our pleasures, but also our standards with regard to art are
social. In all aesthetic appreciation we can distinguish two phases, a primary
phase of direct pleasure in what is offered us, and a secondary phase that
arises through the fact that the work of art meets the standards which we
bring to bear upon it. Without the direct appeal, the work of art is in-
effective; but unless, besides, it measures up to our expectations, we are disappointed and disturbed. We come to every work of art with a fairly definite
idea of what a work of art of that kind should be like; our approach is not
naive, but critical and sophisticated. A good picture, a good play, a good
musical composition, must be so and so; or so and so. In this respect, to be
sure, art is not peculiar; for we bring to every type of experience a preconceived idea of excellence. Every smoker has his own idea of what makes
a good smoke. For one, it is a briar pipe, with a certain brand of tobacco;
for another, it is a fine Havana cigar; for a third, a Lucky Strike; for a fourth,
a Camel. What is peculiar about art in comparison with, say, smoking, is
that we claim for our standards social validity. If you like Camels, while I
like Luckies; well, it is all right with me; we will agree to disagree, and
that's the end of it; but if you don't like John Marin, I shall feel that there
is something wrong with you, and I may call you a Philistine, and tell you
that you are sadly in need of aesthetic education. And what you think of
James Joyce is not a matter of indifference to me. If you give me provoca-
tion, I shall dispute with you about it until midnight. And unlike our standards of smoking, our standards for art are formed not merely on a basis of
personal experience and comparison, but like our standards of manners and
morals, on a basis of tradition and education. An aesthetic value is not a
given thing, to take or to leave, but something to be educated into. What
a long way we are from the mere dream! A work of art is part of the history
and culture of a people, a dream is a transitory and trivial happening in an
isolated brain. It would be an indignity to mention such commonplaces,
were they not so flagrantly contradicted by certain "authorities."

Moreover, art is social not only for the appreciator, but also for the artist. A really fatal misunderstanding about this matter has arisen in certain quarters, in connection with the definition of art as "expression." That art is expression or self-expression, no one would deny. It is a free creation of an imaginary world through which the artist finds surcease for his desires and a solution for his problems. But art is not self-expression the way a baby's cry or a bird's song is; it is not even what Wordsworth called poetry, a spontaneous overflow of powerful feelings. No genuine artist is content merely to give form to his feelings, burning desire clean in creation, and out of its flame warming his heart with a merely private joy. On the contrary, he is building something for his group from whom he demands sympathy and understanding. He is not trying to please the group; that is the last thing he wishes to do; rather he is insisting that his group find pleasure in what pleases him. The idea that art is mere expression is valid only for the work of amateurs and dilettantes. Such people are, in fact, just expressing themselves for the sake of expression; amusing, pleasing themselves. They do not care whether anyone likes what they do or not; that is no part of their purpose. The improviser does not need an audience; the amateur painter will not show his work except perhaps and grudgingly to his wife or intimate friend. How different is the artist! He stands for something in a group and insists that what he creates shall be known and valued as he values it.

A final implication of the social character of art is the necessity that imagination shall be embodied in some physical thing by means of which it may be reproduced in many minds and at many moments. So close in fact is the connection between imagination and physical embodiment that common sense hardly knows how to distinguish between them. The unphilosophical mind means by the *Mona Lisa,* a canvas that hangs on a wall in the Louvre; by the *Venus de Milo* a sculptured block of marble set up in another room of the palace; and by a poem something he can find written on a certain page of a certain book. He is like the Pagan who believes that God can be found in a certain temple or even in a certain piece of wood in a shrine. If you remind him that the same poem can be found in many books; the same statue in many blocks of marble, of which the one in the Louvre was probably not the original; or ask how a landscape can hang on a wall, or Venus who dwells on Olympus can live in a museum; and enquire how it happens that the same music may be heard in Budapest that he is hearing in New York, he would probably be as much puzzled as the Pagan nurtured in a creed outworn would be if you were to ask him how God can inhabit so many shrines and temples at once. The solution of the prob-

lem is, of course, as follows: just as the theologian distinguishes between
God, whom no man hath seen at any time, and the temple, shrine or icon,
where God may be supposed to "appear"; so we can distinguish between the
aesthetic object or experience—a sensuous form, together with meanings
underlying the form, which exists only in the imagination, and what I
would call the *aesthetic instrument,* which is the vehicle for the imagination,
and a part of the physical world. The *Mona* Lisa as a pattern of color and
shape, and a system of meanings that may enter the same into the minds
of thousands, is what I am calling the aesthetic object; while the painted
canvas that one can dust and carry about and steal and recover is the
aesthetic instrument; the *Waste Land,* as a system of words and meanings
that you and I and the generations after may hear and, with sufficient pains,
understand, is an aesthetic object, while any printed page upon which the
poem is written is an aesthetic instrument; the *Venus de Milo,* a gracious
form beheld and adored by countless worshippers, is an aesthetic object, but
the blocks of marble in which this form is incarnate are aesthetic instruments. But while it is important that this distinction be made and its validity
recognized, one must not go the lengths of a Croce in affirming that the
instrument has nothing to do with art. For the appreciator, the instrument
is essential, because it makes the aesthetic experience communicable; and
preserves it for future generations. Without the instrument it would be a
mere dream, unknowable and ephemeral. Imagination and physical embodiment are two aspects of a single fact.

The physical aspect of a work of art is of supreme importance to the
artist, also. It was said of Raphael that he painted with his mind, not with
his hands; but however much truth this paradox contains, like all paradoxes,
it conceals an equal amount of falsehood. For every painter knows that
unless he has his vision in his fingers he cannot have it in his mind. His long
effort to conquer the physical medium of his art is essential to the growth of
his imagination. Michelangelo's conception of the form as lying sleeping in
the marble was, as Bosanquet remarked, a truer account of the facts regarding sculpture than ever Vasari's was regarding painting. And what of the
relation of the violinist to his instrument or the dancer's to hers—her own
body? Does not the instrument enter into the very meaning of their art
for them? There are, it is true, certain arts where it almost seems as if the
creative, as distinguished from the merely receptive phase of the art, had
acquired independence of the instrument, even as Aristotle thought that
intellect could free itself of the body and so become immortal: poetry,
where the use of pen and paper, or perhaps today the typewriter, appears
so irrelevant; the poet sometimes composing his verses entirely in his head,

as Goethe composed his *Wanderers Nachtlied* during a walk; the music of the composer, as contrasted with the music of the performer, which may be born complete in the head of a Mozart; for which reason every Platoniz-ing philosopher has felt that these two arts were superior to such arts as painting, sculpture, and dancing, where the relation of the artist to his instrument seems to be essential, and where the activity of the artist, since it involves manual skill no less than imagination places him among the handicraftsmen. And following out this relationship between imagination and instrument, we might go on to distinguish between these same arts of poetry and music, on the one hand, where the preservation and com-munication of imagination depend indeed upon a physical instrument—the score of a sonata or the page of a book of poetry—yet may be multiplied a millionfold; and the beauty of a building or a dance, on the other hand, that are tied once and for all to unique materials of stone and steel, or of flesh and bones, and die with them; then, such intermediate arts as painting and sculpture, where reproduction is possible, but always imperfect. But interesting as these distinctions are, they are not important; the important matter is the fact that the full meaning of art includes its social and historical significance, which would be impossible without the material aesthetic instrument.

We come finally to the last of the marks by means of which I am seek-ing to define and distinguish art. There are a number of words, more or less synonymous, which have been used to designate what I have in mind—*harmony, form, pattern, design.* This is an absolutely universal characteristic of all works of art, of every kind. But while design is a necessary mark of art, it is not sufficient, for it is not a distinguishing mark. There are other things besides works of art that possess design. The human body possesses its design, so does any machine, an airplane or a motor car. Yet while this is true, it deserves to be pointed out that there are certain differences be-tween the form of the human body and the machine, on the one hand, and the form of a work of art, on the other hand. In order to make this clear, I wish to distinguish between two types of design in aesthetic objects, which I shall call intrinsic form and extrinsic or representational form, respectively. By representational form, I mean structure that is determined by the mean-ings that underlie the sensuous surface. I can make this clear by asking whether even the most radical post-impressionist would be willing to have the part of a statue that represents a head attached to the part that repre-sents the ankle; or in a picture whether he would be willing to have the shapes that represent the sky below those that represent the earth, and the tree tops touching the ground, with the trunks in the air. Whether, not in a fairy story, but in a novel, he would be willing to have the men look like women, the babes talk and the grown-ups babble; or whether in a line of verse, for example,

> Shall I compare thee to a summer's day?

it would be just as well to write,

> I shall compare thee to a summer's day.

In all such cases it is plain that part of the pattern of the work is determined by connections between meanings, reproduced from nature and human life and thought. In other words, we demand of a work of art that represents nature or human life and thought, an analogous pattern of its parts. Now so far as this type of form in works of art is concerned, it is obviously closely similar to the form found in machines and the organism. Just as the purpose to represent a human body requires that such and such parts of a statue represent such and such portions of the human body, and with a certain comparable arrangement; so the embodied purposes of the organism itself demand the parts and organs necessary for the carrying out of this purpose. But notice that there is a difference. For whereas in the case of the human body or the machine, the various parts are meaningless and functionless, except with relation to an environment in which they operate—a foot in relation to the ground; an eye in relation to things to be seen; a mouth in relation to food; the wheel of an automobile in relation to a road; the seat in relation to passengers; on the other hand, in the case of a work of art, there is no relation of parts to an environment, but only of parts to parts within a whole. The foot of the statue rests, not on the ground, but on a pedestal; and while its eyes may be said to see, there is nothing for them to see, and if its mouth may be said to speak, there is no one to listen to what is said. Spencer defined life as a continual adjustment of inner relations to outer relations; and he might have defined a machine in much the same way. In a work of art, however, there are internal relations only; a part refers to other parts, within the whole, in accordance with the idea that is expressed there, but does not refer to anything outside itself. It is a microcosm, a self-sufficient little world of embodied, interrelated meanings, in need of nothing to give it life and significance, save only the mind of the spectator.

One might hope to make out a better case for the uniqueness of aesthetic form in regard to what I have been calling intrinsic form. This type of form is significant in complete independence of meanings. Absolute music is the best example, for there all form is intrinsic form. The rhythmic and harmonic structure of music is effective and intelligible wholly by itself; we understand why certain harmonies are present or certain dissonances resolved without any reference to the objects and events in nature or human life. In the same way we understand why in a picture a certain color demands its contrasting and complementary color, or a certain line its balancing line, independent of what the color is the color of, or the line the line of. In a poem, we know that a word of a certain length and sound texture is demanded, independent of its meaning, because of the necessities of rime and rhythm. And even in a statue, where it might seem as if every part had to be just what it is because of the laws of anatomy, there are relations of harmony and balance of line and mass that cannot be understood in *that* way, but are intelligible in their own way. I do not mean to imply that intrinsic and extrinsic form are as separate in any work of art as might appear from my discussion; for, on the contrary, there must be a fine adaptation of one to the other, for beauty. Yet I would insist that they are two very different types of form, springing from different roots; the one type following the objective laws of nature, and so creating in every work of art some semblance of truth; the other based on those subjective principles of human nature upon which depend all value or satisfaction. Elsewhere[5] I have tried to formulate these laws; but I have no room to go into the matter here. What is of immediate concern to us is the possibility of defining art in terms of intrinsic form. That intrinsic form is a universal factor in works of art, and for that reason belongs among the indispensable elements in any definition, can I think be proved. But that it is no exclusive characteristic, and cannot therefore function as a sufficient criterion, can also be shown. For all the activities of man, so far as they are valuable, display it. His walk is rhythmic, when he enjoys it; his body is beautiful to him when harmonious and well-balanced; even his life as a whole is happy when it possesses intrinsic form. It is true, I think, that intrinsic form is most perfect in works of art; because imagination is of all spheres the most plastic to desire, and because the technique of expression of the imagination in the medium of the arts, being vastly simpler than the technique of business or politics, has achieved a perfection there unmatched anywhere, except perhaps in mathematics. For this reason art will always seem to be the superlative example of form, even though, as has been shown, it be not the sole example.

In conclusion, let me summarize the chief points I have been making in regard to the definition of art. I have tried to show that there is no single and sufficient criterion by means of which art may be defined. There are single characteristics which apply to all works of art, but none which applies exclusively to art. The definition of art must therefore be in terms of a complex of characteristics. Failure to recognize this has been the fault of

[5] *The Analysis of Art.* Yale University Press.

all the well-known definitions. The definition which I have proposed contains three parts: the provision of satisfaction through the imagination, social significance, and harmony. I am claiming that nothing except works of art possesses all three of these marks. By imagination is meant the whole realm of given experience, inclusive of sensations and meanings as well as of images, so far as it is under the control of desire, and capable of being viewed in independence of action and reality. By the social significance of art I have meant the fact that the satisfaction which art provides does not depend upon factors peculiar to the individual, but upon patterns of sensations and meanings which may become parts of the experience of many minds, and the further fact that an important element of aesthetic satisfaction comes from knowledge that other minds are having or may have a like satisfaction. We saw, in addition, that the possibility of the social significance of art depends upon the fashioning of relatively permanent physical objects, called by us *aesthetic instruments,* which function as stimuli of the aesthetic experience for many minds and vehicles for its transmission to future generations. It is a peculiarity of the imagination of the artist that, despite its freedom, it seeks a local habitation, and a deathless name, in these instruments, and in creating them, the artist acts as both dreamer and artisan. What we call a work of art is on the one hand a thing; on the other hand, an experience. If we are asked to express the nature of this experience in a single sentence, we may venture to say of it that it is satisfaction of desire through a harmonious and socially significant imaginative object which, because it is superlatively harmonious and of more than personal significance, becomes the symbol of all order and all goodness.

Jacques Maritain

ART AS A VIRTUE OF THE PRACTICAL INTELLECT*

THE PRACTICAL INTELLECT

1. Before sewing one must cut. A philosopher who is in search of the nature of things is obliged to begin with sharp distinctions. These distinc-

* From Jacques Maritain's *Creative Intuition in Art and Poetry,* Ch. II. Copyright, 1953, by The Bollingen Foundation, Inc. Reprinted by permission of The Bollingen Foundation.

Jacques Maritain (1882-   ), one of the leading Thomist thinkers in contemporary thought, has written on many philosophical topics, including aesthetics.

tions may seem brutal. They simply deal with certain essences taken in themselves: and how could we bring out otherwise the intelligibility of things from the confused flux of existence? To isolate an essence does not imply any disregard for the complexity and continuity of the real. It is indispensable in order to analyze this complexity and continuity in a correct manner—and finally to become aware of their very richness and meaning.

In this chapter I shall limit myself to the consideration of art—art in its most basic and primordial form, or in its fundamental nature, which is, in one sense, contradistinguished to poetry. For it is in the useful arts that we may discover the most obvious and typical characteristics of art in so far as it is art, and its most universal significance as a root activity of the human race. In prehistoric ages, it seems that the search for beauty and adornment was contemporary with the search for contriving tools and weapons, and that the painting and carving activity of the primitive man was not always, nor even from the very beginning, directed toward magical purposes.[1] The fact remains, nevertheless, that the "pleasure of imitation" and the poetic impulse were but one with the effort to satisfy some need of human life— even if it was the need for adornment and ornamentation, in which beauty is, no doubt, instinctively sought for but not for its own sake (the intended aim being to make woman more attractive or man more formidable, or the human dwelling place more stamped with the mark of man and of his vision). With regard to the natural development of its potentialities, art does not begin with freedom and beauty for beauty's sake. It begins with making instruments for human life, canoes, vases, arrows, necklaces, or wall paintings destined to subject, through magical or nonmagical signs, the human environment to the mastery of man. Art must never forget its origins. Man is *homo faber* and *homo poeta* together. But in the historical evolution of mankind the *homo faber* carries on his shoulders the *homo poeta*. Thus I shall point, first of all, to the art of the craftsman and, secondarily, compare the universe of this art of the craftsman with the universe of the art of those for whom, since the Renaissance and its demi-gods, we reserve the name of artists.

[1] Cf. G. H. Luquet, *L'Art et la Religion des Hommes fossiles* (Paris: Masson, 1926). The author insists in an illuminating manner on the genuinely aesthetic and poetic sense which permeated the art of the primitive man. But his vocabulary is sometimes confused, and he leaves blurred, in my opinion, the fact that this art, while being instinctively interested in beauty, was always and primarily, at the same time, subservient to the needs of human life. (I do not say limited to utilitarian aims in the too strict sense of this word in our civilized language. The truth of the matter is, I think, that the art of the primitive man was undifferentiated—more disinterested than our useful arts, and more subservient to human needs than our fine arts. We may safely assume, moreover, that this destination of satisfying the needs of human life was prevalent in the *consciousness* of the primitive artist.)

2. Aristotle has shown—this is an example of an acquisition definitively made by philosophy (at least, if philosophers were aware of their own treasures)—that the absolutely first and primordial division to be recognized with respect to the activity of the intellect is the division between the speculative or theoretical intellect and the practical intellect. This does not mean a distinction between two separate powers but a distinction between two basically different ways in which the same power of the soul—the intellect or reason—exercises its activity.

The speculative intellect knows only for the sake of knowledge. It longs to see, and only to see. Truth, or the grasping of that which is, is its only goal, and its only life.

The practical intellect knows for the sake of action. From the very start its object is not Being to be grasped, but human activity to be guided and human tasks to be achieved. It is immersed in creativity. To mold intellectually that which will be brought into being, to judge about ends and means, and to direct or even command our powers of execution—these are its very life.

Such a distinction does not deal with accidental circumstances. It is an essential distinction. For the entire dynamism of the intellect and its typical approach to its object depend on this very object, and they are basically different when the object is merely knowledge and when the object is action.

3. We see this more clearly if we take into account two fundamental points: first, the part played by the *appetite;* and second, the nature of *truth* —either when it comes to the activity of the speculative intellect or when it comes to the activity of the practical intellect. The difference between these two kinds of intellectual activity is so deep that neither the vital relation between the intellect and the appetite nor even what truth consists of are the same in the two cases in question.

In the case of the speculative intellect, the appetite—that is to say, the will, but not in the sense of a mere power of decision, rather in the larger sense of man's energy of desire and love, intent on some existential good—the appetite intervenes only to bring the intellect to the exercise of its own power, say, to embark on and pursue a mathematical problem or an anthropological inquiry. But once the intellect is at work, the appetite has nothing to do with this work, which depends only, as far as normal knowledge through concepts is concerned, on the weapons of reason.

On the other hand, in the case of the practical intellect, the appetite plays an essential part in the very work of knowledge. In one way or another, and to quite various degrees (for practicality admits of a vast scale of varying degrees), reason, then, operates in conjunction with the will.

For the intellect taken in itself tends uniquely to grasp Being; and it is only as permeated, in one way or another, by the movement of the appetite toward its own ends that the intellect concerns itself, not with Being to be grasped, but with action to be brought about.

As a result, truth, in speculative knowledge, is the adequation or conformity of the intellect with Being, with what things are. But in practical knowledge how could this be so? In practical or creative knowledge there is no previously existing thing with which the intellect can make itself consonant. The thing does not yet exist, it is to be brought into being. It is not with being, it is with the straight tendential dynamism of the human subject with regard to this thing not yet existing, but to be created, that the intellect must make itself consonant. In other words, truth, in practical knowledge, is the adequation or conformity of the intellect with the straight appetite, with the appetite as straightly tending to the ends with respect to which the thing that man is about to create will exist. This statement, basic in Thomist philosophy, applies to the various fields of practical knowledge in the most diversified ways, and in an analogous, not univocal manner. But it holds true for the whole realm of practical knowledge.

THE VIRTUE OF ART

4. Now there is a second essential division to be taken into consideration, this time in practical knowledge itself. The activity of the practical intellect divides into human actions to be done (within the universe of man's destiny) and works to be made (by man, but within the universe of things, outside the universe of man's destiny); in other words, it divides into moral activity and artistic activity.

Morality is concerned with what the Schoolmen called *agibilia,* or what pertains to doing: that is, the very use of human free will, on which depends the fact of a man's being good or bad. Art is concerned with what the Schoolmen called *factibilia,* or what pertains to making: that is, the making of a work, on which depends the fact of this very work's being good or bad.

Thus prudence, the moral virtue par excellence (I mean old *prudentia* in its genuine sense, practical wisdom at the highest degree of practicality, the virtue through which the Bold make an infallible decision, not our bourgeois and timorous prudence)—prudence is the straight intellectual determination of actions to be done. Art, on the contrary, is the straight intellectual determination of works to be made.[2]

[2] As a rule the thing to be made, or the work to be done, refers to the realm of knowledge for the sake of action, not of knowledge for the sake of knowledge. That is why it is said in a general way that art belongs to the sphere of the practical intellect. Yet

Art resides in the soul and is a certain perfection of the soul. It is what Aristotle called an ἕξις, in Latin a *habitus,* an inner quality or stable and deep-rooted disposition that raises the human subject and his natural powers to a higher degree of vital formation and energy—or that makes him possessed of a particular strength of his own: when a *habitus,* a "state of possession"[3] or master quality, an inner demon if you prefer—has developed in us, it becomes our most treasured good, our most unbending strength, because it is an ennoblement in the very kingdom of human nature and human dignity.

Art is a virtue—not a moral virtue (it is contradistinguished to moral virtues). Art is a virtue in the larger and more philosophical sense the ancients gave to this word: a *habitus* or "state of possession," an inner strength developed in man, which perfects him with regard to his ways of acting, and makes him—to the extent to which he uses it—undeviating in a given activity. The virtuous man is not infallible, because often, while acting, he does not use his virtue; but virtue, of itself, is never wrong. The man who possesses the virtue of art is not infallible in his work, because often, while acting, he does not use his virtue. But the virtue of art is, of itself, never wrong.

Art is a virtue of the practical intellect—that particular virtue of the practical intellect which deals with the creation of objects to be made.

We see, then, how essential is the relationship between art and reason. Art is intellectual by essence, as the odor of the rose pertains to the rose, or spark to fire. Art, or the proper virtue of working reason, is—in the realm of making—an intrinsic perfection of the intellect. Not in Phidias and Praxiteles only, but in the village carpenter and blacksmith as well, the Doctors of the Middle Ages acknowledged an intrinsic development of reason, a nobility of the intellect. The virtue of the craftsman was not, in their eyes,

---

there are certain categories of works and, consequently, certain categories of arts which do not belong to this sphere, but to the speculative one; there are speculative arts, such as Logic is for instance. (Cf. *Sum. theol.* II-II, 47, 2, ad 3.) Such arts perfect the speculative Intellect, not the practical Intellect: but the kind of knowledge involved is still akin to the practical in its *mode,* and it constitutes an *art* only because it implies the *making of a work*—this time a work wholly within the mind, and whose sole object is the achievement of knowledge, a work which consists for instance in shaping an idea or a definition, in setting our concepts in order, in framing a proposition or a reasoning. The fact remains, therefore, that wherever we find *art* we find some productive operation to be contrived, some work to be made. Cf. *Art and Scholasticism* (New York: Scribner, 1930), Chapter II.

Given the abstractive and discursive nature of man's intellect, the part of the making, the manufacture of the tools of science, is (unfortunately) essential and necessary, and immense, in the immanent operations of knowledge and the inner life of the mind. But when all this is not vivified by intuition and actual knowledge, we are tempted to see in it, as Faust did, only "Skeletons of animals and bones of the dead."

[3] "State of possession" renders *habitus* (ἕξις) better, it seems to me, than the expression "state of capacity" used by W. D. Ross in his translation.

strength of muscle or nimbleness of fingers. It was a virtue of the intellect, and endowed the humblest artisan with a certain perfection of the spirit.[4]

5. But, in contradistinction to prudence, which is also a perfection of the practical intellect, art is concerned with the good of the work, not with the good of man. The ancients took pleasure in laying stress on this difference, in their thorough-going comparison of art and prudence. If only he contrives a good piece of woodwork or jewelwork, the fact of a craftsman's being spiteful or debauched is immaterial, just as it is immaterial for a geometer to be a jealous or wicked man, if only his demonstrations provide us with geometrical truth. As Thomas Aquinas put it, art, in this respect, resembles the virtues of the speculative intellect: it causes man to act in a right way, not with regard to the use of man's own free will, and to the rightness of the human will, but with regard to the rightness of a particular operating power. The good that art pursues is not the good of the human will but the good of the very artifact. Thus, art does not require, as a necessary precondition, that the will or the appetite should be undeviating with respect to its own nature and its own—human or moral—ends and dynamism, or in the line of human destiny. Oscar Wilde was but a good Thomist when he wrote: "The fact of a man being a poisoner is nothing against his prose."

[4] Cf. *Art and Scholasticism*, p. 20.—In the Scholastic vocabulary "art" is synonymous with "practical science," in the sense that it is a kind of science which is practical in its very essence or its very way of knowing, and practical from the very start—science of the work to be made.

Practical science in this genuine sense is entirely different from applied science, that is, from a science which is theoretical in essence—and then particularized or applied (by art or practical science) in order to achieve a practical result.

A greater or less amount of theoretical science (the science of anatomy, for instance) is indeed involved in art (in medicine for instance) as *presupposed* by it, and *applied* by it. But it would be a fundamental error to mistake practical science for applied theoretical science: Medicine is not applied science of anatomy, it applies in its own way and in its own light the science of anatomy.

Sayings like "L'art c'est la science faite chair" (Jean Cocteau, "Le Secret professionel," in *Le Rappel à l'Ordre*, Paris: Stock, 1930) or "L'art ce n'est que la science humanisée" (Gino Severini, *Du Cubisme au Classicisme*, Paris: Povolozky, 1921) are therefore inaccurate if they relate to theoretical science as embodied in the work. Mathematics may be considered a basic *pre-required* discipline for the painter, yet painting is not humanized mathematics. Painting applies mathematics—it is not applied mathematics.

But such sayings take on fully true meaning if they relate to that knowledge which is implied in the very essense of fine arts, namely to poetic knowledge (See Chapter IV, §§ 6 and 7, and Chapter V, § 9). We must thus admit, if we get rid of our "scienticist" modern prejudices, the existence of a poetic science which differs *toto coelo* from theoretical sciences, and which is however a real knowledge, attained through creative intuition. Its object is neither the essential structure of the object known nor the laws of phenomena; it is real nevertheless—the existential aspects and relations of things grasped through emotion and connaturality. Thus the painter has a real knowledge or "science" of "Nature," or the world of visible matter—a knowledge or "science" which has nothing to do either with mathematics or with physics, the theoretical science of nature (though the art of painting, in its ways and means of execution, has to apply certain mathematical and certain physical, especially optical, laws).

Here we are confronted with a problem which is beyond the subject of this book, but about which it is perhaps not irrelevant to say a few words, parenthetically. As I observed at the beginning, the prime obligation of philosophy is to bring out and circumscribe the nature or essence of the given thing, taken in itself, which it considers: for instance the nature or essence of art taken in itself or in its own basic and constitutive requirements. Yet the trouble is that in actual existence we do not deal with essences taken in themselves, but with essences embodied in concrete reality. Art in itself pertains to a sphere separate from, and independent of, the sphere of morality. It breaks into human life and human affairs like a moon prince or a mermaid into a custom office or a congregation; it will always make trouble and arouse suspicion. But art exists in a human being—the artist. As a result, though the fact of a man's being a poisoner is nothing against his prose, the fact of a man's being a drug addict can be, in the long run, something harmful to his prose. Baudelaire himself has warned us against the exclusive passion for art, which progressively destroys the human subject and finally—through an indirect repercussion, owing to material or subjective causality—destroys art itself: for once a man is through, his art is through also.

But things are still more complicated, because of the fact that the artist is aware of this kind of impact of his own moral life on his art, and therefore is tempted, when he totally yields to his cherished demon, to develop, for the sake of his art, a peculiar morality and peculiar moral standards of his own, directed to the good of the work, not of his soul. Then he will endeavor to taste all the fruits and silts of the earth, and will make curiosity or recklessness in any new moral experiment or vampiric singularity his supreme moral virtue, in order to feed his art. And the undertaking will finally prove to be a miscalculation, for in this adventure he will warp in a more subtle manner—and in a manner more closely connected with the sphere of creativity—that general temperament of thought and sensibility, and that general relationship of the sense and the intellect to reality, which are the human ambiance of the activity of art.

Yet he can still remain an artist—even a great artist, however injured in some respects: the fact is that his very being has been offered in self-sacrifice to the all-devouring glory of art;—well, to the glory of this world also, and to our own delights, and to the spiritual welfare of mankind. For St. Teresa of Avila said that without poetry life would not be tolerable—even for contemplatives. We do not have to judge him. God will work it out with him, somehow or other.

USEFUL ARTS AND FINE ARTS

6. It is a basic maxim in Aristotelian philosophy that the practical intellect works always, in one way or another, in conjunction with the will, and that, in practical knowledge, truth is the conformity of the intellect with the straight appetite. This statement applies to art and prudence in totally different manners. In the case of prudence, it is in so far as the appetite tends to the ends of human life that it plays an indispensable part in practical knowledge; and truth is conformity with the straight will or appetite in so far as the appetite has been made straight by moral virtues.

But in the case of art, the will plays its part in so far as it tends to the work; and the fact of the will's or appetite's being straight means that it tends to the good of the work as it is to be brought into existence by means of the rules discovered by the intellect; so that the judgment of the artist about each of the movements his fingers have to make is true when it is in conformity with the appetite straightly tending to the production of the work through the appropriate rules born out of the intellect. Thus, in the last analysis, the main part is played by the intellect, and art is much more intellectual than prudence.

Let us think (purposely using an oversimplified imagery) of the first boat invented by men, on a day when neither the word nor the idea of boat yet existed. Nothing was present except a will to satisfy a certain need— the need of crossing a river or an arm of the sea. This need to be satisfied —this was the only rule or ruler for the operation of the inventor's intellect. When, by using certain bits of knowledge previously acquired (men had seen trunks of trees floating on the water), and by putting them together into a newborn idea, the intellect contrived a first appropriate means, its judgment was true because it was in conformity with the first rule.

The first contrived raft was probably something quite defective and clumsy. It had to be improved. Now the intellect had to heed two rules: the first and primary rule (the need, grasped by the intellect, the satisfying of which was wanted by the appetite), a rule in conformity with which the first raft had been contrived; and a second rule, the newborn rule of making which the intellect had just discovered in the very process of creating the first raft. The second raft was thus contrived in conformity with these two rules; and at the same time a third newborn rule of making, dealing with the improvement brought about in the making of this second raft, was discovered—and kept in memory. And so the process continued, both by the intellect heeding previously discovered rules, and discovering newborn rules. We have the same story with the invention and progressive improvement of the airplane, the cyclotron, the calculating machine, etc.

I hope I shall be pardoned the excessive simplicity of the example I have just used. It helps us to bring out some truths which are also quite simple indeed, but basic for our purpose. The first one is that even in the useful arts, the rules are not ready-made recipes, taught by professors in schools and museums, but vital ways of operating discovered by the creative eyes of the intellect in its very labor of invention. Once discovered, they tend, it is true, to become recipes; but then they become obstacles as well as aids to the life of art.[5]

Another basic truth is that whatever the more and more refined and more and more ingenious rules discovered by the craftsman may be, his primary obligation remains to obey the primary rule—the need to be satisfied, toward which, from the very start, his will basically tends.

Finally, to sum up, let us say that in the useful arts, what the will or appetite demands is the satisfying of a particular need; and the straightness of the appetite means that it tends to the satisfying of this particular need by means of the rules discovered by the intellect, the first of which is this very need as grasped by intelligence.

7. Now what about those arts which are designated (I shall say later on why I distrust the expression) as the fine arts? Here I would say that in the fine arts what the will or appetite demands is the release of the pure creativity of the spirit, in its longing for beauty—for that enigmatic beauty whose love affairs and quarrels with poetry will occupy us in a further chapter.

And the straightness of the appetite means that it tends to this aim as to be achieved by means of the rules discovered by the intellect, the first of which is the creative intuition from which the whole work originates. Creativity, or the power of engendering, does not belong only to material organisms, it is a mark and privilege of life in spiritual things also. "To be fertile, so as to manifest that which one possesses within oneself," John of St. Thomas wrote, "is a great perfection, and it essentially belongs to the intellectual nature."[6] The intellect in us strives to engender. It is anxious

---

[5] Be it noted, furthermore, that the truth of the creative judgment does not consist in judging of the work in conformity with the rules (theoretically known); it consists in judging of the work in conformity with the appetite straightly tending to the production of this work through the appropriate rules. So are—*recta ratio factibilium*—is a virtue of working reason. But an element of knowledge through connaturality, a certain "instinct" developed in reason, is already involved in the basic notion of the truth of the artistic judgment, since this truth is conformity *with the appetite* intent on the use of the appropriate rules.

[6] *Cursus theol.*, t. IV, disp. 12, a. 6, § 21.

to produce, not only the inner word, the concept, which remains inside us, but a work at once material and spiritual, like ourselves, and into which something of our soul overflows. Through a natural super-abundance the intellect tends to express and utter *outward*, it tends to sing, to manifest itself in a work. This natural desire, because it goes beyond the boundaries of the intellect, can be implemented only through the movement of the will and the appetitive powers, which make the intellect go out for itself—in accordance with its own natural aspiration—and which determine thereby the operative practicality of intelligence, in its most primordial and general impulse.

This creativity of the spirit is the first ontological root of the artistic activity. And in fine arts it is pure, cleared of all adventitious elements. And the pure creativity of spiritual intelligence tends to achieve something in which spiritual intelligence finds its own delight, that is, to produce an object in beauty. Left to the freedom of its spiritual nature, the intellect strives to engender in beauty.[7]

Such is, in its longing for beauty, that pure creativity of the spirit, to the release of which the appetite basically tends, together with the intellect, in the vital dynamism of fine arts.

Here we do not have a demand for the satisfying of a particular need in human life. We are beyond the realm of the useful. The need is not extraneous to the intellect, it is one with the intellect. We have a demand for the participation, through the object created, in something which is itself spiritual in nature. For beauty, which is of no use, is radiant with intelligence and is as transcendental and infinite as the universe of the intellect. Thus the very end—transcendent end—intended pertains to the realm of the intellect, of its exultation and joy, not to the world of utility, and the intellectuality of art is in the fine arts (though more bound there with the sensitive and emotional powers) at a much higher degree than in the arts of the craftsman. The need of the intellect to manifest externally what is grasped within itself, in creative intuition, and to manifest it in beauty, is simply the essential thing in the fine arts.

From this point of view we may perceive how short of the mark inevitably fall all the explanations and theories of art offered by psychological or sociological, materialist, empiricist, logical-empiricist, or pragmatist positivism, or by those who, as Allen Tate[8] puts its, explain to us "how the *stimuli* of poems elicit *responses* in such a way as to *organize our impulses* toward action," and who tell us that "poetry is a kind of applied psychology," or else

[7] The phrase "engendering in beauty" is Platonic in origin. Cf. *Symposium*, 206.
[8] *On the Limits of Poetry* (New York: The Swallow Press and William Morrow, 1948), pp. 9, 15.

(this is logical positivism) that it is "only *amiable insanity*," because "it 'designates' but it does not denote anything *real*."

8. Let us come now to that with which the creative judgment, if it is true, comes into accordance, namely the rules—or the straight appetite tending toward beauty to be participated in by a work produced according to the appropriate rules.

This very notion of rule, in the fine arts, is transfigured, through the impact of beauty on the activity of art.

First, the rules, in fine arts, are subjected to a law of perpetual renewal infinitely more exacting than in useful arts. They must be perpetually new-born rules, not only with respect to a given subject—boat, vase, or calculating machine—to be improved, but with respect to beauty to be participated in; and beauty is infinite. Outside any particular style or lineage of masterworks, there is always an infinity of other ways to achieve participation in beauty. No form of art, however perfect, can encompass beauty within its limits. The artist is faced with an immense and desert sea.

> *. . . sans mâts, sans mâts, ni fertiles îlots,*

and the mirror he holds up to it is no bigger than his own heart. He is bound to go hunting a new analogate, a new typically different participation in beauty; and this new participation in beauty will involve and require new ways of making—either a new adaptation of the fundamental and perennial rules, or the use of rules not hitherto employed, which are simply new, and which at first disconcert people. It seems relevant, moreover, to lay stress at this point on the spiritual universality of what I just called the fundamental and perennial rules of art—or, better, the eternal laws of art. These eternal laws of art are not to be found at the level of the particular rules of making, say, the famous Golden Number. They exist only at the supremely universal level of philosophy, and of that wisdom (more lived than conceptualized) which is concealed in the roots of the virtue of art. They are in the artist the spiritual, and general, foundations of his intellectual virtue, prior to any particular, technical manifestation of this virtue. And it is through an infinite diversity in application that they are exemplified by the great works of any epoch and any style.

In the second place, the work to be made, in the case of the fine arts, is an end in itself, and an end totally singular, absolutely unique. Then, every time and for every single work, there is for the artist a new and unique way to strive after the end, and to impose on matter the form of the mind. As a result, the rules of making—which, as concerns art in general, are fixed and determined, as opposed to the rules used by prudence—come in the fine arts to share in the infinite suppleness and adaptability of the rules used by prudence, because they deal every time with the utter singularity of a new case, which is, in actual fact, unprecedented. It is, then, with prudential rules not fixed beforehand but determined according to the contingency of singular cases, it is with the virtues proper to prudence—perspicacity, circumspection, precaution, industry, boldness, shrewdness, and guile—that the craftsmanship of the artist succeedes in engendering in beauty.

In the third place, and also because the work to be made is an end in itself and a certain singular and original, totally unique participation in beauty, reason alone is not enough for the artist to form and conceive this work within himself in an infallible creative judgment. For, as Aristotle put it, "as everyone is, so does the end appear to him." Everyone judges of his own ends, when they engage his own self, in accordance with what he himself actually is. And since the final transcendent end is beauty—not a particular need to be satisfied, but beauty to be seduced—such a spiritual and transcendental, self-sufficient, absolute, all-exacting end demands that the very self and subjectivity of the artist should be committed to it. As a result, in order for the artist to form and conceive his work within himself in an infallible creative judgment, it is necessary that his subjective dynamism, his will and appetite straightly tend to beauty. At this point the statement that the truth of the practical intellect consists in conformity with the straight appetite takes on a new meaning. And we see that the fine arts, though they are more fully intellectual than the useful arts, imply, however, a much greater and more essential part played by the appetite, and require that the love for beauty should make the intellect co-natured with beauty. Because, in the last analysis, in art as in contemplation, intellectuality at its peak goes beyond concepts and discursive reason, and is achieved through a congeniality or connaturality with the object, which love alone can bring about. To produce in beauty the artist must be in love with beauty. Such undeviating love is a supra-artistic rule—a precondition, not sufficient as to the ways of making, yet necessary as to the vital animation of art—which is presupposed by all the rules of art.

9. The most significant point remains to be made. In speaking of the useful arts, we have observed that however important and necessary the secondary, more and more refined rules discovered by the craftsman may be, his primary obligation is to the primary rule, which is, in his case, the satisfying of a certain need, toward which, from the very start, his will basically tends. A splendid house with no doorway is not a good piece of architecture.

Now what is this primary rule in the case of the fine arts? I have said that in this case the appetite, together with the intellect, basically tends to the release of the pure creativity of the spirit, in its longing for beauty.

Consequently, the primary rule is the vital actuation or determination through which this free creativity of the spirit expresses itself first and foremost—and to which, therefore, the mind and the hand of the artist must first of all be loyal.

Thus for the apprentice as a painter or as a composer the primary rule is to follow purely the pleasure of his eyes or ears in the colors or sounds he will be responsible for; to respect this pleasure, and pay total attention to it; at every instant to produce nothing but what the senses are fully pleased with. For the creativity of the spirit, in its longing for beauty, passes through the senses, and is first vigilant in them, in a fragile way. Moreover, as soon as a tyro begins to discover, or to be taught, a particular rule of making, he happens more often than not to lose these fragile, inchoate awakenings of art, because he lacks the inner strength to master the particular rule in question, which then becomes a recipe and mars, along with his fidelity to his pleasure, the primary rule of art.

But with all that the threshold of art has not yet been crossed. It is crossed when the making of a work passes under the regime, no longer of the pleasure of intelligence-permeated senses, but of the creative intuition, which is born in the deepest depths of the Intellect. For the really genuine vital actuation through which the free creativity of the spirit expresses itself first and foremost is this creative or poetic intuition, to which the entire work to be engendered in beauty, in its perfect singularity as a kind of unique cosmos, is appendent. I shall have to discuss creative intuition in a subsequent chapter; I am only mentioning it now.

What I should like to stress is the fact that in creative intuition we have the primary rule to which, in the case of the fine arts, the whole fidelity, obedience, and heedfulness of the artist must be committed. I also should like to stress the fact that between this primary, primordial, primitive rule and all the other rules of making, however indispensable they may be, there exists an essential difference, so to speak infinite, as between heaven and earth. All other rules are of the earth, they deal with particular ways of operation in the making of the work. But this primary rule is a heavenly rule, because it deals with the very conception, in the bosom of the spirit, of the work to be engendered in beauty. If creative intuition is lacking, a work can be perfectly made, and it is nothing; the artist has nothing to say. If creative intuition is present, and passes, to some extent, into the work, the work exists and speaks to us, even if it is imperfectly made and proceeds from a man

c'ha l'habito de l'arte e man che trema,

—who has the habit of art and a hand which shakes.

At the summit of artistic activity, and for the one who has long traveled along the road of the rules, finally there is no longer any road. For the sons of God are under no law. Just as finally the unique law of the perfect soul, according to the saying of St. Augustine (not literally of him, but it does not matter), is *"ama et fac quod vis"*—love and do what you want—so the unique rule of the perfect artist is finally: "Cling to your creative intuition, and do what you want." "This kind of excellence . . . we recognize in a person in whom we are aware of a rare presence, a pure creative force, or an untrammeled spirit."[9]

TRANSCENDENCE OF THE FINE ARTS

10. The division between the useful arts and the fine arts must not be understood in too absolute a manner.[10] In the humblest work of the craftsman, if art is there, there is a concern for beauty, through a kind of indirect repercussion that the requirements of the creativity of the spirit exercise upon the production of an object to serve human needs. Furthermore, especially in works produced by our industrial age, in the various kinds of machines, or machinelike objects, contrived by the art of engineering or by our modern engineering-minded arts, the mere search for the pure technical exigencies of the utility, the solidity, and the good functioning of the thing made, without any search for beauty, naturally results in a beauty of its own. Our modern steamships, constructed only with a view to speed and utility, do not need the ornamentation of ancient galleys to provide a joy of the eyes and the mind by their perfect shape. I do not think that Brooklyn Bridge was built with any intention of beauty; and it was able to stir the deepest emotions of Hart Crane, and is bound forever to his lines. The chaos of bridges and skyways, desolated chimneys, gloomy factories, queer industrial masts and spars, infernal and stinking machinery which surrounds New York is one of the most moving—and beautiful—spectacles in the world.

All that is true. But for all that I consider the theories of Le Corbusier to be faulty dogmatism, and any system of aesthetics which gets clear of beauty for the sake of mechanical adjustment to be puritanism of forms and spurious austerity. For the kind of beauty I just described exists indeed: but as an accidental occurrence, a quite peculiar case in the whole universe of art, and I even wonder whether the delight we find in it does not flatter, perhaps, some perverse instinct of our too civilized eyes. In actual

[9] George Rowley, *Principles of Chinese Painting*, p. 80.
[10] Even, as we shall see further, the stock phrases "useful arts" and "fine arts," which I am using now to conform to the accepted vocabulary, are not, in my opinion, philosophically well grounded. I would prefer to say "subservient arts" and "free" or "self-sufficient arts."

fact, nature does not follow the teachings of Le Corbusier. Flowers, insects, and birds are not constructed with a view to the mere necessities of living; they display an amazing extravagance of ornament and luxury. And the beauty of the baroque also exists. And finally the same concern for beauty which was present in the craftsman, the same repercussion of the requirements of the creativity of the spirit, surreptitiously creeps into the very construction of machines and the very art of engineering. The beauty of the lines of an automobile is not indifferent to the engineers who draw its blueprint. And I doubt whether the engineers who built the George Washington Bridge or the Delaware Memorial Bridge were mere puritans of utility.

As to the great artists who take pleasure in describing themselves as mere engineers in the manufacturing of an artifact of words or sounds, as Paul Valéry did, and as Stravinsky does, I think that they purposely do not tell the truth, at least completely. In reality the spiritual content of a creative intuition, with the poetic or melodic sense it conveys, animates their artifact, despite their grudge against inspiration. And they are well aware of the vital value of this God-given element. But because it is scanty in them, or arises only from some secret stir in the working reason of a touchy Muse, they make good this very aridity, and manage to sidetrack us, by magnifying it, so as to glory in what they falsely describe as a total lack—lack of a quality that Plato has supposedly invented, and which is nothing, they say, for real art. For all that, Stravinsky is not a narcissist but a genuine creator, "a ferocious intellect which has fallen in love with the song of the daughters of man."[11]

11. Now the essential thing I should like to point out in our present comparison between useful arts and fine arts is contained in this twofold assertion: First, the fine arts, because of their immediate relation to beauty and to the pure creativity of the spirit, are free—with the very freedom of the spirit. They belong, therefore, in actual fact, to the world of liberal arts: a truth which the ancients did not recognize with respect to most of the fine arts, because any manual labor bore in their eyes the stamp of the servile condition. And this spiritual freedom of the fine arts causes them to dwell in a place which admits of no common, univocal measure with the useful arts. Everything said about art in general is to be transfigured when applied to them. They are virtues of the practical intellect; but, as we shall see in our further chapters, the intellect or reason which plays the principal and royal part in them is not conceptual, discursive, logical reason, nor even working reason. It is intuitive reason, in the obscure and high regions which

11 "The Freedom of Song," in my *Art and Poetry* (New York: Philosophical Library, 1943), p. 72.

are near the center of the soul, and in which the intellect exercises its activity at the single root of the soul's powers and conjointly with them. Thus it is that the fine arts are transcendent with regard to the useful arts.

Yet—this is my second point—the fine arts, from the very fact that they belong in the generic nature of art, participate in the law of the useful arts. Thus the conceptual, discursive, logical reason, or better (since we are in the practical order), the working reason, plays an essential and necessary— though secondary—part in the fine arts. This part, which relates to the particular ways of the making of an object, and of the realization of a creative intuition in matter, is an instrumental part: not only secondary, but merely instrumental. As soon as it gets the upper hand, the work is but a corpse of a work of art—a product of academicism. But when the resourcefulness of discursive reason, and the rules involved—which I called a moment ago the secondary rules—are used as instruments of a master *habitus*, and as the fingers, so to speak, of creative intuition, they compose the indispensable arsenal of prudence, shrewdness, and cleverness of the life of art. Degas pointed at all that when he said: "A painting is a thing which requires as much cunning, rascality, and viciousness as the perpetration of a crime."[12] To make fun of the rules, in proclaiming the liberty of art, is just an excuse provided by foolishness to mediocrity. "It is clear," Baudelaire wrote, "that systems of rhetoric and prosodies are not forms of tyranny arbitrarily devised, but a collection of rules required by the very organization of the spiritual being: never have prosodies and systems of rhetoric prevented originality from manifesting itself distinctly. The opposite would be far more true, that they have been a help to the blossoming forth of originality."[13] And Coleridge's sentence is still more to the point: "As it must not, so genius cannot, be lawless; for it is even this that constitutes it genius—the power of acting creatively under laws of its own origination."[14]

12. Two final remarks must be made. I have tried to bring out, and to lay stress upon, the pure essentials of art in its very nature, as operative virtue of the practical intellect. But obviously no virtue of the intellect can live in isolation. Since art is a virtue of the intellect, it demands to communicate with the entire universe of the intellect. Hence it is that the normal climate of art is intelligence and knowledge: its normal soil, the civilized heritage of a consistent and integrated system of beliefs and values; its

[12] Quoted by Etienne Charles in *Renaissance de l'Art français*, April, 1918.—Cf. *Artists on Art*, p. 308.

[13] "L'Œuvre et la vie d'Eugène Delacroix," in *L'Art romantique* (Paris: Calmann-Lévy, 1885), p. 13.

[14] *Lectures and Notes on Shakespeare and Other Dramatists* (New York: Harper, 1853), p. 54.

normal horizon, the infinity of human experience enlightened by the passionate insights of anguish or the intellectual virtues of a contemplative mind. The worshipping of ignorance and rudeness is for an artist but a sign of inner weakness. Yet, the fact remains that all the treasures of the earth are profitable to art only if it is strong enough to master them and make them a *means* for its own operation, an aliment for its own spark. And not all poets have the strength of a Dante.

On the other hand, the intellect is reflective by nature; so, no virtue of the intellect, even practical virtues, can genuinely develop in its own particular sphere without a more or less simultaneous development of reflectivity. Now what is the name of reflective intelligence in the domain of art? Its name is critical reason. Baudelaire wrote in this connection: "It would be quite a new departure in the history of the arts for a critic" (Baudelaire meant a critic who is born with *only* the gifts of a critic—which is, in my opinion, a nonsensical assumption) "to turn poet, a reversal of all psychological laws, a monstrosity; on the contrary, every great poet becomes naturally, inevitably, a critic. I am sorry for poets who are guided by instinct alone; I consider them incomplete. In the spiritual life of great poets a crisis infallibly arises, in which they want to reason out their art, to discover the obscure laws by virtue of which they have produced, and to derive from such a scrutiny a set of precepts whose divine aim is infallibility in poetic production. It would be a prodigy for a critic to turn poet and it is impossible for a poet not to contain a critic within himself."[15] These views are, I think, simply true as regards the poet. As regards the critic, they must be qualified, as we shall have an opportunity to see in a further chapter.

To conclude, let us observe that if it is true that art is a creative virtue of the intellect, which tends to engender in beauty, and that it catches hold, in the created world, of the secret workings of nature in order to produce its own work—a new creature—the consequence is that art continues in its own way the labor of divine creation. It is therefore true to say with Dante that our human art is, as it were, the grandchild of God—

Si che vostr' arte a Dio quasi è nipote.

[15] "Richard Wagner et Tannhauser," in op. cit., p. 229.

Benedetto Croce

ART AS INTUITION*

INTUITION AND EXPRESSION

Knowledge has two forms: it is either *intuitive* knowledge or *logical* knowledge; knowledge obtained through the *imagination* or knowledge obtained through the *intellect;* knowledge of the *individual* or knowledge of the *universal;* of *individual things* or of the *relations* between them: it is, in fact, productive either of *images* or of *concepts.*

In ordinary life, constant appeal is made to intuitive knowledge. It is said that we cannot give definitions of certain truths; that they are not demonstrable by syllogisms; that they must be learnt intuitively. The politician finds fault with the abstract reasoner, who possesses no lively intuition of actual conditions; the educational theorist insists upon the necessity of developing the intuitive faculty in the pupil before everything else; the critic in judging a work of art makes it a point of honour to set aside theory and abstractions, and to judge it by direct intuition; the practical man professes to live rather by intuition than by reason.

But this ample acknowledgment granted to intuitive knowledge in ordinary life, does not correspond to an equal and adequate acknowledgment in the field of theory and of philosophy. There exists a very ancient science of intellectual knowledge, admitted by all without discussion, namely, Logic: but a science of intuitive knowledge is timidly and with difficulty asserted by but a few. Logical knowledge has appropriated the lion's share and if she does not slay and devour her companion outright, yet yields to her but grudgingly the humble place of maid-servant or doorkeeper.—What can intuitive knowledge be without the light of intellectual knowledge? It is a servant without a master; and though a master find a servant useful, the master is a necessity to the servant, since he enables him to gain his livelihood. Intuition is blind; intellect lends her eyes.

Now, the first point to be firmly fixed in the mind is that intuitive knowledge has no need of a master, nor to lean upon any one; she does not need

---

* From Benedetto Croce's *Aesthetic*, trans., Douglas Ainslie, Chapters I-II. Copyright, 1909, by The Macmillan Company, Ltd. Reprinted by permission of Mrs. Gladys C. Quinton.

Benedetto Croce (1866-1952), Italian Idealist philosopher, wrote many books on philosophical problems, including his *Aesthetic* (1902), which became one of the leading works in twentieth century philosophy of art and criticism.

to borrow the eyes of others, for she has excellent eyes of her own. Doubt-less it is possible to find concepts mingled with intuitions. But in many other intuitions there is no trace of such a mixture, which proves that it is not necessary. The impression of a moonlight scene by a painter; the out-line of a country drawn by a cartographer; a musical motive, tender or en-ergetic; the words of a sighing lyric, or those with which we ask, command and lament in ordinary life, may well all be intuitive facts without a shadow of intellectual relation. But, think what one may of these instances, and ad-mitting further the contention that the greater part of the intuitions of civilized man are impregnated with concepts, there yet remains to be ob-served something more important and more conclusive. Those concepts which are found mingled and fused with the intuitions are no longer con-cepts, in so far as they are really mingled and fused, for they have lost all independence and autonomy. They have been concepts, but have now be-come simple elements of intuition. The philosophical maxims placed in the mouth of a personage of tragedy or of comedy, perform there the function, not of concepts, but of characteristics of such personage; in the same way as the red in a painted face does not there represent the red colour of the physicists, but is a characteristic element of the portrait. The whole is that which determines the quality of the parts. A work of art may be full of philosophical concepts; it may contain them in greater abundance and they may there be even more profound than in a philosophical dissertation, which in its turn may be rich to overflowing with descriptions and intuitions. But notwithstanding all these concepts the total effect of the work of art is an intuition and notwithstanding all those intuitions, the total effect of the philosophical dissertation is a concept. The *Promessi Sposi* contains copi-ous ethical observations and distinctions, but does not for that reason lose as a whole its character of simple story or intuition. In like manner the anecdotes and satirical effusions to be found in the works of a philosopher like Schopenhauer do not deprive those works of their character of intel-lectual treatises. The difference between a scientific work and a work of art, that is, between an intellectual fact and an intuitive fact, lies in the difference of the total effect aimed at by their respective authors. This it is that de-termines and rules over the several parts of each, not these parts separated and considered abstractly in themselves.

But to admit the independence of intuition as regards concept does not suffice to give a true and precise idea of intuition. Another error arises among those who recognize this, or who at any rate do not explicitly make intuition dependent upon the intellect, to obscure and confuse the real nature of intui-tion. By intuition is frequently understood *perception*, or the knowledge of actual reality, the apprehension of something as *real*.

Certainly perception is intuition: the perceptions of the room in which I am writing, of the ink-bottle and paper that are before me, of the pen I am using, of the objects that I touch and make use of as instruments of my person, which, if it write, therefore exists;—these are all intuitions. But the image that is now passing through my brain of a me writing in another room, in another town, with different paper, pen and ink, is also an intuition. This means that the distinction between reality and non-reality is extraneous, secondary, to the true nature of intuition. If we imagine a human mind having intuitions for the first time, it would seem that it could have intuitions of actual reality only, that is to say, that it could have perceptions of nothing but the real. But since knowledge of reality is based upon the distinction between real images and unreal images, and since this distinction does not at the first moment exist, these intuitions would in truth not be intuitions either of the real or of the unreal, not perceptions, but pure intuitions. Where all is real, nothing is real. The child, with its difficulty of distinguishing true from false, history from fable, which are all one to childhood, can furnish us with a sort of very vague and only remotely approximate idea of this ingenuous state. Intuition is the undifferentiated unity of the perception of the real and of the simple image of the possible. In our intuitions we do not oppose ourselves as empirical beings to external reality, but we simply objectify our impressions, whatever they be.

Those, therefore, who look upon intuition as sensation formed and arranged simply according to the categories of space and time, would seem to approximate more nearly to the truth. Space and time (they say) are the forms of intuition; to have an intuition is to place it in space and in temporal sequence. Intuitive activity would then consist in this double and concurrent function of spatiality and temporality. But for these two categories must be repeated what was said of intellectual distinctions, when found mingled with intuitions. We have intuitions without space and without time: the colour of a sky, the colour of a feeling, a cry of pain and an effort of will, objectified in consciousness: these are intuitions which we possess, and with their making space and time have nothing to do. In some intuitions, spatiality may be found without temporality, in others, *vice versa*; and even where both are found, they are perceived by later reflexion: they can be fused with the intuition in like manner with all its other elements: that is, they are in it *materialiter* and not *formaliter*, as ingredients and not as arrangement. Who, without an act or reflexion which for a moment breaks in upon his contemplation, can think of space while looking at a drawing or a view? Who is conscious of temporal sequence while listening to a story or a piece of music without breaking into it with a similar act of reflexion? What intuition reveals in a work of art is not space and time, but *character, in-*

dividual physiognomy. The view here maintained is confirmed in several quarters of modern philosophy. Space and time, far from being simple and primitive functions, are nowadays conceived as intellectual constructions of great complexity. And further, even in some of those who do not altogether deny to space and time the quality of formative principles, categories and functions, one observes an effort to unite them and to regard them in a different manner from that in which these categories are generally conceived. Some limit intuition to the sole category of spatiality, maintaining that even time can only be intuited in terms of space. Others abandon the three dimensions of space as not philosophically necessary, and conceive the function of spatiality as void of all particular spatial determination. But what could such a spatial function be, a simple arrangement that should arrange even time? It represents, surely, all that criticism and refutation have left standing—the bare demand for the affirmation of some intuitive activity in general. And is not this activity truly determined, when one single function is attributed to it, not spatializing nor temporalizing, but characterizing? Or rather, when it is conceived as itself a category or function which gives us knowledge of things in their concreteness and individuality?

Having thus freed intuitive knowledge from any suggestion of intellectualism and from every later and external addition, we must now explain it and determine its limits from another side and defend it from a different kind of invasion and confusion. On the hither side of the lower limit is sensation, formless matter, which the spirit can never apprehend in itself as simple matter. This it can only possess with form and in form, but postulates the notion of it as a mere limit. Matter, in its abstraction, is mechanism, passivity; it is what the spirit of man suffers, but does not produce. Without it no human knowledge or activity is possible but mere matter produces animality, whatever is brutal and impulsive in man, not the spiritual dominion, which is humanity. How often we strive to understand clearly what is passing within us! We do catch a glimpse of something, but this does not appear to the mind as objectified and formed. It is in such moments as these that we best perceive the profound difference between matter and form. These are not two acts of ours, opposed to one another; but the one is outside us and assaults and sweeps us off our feet, while the other inside us tends to absorb and identify itself with that which is outside. Matter, clothed and conquered by form, produces concrete form. It is the matter, the content, which differentiates one of our intuitions from another: the form is constant: it is spiritual activity, while matter is changeable. Without matter spiritual activity would not forsake its abstractness to become concrete and real activity, this or that spiritual content, this or that definite intuition.

It is a curious fact, characteristic of our times, that this very form, this very activity of the spirit, which is essentially ourselves, is so often ignored or denied. Some confound the spiritual activity of man with the metaphorical and mythological activity of what is called nature, which is mechanism and has no resemblance to human activity, save when we imagine, with Aesop, that *"arbores loquuntur non tantum ferae."* Some affirm that they have never observed in themselves this "miraculous" activity, as though there were no difference, or only one of quantity, between sweating and thinking, feeling cold and the energy of the will. Others, certainly with greater reason, would unify activity and mechanism in a more general concept, though they are specifically distinct. Let us, however, refrain for the moment from examining if such a final unification be possible, and in what sense, but admitting that the attempt may be made, it is clear that to unify two concepts in a third implies to begin with the admission of a difference between the two first. Here it is this difference that concerns us and we set it in relief.

Intuition has sometimes been confused with simple sensation. But since this confusion ends by being offensive to common sense, it has more frequently been attenuated or concealed with a phraseology apparently designed at once to confuse and to distinguish them. Thus, it has been asserted that intuition is sensation, but not so much simple sensation as *association* of sensations. Here a double meaning is concealed in the word "association." Association is understood, either as memory, mnemonic association, conscious recollection, and in that case the claim to unite in memory elements which are not intuited, distinguished, possessed in some way by the spirit and produced by consciousness, seems inconceivable: or it is understood as association of unconscious elements, in which case we remain in the world of sensation and of nature. But if with certain associations we speak of an association which is neither memory nor flux of sensations, but a *productive* association (formative, constructive, distinguishing); then our contention is admitted and only its name is denied to it. For productive association is no longer association in the sense of the sensationalist, but *synthesis*, that is to say, spiritual activity. Synthesis may be called association but with the concept of productivity is already posited the distinction between passivity and activity, between sensation and intuition.

Other psychologists are disposed to distinguish from sensation something which is sensation no longer, but is not yet intellectual concept: the *representation* or *image*. What is the difference between their representation or image and our intuitive knowledge? Everything and nothing: for "representation" is a very equivocal word. If by representation be understood something cut off and standing out from the psychic basis of the sensations, then representation is intuition. If, on the other hand, it be conceived as complex sensation we are back once more in crude sensation, which does not vary in quality according to its richness or poverty, or according to whether the organism in which it appears is rudimentary or highly developed and full of traces of past sensations. Nor is the ambiguity remedied by defining representation as a psychic product of secondary degree in relation to sensation, defined as occupying the first place. What does secondary degree mean here? Does it mean a qualitative, formal difference? If so, representation is an elaboration of sensation and therefore intuition. Or does it mean greater complexity and complication, a quantitative, material difference? In that case intuition is once more confused with simple sensation.

And yet there is a sure method of distinguishing true intuition, true representation, from that which is inferior to it: the spiritual fact from the mechanical, passive, natural fact. Every true intuition or representation is also *expression*. That which does not objectify itself in expression is not intuition or representation, but sensation and mere natural fact. The spirit only intuites in making, forming, expressing. He who separates intuition from expression never succeeds in reuniting them.

Intuitive activity possesses intuitions to the extent that it expresses them. Should this proposition sound paradoxical, that is partly because, as a general rule, a too restricted meaning is given to the word "expression." It is generally restricted to what are called verbal expressions alone. But there exist also non-verbal expressions, such as those of line, colour and sound, and to all of these must be extended our affirmation, which embraces therefore every sort of manifestation of the man, as orator, musician, painter, or anything else. But be it pictorial, or verbal, or musical, or in whatever other form it appear, to no intuition can expression in one of its forms be wanting; it is, in fact, an inseparable part of intuition. How can we really possess an intuition of a geometrical figure, unless we possess so accurate an image of it as to be able to trace it immediately upon paper or on the blackboard? How can we really have an intuition of the contour of a region, for example of the island of Sicily, if we are not able to draw it as it is in all its meanderings? Every one can experience the internal illumination which follows upon his success in formulating to himself his impressions and feelings, but only so far as he is able to formulate them. Feelings or impressions, then, pass by means of words from the obscure region of the soul into the clarity of the contemplative spirit. It is impossible to distinguish intuition from expression in this cognitive process. The one appears with the other at the same instant, because they are not two, but one.

The principal reason which makes our view appear paradoxical as we maintain it, is the illusion or prejudice that we possess a more complete intuition of reality than we really do. One often hears people say that they have many great thoughts in their minds, but that they are not able to express them. But if they really had them, they would have coined them into just so many beautiful, sounding words, and thus have expressed them. If these thoughts seem to vanish or to become few and meagre in the act of expressing them, the reason is that they did not exist or really were few and meagre. People think that all of us ordinary men imagine and intuite countries, figures and scenes like painters, and bodies like sculptors; save that painters and sculptors know how to paint and carve such images, while we bear them unexpressed in our souls. They believe that any one could have imagined a Madonna of Raphael; but that Raphael was Raphael owing to his technical ability in putting the Madonna upon canvas. Nothing can be more false than this view. The world which as a rule we intuite is a small thing. It consists of little expressions, which gradually become greater and wider with the increasing spiritual concentration of certain moments. They are the words we say to ourselves, our silent judgments: "Here is a man, here is a horse, this is heavy, this is sharp, this pleases me," etc. It is a medley of light and colour, with no greater pictorial value than would be expressed by a haphazard splash of colours, from among which one could barely make out a few special, distinctive traits. This and nothing else is what we possess in our ordinary life; this is the basis of our ordinary action. It is the index of a book. The labels tied to things (it has been said) take the place of the things themselves. This index and these labels (themselves expressions) suffice for small needs and small actions. From time to time we pass from the index to the book, from the label to the thing, or from the slight to the greater intuitions, and from these to the greatest and most lofty. This passage is sometimes far from easy. It has been observed by those who have best studied the psychology of artists that when, after having given a rapid glance at any one, they attempt to obtain a real intuition of him, in order, for example, to paint his portrait, then this ordinary vision, that seemed so precise, so lively, reveals itself as little better than nothing. What remains is found to be at the most some superficial trait, which would not even suffice for a caricature. The person to be painted stands before the artist like a world to discover. Michael Angelo said, "One paints, not with the hands, but with the brain." Leonardo shocked the prior of the Convent of the Graces by standing for days together gazing at the "Last Supper," without touching it with the brush. He remarked of this attitude: "The minds of men of lofty genius are most active in invention when they are doing the least external work." The painter is a painter, because he sees what others only feel or catch a glimpse of, but do not see. We think we see a smile, but in reality we have only a vague impression of it, we do not perceive all the characteristic traits of which it is the sum, as the painter discovers them after he has worked upon them and is thus able to fix them on the canvas. We do not intuitively possess more even of our intimate friend, who is with us every day and at all hours, than at most certain traits of physiognomy which enable us to distinguish him from others. The illusion is less easy as regards musical expression; because it would seem strange to every one to say that the composer had added or attached notes to a motive which was already in the mind of him who is not the composer; as if Beethoven's Ninth Symphony were not his own intuition and his intuition the Ninth Symphony. Now, just as one who is deluded as to the amount of his material wealth is confuted by arithmetic, which states its exact amount, so he who nourishes delusions as to the wealth of his own thoughts and images is brought back to reality, when he is obliged to cross the *Pons Asinorum* of expression. Let us say to the former, count; to the latter, speak; or, here is a pencil, draw, express yourself.

Each of us, as a matter of fact, has in him a little of the poet, of the sculptor, of the musician, of the painter, of the prose writer: but how little, as compared with those who bear those names, just because they possess the most universal dispositions and energies of human nature in so lofty a degree! How little too does a painter possess of the intuitions of a poet! And how little does one painter possess those of another painter! Nevertheless, that little is all our actual patrimony of intuitions or representations. Beyond these are only impressions, sensations, feelings, impulses, emotions, or whatever else one may term what still falls short of the spirit and is not assimilated by man; something postulated for the convenience of exposition, while actually non-existent, since to exist also is a fact of the spirit.

We may thus add this to the various verbal descriptions of intuition, noted at the beginning: intuitive knowledge is expressive knowledge. Independent and autonomous in respect to intellectual function; indifferent to later empirical discriminations, to reality and to unreality, to formations and apperceptions of space and time, which are also later: intuition or representation is distinguished as *form* from what is felt and suffered, from the flux or wave of sensation, or from psychic matter; and this form, this taking possession, is expression. To intuite is to express; and nothing else (nothing more, but nothing less) than *to express*.

INTUITION AND ART

Before proceeding further, it may be well to draw certain consequences from what has been established and to add some explanations.

We have frankly identified intuitive or expressive knowledge with the
aesthetic or artistic fact, taking works of art as examples of intuitive knowledge and attributing to them the characteristics of intuition, and *vice versa*.
But our identification is combated by a view held even by many philosophers,
who consider art to be an intuition of an altogether special sort. "Let us
admit" (they say) "that art is intuition; but intuition is not always art:
artistic intuition is a distinct species differing from intuition in general by
something *more*."

But no one has ever been able to indicate of what this something more
consists. It has sometimes been thought that art is not a simple intuition,
but an intuition of an intuition, in the same way as the concept of science
has been defined, not as the ordinary concept, but as the concept of a
concept. Thus man would attain to art by objectifying, not his sensations,
as happens with ordinary intuition, but intuition itself. But this process of
raising to a second power does not exist; and the comparison of it with the
ordinary and scientific concept does not prove what is intended, for the
good reason that it is not true that the scientific concept is the concept of
a concept. If this comparison proves anything, it proves just the opposite.
The ordinary concept, if it be really a concept and not a simple representation, is a perfect concept, however poor and limited. Science substitutes
concepts for representations; for those concepts that are poor and limited
it substitutes others, larger and more comprehensive; it is ever discovering
new relations. But its method does not differ from that by which is formed
the smallest universal in the brain of the humblest of men. What is generally
called *par excellence* art, collects intuitions that are wider and more complex
than those which we generally experience, but these intuitions are always of
sensations and impressions.

Art is expression of impressions, not expression of expression.

For the same reason, it cannot be asserted that the intuition, which is
generally called artistic, differs from ordinary intuition as intensive intuition.
This would be the case if it were to operate differently on the same matter.
But since the artistic function is extended to wider fields, yet does not differ
in method from ordinary intuition, the difference between them is not
intensive but extensive. The intuition of the simplest popular love-song,
which says the same thing, or very nearly, as any declaration of love that
issues at every moment from the lips of thousands of ordinary men, may
be intensively perfect in its poor simplicity, although it be extensively so
much more limited than the complex intuition of a love-song by Leopardi.

The whole difference, then, is quantitative, and as such is indifferent to
philosophy, *scientia qualitatum*. Certain men have a greater aptitude, a

more frequent inclination fully to express certain complex states of the soul. These men are known in ordinary language as artists. Some very complicated and difficult expressions are not often achieved, and these are called works of art. The limits of the expression-intuitions that are called art, as opposed to those that are vulgarly called non-art, are empirical and impossible to define. If an epigram be art, why not a simple word? If a story, why not the news-jottings of the journalist? If a landscape, why not a topographical sketch? The teacher of philosophy in Molière's comedy was right: "whenever we speak, we create prose." But there will always be scholars like Monsieur Jourdain, astonished at having spoken prose for forty years without knowing it, who will have difficulty in persuading themselves that when they call their servant John to bring their slippers, they have spoken nothing less than—prose.

We must hold firmly to our identification, because among the principal reasons which have prevented Aesthetic, the science of art, from revealing the true nature of art, its real roots in human nature, has been its separation from the general spiritual life, the having made of it a sort of special function or aristocratic club. No one is astonished when he learns from physiology that every cell is an organism and every organism a cell or synthesis of cells. No one is astonished at finding in a lofty mountain the same chemical elements that compose a small stone fragment. There is not one physiology of small animals and one of large animals; nor is there a special chemical theory of stones as distinct from mountains. In the same way, there is not a science of lesser intuition as distinct from a science of greater intuition, nor one of ordinary intuition as distinct from artistic intuition. There is but one Aesthetic, the science of intuitive or expressive knowledge, which is the aesthetic or artistic fact. And this Aesthetic is the true analogue of Logic, which includes, as facts of the same nature, the formation of the smallest and most ordinary concept and the most complicated scientific and philosophical system.

Nor can we admit that the word *genius* or artistic genius, as distinct from the non-genius of the ordinary man, possesses more than a quantitative signification. Great artists are said to reveal us to ourselves. But how could this be possible, unless there were identity of nature between their imagination and ours, and unless the difference were only one of quantity? It were better to change *poeta nascitur* into *homo nascitur poeta*: some men are born great poets, some small. The cult of the genius with all its attendant superstitions has arisen from this quantitative difference having been taken as a difference of quality. It has been forgotten that genius is not something that has fallen from heaven, but humanity itself. The man of genius who poses or is represented as remote from humanity finds this punishment in becoming or appearing somewhat ridiculous. Examples of this are the *genius* of the romantic period and the *superman* of our time.

But it is well to note here, that those who claim unconsciousness as the chief quality of an artistic genius, hurl him from an eminence far above humanity to a position far below it. Intuitive or artistic genius, like every form of human activity, is always conscious; otherwise it would be blind mechanism. The only thing that can be wanting to artistic genius is the *reflective* consciousness, the superadded consciousness of the historian or critic, which is not essential to it.

The relation between matter and form, or between *content* and *form,* as is generally said, is one of the most disputed questions in Aesthetic. Does the aesthetic fact consist of content alone, or of form alone, or of both together? This question has taken on various meanings, which we shall mention, each in its place. But when these words are taken as signifying what we have above defined, and matter is understood as emotionally not aesthetically elaborated, or impressions, and form as intellectual activity and expression, then our view cannot be in doubt. We must, that is to say, reject both the thesis that makes the aesthetic fact to consist of the content alone (that is, the simple impressions), and the thesis which makes it to consist of a junction between form and content, that is, of impressions plus expressions. In the aesthetic fact, expressive activity is not added to the fact of the impressions, but these latter are formed and elaborated by it. The impressions reappear as it were in expression, like water put into a filter, which reappears the same and yet different on the other side. The aesthetic fact, therefore, is form, and nothing but form.

From this was inferred not that the content is something superfluous (it is, on the contrary, the necessary point of departure for the expressive fact); but that *there is no passage* from the qualities of the content to those of the form. It has sometimes been thought that the content, in order to be aesthetic, that is to say, transformable into form, should possess some determined or determinable qualities. But were that so, then form and content, expression and impression, would be the same thing. It is true that the content is that which is convertible into form, but it has no determinable qualities until this transformation takes place. We know nothing about it. It does not become aesthetic content before, but only after it has been actually transformed. The aesthetic content has also been defined as the *interesting*. That is not an untrue statement; it is merely void of meaning. Interesting to what? To the expressive activity? Certainly the expressive activity would not have raised the content to the dignity of form, had it not been interested in it. Being interested is precisely the raising of the content to the dignity of form. But the word "interesting" has also been employed in another and an illegitimate sense, which we shall explain further on.

The proposition that art is *imitation of nature* has also several meanings. Sometimes truths have been expressed or at least shadowed forth in these words, sometimes errors have been promulgated. More frequently, no definite thought has been expressed at all. One of the scientifically legitimate meanings occurs when "imitation" is understood as representation or intuition of nature, a form of knowledge. And when the phrase is used with this intention, and in order to emphasize the spiritual character of the process, another proposition becomes legitimate also: namely, that art is the *idealization* or *idealizing* imitation of nature. But if by imitation of nature be understood that art gives mechanical reproductions, more or less perfect duplicates of natural objects, in the presence of which is renewed the same tumult of impressions as that caused by natural objects, then the proposition is evidently false. The coloured waxen effigies that imitate the life, before which we stand astonished in the museums where such things are shown, do not give aesthetic intuitions. Illusion and hallucination have nothing to do with the calm domain of artistic intuition. But on the other hand if an artist paint the interior of a wax-work museum, or if an actor give a burlesque portrait of a man-statue on the stage, we have work of the spirit and artistic intuition. Finally, if photography have in it anything artistic, it will be to the extent that it transmits the intuition of the photographer, his point of view, the pose and grouping which he has striven to attain. And if photography be not quite an art, that is precisely because the element of nature in it remains more or less unconquered and ineradicable. Do we ever, indeed, feel complete satisfaction before even the best of photographs? Would not an artist vary and touch up much or little, remove or add something to all of them?

The statements repeated so often, that art is not knowledge, that it does not tell the truth, that it does not belong to the world of theory, but to the world of feeling, and so forth, arise from the failure to realize exactly the theoretic character of simple intuition. This simple intuition is quite distinct from intellectual knowledge, as it is distinct from perception of the real; and the statements quoted above arise from the belief that only intellectual cognition is knowledge. We have seen that intuition is knowledge, free from concepts and more simple than the so-called perception of the real. Therefore art is knowledge, form; it does not belong to the world of feeling or to psychic matter. The reason why so many aestheticians have so often insisted that art is *appearance* (*Schein*), is precisely that they have felt the necessity of distinguishing it from the more complex fact of perception, by maintaining its pure intuitiveness. And if for the same reason it has been claimed that art is *feeling* the reason is the same. For if the concept as content of art, and historical reality as such, be excluded from the sphere of art, there remains no other content than reality apprehended in all its ingenuousness and immediacy in the vital impulse, in its *feeling*, that is to say again, pure intuition.

The theory of the *aesthetic senses* has also arisen from the failure to establish, or from having lost to view, the character of expression as distinct from impression, of form as distinct from matter.

This theory can be reduced to the error just indicated of wishing to find a passage from the qualities of the content to those of the form. To ask, in fact, what the aesthetic senses are, implies asking what sensible impressions are able to enter in aesthetic expressions, and which must of necessity do so. To this we must at once reply, that all impressions can enter into aesthetic expressions or formations, but that none are bound to do so of necessity. Dante raised to the dignity of form not only the "sweet colour of the oriental sapphire" (visual impressions), but also tactual or thermic impressions, such as the "dense air" and the "fresh rivulets" which "parch the more" the throat of the thirsty. The belief that a picture yields only visual impressions is a curious illusion. The bloom on a cheek, the warmth of a youthful body, the sweetness and freshness of a fruit, the edge of a sharp knife, are not these, too, impressions obtainable from a picture? Are they visual? What would a picture mean to an imaginary man, lacking all or many of his senses, who should in an instant acquire the organ of sight alone? The picture we are looking at and believe we see only with our eyes would seem to his eyes to be little more than an artist's paint-smeared palette.

Some who hold firmly to the aesthetic character of certain groups of impressions (for example, the visual and auditive), and exclude others, are nevertheless ready to admit that if visual and auditive impressions enter *directly* into the aesthetic fact, those of the other senses also enter into it, but only as *associated*. But this distinction is altogether arbitrary. Aesthetic expression is synthesis, in which it is impossible to distinguish direct and indirect. All impressions are placed by it on a level, in so far as they are aestheticized. A man who absorbs the subject of a picture or poem does not have it before him as a series of impressions, some of which have prerogatives and precedence over the others. He knows nothing as to what has happened prior to having absorbed it, just as, on the other hand, distinctions made after reflexion have nothing whatever to do with art as such.

The theory of the aesthetic senses has also been presented in another way; as an attempt to establish what physiological organs are necessary for the aesthetic fact. The physiological organ or apparatus is nothing but a group of cells, constituted and disposed in a particular manner; that is to say, it is a merely physical and natural fact or concept. But expression does not know physiological facts. Expression has its point of departure in the impressions, and the physiological path by which these have found their way to the mind is to it altogether indifferent. One way or another comes to the same thing: it suffices that they should be impressions.

It is true that the want of given organs, that is, of certain groups of cells, prevents the formation of certain impressions (when these are not otherwise obtained through a kind of organic compensation). The man born blind cannot intuite and express light. But the impressions are not conditioned solely by the organ, but also by the stimuli which operate upon the organ. One who has never had the impression of the sea will never be able to express it, in the same way as one who has never had the impression of the life of high society or of the political arena will never express either. This, however, does not prove the dependence of the expressive function on the stimulus or on the organ. It merely repeats what we know already: expression presupposes impression, and particular expressions particular impressions. For the rest, every impression excludes other impressions during the moment in which it dominates; and so does every expression.

Another corollary of the conception of expression as activity is the *indivisibility* of the work of art. Every expression is a single expression. Activity is a fusion of the impressions in an organic whole. A desire to express this has always prompted the affirmation that the work of art should have *unity*, or, what amounts to the same thing, *unity in variety*. Expression is a synthesis of the various, or multiple, in the one.

The fact that we divide a work of art into parts, a poem into scenes, episodes, similes, sentences, or a picture into single figures and objects, background, foreground, etc., may seem opposed to this affirmation. But such division annihilates the work, as dividing the organism into heart, brain, nerves, muscles and so on, turns the living being into a corpse. It is true that there exist organisms in which division gives rise to other living beings, but in such a case we must conclude, maintaining the analogy between the organism and the work of art, that in the latter case too there are numerous germs of life each ready to grow, in a moment, into a single complete expression.

It may be said that expression sometimes arises from other expressions. There are simple and there are *compound* expressions. One must surely admit some difference between the *eureka*, with which Archimedes expressed all his joy at his discovery, and the expressive act (indeed all the five acts) of a regular tragedy.—Not in the least: expression always arises directly from impressions. He who conceives a tragedy puts into a crucible a great quantity, so to say, of impressions: expressions themselves, conceived on other occasions, are fused together with the new in a single mass, in the same way as we can cast into a melting furnace formless pieces of bronze and choicest statuettes. Those choicest statuettes must be melted just like the pieces of bronze, before there can be a new statue. The old expressions must descend again to the level of impressions, in order to be synthesized in a new single expression.

By elaborating his impressions, man *frees* himself from them. By objectifying them, he removes them from him and makes himself their superior. The liberating and purifying function of art is another aspect and another formula of its character as activity. Activity is the deliverer, just because it drives away passivity.

This also explains why it is usual to attribute to artists both the maximum of sensibility or *passion,* and the maximum of insensibility or Olympian *serenity.* The two characters are compatible, for they do not refer to the same object. The sensibility or passion relates to the rich material which the artist absorbs into his psychic organism; the insensibility or serenity to the form with which he subdues and dominates the tumult of the sensations and passions.

Ernst Cassirer

ART*

1

Beauty appears to be one of the most clearly known of human phenomena. Unobscured by any aura of secrecy and mystery, its character and nature stand in no need of subtle and complicated metaphysical theories for their explanation. Beauty is part and parcel of human experience; it is palpable and unmistakable. Nevertheless, in this history of philosophical

* From Ernst Cassirer's *An Essay on Man,* Ch. 9. Copyright, 1944, by the Yale University Press. Reprinted by permission of the Yale University Press.

Ernst Cassirer (1874-1945), historian and philosopher, wrote many books on all phases of philosophy and the history of ideas. His most original work is the three volume *Philosophy of Symbolic Forms.* The essay on "Art," reprinted here from *An Essay on Man,* represents one aspect of Cassirer's total philosophy of symbolism.

thought the phenomenon of beauty has always proved to be one of the greatest paradoxes. Up to the time of Kant a philosophy of beauty always meant an attempt to reduce our aesthetic experience to an alien principle and to subject art to an alien jurisdiction. Kant in his *Critique of Judgment* was the first to give a clear and convincing proof of the autonomy of art. All former systems had looked for a principle of art within the sphere either of theoretical knowledge or of the moral life. If art was regarded as the off-spring of theoretical activity it became necessary to analyze the logical rules to which this particular activity conforms. But in this case logic itself was no longer a homogeneous whole. It had to be divided into separate and comparatively independent parts. The logic of the imagination had to be distinguished from the logic of rational and scientific thought. In his *Aesthetica* (1750) Alexander Baumgarten had made the first comprehensive systematic attempt to construct a logic of the imagination. But even this attempt, which in a sense proved to be decisive and invaluable, could not secure for art a really autonomous value. For the logic of the imagination could never command the same dignity as the logic of the pure intellect. If there was a theory of art, then it could only be a *gnoseologia inferior,* an analysis of the "lower," sensuous part of human knowledge. Art could, on the other hand, be described as an emblem of moral truth. It was conceived as an allegory, a figurative expression which under its sensuous form concealed an ethical sense. But in both cases, in its moral as well as in its theoretical interpretation, art possessed no independent value of its own. In the hierarchy of human knowledge and of human life art was only a preparatory stage, a subordinate and subservient means pointing to some higher end.

The philosophy of art exhibits the same conflict between two antagonistic tendencies that we encounter in the philosophy of language. This is of course no mere historical coincidence. It goes back to one and the same basic division in the interpretation of reality. Language and art are constantly oscillating between two opposite poles, an objective and a subjective pole. No theory of language or art could forget or suppress either one of these poles, though the stress may be laid now on the one and now on the other.

In the first case language and art are subsumed under a common heading, the category of imitation; and their principal function is mimetic. Language originates in an imitation of sounds, art is an imitation of outward things. Imitation is a fundamental instinct, an irreducible fact of human nature. "Imitation," says Aristotle, "is natural to man from childhood, one of his advantages over the lower animals being this, that he is the most imitative creature in the world, and learns at first by imitation." And imitation is also an inexhaustible source of delight, as is proved by the fact that, though the objects themselves may be painful to see, we delight nevertheless in viewing the most realistic representations of them in art—the forms, for example, of the lowest animals and of dead bodies. Aristotle describes this delight rather as a theoretical than as a specifically aesthetic experience. "To be learning something," he declares, "is the greatest of pleasures not only to the philosopher but also to the rest of mankind, however small their capacity for it; the reason of the delight in seeing the picture is that one is at the same time learning—gathering the meaning of things, e.g., that the man there is so-and-so."[1] At first sight this principle seems only to apply to the representative arts. It could, however, easily be transferred to all the other forms. Music itself became a picture of things. Even flute playing or dancing are, after all, nothing but imitations; for the flute player or the dancer represents by his rhythms men's characters as well as what they do and suffer.[2] And the whole history of poetics was influenced by the device of Horace, "*ut pictura poesis*," and by the saying of Simonides, "painting is mute poetry and poetry a speaking picture." Poetry is differentiated from painting by the mode and means, but not by the general function of imitation.

But it should be observed that the most radical theories of imitation were not intended to restrict the work of art to a merely mechanical reproduction of reality. All of them had to make allowance to a certain extent for the creativeness of the artist. It was not easy to reconcile these two demands. If imitation is the true aim of art, it is clear that the spontaneity, the productive power of the artist is a disturbing rather than a constructive factor. Instead of describing things in their true nature it falsifies the aspect of things. This disturbance introduced by the subjectivity of the artist could not be denied by the classical theories of imitation. But it could be confined within its proper limits and subjected to general rules. Thus the principle *ars simia naturae* could not be maintained in a strict and uncompromising sense. For not even nature itself is infallible, nor does it always attain its end. In such a case art must come to the aid of nature and actually correct or perfect it.

> But Nature mars—wherein she doth resemble
> The craftsman who about his labour goes
> And keeps the knack, although his fingers tremble.[3]

If "all beauty is truth," all truth is not necessarily beauty. In order to reach

---

[1] Aristotle, *Poetics*, 4. 1448[b] 5–17. In *Aristotle on the Art of Poetry*, ed. by Ingram Bywater (Oxford, 1909), pp. 8–11.

[2] *Idem*, 1. 1447[a] 26. Ed. Bywater, pp. 2–5.

[3] Dante, *Paradiso*, XIII, v. 76. English trans. by Melville Best Anderson, *The Divine Comedy* (World Book Co., 1921), p. 357.

the highest beauty it is just as essential to deviate from nature as to reproduce nature. To determine the measure, the right proportion, of this deviation, became one of the principal tasks of a theory of art. Aristotle had asserted that for the purposes of poetry a convincing impossibility is preferable to an unconvincing possibility. To the objection of a critic that Zeuxis had painted men such as could never exist in reality, the right answer is that it is *better* they should be like that, for the artist *ought* to improve on his model.[4]

The neoclassicists—from the Italians of the sixteenth century to the work of Abbé Batteux, *Les beaux arts reduits à un même principe* (1747)— took their point of departure from the same principle. Art does not reproduce nature in a general and indiscriminate sense; it reproduces *"la belle nature."* But if imitation is the real purpose of art the very concept of any such "beautiful nature" is highly questionable. For how can we improve on our model without disfiguring it? How can we transcend the reality of things without trespassing against the laws of truth? From the point of view of this theory poetry and art in general never can be anything but an agreeable falsity.

The general theory of imitation seemed to hold its ground and to defy all attacks up to the first half of the eighteenth century. But even in the treatise of Batteux, who was perhaps the last resolute champion of this theory,[5] we feel a certain uneasiness with regard to its universal validity. The stumbling block for this theory had always been the phenomenon of lyrical poetry. The arguments by which Batteux attempted to include lyrical poetry under the general scheme of imitative art are weak and inconclusive. And indeed all these superficial arguments were suddenly swept away by the appearance of a new force. Even in the field of aesthetics the name of Rousseau marks a decisive turning point in the general history of ideas. Rousseau rejected the whole classical and neoclassical tradition of the theory of art. To him art is not a description or reproduction of the empirical world but an overflow of emotions and passions. Rousseau's *Nouvelle Héloise* proved to be a new revolutionary power. The mimetic principle that had prevailed for many centuries had, henceforward, to give way to a new conception and a new ideal—to the ideal of "characteristic art." From this point we can trace the triumph of a new principle throughout the whole of European literature. In Germany Herder and Goethe followed the example of Rousseau. Thus the whole theory of beauty had to assume a new shape.

[4] Aristotle, *op. cit.*, 25. 1461[b]. Ed. Bywater, pp. 86–87.
[5] To be sure, even in the nineteenth century the general theory of imitation still played an important role. It is, for instance, maintained and defended in Taine's *Philosophie de l'art*.

Beauty in the traditional sense of the term is by no means the only aim of art; it is in fact but a secondary and derivative feature. "Do not let a misconception come between us"; Goethe admonishes his reader in his paper "Von deutscher Baukunst"; "do not let the effeminate doctrine of the modern beauty-monger make you too tender to enjoy significant roughness, lest in the end your enfeebled feeling should be able to endure nothing but unmeaning smoothness. They try to make you believe that the fine arts arose from our supposed inclination to beautify the world around us. That is not true. . . .

"Art is formative long before it is beautiful, and yet it is then true and great art, very often truer and greater than beautiful art itself. For man has in him a formative nature, which displays itself in activity as soon as his existence is secure; . . . And so the savage remodels with bizarre traits, horrible forms and coarse colors, his 'cocos,' his feathers, and his own body. And though this imagery consists of the most capricious forms, yet without proportions of shape, its parts will agree together, for a single feeling has created them into a characteristic whole.

"Now this characteristic art is the only true art. When it acts on what lies round it from inward, single, individual, original, independent feeling, careless and even ignorant of all that is alien to it, then, whether born of rude savagery or of cultivated sensibility, it is whole and living."[6]

With Rousseau and Goethe there began a new period of aesthetic theory. Characteristic art has gained a definitive victory over imitative art. But in order to understand this characteristic art in its true sense we must avoid a one-sided interpretation. It is not enough to lay the stress upon the emotional side of the work of art. It is true that all characteristic or expressive art is "the spontaneous overflow of powerful feelings." But if we were to accept this Wordsworthian definition without reserve, we should only be led to a change of sign, not to a decisive change of meaning. In this case art would remain reproductive, but, instead of being a reproduction of things, of physical objects, it would become a reproduction of our inner life, of our affections and emotions. Using once more our analogy with the philosophy of language, we might say that in this case we had only exchanged an onomatopoetic theory of art for an interjectional theory. But this is not the sense in which the term "characteristic art" was understood by Goethe. The passage cited above was written in 1773, in Goethe's youthful "*Sturm und Drang*" period. Yet in no period of his life could he ever neglect the objective pole of his poetry. Art is indeed expressive, but it cannot be

[6] Goethe, "Von deutscher Baukunst," "Werke," XXXVII, 148 f. English trans. by Bernard Bosanquet in *Three Lectures on Aesthetic* (London, Macmillan, 1923), pp. 114 ff.

expressive without being formative. And this formative process is carried out in a certain sensuous medium. "As soon as he is free from care and fear," writes Goethe, "the demigod, creative in repose, gropes round him for matter into which to breathe his spirit." In many modern aesthetic theories—especially that of Croce and his disciples and followers—this material factor is forgotten or minimized. Croce is interested only in the fact of expression, not in the mode. The mode he takes to be irrelevant both for the character and for the value of the work of art. The only thing which matters is the intuition of the artist, not the embodiment of this intuition in a particular material. The material has a technical but not an aesthetical importance. Croce's philosophy is a philosophy of the spirit emphasizing the purely spiritual character of the work of art. But in his theory the whole spiritual energy is contained and expended in the formation of the intuition alone. When this process is completed the artistic creation has been achieved. What follows is only an external reproduction which is necessary for the communication of the intuition but meaningless with respect to its essence. But for a great painter, a great musician, or a great poet, the colors, the lines, rhythms, and words are not merely a part of his technical apparatus; they are necessary moments of the productive process itself.

This is just as true of the specifically expressive arts as of the representative arts. Even in lyrical poetry emotion is not the only and decisive feature. It is of course true that the great lyrical poets are capable of the deepest emotions and that an artist who is not endowed with powerful feelings will never produce anything except shallow and frivolous art. But from this fact we cannot conclude that the function of lyrical poetry and of art in general can be adequately described as the artist's ability "to make a clean breast of his feelings." "What the artist is trying to do," says R. G. Collingwood, "is to express a given emotion. To express it, and to express it well, are the same thing. . . . Every utterance and every gesture that each one of us makes is a work of art."[7] But here again the whole constructive process which is a prerequisite both of the production and of the contemplation of the work of art is entirely overlooked. Every gesture is no more a work of art than every interjection is an act of speech. Both the gesture and the interjection are deficient in one essential and indispensable feature. They are involuntary and instinctive reactions; they possess no real spontaneity. The moment of purposiveness is necessary for linguistic and artistic expression. In every act of speech and in every artistic creation we find a definite teleological structure. An actor in a drama really "acts" his part. Each individual utterance is

[7] R. G. Collingwood, *The Principles of Art* (Oxford, Clarendon Press, 1938), pp. 279, 282, 285.

a part of a coherent structural whole. The accent and rhythm of his words, the modulation of his voice, the expressions of his face, and the postures of his body all tend to the same end—to the embodiment of human character. All this is not simply "expression"; it is also representation and interpretation. Not even a lyric poem is wholly devoid of this general tendency of art. The lyric poet is not just a man who indulges in displays of feeling. To be swayed by emotion alone is sentimentality, not art. An artist who is absorbed not in the contemplation and creation of forms but rather in his own pleasure or in his enjoyment of "the joy of grief" becomes a sentimentalist. Hence we can hardly ascribe to lyric art a more subjective character than to all the other forms of art. For it contains the same sort of embodiment, and the same process of objectification. "Poetry," wrote Mallarmé, "is not written with ideas, it is written with words." It is written with images, sounds, and rhythms which, just as in the case of dramatic poetry and dramatic representation, coalesce into an indivisible whole. In every great lyrical poem we find this concrete and indivisible unity.

Like all the other symbolic forms art is not the mere reproduction of a ready-made, given reality. It is one of the ways leading to an objective view of things and of human life. It is not an imitation but a discovery of reality. We do not, however, discover nature through art in the same sense in which the scientist uses the term "nature." Language and science are the two main processes by which we ascertain and determine our concepts of the external world. We must classify our sense perceptions and bring them under general notions and general rules in order to give them an objective meaning. Such classification is the result of a persistent effort toward simplification. The work of art in like manner implies such an act of condensation and concentration. When Aristotle wanted to describe the real difference between poetry and history he insisted upon this process. What a drama gives us, he asserts, is a single action (*mia praxis*) which is a complete whole in itself, with all the organic unity of a living creature; whereas the historian has to deal not with one action but with one period and all that happened therein to one or more persons, however disconnected the several events may have been.[8]

In this respect beauty as well as truth may be described in terms of the same classical formula: they are "a unity in the manifold." But in the two cases there is a difference of stress. Language and science are abbreviations of reality; art is an intensification of reality. Language and science depend upon one and the same process of abstraction; art may be described as a continuous process of concretion. In our scientific description of a given

[8] Aristotle, *op. cit.*, 23. 1459ª 17–29. Ed. Bywater, pp. 70–73.

object we begin with a great number of observations which at first sight are only a loose conglomerate of detached facts. But the farther we proceed the more these individual phenomena tend to assume a definite shape and become a systematic whole. What science is searching for is some central features of a given object from which all its particular qualities may be derived. If a chemist knows the atomic number of a certain element he possesses a clue to a full insight into its structure and constitution. From this number he may deduce all the characteristic properties of the element. But art does not admit of this sort of conceptual simplification and deductive generalization. It does not inquire into the qualities or causes of things; it gives us the intuition of the form of things. But this too is by no means a mere repetition of something we had before. It is a true and genuine discovery. The artist is just as much a discoverer of the forms of nature as the scientist is a discoverer of facts or natural laws. The great artists of all times have been cognizant of this special task and special gift of art. Leonardo da Vinci spoke of the purpose of painting and sculpture in the words *"saper vedere."* According to him the painter and sculptor are the great teachers in the realm of the visible world. For the awareness of pure forms of things is by no means an instinctive gift, a gift of nature. We may have met with an object of our ordinary sense experience a thousand times without ever having "seen" its form. We are still at a loss if asked to describe not its physical qualities or effects but its pure visual shape and structure. It is art that fills this gap. Here we live in the realm of pure forms rather than in that of the analysis and scrutiny of sense objects or the study of their effects.

From a merely theoretical point of view we may subscribe to the words of Kant that mathematics is the "pride of human reason." But for this triumph of scientific reason we have to pay a very high price. Science means abstraction, and abstraction is always an impoverishment of reality. The forms of things as they are described in scientific concepts tend more and more to become mere formulae. These formulae are of a surprising simplicity. A single formula, like the Newtonian law of gravitation, seems to comprise and explain the whole structure of our material universe. It would seem as though reality were not only accessible to our scientific abstractions but exhaustible by them. But as soon as we approach the field of art this proves to be an illusion. For the aspects of things are innumerable, and they vary from one moment to another. Any attempt to comprehend them within a simple formula would be in vain. Heraclitus' saying that the sun is new every day is true for the sun of the artist if not for the sun of the scientist. When the scientist describes an object he characterizes it by a set of numbers, by its physical and chemical constants. Art has not only a different aim but a different object. If we say of two artists that they paint "the same" landscape we describe our aesthetic experience very inadequately. From the point of view of art such a pretended sameness is quite illusory. We cannot speak of one and the same thing as the subject matter of both painters. For the artist does not portray or copy a certain empirical object— a landscape with its hills and mountains, its brooks and rivers. What he gives us is the individual and momentary physiognomy of the landscape. He wishes to express the atmosphere of things, the play of light and shadow. A landscape is not "the same" in early twilight, in midday heat, or on a rainy or sunny day. Our aesthetic perception exhibits a much greater variety and belongs to a much more complex order than our ordinary sense perception. In sense perception we are content with apprehending the common and constant features of the objects of our surroundings. Aesthetic experience is incomparably richer. It is pregnant with infinite possibilities which remain unrealized in ordinary sense experience. In the work of the artist these possibilities become actualities; they are brought into the open and take on a definite shape. The revelation of this inexhaustibility of the aspects of things is one of the great privileges and one of the deepest charms of art.

The painter Ludwig Richter relates in his memoirs how once when he was in Tivoli as a young man he and three friends set out to paint the same landscape. They were all firmly resolved not to deviate from nature; they wished to reproduce what they had seen as accurately as possible. Nevertheless the result was four totally different pictures, as different from one another as the personalities of the artists. From this experience the narrator concluded that there is no such thing as objective vision, and that form and color are always apprehended according to individual temperament.[9] Not even the most determined champions of a strict and uncompromising naturalism could overlook or deny this factor. Émile Zola defines the work of art as *"un coin de la nature vu à travers un tempérament."* What is referred to here as temperament is not merely singularity or idiosyncrasy. When absorbed in the intuition of a great work of art we do not feel a separation between the subjective and the objective worlds. We do not live in our plain commonplace reality of physical things, nor do we live wholly within an individual sphere. Beyond these two spheres we detect a new realm, the realm of plastic, musical, poetical forms; and these forms have a real universality. Kant distinguishes sharply between what he calls *"aesthetic* universality" and the "objective validity" which belongs to our logical and scientific judgments.[10] In our aesthetic judgments, he contends, we are not concerned

---

[9] I take this account from Heinrich Wölfflin's *Principles of Art History.*

[10] In Kant's terminology the former is called Gemeingültigkeit whereas the latter is called Allgemeingültigkeit—a distinction which is difficult to render in corresponding English terms. For a systematic interpretation of the two terms see H. W. Cassirer, *A Commentary on Kant's "Critique of Judgment"* (London, 1938), pp. 190 ff.

with the object as such but with the pure contemplation of the object. Aesthetic universality means that the predicate of beauty is not restricted to a special individual but extends over the whole field of judging subjects. If the work of art were nothing but the freak and frenzy of an individual artist it would not possess this universal communicability. The imagination of the artist does not arbitrarily invent the forms of things. It shows us these forms in their true shape, making them visible and recognizable. The artist chooses a certain aspect of reality, but this process of selection is at the same time a process of objectification. Once we have entered into his perpective we are forced to look on the world with his eyes. It would seem as if we had never before seen the world in this peculiar light. Yet we are convinced that this light is not merely a momentary flash. By virtue of the work of art it has become durable and permanent. Once reality has been disclosed to us in this particular way, we continue to see it in this shape.

A sharp distinction between the objective and the subjective, the representative and the expressive arts is thus difficult to maintain. The Parthenon frieze or a Mass by Bach, Michelangelo's "Sistine Chapel" or a poem of Leopardi, a sonata of Beethoven or a novel of Dostoievski are neither merely representative nor merely expressive. They are symbolic in a new and deeper sense. The works of the great lyrical poets—of Goethe or Hölderlin, of Wordsworth or Shelley—do not give us *disjecti membra poetae,* scattered and incoherent fragments of the poet's life. They are not simply a momentary outburst of passionate feeling; they reveal a deep unity and continuity. The great tragic and comic writers on the other hand—Euripides and Shakespeare, Cervantes and Molière—do not entertain us with detached scenes from the spectacle of life. Taken in themselves these scenes are but fugitive shadows. But suddenly we begin to see behind these shadows and to envisage a new reality. Through his characters and actions the comic and the tragic poet reveals his view of human life as a whole, of its greatness and weakness, its sublimity and its absurdity. "Art," wrote Goethe, "does not undertake to emulate nature in its breadth and depth. It sticks to the surface of natural phenomena; but it has its own depth, its own power; it crystallizes the highest moments of these superficial phenomena by recognizing in them the character of lawfulness, the prefection of harmonious proportion, the summit of beauty, the dignity of significance, the height of passion."[11] This fixation of the "highest moments of phenomena" is neither an imitation of physical things nor a mere overflow of powerful feelings. It is an interpretation of reality—not by concepts but by intuitions; not through the medium of thought but through that of sensuous forms.

[11] Goethe, Notes to a translation of Diderot's "Essai sur la peinture," "Werke," XLV, 260.

From Plato to Tolstoi art has been accused of exciting our emotions and thus of disturbing the order and harmony of our moral life. Poetical imagination, according to Plato, waters our experience of lust and anger, of desire and pain, and makes them grow when they ought to starve with drought.[12] Tolstoi sees in art a source of infection. "Not only is infection," he says, "a sign of art, but the degree of infectiousness is also the sole measure of excellence in art." But the flaw in this theory is obvious. Tolstoi suppresses a fundamental moment of art, the moment of form. The aesthetic experience—the experience of contemplation—is a different state of mind from the coolness of our theoretical and the sobriety of our moral judgment. It is filled with the liveliest energies of passion, but passion itself is here transformed both in its nature and in its meaning. Woodsworth defines poetry as "emotion recollected in tranquillity." But the tranquillity we feel in great poetry is not that of recollection. The emotions aroused by the poet do not belong to a remote past. They are "here"—alive and immediate. We are aware of their full strength, but this strength tends in a new direction. It is rather seen than immediately felt. Our passions are no longer dark and impenetrable powers; they become, as it were, transparent. Shakespeare never gives us an aesthetic theory. He does not speculate about the nature of art. Yet in the only passage in which he speaks of the character and function of dramatic art the whole stress is laid upon this point. "The purpose of playing," as Hamlet explains, "both at the first and now, was and is, to hold, as 'twere, the mirror up to nature; to show virtue her own feature, scorn her own image, and the very age and body of the time his form and pressure." But the image of a passion is not the passion itself. The poet who represents a passion does not infect us with this passion. At a Shakespeare play we are not infected with the ambition of Macbeth, with the cruelty of Richard III, or with the jealousy of Othello. We are not at the mercy of these emotions; we look through them; we seem to penetrate into their very nature and essence. In this respect Shakespeare's theory of dramatic art, if he had such a theory, is in complete agreement with the conception of the fine arts of the great painters and sculptors of the Renaissance. He would have subscribed to the words of Leonardo da Vinci that "*saper vedere*" is the highest gift of the artist. The great painters show us the forms of outward things; the great dramatists show us the forms of our inner life. Dramatic art discloses a new breadth and depth of life. It conveys an awareness of human things and human destinies, of human greatness and misery, in comparison to which our ordinary existence appears poor and trivial. All of us feel, vaguely and dimly, the infinite potentialities of life, which silently await the moment when they are to be called forth from

[12] Plato, *Republic*, 606D (Jowett trans.).

dormancy into the clear and intense light of consciousness. It is not the degree of infection but the degree of intensification and illumination which is the measure of the excellence of art.

If we accept this view of art we can come to a better understanding of a problem first encountered in the Aristotelian theory of catharsis. We need not enter here into all the difficulties of the Aristotelian term or into the innumerable efforts of the commentators to clear up these difficulties.[13] What seems to be clear and what is now generally admitted is that the cathartic process described by Aristotle does not mean a purification or a change in the character and quality of the passions themselves but a change in the human soul. By tragic poetry the soul acquires a new attitude toward its emotions. The soul experiences the emotions of pity and fear, but instead of being disturbed and disquieted by them it is brought to a state of rest and peace. At first sight this would seem to be a contradiction. For what Aristotle looks upon as the effect of tragedy is a synthesis of two moments which in real life, in our practical existence, exclude each other. The highest intensification of our emotional life is thought of as at the same time giving us a sense of repose. We live through all our passions feeling their full range and highest tension. But what we leave behind when passing the threshold of art is the hard pressure, the compulsion of our emotions. The tragic poet is not the slave but the master of his emotions; and he is able to transfer this mastery to the spectators. In his work we are not swayed and carried away by our emotions. Aesthetic freedom is not the absense of passions, not Stoic apathy, but just the contrary. It means that our emotional life acquires its greater strength, and that in this very strength it changes its form. For here we no longer live in the immediate reality of things but in a world of pure sensuous forms. In this world all our feelings undergo a sort of transubstantiation with respect to their essence and their character. The passions themselves are relieved of their material burden. We feel their form and their life but not their encumbrance. The calmness of the work of art is, paradoxically, a dynamic, not a static calmness. Art gives us the motions of the human soul in all their depth and variety. But the form, the measure and rhythm, of these motions is not comparable to any single state of emotion. What we feel in art is not a simple or single emotional quality. It is the dynamic process of life itself—the continuous oscillation between opposites poles, between joy and grief, hope and fear, exultation and despair. To give aesthetic form to our passions is to transform

[13] For details see Jakob Bernays, *Zwei Abhandlungen über die Aristotelische Theorie des Dramas* (Berlin, 1880) and Ingram Bywater, *Aristotle on the Art of Poetry* (Oxford, 1909), pp. 152 ff.

them into a free and active state. In the work of the artist the power of passion itself has been made a formative power.

It may be objected that all this applies to the artist but not to ourselves, the spectators and auditors. But such an objection would imply a misunderstanding of the artistic process. Like the process of speech the artistic process is a dialogical and dialectic one. Not even the spectator is left to a merely passive role. We cannot understand a work of art without, to a certain degree, repeating and reconstructing the creative process by which it has come into being. By the nature of this creative process the passions themselves are turned into actions. If in real life we had to endure all those emotions through which we live in Sophocles' *Oedipus* or in Shakespeare's *King Lear* we should scarcely survive the shock and strain. But art turns all these pains and outrages, these cruelties and atrocities, into a means of self-liberation, thus giving us an inner freedom which cannot be attained in any other way.

The attempt to characterize a work of art by some particular emotional feature must, therefore, inevitably fail to do it justice. If what art tries to express is no special state but the very dynamic process of our inner life, then any such qualification could hardly be more than perfunctory and superficial. Art must always give us motion rather than mere emotion. Even the distinction between tragic and comic art is much more a conventional than a necessary one. It relates to the content and motives but not to the form and essence of art. Plato had long since denied the existence of these artificial and traditional boundaries. At the end of the *Symposium* he describes Socrates as engaged in a conversation with Agathon, the tragic poet, and Aristophanes, the comic poet. Socrates compels the two poets to admit that the true tragedian is the true artist in comedy, and vice versa.[14] A commentary on this passage is given in the *Philebus*. In comedy as well as in tragedy, Plato maintains in this dialogue, we always experience a mixed feeling of pleasure and pain. In this the poet follows the rules of nature itself since he portrays "the whole comedy and tragedy of life."[15] In every great poem— in Shakespeare's plays, in Dante's *Commedia*, in Goethe's *Faust*—we must indeed pass through the whole gamut of human emotions. If we were unable to grasp the most delicate nuances of the different shades of feeling, unable to follow the continuous variations in rhythm and tone, if unmoved by sudden dynamic changes, we could not understand and feel the poem. We may speak of the individual temperament of the artist, but the work of art, as such, has no special temperament. We cannot subsume it under any traditional psychological class concept. To speak of Mozart's music as cheerful

[14] Plato, *Symposium*, 223 (Jowett trans.).
[15] *Philebus*, 48 ff. (Jowett trans.).

or serene, of Beethoven's as grave, somber, or sublime would betray an unpenetrating taste. Here too the distinction between tragedy and comedy becomes irrelevant. The question whether Mozart's *Don Giovanni* is a tragedy or an *opera buffa* is scarcely worth answering. Beethoven's composition based on Schiller's "Hymn to Joy" expresses the highest degree of exultation. But when listening to it we do not for a moment forget the tragic accents of the Ninth Symphony. All these contrasts must be present and they must be felt in their full strength. In our aesthetic experience they coalesce into one indivisible whole. What we hear is the whole scale of human emotions from the lowest to the highest note; it is the motion and vibration of our whole being. The greatest comedians themselves can by no means give us an easy beauty. Their work is often filled with great bitterness. Aristophanes is one of the sharpest and sternest critics of human nature; Molière is nowhere greater than in his *Misanthrope* or *Tartuffe*. Nevertheless the bitterness of the great comic writers is not the acerbity of the satirist or the severity of the moralist. It does not lead to a moral verdict upon human life. Comic art possesses in the highest degree that faculty shared by all art, sympathetic vision. By virtue of this faculty it can accept human life with all its defects and foibles, its follies and vices. Great comic art has always been a sort of *encomium moriae*, a praise of folly. In comic perspective all things begin to take on a new face. We are perhaps never nearer to our human world than in the works of a great comic writer—in Cervantes' *Don Quixote*, Sterne's *Tristram Shandy*, or in Dickens' *Pickwick Papers*. We become observant of the minutest details; we see this world in all its narrowness, its pettiness, and silliness. We live in this restricted world, but we are no longer imprisoned by it. Such is the peculiar character of the comic catharsis. Things and events begin to lose their material weight; scorn is dissolved into laughter and laughter is liberation.

That beauty is not an immediate property of things, that it necessarily involves a relation to the human mind, is a point which seems to be admitted by almost all aesthetic theories. In his essay "Of the Standard of Taste" Hume declares: "Beauty is no quality in things themselves: it exists merely in the mind which contemplates them." But this statement is ambiguous. If we understand mind in Hume's own sense, and think of self as nothing but a bundle of impressions, it would be very difficult to find in such a bundle that predicate which we call beauty. Beauty cannot be defined by its mere *percipi*, as "being perceived"; it must be defined in terms of an activity of the mind, of the function of perceiving and by a characteristic direction of this function. It does not consist of passive percepts; it is a mode, a process of perceptualization. But this process is not merely subjective in character; on the contrary, it is one of the conditions of our intuition of an objective world. The artistic eye is not a passive eye that receives and registers the impression of things. It is a constructive eye, and it is only by constructive acts that we can discover the beauty of natural things. The sense of beauty is the suceptibility to the dynamic life of forms, and this life cannot be apprehended except by a corresponding dynamic process in ourselves.

To be sure, in the various aesthetic theories this polarity, which as we have seen is an inherent condition of beauty, has led to diametrically opposed interpretations. According to Albrecht Dürer the real gift of the artist is to "elicit" beauty from nature. "Denn wahrhaftig steckt die Kunst in der Natur, wer sie heraus kann reissen, der hat sie."[16] On the other hand we find spiritualistic theories which deny any connection between the beauty of art and the so-called beauty of nature. The beauty of nature is understood as merely a metaphor. Croce thinks it sheer rhetoric to speak of a beautiful river or tree. Nature to him is stupid when compared with art; she is mute save when man makes her speak. The contradiction between these conceptions may perhaps be resolved by distinguishing sharply between organic beauty and aesthetic beauty. There are many natural beauties with no specific aesthetic character. The organic beauty of a landscape is not the same as that aesthetic beauty which we feel in the works of the great landscape painters. Even we, the spectators, are fully aware of this difference. I may walk through a landscape and feel its charms. I may enjoy the mildness of the air, the freshness of the meadows, the variety and cheerfulness of the coloring, and the fragrant odor of the flowers. But I may then experience a sudden change in my frame of mind. Thereupon I see the landscape with an artist's eye—I begin to form a picture of it. I have now entered a new realm—the realm not of living things but of "living forms." No longer in the immediate reality of things, I live now in the rhythm of spatial forms, in the harmony and contrast of colors, in the balance of light and shadow. In such absorption in the dynamic aspect of form consists the aesthetic experience.

2

All the controversies between the various aesthetic schools may in a sense be reduced to one point. What all these schools have to admit is that art is an independent "universe of discourse." Even the most radical de-

[16] "For art standeth firmly fixed in Nature—and who can rend her from thence, he only possesseth her." See William M. Conway, *Literary Remains of Albrecht Dürer* (1889), p. 182.

fenders of a strict realism who wished to limit art to a mimetic function alone have had to make allowance for the specific power of the artistic imagination. But the various schools differed widely in their evaluation of this power. The classical and neoclassical theories did not encourage the free play of imagination. From their point of view the imagination of the artist is a great but rather questionable gift. Boileau himself did not deny that, psychologically speaking, the gift of imagination is indispensable for every true poet. But if the poet indulges in the mere play of this natural impulse and instinctive power, he will never achieve perfection. The poet's imagination must be guided and controlled by reason and subjected to its rules. Even when deviating from the natural the poet must respect the laws of reason, and these laws restrict him to the field of the probable. French classicism defined this field in purely objective terms. The dramatic unities of space and time became physical facts measurable by a linear standard or by a clock.

An entirely different conception of the character and function of poetic imagination was introduced by the romantic theory of art. This theory is not the work of the so-called "romantic school" in Germany. It had been developed much earlier and had begun to play a decisive role in both French and English literature during the eighteenth century. One of the best and most concise expressions of this theory is to be found in Edward Young's *Conjectures on Original Composition* (1759). "The pen of an original writer," says Young, "like Armida's wand out of a barren waste calls a blooming spring." From this time on the classical views of the probable were supplanted more and more by their opposite. The marvelous and miraculous are now believed to be the only subjects that admit of true poetical portraiture. In eighteenth-century aesthetics we can trace step by step the rise of this new ideal. The Swiss critics Bodmer and Breitinger appeal to Milton in justification of the "wonderful in poetry."[17] The wonderful gradually outweighs and eclipses the probable as a literary subject. The new theory seemed to be embodied in the works of the greatest poets. Shakespeare himself had illustrated it in his description of the poet's imagination:

> The lunatic, the lover, and the poet
> Are of imagination all compact:
> One sees more devils than vast hell can hold,
> That is, the madman; the lover, all as frantic,
> Sees Helen's beauty in a brow of Egypt:
> The poet's eye, in a fine frenzy rolling,
> Doth glance from heaven to earth, from earth to heaven;
> And, as imagination bodies forth

[17] Cf. Bodmer and Breitinger, *Diskurse der Maler* (1721–23).

The forms of things unknown, the poet's pen
Turns them to shapes, and gives to airy nothing
A local habitation and a name.[18]

Yet the romantic conception of poetry found no solid support in Shakespeare. If we stood in need of proof that the world of the artist is not a merely "fantastic" universe, we could find no better, no more classical, witness than Shakespeare. The light in which he sees nature and human life is no mere "fancy light in fancy caught." But there is still another form of imagination with which poetry seems to be indissolubly connected. When Vico made his first systematic attempt to create a "logic of the imagination" he turned back to the world of myth. He speaks of three different ages: the age of gods, the age of heroes, and the age of man. It is in the two former ages, he declared, that we have to look for the true origin of poetry. Mankind could not begin with abstract thought or with a rational language. It had to pass through the era of the symbolic language of myth and poetry. The first nations did not think in concepts but in poetic images; they spoke in fables and wrote in hieroglyphs. The poet and the maker of myth seem, indeed, to live in the same world. They are endowed with the same fundamental power, the power of personification. They cannot contemplate any object without giving to it an inner life and a personal shape. The modern poet often looks back at the mystical, the "divine" or "heroic" ages, as at a lost paradise. In his poem "The Gods of Greece" Schiller expressed this feeling. He wished to recall the times of the Greek poets, for whom myth was not an empty allegory but a living power. The poet yearns for this golden age of poetry in which all things were still full of gods, in which every hill was the dwelling place of an oread, every tree the home of a dryad.

But this complaint of the modern poet appears to be unfounded. For it is one of the greatest privileges of art that it can never lose this "divine age." Here the source of imaginative creation never dries up, for it is indestructible and inexhaustible. In every age and in every great artist the operation of the imagination reappears in new forms and in new force. In the lyrical poets, first and foremost, we feel this continuous rebirth and regeneration. They cannot touch a thing without imbuing it with their own inner life. Wordsworth has described this gift as the inherent power of his poetry:

To every natural form, rock, fruits or flower,
Even the loose stones that cover the highway,
I gave a moral life: I saw them feel,
Or linked them to some feeling: the great mass

[18] *Midsummer Night's Dream*, Act V, sc. 1.

Lay imbedded in a quickening soul, and all
That I beheld respired with inward meaning.[19]

But with these powers of invention and of universal animation we are
only in the anteroom of art. The artist must not only feel the "inward meaning" of things and their moral life, he must externalize his feelings. The
highest and most characteristic power of artistic imagination appears in
this latter act. Externalization means visible or tangible embodiment not
simply in a particular material medium—in clay, bronze, or marble—but in
sensuous forms, in rhythms, in color pattern, in lines and design, in plastic
shapes. It is the structure, the balance and order, of these forms which affects
us in the work of art. Every art has its own characteristic idiom, which is
unmistakable and unexchangeable. The idioms of the various arts may be
interconnected, as, for instance, when a lyric is set to music or a poem is
illustrated; but they are not translatable into each other. Each idiom has
a special task to fulfill in the "architectonic" of art. "The problems of form
arising from this architectonic structure," states Adolf Hildebrand, "though
they are not given us immediately and self-evidently by Nature, are yet the
true problems of art. Material acquired through a direct study of Nature is,
by the architectonic process, transformed into an artistic unity. When we
speak of the imitative aspect of art, we are referring to material which has
not yet been developed in this manner. Through architectonic development,
then, sculpture and painting emerge from the sphere of mere naturalism into
the realm of true art."[20] Even in poetry we find this architectonic development. Without it poetical imitation or invention would lose its force. The
horrors of Dante's *Inferno* would remain unalleviated horrors, the raptures
of his *Paradiso* would be visionary dreams were they not molded into a
new shape by the magic of Dante's diction and verse.

In his theory of tragedy Aristotle stressed the invention of the tragic
plot. Of all the necessary ingredients of tragedy—spectacle, characters, fable,
diction, melody, and thought—he thought the combination of the incidents
of the story (*hê tôn pragmatôn systasis*) the most important. For tragedy
is essentially an imitation not of persons but of action and life. In a play the
persons do not act in order to portray the characters; the characters are
represented for the sake of the action. A tragedy is impossible without action,
but there may be tragedy without character.[21] French classicism adopted
and emphasized this Aristotelian theory. Corneille in the prefaces to his plays

[19] *Prelude*, III, 127–132.
[20] Adolpf Hildebrand, *Das Problem der Form in der bildenden Kunst*. English trans. by
Max Meyer and R. M. Ogden, *The Problem of Form in Painting and Sculpture* (New
York, G. E. Stechert Co., 1907), p. 12.
[21] Aristotle, *op. cit.*, 6. 1450[a] 7–25. Ed. Bywater, pp. 18–19.

everywhere insists upon this point. He speaks with pride of his tragedy *Heraclius* because here the plot was so complicated that it needed a special intellectual effort to understand and unravel it. It is clear, however, that this sort of intellectual activity and intellectual pleasure is no necessary element of the artistic process. To enjoy the plots of Shakespeare—to follow with the keenest interest "the combination of the incidents of the story" in *Othello, Macbeth,* or *Lear*—does not necessarily mean that one understands and feels the tragic art of Shakespeare. Without Shakespeare's language, without the power of his dramatic diction, all this would remain unimpressive. The context of a poem cannot be separated from its form—from the verse, the melody, the rhythm. These formal elements are not merely external or technical means to reproduce a given intuition; they are part and parcel of the artistic intuition itself.

In romantic thought the theory of poetic imagination had reached its climax. Imagination is no longer that special human activity which builds up the human world of art. It now has universal metaphysical value. Poetic imagination is the only clue to reality. Fichte's idealism is based upon his conception of "productive imagination." Schelling declared in his *System of Transcendental Idealism* that art is the consummation of philosophy. In nature, in morality, in history we are still living in the propylaeum of philosophical wisdom; in art we enter into the sanctuary itself. Romantic writers in both verse and prose expressed themselves in the same vein. The distinction between poetry and philosophy was felt to be shallow and superficial. According to Friedrich Schlegel the highest task of a modern poet is to strive after a new form of poetry which he describes as "transcendental poetry." No other poetic genre can give us the essence of the poetic spirit, the "poetry of poetry."[22] To poeticize philosophy and to philosophize poetry—such was the highest aim of all the romantic thinkers. The true poem is not the work of the individual artist; it is the universe itself, the one work of art which is forever perfecting itself. Hence all the deepest mysteries of all the arts and sciences appertain to poetry.[23] "Poetry," said Novalis, "is what is absolutely and genuinely real. That is the kernel of my philosophy. The more poetic, the more true."[24]

By this conception poetry and art seemed to be elevated to a rank and dignity they had never before possessed. They became a *novum organum* for discovering the wealth and depth of the universe. Nevertheless this exu-

[22] Cf. Schlegel, "Athenäumsfragmente," 238, in *Prosaische Jugendschriften,* ed. by J. Minor (2d ed. Vienna, 1906), II 242.
[23] Schlegel, "Gespräch über die Poesie" (1800), *op. cit.,* II, 364.
[24] Novalis, ed. J. Minor, III, 11. Cf. O. Walzel, *German Romanticism,* English trans. by Alma E. Lussky (New York, 1932), p. 28.

berant and ecstatic praise of poetic imagination had its strict limitations. In order to achieve their metaphysical aim the romanticist had to make a serious sacrifice. The infinite had been declared to be the true, indeed the only, subject of art. The beautiful was conceived as a symbolic representation of the infinite. He only can be an artist, according to Friedrich Schlegel, who has a religion of his own, an original conception of the infinite.[25] But in this event what becomes of our finite world, the world of sense experience? Clearly this world as such has no claim to beauty. Over against the true universe, the universe of the poet and artist, we find our common and prosaic world deficient in all poetic beauty. A dualism of this kind is an essential feature in all romantic theories of art. When Goethe began to publish *Wilhelm Meister's Lehrjahre* the first romantic critics hailed the work with extravagant expressions of enthusiasm. Novalis saw in Goethe "the incarnation of the poetic spirit on earth." But as the work continued, as the romantic figure of Mignon and the harpist were overshadowed by more realistic characters and more prosaic events, Novalis grew deeply disappointed. He not only revoked his first judgment; he went so far as to call Goethe a traitor to the cause of poetry. *Wilhelm Meister* came to be looked upon as a satire, a "*Candide* against poetry." When poetry loses sight of the wonderful, it loses its significance and justification. Poetry cannot thrive in our trivial and commonplace world. The miraculous, the marvelous, and the mysterious are the only subjects that admit of a truly poetic treatment.

This conception of poetry is, however, rather a qualification and limitation than a genuine account of the creative process of art. Curiously enough the great realists of the nineteenth century had in this respect a keener insight into the art process than their romantic adversaries. They maintained a radical and uncompromising naturalism. But it was precisely this naturalism which led them to a more profound conception of artistic form. Denying the "pure forms" of the idealistic schools they concentrated upon the material aspect of things. By virtue of this sheer concentration they were able to overcome the conventional dualism between the poetic and the prosaic spheres. The nature of a work of art, according to the realists, does not depend on the greatness or smallness of its subject matter. No subject whatever is imimpermeable to the formative energy of art. One of the greatest triumphs of art is to make us see commonplace things in their real shape and in their true light. Balzac plunged into the most trifling features of the "human comedy," Flaubert made profound analyses of the meanest characters. In some of Émile Zola's novels we discover minute descriptions of the structure of a locomotive, of a department store, or of a coal mine. No technical detail,

[25] Ideen, 13, in *Prosaische Jugendschriften*, II, 290.

however insignificant, was omitted from these accounts. Nevertheless, running through the works of all these realists great imaginative power is observable, which is by no means inferior to that of the romantic writers. The fact that this power could not be openly acknowledged was a serious drawback to the naturalistic theories of art. In their attempts to refute the romantic conceptions of a transcendental poetry they reverted to the old definition of art as an imitation of nature. In so doing they missed the principal point, since they failed to recognize the symbolic character of art. If such a characterization of art were admitted, there seemed to be no escape from the metaphysical theories of romanticism. Art is, indeed, symbolism, but the symbolism of art must be understood in an immanent, not in a transcendent sense. Beauty is "The Infinite finitely presented" according to Schelling. The real subject of art is not, however, the metaphysical Infinite of Schelling, nor is it the Absolute of Hegel. It is to be sought in certain fundamental structural elements of our sense experience itself—in lines, design, in architectural, musical forms. These elements are, so to speak, omnipresent. Free of all mystery, they are patent and unconcealed; they are visible, audible, tangible. In this sense Goethe did not hesitate to say that art does not pretend to show the metaphysical depth of things, it merely sticks to the surface of natural phenomena. But this surface is not immediately given. We do not know it before we discover it in the works of the great artists. This discovery, however, is not confined to a special field. To the extent that human language can express everything, the lowest and the highest things, art can embrace and pervade the whole sphere of human experience. Nothing in the physical or moral world, no natural thing and no human action, is by its nature and essence excluded from the realm of art, because nothing resists its formative and creative process. "Quicquid essentia dignum est," says Bacon in his *Novum Organum,* "id etiam scientia dignum est."[26] This dictum holds for art as well as for science.

3

The psychological theories of art have a clear and palpable advantage over all the metaphysical theories. They are not obliged to give a general theory of beauty. They limit themselves to a narrower compass, for they are concerned only with the fact of beauty and with a descriptive analysis of this fact. The first task of psychological analysis is to determine the class of phenomena to which our experience of beauty belongs. This problem entails no difficulty. No one could ever deny that the work of art gives us the highest

[26] Bacon, *Novum Organum,* Liber I, Aphor. CXX.

pleasure, perhaps the most durable and intense pleasure of which human nature is capable. As soon as we choose this psychological approach the secret of art seems, therefore, to be solved. There is nothing less mysterious than pleasure and pain. To call into question these best-known phenomena—phenomena not merely of human life but of life in general—would be absurd. Here if anywhere we find a *dos moi pou stô*, a fixed and immovable place to stand. If we succeed in connecting our aesthetic experience with this point there can no longer be any uncertainty as to the character of beauty and art.

The utter simplicity of this solution appears to recommend it. On the other hand all the theories of aesthetic hedonism have the defects of their qualities. They begin with the statement of a simple, undeniable, obvious fact; but after the first few steps they fall short of their purpose and come to a sudden standstill. Pleasure is an immediate datum of our experience. But when taken as a psychological principle its meaning becomes vague and ambiguous in the extreme. The term extends over such a large field as to cover the most diverse and heterogeneous phenomena. It is always tempting to introduce a general term broad enough to include the most disparate references. Yet if we yield to this temptation we are in danger of losing sight of significant and important differences. The systems of ethical and aesthetic hedonism have always been prone to obliterate these specific differences. Kant stresses this point in a characteristic remark in the *Critique of Practical Reason*. If the determination of our will, Kant argues, rests upon the feeling of agreeableness or disagreeableness which we expect from any cause, then it is all the same to us by what sort of ideas we are to be affected. The only thing that concerns us in making our choice is how great, how long continued, how easily obtained, and how often repeated this agreeableness is.

"Just as to the man who wants money to spend, it is all the same whether the gold was dug out of the mountain or washed out of the sand, provided it is everywhere accepted at the same value; so the man who cares only for the enjoyment of life does not ask whether the ideas are of the understanding or of the senses, but only *how much* and *how great* pleasure they will give us for the longest time."[27] If pleasure is the common denominator it is only the degree, not the kind, which really matters—all pleasures whatever are on the same level and may be traced back to a common psychological and biological origin.

In contemporary thought the theory of aesthetic hedonism has found its clearest expression in the philosophy of Santayana. According to Santayana beauty is pleasure regarded as a quality of things; it is "pleasure ob-

[27] *Critique of Practical Reason*, trans. by T. K. Abbott (6th ed., New York, Longmans, Green & Co., 1927); p. 110.

jectified." But this is begging the question. For how can pleasure—the most subjective state of our mind—ever be objectified? Science, says Santayana, "is the response to the demand for information, and in it we ask for the whole truth and nothing but the truth. Art is the response to the demand for entertainment, . . . and truth enters into it only as it subserves these ends."[28] But if this were the end of art we should be bound to say that art, in its highest achievements, fails to attain its real end. The "demand for entertainment" may be satisfied by much better and cheaper means. To think that the great artists worked for this purpose, that Michelangelo constructed Saint Peter's Cathedral, that Dante or Milton wrote their poems, for the sake of entertainment, is impossible. They would undoubtedly have subscribed to Aristotle's dictum that "to exert oneself and work for the sake of amusement seems silly and utterly childish."[29] If art is enjoyment it is not the enjoyment of things but the enjoyment of forms. Delight in forms is quite different from delight in things or sense impressions. Forms cannot simply be impressed on our minds; we must produce them in order to feel their beauty. It is a common flaw of all the ancient and modern systems of aesthetic hedonism that they offer us a psychological theory of aesthetic pleasure which completely fails to account for the fundamental fact of aesthetic creativeness. In aesthetic life we experience a radical transformation. Pleasure itself is no longer a mere affection; it becomes a function. For the artist's eye is not simply an eye that reacts to or reproduces sense impressions. Its activity is not confined to receiving or registering the impressions of outward things or to combining these impressions in new and arbitrary ways. A great painter or musician is not characterized by his sensitiveness to color or sounds but by his power to elicit from his static material a dynamic life of forms. Only in this sense, then, can the pleasure we find in art be objectified. To define beauty as "pleasure objectified" contains, therefore, the whole problem in a nutshell. Objectification is always a constructive process. The physical world —the world of constant things and qualities—is no mere bundle of sense data, nor is the world of art a bundle of feelings and emotions. The first depends upon acts of theoretical objectification, objectification by concepts and scientific constructs; the second upon formative acts of a different type, acts of contemplation.

Other modern theories protesting against all attempts to identify art and pleasure lie open to the same objection as the theories of aesthetic hedonism. They try to find the explanation of the work of art by connecting it with other well-known phenomena. These phenomena are, however, on an entirely

[28] *The Sense of Beauty* (New York, Charles Scribner's Sons, 1896), p. 22.
[29] Aristotle, *Nicomachean Ethics*, 1776ᵇ 33.

different level; they are passive, not active states of mind. Between the two classes we may find some analogies but we cannot trace them back to one and the same metaphysical or psychological origin. It is the struggle against the rationalist and intellectualist theories of art which is a common feature and a fundamental motive of these theories. French classicism had in a sense turned the work of art into an arithmetical problem which was to be solved by a sort of rule of three. The reaction against this conception was necessary and beneficial. But the first romantic critics—especially the German romanticists—went immediately to the opposite extreme. They declared the abstract intellectualism of the enlightenment to be a travesty upon art. We cannot understand the work of art by subjecting it to logical rules. A textbook on poetics cannot teach us how to write a good poem. For art arises from other and deeper sources. In order to discover these sources we must first forget our common standards, we must plunge into the mysteries of our unconscious life. The artist is a sort of somnambulist who must pursue his way without the interference or control of any conscious activity. To awake him would be to destroy his power. "It is the beginning of all poetry," said Friedrich Schlegel, "to abolish the law and method of the rationally proceeding reason and to plunge us once more into the ravishing confusion of fantasy, the original chaos of human nature."[30] Art is a waking dream to which we voluntarily surrender ourselves. This same romantic conception has left its mark upon contemporary metaphysical systems. Bergson gave a theory of beauty which was intended as the last and most conclusive proof of his general metaphysical principles. According to him there is no better illustration of the fundamental dualism, of the incompatibility, of intuition with reason than the work of art. What we call rational or scientific truth is superficial and conventional. Art is the escape from this shallow and narrow conventional world. It leads us back to the very sources of reality. If reality is "creative evolution" it is in the creativeness of art that we must seek the evidence for and the fundamental manifestation of the creativeness of life. At first sight this would appear to be a truly dynamic or energetic philosophy of beauty. But the intuition of Bergson is not a really active principle. It is a mode of receptivity, not of spontaneity. Aesthetic intuition, too, is everywhere described by Bergson as a passive capability, not as an active form. ". . . the object of art," writes Bergson, "is to put to sleep the active or rather resistant powers of our personality, and thus to bring us into a state of perfect responsiveness, in which we realize the idea that is suggested to us and sympathize with the feeling that is expressed. In the

---

[30] For a fuller documentation and for a criticism of these early romantic theories of art see Irving Babbitt, *The New Laokoon*, chap. iv.

processes of art we shall find, in a weakened form, a refined and in some measure spiritualized version of the processes commonly used to induce the state of hypnosis. . . . The feeling of the beautiful is no specific feeling . . . every feeling experienced by us will assume an aesthetic character, provided that it has been *suggested,* and not *caused.* . . . There are thus distinct phases in the progress of an aesthetic feeling, as in the state of hypnosis . . ."[31] Our experience of beauty is not, however, of such a hypnotic character. By hypnosis we may prompt a man to certain actions or we may force upon him some sentiment. But beauty, in its genuine and specific sense, cannot be impressed upon our minds in this way. In order to feel it one must co-operate with the artist. One must not only sympathize with the artist's feelings but also enter into his creative activity. If the artist should succeed in putting to sleep the active powers of our personality he would paralyze our sense of beauty. The apprehension of beauty, the awareness of the dynamism of forms, cannot be communicated in this way. For beauty depends both on feelings of a specific kind and on an act of judgment and contemplation.

One of the great contributions of Shaftesbury to the theory of art was his insistence on this point. In his "Moralists" he gives an impressive account of the experience of beauty—an experience which he regarded as a specific privilege of human nature. "Nor will you deny beauty," writes Shaftesbury, "to the wild field, or to these flowers which grow around us, on this verdant couch. And yet, as lovely as are these forms of nature, the shining grass or silvered moss, the flowry thyme, wild rose, or honey-suckle; 'tis not their beauty allures the neighboring herds, delights the brouzing fawn, or kid and spreads the joy we see amidst the feeding flocks: 'Tis not the *Form* rejoices; but that which is beneath the form: 'tis savouriness attracts, hunger impels; . . . for never can the *Form* be of real force where it is uncontemplated, unjudged of, unexamined, and stands only as the accidental note or token of what appeases provoked sense. . . . If brutes therefore . . . be incapable of knowing and enjoying beauty, as being brutes, and having sense only . . . for their own share; it follows, that neither can man by the same *sense* . . . conceive or enjoy *beauty:* but all the *beauty* . . . he enjoys, is in a nobler way, and by the help of what is noblest, his mind and reason."[32] Shaftesbury's praise of mind and reason was very far from the intellectualism of the enlightenment. His rhapsody on the beauty and infinite creative power of nature was an entirely new feature of eighteenth-century intellectual history. In this respect he was one of the first champions of romanticism. But Shaftesbury's romanticism was of a Platonic type. His theory of aesthetic

[31] Bergson, *Essai sur les données immédiates de la conscience.* English trans. by R. L. Pogson, *Time and Free Will* (London, Macmillan, 1912), pp. 14 ff.

[32] Shaftesbury, "The Moralists," sec. 2, Pt. III. See *Characteristics* (1714), II, 424 f.

form was a Platonic conception by virtue of which he was led to react and protest against the sensationalism of the English empiricists.[33]

The objection raised against the metaphysics of Bergson holds also for the psychological theory of Nietzsche. In one of his first writings, *The Birth of Tragedy from the Spirit of Music,* Nietzsche challenged the conceptions of the great classicists of the eighteenth century. It is not, he argues, the ideal of Winckelmann that we find in Greek art. In Aeschylus, in Sophocles or Euripides we seek in vain for "noble simplicity and quiet grandeur." The greatness of Greek tragedy consists in the depth and extreme tension of violent emotions. Greek tragedy was the offspring of a Dionysiac cult; its power was an orgiastic power. But orgy alone could not produce Greek drama. The force of Dionysus was counterbalanced by the force of Apollo. This fundamental polarity is the essence of every great work of art. Great art of all times has arisen from the interpenetration of two opposing forces— from an orgiastic impulse and a visionary state. It is the same contrast as exists between the dream state and the state of intoxication. Both these states release all manner of artistic powers from within us, but each unfetters powers of a different kind. Dream gives us the power of vision, of association, of poetry; intoxication gives us the power of grand attitudes, of passion, of song and dance.[34] Even in this theory of its psychological origin one of the essential features of art has disappeared. For artistic inspiration is not intoxication, artistic imagination is not dream or hallucination. Every great work of art is characterized by a deep structural unity. We cannot account for this unity by reducing it to two different states which, like the dream state and the state of intoxication, are entirely diffused and disorganized. We cannot integrate a structural whole out of amorphous elements.

Of a different type are those theories which hope to elucidate the nature of art by reducing it to the function of play. To these theories one cannot object that they overlook or underrate the free activity of man. Play is an active function; it is not confined within the boundaries of the empirically given. On the other hand the pleasure we find in play is completely disinterested. None of the specific qualities and conditions of the work of art seems, therefore, to be missing in play activity. Most of the exponents of the play theory of art have, indeed, assured us that they were quite unable to find any difference between the two functions.[35] They have declared that there is not a single characteristic of art which does not apply to games of

[33] For a detailed discussion of Shaftesbury's place in the philosophy of the eighteenth century, see Cassirer, *Die platonische Renaissance in England und die Schule von Cambridge* (Leipzig, 1932), chap. vi.

[34] Cf. Nietzsche, *The Will to Power.* English trans. by A. M. Ludovici (London, 1910), p. 240.

[35] See, for instance Konrad Lange, *Das Wesen der Kunst* (Berlin 1901). 2 vols.

illusion, and no characteristic of such games which could not also be found in art. But all the arguments that may be alleged for this thesis are purely negative. Psychologically speaking, play and art bear a close resemblance to each other. They are nonutilitarian and unrelated to any practical end. In play as in art we leave behind us our immediate practical needs in order to give our world a new shape. But this analogy is not sufficient to prove a real identity. Artistic imagination always remains sharply distinguished from that sort of imagination which characterizes our play activity. In play we have to do with simulated images which may become so vivid and impressive as to be taken for realities. To define art as a mere sum of such simulated images would indicate a very meager conception of its character and task. What we call *"aesthetic* semblance" is not the same phenomenon that we experience in games of illusion. Play gives us illusive images; art gives us a new kind of truth—a truth not of empirical things but of pure forms.

In our aesthetic analysis above we distinguished between three different kinds of imagination: the power of invention, the power of personification, and the power to produce pure sensuous forms. In the play of a child we find the two former powers, but not the third. The child plays with *things,* the artist plays with *forms,* with lines and designs, rhythms and melodies. In a playing child we admire the facility and quickness of transformation. The greatest tasks are performed with the scantiest means. Any piece of wood may be turned into a living being. Nevertheless, this transformation signifies only a metamorphosis of the objects themselves; it does not mean a metamorphosis of objects into forms. In play we merely rearrange and redistribute the materials given to sense perception. Art is constructive and creative in another and deeper sense. A child at play does not live in the same world of rigid empirical facts as the adult. The child's world has a much greater mobility and transmutability. Yet the playing child, nevertheless, does no more than exchange the actual things of his environment for other possible things. No such exchange as this characterizes genuine artistic activity. Here the requirement is much more severe. For the artist dissolves the hard stuff of things in the crucible of his imagination, and the result of this process is the discovery of a new world of poetical, musical, or plastic forms. To be sure, a great many ostensible works of art are very far from satisfying this requirement. It is the task of the aesthetic judgment or of artistic taste to distinguish between a genuine work of art and those other spurious products which are indeed playthings, or at most "the response to the demand for entertainment."

A closer analysis of the psychological origin and psychological effects of play and art leads to the same conclusion. Play gives us diversion and recreation but it also serves a different purpose. Play has a general biological relevance in so far as it anticipates future activities. It has often been pointed out that the play of a child has a propaedeutic value. The boy playing war and the little girl dressing her doll are both accomplishing a sort of preparation and education for other more serious tasks. The function of fine art cannot be accounted for in this manner. Here is neither diversion nor preparation. Some modern aestheticians have found it necessary to distinguish sharply between two types of beauty. One is the beauty of "great" art; the other is described as "easy" beauty.[36] But, strictly speaking, the beauty of a work of art is never "easy." The enjoyment of art does not originate in a softening or relaxing process but in intensification of all our energies. The diversion which we find in play is the very opposite of that attitude which is a necessary prerequisite of aesthetic contemplation and aesthetic judgment. Art demands the fullest concentration. As soon as we fail to concentrate and give way to a mere play of pleasurable feelings and associations, we have lost sight of the work of art as such.

The play theory of art has developed in two entirely different directions. In the history of aesthetics Schiller, Darwin, and Spencer are usually regarded as the outstanding representatives of this theory. Yet it is difficult to find a point of contact between the views of Schiller and modern biological theories of art. In their fundamental tendency these views are not only divergent but in a sense incompatible. The very term "play" is understood and explained in Schiller's accounts in a sense quite different from that of all the subsequent theories. Schiller's is a transcendental and idealistic theory; Darwin's and Spencer's theories are biological and naturalistic. Darwin and Spencer regard play and beauty as general natural phenomena, while Schiller connects them with the world of freedom. And, according to his Kantian dualism, freedom does not signify the same thing as nature; on the contrary, it represents the opposite pole. Both freedom and beauty belong to the intelligible, not to the phenomenal world. In all the naturalistic variants of the play theory of art the play of animals was studied side by side with that of men. Schiller could not admit any such view. For him play is not a general organic activity but a specifically human one. "Man only plays when in the full meaning of the word he is a man, and *he is only completely a man when he plays*."[37] To speak of an analogy, let alone an identity, between human and animal play or, in the human sphere, between the play of art and the

---

[36] See Bernard Bosanquet, *Three Lectures on Aesthetics,* and S. Alexander, *Beauty and Other Forms of Value.*

[37] Schiller, *Briefe über die ästhetische Erziehung des Menschen* (1795), Letter XV. English trans., *Essays Aesthetical and Philosophical* (London, George Bell & Sons, 1916), p. 71.

so-called games of illusion, is quite alien to the theory of Schiller. To him this analogy would have appeared to be a basic misconception.

If the historical background of Schiller's theory is taken into consideration his viewpoint is easily understandable. He did not hesitate to connect the "ideal" world of art with the play of a child because in his mind the world of the child had undergone a process of idealization and sublimation. For Schiller spoke as a pupil and admirer of Rousseau, and he saw the life of the child in the new light in which the French philosopher had placed him. "There is deep meaning in the play of a child," Schiller asserted. Yet even though we admit this thesis it must be said that the "meaning" of play is different from that of beauty. Schiller himself defines beauty as "living form." To him the awareness of living forms is the first and indispensable step which leads to the experience of freedom. Aesthetic contemplation or reflection, according to Schiller, is the first liberal attitude of man toward the universe. "Whereas desire seizes at once its object, reflection removes it to a distance and renders it inalienably her own by saving it from the greed of passion."[38] It is precisely this "liberal," this conscious and reflective attitude which is lacking in a child's play, and which marks the boundary line between play and art.

On the other hand this "removal to a distance" which is here described as one of the necessary and most characteristic features of the work of art has always proved to be a stumbling block for aesthetic theory. If this be true, it was objected, art is no longer something really human, for it has lost all connection with human life. The defenders of the principle *l'art pour l'art* did not, however, fear this objection; on the contrary they openly defied it. They held it to be the highest merit and privilege of art that it burns all bridges linking it with commonplace reality. Art must remain a mystery inaccessible to the *profanum vulgus*. "A poem," said Stéphane Mallarmé, "must be an enigma for the vulgar, chamber-music for the initiated."[39] Ortega y Gasset has written a book in which he foretells and defends the "dehumanization" of art. In this process he thinks that the point will at last be reached at which the human element will almost vanish from art.[40] Other critics have supported a diametrically opposed thesis. "When we look at a picture or read a poem or listen to music," I. A. Richards insists, "we are not doing something quite unlike what we were doing on our way to the Gallery or when we dressed in the morning. The fashion in which the experience is caused in us is different, and as a rule the experience is more com-

[38] Schiller, *op. cit.*, Letter XXV. English trans., p. 102.

[39] Quoted from Katherine Gilbert, *Studies in Recent Aesthetic* (Chapel Hill, 1927), p. 18.

[40] Ortega y Gasset, *La dezhumanización del' arte* (Madrid, 1925).

plex and, if we are successful, more unified. But our activity is not of a fundamentally different kind."[41] But this theoretical antagonism is no real antinomy. If beauty according to Schiller's definition is "living form" it unites in its nature and essence the two elements which here stand opposed. To be sure, it is not the same thing to live in the realm of forms as to live in that of things, of the empirical objects of our surroundings. The forms of art, on the other hand, are not empty forms. They perform a definite task in the construction and organization of human experience. To live in the realm of forms does not signify an evasion of the issues of life; it represents, on the contrary, the realization of one of the highest energies of life itself. We cannot speak of art as "extrahuman" or "superhuman" without overlooking one of its fundamental features, its constructive power in the framing of our human universe.

All aesthetic theories which attempt to account for art in terms of analogies taken from disordered and disintegrated spheres of human experience—from hypnosis, dream, or intoxication—miss the main point. A great lyrical poet has the power to give definite shape to our most obscure feelings. This is possible only because his work, though dealing with a subject which is apparently irrational and ineffable, possesses a clear organization and articulation. Not even in the most extravagant creations of art do we ever find the "ravishing confusions of fantasy," the "original chaos of human nature." This definition of art, given by the romantic writers,[42] is a contradiction in terms. Every work of art has an intuitive structure, and that means a character of rationality. Every single element must be felt as part of a comprehensive whole. If in a lyrical poem we change one of the words, an accent or a rhythm, we are in danger of destroying the specific tone and charm of the poem. Art is not fettered to the rationality of things or events. It may infringe all those laws of probability which classical aestheticians declared to be the constitutional laws of art. It may give us the most bizarre and grotesque vision, and yet retain a rationality of its own—the rationality of form. We may in this way interpret a saying of Goethe's which at first sight looks paradoxical, "Art: a second nature; mysterious too, but more understandable, for it originates in the understanding."[43]

Science gives us order in thoughts; morality gives us order in actions; art gives us order in the apprehension of visible, tangible, and audible appearances. Aesthetic theory was very slow indeed to recognize and fully

[41] I. A. Richards, *Principles of Literary Criticism* (New York, Harcourt, Brace, 1925), pp. 16–17.

[42] See above, p. 161.

[43] "Kunst: eine andere Natur, auch geheimnisvoll, aber verständlicher; denn sie entspringt aus dem Verstande." *See Maximen und Reflexionen,* ed. Max Hecker, in "Schriften der Goethe-Gesellschaft," XXI (1907), 229.

realize these fundamental differences. But if instead of seeking a meta-physical theory of beauty we simply analyze our immediate experience of the work of art we can hardly miss the mark. Art may be defined as a symbolic language. But this leaves us only with the common genus, not the specific difference. In modern aesthetics the interest in the common genus seems to prevail to such a degree as almost to eclipse and obliterate the specific difference. Croce insists that there is not only a close relation but a complete identity between language and art. To his way of thinking it is quite arbitrary to distinguish between the two activities. Whoever studies general linguistics, according to Croce, studies aesthetic problems—and vice versa. There is, however, an unmistakable difference between the symbols of art and the linguistic terms of ordinary speech or writing. These two activities agree neither in character nor purpose; they do not employ the same means, nor do they tend toward the same ends. Neither language nor art gives us mere imitation of things or actions; both are representations. But a representation in the medium of sensuous forms differs widely from a verbal or conceptual representation. The description of a landscape by a painter or poet and that by a geographer or geologist have scarcely anything in common. Both the mode of description and the motive are different in the work of a scientist and in the work of an artist. A geographer may depict a landscape in a plastic manner, and he may even paint it in rich and vivid colors. But what he wishes to convey is not the vision of the landscape but its empirical concept. To this end he has to compare its form with other forms; he has to find out, by observation and induction, its characteristic features. The geologist goes a step farther in this empirical delineation. He does not content himself with a record of physical facts, for he wishes to divulge the origin of these facts. He distinguishes the strata by which the soil has been built up, noting chronological differences; and he goes back to the general causal laws according to which the earth has reached its present shape. For the artist all these empirical relations, all these comparisons with other facts, and all this research into causal relations do not exist. Our ordinary empirical concepts may be, roughly speaking, divided into two classes according as they have to do with practical or theoretical interests. The one class is concerned with the use of things and with the question "What is that for?" The other is concerned with the causes of things and with the question "Whence?" But upon entering the realm of art we have to forget all such questions. Behind the existence, the nature, the empirical properties of things, we suddenly discover their forms. These forms are no static elements. What they show is a mobile order, which reveals to us a new horizon of nature. Even the greatest admirers of art have often spoken of it as if it were

a mere accessory, an embellishment or ornament, of life. But this is to underrate its real significance and its real role in human culture. A mere duplicate
of reality would always be of a very questionable value. Only by conceiving
art as a special direction, a new orientation, of our thoughts, our imagination, and our feelings, can we comprehend its true meaning and function.
The plastic arts make us see the sensible world in all its richness and multi-
fariousness. What would we know of the innumerable nuances in the aspect
of things were it not for the works of the great painters and sculptors?
Poetry is, similarly, the revelation of our personal life. The infinite potentialities of which we had but a dim and obscure presentiment are brought to
light by the lyric poet, by the novelist, and by the dramatist. Such art is in
no sense mere counterfeit or facsimile, but a genuine manifestation of our
inner life.

So long as we live in the world of sense impressions alone we merely
touch the surface of reality. Awareness of the depth of things always requires an effort on the part of our active and constructive energies. But
since these energies do not move in the same direction, and do not tend
toward the same end, they cannot give us the same aspect of reality. There
is a conceptual depth as well as a purely visual depth. The first is discovered by science; the second is revealed in art. The first aids us in understanding the reasons of things; the second in seeing their forms. In science
we try to trace phenomena back to their first causes, and to general laws
and principles. In art we are absorbed in their immediate appearance, and
we enjoy this appearance to the fullest extent in all its richness and variety.
Here we are not concerned with the uniformity of laws but with the multi-
formity and diversity of intuitions. Even art may be described as knowledge,
but art is knowledge of a peculiar and specific kind. We may well subscribe
to the observation of Shaftesbury that "all beauty is truth." But the truth of
beauty does not consist in a theoretical description or explanation of things;
it consists rather in the "sympathetic vision" of things.[44] The two views of
truth are in contrast with one another, but not in conflict or contradiction.
Since art and science move in entirely different planes they cannot contradict or thwart one another. The conceptual interpretation of science does
not preclude the intuitive interpretation of art. Each has its own perspective
and, so to speak, its own angle of refraction. The psychology of sense perception has taught us that without the use of both eyes, without a binocular

[44] See De Witt H. Parker, *The Principles of Aesthetics*, p. 39: "Scientific truth is the
fidelity of a description to the external objects of experience; artistic truth is sympathetic
vision—the organization into clearness of experience itself." The difference between
scientific and aesthetic experience has recently been illustrated in a very instructive article
by Prof. F. S. C. Northrup in the review *Furioso*, I, No. 4, 71 ff.

vision, there would be no awareness of the third dimension of space. The depth of human experience in the same sense depends on the fact that we are able to vary our modes of seeing, that we can alternate our views of reality. *Rerum videre formas* is a no less important and indispensable task than *rerum cognoscere causas.* In ordinary experience we connect phenomena according to the category of causality or finality. According as we are interested in the theoretical reasons or the practical effects of things, we think of them as causes or as means. Thus we habitually lose sight of their immediate appearance until we can no longer see them face to face. Art, on the other hand, teaches us to visualize, not merely to conceptualize or utilize, things. Art gives us a richer, more vivid and colorful image of reality, and a more profound insight into its formal structure. It is characteristic of the nature of man that he is not limited to one specific and single approach to reality but can choose his point of view and so pass from one aspect of things to another.

SELECTED BIBLIOGRAPHY

I.   Other Theories:
1. Immanuel Kant, *Critique of Judgment,* Part I, #43-46; 51-53. These sections contain Kant's views on the nature of art.
2. G. F. Hegel, *The Philosophy of Art,* especially "Introduction." (Available in either Modern Library or Scribner's *Selections.*)
3. Arthur Schopenhauer, *The World as Will and Idea,* Book III.
4. Leo Tolstoy, *What Is Art?* The classic statement of Emotionalism; the relevant parts of this view are reprinted in Chapter V below, especially as they relate to aesthetic response. (Available as Oxford Classic edition.)

II. Some Explanatory Writings:
1. Richard McKeon, "Literary Criticism and the Concept of Imitation in Antiquity," in R. Crane (ed.), *Critics and Criticism: Ancient and Modern,* University of Chicago Press, 1952. A discussion of 'mimesis' in Greek thought.
2. Erwin Panofsky, "The Neoplatonic Movement and Michelangelo," *Studies in Iconology,* pp. 171-230, Oxford University Press, 1939. A remarkable analysis of the influence of Plotinus on Ficino and the Platonic Academy in Florence and, consequently, on the art of Michelangelo.
3. John Hospers, "The Croce-Collingwood Theory of Art," *Philosophy,* 1956. A clear, critical account of the Expression Theory of Art.

Thus an artists picture
is an attempt to find
an order in ~~relation~~ a ~~in~~
disorder

That which is beautiful can
only be that which
is appealing to
man — man is most
appealing to man

Religious picture
Jesus Christ
is merely the highest
expression of
order in mankind
he is order

Beauty is ~~truth~~

~~truth~~ is unified knowledge

unified knowledge is the ~~knowledge~~ knowledge
of the order of a
part of reality

Thus beauty is the ~~attempt to~~
find expression of order ~~and~~ in
~~#~~ reality

II

Some Basic Concepts and Problems

our Lady — expression
of abstract concept of order
in
human
being
~~spiritual~~ reality

Beauty to man is the
imitation of himself
order in ~~disorder~~

our ~~lady~~ is ~~relief~~
of the spiritual / order

Michael Angelo
tried to put our order
pagan + christian
together

Introduction

This Part contains discussions of some major problems revolving around the first one, "what is art?" or "what do works of art have in common?" Seven distinct questions are raised, each one of which is dealt with by one or more selections. Involved in each question are one or more concepts that are often employed in our thinking and talking about art, and about which there is still much debate. The questions and their relevant concepts are these: (1) Can "art" be defined?; (2) What, if anything, are the form and content of a work of art?; (3) Does a work of art express anything and, if it does, what?; (4) Is art a language; does it have meanings?; (5) What are the nature and role of the medium in art?; (6) What is style in a work of art?; and (7) In order to appreciate fully any work of art, must we know what the artist intended when he created it and, if we must, how do we find out what his intention was?

Before these questions can be intelligently discussed, their basic concepts must be clarified and understood. For example, if we are to answer, say, the traditional question, "does music mean anything?," we must first come to terms with the concept of meaning itself. And the same point holds for all the above questions: The concepts of definition, form and content, expression, language, meaning, medium, style, and intention must be clarified. Hence, each of the readings of the separate sections of this chapter purports to be an elucidation of the relevant concept and a statement and solution of a particular problem about works of art.

CAN "ART" BE DEFINED?

The first selection, "The Role of Theory in Aesthetics," raises some fundamental questions about the factual and logical difficulties of any attempt to state the defining properties of art and, hence, to give an adequate answer to the question, "what is art?" It also goes on to reassess the role of traditional aesthetic theory in the light of these difficulties.

Erich Kahler wrote the second essay, "What is Art?," especially for this volume. It illustrates the sort of reply that can be made to the first selection, and, in addition, it incorporates Kahler's own, humanistic, definition of art. Taken together, the two essays show forth some of the basic issues between the traditional and the more modern, "linguistic" approaches to aesthetics.

Morris Weitz

THE ROLE OF THEORY IN AESTHETICS*

Theory has been central in aesthetics and is still the preoccupation of the philosophy of art. Its main avowed concern remains the determination of the nature of art which can be formulated into a definition of it. It construes definition as the statement of the necessary and sufficient properties

* From Morris Weitz's "The Role of Theory in Aesthetics," from *The Journal of Aesthetics and Art Criticism*, Vol. XV, No. 1, September, 1956, 27–35. Reprinted by permission of *The Journal of Aesthetics and Art Criticism*.

Morris Weitz (1916–   ), professor of philosophy at The Ohio State University, is author of *Philosophy of the Arts*.

of what is being defined, where the statement purports to be a true or false claim about the essence of art, what characterizes and distinguishes it from everything else. Each of the great theories of art—Formalism, Voluntarism, Emotionalism, Intellectualism, Intuitionism, Organicism—converges on the attempt to state the defining properties of art. Each claims that it is the true theory because it has formulated correctly into a real definition the nature of art; and that the others are false because they have left out some necessary or sufficient property. Many theorists contend that their enterprise is no mere intellectual exercise but an absolute necessity for any understanding of art and our proper evaluation of it. Unless we know what art is, they say, what are its necessary and sufficient properties, we cannot begin to respond to it adequately or to say why one work is good or better than another. Aesthetic theory, thus, is important not only in itself but for the foundations of both appreciation and criticism. Philosophers, critics, and even artists who have written on art, agree that what is primary in aesthetics is a theory about the nature of art.

Is aesthetic theory, in the sense of a true definition or set of necessary and sufficient properties of art, possible? If nothing else does, the history of aesthetics itself should give one enormous pause here. For, in spite of the many theories, we seem no nearer our goal today than we were in Plato's time. Each age, each art-movement, each philosophy of art, tries over and over again to establish the stated ideal only to be succeeded by a new or revised theory, rooted, at least in part, in the repudiation of preceding ones. Even today, almost everyone interested in aesthetic matters is still deeply wedded to the hope that the correct theory of art is forthcoming. We need only examine the numerous new books on art in which new definitions are proffered; or, in our own country especially, the basic textbooks and anthologies to recognize how strong the priority of a theory of art is.

In this essay I want to plead for the rejection of this problem. I want to show that theory—in the requisite classical sense—is *never* forthcoming in aesthetics, and that we would do much better as philosophers to supplant the question, "What is the nature of art?," by other questions, the answers to which will provide us with all the understanding of the arts there can be. I want to show that the inadequacies of the theories are not primarily occasioned by any legitimate difficulty such e.g., as the vast complexity of art, which might be corrected by further probing and research. Their basic inadequacies reside instead in a fundamental misconception of art. Aesthetic theory—all of it—is wrong in principle in thinking that a correct theory is possible because it radically misconstrues the logic of the concept of art. Its main contention that "art" is amenable to real or any kind of true definition is false. Its attempt to discover the necessary and sufficient properties of art is logically misbegotten for the very simple reason that such a set and, consequently, such a formula about it, is never forthcoming. Art, as the logic of the concept shows, has no set of necessary and sufficient properties, hence a theory of it is logically impossible and not merely factually difficult. Aesthetic theory tries to define what cannot be defined in its requisite sense. But in recommending the repudiation of aesthetic theory I shall not argue from this, as too many others have done, that its logical confusions render it meaningless or worthless. On the contrary, I wish to reassess its role and its contribution primarily in order to show that it is of the greatest importance to our understanding of the arts.

Let us now survey briefly some of the more famous extant aesthetic theories in order to see if they do incorporate correct and adequate statements about the nature of art. In each of these there is the assumption that it is the true enumeration of the defining properties of art, with the implication that previous theories have stressed wrong definitions. Thus, to begin with, consider a famous version of Formalist theory, that propounded by Bell and Fry. It is true that they speak mostly of painting in their writings but both assert that what they find in that art can be generalized for what is "art" in the others as well. The essence of painting, they maintain, is the plastic elements in relation. Its defining property is significant form, i.e., certain combinations of lines, colors, shapes, volumes—everything on the canvas except the representational elements—which evoke a unique response to such combinations. Painting is definable as plastic organization. The nature of art, what it *really* is, so their theory goes, is a unique combination of certain elements (the specifiable plastic ones) in their relations. Anything which is art is an instance of significant form; and anything which is not art has no such form.

To this the Emotionalist replies that the truly essential property of art has been left out. Tolstoy, Ducasse, or any of the advocates of this theory, find that the requisite defining property is not significant form but rather the expression of emotion in some sensuous public medium. Without projection of emotion into some piece of stone or words or sounds, etc., there can be no art. Art is really such embodiment. It is this that uniquely characterizes art, and any true, real definition of it, contained in some adequate theory of art, must so state it.

The Intuitionist disclaims both emotion and form as defining properties. In Croce's version, for example, art is identified not with some physical, public object but with a specific creative, cognitive and spiritual act. Art is really a first stage of knowledge in which certain human beings (artists) bring their images and intuitions into lyrical clarification or expression. As such, it is an awareness, non-conceptual in character, of the unique individuality of things; and since it exists below the level of conceptualization or action, it is without scientific or moral content. Croce singles out as the defining essence of art this first stage of spiritual life and advances its identification with art as a philosophically true theory or definition.

The Organicist says to all of this that art is really a class of organic wholes consisting of distinguishable, albeit inseparable, elements in their causally efficacious relations which are presented in some sensuous medium. In A. C. Bradley, in piece-meal versions of it in literary criticism, or in my own generalized adaptation of it in my *Philosophy of the Arts*, what is claimed is that anything which is a work of art is in its nature a unique complex of interrelated parts—in painting, for example, lines, colors, volumes, subjects, etc., all interacting upon one another on a paint surface of some sort. Certainly, at one time at least it seemed to me that this organic theory constituted the one true and real definition of art.

My final example is the most interesting of all, logically speaking. This is the Voluntarist theory of Parker. In his writings on art, Parker persistently calls into question the traditional simple-minded definitions of aesthetics. "The assumption underlying every philosophy of art is the existence of some common nature present in all the arts."[1] All the so popular brief definitions of art—'significant form,' 'expression,' 'intuition,' 'objectified pleasure'—are fallacious, either because, while true of art, they are also true of much that is not art, and hence fail to differentiate art from other things; or else because they neglect some essential aspect of art."[2] But instead of inveighing against the attempt at definition of art itself, Parker insists that what is needed is a complex definition rather than a simple one. "The definition of art must therefore be in terms of a complex of characteristics. Failure to recognize this has been the fault of all the well-known definitions."[3] His own version of Voluntarism is the theory that art is essentially three things: embodiment of wishes and desires imaginatively satisfied, language, which characterizes the public medium of art, and harmony, which unifies the language with the layers of imaginative projections. Thus, for Parker, it is a true definition to say of art that it is "... the provision of satisfaction through the imagination, social significance, and harmony. I am claiming that nothing except works of art possesses all three of these marks."[4]

Now, all of these sample theories are inadequate in many different

---

[1] D. Parker, "The Nature of Art," reprinted in Part I.
[2] *Ibid.*
[3] *Ibid.*
[4] *Ibid.*

ways. Each purports to be a complete statement about the defining features of all works of art and yet each of them leaves out something which the others take to be central. Some are circular, e.g., the Bell-Fry theory of art as significant form which is defined in part in terms of our response to significant form. Some of them, in their search for necessary and sufficient properties, emphasize too few properties, like (again) the Bell-Fry definition which leaves out subject-representation in painting, or the Croce theory which omits inclusion of the very important feature of the public, physical character, say, of architecture. Others are too general and cover objects that are not art as well as works of art. Organicism is surely such a view since it can be applied to *any* causal unity in the natural world as well as to art.[5] Still others rest on dubious principles, e.g., Parker's claim that art embodies imaginative satisfactions, rather than real ones; or Croce's assertion that there is nonconceptual knowledge. Consequently, even if art has one set of necessary and sufficient properties, none of the theories we have noted or, for that matter, no aesthetic theory yet proposed, has enumerated that set to the satisfaction of all concerned.

Then there is a different sort of difficulty. As real definitions, these theories are supposed to be factual reports on art. If they are, may we not ask, Are they empirical and open to verification or falsification? For example, what would confirm or disconfirm the theory that art is significant form or embodiment of emotion or creative synthesis of images? There does not even seem to be a hint of the kind of evidence which might be forthcoming to test these theories; and indeed one wonders if they are perhaps honorific definitions of "art," that is, proposed redefinitions in terms of some *chosen* conditions for applying the concept of art, and not true or false reports on the essential properties of art at all.

But all these criticisms of traditional aesthetic theories—that they are circular, incomplete, untestable, pseudo-factual, disguised proposals to change the meaning of concepts—have been made before. My intention is to go beyond these to make a much more fundamental criticism, namely, that aesthetic theory is a logically vain attempt to define what cannot be defined, to state the necessary and sufficient properties of that which has no necessary and sufficient properties, to conceive the concept of art as closed when its very use reveals and demands its openness.

The problem with which we must begin is not "What is art?," but "What sort of concept is 'art'?" Indeed, the root problem of philosophy itself is to explain the relation between the employment of certain kinds of con-

---

[5] See M. Macdonald's review of my *Philosophy of the Arts, Mind*, Oct., 1951, pp. 561–564, for a brilliant discussion of this objection to the Organic theory.

cepts and the conditions under which they can be correctly applied. If I may paraphrase Wittgenstein, we must not ask, What is the nature of any philosophical x?, or even, according to the semanticist, What does "x" mean?, a transformation that leads to the disastrous interpretation of "art" as a name for some specifiable class of objects; but rather, What is the use or employment of "x"? What does "x" do in the language? This, I take it, is the initial question, the begin-all if not the end-all of any philosophical problem and solution. Thus, in aesthetics, our first problem is the elucidation of the actual employment of the concept of art, to give a logical description of the actual functioning of the concept, including a description of the conditions under which we correctly use it or its correlates.

My model in this type of logical description or philosophy derives from Wittgenstein. It is also he who, in his refutation of philosophical theorizing in the sense of constructing definitions of philosophical entities, has furnished contemporary aesthetics with a starting point for any future progress. In his new work, *Philosophical Investigations*,[6] Wittgenstein raises as an illustrative question, What is a game? The traditional philosophical, theoretical answer would be in terms of some exhaustive set of properties common to all games. To this Wittgenstein says, let us consider what we call "games": "I mean board-games, card-games, ball-games, Olympic games, and so on. What is common to them all?—Don't say: 'there *must* be something common, or they would not be called "games"' but *look and see* whether there is anything common to all.—For if you look at them you will not see something that is common to *all*, but similarities, relationships, and a whole series of them at that . . ."

Card games are like board games in some respects but not in others. Not all games are amusing, nor is there always winning or losing or competition. Some games resemble others in some respects—that is all. What we find are no necessary and sufficient properties, only "a complicated network of similarities overlapping and crisscrossing," such that we can say of games that they form a family with family resemblances and no common trait. If one asks what a game is, we pick out sample games, describe these, and add, "This and *similar things* are called 'games'." This is all we need to say and indeed all any of us knows about games. Knowing what a game is is not knowing some real definition or theory but being able to recognize and explain games and to decide which among imaginary and new examples would or would not be called "games."

The problem of the nature of art is like that of the nature of games, at

---

[6] L. Wittgenstein, *Philosophical Investigations*, (Oxford, 1953), tr. by E. Anscombe; see esp. Part I, Sections 65–75. All quotations are from these sections.

least in these respects: If we actually look and see what it is that we call "art," we will also find no common properties—only strands of similarities. Knowing what art is is not apprehending some manifest or latent essence but being able to recognize, describe, and explain those things we call "art" in virtue of these similarities.

But the basic resemblance between these concepts is their open texture. In elucidating them, certain (paradigm) cases can be given, about which there can be no question as to their being correctly described as "art" or "game," but no exhaustive set of cases can be given. I can list some cases and some conditions under which I can apply correctly the concept of art but I cannot list all of them, for the all-important reason that unforeseeable or novel conditions are always forthcoming or envisageable.

A concept is open if its conditions of application are emendable and corrigible; i.e., if a situation or case can be imagined or secured which would call for some sort of *decision* on our part to extend the use of the concept to cover this, or to close the concept and invent a new one to deal with the new case and its new property. If necessary and sufficient conditions for the application of a concept can be stated, the concept is a closed one. But this can happen only in logic or mathematics where concepts are constructed and completely defined. It cannot occur with empirically-descriptive and normative concepts unless we arbitrarily close them by stipulating the ranges of their uses.

I can illustrate this open character of "art" best by examples drawn from its sub-concepts. Consider questions like "Is Dos Passos' *U. S. A.* a novel?," "Is V. Woolf's *To the Lighthouse* a novel?," "Is Joyce's *Finnegan's Wake* a novel?" On the traditional view, these are construed as factual problems to be answered yes or no in accordance with the presence or absence of defining properties. But certainly this is not how any of these questions is answered. Once it arises, as it has many times in the development of the novel from Richardson to Joyce (e.g., "Is Gide's *The School for Wives* a novel or a diary?"), what is at stake is no factual analysis concerning necessary and sufficient properties but a decision as to whether the work under examination is similiar in certain respects to other works, already called "novels," and consequently warrants the extension of the concept to cover the new case. The new work is narrative, fictional, contains character delineation and dialogue but (say) it has no regular time-sequence in the plot or is interspersed with actual newspaper reports. It is like recognized novels, A, B, C . . . , in some respects but not like them in others. But then neither were B and C like A in some respects when it was decided to extend the concept applied to A to B and C. Because work N + 1 (the brand new work) is like A, B, C . . . N in certain respects—has strands of similarity to them—the concept is extended and a new phase of the novel engendered. "Is N + 1 a novel?," then, is no factual, but rather a decision problem, where the verdict turns on whether or not we enlarge our set of conditions for applying the concept.

What is true of the novel is, I think, true of every sub-concept of art: "tragedy," "comedy," "painting," "opera," etc., of "art" itself. No "Is X a novel, painting, opera, work of art, etc.?" question allows of a definitive answer in the sense of a factual yes or no report. "Is this *collage* a painting or not?" does not rest on any set of necessary and sufficient properties of painting but on whether we decide—as we did!—to extend "painting" to cover this case.

"Art," itself, is an open concept. New conditions (cases) have constantly arisen and will undoubtedly constantly arise; new art forms, new movements will emerge, which will demand decisions on the part of those interested, usually professional critics, as to whether the concept should be extended or not. Aestheticians may lay down similarity conditions but never necessary and sufficient ones for the correct application of the concept. With "art" its conditions of application can never be exhaustively enumerated since new cases can always be envisaged or created by artists, or even nature, which would call for a decision on someone's part to extend or to close the old or to invent a new concept. (E.g., "It's not a sculpture, it's a mobile.")

What I am arguing, then, is that the very expansive, adventurous character of art, its ever-present changes and novel creations, makes it logically impossible to ensure any set of defining properties. We can, of course, choose to close the concept. But to do this with "art" or "tragedy" or "portraiture," etc., is ludicrous since it forecloses on the very conditions of creativity in the arts.

Of course there are legitimate and serviceable closed concepts in art. But these are always those whose boundaries of conditions have been drawn for a *special* purpose. Consider the difference, for example, between "tragedy" and "(extant) Greek tragedy." The first is open and must remain so to allow for the possibility of new conditions, e.g., a play in which the hero is not noble or fallen or in which there is no hero but other elements that are like those of plays we already call "tragedy." The second is closed. The plays it can be applied to, the conditions under which it can be correctly used are all in, once the boundary, "Greek," is drawn. Here the critic can work out a theory or real definition in which he lists the common properties at least of the extant Greek tragedies. Aristotle's definition, false as it is as a theory of all the plays of Aeschylus, Sophocles, and Euripides, since it does not cover some of them,[7] properly called "tragedies," can be interpreted as a real (albeit incorrect) definition of this closed concept; although it can also be, as it unfortunately has been, conceived as a purported real definition of "tragedy," in which case it suffers from the logical mistake of trying to define what cannot be defined—of trying to squeeze what is an open concept into an honorific formula for a closed concept.

What is supremely important, if the critic is not to become muddled, is to get absolutely clear about the way in which he conceives his concepts; otherwise he goes from the problem of trying to define "tragedy," etc., to an arbitrary closing of the concept in terms of certain preferred conditions or characteristics which he sums up in some linguistic recommendation that he mistakenly thinks is a real definition of the open concept. Thus, many critics and aestheticians ask, "What is tragedy?," choose a class of samples for which they may give a true account of its common properties, and then go on to construe this account of the chosen closed class as a true definition or theory of the whole open class of tragedy. This, I think, is the logical mechanism of most of the so-called theories of the subconcepts of art: "tragedy," "comedy," "novel," etc. In effect, this whole procedure, subtly deceptive as it is, amounts to a transformation of correct criteria for *recognizing* members of certain legitimately closed classes of works of art into recommended criteria for *evaluating* any putative member of the class.

The primary task of aesthetics is not to seek a theory but to elucidate the concept of art. Specifically, it is to describe the conditions under which we employ the concept correctly. Definition, reconstruction, patterns of analysis are out of place here since they distort and add nothing to our understanding of art. What, then, is the logic of "X is a work of art"?

As we actually use the concept, "Art" is both descriptive (like "chair") and evaluative (like "good"); i.e., we sometimes say, "This is a work of art," to describe something and we sometimes say it to evaluate something. Neither use surprises anyone.

What, first, is the logic of "X is a work of art," when it is a descripitve utterance? What are the conditions under which we would be making such an utterance correctly? There are no necessary and sufficient conditions but there are the strands of similarity conditions, i. e., bundles of properties, none of which need be present but most of which are, when we describe things as works of art. I shall call these the "criteria of recognition" of works of art. All of these have served as the defining criteria of the individual traditional theories of art; so we are already familiar with them. Thus, mostly, when we

---

[7] See H. D. F. Kitto, *Greek Tragedy*, (London, 1939), on this point.

describe something as a work of art, we do so under the conditions of there being present some sort of artifact, made by human skill, ingenuity, and imagination, which embodies in its sensuous, public medium—stone, wood, sounds, words, etc.—certain distinguishable elements and relations. Special theorists would add conditions like satisfaction of wishes, objectification or expression of emotion, some act of empathy, and so on; but these latter conditions seem to be quite adventitious, present to some but not to other spectators when things are described as works of art. "X is a work of art and contains *no* emotion, expression, act of empathy, satisfaction, etc.," is perfectly good sense and may frequently be true. "X is a work of art and . . . was made by no one," or . . . "exists only in the mind and not in any publicly observable thing," or . . . "was made by accident when he spilled the paint on the canvas," in each case of which a normal condition is denied, are also sensible and capable of being true in certain circumstances. None of the criteria of recognition is a defining one, either necessary or sufficient, because we can sometimes assert of something that it is a work of art and go on to deny any one of these conditions, even the one which has traditionally been taken to be basic, namely, that of being an artifact: Consider, "This piece of driftwood is a lovely piece of sculpture." Thus, to say of anything that it is a work of art is to commit oneself to the presence of *some* of these conditions. One would scarcely describe X as a work of art if X were not an artifact, or a collection of elements sensuously presented in a medium, or a product of human skill, and so on. If none of the conditions were present, if there were no criteria present for recognizing something as a work of art, we would not describe it as one. But, even so, no one of these or any collection of them is either necessary or sufficient.

The elucidation of the descriptive use of "Art" creates little difficulty. But the elucidation of the evaluative use does. For many, especially theorists, "This is a work of art" does more than describe; it also praises. Its conditions of utterance, therefore, include certain preferred properties or characteristics of art. I shall call these "criteria of evaluation." Consider a typical example of this evaluative use, the view according to which to say of something that it is a work of art is to imply that it is a *successful* harmonization of elements. Many of the honorific definitions of art and its sub-concepts are of this form. What is at stake here is that "Art" is construed as an evaluative term which is either identified with its criterion or justified in terms of it. "Art" is defined in terms of its evaluative property, e.g., successful harmonization. On such a view, to say "X is a work of art" is (1) to say something which is taken *to mean* "X is a succesful harmonization" (e.g., "Art *is* significant form") or (2) to say something praiseworthy *on the basis* of its successful harmonization.

Theorists are never clear whether it is (1) or (2) which is being put forward. Most of them, concerned as they are with this evaluative use, formulate (2), i.e., that feature of art that *makes* it art in the praise-sense, and then go on to state (1), i.e., the definition of "Art" in terms of its art-making feature. And this is clearly to confuse the conditions under which we say something evaluatively with the meaning of what we say. "This is a work of art," said evaluatively, cannot mean "This is a successful harmonization of elements"— except by stipulation—but at most is said in virtue of the art-making property, which is taken as a (the) criterion of "Art," when "Art" is employed to assess, "This is a work of art," used evaluatively, serves to praise and not to affirm the reason why it is said.

The evaluative use of "Art," although distinct from the conditions of its use, relates in a very intimate way to these conditions. For, in every instance of "This is a work of art" (used to praise), what happens is that the criterion of evaluation (e.g., successful harmonization) for the employment of the concept of art is converted into a criterion of recognition. This is why, on its evaluative use, "This is a work of art" implies "This has P," where "P" is some chosen art-making property. Thus, if one chooses to employ "Art" evaluatively, as many do, so that "This is a work of art and not (aesthetically) good" makes no sense, he uses "Art" in such a way that he refuses to *call* anything a work of art unless it embodies his criterion of excellence.

There is nothing wrong with the evaluative use; in fact, there is good reason for using "Art" to praise. But what cannot be maintained is that theories of the evaluative use of "Art" are true and real definitions of the necessary and sufficient properties of art. Instead they are honorific definitions, pure and simple, in which "Art" has been redefined in terms of chosen criteria.

But what makes them—these honorific definitions—so supremely valuable is not their disguised linguistic recommendations; rather it is the *debates* over the reasons for changing the criteria of the concept of art which are built into the definitions. In each of the great theories of art, whether correctly understood as honorific definitions or incorrectly accepted as real definitions, what is of the utmost importance are the reasons proffered in the argument for the respective theory, that is, the reasons given for the chosen or preferred criterion of excellence and evaluation. It is this perennial debate over these criteria of evaluation which makes the history of aesthetic theory the important study it is. The value of each of the theories resides in its attempt to state and to justify certain criteria which are either neglected or distorted by previous theories. Look at the Bell-Fry theory again. Of course, "Art is significant form" cannot be accepted as a true, real definition of art; and most certainly it actually functions in their aesthetics as a redefinition of art in terms of the chosen condition of significant form. But what gives it its aesthetic importance is what lies behind the formula: In an age in which literary and representational elements have become paramount in painting, *return* to the plastic ones since these are indigenous to painting. Thus, the role of the theory is not to define anything but to use the definitional form, almost epigrammatically, to pin-point a crucial recommendation to turn our attention once again to the plastic elements in painting.

Once we, as philosophers, understand this distinction between the formula and what lies behind it, it behooves us to deal generously with the traditional theories of art; because incorporated in every one of them is a debate over and argument for emphasizing or centering upon some particular feature of art which has been neglected or perverted. If we take the aesthetic theories literally, as we have seen, they all fail; but if we reconstrue them, in terms of their function and point, as serious and argued-for recommendations to concentrate on certain criteria of excellence in art, we shall see that aesthetic theory is far from worthless. Indeed, it becomes as central as anything in aesthetics, in our understanding of art, for it teaches us what to look for and how to look at it in art. What is central and must be articulated in all the theories are their debates over the reasons for excellence in art—debates over emotional depth, profound truths, natural beauty, exactitude, freshness of treatment, and so on, as criteria of evaluation—the whole of which converges on the perennial problem of what makes a work of art good. To understand the role of aesthetic theory is not to conceive it as definition, logically doomed to failure, but to read it as summaries of seriously made recommendations to attend in certain ways to certain features of art.

Erich Kahler

WHAT IS ART?*
An answer to Morris Weitz's "The Role of Theory in Aesthetics"

I

In the essay under consideration, Professor Weitz attempts to demonstrate that theory has no legitimate role in aesthetics and that art is not amenable to any kind of true definition because it "has no set of necessary and sufficient properties" on which to base a definition.

His argument runs as follows:

1) There exists a great variety of definitions, or theories, of art, but none of them is quite adequate or sufficient: "Even if art has one set of necessary and sufficient properties, . . . no aesthetic theory yet proposed has enumerated that set to the satisfaction of all concerned."

2) "As real definitions, these theories are supposed to be factual reports on art. If they are, may we not ask, Are they empirical and open to verification or falsification?"

3) According to Wittgenstein's train of thought from which Weitz derives his scepticism, any concept, theory, or definition, based on common properties is questionable, except logical or mathematical concepts which "are constructed and completely defined," and therefore "closed concepts." If you look at a group of phenomena denoted by a common name, say games, "you will not see something that is common to *all*, but similarities, relationships, and a whole series of them at that." This is said to be true particularly of art in which we not only find "no common properties— only strands of similarities," but whose "very expansive, adventurous character," whose "ever-present changes and novel creations" make it especially "logically impossible to ensure any set of defining properties." To "close the concept" is "ludicrous since it forecloses on the very conditions of creativity in the arts."

4) In our use of the term "art," there is no clear distinction between description and evaluation. When we say "This is a work of art," "the

---

* Erich Kahler's "What Is Art?" was written especially for this volume, at the request of the Editor. It is printed here by the kind permission of the author.

Erich Kahler (1885–   ), author of *Man the Measure*, and the recently published *The Tower and the Abyss*, is one of the great contemporary humanists. He is at present in residence at Princeton.

criterion of evaluation . . . is converted into a criterion of recognition. . . . Thus, if one chooses to employ 'art' evaluatively, as many do, so that 'This is a work of art and not (aesthetically) good' makes no sense, he uses 'art' in such a way that he refuses to *call* anything a work of art unless it embodies his criterion of excellence."

From all these premises Professor Weitz concludes that "aesthetic theory is a logically vain attempt to define what cannot be defined, to state the necessary and sufficient properties of that which has no necessary and sufficient properties. . . ." "Art" is an "open concept." "In elucidating [it], certain (paradigm) cases can be given, about which there can be no question as to their being correctly described as "art". . . , but no exhaustive set of cases can be given . . . for the all-important reason that unforeseeable or novel conditions are always forthcoming or envisageable." All we can do and should do in regard to theories of art is to take them as guides for evaluation, as "serious and argued-for recommendations to concentrate on certain criteria of excellence in art," "debates over the reasons for excellence in art." If used in this aspect, they may teach us "what to look for and how to look at it in art" and to find out "what makes a work of art good."

II

Certainly, Professor Weitz has to be given credit for his reminding professional aestheticists of the fact that their discipline is not a science and that their definitions lack the foolproof exactitude and closedness of logical and mathematical formulas. But then, this may be said of all definitions in whatever field concerning reality and not constructed models. If we insist on mathematical exactitude we may just as well give up any inquiry into the nature of a real entity, indeed any serious communication.

Any real entities or phenomena are to a certain degree fluid and "open," structurally as well as temporally. None of their properties, taken separately, is exclusively their own, none of their "set of properties" exhausts their character, none of such combinations of characteristics is *completely* verifiable. No historical personality, or event, is fully defined by their verifiable data, nor is a social phenomenon by its statistics. As to biology, we read in the most recent standard work *Life* by G. G. Simpson, C. S. Pittendrigh, and I. H. Tiffany (New York: Harcourt Brace, 1957, pp. 427 ff.): "All organisms are classified into species. All sorts of biologists . . . recognize that a species is a very special sort of thing and one with fundamental significance for the study of life. All biologists think that they have a pretty good idea of what a species is . . . yet for centuries biologists have been battling and baffling each other about the . . . problem . . . to produce a clear, fully satisfactory answer to the question 'What is a species?' . . . It is one of the facts of life that an exact definition of a species applicable without question to all sorts of organisms is inherently impossible. . . . Natural populations are not static things that stay put neatly within the confines of rigid definitions . . . It is a waste of time to try to agree on one, infallible definition of species." But "it is no waste of time to discuss what species are; on the contrary, that is one of the most important subjects in the whole science of biology." Even in nuclear physics, a perfectly valid definition of a particle will be difficult to obtain, although this entity forms an integral part of modern physical concepts and operations. As to verification, we have learned that even practical applicability is no guarantee for the correctness of the picture of reality from which it was derived.

What this situation in the real, the incontestably empirical sciences shows is the precariousness, inherent incompleteness, and insufficient verifiability of *all* definition, or theory, concerned with reality, but, on the other hand, the indispensability of these tentative definitions and theories and the necessity to search relentlessly for an approximative elucidation of such intuitively identified entities that form the elements of our dealings with reality.

The dynamic nature of our world is all-pervasively established by now and physical, biological, historical, sociological entities are no less fluid and subject to change than the artistic ones. In all these domains processes of creativity are involved; nor are artistic creations as imaginatively free and unconditioned as they are commonly held to be; they are in part determined by the human stage, the problems and techniques of their particular epochs.

Thus, while the general situation of our learning confirms Weitz's (and Wittgenstein's) assertion that any stable, entirely satisfactory definition of real entities and phenomena, and so of art, is impossible, we still, I contend, cannot dispense with the search for approximately comprehensive and valid definitions of anything we are dealing with. The terminological confusion, in our disciplines no less than in our conversation, is staggering, and no discussion can be fruitful unless we make perfectly clear from the outset what exactly we are talking about. So when we go about discussing problems of art seriously, this imposes on us the duty to state, be it ever so tentatively and transitorily, what we understand by the term "art." Just as biologists are not satisfied with their vague feeling and consensus concerning the nature of a species, but keep trying descriptively to elucidate this common feeling, so, in dealing with art, we should not give up seeking a clarification of what art really is. If we carefully take account of the artistic achievements and experiences up to our time, we may even reach a less than personally or doctrinally subjective, but a merely epochally subjective, conception; that is to say, a concept that, by assembling the principal features of art as developed up to the present stage, may claim an approximate general validity *as of today.* If we succeed in making use of all the artistic material, all individual and group efforts up to now, such a concept should be more inclusive than any previous concept. As to verifiability, we shall see that there exist certain artistic properties that are no less verifiable and documentable than any relevant historical event or personality, all of which are to some degree liable to interpretation.

III

Let us first test the conclusiveness of Weitz's argument on three points. The first one refers to Wittgenstein's "Investigations" which it would lead too far to consider in our context; I confine myself to Weitz's text. Wittgenstein is quoted as saying with respect to games: "What we find are no necessary and sufficient properties only 'a complicated network of similarities overlapping and crisscrossing' such that we can say of games that they form a family with family resemblances and no common trait." "The problem of the nature of art," Professor Weitz concludes, "is like that of the nature of games . . . If we actually look and see what it is that we call 'art,' we will also find no common properties—only strands of similarities."

Now family resemblances, being genotypical, not phenotypical similarities, are genuinely common traits: they spring from common genes and traditions. That they do not all of them visibly pertain to all members of the family does not detract from their being common traits and belonging to a hereditary group essence. Art is not easily comparable to a family, since its "members" are not organically grown beings, but works, "artifacts," achievements, products of consciously controlled efforts. What links them together are impulses or aims, not just origins. And if there exist, according to Weitz, "certain (paradigm) cases . . . about which there can be no question as to their being correctly described as 'art,'" paradigm cases may be found which, unlike members of a family, and due to the work-character of art, assemble all detectable features of artistic endeavor up to the present time and may very well serve as natural models by which to demonstrate the "set of properties" of art. If there exist "paradigm cases," this means that there exists a definite consensus of feeling as to their being true works of art. And if there exists such a consensus of feeling (as in the case of the biological species) we may, indeed we must, ask ourselves what is the substratum of this feeling. It should be possible to express in words what makes us feel that, unquestionably, these works are art.

IV

Professor Weitz wants aesthetic theories to be considered not as explanations of the nature of art, which, to him, is an impossible task, but as "recommendations to concentrate on certain criteria of excellence in art," teaching us "what to look for and how to look at it in art." This in fact is a *petitio principii*. How can we determine what is excellent in art as long as we have not established a clear notion of the distinct character of art? Wherefrom can we derive the criteria of artistic excellence if not from the artistic performance itself? "Emotional depth," "profound truths," "natural beauty," "exactitude"—any of this can also be found elsewhere, in personal utterances and acts, in nature, in science; none of it affords a specifically artistic criterion; none of it taken by itself, nor all of it taken together, "makes a work of art good."

The attempt to establish specifically artistic values, a distinctive artistic excellence, inevitably refers us back to the recognition of the specific nature of art. Here is where a third point in Weitz's argument comes in which appears to me questionable.

Weitz maintains that in art any possible criterion of recognition is basically a criterion of evaluation. "In every instance of 'This is a work of art' (used to praise), what happens is that the criterion of evaluation . . . is converted into a criterion of recognition . . . 'This is a work of art' implies 'This has P,' where P is some chosen art-making property."

However, the relation between recognition and evaluation in art is not as simple as it is presented by Weitz. Art is, first of all, a form of human activity. When we ask "What distinguishes this particular human activity from other human activities, as f.i. craftwork, science, philosophy, all of which are neighboring fields and have certain features in common with art?," when we try contrastingly to single out the distinguishing features of this activity "art," what we are seeking is clearly a criterion of recognition, which does not lend itself to being confounded with evaluation. Such differentiation is in no way more susceptible to substantial praise than, say, the distinction between economy and politics.

To be sure, any recognition of the specific character of a human activity entails potential evaluation. This is true of science, or diplomacy, or business no less than of art. An act of diplomacy, a piece of scientific research, is good or bad according to the degree in which it fills the necessary requirements of the specific task of diplomacy or science. The more it is diplomacy, or science, the better it is. When we say of a man "He is a real businessman," we mean by this "He is a good businessman." Any human activity is liable to evaluation inasmuch as it is a conscious act and effort toward a specific end. A creature or object of nature, being a piece of sheer existence, f.i., a tree, or a tiger, cannot be more or less of a tree, or a tiger. But any human being in his capacity as a consciously willing and acting person is always more or less of what he intends to be or to do. In his activity a discrepancy inheres between end and fulfilment. The degree of achievement, of approximation to his specific task, invites evaluation. But clearly, it is not evaluation that clarifies the nature of a specific activity. On the contrary, evaluation is based on the greater or lesser approximation to a specific task. This is true of art no less than of all other activities. Evaluation cannot help us to a better understanding of the nature of art. Evaluation *derives* from the understanding and the description of the specific nature of art.

V

Let me finally venture a *definition of art,* as precise and comprehensive as possible.

Two requirements have to be observed for achieving a valid definition: (1) The definition has to be *strictly specific*; that is to say the combination of properties of the entity to be described has to be distinctively and exclusively its own, shared by no other entity. (2) Distinctions have to be made *by centers, not by boundaries*[1] because there is no real entity without fluid boundaries. If we try to establish peripheral distinctions we arrive at conclusions such as those of the British historian Geoffrey Barraclough who in an essay dealing with *Europe in the Middle Ages* ended up by stating that there is no Europe and there are no middle ages, since no exact confines can be determined for either sphere of existence. Europe passes over into Asia and Africa, and no rigorously fixed data can be established for the beginning and the end of the medieval period. And yet, to deny on such grounds the real validity of these two concepts is equivalent to denying the existence of any discrete physical body which also peripherically mingles with its surroundings.

As has been stated before, art is primarily a special kind of *human activity* that like other human activities evolved historically into a separate, distinct sphere and manner of work. In the course of its evolution it de-

[1] This is the error underlying all application of strict logicity to objects of reality, and so that of Wittgenstein. Cf., "Philosophical Investigations" (New York: The Macmillan Co. 1953) pp. 68–70, 77.

veloped an ever-growing *body of work results,* i.e., works of art, a residue that we also have come to denote by the name of art. Finally, in more recent times when in all artistic fields a commercialization and mechanization of production, a mass-production set in, "art" assumed a more restricted sense, differentiating a *special kind of creation,* unaffected by mechanization and commercialization, from the products and practices of conventional fabrication. It is this restrictive sense of art which inevitably carries a value connotation and invites that confusion of recognition and evaluation which is said to invalidate all definition of art. As will be shown, however, even in this sense a neatly descriptive identification of art is possible.

VI

When we now first contemplate art as a specific human activity, the very fact of its being an activity implies a sharp distinction between natural and artistic phenomena. The word *Ars* itself deriving from an Aryan root "ar," signifying "join, put together," connected with Greek "artizein," "to prepare" and "arariskein" "to put together," means originally a "fitting, adjusting, joining."[2] It has commonly been used in contradistinction to nature. Therefore, sentences like those quoted by Weitz: "X is a work of art and . . . was made by no one" or ". . . was made by accident when he spilled the paint on the canvas" are under no circumstances "sensible and capable of being true." A piece of driftwood or a sea shell, be it ever so characteristically depictive or charming, may remind us of art, but is never itself a piece of art, because it is not made by man through a consciously controlled impulse or effort.[3] This is a basic premise of all art.

[2] Cf., the articles *Ars* and *Art* in *Thesaurus Linguae Latinae,* Grandsaigne d' Hauterive, *Dictionnaire des racines des langues européennes* (Paris, 1949), H. C. Wyld, *The Universal English Dictionary* (London, 1952).

[3] To be sure, a work of art is never completely a result of conscious effort. A considerable part of creation, larger or lesser in different artists, goes on in the unconscious. Picasso said of his manner of producing: "A picture comes to me from miles away: who is to say from how far away I sensed it, saw it, painted it . . . how can anyone enter into my dreams, my instincts, my thoughts which have taken a long time to mature and to come out into the daylight, and above all grasp from them what I have been about— perhaps against my own will?" And again: "When I paint, my object is to show what I have found and not what I am looking for." (from Alfred Barr, *Picasso,* Museum of Modern Art, New York 1946). Rilke's most rarefied, analytically sensitive poetry erupted precipitately from a long, almost vegetative process of unconscious, or half-conscious, formation, of which he had hardly any command. And yet, there was, in Picasso, an "I" to sense, see and paint, and be about something, however hidden in the dark of the unconscious or subconscious, and set against his conscious will; there was a conscious control of what he has found, an "object to show it." There was, in Rilke, a most subtly discerning mind residing deep below the surface of consciousness and directing the structure of the poem. Even in such cases—and there are others where the conscious effort is foremost, as in Flaubert's and Cézanne's artistry—what is taking place is guided creation, not accidental growth.

As an activity, art borders on other human activities with which it has, in part or as a whole, certain traits in common: craftwork, science, philosophy, historiography. Painting, sculpture, architecture are connected with handicraft (indeed technology), and even music and literary work of all kind are partly constituted by techniques. With science art has in common the exploratory character of its work, the intent of ever expanding cognition; with philosophy its conceptual nature, its concern in ideas; with historiography its descriptive element. Art differs, however, from every one of these activities by specific variances of mode of these common properties, by its special combination of properties, and by additional properties which are exclusively its own.

Everybody will agree that the aim and activity of science consists in the acquisition of ever wider and deeper knowledge of the nature of reality. The same can be said of philosophy. And it is no less true of art, only here this is not so easily recognizable because another property of art tends to conceal it.

The manner of such exploration varies in the three activities. *Science* deals with a directly apparent, unmediated, surface, form of reality, i.e., factuality. It deals with it collectively; the advances made by single geniuses notwithstanding, it has come to be increasingly collective work, teamwork on a grand scale, where the individual works on an ever narrower, ever more specialistic segment of factual reality and is tied up with a rank and file of students of collectively, quasi-objectively developed sets of problems. Accordingly, the kind of knowledge produced by science is always on the move, advancing on a wide and uncontrolled front, always fragmentary, provisional, open to correction and even replacement; it is never at rest, it never reaches an even transient state of completion. *Philosophy* was in previous periods of less developed empirical learning the attempt to integrate the whole of immediate reality, to grasp it by rational means. The immense expansion of the sciences reduced it to the task of investigating the epistemological, ontological, logico-linguistic foundations or premises of knowledge. In general, its analytical explorations have by now assumed a scientistic, if scientific character. But even where an attempt has been made by recent philosophers, as, f.i., Whitehead, to search for the links, and in this way integrate the whole, of present reality, as presented by the findings of the modern sciences, this attempted integration has been concerned with immediate, factual reality which was intended to be grasped by strictly rational means.

Art too is involved in the exploration of reality, the penetration of an ever wider and deeper range and increased complexity of reality, and in this respect it has a demonstrable evolution, just as science has. This is an evolution of the nature and scope of reality rendered, and implicitly of the forms of rendering, the modes of expression. A newly detected reality involves new forms and techniques of expression. "Content" and "form," as it is well established by now, are but two aspects of one and the same thing. New "contents" call for new "forms" of presentation, they are not expressible, they simply do not exist without their new appropriate form. And just as science, through its new findings, broadens and changes the picture of our reality and in this way, as well as through the application of its findings, changes our reality itself, so art, through its reaching into new complexities and levels of reality, extends the scope and changes the nature of our consciousness, and by this means of our reality itself.

In science the crucial importance of novelty is quite evident. What else does science seek than additional knowledge, better knowledge, and that is new fact-finding, new knowledge. As far as art is concerned, however, scarcely any explicit attention has been given to the just as essential role which the search for the new plays in it. Here, the search for the new, the impulse toward the new, means even more than sheer innovation, additional material, increased profundity and complexity. It implies other properties which we, more or less consciously, sense and admire in any "paradigm" work of art, such as freshness, vitality, vigor, authenticity, expressiveness, precision, truth, and even emotional impact. All such properties and, as we shall see, even more, are inherent in that one characteristic of art: its thrusting out into the sphere of the unknown, the hitherto unachieved, "the ground that never a word has trod," as Rilke put it, and, we may add, "never a stroke of the brush, or a conventional sound."[4] For it is this effort

[4] The experience of this pioneer quality of art has been expressed by many artists since *Lucretius*, who writes in his *De Rerum Natura*: "Not that I am unaware how obscure these matters are: but the high hope of renown has struck into my heart sweet love of the Muses, thrilled by which now in lively thought I traverse pathless tracts of the Pierides never yet trodden by any foot. I love to approach virgin springs and there to drink; I love to pluck fresh flowers, and to seek an illustrious chaplet for my head from fields whence ere this the Muses have crowned the brows of none: first because my teaching is of high matters, and I proceed to unloose the mind from the close knots of religion; next because the subject is so dark and the lines I write so clear, as I touch all with the Muses' grace." (I, 922–934, tr. by W. H. D. Rouse, Loeb Class. Lib; cf., also IV, 1–5). Other artists felt their frontier venture either as limits or as feats of their strained expression. *Dante: Divina Commedia, Paradiso* XXX, 31ff: "But now my poetic pursuit lagging behind her beauty must halt, as every artist has to at his utmost." ("Ma or convien che mio seguir desista/Più dietro a sua bellezza poetando/Come all'ultimo suo ciascuno artista . . ."); *Milton* in *Paradise Lost* I, 16: "Things unattempted yet in Prose or Rhyme"; *Goethe*: "Art is the conveyor of the inexpressible." *Dürer, On Human Proportion*, III: "For indeed art is hidden in nature; he who can tear it out has it." *Degas*: "There is courage indeed in launching a frontal attack upon the main structure and the main lines of nature . . . art is really a battle." *Klee*: "One learns to look behind the façade, to grasp the root of things. One learns to recognize the undercurrents, the ante-

to express something heretofore inexpressible, to grasp and to shape something for the first time, it is this *"for the first time"* that gives a work of art its lasting freshness and vitality, its genuineness of language, its convincing vigor, so that ancient works, whose scopes and styles are by now utterly familiar to us and in one way or another left behind by the endeavors of our age, are still fully alive, and we are able to enjoy them as if they were created today. The trace of that ultimate effort that created them persists in them, the longing, the struggle, the suffering, the immediacy of all primal creation. When we feel certain works to be of secondary quality it is because all this is lacking in them; they echo, iterate and imitate the achievements of masters.[5]

VII

It is this drive toward the conquest of the unknown and inexpressible which also makes for the evolutionary and sometimes revolutionary character of artistic activity; which causes the expansion of scope, the growth of complexity, the development of new dimensions, forms and techniques, traceable throughout the history of the arts.

There is a further most important property of art, which derives from the same source. By penetrating into new spheres and dimensions of experience, developing new forms, creating new reality, artists like Masaccio, Giotto, Leonardo, Titian, Rembrandt, the Impressionists, Cézanne, van Gogh, Picasso, or Dante, Shakespeare, Cervantes, Goethe, the romanticists and the symbolists, Flaubert, Proust, Joyce, Kafka, or Monteverdi, Bach, Mozart, Beethoven, Wagner, Stravinsky, Schönberg—to mention only a few

cedents of the visible. One learns to dig down, to uncover. . . ." *Beckmann*: "What I want to show in my work is the idea which hides itself behind so-called reality. I am seeking for the bridge which leads from the visible to the invisible, like the famous cabalist who once said: 'If you wish to get hold of the invisible you must penetrate as deeply as possible into the visible.'" (Quotations of Degas, Klee and Beckmann taken from *Artists on Art*, ed., R. Goldwater and M. Treves, New York: Pantheon Books, Inc. 1949).

[5] There was an evolutionary stage of man, an early stage, in which repetition had not a deadening but an inspiring effect. Primeval art is tribal art, that is to say, the individual is hardly developed as yet and remains creatively anonymous. Certain basic forms are traditionally, ritually repeated with slightest variations, but repetition is predominant and has the character of a driving force, a resurgence of life from a common tribal source. In this stage, art has not yet developed into a specialized form of expression, it is a straight magic act of undivided life and springs immediately from existential fears and visions. What manifests itself in it is the tribe with its relations to the forces of nature, and in every single member of the tribe, who shapes his visions and conjurations, the tribal stir rises anew. In the constant presence in which these people live the customary is ever new, freshness is not separated from traditionality. This keeps repetition from becoming stale, as it is in purely individual imitation; indeed repetition has here an intensifying, trance-producing effect, and at a certain climactic point it may rise to become the very moving force that produces the individual transgressions of the traditional.

of the most decisive figures—such artists did not just indulge in an arbitrary play of their imagination, they were pushed along or guided in a certain direction by the human condition, the stage of perception and experience, and implicitly techniques of expression, of their specific period; and the new experience of reality, indeed the new reality itself they reached was a reality in the making, that lay hidden under the conventions of the epoch. They presented a human condition, they liberated forms and experiences that were to become *the* reality of the next age. That means: whatever they presented was not just this or that individual story, portrait, scenery, phenomenal structure, or combination of sounds; it reflected a human condition in transition. When we admire in a portrait by Titian, Dürer, or Holbein the deep physiognomical grasp of an individual personality, what strikes us is not only the visual elucidation of this specific character, but implicitly the close, meticulous and yet synoptical accuracy of rendering as such, which these Renaissance masters have achieved. Here, likeness represents the last frontier of visual exploration. Again, when we turn from these portraits to portraits by, say, van Gogh or Kokoschka, we are confronted not merely with a peculiarly sharpened and intensified characterization of the specific person depicted, but with a new structural and psychic depth of appearance which has been revealed by these artists. New phenomenal vistas have been opened up, uncovering the new reality of our age. The same applies to the progression from a scene or scenery presented by a Renaissance painter to one by Rembrandt, by Claude Lorrain, and by Constable, and further on one by Monet, and by Cézanne. What a modern "non-objective" painting expresses in its line-and-color construction is not just this particular formal combination but implicitly phenomenal relationships of a more general order. In literature we need only trace the corresponding development from the baroque novel to those of Flaubert, Proust, and Joyce, in music the steps from Haydn to Beethoven, to Wagner, to Stravinsky and Schönberg. By virtue of their frontier character, of their acts of revelation, these works bear a generally human significance. Their presenting in, and effecting through, a singular selective unit a coherency of the broadest import establishes their *symbolic* quality. Thus the special creativity of art implies its inherently symbolic quality.

It is this symbolic quality which distinguishes art from science. Both activities have in common the search for the nature of reality, their disclosure of new reality. But the manner of this search and the dimension of reality it reaches are characteristically different in one and the other activity. While science deals with factual reality and approaches it in a direct, immediate way, art proceeds in a symbolic or metaphoric fashion. It presents

single individual entities carrying a general purport. The abstraction and
generalization of science is extrinsic, it seeks to arrive at strict or statistical
laws which call for mathematical expression; the abstraction and generalization of art is intrinsic, it shows macrocosmic through microcosmic coherences,
and its form of expression is therefore symbolically or metaphoncally variable. It is in the nature of this kind of endeavor, which is aiming at the presentation of a whole, that each work of art is complete in itself, or supposed
to be complete in itself, and that it is, accordingly, individual work. This
characteristic of art, that each of its works is complete in itself, has blurred
the recognition of the fact that art also has a definite evolution.

VIII

The disposition of art to present a whole (reflecting a broader whole)
and to advance by works, exery one of which is a whole in itself, entails,
indeed demands, that strict organization and integration that constitutes
completeness. It is the property usually referred to as "organicism," or "perfection," or "harmonization," certainly the one which has the longest record
of recognition, having been established by Aristotle: "For, as in [the other
imitative arts] . . . painting and the rest, so in poetry, the object of the
imitation is a unit; therefore . . . the plot . . . must represent an action that
is organically unified, the structural order of the incidents being such that
transposing or removing any one of them will dislocate and disorganize the
whole. Every part must be necessary and in its place; for a thing whose
presence or absence makes no perceptible difference is no organic part of
the whole." (*Peri Poietikes,* VIII, 4, trans. Lane Cooper, Cornell University
Press, 1947).

It has been remarked, and so by Weitz himself (*loc. cit.,* p. 29), that
"Organicism . . . can be applied to *any* causal unity in the natural world
as well as to art," which is said to eliminate it as a specific characteristic of
art. But what this objection ignores is the premise that are is a *human
activity* and that therefore the artistic organicity is the result of *work,* not
of natural growth—which entails other essential differences between natural
and artistic organicity.

In contemplating this artistic property of organic wholeness we touch
upon the concept of *beauty,* which is used widely in a rather vague and
indiscriminate sense. The clarification of this problematic term would require a separate study. In our context, I must confine myself to a few indications.

First of all, "beauty," in common usage, is by no means plainly identical
with "harmony." As far as natural objects are concerned, the term "beauty"

may sometimes designate "harmony"—f.i., when we contemplate a "beautiful" body—but in other cases it may mean just the opposite: extreme *dis*harmony—as in the romantic admiration of the savage contrastfulness, boundless expressiveness and elemental grandeur of an excessive landscape or natural scene (as a thunderstorm). Anything colorful, anything sensational, strongly evocative is often called "beautiful." Moreover, this confused concept abounds with emotional overtones induced by most diverse motivations. Some people, in some particular mood, harassed by the turbulence of inner troubles, or just modern life, will find a calm, idyllic scenery "beautiful"; others may want to loosen and lose themselves in a feeling of infinity, eternity, and will, accordingly, call natural phenomena "beautiful" just because of their vast, mute, mysterious impenetrability.

The same fluctuation of meaning prevails in people's notion of "beauty" in art. Certain works of art strike us as "beautiful" because of their vigorous expressiveness, their sensitive precision of expression; others because of their ingeniously consummate integration, "harmonization" of a rich variety of elements. To be sure, our feeling of "beauty" will be most intense when a work combines both qualities. In speaking of "harmony," it is important to bear in mind that this concept is by no means static; it has, in our modern experience, by far exceeded the meaning of a balance of simple proportions such as the classical ones. Art has, in the course of its evolution, through gradual expansion of scope, in width and in depth, and inclusion of more and more, and ever more diverse, elements of reality, broken through the bounds of traditional "harmony." The breaking of these bounds, the dissolution of the old "harmony," necessarily meant disharmony, overemphasis of newly discovered elements at the expense of other elements of reality; and these new disparities and dissonances had to be reintegrated in a wider and deeper, more comprehensive "harmony." Indeed the whole evolution of art may be seen as consisting in an alternate progression from dissolution of a worn harmony to formation of a new, more comprehensive harmony, i.e., in ever recurring stages of expressiveness and integration. Therefore, the prevalence of expressiveness over integration in certain works of art appears to be an intermediary stage on the way to the formation of a new, more comprehensive harmony.

Philosophy, inasmuch as it also attempts to interpretatively synthesize the reality of our world into an integrated whole, is distinguished from art by its rational dealing with immediate reality. Art operates extra– or suprarationally, not by argument, but by vision. What it wants to achieve is rendering a whole through visional simultaneity. Even in the dynamic arts, those compelled to representation by flux, such as drama, epics, poetry, music, the ultimate goal is the grasp of an entity as a visional whole. In music too, in spite of its apparently purely motional character, the final, intrinsic intent is the visional (not visual) unity of a structural piece. This visional character of art is implicated in its symbolic or metaphoric quality.

What distinguishes art from *historiography*, where the two border on each other, is obviously again its metaphoric, symbolic quality with all that it implies. And it is the same symbolic quality, particularly its source, the conquest of new reality, that marks the difference between art and *craftwork*. Craftwork, good or bad, is routine work adapted to practical uses, and whatever innovation it carries is purely technical. To be sure, technology and techniques also change our reality, but these changes are just the external exploitation of the findings of science and the ventures of art. They lack all cognitive purport.[6]

IX

With the distinction between art and craftwork we have reached a point where the boundaries between description and evaluation seem to become fluid. We have up to now considered art as a human activity clearly and describably differing from other human activities. However, as has been stated before, the mechanization and commercialization that has seized upon all human activities has given rise to a distinction between art and craftwork *within* the domain of activity that is commonly regarded as art; that is to say, a distinction between art in an uncompromisingly strict and restricted sense, and the routine production of novels, plays, poetry, paintings, or music, the best-sellers and "hits" that flood the markets.

A concept of art derived from such distinction alone would indeed be most precarious, and in this case the suspicion that the criterion of recognition is actually a criterion of evaluation would be entirely justified. Few people who have acquired some familiarity with art will deny that Joyce's *Ulysses* is a work of art, but a story of Mickey Spillane is not. But even in such a case of striking evidence this evidence cannot easily be substantiated without applying a criterion of art that has been established beforehand on more solid grounds than just a vague feeling of "excellence" whatever that may be interpreted to be.

In the present investigation I have attempted to show that an approxi-

[6] Architecture, due to its regard for practical uses, is particularly involved in craftwork and technology, but within these limitations all that has been said here of the properties of art also obtains of the art of building (cf., in this connection, Erwin Panofsky's admirable study on *Gothic Architecture and Scholasticism*, now available in a Meridian Books edition). In previous, non-technological ages (and in rare cases of modern artistic handicraft) a piece of craftwork could also be a work of art in-as-much as it was (or is) individual work, and the dictate of practical uses and arbitrary commercial fashions did not so strongly prevail over the formal expression of a style, or idea, of life.

mately reliable recognition of the nature of art is very well possible when we consider art as a human activity characteristically different from other human activities. We have found that the special creativity of art consists in the discovery, and that means implicitly creation, of new reality, reality that has not been raised into our consciousness before; that expressing something for the first time is a crucial feature of art which appears to be the primary source of other qualities, less strictly identifiable and rather felt than clearly recognized, such as vitality, authenticity, precision, truth etc; that art reaches the new reality in a suprarational, visional, metaphoric way, and that accordingly the reality it presents is a microcosmic whole reflecting a macrocosmic whole—which establishes the symbolic quality of art; that this very same manner of proceeding and presentation calls for another crucial property of art: its aiming at organic wholeness, integration, "harmonization" of an ever more complex and discordant reality. In those works of art which, by venturing into new spheres and dimensions of reality, break down worn, conventional harmonies, the emphasis is on intensity, vigor and accuracy of expression. Such works are the pioneers, preparing the path for other works which attempt to rally these gains in a new, more broadly balanced whole and to achieve completion and perfection on a larger scale. The correspondences and convergences of parts, elements and symbols which constitute such a work of art are amenable to accurate demonstration, which means a, however limited, verification of art.

Equipped with these distinctions we should be able to safely recognize a true work of art and distinguish it from current and futile craftwork even within the domain of artistic performance.

As a summary definition of art I propose the following: Art is a human activity which explores, and hereby creates, new reality in a suprarational, visional manner and presents it symbolically or metaphoncally, as a microcosmic whole signifying a macrocosmic whole.

SELECTED BIBLIOGRAPHY

1. Stephen Pepper, *The Work of Art*, Ch. I, Indiana University Press, 1955.
2. R. Wellek and A. Warren, *Theory of Literature*, Ch. 12, Harcourt, Brace and Company, 1942. A good statement of the 'ontological' problem of a work of art. (Available as Harvest paperback.)
3. Charles L. Stevenson, "On 'What Is a Poem'?," *The Philosophical Review*, 1957. A reply to (2) and an independent attempt at locating the problem of defining "art."
4. Margaret Macdonald, "Art and Imagination," *Proceedings of the Aristotelian Society*, 1953. Another version of the dissolution of the problem of defining "art."

FORM AND CONTENT

The concepts of form and content are as variegated as they are traditional. Works of art have been analyzed into these two sometimes separable but always distinguishable aspects by critics and philosophers since Plato. But the words used to represent these general ideas, and many others, are not univocal in meaning; there are many and competing uses of these terms in aesthetics and criticism. Even seemingly fundamental disputes between Formalists, like Clive Bell and Roger Fry, and their numerous critics range around completely different conceptions of form as against content. The extreme vagueness of the terms and especially the specious character of the disputes their application has sometimes engendered have led certain theorists to plead for the rejection of both the terms and the distinction they express. But on the whole the use of the terms persists, and the form-content distinction remains for most theorists and critics a serviceable one. Roger Fry, in his form-content analysis of Raphael's "Transfiguration," our first selection, is a case in point. DeWitt Parker's further probing of the concept of form alone, which has already achieved the status of a classic in aesthetics, is the second selection, and another example of the acceptance of the distinction. Together, Fry and Parker raise provoking questions about the clarificatory character of the form and content concepts and distinction.

Roger Fry

THE FORM-CONTENT DISTINCTION*

Let us take as an example of what I mean Raphael's "Transfiguration," which a hundred years ago was perhaps the most admired picture in the world, and twenty years ago was one of the most neglected. It is at once apparent that this picture makes a very complex appeal to the mind and feelings. To those who are familiar with the Gospel story of Christ it brings together in a single composition two different events which occurred simultaneously at different places, the Transfiguration of Christ and the unsuccessful attempt of the Disciples during His absence to heal the lunatic boy. This at once arouses a number of complex ideas about which the intellect and feelings may occupy themselves. Goethe's remark on the picture is instructive from this point of view. "It is remarkable," he says, "that any one has ever ventured to query the essential unity of such a composition. How can the upper part be separated from the lower? The two form one whole. Below the suffering and the needy, above the powerful and helpful—mutually dependent, mutually illustrative."

It will be seen at once what an immense complex of feelings interpenetrating and mutually affecting one another such a work sets up in the mind of a Christian spectator, and all this merely by the content of the picture, its subject, the dramatic story it tells.

Now if our Christian spectator has also a knowledge of human nature he will be struck by the fact that these figures, especially in the lower group, are all extremely incongruous with any idea he is likely to have formed of the people who surrounded Christ in the Gospel narrative. And according to his prepossessions he is likely to be shocked or pleased to find instead of the poor and unsophisticated peasants and fisherfolk who followed Christ, a number of noble, dignified, and academic gentlemen in improbable garments and purely theatrical poses. Again the representation merely as representation, will set up a number of feelings and perhaps of critical thoughts dependent upon innumerable associated ideas in the spectator's mind.

Now all these reactions to the picture are open to any one who has enough understanding of natural form to recognize it when represented

---

* From Roger Fry's "Retrospect," in *Vision and Design*, pp. 239–242 of the Pelican Edition, 1937. Copyright, 1920, by Chatto & Windus, Ltd. Reprinted by permission of Chatto & Windus, Ltd.

adequately. There is no need for him to have any particular sensibility to form as such.

Let us now take for our spectator a person highly endowed with the special sensibility to form, who feels the intervals and relations of forms as a musical person feels the intervals and relations of tones, and let us suppose him either completely ignorant of, or indifferent to, the Gospel story. Such a spectator will be likely to be immensely excited by the extraordinary power of co-ordination of many complex masses in a single inevitable whole, by the delicate equilibrium of many directions of line. He will at once feel that the apparent division into two parts is only apparent, that they are co-ordinated by a quite peculiar power of grasping the possible correlations. He will almost certainly be immensely excited and moved, but his emotion will have nothing to do with the emotions which we have discussed hitherto, since in this case we have supposed our spectator to have no clue to them.

It is evident then that we have the possibility of infinitely diverse reactions to a work of art. We may imagine, for instance, that our pagan spectator, though entirely unaffected by the story, is yet conscious that the figures represent men, and that their gestures are indicative of certain states of mind and, in consequence, we may suppose that according to an internal bias his emotion is either heightened or hindered by the recognition of their rhetorical insincerity. Or we may suppose him to be so absorbed in purely formal relations as to be indifferent even to this aspect of the design as representation. We may suppose him to be moved by the pure contemplation of the spatial relations of plastic volumes. It is when we have got to this point that we seem to have isolated this extremely elusive aesthetic quality which is the one constant quality of all works of art, and which seems to be independent of all the prepossessions and associations which the spectator brings with him from his past life.

A person so entirely pre-occupied with the purely formal meaning of a work of art, so entirely blind to all the overtones and associations of a picture like the Transfiguration is extremely rare. Nearly every one, even if highly sensitive to purely plastic and spatial appearances, will inevitably entertain some of those thoughts and feelings which are conveyed by implication and by reference back to life. The difficulty is that we frequently give wrong explanations of our feelings. I suspect, for instance, that Goethe was deeply moved by the marvellous discovery of design, whereby the upper and lower parts cohere in a single whole, but the explanation he gave of this feeling took the form of a moral and philosophical reflection.

It is evident also that owing to our difficulty in recognizing the nature of our own feelings we are liable to have our aesthetic reaction interfered with by our reaction to the dramatic overtones and implications. I have chosen this picture of the Transfiguration precisely because its history is a striking example of this fact. In Goethe's time rhetorical gesture was no bar to the appreciation of aesthetic unity. Later on in the nineteenth century, when the study of the Primitives had revealed to us the charm of dramatic sincerity and naturalness, these gesticulating figures appeared so false and unsympathetic that even people of aesthetic sensibility were unable to disregard them, and their dislike of the picture as illustration actually obliterated or prevented the purely aesthetic approval which they would probably otherwise have experienced. It seems to me that this attempt to isolate the elusive element of the pure aesthetic reaction from the compounds in which it occurs has been the most important advance of modern times in practical aesthetic.

The question which this simile suggests is full of problems; do these form chemical compounds, as it were, in the case of the normal aesthetically gifted spectator, or are they merely mixtures due to our confused recognition of what goes on in the complex of our emotions? The picture I have chosen is also valuable, just at the present time, from this point of view. Since it presents in vivid opposition for most of us a very strong positive (pleasurable) reaction on the purely aesthetic side, and a violently negative (painful) reaction in the realm of dramatic association.

DeWitt H. Parker

THE PROBLEM OF AESTHETIC FORM*

We must first consider the general characteristics of aesthetic form. These I shall try to reduce to their simplest principles, hoping to provide the elements of what might be called a logic of aesthetic form. These principles are, I think, very few; as few, indeed, as six: the principle of organic unity, or unity in variety, as it has been called; the principle of the theme; the principle of thematic variation; balance; the principle of hierarchy; and evolution. I do not assert that there are no more principles, but I at least have been unable to find any of equal generality. Others that have been suggested can be shown either to be identical with the six mentioned or to be special cases of them. I shall consider each at some length.

First, the long-established principle of organic unity. By this is meant

* From DeWitt H. Parker's *The Analysis of Art*, Ch. II. Copyright, 1926, by the Yale University Press. Reprinted by permission of the Yale University Press.

the fact that each element in a work of art is necessary to its value, that it contains no elements that are not thus necessary, and that all that are needful are there. The beautiful object is organized all through, "baked all through like a cake." Since everything that is necessary is there, we are not led to go beyond it to seek something to complete it; and since there are no unnecessary elements, there is nothing present to disturb its value. Moreover, the value of the work as a whole depends upon the reciprocal relations of its elements: each needs, responds to, demands, every other element. For example, in the Young Woman with a Water Jug (by Johannes Vermeer: Metropolitan Museum), the cool green needs the warm yellow and both need the red; the casement demands the table, the map requires the dark shadow under the casement, to balance it. In a melody, each tone requires its successor to continue the trend that is being established. In short, the meaning of the whole is not something additional to the elements of the work of art, but their coöperative deed.

This principle cannot, however, be described in so external a fashion. For the unity of a work of art is the counterpart of a unity within the experience of the beholder. Since the work of art becomes an embodiment not only of the imagination of the artist, but of the imagination of the spectator as well, his own experience is, for the moment, concentrated there. He is potentially as completely absorbed in it as he is in a dream; it is for the moment, in fact, his dream. And he can and does remain in the dream because the artist has so fashioned his work that everything there tends to continue and deepen it, and nothing to disturb and interrupt it. Art is the expression of the whole man, because it momentarily makes of man a whole. The "isolation" of the esthetic experience of Hugo Münsterberg[1] and the "repose in the object" of Ethel Puffer[2] are descriptions of the fact to which I am calling attention. This does not mean, of course, that the work of art is not related to other things or that it is actually isolated; but only that its relations are irrelevant to its value, and that it cuts itself off from the rest of the world during appreciation; and this it does, first, because it embodies my dream and, second, because it is so constructed as to make me dream on. The marble of which the statue is made comes from a certain quarry and has an interesting geological history there; it stands in a certain part of space, and hence is related to other parts of space; but all such facts are of no account to its beauty. By placing the statue on a pedestal, we indicate its isolation from the space of the room, as by putting a frame around a picture we isolate it, too, from everything else in the world. It is true that,

---

[1] *The Eternal Values*, chap. IX.
[2] *The Psychology of Beauty*, chap. III.

in order to understand a work of art in its historical relations, I must connect it with the artist's personality, with other works of his, with the "moral temperature" of the age, with the development of artistic styles, and the full appreciation of its beauty depends upon acquaintance with its spiritual background. Who, for example, can appreciate the whole meaning of Signorelli's Pan without some knowledge of classical antiquity and the Italian Renaissance? Yet at the moment of appreciation, all such knowledge becomes focused in the work of art, gathered and contained there like rays in a prism, and does not divert us from it.

The ancient law of organic unity is the master principle of esthetic form; all the other principles serve it. First among them is what I would call the principle of the theme. This corresponds to the "dominant character" or *idee mère* of Taine.[3] In every complex work of art there is some one (or there may be several) preëminent shape, color, line, melodic pattern or meaning, in which is concentrated the characteristic value of the whole. It contains the work of art in little; represents it; provides the key to our appreciation and understanding of it. Thus every good pattern is built up of one or more shapes, the disposition of which constitutes the design. When there is color as well as shape, there is some dominant color that appears again and again or in related degrees of saturation, or else there is a color chord that is similarly repeated or is analyzed. In architecture, each style has its characteristic shape, line, or volume, as the pointed arch of the Gothic, the round arch of the Roman, the ellipse of the baroque. In music, there are the one or more themes that express the essential significance of each composition. Likewise, every sculptor, every draughtsman, has his unique and inimitable line. In every poem, there is a peculiar inflection and a regnant idea which constitute the basis of the design. In the drama or the novel, there is some one, or there may be several persons, whose character and fate create the plot.

The third principle is thematic variation. It is not sufficient to state the theme of a work of art; it must be elaborated and embroidered. One of the prominent ways of doing this is to make it echo and reëcho in our minds. Usually, if the theme can be repeated once only we are better pleased than with a single appearance. Yet to find the same thing barely repeated is monotonous; hence what we want is the same, to be sure, but the same with a difference: thematic variation. The simplest type of thematic variation is recurrence of the theme, as in any pattern built upon a repeat. Here is the maximum of sameness with the minimum of difference: mere difference of spatial or temporal position. A slight acquaintance with primitive

[3] *Philosophie de l'art,* part I, p. 5.

art is sufficient to convince one of the overwhelming importance of recurrence there. Yet it is needless to say that recurrence is not confined to
primitive art. We find it in all civilized art: the recurrence of the same
shape and proportions in architecture and sculpture; the recurrence of the
theme in music; the recurrence of the same type of foot in meter; repetition
of the same color in painting; recurrence of lines and directions of lines
(parallelism) in painting and sculpture and architecture; the refrain in
poetry; the reappearance of the hero in different scenes in the drama and
novel. However, because of the monotony of mere repetition, recurrence
gives place to what may be called, in a generalized sense, transposition of
theme, as when a melody is transposed to another key or tempo; or when in
a design the same shape appears in a different color, or a color appears in
different degrees of saturation or brightness; or in architecture, where a
shape occurs in different sizes or members—in doors, windows, gables,
choir-stalls, and the like. Still another kind of thematic variation is alternation, which requires, of course, more than one theme, or at least two different transpositions of the same theme. Of this, again, the illustrations are
legion. Finally, there is inversion of theme, as when melody is inverted or,
in painting or sculpture, a curve is reversed. These are not all the possible
types of thematic variation, but they are, I think, the most important and
usual.

Another principle of esthetic form is balance. Balance is equality of
opposing or contrasting elements. Balance is one kind of esthetic unity, for
despite the opposition of the elements in balance, each needs the other and
together they create a whole. Thus the blue demands the gold and the
gold the blue, and together they make a new whole, gold-and-blue. Opposition or contrast is never absent from balance, for even in symmetry, where
the balancing elements are alike, the directions of these elements are opposed, right and left. But contrast is never by itself esthetically satisfactory,
for the contrasting elements must offset each other, they must balance.
In color, the warm offsets the cold; in a picture, the small object, properly
placed, offsets the large one. Hence, just as only equal weights will balance
in a scale pan, so only elements that are somehow equal in value, despite
their opposition, will balance esthetically. Not every tint of blue will balance
every shade of yellow; that depth of blue must reappear in a corresponding
depth of yellow; a light, superficial blue would never balance a deep
yellow. But the identity of the opposites is even greater than this. For,
as has been remarked, the elements of a balanced unity demand each
other; the blue demands the yellow; the line which falls in one direction demands the line that falls in the opposite direction. Now the demand which

the color or line makes for its opposite is itself a foreshadowing of the latter; in its demand it already contains the prophecy of its opposite. And even when, as may occur in painting, there is balance between elements of unlike quality—balance, say, of brightness of color against distance or size—the attention value of each must be the same, though opposed in direction. The essential thing about balance is equality of opposed values, however unlike be the things that embody or carry the values.

The pervasiveness of the principle of balance is too generally recognized to need much illustration or argument. In painting we expect, with a reservation that I shall consider in a moment, a threefold balance: horizontal, perpendicular, and radial or diagonal—between the right and left sides, the upper and lower portions, and between what may roughly be called the corners. This last has not received the attention which it deserves; but in many pictures, as for example, Tintoretto's Mercury and the Three Graces, the diagonal axis is the main axis; and in all cases of circular composition, radial balance is fundamental. In architecture, we find balance between right and left, and often between upper and lower parts. In music, there is not seldom a balance between earlier and later parts of a composition, or between opposing themes. In sculpture, there is the balance characteristic of the human body made more perfect by the artist.

Pervasive as balance is, its universality has not stood unquestioned. Nevertheless, many apparent exceptions can be explained away, as is well known, as cases of disguised or subtle balance. The older interpretation of balance after the analogy of symmetry—the balance of like parts—is only a special kind of balance, and has to be supplemented by the wider conception of balance of unlike parts.[4] With this richer conception in mind, we can understand the balance—as in Bruegel's Harvesters—between prominent objects in the right-hand part and little except a vista on the left. Similarly, there is a balance—as in the same picture—between the upper and lower halves of a painting, even when the horizon line is high, and the upper part seems therefore to be relatively empty of masses; for the distance values in the sky balance the heavier lower part. No more difficult of explanation are some cases where asymmetry appears to be definitely sought, as when a girl will put a patch on one cheek but not on another, or will tie the lock of hair on the right with a ribbon, but not the lock on the left. For the piquancy of this procedure comes from the fact that there is a background of decisive symmetry, against which the asymmetrical element stands out. This is quite different from absolute lack of balance. One finds similar eccentric elements

[4] Compare Ethel Puffer, "Studies in Symmetry," *Harvard Psychological Studies*, vol. I, 1902.

in all complex patterns; but always with a background of emphatic balance. And if it is true that such elements disturb symmetry, it is equally true that they serve to emphasize it. The triangle of passion is another illustration; for there also a balanced relationship is the background against which the unbalanced derives its interest.

There are, however, more difficult cases to consider. Many works of art, of the temporal arts in particular, are superficially considered rhythmical rather than balanced, and rhythm may seem to be opposed to balance. Yet an analysis of rhythm shows it to be built upon the two fundamental esthetic forms, thematic repetition and balance. For what are the typical characteristics of rhythm? Every rhythm is a motion of waves, all of a relatively constant or lawfully varying shape and temporal and spatial span, with balancing crests and troughs. The crest may be an accent or the swing up of a line; the trough may be one or more unaccented syllables, a pause, or the swing back of a line in the opposite direction. The rhythm may begin with the trough, as in iambic meter. The swing up and the swing back may both be very complex, as in free verse, yet the fundamental pattern, as it has just been described, is maintained: in every case there is the recurrence of a certain type of wave form, and the opposition—and balance —between the rising and falling swings. The simplest repeat, if you take its elements in succession, is a rhythm. In the diaper pattern, for example, there is the recurrence of the rising and falling lines, and their opposition and balance, two by two. Or a colonnade, as you apprehend the columns in succession, is a rhythm of identical and balancing filled and empty spaces, the columns corresponding to the arsis, and the spatial interval to the thesis.

Hence when balance seems to be replaced by rhythm, balance is still present, only it is not the simple type of balance so easily recognized, but balance as an element in the complex structure we call rhythm. This more subtle type of balance exists oftentimes in pictorial composition—in "open" as opposed to "closed" forms—where the ordinary mode of balance is rejected. I remember one of Monet's Lily Ponds, in which I searched vainly for the usual type of balance with reference to some axis, only to find that the elements of the picture were arranged in a clear-cut rhythm. Rhythm often replaces right-and-left balance in wall paintings, as in those of Puvis de Chavannes. In the Metropolitan Museum he has two paintings, both decorative sketches, which illustrate this: Inter Artes et Naturam and The River. In the former, notice how we do not view the picture from a vertical central axis, but rather from left or right, taking each group of figures in turn as an element in a rhythmically disposed sequence of filled and empty spaces. In The River, the rhythmical arrangement is in deep space.

Another and last type of unity I call evolution. By this I mean the unity of a process when the earlier parts determine the later, and all together create a total meaning. For illustrations, one naturally turns first to the temporal arts. The course of a well-fashioned story is a good example, for each incident determines its follower and all the incidents determine the destiny of the characters involved. The drama offers similar illustrations: the form is the same, only transposed to theatrical presentation. In the older, orthodox story or play there were three stages in the development, an initial one of introduction of characters, a second stage of complication, ending in the climax, and then the unraveling. But these stages may be compressed. The story may begin with the complication already there; the play may begin with the climax and proceed to the unraveling, and go back, as in Ibsen, to the preparation. But in every case, there is a necessary relation between means and consequences, causes and effects, and a total resulting meaning. Illustrations of this type of unity abound also in the static arts. Any line which we appreciate as having a beginning, middle, and end, and any composition of figures where we are led on from one figure or group of figures to another, is an illustration; for there, too, although the figures be physically static, our appreciation of them is a process in time, and through the process the meaning of the whole is evolved. Of all painters, I think El Greco offers the best illustrations of evolution, as in the Crucifixion (Prado museum), where we follow an intensely dramatic movement from the lower to the upper part of the picture.

Is evolution a genuinely distinct type of esthetic unity? Can it be reduced to one or more of the preceding forms? The most closely allied form is rhythm; yet that evolution is distinct from rhythm can easily be seen. For in rhythm, unless combined with evolution, there is no obvious development, no tendency toward a goal. Rhythm is recurrence and balance of systole and diastole, with no growth from one phase to another. It is true that we sometimes speak of any movement of growth as a rhythm, as when we talk of the rhythm of life, but in such cases rhythm exists in combination with evolution. For there is, of course, a rhythm in all life—birth and death, sleep and waking, activity and repose. And if life be taken generically or historically, there are other equally well-known rhythms, as in the history of art, with the alternation of the opposed directions from realism to romanticism. In melody also, except in the most eccentric types of music, harmonic evolution is joined with an accentual or time rhythm. Moreover, even in the most mechanical types of rhythm, like the simple repeat, provided they be esthetic, there is some felt growth of value through the recurrence and balance of parts, and some, however slight, looking forward to the end term as a goal.

Only in purely natural rhythms, as of the tides, is there no growth at all, but these, unless they enter into the mind and emotion of man, are not esthetic in character. Nevertheless, although there is always some evolution in every esthetic rhythm, evolution is not itself necessarily rhythmical. In literature, the rhythm of prose and poetry overlies a development of meanings which does not itself have a quasi-mechanical character of rhythm; the rhythm of time and accent is united with the melodic development of the musical theme, but does not constitute it. The essential character of evolution is, as Bergson has shown, growth or accumulation of meaning, which need not be rhythmical.

Two different types of evolutionary unity must be discriminated, the dramatic and the non-dramatic. In the dramatic type there is an element of overshadowing importance, the climax or goal; in the other type, this element is lacking. To be sure, every process must have an end, and the end has a distinctive importance as such, but it is not always true that the end has a greater importance than some other element or elements. The consummation of the meaning may occur through the agency of all parts evenly, rather than through a particular one. Many stories are of this character; there is an unfolding, a working out of something, with no obvious high points. Here and there the meaning rises, but there is no place where it becomes so central that we feel that the whole story depends upon it. And, if I mistake not, there is much music of this character; there is a definite drift or unfolding, but no climax or finale.

Closeness of connection, yet ultimate difference, marks the relation between evolution and the other types of esthetic unity, balance and thematic variation. The static character of balance is opposed to the dynamic character of evolution; indeed, all movement depends upon the upsetting of an established equilibrium. Yet seldom, even in the static arts, is balance found without movement; for there exists a tendency to proceed from one to another of the balanced elements. In a simple color contrast, for example, there is ever so slight a movement from the cold to the warm color. And, on the other hand, there is often a balance within evolution, between the complication and the unraveling of the plot, or the earlier and later parts of a musical theme. But the union of evolution and balance does not militate against the uniqueness of either. There remains for comparison, thematic variation. This form, too, might seem at first sight to be opposed to evolution, yet not so, for there is probably no case of variation in which the evolutionary element is not present. For the series of variations is not fruitless; each contributes something to a meaning which accumulates and is complete when the variations are over. So many, and no more, exist as are necessary to this end. In so far as, in this way, a meaning is worked out, evolution and thematic variation approach and meet. Yet a difference remains. For the mode of the creation of the meaning is different. In the one case, it occurs through the recurrence of the central meaning in new shapes; in the other, through the realization of some single dominant idea, which extends over the entire work and is expressed once and once only. In the one case, we start with an idea already given, and work it out by repetition; in the other, we have no definite, but only a very vague idea to start with, and construct it step by step. The one method may be called analytic, the other synthetic. For example, we do not know what a musical theme is like until we have heard it entire; building it up is one thing; then, having got it, it is another thing to modulate, invert, and vary it. The same is true of a line.

Nevertheless, in the construction of a theme, both thematic variation and balance may be employed. For example, in building a melody, we may proceed from tone to tone consonant with a given tone, thus repeating the fundamental psychophysical rhythm of the two tones which is the basis of their harmony; or we may proceed through opposition by introducing dissonances. Again, in constructing a linear theme, it is possible to proceed either by repeating or continuing the curve with which we start, or else by introducing opposing and balancing lines. Or for the elucidation of a story it may be expedient to place the persons in various situations, in order that they may manifest their characters—the method of thematic variation— or to balance them against unlike characters. Yet by themselves neither mere variation of theme nor balance of opposites will create evolution.

Thematic variation, balance, and evolution remain, therefore, the fundamental and irreducible types of esthetic unity. I personally have been unable to find other types. Types which seem to be different, like rhythm or circular composition, can easily be shown to be species of one or another of these preëminent forms. The reduction of rhythm has already been effected. As for circular composition, it is evidently a case of evolution; for there is always a beginning and an end; but evolution is combined with repetition, for the beginning and the end are the same. A melody that begins and ends on the tonic is a simple illustration. I have shown that all three forms are intermingled; and most works of art contain all three; yet they remain, nevertheless, distinct.[5]

The principle of hierachy is not so much a mode of organic unity, like thematic variation, balance, and evolution, as rather a species of organization of elements in each of these modes. Sometimes, although not always, there is some one element, or there may be more, of a complex work of art which

[5] I am reminded by my friend, Miss Shio Sakanishi, that in many forms of Japanese art symmetry and repetition are carefully avoided, yet balance is scrupulously observed.

occupies a position of commanding importance there. These elements always embody the theme in an emphatic way, and have a significance far greater than any of the other elements. Thus, in a portrait, the figure is more important than the background, and the face is more significant than anything else. In a novel or drama there may be a scene of unusual significance for the development of the plot, or in a musical composition a single passage, like the Liebestod in Tristan, which overshadows the remainder of the composition or is the climax of its movement. Every dramatic species of evolution illustrates this, as we have seen. In balance also, as again we have already observed, one or the other of the elements may dominate, though slightly. However, dominance is a relative matter, and an element, not itself of unusual importance in the whole, may nevertheless overshadow another element, relatively. Thus, in the Young Woman with a Water Jug of Vermeer, the pitcher is more prominent than the box. Any quality whatever—large size, unusual brightness, richness of elaboration, central position, fullness of meaning—that attracts the attention to itself more strongly than the attention is attracted to other elements, creates relative dominance. However, there may be no elements of outstanding importance in the whole, as is the case in many a landscape painting and in the nondramatic types of evolution, but only varying degrees of importance among all the elements.

SELECTED BIBLIOGRAPHY

1. C. J. Ducasse, *Philosophy of Art*, Ch. XIII, The Dial Press, 1929.
2. Benedetto Croce, *Aesthetic*, Ch. II, The Macmillan Co. Ltd., 1909. (Reprinted in Part I of this anthology.)
3. John Dewey, *Art as Experience*, Ch. VI, Minton, Balch & Company, 1934.
4. A. C. Bradley, "Poetry for Poetry's Sake," *Oxford Lectures on Poetry*, The Macmillan Co., Ltd., 1909. Bradley's distinction between "subject" and "poem"; and "substance" and "form" as "versification" is an attempt at mitigation of the difficulties of a too sharp separation between form and content.
5. Morris Weitz, *Philosophy of the Arts*, Ch. III, Harvard University Press, 1950. A plea for the repudiation of "form" and "content" and the distinction altogether.
6. Erwin Panofsky, "Introductory," *Studies in Iconology*, Oxford University Press, 1939. Reprinted in *Meaning in the Visual Arts*, Anchor paperback, Ch. I. An excellent defense of the form-content distinction.
7. Arnold Isenberg, "Perception, Meaning, and the Subject-Matter of Art," *The Journal of Philosophy*, 1944. An incisive analysis of form and content as applied to the problem of representation in art.
8. Cleanth Brooks, *The Well Wrought Urn*, Ch. 4, Reynal and Hitchcock, 1947. A fine example of the identification of the "how" and "what" of poetic utterance with especial reference to Herrick's "Corinna's Going A-Maying." (Available as a Harvest Paperback.)

EXPRESSION

The concept of expression is a central one in much of modern aesthetics. For some, for example, Croce and Collingwood, it has served as a defining property of art, where art itself has been identified with the activity of making it. For others, Hospers, Parker, Ducasse, and Santayana, to mention only a few, expression has been regarded at least as an important characteristic of many works of art. Almost everyone agrees that in *some* sense it is an intelligible, illuminating and even verifiable way of speaking to say of a particular work of art that it expresses, say, sadness. One aesthetic problem, then, is this: "What does it mean to say of a work of art that it expresses something?"

Our two selections converge on this problem. The first, by R. G. Collingwood, although it is mostly concerned with the clarification of the artist's act of expressing himself as against his merely feeling something, or arousing emotions in his audience, argues that the work of art *is* the expression of the artist who created it. For Collingwood, expression is the artist making clear to himself just what his emotions are, which process, because it involves the use of language, is the work of art.

John Hospers, in our second selection, denies Collingwood's thesis that the act of expression is identical with the work of art. In his penetrating analysis, his distinguishes between expression as the artist's act of expressing himself and the property of expression which we sometimes attribute to works of art.

He also distinguishes between the various uses of "express," "expressive," and "expression," in an attempt to clarify the whole problem of expression in art.

Taken together, these selections should open up some fundamental questions in aesthetics: "Does the artist express himself when he creates a work of art?" "Does every work of art express something?" "Is the work of art identical with the act of expression of the artist?" None of these questions about expression in art has been fully answered, and there is further probing that needs to be done, even to try to explain what is involved in the seemingly simple remark, "this piece of music is sad."

Robin G. Collingwood

EXPRESSION IN ART*

EXPRESSING EMOTION AND AROUSING EMOTION

Our first question is this. Since the artist proper has something to do with emotion, and what he does with it is not to arouse it, what is it that he does? It will be remembered that the kind of answer we expect to this question is an answer derived from what we all know and all habitually say; nothing original or recondite, but something entirely commonplace.

Nothing could be more entirely commonplace than to say he expresses them. The idea is familiar to every artist, and to every one else who has any acquaintance with the arts. To state it is not to state a philosophical theory or definition of art; it is to state a fact or supposed fact about which, when we have sufficiently identified it, we shall have later to theorize philosophically. For the present it does not matter whether the fact that is alleged, when it is said that the artist expresses emotion, is really a fact or only supposed to be one. Whichever it is, we have to identify it, that is, to decide what it is that people are saying when they use the phrase. Later on, we shall have to see whether it will fit into a coherent theory.

They are referring to a situation, real or supposed, of a definite kind. When a man is said to express emotion, what is being said about him comes to this. At first, he is conscious of having an emotion, but not conscious of what this emotion is. All he is conscious of is a perturbation or excitement, which he feels going on within him, but of whose nature he is ignorant. While in this state, all he can say about his emotion is: "I feel. . . . I don't know what I feel." From this helpless and oppressed condition he extricates

---

* From Robin G. Collingwood's *The Principles of Art*, pp. 109–115; 121–124. Copyright, 1938, by The Clarendon Press. Reprinted by permission of The Clarendon Press.

Robin G. Collingwood (1889–1943), English historian and philosopher, wrote on a variety of subjects including problems of art and criticism.

himself by doing something which we call expressing himself. This is an activity which has something to do with the thing we call language: he expresses himself by speaking. It has also something to do with consciousness: the emotion expressed is an emotion of whose nature the person who feels it is no longer unconscious. It has also something to do with the way in which he feels the emotion. As unexpressed, he feels it in what we have called a helpless and oppressed way; as expressed, he feels it in a way from which this sense of oppression has vanished. His mind is somehow lightened and eased.

This lightening of emotions which is somehow connected with the expression of them has a certain resemblance to the "catharsis" by which emotions are earthed through being discharged into a make-believe situation; but the two things are not the same. Suppose the emotion is one of anger. If it is effectively earthed, for example by fancying oneself kicking some one down stairs, it is thereafter no longer present in the mind as anger at all: we have worked it off and are rid of it. If it is expressed, for example by putting it into hot and bitter words, it does not disappear from the mind; we remain angry; but instead of the sense of oppression which accompanies an emotion of anger not yet recognized as such, we have that sense of alleviation which comes when we are conscious of our own emotion as anger, instead of being conscious of it only as an unidentified perturbation. This is what we refer to when we say that it "does us good" to express our emotions.

The expression of an emotion by speech may be addressed to some one; but if so it is not done with the intention of arousing a like emotion in him. If there is any effect which we wish to produce in the hearer, it is only the effect which we call making him understand how we feel. But, as we have already seen, this is just the effect which expressing our emotions has on ourselves. It makes us, as well as the people to whom we talk, understand how we feel. A person arousing emotion sets out to affect his audience in a way in which he himself is not necessarily affected. He and his audience stand in quite different relations to the act, very much as physician and patient stand in quite different relations towards a drug administered by the one and taken by the other. A person expressing emotion, on the contrary, is treating himself and his audience in the same kind of way: he is making his emotions clear to his audience, and that is what he is doing to himself.

It follows from this that the expression of emotion, simply as expression, is not addressed to any particular audience. It is addressed primarily to the speaker himself, and secondarily to any one who can understand. Here again, the speaker's attitude towards his audience is quite unlike that of a person desiring to arouse in his audience a certain emotion. If that is what he wishes to do, he must know the audience he is addressing. He must know what type of stimulus will produce the desired kind of reaction in people of that particular sort; and he must adapt his language to his audience in the sense of making sure that it contains stimuli appropriate to their pecularities. If what he wishes to do is to express his emotions intelligibly, he has to express them in such a way as to be intelligible to himself; his audience is then in the position of persons who overhear him doing this. Thus the stimulus-and-reaction terminology has no applicability to the situation.

The means-and-end, or technique, terminology too is inapplicable. Until a man has expressed his emotion, he does not yet know what emotion it is. The act of expressing it is therefore an exploration of his own emotions. He is trying to find out what these emotions are. There is certainly here a directed process: an effort, that is, directed upon a certain end; but the end is not something foreseen and preconceived, to which appropriate means can be thought out in the light of our knowledge of its special character. Expression is an activity of which there can be no technique.

EXPRESSION AND INDIVIDUALIZATION

Expressing an emotion is not the same thing as describing it. To say "I am angry" is to describe one's emotion, not to express it. The words in which it is expressed need not contain any reference to anger as such at all. Indeed, so far as they simply and solely express it, they cannot contain any such reference. The curse of Ernulphus, as invoked by Dr. Slop on the unknown person who tied certain knots, is a classical and supreme expression of anger; but it does not contain a single word descriptive of the emotion it expresses.

This is why, as literary critics well know, the use of epithets in poetry, or even in prose where expressiveness is aimed at, is a danger. If you want to express the terror which something causes, you must not give it an epithet like "dreadful." For that describes the emotion instead of expressing it, and your language becomes frigid, that is inexpressive, at once. A genuine poet, in his moments of genuine poetry, never mentions by name the emotions he is expressing.

Some people have thought that a poet who wishes to express a great variety of subtly differentiated emotions might be hampered by the lack of a vocabulary rich in words referring to the distinctions between them; and that psychology, by working out such a vocabulary, might render a valuable service to poetry. This is the opposite of the truth. The poet needs no such words at all; the existence or nonexistence of a scientific terminology describing the emotions he wishes to express is to him a matter of perfect indifference. If such a terminology, where it exists, is allowed to affect his own use of language, it affects it for the worse.

The reason why description, so far from helping expression, actually damages it, is that description generalizes. To describe a thing is to call it a thing of such and such a kind: to bring it under a conception, to classify it. Expression, on the contrary, individualizes. The anger which I feel here and now, with a certain person, for a certain cause, is no doubt an instance of anger, and in describing it as anger one is telling truth about it; but it is much more than mere anger: it is a peculiar anger, not quite like any anger that I ever felt before, and probably not quite like any anger I shall ever feel again. To become fully conscious of it means becoming conscious of it not merely as an instance of anger, but at this quite peculiar anger. Expressing it, we saw, has something to do with becoming conscious of it; therefore, if being fully conscious of it means being conscious of all its peculiarities, fully expressing it means expressing all its peculiarities. The poet, therefore, in proportion as he understands his business, gets as far away as possible from merely labelling his emotions as instances of this or that general kind, and takes enormous pains to individualize them by expressing them in terms which reveal their difference from any other emotion of the same sort.

This is a point in which art proper, as the expression of emotion, differs sharply and obviously from any craft whose aim it is to arouse emotion. The end which a craft sets out to realize is always conceived in general terms, never individualized. However accurately defined it may be, it is always defined as the production of a thing having characteristics that could be shared by other things. A joiner, making a table out of these pieces of wood and no others, makes it to measurements and specifications which, even if actually shared by no other table, might in principle be shared by other tables. A physician treating a patient for a certain complaint is trying to produce in him a condition which might be, and probably has been, often produced in others, namely, the condition of recovering from that complaint. So an "artist" setting out to produce a certain emotion in his audience is setting out to produce not an individual emotion, but an emotion of a certain kind. It follows that the means appropriate to its production will be not individual means but means of a certain kind: that is to say, means which are always in principle replaceable by other similar means. As every good craftsman insists, there is always a "right way" of performing any operation. A "way" of acting is a general pattern to which various individual actions may conform. In order that the "work of art" should produce its intended psychological effect, therefore, whether this effect be magical or merely amusing, what is necessary is that it should satisfy certain conditions, possess certain characteristics: in other words be, not this work and no other, but a work of this kind and of no other.

This explains the meaning of the generalization which Aristotle and others have ascribed to art. We have already seen that Aristotle's *Poetics* is concerned not with art proper but with representative art, and representative art of one definite kind. He is not analyzing the religious drama of a hundred years before, he is analyzing the amusement literature of the fourth century, and giving rules for its composition. The end being not individual but general (the production of an emotion of a certain kind) the means too are general (the portrayal, not of this individual act, but of an act of this sort; not, as he himself puts it, what Alcibiades did, but what anybody of a certain kind would do). Sir Joshua Reynold's idea of generalization is in principle the same; he expounds it in connexion with what he calls "the grand style," which means a style intended to produce emotions of a certain type. He is quite right; if you want to produce a typical case of a certain emotion, the way to do it is to put before your audience a representation of the typical features belonging to the kind of thing that produces it: make your kings very royal, your soldiers very soldierly, your women very feminine, your cottages very cottagesque, your oak-trees very oakish, and so on.

Art proper, as expression of emotion, has nothing to do with all this. The artist proper is a person who, grappling with the problem of expressing a certain emotion, says, "I want to get this clear." It is no use to him to get something else clear, however like it this other thing may be. Nothing will serve as a substitute. He does not want a thing of a certain kind, he wants a certain thing. This is why the kind of person who takes his literature as psychology, saying "How admirably this writer depicts the feelings of women, or bus-drivers, or homosexuals . . . ," necessarily misunderstands every real work of art with which he comes into contact, and takes for good art, with infallible precision, what is not art at all.

EXPRESSING EMOTION AND BETRAYING EMOTION

Finally, the expression of emotion must not be confused with what may be called the betraying of it, that is, exhibiting symptoms of it. When it is said that the artist in the proper sense of that word is a person who expresses his emotions, this does not mean that if he is afraid he turns pale and stammers; if he is angry he turns red and bellows; and so forth. These things are no doubt called expressions; but just as we distinguish proper and improper senses of the word "art," so we must distinguish proper and improper senses of the word 'expression,' and in the context of a discussion about art this sense of expression is an improper sense. The characteristic mark of expression proper is lucidity or intelligibility; a person who expresses something thereby becomes conscious of what it is that he is expressing, and enables others to become conscious of it in himself and in them. Turning pale and stammering is a natural accompaniment of fear, but a person who in addition to being afraid also turns pale and stammers does not thereby become conscious of the precise quality of his emotion. About that he is as much in the dark as he would be if (were that possible) he could feel fear without also exhibiting these symptoms of it.

Confusion between these two senses of the word 'expression' may easily lead to false critical estimates, and so to false aesthetic theory. It is sometimes thought a merit in an actress that when she is acting a pathetic scene she can work herself up to such an extent as to weep real tears. There may be some ground for that opinion if acting is not an art but a craft, and if the actress's object in that scene is to produce grief in her audience; and even then the conclusion would follow only if it were true that grief cannot be produced in the audience unless symptoms of grief are exhibited by the performer. And no doubt this is how most people think of the actor's work. But if his business is not amusement but art, the object at which he is aiming is not to produce a preconceived emotional effect on his audience but by means of a system of expressions, or language, composed partly of gesture, to explore his own emotions: to discover emotions in himself of which he was unaware, and, by permitting the audience to witness the discovery, enable them to make a similar discovery about themselves. In that case it is not her ability to weep real tears that would mark her out a good actress; it is her ability to make it clear to herself and her audience what the tears are about.

This applies to every kind of art. The artist never rants. A person who writes or paints or the like in order to blow off steam, using the traditional materials of art as means for exhibiting the symptoms of emotion, may deserve praise as an exhibitionist, but loses for the moment all claim to the title of artist. Exhibitionists have their uses; they may serve as an amusement, or they may be doing magic. The second category will contain, for example, those young men who, learning in the torment of their own bodies and minds what war is like, have stammered their indignation in verses, and published them in the hope of infecting others and causing them to abolish it. But these verses have nothing to do with poetry.

Thomas Hardy, at the end of a fine and tragic novel in which he has

magnificently expressed his sorrow and indignation for the suffering in-
flicted by callous sentimentalism on trusting innocence, spoils everything by
a last paragraph fastening his accusation upon 'the president of the im-
mortals'. The note rings false, not because it is blasphemous (it offends
against no piety worthy of the name) but because it is rant. The case against
God, so far as it exists, is complete already. The concluding paragraph
adds nothing to it. All it does is to spoil the effect of the indictment by
betraying a symptom of the emotion which the whole book has already
expressed; as if a prosecuting counsel, at the end of his speech, spat in the
prisoner's face.

The same fault is especially common in Beethoven. He was confirmed
in it, no doubt, by his deafness; but the cause of it was not his deafness
but a temperamental inclination to rant. It shows itself in the way his music
screams and mutters instead of speaking, as in the soprano part of the
Mass in D, or the layout of the opening pages of the *Hammerklavier* Sonata.
He must have known his failing and tried to overcome it, or he would
never have spent so many of his ripest years among string quartets, where
screaming and muttering are almost, one might say, physically impossible.
Yet even there, the old Adam struts out in certain passages of the *Grosse
Fuge*.

It does not, of course, follow that a dramatic writer may not rant in
character. The tremendous rant at the end of *The Ascent of F6*, like the
Shakespearian[1] ranting on which it is modelled, is done with tongue in
cheek. It is not the author who is ranting, but the unbalanced character
he depicts; the emotion the author is expressing is the emotion with which
he contemplates that character; or rather, the emotion he has towards that
secret and disowned part of himself for which the character stands.

---

[1] Shakespeare's characters rant (1) when they are characters in which he takes no
interest at all, but which he simply uses as pegs on which to hang what the public wants,
like Henry V; (2) when they are meant to be despicable, like Pistol; or (3) when they
have lost their heads, like Hamlet in the graveyard.

John Hospers

THE CONCEPT OF ARTISTIC EXPRESSION*

The expression theory of art, in one form or another, has dominated the esthetic scene for the past two centuries as much, perhaps, as the imitation theory had done previously. It is often assumed without question that the distinctive function of the artist is to express emotions; that if the artist does not express in his work, what he does is to that extent less entitled to be called art; and that all art must be expressive of something or other, so much so that a non-expressive work of art is a contradiction in terms. Nor has the predominance of expression been limited to art; it has been extended to all objects of beauty. It is said that all truly beautiful objects are expressive, and some have even asserted their identity: beauty *is* expression.

In all this the terms "express," "expressive," and "expression" are, of course, all-important. It is of the utmost consequence, then, that we know what these terms are being used to mean. What is artistic expression? what does an artist do when he expresses? what is it for a work of art to be expressive? In this paper I shall try to do no more than give a brief critical examination of the principal senses which can be given to the notion of expression as it occurs in the literature of esthetics.

I. EXPRESSION AS A PROCESS

What, then, is expression? One answer seems obvious, though we shall see that it is not the only possible one: expression is an activity of the artist in the process of artistic creation; expressing is something that the artist *does*. What precisely is it that the artist does when he expresses? On this point accounts differ from one another considerably, and I can do no more than mention a few main points to indicate briefly the area in which esthetic philosophers are working when they discuss expression.

* From John Hosper's "The Concept of Artistic Expression," *Proceedings of the Aristotelian Society*, pp. 313–344, 1954–1955. Copyright, 1954–1955, by the Aristotelian Society. Reprinted, with some changes by the author, by permission of the author and the Aristotelian Society.

John Hospers (1918–   ), at present Professor of Philosophy at Brooklyn College, has taught at the University of Minnesota and in England. He is author of *Meaning and Truth in the Arts* and articles on aesthetic matters as well as of other works in various fields of philosophy.

Most accounts of the expressive process emphasize the confusion and chaos with which the process begins in the artist's mind; gradually replaced by clarity and order as it approaches completion. Collingwood, for example, says:

> When a man is said to express emotion, what is being said about him comes to this. At first, he is conscious of having an emotion, but not conscious of what that emotion is. All he is conscious of is a perturbation or excitement, which he feels going on within him, but of whose nature he is ignorant. While in this state, all he can say about his emotion is: "I feel . . . I don't know what I feel." From this helpless and oppressed condition he extricates himself by doing something which we call expressing himself. (R. G. Collingwood, *The Principles of Art*, p. 109.)

At this point, he writes, he paints, or he carves in stone, and from doing this his emotions become channeled in the exercise of a medium, and his oppressed state is relieved; his inner turbulence ceases, and what was inchoate becomes clear and articulate.

Although Collingwood does not make clear what sense of the phrase "what it is" he is employing when he says that the artist does not know what his emotion is, let us assume that the process he is describing is in general clear enough and turn to another aspect of the expressive process which is usually included, namely, its springs in the artist's unconscious life. William James says:

> A man's conscious wit and will are aiming at something only dimly and inaccurately imagined. Yet all the while the forces of organic ripening within him are going on to their own prefigured result, and his conscious strainings are letting loose subconscious allies behind the scenes which in their way work toward rearrangement, and the rearrangement toward which all these deeper forces tend is pretty surely definite, and definitely different from what he consciously conceives and determines. It may consequently be actually interfered with (jammed as it were) by his voluntary efforts slanting toward the true direction. When the new center of energy has been subconsciously incubated so long as to be just ready to burst into flower, "hands off" is the only word for us; it must burst forth unaided.

In all this, the expression of feeling or emotion is to be distinguished sharply from the deliberate *arousing* of it; accounts are fairly unanimous on this point. A writer of fiction, for example, may deliberately attempt to arouse feelings in his readers, which he does not experience himself. In this case he is expressing nothing, but cold-bloodedly adopting what devices he can to arouse feelings in others, remaining himself unmoved. Because the artist, while expressing his feeling, is clarifying it to himself, he cannot before expressing it know or state what he is going to express; therefore he cannot *calculate* in advance what effects he wants to produce and then proceed to produce them. If he could, he would have no need to express, since the emotion would already be clear to him. "Until a man has expressed his emotion," says Collingwood (p. 111), "he does not yet know what emotion it is. The act of expressing it is therefore an exploration of his own emotions. He is trying to find out what these emotions are." The novelist who tries deliberately and consciously to arouse a certain emotion in his audience cannot, on the expression theory, be an artist; expression is the activity of an artist, while arousal is the activity of a clever craftsman or a trained technician.

In the foregoing characterization of the expressive process, attention has been given primarily to what is going on in the artist; and this, indeed, is the center of emphasis in the Croce-Collingwood school of aesthetics. Though they do talk about the artistic medium, and insist that what the artist expresses must be conceived in the medium the artist is going to use—be it words or paints or musical tones—they tend to view the artist's actual manipulation of a physical medium outside himself as an accident or an afterthought. That such a bias, though perhaps affecting most accounts of expression, is no essential part of the expression theory is brought out most clearly by John Dewey in his account of expression in *Art as Experience*. Dewey conceives expression, as (one is tempted to add) he conceives of everything else, as an interaction between the organism and its environment: more specifically, in the case of art, as the recalcitrance of the medium and the artist's attempt to bend the medium to his will. To talk about expression in terms of the artist alone is to omit half the story; no amount of talk about the artist's inner experiences is enough.

> There is no expression without excitement, without turmoil. Yet an inner agitation that is discharged at once in a laugh or a cry, passes away with its utterance. To discharge is to get rid of, to dismiss; to express is to stay by, to carry forward in development, to work out to completion. A gush of tears may bring relief, a spasm of destruction may give outlet to inward rage. But where there is no administration of objective conditions, no shaping of materials in the interest of embodying the excitement, there is no expression. What is sometimes called an act of self-expression might better be termed one of self-exposure; it discloses character—or lack of character—to others. In itself, it is only a spewing forth. (John Dewey, *Art as Experience*, pages 61-62.)

We have already distinguished expressing from arousing; Dewey asks us now to make another distinction, from the opposite direction, between expressing and discharging, getting rid of, or as Dewey puts it, "spewing forth." Esthetic theory, says Dewey, has made the mistake of supposing that the mere giving way to an impulsion, native or habitual, constitutes expression. Such an act is expressive not in itself but only in reflective interpretation on the part of some observer—as the nurse may interpret a sneeze as the sign of an impending cold. As far as the act itself is concerned, it is, if purely impulsive, just a boiling over. While there is no expression, unless there is urge from within outwards, the welling up must be clarified and ordered by taking into itself the values of prior experiences before it can be an act of expression. And these values are not called into play save through objects of the environment that offer resistance to the direct discharge of emotion and impulse. Emotional discharge is a necessary but not a sufficient condition of expression. (Page 61.)

There are many questions which one might ask of the above accounts as descriptions of what goes on when artists create. But as a psychological account I shall leave it largely unquestioned. It becomes of interest for the philosopher when it is presented, as it often is, as a theory of art. And as such there are a few questions which should be put to it:

1. Expression theories usually speak of *emotions* as what is being expressed, although sometimes the phrase "expression of *feelings*" is used; but the meaning of these two terms, and their relation to one another, is not usually made clear. But let that pass: cannot other things be expressed as well, such as ideas? One wants to know more about *what* it is that the artist *qua* artist is expressing, and, if some things are appropriate for artistic expression and not others, why.

2. But no matter what the artist is said to be expressing, why should one assume that the artist in his distinctively artistic activity is always expressing? Why not say that he is sometimes representing, for example, or just playing around with tones or colors? Many composers do not begin with emotions or feelings at all, but with fragments of melody which they then develop. For them feelings do not particularly enter the picture at all, except possibly feelings of frustration at delays and jubilation at having finished the job. Artists have been creating great works of art for many centuries, yet only in the last two centuries or less would it have been customary, or even seemed natural, to say that *the* distinctive activity of the artist was that of expression.

Indeed, if we accept as being artists those men who have created unquestionably great works of art—Bach, Shakespeare, Cézanne, and so on —it is by no means clear that the creative processes through which they passed can be adequately labeled under the heading of "expression." In the first place, in the case of most artists we have very little idea of what their creative processes were like, since we have no record of them. And in the second place, even when we have such records, whether by the artist himself or his biographers, they do not always point to the kind of thing set forth by the expression theory. For example, what was Shakespeare doing—was he, necessarily and always, expressing? There are doubtless creative experiences in the life of every artist which could be described by talking about an inner turbulence gradually becoming clarified and ordered, and emotions being released through the manipulation of an artistic medium; but I suspect that, as a general description of artistic activity, this is far too narrow, and is a bit too reminiscent of the mystical concept of genius fostered by the Romantic era. I doubt whether Shakespeare was always expressing feelings; sometimes he probably wrote, although he did not feel like it, to meet a deadline, or to have money coming in for the next month, or because the plot he had borrowed from somewhere else intrigued him and he wondered how he could incorporate it into a five-act drama. The motivation, the ends and aims, as well as the inner springs of artistic activity are, I am sure, a very mixed lot; and to assume that the artist *qua* artist is always expressing seems just as one-sided as the earlier assumption that he is always imitating nature or human action.

The written records left by artists, when we have them, sometimes seem flatly to contradict the expression theory—even though artists as a whole probably tend to glamorize themselves and like to leave the impression that they are solitary geniuses engaged in mysterious acts of self-expression. Thus, Poe gives us an account of cold-blooded calculation in the composition of his poem "The Raven," which is such a far cry from the description of the artistic process given us by the expression theory that it would be difficult to make it fit in at any point. And T. S. Eliot said in *The Sacred Wood* that "poetry is not a turning loose of emotion but an escape from emotion." One may, of course, say that if these men did not go through the process described by the theory, they were therefore not true artists; but this is surely to allow an *a priori* dogma to take precedence over cold facts. It is, I think, more certain that these men were artists than that any single theory of art, such as the expression theory, is true. And if the theory is presented, not as an *a priori* pronouncement but as an actual account of the creative process in artists, it will have to stand the empirical test, namely: in all cases of admitted works of art, was the process of its creation such as the expression theory describes? And I do not see any evidence that it holds true in all cases.

3. If it is true that not all great art was created in the way the theory

describes, it is, I think, even more plainly true that not everything created in the way the theory describes is great art. Let us assume that Shakespeare, Virgil, Mozart, Rembrandt, and Hokusai all went through the throes of creation as described by the expression theory; the same can be said of any number of would-be poets, painters, and composers whom one has never heard of for the very good reason that they have never produced anything worth looking at twice. I do not mean, now, the deliberate hacks and quacks, the detective-story writers who spin out half a dozen books a year with an eye on next season's market—these could be accused of trying to arouse emotions in others instead of expressing emotions of their own; I mean the host of deeply earnest would-be artists with delusions of grandeur, so dedicated to Art that they would starve if need be to give proper expression to their genius—but who have neither genius nor, sometimes, even talent. The same turmoil and excitement, the same unpredictability of outcome, the feelings of compulsion and dedication, the surcease from emotion from working in a medium, are experienced not alone by the great creators of art but by their hosts of adoring imitators and camp-followers as well as the supreme individualists who sigh and die alone, ignored and unrecognized but devoted still. This is indeed the most disconcerting fact about the expression theory as a criterion of art: that

> all the characteristic phenomena of inspiration are described in undistinguishable terms by good and bad artists alike. Nor has the most penetrating psychological investigation succeeded in detecting any general differences between the mental processes which accompany the creation of a masterpiece and the inspirations of a third-rate botcher. (Harold Osborne, *Aesthetics and Criticism*, p. 161.)

4. In any case, can anything at all relating to the artistic process be validly used as a criterion for evaluating the artistic product? Even if all artists did in fact go through the process described by the expression theory, and even if nobody but artists did this, would it be true to say that the work of art was a good one *because* the artist, in creating it, went through this or that series of experiences in plying his medium? Once the issue is put thus baldly, I cannot believe that anyone could easily reply in the affirmative; it seems much too plain that the merits of a work of art must be judged by what we can find in the work of art, quite regardless of the conditions under which the work of art came into being. Its genesis is strictly irrelevant; what we must judge is the work before us, not the process of the artist who created it. And yet much critical writing seems to be beset by the delusion that the artist's creative processes are relevant to judging his product—that a bad work is excused or a great work enhanced by considera-

tions of how hard he tried or whether the conditions of work were unfavorable or whether he was inspired or in a mystical trance, and so on. And, perhaps, such considerations do excuse the *artist,* but they do not change the value of the work of art. It is a moral condemnation of Fitzgerald that he was lazy and indolent, and could have composed many poems like the *Rubaiyat* but failed to do so; but this is no criticism of the *Rubaiyat* itself; and it may be praise of Mozart's genius that every note in a concerto of his popped into his head in one afternoon, but not praise of his work—the concerto would be just as great if it had taken him ten years to complete. Even Collingwood, when he is distinguishing false art from art proper, does so on the basis of the artistic process: the artist is one who, during creation, expresses emotions formerly unclear to himself, while the false artist is the one who tries to evoke in others emotions which he does not feel. And I cannot emphasize too strongly that, however much this may be a criterion for judging the artist as a man (and I am not saying that it is a good one), it is not a criterion for judging his work. To fudge the distinction between these two is to fall victim to the process-product ambiguity with a vengeance: the word "art" is normally used to name both a process and the product of that process, and because of this fact formulas like "art is expression" can be made to sound true and reasonable; the misfortune here is that this ambiguity, so obvious once it is pointed out, may help to make people think that any considerations about the artistic process can be relevant to judging the merits of the artistic product.

Our conclusion is, then, that when we make a judgment of esthetic value upon a work of art, we are in no way judging the process, including any expressive process, which led to its completion, and therefore the act of expression does not enter into a critical judgment. If we do not know what the process was like, we need not on that account hold our judgment of the work in abeyance; and if we do happen to know what it was like, we should not let this sway our judgment of the work of art. But there *are* times when we *seem* to invoke the process as a criterion of judgment, and these we should now briefly examine. Here is an example from Dewey:

> If one examines into the reason why certain works of art offend us, one is likely to find that the cause is that there is no personally felt emotion guiding the selecting and assembling of the materials presented. We derive the impression that the artist . . . is trying to regulate by conscious intent the nature of the emotion aroused. (*Art as Experience,* p. 68.)

One example of this occurs, I suppose, when we feel that a novel is "plot-ridden"—for example, that the novelist has forced his characters into conformity with the demands of a plot which he had outlined in full before giving much thought to his characters. This feeling, I take it, is familiar enough. But is our criticism here really of the author's creative processes? Are we blaming the novel because he outlined the plot first and then manufactured the characters to fit the plot? I do not think so: we criticize the work because the actions that these characters are made to perform are not such as characters of this kind would do; in other words, they oversimplify and falsify human nature, and it is because of this that we are offended. If the characters strike us as real human beings, we do not care what process the artist went through in creating them: whether he thought of the plot first and the characters afterward, or whatever it may have been.

The same considerations apply in other cases where we seem to make use of the process in criticizing the product. For example, we say, "One must feel that the work of art came out of the artist's own experience, that he himself lived through the things he was describing," or we say, "I don't like this work because I don't feel that the artist was being *sincere* when he wrote it." Now, living through something and being sincere about something are things we say about people; are we not therefore using the process in evaluating the product? Again, I think not. Perhaps we do require that the characters in the drama behave as if the dramatist had personally experienced all their emotions and shared all their fates; but as long as we feel this, must we reverse our judgment if we should subsequently discover that the dramatist had felt none of these things at all, or only a small part of them? Shakespeare could hardly have gone through the experiences of Hamlet, Macbeth, Iago, Cleopatra, Lear, Goneril, Prospero and Coriolanus in one lifetime, but what difference does this make as long as he could present us with a series of vivid, powerful, convincing characterizations? Or suppose we praise a work, say *Uncle Tom's Cabin,* for its sincerity. Does it really change our critical judgment when we know that Mrs. Stowe was weeping tears during many of the hours in which she wrote it, and if we should discover that it was written by a wealthy Southern slaveowner on a wager to prove how well he could present the feelings of "the other side," would it alter our critical judgment of his work? It would alter our judgment about the author, surely; it would change our judgment about the author's sincerity, and it would probably make us attribute to the author much more ingenuity than we now attribute to Mrs. Stowe. But our judgment of the work would not be changed; or, at any rate, I submit, it *should* not—for the novel, after we have made this discovery, would be just the same as before; not a jot or a tittle of it would be changed by our discovery. And as long as it is the *work* which we are judging, surely our judgment should remain unchanged as long as the work is unchanged.

What difference does it make *what* emotions the artist felt, so long as the work of art is a good one? If the artist was clever enough to compose a work of art without expressing emotion in anything like the manner described by the expression theory, or even if he felt nothing at all, this is of no importance so long as we find the work an enduring source of esthetic satisfaction. It may be true as an empirical fact about artists, that *unless* they really feel something, unless they are or have been on fire with emotion, or unless they have deep perturbations which demand resolution, they are not able to create great works of art. This may sometimes be true, though I doubt whether it is true in all cases. But even if it were true in all cases, we need still have no interest in the artist's creative processes as such; knowing facts about the artist's processes would at best be a good indicator of his having created great works of art, which we might then go on to examine, and test the correlation between process and product. To know (supposing it to be true) that a work of art could be produced only when the artist went through this or that kind of creative process would be to know an interesting correlation, but it would not be a means of judging the work of art itself. Even if Bach's Preludes and Fugues had been produced by machinery, would they not be as great as before?—and this in spite of the fact that there were no artist's emotions to be expressed because there was no artist. For appreciating the work of art, the artist's biography is not essential: "by their works shall ye know them."

II EXPRESSION AS EVOCATION

Thus far we have been discussing the sense of "express" in which expressing is something the artist does. Let us now turn to another sense, that in which we say that a work of art expresses something, or is expressive. Here we need not bring in the artist's creative process, which we found to be so damaging to the expression theory of Section I.

1. There is, I think, a sense in which we can bring in the artist even here. We may say, "The music expresses sadness," meaning thereby the sadness which the artist felt; this sense means approximately the same as "reveal." In this sense there *is* a biographical commitment, for if it should turn out that the artist did not feel any sadness, this would falsify our statement that the music expressed the sadness that he felt.

This sense of "express" is easily confused with something we distinguished from expression in Section I, namely giving vent to or releasing emotion as opposed to expressing it. The two are easily confused because they may both be asserted of one and the same person in one and the same situation; they differ only in *from whose point of view* the expressing is done. We may say of the person who is raging that he is expressing rage. In Dewey's sense (considered in Section I) this is false, since he is merely giving vent to rage, not expressing it; but *to us as observers* his actions may be expressive of rage in the sense we are now considering, namely that they *reveal* it. Another example:

> . . . the cry or smile of an infant may be expressive to mother or nurse and yet not be an act of expression of the baby. To the onlooker it is an expression because it tells (reveals) something about the state of the child. But the child is only engaged in doing something directly, no more expressive from his standpoint than is breathing or sneezing—activities that are also expressive to the observer of the infant's condition. (*Art as Experience*, p. 61.)

Whether this "reveal" sense of "express" is much used of art is doubtful. At any rate it is primarily used in speaking of a person's state-of-mind as being expressed (revealed) by his facial expression or gestures. If Jones was not feeling joyful, we would probably retract our statement that his face expressed his joy; but if Mozart was not feeling joy, we would probably not retract our statement that Mozart's rondo expresses joy. This shows that when we make the expression-claim of music we are not involving ourselves in any biographical commitment, anything that could be falsified by knowing more about the composer's biography. We would insist that the music was expressive of joy even if we learned that Mozart hadn't had a joyful moment in his life. Since in this case we do not test our statement by facts about Mozart's life, what *do* we mean when we say that the music expresses, or is expressive of, the emotion?

2. One obvious answer is that to say that the music expresses joy is to say that it *evokes* joy in the listener. (Expression is in this sense a "to me" characteristic: it may express to you and not to me because it evokes sadness in you but not in me.)

But this analysis is at once seen to be too crude to do the job. Music which I say expresses joy may not make me joyful at all, especially if I am in a sour mood today or am tired or have already heard the same composition twenty times this week.

3. Perhaps then we should say, not that it actually *does* make me feel so-and-so, but that when I hear it I have a *disposition* to feel so-and-so, the fulfillment of this disposition depending on the non-occurrence of certain inhibiting factors such as fatigue, boredom, worry, and sleep. In short, in normal circumstances (and we can specify what these are) the music will make me feel so-and-so, but it will not always do so, just as normally

light-waves of a certain character impinging on my retina will make me see red but will not do so if I am drugged, asleep, or color-blind.

4. But this, though an improvement, will not do either. To respond to works of art with emotions, some will say, is not yet to have developed the esthetic attitude toward art-objects. Those who respond to a drama or a novel with tears have not developed esthetic distance; they are responding to the work of art as they would respond to a situation in real life; they are still in the position of the yokel in the gallery who shoots the villain on the stage as he is about to capture the heroine. We should not respond to art with the emotions of life.

One might object also: if "The music expresses sadness" means "I am disposed to feel sad when I hear it," why should I ever wish to hear it? Sad experiences, such as suffering personal bereavement or keen disappointment, are not the kind of thing we wish to repeat or prolong. Yet sad music does not affect us in this way; it may bring relief, pleasure, even happiness. Strange kind of sadness that brings pleasure!

One may, of course, reply to this as follows: Sadness expressed in music is a very different thing from sadness in life; it is only by a kind of analogy that we use the same word for both. Sadness in music is depersonalized; it is taken out of, or abstracted from, the particular personal situation in which we ordinarily feel it, such as the death of a loved one or the shattering of one's hopes. In music we get what is sometimes called the "essence" of sadness without all the accompanying accidents, or causal conditions which usually bring it into being. In view of this, it is said, we can continue to say that music expresses sadness, but we should distinguish the music-sadness, which is a happy experience, from life-sadness, which is not.

Now, this view is not beyond criticism. Why, one might ask, should the experience of sadness come into being when it is cut off from its usual causal conditions? And if it is replied that the experience is after all very different, why call it sadness? is not sadness the kind of experience that accompanies events like bereavement and disappointment? and would it be sadness without these things?

There is both a psychological and a linguistic point involved here. I shall not attempt to discuss the psychological issue: *why* it is that music is able to evoke in us experiences which we describe as sad is a psychological-physiological question of great complexity; it is the kind of question to which the answer lies, as I. A. Richards once said, still hidden in the jungles of neurology. The linguistic point is that however unlike music-sadness and life-sadness may be, and although music-sadness may not deserve the name "emotion" at all, the experiences are sufficiently similar to have received the same name—and not through accidental ambiguity, like the river bank and the Bank of England, but quite spontaneously, so that a person who has experienced sadness in life does not need to learn the application of the same word to music-experiences. And this is enough for our purposes. Let us grant, then, that music-sadness is different from life-sadness, and that whatever the psychological causes of the felt similarity may be, it is the music-sadness and not the life-sadness that the music evokes.

Here, then, is a possible meaning for "The music expresses sadness": "I am disposed, in response to hearing the music, to feel music-sadness." But there are other possible meanings as well:

5. It may be that when we hear the music we do not ourselves *have* or *experience* the sadness, we *imagine* it. Quite surely this often happens; we imagine what we do not feel.

6. Or again, we may not imagine it, but *think* of it. On hearing the music we may feel nothing at all, but say to ourselves, "Oh yes, sadness." I am sure that this often happens, but I am inclined to think that this is a derivative sense: when I say "Oh yes, sadness" I recognize it as the kind of music which under *other* conditions would make me feel or imagine the music-sadness. Unless I had at least once experienced the feeling, I would be unable so to recognize it.

7. I may even say that the music expresses sadness without having ever felt anything in response to it at all; perhaps I am tone-deaf; but I have heard others say that it expressed sadness and I may recognize this composition as similar to other compositions of which I have heard people say this, and therefore say that this one too expresses sadness. Again this is clearly derivative: if I have not experienced the music-sadness, someone else must have. This is strictly a trying-to-keep-up-with-the-Joneses sense: not having a musical sense myself, I disguise the fact by aping the locutions of others.

8. All these are rough characterizations of states of mind evoked in us by the music which may be the criterion for our calling them expressive. But there are other, more demanding and complicated, criteria, which there is no time to discuss in detail. I shall select only one, perhaps the best known, that of Santayana, who says in *The Sense of Beauty* that A (an element in a work of art) does not express B (an emotion) to me unless A and B are confounded with one another in my mind; or, as he says in another passage, A and B are so indissolubly fused together in my mind that I do not think of them as separate entities. The music does not express joy to me unless the joy is felt as being "in the very notes I hear"; if I merely associated joy with the notes, then the one would merely remind me of the other and the

two would not have fused in my mind, and without this fusion there is no expression.

It is not easy to know what to make of this way of putting the matter. (a) If in taking A to express B I am *confounding* A with B, then our entire talk about expression depends on a delusion: a false identification between the A and B which are clearly not identical things. It is difficult to believe that when I take A to express B I am confusing two things which in my soberer moments I know very well should not be confused—a case of mistaken identity. (b) But if, in taking A to express B, I am said to be *fusing* A with B, I am not clear about what I am supposed to be doing. I know what it is like for two metals to be fused together in intense heat, but talking about two such different kinds of thing as notes and emotions as being fused together seems just as mysterious as talking about two railway cars as being connected, not by a coupling, but by the *thought* of a coupling. It may be, of course, that this kind of language is not meant to be taken literally; perhaps it refers merely to the kind of experience which would lead us to say such curious things. But this, of course, leaves the rest of us, who are not moved to say these things, in the dark about what this experience is like.

The words "express" and "expressive," however, can be variously used, as we have already seen; and if anyone finds in his experience anything which leads him to use the combination of words which Santayana employs, and wants to use the word "express" to refer to it, he is welcome to do so. Since the word "express" in the context of evocation has numerous related meanings, I suppose it will not be fatal to add still another to the list.

In this section we have been speaking of A expressing B, or A being expressive of B, if A evokes or tends to evoke in us a feeling of kind B—with the variations and complications we have now reviewed. Let us now pause for a moment to examine the question, How does the expression theory of art stand up when we use *this* kind of meaning for the term "expression"?

Personally, I am not inclined to say either that a work is better art, or that it is more beautiful, when I say that it is expressive of something.[1] (1) When I hear several compositions and say what they express to me, and then hear some entirely different, non-descriptive compositions (a Mozart quintet, a Bach fugue) and cannot say what they seem to me expressive of, in fact I cannot honestly say I find them expressive of anything at all, I do not value them any the less as music on this account. My judgment of their merit as music remains unchanged by whether I do or do not attribute to them any expressive character. I can say that some passages of *Tristan and Isolde*

[1] Some of the following arguments are drawn from Edmund Gurney, *The Power of Sound.*

express longing but I cannot say that the *Prelude and Fugue in G Minor* is expressive of anything, but I still prefer the *Prelude and Fugue* for all that. (2) When I say that a composition expresses this or that, I do not think that its beauty or its merit as music depends on this. I may find many mediocre compositions also expressive of the same emotion. Expressiveness is one thing and beauty is another; as Gurney said, why should expressiveness be any more an indicator of beauty in a tune than in a face? Just as there may be faces which are expressive but not beautiful, so also with works of art. (3) On those occasions when I hold the same composition to be both beautiful and expressive, I do not mean to imply that it is beautiful *because* it is expressive. Its beauty seems to depend on an extremely complex, subtle, and delicate combination of tones; and while I cannot say why I find this melody beautiful and another one, almost exactly like it, repulsive, I find the recourse to expressiveness quite unhelpful in explaining the difference. Indeed, when I say that it expresses so-and-so, the expressiveness seems to be as far from constituting its beauty, or even being an explanation of its beauty, as a heap of scattered clothes on the floor constitutes or explains the living beauty of face and form. (4) The expressive quality attributed to a composition by a person or a generation of people may alter, while leaving the attribution of beauty and musical merit unchanged. When Mozart's compositions first appeared, they struck the public as being full of storm and stress as opposed to the serenity and peace characterizing the works of Haydn. When Beethoven appeared on the scene, the compositions of Mozart joined those of Haydn in the Olympian realm of calm. And when Beethoven was followed by Brahms, Wagner, and Mahler, the expressive qualities attributed to the works of music again shifted. In all this the attribution of musical merit remained fairly stable; the beauty of Mozart's compositions, for example, was nowhere questioned. Again: Hanslick reports that he found the opening passage of the great E flat trio by Schubert "the *ne plus ultra* of energy and passion," while Schuman called that same passage "tender, girlish, and confiding." Yet these two sensitive listeners did not disagree in their judgments about its beauty; if they had been called upon to make a list of all Schubert's works in order of merit, they might well have constructed identical lists. I am not trying to show here that our verdict of expressiveness has nothing to do with our verdict of beauty, but that it is far from being the only thing. At the very least it should lead us to reject the notion that beauty *is* expressiveness. Even if we held that all beautiful works were *also* expressive (or vice versa), the material equivalence would still not constitute an identity.

Expressiveness, then, as constituting, or even being a reliable indicator of, beauty in a work of art, is a view I would reject. Of course one may simply stipulate the alleged identity in a definition, saying "Beauty = expressiveness." But I see no reason to adopt such a use of terms, and would no more equate them than I would be inclined to say "Blue = solid." If, on the other hand, we tone down the assertion to read, "Whenever you say that something is beautiful, then you will also find that you will want to call that object expressive," then I think we shall find that in many cases this correlation does not hold. In this area, of course, since we are talking about evocation, each person can speak only in terms of what is evoked in him; if anyone honestly says that all those things he finds beautiful he also finds expressive, and vice versa, then I cannot deny what he says, but would still remind him that what he is uttering, at most, is a correlation which he has found to hold thus far in his experience between two different things—a correlation which could conceivably be upset by the next instance that appeared. This indeed is the possible fate of any contingent connection.

III EXPRESSION AS COMMUNICATION

But we may long since have become impatient with the line of reasoning pursued in Section II. What we have been talking about all through it (it will be said) is evocation—trying to analyze expression in terms of certain effects, of whatever kind, evoked in the listener or reader or observer. And whatever expression is, it is not evocation; no theory of expression is merely a theory about evocation. So we shall have to look elsewhere if we want a sensible meaning for the term "expression," when used to characterize not artistic processes but works of art.

Why is this evocation-talk inadequate, one might ask, to deal with expression? One could imagine the following reply: To say that a work of art expresses something is not to say that the artist underwent certain creative processes, such as described in Section I, nor to say that the listener had certain experiences, such as described in Section II. Rather, it is to say that the artist has communicated something *to* the listener by means of his work. Expression is not just something evoked in us, it is something which the artist *did* which he then *communicated* to us. Thus far we have dealt with the two aspects—artist and audience—in isolation from each other; but we should have considered them both together; this has been our error. Let us pursue this line of thought a little.

The typical kind of view here is one hallowed by tradition; we might describe it roughly as follows: The artist feels a powerful emotion which he expresses by creating a work of art, in such a way that we, the audience, on

reading or seeing or hearing the work of art, feel the same emotion ourselves. Whether the artist did this by intent—i.e., whether in creating he
wanted us to feel this emotion, which is what Collingwood denies that a true
artist will do—or whether he was working something out within himself
without thinking of an audience, does not matter at this point; the important
thing is that, whether by intent or not, whether he created with an audience
in mind or only to express what he felt, the artist put something into his
work which we, the audience, can get out of it; and what we get out is the
same thing that he put in. In this way whatever it is that he put in is communicated to us who get it out. Expression is thus a "two-way deal" involving both the artist and his audience.

The language used just now in characterizing the view is deliberately
crude, for I do not know how else to describe it with any accuracy. Indeed,
this is the very feature of it which makes it, on reflection, extremely difficult
to defend. Nor is it easy to remedy it by employing a more sophisticated
language in formulating it, for the sophisticated terms usually turn out to
be metaphorical. Yet these metaphors seem to be basic to the theory.

For example, it is said that the artist, by means of his work, *transmits*
his emotion to us. But what is meant by "transmit" here? When water is
transmitted through a pipe, the same water that comes into the pipe at one
end comes out at the other; this is perhaps a paradigm case of transmission.
When we speak of electricity as being transmitted through a wire, there is
not in the same sense something that comes in at one end and out at the
other, but at any rate there is a continuous flow of electricity; or if the word
"flow" is itself metaphorical, it is perhaps enough to remark that at any
point between its two ends the wire will affect instruments and produce
shocks. When we transfer this talk about transmission from these contexts
to works of art, we may tend to imagine a kind of wire connecting the work
of art with the artist at one end and with the audience at the other; or, if we
do not actually have such an image, at any rate the term "transmit" takes its
meaning from situations such as we have just described; and the question
arises, what does it mean in the very different context of art? If it is not like
these orthodox cases of transmission, what makes it transmission? what is
one committing himself to when he says that in art emotion is transmitted?

A metaphor that may seem to do better justice to the theory is that of
deposition. The artist has, as it were, *deposited* his emotion in the work of
art, where we can withdraw it at any time we choose. It is somewhat like
the dog burying a bone, which another dog may dig up at his own pleasure.
But of course, the artist has not literally buried or deposited emotion in his
work; he has, rather, with or without the divine agonies of inspiration,

painted in oils or written a complicated set of notes on paper. It is true that on seeing the one or hearing the other performed we may have certain feelings; but in no literal sense has the artist *put* them there in the way that we put money into the bank to withdraw at a later time. Moreover, the bone that is dug up is one and the same bone that was previously buried; whereas the emotion which we feel (I shall not say "extract") when we hear or see the work of art cannot be one and the same numerical emotion as the one which the artist felt (I shall not say "put in").

Let us then substitute the metaphor of *conveying*. Whatever it is that the artist is said to be conveying to his audience, of what does such conveyance consist? One person conveys the ball to another by throwing it; the postman conveys letters from the postoffice to one's door. Is a material continuum necessary for conveyance—the postman between the postoffice and the house, the moving conveyor-belt for trays and machinery? If something mysteriously disappeared at one place and reappeared at another, would it be said to be conveyed? If the emotion ceases in the artist and turns up in the audience when they examine his work, has the artist's emotion been conveyed? Again it is not clear exactly what is involved in the talk about conveying. And even if the emotion ceased in the artist and thereupon occurred in the audience, would it be the same emotion that occurred in the two? In all the cases of conveyance—the ball, the letter, the water through the pipe—it is one and the same thing that is conveyed from the one person or place to the other. This condition is not fulfilled in the case of emotion. One and the same emotion could no more occur in both artist and observer than the same pain can be passed along from one person to another by each person in a row successively pricking his finger with the same pin.

Though the language of the expression theory leaves the impression that it is one and the same emotion which occurs in both artist and observer, on the analogy with the other examples, this is surely not essential to the theory; perhaps it is enough that they be two emotions of the same kind or class. It may be enough that the artist in composing may feel an emotion of kind X, and the observer on seeing it may feel another emotion of kind X. This probably occurs often enough. But suppose it does; is *this* sufficient for saying that X is conveyed from the one to the other? Is this watered-down formulation really what the theory means when it says that art expresses emotion?

Let us, then, speak simply of "communication." The word "communicate" is somewhat more elastic than the previous ones—people can communicate in person, by wireless, even telepathically—but it is also more vague and difficult to pin down. We could spend many hours discussing criteria for communication. Since we cannot do this here, let us take an example in which we would probably agree that communication had occurred. A student summarizes the contents of a difficult essay, and the author looks at the summary and says, "That's it exactly!" Similarly, one might say that an emotion had been communicated if the listener to a symphony described a movement as "haunting, tinged with gentle melancholy, becoming by degrees hopeful, ending on a note of triumph" and the composer said, "Exactly so! that's just what I meant to communicate."

I have some doubts about whether even this last example would satisfy us as being a "communication of emotion." At any rate, what the listener did here was intellectual, not emotional—he *recognized* the emotions rather than experiencing them himself; and perhaps this suffices for communication, but it is worth pointing out that in the traditional expression theory the listener does not merely recognize the feeling, he himself *has* the feeling. But, so as not to spend more time tinkering with the highly vulnerable terminology of the expression theory (in the form we are considering in this section), let me state some objections that could be raised to any formulation of it known to me.

1. There are many experiences which the artist undergoes in the process of creation—the divine agonies of inception, the slow working through of ideas to fruition, and the technical details of execution—which the audience need not and probably should not share. This part of the artist's creative activity need in no sense be communicated. For example, much of the creative process may be agonizing or even boring, but the audience on viewing or hearing the work of art should not feel either agonized or bored. At most, then, it is only a selection of the artist's experiences in creation that should be communicated. One should not speak as if somehow the artist's whole experience in creation were somehow transferred bodily to the observer or listener.

2. Even for the part that the artist wants to communicate to his audience, it is not necessary that he be feeling this at the time of creation, as the theory so often seems to imply. When the artist is under the sway or spell of an emotion, he is all too inclined to be victim and not master of it, and therefore not to be in a good position to create a work of art, which demands a certain detachment and distance as well as considerable lucidity and studied self-discipline. Wordsworth himself said that the emotion should be recollected in tranquillity; and others, such as Eliot, have gone further and expunged emotion from the account altogether. Perhaps, then, it might be held essential only that the artist *have had* the emotion at some time or

other. But if all that is required is that the artist have some emotion or other of type X, then, since most people of any sensitivity have experienced a considerable part of the gamut of human emotions, including some from type X or any other one chooses to mention, this feature in no way distinguishes the artist from other people, and the theory loses all its punch; it becomes innocuous and, like all highly diluted solutions, uninteresting and undistinctive.

3. To say that the audience should feel the same kind of emotion as the artist seems often to be simply not true. Perhaps, in lyric poems and some works of music, the listener may feel an emotion of the same kind as the artist once felt; but in many cases this is not so at all. Even when we do feel emotions in response to works of art (and most of the time what we experience should not, I think, be called "emotions" at all, at least if our attitude is esthetic), they are often of a quite different sort: if the author has expressed anger, we feel not anger but (perhaps) horror or repulsion; if he has expressed anguish, we may feel not anguish but pity.

Often it seems quite clear that the audience emotion should be quite different from anything that was or sometimes even could have been in the mind of the artist. We may experience fascination, horror, or sympathy when seeing *Hamlet* because of what we feel is the oedipal conflict unconsciously motivating his inaction; but this response, a result of Freudian psychology, could hardly have been in the mind of Shakespeare. And why indeed should it have been? It is enough that his drama can be consistently interpreted in this way, perhaps even giving it an added coherence; it is enough that he wrote a drama capable of arousing such feelings; it is not necessary that he have experienced them himself.

4. Epistemologically the most ticklish point for the expression theory is simply this: how can we ever know for sure that the feeling in the mind of the artist was anything like the feeling aroused in a listener or observer? Our judgments on this point, in cases where we do have evidence, have notoriously often been mistaken. We might feel absolutely certain that Mozart felt joy when he composed the Haffner Symphony, and be amazed to discover that during this whole period of his life he was quite miserable, full of domestic dissension, poverty, and disease. A happy composition does not imply a happy composer. Strictly speaking the only way we can know how a composer felt is to ask him, and then only if he is not lying. If he is dead, we have to consult his autobiography, if any, or other written records, if any, and hope that they do not misrepresent the facts and that they do not tell us what the composer or biographer wanted us to think rather than what really was the case. And of course they often do this: "Artists who are

dead have rarely left satisfactory psychological records, and the difficulties of appealing to living artists, whose motives and intentions are often mixed and their powers of introspective analysis small, are overwhelming." (Harold Osborne, *Aesthetics and Criticism,* p. 153.)

This consequence is fatal if the expression theory is made a criterion of good art. For it would follow that if we do not know whether the emotion experienced by a listener is of the same kind as that experienced by the artist, we do not know whether or not this is a good work of art. Therefore in those cases where we have no records or they are of dubious value, we must hold our judgment of the work of art in abeyance. And such a consequence, it would seem, makes the theory in this form pass the bounds of the ridiculous.

"But," it may be said, "we don't have to find out from the artist himself or from written records what emotion the artist felt—we can tell this from seeing or hearing the work of art." But this is precisely what we cannot do. Though in this area conviction is strong and subjective feelings of certainty run high, our inferences from works of art to artists are as likely as not to be mistaken. We cannot tell from just listening to the symphony how Mozart felt; the work simply provides no safe clue to this. The best we can do is guess, after hearing the composition, what he was feeling; and then, if the available evidence should point to the conclusion that he actually was feeling so at the time, our inference would have been correct for at least this instance. But once we do this, we are already checking our inference (made from hearing the work) against the empirical evidence, and it is the evidence that is decisive.

We might, in the light of these objections, wish to revise the theory so as not to require that the audience should feel what the artist felt, but only what the artist wanted or *intended* the audience to feel. But when this is done, difficulties again confront us: (1) The same difficulties that attend our knowing how the artist felt are also present, though sometimes in lesser degree, in knowing what he intended. (2) The artist's whole intention may have misfired; he may have intended us to feel one thing, but if even the most careful and sensitive listeners for generations fail to feel anything like this when they hear his composition, shall we still say that we should feel what the artist intended us to feel? (3) The moment we abandon the stipulation that the audience should feel, not as the artist felt but as the artist intended the audience to feel, we seem to abandon anything that could be called the expression theory. For it is characteristic of the expression theory that the artist must have felt something which he "conveys" through his work and which we on observing the work also feel; if he did not feel it, but only tried to make us feel it or intended us to feel it, this is no longer an expression of feeling on his part but a deliberate attempt to evoke it in others—in other words, not expressing but arousing.

It may seem that in the last few pages we have been flogging a dead horse; yet if one examines much critical writing he must be aware how far from dead this horse is. Critics and laymen alike are dominated, quite unconsciously, by the metaphors of transmission, conveyance, and the like, the emotion in the analogy being usually a kind of liquid that is transmitted bodily from artist to audience. Although when made explicit this kind of formulation would doubtless be rejected, it is precisely these metaphors which are at the very roots (to use another metaphor) of the expression theory in the form we have been considering in this section. And the very strong objections to the theory seem seldom to be realized.

But then, one might say, why should the expression theory be held in any such form as this? What we have been discussing in this section concerns communication between artist and audience; and a theory of communication, one might say, is no more a theory of expression than a theory of evocation is. For an artist to *express* something, however irrelevant this may be to a judgment of its value, is one thing; for him to *communicate* it to an audience is another. For a work to be expressive is one thing; for an audience to feel so-and-so is another. If this is so—if reference to an audience has no place in a theory of expression—it immediately rules out both the evocation forms of the theory which we discussed in Section II, and the communication forms which we have been discussing in Section III.

IV EXPRESSION AS A PROPERTY OF THE WORK OF ART

Is there yet another possibility? We have now discussed expression as an activity of the artist, expression as evocation in an audience, and expression as communication between artist and audience. But we may be dissatisfied with all of these. "To say," we might object, "that the artist went through a certain series of experiences, or (if you prefer) interactions with his artistic medium, is indeed to talk about expression, in the sense of the expressive *process;* but this is chiefly of importance if we are interested in the psychology of artistic creation; it says nothing about the expressive *product.* The attempt to talk about the expressive product in terms of what feelings it evokes in an audience is, I suspect, a mistake; and so is the attempt to talk about it as a transaction between the artist and the audience. It is neither the artist nor the audience that matters here; it is the work of art itself. It is *the music* that is expressive; and the music may be expressive even if the artist had no emotions when he wrote it, and even if the audience is composed of such dull insensitive clods that they feel nothing when they hear it. Surely we do not want expression to depend in its very definition on the reliability or unreliability of audience response. The expressiveness of the music is dependent on neither the experiences of the artist nor the experiences of the audience."

This way of looking at the matter probably strikes a responsive chord in most of us. If somebody said to us that the last movement of Beethoven's Ninth Symphony, which we take to be expressive of joy or exultation, was mournful, dour, and depressing, we would probably dismiss his claim as absurd and assert with complete confidence that he had not even begun to listen to the music. We are inclined to feel that the music *does* express so-and-so just as objectively as it contains so-and-so many measures; and that if the audience is so stupid as not to respond appropriately to it, so much the worse for the audience.

Yet how are we in the final analysis to defend such a claim? If our opponent in the controversy has just as long an experience of music as we have, and is just as learned, sincere, and intelligent, and after repeated hearings he retains his conviction, what now can we do? Shall we simply say, "Now ends the argument and begins the fight?" Or is there some way in which we can defend the view that the music *really does* express what we say it does?

Let us try. We may take pains to define the music's expressive character in terms of certain configurations of tones or rhythmic patterns in the music. We may say, for example, that music is expressive of sadness if it falls within a certain range of (rather slow) tempo, is in the minor key, has more than a certain proportion of descending notes, a certain proportion of sixths or diminished thirds among its intervals, etc. The formula will have to be extremely complex, for the characteristics of music which make us say that a composition expresses sadness are extremely numerous. Moreover, it may be that no single one of them is necessary; for example, sad music does not *have* to be in the minor key; it is only necessary that some of the characteristics be present. We shall doubtless end up with something of this sort: "Music expressive of sadness has features ABCD or ABDE or BEFG or . . ." etc. But it is at least conceivable that we might, with some patience, be able to track down all of what I shall call the sad-making features of the music and formulate them in a precise way, entirely in terms of what is to be found on the musical score. (And similarly for the other arts.) If this happened, we could say to our opponent, "Music that has features ABCD expresses sadness; this music has those features, as I can prove to you by showing you the score; therefore this music *is* expressive of sadness, and you are wrong when you say it isn't." We could then do the same with as many emotions or states of feeling as we wished: "Musical pattern of type 3856; this means emotion # 3856, gentle melancholy tinged with doubt"—and so on.

The reason why this suggestion may not be helpful is, of course, that our opponents may reject these patterns of notes as expressive of sadness. He will perhaps present a counter-list of sad-making features. The difficulty is that which features of the music we are willing to include on our list of sad-making features is dependent on which features of the music make us feel the music-sadness, or at any rate make us inclined to say that the music is sad. And those features in virtue of which you call the music sad *may* be different from those in virtue of which I call it sad. And when this happens, what are we to do?

But now, it will be said, the case is not quite so hopeless as this. For there *are* times when we can say that, quite objectively, this expresses that. We can do it with regard to human facial expressions and gestures; this one expresses grief, another expresses perturbation, another jubilation, and so on. We know that this facial configuration expresses grief because when we feel grief we behave so-and-so and have such-and-such facial features. When we feel joy or disturbance we have other facial features. And this is quite objective: everyone recognizes in general what facial features are expressive of what inner states. Tears go with sadness and smiles with gladness, and this is just an objective fact. Anyone who said that furrowed brows and menacing gestures were expressive of joy or relaxation would be wrong. Now, if publicly observable facial features and gestures can be expressive, why cannot publicly observable patterns of sounds or colors also be so?

But let us examine this comparison for a moment. My facial features and general demeanor express my disturbed state of mind; that is to say, they reveal it to others; they express in the sense of "reveal." What then do these musical tones reveal? That the composer was in a certain state of mind? But we have already sought to attack this notion; first, because the pattern of notes does not enable us to know this, or even infer it with great probability; and second, because even if it did, it would not be particularly relevant anyway, unless we are psychologists trying to get at the composer's state of mind. Surely this is not what we want. Yet the analogy of music with facial features here permits no more than this; if a person's facial features express his feeling in the sense of revealing it, then the musical tones, even if the argument from analogy is here accepted, do no more than express in the same sense.

Perhaps another consideration may help the situation: The person *need* not feel the emotion his face expresses. Ordinarily he does, else we would never have arrived at the connection between the facial features and what they express; but in some cases it may not—if the man is an actor his face may express grief, but on the stage he does not feel the grief which his face expresses. And so too the composer may not feel the grief which his composition expresses. It may express grief regardless of what he really feels, if indeed he feels anything.

Very well; but having reached this point, how far does it take us? Pursuing still the analogy of the musical notes with the facial features, we are only permitted to say that whereas usually when a person shows facial features X he also feels X', this is sometimes not so, and that similarity when music expresses X the composer usually felt X', though sometimes not. The link with the composer is still a usual one though not an exceptionless one; and we want it to be not usual but nonexistent: we want music to be expressive of X' even if the composer felt not X' but Y' or even nothing at all.

And how are we to do this? If we can do it at all, it is surely on the basis of some *similarity* between what exists in the musical tones and what exists in a person's facial features and behavior. Thus, as Professor Bouwsma says ("The Expression Theory of Art," in W. Elton, *Aesthetics and Language*, p. 99), "sad music has some of the characteristics of people who are sad. It will be slow, not tripping; it will be low, not tinkling. People who are sad move more slowly, and when they speak, they speak softly and low."

Now, I venture to suggest than any theory of musical expression must be based on some such resemblance as this. But it is not so easy as it sounds. (1) The properties by virtue of which we call musical patterns sad or tense or exultant or profound are often, it would seem, not the properties by virtue of which we call people these things. For example, if there are any passages in music which I would call tense, it would be such passages as occur in Strauss' *Salome* and *Elektra* in which, for instance, after a sudden silence followed by a soft intermittent and irregular drumbeat, there is a quick piercing shriek from the piccolo, silence, then a wail from the bassoon, playing alone, coupled a moment later with small fragments of tonality from the tuba (and with a large range of octaves between). And yet these "tense-making" properties of the music cannot be attributed to a person when he is tense in daily life; one cannot truly say of Jones when he feels tense after a quarrel with his wife that there is a large tonal interval between his upper and lower registers.

(2) When we ask ourselves, Quite literally, what features are possessed in common by the music and the person? there turns out, I think, to be much less than we might at first have thought. And let us remember that

we cannot take the easy way and say that just as a person is excited or melancholy, so music may be excited or melancholy; for this would be to read into the music the very expressive character we were setting out to analyze. What we want to know is what features there are in the tones and tone-relationships themselves which are quite literally like features we attribute to human beings when we say that they are excited or melancholy. Thus, to return to Professor Bouwsma's example, sad music really *is* slow and sad people really do tend to move slowly—here is a real and objective similarity; but when he goes on to say that sad music is low, we cannot apply this adjective to human beings in the same sense, for the word "low" in music refers to pitch, and if we say that sad people are low this probably means something like "feeling low," which is a very different (and metaphorical) sense of the word.

(3) In any case, there will again be difficulty in defending our judgment of expressiveness against others. Let us assume that we agree pretty well about the claim that a given work of music is sad. But what about more complex claims, especially when disagreement continues? How would we defend against attack our judgment that this is after all not joyful, as we had always thought, but a bit frenzied, and that its rapidity is that of tension rather than of exuberance? or that a composition which we had always thought to be highly dramatic in character is not really so but pompous, ostentatious, and posed? It may be that these examples too could be handled along the same general lines as the sadness example; but in the field of esthetics, where there are probably more promises and fewer fulfillments than anywhere else in philosophy, I am impelled to be suspicious of the promissory note, especially when the date due is repeatedly postponed, and to be content only with the cold hard cash of fulfillment.

SELECTED BIBLIOGRAPHY

1. O. K. Bouwsma, "The Expression Theory of Art," in M. Black (ed.), *Philosophical Analysis*, Cornell University Press, 1950; reprinted in W. Elton (ed.), *Aesthetics and Language*, Blackwell, 1954. A brilliant exposition of "expression" in its many, quite different uses in talk about art and life. Highly entertaining, highly recommended.
2. George Santayana, *The Sense of Beauty*, Scribner's Sons, 1936, Part Four. A classic statement.
3. David Prall, *Aesthetic Judgment*, Ch. XI, Thomas Y. Crowell, 1929.
4. D. W. Gotshalk, *Art and the Social Order*, Ch. VI, University of Chicago Press, 1947.
5. Harold Osborne, *Aesthetics and Criticism*, Ch. VII, Philosophical Library, 1955. Good especially on "expression" and literature.

LANGUAGE AND MEANING

The doctrines that art is a language and has meaning, or that art is not a language and has no meaning, or that art is a certain kind of symbol but not a language have been put forth from time to time in the history of aesthetics. Some very important specific issues converge on these doctrines—"Is music a language?," "Does abstract painting mean anything?" Central in these disputes and the general views they inspire are the concepts of language and meaning. Indeed, these two concepts have become major subjects of inquiry in much of contemporary philosophy, and the last word on them is far from having been spoken. Two separate discussions of language and meaning, one by Susanne Langer, in which she explores the whole field of signs, symbols, language and meaning, the other by John Hospers on the problem of meaning alone, are reproduced here. Taken together, they survey at least one major trend in the philosophy of language and meaning.

218

Susanne K. Langer

LANGUAGE AND SYMBOLISM*

THE LOGIC OF SIGNS AND SYMBOLS

So much work has already been done on the logic of meaning that it is not necessary to present long arguments in support of the theory here employed; let it suffice to outline the facts, or if you will, the assumptions, on which my further considerations are to rest.

Meaning has both a logical and a psychological aspect. Psychologically, any item that is to have meaning must be *employed* as a sign or a symbol; that is to say, it must be a sign or a symbol *to* someone. Logically, it must be *capable* of conveying a meaning, it must be the sort of item that can be thus employed. In some meaning-relations this logical requirement is trivial, and tacitly accepted; in others it is of the utmost importance, and may even lead us a merry chase through the labyrinths of nonsense. These two aspects, the logical and the psychological, are thoroughly confounded by the ambiguous verb "to mean"; for sometimes it is proper to say "*it* means," and sometimes "*I* mean." Obviously, a word—say, "London"—does not "mean" a city in just the same sense that a person employing the word "means" the place.

Both aspects, the logical and the psychological, are always present, and their interplay produces the great variety of meaning-relations over which philosophers have puzzled and fought for the last fifty years. The analysis of "meaning" has had a peculiarly difficult history; the word is used in many different ways, and a good deal of controversy has been wasted on the subject of *the* correct way, *the* meaning of "meaning." Whenever people find several species of a genus, they look for the prime form, the archetype that is supposed to be differently disguised in each special case; so, for a long time, philosophers hoped to find the true quality of meaning by collecting all its various manifestations and looking for a common ingredient. They talked more and more generally about "symbol-situations," believing that by generalization they might attain to the essential quality which all such situations had in common. But generalizing from vague and muddled special theories can never give us a clear general theory. The sort of generalization that

* Reprinted by permission of the publishers from Susanne K. Langer's *Philosophy in a New Key: A Study in the Symbolism of Reason, Rite and Art*, Cambridge, Mass.: Harvard University Press, Copyright, 1942, 1951, 1957 by the President and Fellows of Harvard College.

Susanne K. Langer (1895–   ) is the author of many books, including *Feeling and Form* and *Problems of Art*, in the area of aesthetics.

merely substitutes "symbol-situation" for "denotation-or-connotation-or-sig-
nification-or-association-etc." is scientifically useless; for the whole purpose of
general concepts is to make the distinctions between special classes clear,
to relate all subspecies to each other in definite ways; but if such general
concepts are simply composite photographs of all known types of meaning,
they can only blur, not clarify, the relations that obtain among specialized
senses of the word.

Charles Peirce, who was probably the first person to concern himself
seriously with semantics, began by making an inventory of all "symbol-
situations," in the hope that when all possible meanings of "meaning" were
herded together, they would show empirical differentiae whereby one could
divide the sheep from the goats. But the obstreperous flock, instead of falling
neatly into a few classes, each according to its kind, divided and subdivided
into the most terrifying order of icons, qualisigns, legisigns, semes, phemes,
and delomes, and there is but cold comfort in his assurance that his original
59,049 types can really be boiled down to a mere sixty-six.[1]

A few further attempts were made to grasp the essential quality of meaning by empirical methods, but the more varieties could be found, the less
did they promise to reveal a common essence. Husserl, distinguishing each
type of meaning as a special notion, ended with as many theories as there
are "meanings."[2] But we have still the sheep and the goats and all their
several relatives, and are still left wondering why one family name, Meaning,
should apply where no family likeness can be detected.

There is in fact no quality of meaning; its essence lies in the realm of
logic, where one does not deal with qualities, but only with relations. It
is not fair to say: "Meaning is a relation," for that suggests too simple a
business. Most people think of a relation as a two-termed affair—"A-in-
relation-to-B"; but meaning involves several terms, and different types of
meaning consist of different types and degrees of relationship. It is better,
perhaps, to say: "Meaning is not a quality, but a *function* of a term." A
function is a *pattern* viewed with reference to one special term round which
it centers; this pattern emerges when we look at the given term *in its total
relation to the other terms about it.* The total may be quite complicated.
For instance, a musical chord may be treated as a function of one note,
known as the "written bass," by writing this one note and indicating its relation to all the other notes that are to go above it. In old organ music, the chord

[1] From two letters to Lady Welby, 1904 and 1908 respectively, first cited by Ogden
and Richards in *The Meaning of Meaning* (App. D, pp. 435-444), and now published in
The Collected Papers of Charles S. Peirce (Cambridge, Mass.: Harvard University Press,
1932), II: "Elements of Logic," p. 330.

[2] Edmund Husserl, *Logische Untersuchungen*, 2 vols. (Halle a/S., 1913 and 1921), vol.
II, part I, *passim.*

(a) ⁶₄₃   would be written: (b) , which means: "The A-chord with the sixth, the fourth, and the third notes above A." The chord is treated as *a pattern surrounding and including* A. It is expressed as a function of A.

The meaning of a term is, likewise, a function; it rests on a pattern, in which the term itself holds the key-position. Even in the simplest kinds of meaning there must be at least two other things related to the term that "means"—an object that is "meant," and a subject who uses the term; just as in a chord there must be at least two notes besides the "written bass" to determine what the chord is (one of these may be merely "understood" by musicians, but without it the combination would not be a determinate chord). The same may be said for a term with a meaning; the existence of a subject is often tacitly accepted, but if there is not at least one thing meant and one mind for which it is meant, then there is not a complete meaning—only a partial pattern which might be completed in different ways.

Any term in a pattern may be taken as a key-term to which the others are related. For instance, the chord (a) ⁶₄₃ may be regarded as a function of its lowest note, and expressed by the description (b) ; or it may be treated with reference to the note on which it is built harmonically, which happens to be D. A musician analyzing the harmony would call this chord "the second inversion of the seventh-chord on the dominant, in the key of G." The "dominant" of that key is D, not A. He would treat the whole pattern as *a function of D*; that sounds more complicated than the other treatment, which fixed the notes from the A upward, but of course it is not really so, because it comes to just the same pattern.

Similarly, we may view a meaning-pattern from the point of view of any term in it, and our descriptions of the same pattern will differ accordingly. We may say that a certain symbol "means" an object to a person, or that the person "means" the object by the symbol. The first description treats meaning in the logical sense, the second in the psychological sense. The former takes the symbol as the key, and the latter the subject.[3] So, the two most controversial kinds of meaning—the logical and the psychological—are

---

[3] Where the object is taken as the key, the resulting description begins with the "knowledge-content" postulated in some epistemologies.

distinguished and at the same time related to each other, by the general principle of viewing meaning *as a function, not a property, of terms.*

In the further analyses that follow, "meaning" will be taken in the objective sense, unless some other is specified; that is to say, I shall speak of terms (such as words) as "meaning" something, not of people as "meaning" this or that. Later we shall have to distinguish various subjective functions; but at present let us consider the *relations of terms to their objects.* What *relates* the terms to their objects is, of course, a subject; that is always to be understood.

There are, first of all, two distinct functions of terms, which have both a perfectly good right to the name "meaning": for a significant sound, gesture, thing, event (e.g. a flash, an image), may be either a *sign* or a *symbol.*

A sign indicates the existence—past, present, or future—of a thing, event, or condition. Wet streets are a sign that it has rained. A patter on the roof is a sign that it is raining. A fall of the barometer or a ring round the moon is a sign that it is going to rain. In an unirrigated place, abundant verdure is a sign that it often rains there. A smell of smoke signifies the presence of fire. A scar is a sign of a past accident. Dawn is a herald of sunrise. Sleekness is a sign of frequent and plentiful food.

All the examples here adduced are *natural signs.* A natural sign is a part of a greater event, or of a complex condition, and to an experienced observer it signifies the rest of that situation of which it is a notable feature. It is a *symptom* of a state of affairs.[4]

The logical relation between a sign and its object is a very simple one: they are associated, somehow, to form a *pair;* that is to say, they stand in a one-to-one correlation. To each sign there corresponds one definite item which is its object, the thing (or event, or condition) signified. All the rest of that important function, signification, involves the third term, the subject, which *uses* the pair of items; and the relation of the subject to the other two terms is much more interesting than their own bare logical coupling. The subject is related, essentially, to the other two terms *as a pair.* What characterizes them is the fact that they are paired. Thus, a white bump on a person's arm, as a mere sense-datum, would probably not be interesting enough even to have a name, but such a datum *in its relation to the past* is noted and called a "scar." Note, however, that although the subject's relation

---

[4] There is a fine distinction between sign and symptom, in that the object signified by a symptom is the *entire condition* of which the symptom is a proper part; e.g., red spots are a symptom of measles, and "measles" is the entire condition begetting and including the red spots. A sign, on the other hand, may be one part of a total condition, which we associate with another separate part. Thus a ring round the moon is part of a weather condition, but what it signifies is rain—another proper part—and not the entire state of "low-pressure" weather.

is to the *pair* of other terms, he has also a relation to each one of them individually, which makes one of them the sign and the other the object. What is the difference between a sign and its object, by virtue of which they are not interchangeable? Two terms merely associated as a pair, like two socks, two balances of a scale, two ends of a stick, etc., could be interchanged without any harm.

The difference is, that the subject for which they constitute a pair must *find one more interesting than the other, and the latter more easily available than the former*. If we are interested in tomorrow's weather, the events now present, if coupled with tomorrow's weather-phenomena, are signs for us. A ring round the moon, or "mares' tails" in the sky, are not important in themselves; but as visible, present items coupled with something important but not yet present, they have "meaning." If it were not for the subject, or *interpretant*, sign and object would be interchangeable. Thunder may just as well be a sign that there has been lightning, as lightning may signify that there will be thunder. In themselves they are merely correlated. It is only where one is perceptible and the other (harder or impossible to perceive) is interesting, that we actually have a case of *signification belonging to a term*.[5]

Now, just as in nature certain events are correlated, so that the less important may be taken as signs of the more important, so we may also *produce* arbitrary events purposely correlated with important ones that are to be their meanings. A whistle means that the train is about to start. A gunshot means that the sun is just setting. A crêpe on the door means someone has just died. These are artificial signs, for they are not part of a condition of which they naturally signify the remainder or something in the remainder. Their logical relation to their objects, however, is the same as that of natural signs—a one-to-one correspondence of sign and object, by virtue of which the interpretant, who is interested in the latter and perceives the former, may apprehend the existence of the term that interests him.

The interpretation of signs is the basis of animal intelligence. Animals presumably do not distinguish between natural signs and artificial or fortuitous signs; but they use both kinds to guide their practical activities. We do the same thing all day long. We answer bells, watch the clock, obey warning signals, follow arrows, take off the kettle when it whistles, come at the baby's cry, close the windows when we hear thunder. The logical basis of all these interpretations, the mere correlation of trivial events with important ones, is really very simple and common; so much so that there is no limit to what a sign may mean. This is even more obviously true of artificial signs than of natural ones. A shot may mean the beginning of a race, the rise of the sun,

[5] Cf. Whitehead, *Symbolism*, (New York: The Macmillan Co., 1927), pp. 9–13.

the sighting of danger, the commencement of a parade. As for bells, the world is mad with their messages. Somebody at the front door, the back door, the side door, the telephone—toast is ready—typewriter line is ended—school begins, work begins, church begins, church is over—street car starts—cashbox registers—knife grinder passes—time for dinner, time to get up—fire in town!

Because a sign may mean so many things, we are very apt to misinterpret it, especially when it is artificial. Bell signals, of course, may be either wrongly associated with their objects, or the sound of one bell may actually be confused with that of another. But natural signs, too, may be misunderstood. Wet streets are not a reliable sign of recent rain if the sprinkler wagon has passed by. The misinterpretation of signs is the simplest form of *mistake.* It is the most important form, for purposes of practical life, and the easiest to detect; for its normal manifestation is the experience called *disappointment.*

Where we find the simplest form of error, we may expect to find also, as its correlate, the simplest form of knowledge. This is, indeed, the interpretation of signs. It is the most elementary and most tangible sort of intellection; the kind of knowledge that we share with animals, that we acquire entirely by experience, that has obvious biological uses, and equally obvious criteria of truth and falsehood. Its mechanism may be conceived as an elaboration of the conditioned-reflex arc, with the brain doing switchboard duty, and getting the right or the wrong number for the sense organ that called up the musculature and expects an answer in terms of altered sensations. It has all those virtues of simplicity, componability, and intelligibility that recommend a concept for scientific purposes. So it is not surprising that students of genetic psychology have seized upon sign interpretation as the archetype of all knowledge, that they regard *signs* as the original bearers of meaning, and treat all other terms with semantic properties as subspecies—"substitute signs," which act as proxy for their objects and evoke conduct appropriate to the latter instead of to themselves.

But "substitute signs," though they may be classed with symbols, are of a very specialized sort, and play only a meagre and restricted part in the whole process of mental life. I shall return to them later, in discussing the relationship between symbols and signs, for they do stand with a foot in either domain. First, however, the characteristics of symbols in general, and their essential difference from signs, must go on record.

A term which is used symbolically and not signally does *not* evoke action appropriate to the presence of its object. If I say: "Napoleon," you do not bow to the conqueror of Europe as though I had introduced him, but merely think of him. If I mention a Mr. Smith of our common acquaintance, you may be led to tell me something about him "behind his back," which is just what you would *not* do in his presence. Thus the symbol for Mr. Smith—his name—may very well initiate an act appropriate peculiarly to his absence. Raised eyebrows and a look at the door, interpreted as a *sign* that he is coming, would stop you in the midst of your narrative; *that* action would be directed toward Mr. Smith in person.

Symbols are not proxy for their objects, but are *vehicles for the conception of objects*. To conceive a thing or a situation is not the same thing as to "react toward it" overtly, or to be aware of its presence. In talking *about* things we have conceptions of them, not the things themselves; and *it is the conceptions, not the things, that symbols directly "mean."* Behavior toward conceptions is what words normally evoke; this is the typical process of thinking.

Of course a word may be used as a sign, but that is not its primary role. Its significant character has to be indicated by some special modification—by a tone of voice, a gesture (such as pointing or staring), or the location of a placard bearing the word. In itself it is a symbol, associated with a conception.[6] not directly with a public object or event. The fundamental difference between signs and symbols is this difference of association, and consequently of their *use* by the third party to the meaning function, the subject; signs *announce* their objects to him, whereas symbols *lead him to conceive* their objects. The fact that the same item—say, the little mouthy noise we call a "word"—may serve in either capacity, does not obliterate the cardinal distinction between the two functions it may assume.

The simplest kind of symbolistic meaning is probably that which belongs to proper names. A personal name evokes a conception of something given as a unit in the subject's experience, something concrete and therefore easy to recall in imagination. Because the name belongs to a notion so obviously and unequivocally derived from an individual object, it is often supposed to "mean" that object as a sign would "mean" it. This belief is reinforced by the fact that a name borne by a living person always is at once a symbol by which we think of the person, and a call-name by which we signal him. Through a confusion of these two functions, the proper name is often deemed the bridge from animal semantic, or sign-using, to human language, which is symbol-using. Dogs, we are told, understand names—not only their own,

---

[6] Note that I have called the terms of our thinking conceptions, not concepts. Concepts are abstract forms embodied in conceptions; their bare presentation may be approximated by so-called "abstract thought," but in ordinary mental life they no more figure as naked factors than skeletons are seen walking the street. Concepts, like decent living skeletons, are always embodied—sometimes rather too much. I shall return to the topic of pure concepts later on, in discussing communication.

but their masters'. So they do, indeed; but they understand them *only in the capacity of call-names.* If you say "James" to a dog whose master bears that name, the dog will interpret the sound as a sign, and *look for* James. Say it to a person who knows someone called thus, and he will ask: "What about James?" That simple question is forever beyond the dog; signification is the only meaning a name can have for him—a meaning which the master's name shares with the master's smell, with his footfall, and his characteristic ring of the doorbell. In a human being, however, the name evokes the *conception* of a certain man so called, and prepares the mind for further conceptions in which the notion of that man figures; therefore the human being naturally asks: "What about James?"

There is a famous passage in the autobiography of Helen Keller, in which this remarkable woman describes the dawn of Language upon her mind. Of course she had used signs before, formed associations, learned to expect things and identify people or places; but there was a great day when all sign-meaning was eclipsed and dwarfed by the discovery that a certain datum in her limited sense-world had a *denotation,* that a particular act of her fingers constituted a *word.* This event had required a long preparation; the child had learned many finger acts, but they were as yet a meaningless play. Then, one day, her teacher took her out to walk—and there the great advent of Language occurred.

"She brought me my hat," the memoir reads, "and I knew I was going out into the warm sunshine. This thought, if a wordless sensation may be called a thought, made me hop and skip with pleasure.

"We walked down the path to the well-house, attracted by the fragrance of the honeysuckle with which it was covered. Some one was drawing water and my teacher placed my hand under the spout. As the cool stream gushed over my hand she spelled into the other the word *water,* first slowly, then rapidly. I stood still, my whole attention fixed upon the motion of her fingers. Suddenly I felt a misty consciousness as of something forgotten—a thrill of returning thought; and somehow the mystery of language was revealed to me. I knew then that w-a-t-e-r meant the wonderful cool something that was flowing over my hand. That living word awakened my soul, gave it light, hope, joy, set it free! There were barriers still, it is true, but barriers that in time could be swept away.

"I left the well-house eager to learn. Everything had a name, and each name gave birth to a new thought. As we returned to the house every object which I touched seemed to quiver with life. That was because I saw everything with the strange, new sight that had come to me."[7]

---

[7] Helen Keller, *The Story of My Life* (Garden City: Doubleday, Doran & Co., 1936; 1st ed. 1902), pp. 23–24.

This passage is the best affidavit we could hope to find for the genuine difference between sign and symbol. The sign is something to act upon, or a means to command action; the symbol is an instrument of thought. Note how Miss Keller qualifies the mental process just preceding her discovery of words—"This thought, *if a wordless sensation may be called a thought.*" Real thinking is possible only in the light of genuine language, no matter how limited, how primitive; in her case, it became possible with the discovery that "w-a-t-e-r" was not necessarily a sign that water was wanted or expected, but was the *name* of this substance, by which it could be mentioned, conceived, remembered.

Since a name, the simplest type of symbol, is directly associated with a conception, and is employed by a subject to realize the conception, one is easily led to treat a name as a "conceptual sign," an artificial sign which announces the presence of a certain idea. In a sense this is quite justified; yet it strikes a strained and unnatural note, which is usually a fair warning that the attempted interpretation misses the most important feature in its material. In the present case, it misses *the relation of conceptions to the concrete world,* which is so close and so important that it enters into the very structure of "names." A name, above all, *denotes* something. "James" may represent a conception, but *names* a certain person. In the case of proper nouns this relation of the symbol to what it denotes is so striking that denotation has been confused with the direct relation of sign and object, signification. As a matter of fact, "James" does not, without further ado, *signify* a person; it *denotes* him—it is associated with a conception which "fits" the actual person. The relation between a symbol and an object, usually expressed by "S denotes O," is not a simple two-termed relation which S has to O; it is a complex affair: S is coupled, for a certain subject, with a conception that fits O, i.e. with a notion which O satisfies.

In an ordinary sign-function, there are three essential terms: subject, sign, and object. In denotation, which is the simplest kind of symbol-function, there have to be four: subject, symbol, conception and object. The radical difference between sign-meaning and symbol-meaning can therefore be logically exhibited, for it rests on a difference of pattern, it is strictly a different function.[8]

Denotation is, then, the complex relationship which a name has to an object which bears it; but what shall the more direct relation of the name, or symbol, to its associated *conception* be called? It shall be called by its tradi-

[8] If a symbol could be said normally to "signify" anything, its object would be the occurrence of an act of conception. But such a function of a symbol is casual, and crosses with its use *as a symbol.* In the latter function it is not the act of conception, but *what is conceived,* that enters into the meaning-pattern. We shall avoid much confusion and quibbling by recognizing that signification does not figure in symbolization at all.

tional name, *connotation*. The connotation of a word is the conception it conveys. Because the connotation remains with the symbol when the object of its denotation is neither present nor looked for, we are able to *think* about the object without reacting to it overtly at all.

Here, then, are the three most familiar meanings of the one word, "meaning": signification, denotation, and connotation. All three are equally and perfectly legitimate, but in no possible way interchangeable.

In every analysis of sign-using or symbol-using, we must be able to account not only for the genesis of knowledge, but also of that most human characteristic, error. How sign-interpretation can miscarry, has already been shown; but failures of denotation, or confusions of connotation, are unfortunately just as common, and have a claim to our attention, too.

There is a psychological act involved in every case of denotation, which might be called the *application* of a term to an object. The word "water," for instance, denotes a certain substance because people conventionally *apply* it to that substance. Such application has fixed its connotation. We may ask, quite reasonably, whether a certain colorless liquid is or is not water, but hardly whether water "really" means that substance which is found in ponds, falls from the clouds, has the chemical constitution H_2O, etc. The connotation of the word, though derived from an age-long application, is more definite now than some cases of the word's applicability. When we have *misapplied* a term, i.e. applied it to an object that does not satisfy its connotation, we do not say that the term "denoted" that object; one feature in the tetradic meaning-relation is missing, so there is no real denotation—only a psychological act of application, and that was a mistake. The word "water" was never guilty of *denoting* the drink that undid little Willy, in the pathetic laboratory rhyme:

> We had a little Willy,
> Now Willy is no more,
> For what he thought was H_2O
> Was H_8SO_4.

Willy had mistaken one object for another; he *misapplied* a term of which he knew the connotation well enough. But since connotations are normally fixed upon a word, originally, by its application to certain *things*, whose properties are but vaguely known, we may also be mistaken about the connotation, when we use the term as a vehicle of thought. We may know that the symbol "James" applies to our next-door neighbor, and quite mistakenly suppose it connotes a man with all sorts of virtues or frailties. This time we are not mistaking James for someone else, but we are *mistaken about James*.

It is a pecularity of proper names that they have a *different connotation for every denotation.* Because their connotation is not fixed, they can be arbitrarily applied. In itself, a proper name has no connotation at all; sometimes it acquires a very general sort of conceptual meaning—it connotes a gender, or race, or confession (e.g. "Christian," "Wesley," "Israel")—but there is no actual *mistake* involved in calling a boy "Marion," a girl "Frank," a German "Pierre," or a Jew "Luther." In civilized society the connotation of a proper name is not regarded as a meaning applying to the bearer of the name; when the name is used to denote a certain person it takes on the connotation required by that function. In primitive societies this is less apt to be the case; names are often changed because their accepted connotations do not fit the bearer. The same man may in turn be *named* "Lightfoot," "Hawkeye," "Whizzing Death," etc. In an Indian society, the class of men named "Hawkeye" would very probably be a subclass of the class "sharp-eyed men." But in our own communities ladies named "Blanche" do not have to be albinos or even platinum blondes. A word that functions as a proper noun is excused from the usual rules of application.

So much, then, for the venerable "logic of terms." It appears a little more complicated than in the medieval books, since we must add to the long-recognized functions, connotation and denotation, a third one, signification, which is fundamentally different from the other two; and since, moreover, in discussing the semantic functions of terms we have made the rare discovery that they really are *functions,* not powers or mysterious properties or what-not, and have treated them accordingly. The traditional "logic of terms" is really a metaphysic of meaning; the new philosophy of meaning is first of all a logic of terms—of signs and symbols—an analysis of the relational patterns in which "meaning" may be sought.

But a semantic of separate symbols is only a rudimentary foundation for a more interesting aspect of meaning. Everything is mere propaedeutic until we come to *discourse.* It is in discursive thinking that truth and falsehood are born. Before terms are built into propositions, they assert nothing, preclude nothing; in fact, although they may *name* things, and convey ideas of such things, they *say* nothing. I have discussed them at such great length simply because most logicians have given them such cavalier treatment that even so obvious a distinction as that between sign-functions and symbol-functions passed unnoticed; so that careless philosophers have been guilty of letting ambitious genetic psychologists argue them from the conditioned reflex to the wisdom of G. Bernard Shaw, all in one skyrocketing generalization.

The logic of discourse has been much more adequately handled—so well, in fact, that practically nothing I have to say about it is new; yet it must at least be brought to mind here, because an understanding of discursive symbolism, the vehicle of propositional thinking, is essential to any theory of human mentality; for without it there could be no *literal meaning*, and therefore no scientific knowledge.

Anyone who has ever learned a foreign language knows that the study of its vocabulary alone will not make him master of the new tongue. Even if he were to memorize a whole dictionary, he would not be able to make the simplest statement correctly; for he could not form a sentence without certain *principles of grammar*. He must know that some words are nouns and some are verbs; he must recognize some as active or passive forms of verbs, and know the person and number they express; he must know where the verb stands in the sentence in order to make the sense he has in mind. Mere separate names of things (even of actions, which are "named" by infinitives) do not constitute a sentence. A string of words which we might derive by running our eye down the left-hand column in the dictionary—for instance, "especially espouse espringal espry esquire"—does not *say* anything. Each word has meaning, yet the series of words has none.

Grammatical structure, then, is a further source of significance. We cannot call it a symbol, since it is not even a term; but it has a symbolific mission. It ties together several symbols, each with at least a fragmentary connotation of its own, to make one complex term, whose meaning is a special constellation of all the connotations involved. What the special constellation is, depends on the syntactical relations within the complex symbol, or *proposition*.

Propositional structure has commanded more interest among logicians of the present generation than any other aspect of symbolism. Ever since Bertrand Russell[9] pointed out that the Aristotelian metaphysic of substance and attribute is a counterpart of the Aristotelian logic of subject and predicate—that the common-sense view of things and properties, agent and patient, object and action, etc., is a faithful counterpart of that common-sense logic embodied in our parts of *speech*—the ties between expressibility and conceivability, forms of language and forms of experience, propositions and facts, have been drawn closer and closer. It has become apparent that a proposition fits a fact not only because it contains names for the things and actions involved in the fact, but also because it combines them in a pattern analogous, somehow, to the pattern in which the named objects are "in fact" combined. *A proposition is a picture of a structure—the structure of a state of affairs.* The unity of a proposition is the same sort of unity that

---

[9] *A Critical Exposition of the Philosophy of Leibniz* (Cambridge, 1900). See p. 12.

belongs to a picture, which presents one scene, no matter how many items may be distinguishable within it.

What property must a picture have in order to *represent* its object? Must it really share the visual appearance of the object? Certainly not to any high degree. It may, for instance, be black on white, or red on grey, or any color on any other color; it may be shiny whereas the object is dull; it may be much larger or much smaller than the object; it is certainly flat, and although the tricks of perspective sometimes give a perfect illusion of three-dimensionality, a picture without perspective—e.g. an architect's "elevation drawing"—is still unmistakably a picture, representing an object.

The reason for this latitude is that *the picture is essentially a symbol, not a duplicate, of what it represents.* It has certain salient features by virtue of which it can function as a symbol for its object. For instance, the childish outline drawing (fig. 1) . . . is immediately recognized as a rabbit, yet it really looks so unlike one that even a person nearly blind could not

FIG. 1

FIG. 2

for a moment be made to think that he saw a rabbit sitting on the open page of his book. All it shares with the "reality" is a certain *proportion of parts*—the position and relative length of "ears," the dot where an "eye" belongs, the "head" and "body" in relation to each other, etc. Beside it is exactly the same figure with different ears and tail (fig. 2); any child will accept it as a cat. Yet cats don't look like long-tailed, short-eared rabbits, in reality. Neither are they flat and white, with a papery texture and a black outline running round them. But all these traits of the pictured cat are irrelevant, because it is merely a symbol, not a pseudo-cat.[10]

Of course, the more detail is depicted by the image, the more unequiv-

[10] Tolstoi relates a little incident of his childhood which hinges on the sudden ingression of irrelevant factors into consciousness, to the detriment of artistic appreciation; I quote it here because it is quite the most charming record I have found of a semantic muddle:

"We settled ourselves about the round table at our drawing. I had only blue paint; nevertheless, I undertook to depict the hunt. After representing, in very lively style, a blue boy mounted on a blue horse, and some blue dogs, I was not quite sure whether I could paint a blue hare, and ran to Papa in his study to take advice on the matter. Papa was reading; and in answer to my question, 'Are there any blue hares?' he said, without raising his head, 'Yes, my dear, there are.' I went back to the round table and painted a blue hare. . . ." L. N. Tolstoi, *Childhood, Boyhood and Youth.*

ocal becomes the reference to a particular object. A good portrait is "true" to only one person. Yet even good portraits are not duplications. There are styles in portraiture as there are in any other art. We may paint in heightened, warm, melting colors, or in cool pastels; we may range from the clean line drawings of Holbein to the shimmering hues of French impressionism; and all the time the object need not change. Our presentation of it is the variable factor.

The picture is a symbol, and the so-called "medium" is a type of symbolism. Yet there is something, of course, that relates the picture to its original, and makes it represent, say, a Dutch interior and not the crucifixion. What it may represent is dictated purely by its logic—by the arrangement of its elements. The disposition of pale and dark, dull and bright paints, or thin and thick lines and variously shaped white spaces, yield the determination of those *forms* that mean certain objects. They can mean all those and only those objects in which we recognize similar forms. All other aspects of the picture—for instance, what artists call the "distribution of values," the "technique," and the "tone" of the whole work—serve other ends than mere representation. The only characteristic that a picture must have in order to be a picture of a certain thing is an arrangement of elements analogous to the arrangement of salient visual elements in the object. A representation of a rabbit must have long ears; a man must feature arms and legs.

In the case of a so-called "realistic" picture, the analogy goes into great detail, so great that many people believe a statue or a painting to be a *copy* of its object. But consider how we meet such vagaries of style as modern commercial art produces: ladies with bright green faces and aluminum hair, men whose heads are perfect circles, horses constructed entirely of cylinders. We still recognize the objects they depict, as long as we find an element to stand for the head and one for the eye in the head, a white mark to connote a starched bosom, a line placed where it may represent an arm. With amazing rapidity your vision picks up these features and lets the whole fantasy convey a human form.

One step removed from the "styled" picture is the diagram. Here any attempt at *imitating* the parts of an object has been given up. The parts are merely indicated by conventional symbols, such as dots, circles, crosses, or what-not. The only thing that is "pictured" is the relation of the parts to each other. *A diagram is a "picture" only of a form.*

Consider a photograph, a painting, a pencil sketch, an architect's elevation drawing, and a builder's diagram, all showing the front view of one and the same house. With a little attention, you will recognize the house in each representation. Why?

Because each one of the very different images expresses the same relation of parts, which you have fastened on in formulating your conception of the house. Some versions show more such relations than others; they are more detailed. But those which do not show certain details at least show no others in place of these, and so it may be understood that the details are there left out. The things shown in the simplest picture, the diagram, are all contained in the more elaborate renderings. Moreover, they are contained in your conception of the house; so the pictures all answer, in their several ways, to your conception, although the latter may contain further items that are not pictured at all. Likewise, another person's conception of that same house will agree in its essential pattern with the pictures *and with your conception,* however many private aspects it may have.

It is by virtue of such a fundamental *pattern,* which all correct conceptions of the house have in common, that we can talk together about the "same" house despite our private differences of sense-experience, feeling, and purely personal associations. *That which all adequate conceptions of an object must have in common, is the concept of the object.* The same concept is embodied in a multitude of conceptions. It is a *form* that appears in all versions of thought or imagery that can connote the object in question, a form clothed in different integuments of sensation for every different mind. Probably no two people see anything just alike. Their sense organs differ, their attention and imagery and feelings differ so that they cannot be supposed to have identical impressions. But if their respective conceptions of a thing (or event, or person, etc.) embody the same *concept,* they will understand each other.

A concept is all that a symbol really conveys. But just as quickly as the concept is symbolized to us, our own imagination dresses it up in a private, personal *conception,* which we can distinguish from the communicable public concept only by a process of abstraction. Whenever we deal with a concept we must have some particular presentation of it, *through* which we grasp it. What we actually have "in mind" is always *universalium in re.* When we express this *universalium* we use another symbol to exhibit it, and still another *res* will embody it for the mind that sees through our symbol and apprehends the concept in its own way.

The power of understanding symbols, i.e. of regarding everything about a sense-datum as irrelevant except a certain *form* that it embodies, is the most characterisic mental trait of mankind. It issues in an unconscious, spontaneous process of *abstraction,* which goes on all the time in the human mind: a process of recognizing the concept in any configuration given to experience, and forming a conception accordingly. That is the real sense of Aristotle's definition of man as "the rational animal." *Abstractive seeing* is

the foundation of our rationality, and is its definite guarantee long before
the dawn of any conscious generalization or syllogism.[11] It is the function
which no other animal shares. Beasts do not read symbols; that is why they
do not see pictures. We are sometimes told that dogs do not react even to
the best portraits because they live more by smell than by sight; but the
behavior of a dog who spies a motionless real cat through the window glass
belies this explanation. Dogs scorn our paintings because they see colored
canvases, not pictures. A representation of a cat does not make them conceive one.

Since any single sense-datum can, logically, be a symbol for any single
item, any arbitrary mark or counter may connote the conception, or publicly
speaking: the concept, of any single thing, and thus denote the thing itself.
A motion of fingers, apprehended as one unit performance, became the name
of a substance to little deaf-and-blind Helen Keller. A word, likewise taken
as a sound-unit, becomes a symbol to us, for some item in the world. And
now the power of seeing *configurations* as symbols comes into play: we
make patterns of denotative symbols, and they promptly symbolize the very
different, but *analogous,* configurations of denoted things. A temporal order
of words stands for a relational order of things. When pure word-order becomes insufficient, word-endings and prefixes "mean" relationships; from these
are born prepositions and other purely relational symbols.[12] Just as mnemonic dots and crosses, as soon as they denote objects, can also enter into
diagrams or simple pictures, so do sounds, as soon as they are words, enter
into word-pictures, or *sentences.* A sentence is a symbol for a state of affairs,
and pictures its character.

Now, in an ordinary picture, the terms of the represented complex are
symbolized by so many visual items, i.e. areas of color, and their relations
are indicated by relations of these items. So painting, being static, can
present only a momentary state; it may suggest, but can never actually
report, a *history.* We may produce a series of pictures, but nothing in the
pictures can actually guarantee the conjunction of their several scenes in one
serial order of events. Five baby-pictures of the little Dionne sisters in
various acts may be taken either as a series representing successive acts of
one child, or as separate views of five little girls in characteristic activities.
There is no sure way of choosing between these two interpretations without
captions or other indications.

But most of our interests center upon events, rather than upon things in
static spatial relations. Causal connections, activities, time, and change are

[11] Cf. Th. Ribot, *Essai sur l'imagination créatrice* (Paris, 1921; 1st ed. 1900), p. 14.

[12] See Philip Wegener, *Untersuchungen über die Grundfragen des Sprachlebens* (Halle
a/s., 1885), esp. pp. 88–89; also Karl Bühler, *Sprachtheorie* (Jena, 1934), chs. iii and iv.

what we want most of all to conceive and communicate. And to this end pictures are poorly suited. We resort, therefore, to the more powerful, supple, and adaptable symbolism of language.

How are relations expressed in language? For the most part, they are not symbolized by other relations, as in pictures, but are *named*, just like substantives. We name two items, and place the name of a relation between; this means that the relation holds the two items together. "Brutus killed Caesar" indicates that "killing" holds between Brutus and Caesar. Where the relation is not symmetrical, the word-order and the grammatical forms (case, mood, tense, etc.) of the words symbolize its direction. "Brutus killed Caesar" means something different from "Caesar killed Brutus," and "Killed Caesar Brutus" is not a sentence at all. The word-order partly determines the sense of the structure.

The trick of naming relations instead of illustrating them gives language a tremendous scope; one word can thus take care of a situation that would require a whole sheet of drawings to depict it. Consider the sentence, "Your chance of winning is one among a thousand of losing." Imagine a pictorial expression of this comparatively simple proposition! First, a symbol for "you, winning"; another for "you, losing," pictured a thousand times! Of course a thousand anythings would be far beyond clear apprehension on a basis of mere visual *Gestalt*. We can distinguish three, four, five, and perhaps somewhat higher numbers as visible patterns, for instance:

But a thousand becomes merely "a great number." Its exact fixation requires an order of concepts in which it holds a definite place, as each number concept does in our number system. But to denote such a host of concepts and keep their relations to each other straight, we need a symbolism that can express both terms and relationships more economically than pictures, gestures, or mnesic signs.

It was remarked before that symbol and object, having a common logical form, would be interchangeable save for some psychological factors, namely: that the object is interesting, but hard to fixate, whereas the symbol is easy of apprehension though in itself perhaps quite unimportant. Now the little vocal noises out of which we make our words are extremely easy to produce in all sorts of subtle variations, and easy to perceive and distinguish. As Bertrand Russell has put it, "It is of course largely a matter of convenience that we do not use words of other kinds (than vocal). There is the deaf-and-dumb language; a Frenchman's shrug of the shoulders is a word; in fact, any kind of externally perceptible bodily movement may become a word, if social usage so ordains. But the convention which has given the supremacy to speaking is one which has a good ground, since there is no other way of producing a number of perceptively different bodily movements so quickly or with so little muscular effort. Public speaking would be very tedious if statesmen had to use the deaf-and-dumb language, and very exhausting if all words involved as much muscular effort as a shrug of the shoulders.[13] Not only does speech cost little effort, but above all it requires no instrument save the vocal apparatus and the auditory organs which, normally, we all carry about as part of our very selves; so words are *naturally available* symbols, as well as very economical ones.

Another recommendation for words is that they have no value except as symbols (or signs); in themselves they are completely trivial. This is a greater advantage than philosophers of language generally realize. A symbol which interests us *also* as an object is distracting. It does not convey its meaning without obstruction. For instance, if the word "plenty" were replaced by a succulent, ripe, real peach, few people could attend entirely to the mere concept of *quite enough* when confronted with such a symbol. The more barren and indifferent the symbol, the greater is its semantic power. Peaches are too good to act as words; we are too much interested in peaches themselves. But little noises are ideal conveyors of concepts, for they give us nothing but their meaning. That is the source of the "transparency" of language, on which several scholars have remarked. Vocables in themselves are so worthless that we cease to be aware of their physical presence at all, and become conscious only of their connotations, denotations, or other meanings. Our conceptual activity seems to flow *through* them, rather than merely to accompany them, as it accompanies other experiences that we endow with significance. They fail to impress us as "experiences" in their own right, unless we have difficulty in using them as words, as we do with a foreign language or a technical jargon until we have mastered it.

But the greatest virtue of verbal symbols is, probably, their tremendous readiness to enter into *combinations*. There is practically no limit to the selections and arrangements we can make of them. This is largely due to the economy Lord Russell remarked, the speed with which each word is produced and presented and finished, making way for another word. This makes it possible for us to grasp whole groups of meanings at a time, and make a new, total, complex concept out of the separate connotations of rapidly passing words.

[13] Bertrand Russell, *Philosophy* (New York: W. W. Norton & Co., 1927), p. 44.

Herein lies the power of language to embody concepts not only of things, but of things in combination, or *situations*. A combination of words connoting a situation-concept is a descriptive phrase; if the relation-word in such a phrase is given the grammatical form called a "verb," the phrase becomes a sentence. Verbs are symbols with a double function; they express a relation, and also *assert that the relation holds,* i.e. that the symbol has a denotation."[14] Logically they combine the meaning of a function, ϕ, and an assertion-sign; a verb has the force of "assert ϕ ( )."

When a word is given an arbitrary denotation (which may be a simple thing, or a complex affair), it is simply a name; for instance, in a language of my invention "Moof" might mean a cat, a state of mind, or the government of a country. I may give that name to anything I like. A name may be awkward or convenient, ugly or pretty, but in itself it is never *true* or *false*. But if it already has a connotation, then it cannot be given an arbitrary denotation, nor vice versa. I cannot use the word "kitten" *with its accepted connotation* to denote an elephant. The application of *a word with its connotation* is the equivalent of a statement: "This is a such-and-such." To call an elephant "kitten," not as a proper name but as a common noun, is a mistake, because he does not exemplify the connoted concept. Similarly a word with a fixed denotation cannot be given an arbitrary connotation, for once the word is a name (common or proper), to give it a certain connotation is to *predicate* the connoted concept of whatever bears the name. If "Jumbo" denotes an elephant, it cannot be given the connotation "something furry," because Jumbo is presumably not furry.

The relation between connotation and denotation is, therefore, the most obvious seat of *truth and falsity*. Its conventional expressions are sentences asserting that something is a such-and-such, or that something has such-and-such a property; in technical language, propositions of the forms "$\chi \in \hat{y} \ (\phi y)$," and "$\phi\chi$." The distinction between these two forms lies simply in *which aspect of the name we have first determined,* its connotation or its denotation; truth and falsity have the same basis for both kinds of proposition.

In a complex symbolic structure, such as a sentence connecting several elements with each other by a verb that expresses an elaborate pattern of relations, we have a "logical picture" whose applicability depends on the denotations of many words and the connotations of many relation-symbols (word-order, particles, cases, etc.). If the names have denotations, the sentence is about *something;* then its truth or falsity depends on whether any

[14] A more detailed discussion of this double function may be found in my article, "A Logical Study of Verbs," *The Journal of Philosophy,* XXIV (1927), 5: 120–129.

relations actually holding among the denoted things exemplify the relational concepts expressed by the sentence, i.e. whether the pattern of things (or properties, events, etc.) denoted is analogous to the syntactical pattern of the complex symbol.

There are many refinements of logic that give rise to special symbol-situations, to ambiguities and odd mathematical devices, and to the legion of distinctions which Charles Peirce was able to make. But the main lines of logical structure in all meaning-relations are those I have just discussed; the correlation of signs with their meanings by a selective mental process; the correlation of symbols with concepts and concepts with things, which gives rise to a "short-cut" relation between names and things, known as denotation; and the assignment of elaborately patterned symbols to certain analogues in experience, the basis of all interpretation and thought. These are, essentially, the relationships we use in weaving the intricate web of meaning which is the real fabric of human life.

DISCURSIVE AND PRESENTATIONAL FORMS

Visual forms—lines, colors, proportions, etc.—are just as capable of *articulation*, i.e. of complex combination, as words. But the laws that govern this sort of articulation are altogether different from the laws of syntax that govern language. The most radical difference is that *visual forms are not discursive*. They do not present their constituents successively, but simultaneously, so the relations determining a visual structure are grasped in one act of vision. Their complexity, consequently, is not limited, as the complexity of discourse is limited, by what the mind can retain from the beginning of an apperceptive act to the end of it. Of course such a restriction on discourse sets bounds to the complexity of speakable ideas. An idea that contains too many minute yet closely related parts, too many relations within relations, cannot be "projected" into discursive form; it is too subtle for speech. A language-bound theory of mind, therefore, rules it out of the domain of understanding and the sphere of knowledge.

But the symbolism furnished by our purely sensory appreciation of forms is a *non-discursive symbolism*, peculiarly well suited to the expression of ideas that defy linguistic "projection." Its primary function, that of conceptualizing the flux of sensations, and giving us concrete *things* in place of kaleidoscopic colors or noises, is itself an office that no language-born thought can replace. The understanding of space which we owe to sight and touch could never be developed, in all its detail and definiteness, by a discursive knowledge of geometry. Nature speaks to us, first of all, through our senses; the forms and qualities we distinguish, remember, imagine, or recognize are symbols of entities which exceed and outlive our momentary experience. Moreover, the same symbols—qualities, lines, rhythms—may occur in innumerable presentations; they are abstractable and combinatory. It is quite natural, therefore, that philosophers who have recognized the symbolical character of so-called "sense-data," especially in their highly developed uses, in science and art, often speak of a "language" of the senses, a "language" of musical tones, of colors, and so forth.

Yet this manner of speaking is very deceptive. Language is a special mode of expression, and not every sort of semantic can be brought under this rubric; by generalizing from linguistic symbolism to symbolism as such, we are easily led to misconceive all other types, and overlook their most interesting features. Perhaps it were well to consider, here, the salient characteristics of true language, or discourse.

In the first place, *every language has a vocabulary and a syntax*. Its elements are words with fixed meanings. Out of these one can construct, according to the rules of the syntax, composite symbols with resultant new meanings.

Secondly, in a language, some words are equivalent to whole combinations of other words, so that most meanings can be expressed in several different ways. This makes it possible *to define the meanings of the ultimate single words,* i.e. to construct a dictionary.

Thirdly, there may be alternative words for the same meaning. When two people systematically use different words for almost everything, they are said to speak different languages. But the two languages are roughly equivalent; with a little artifice, an occasional substitution of a phrase for a single word, etc., the propositions enunciated by one person, in his system, may be *translated* into the conventional system of the other.

Now consider the most familiar sort of non-discursive symbol, a picture. Like language, it is composed of elements that represent various respective constituents in the object; but these elements are not units with independent meanings. The areas of light and shade that constitute a portrait, a photograph for instance, have no significance by themselves. In isolation we would consider them simply blotches. Yet they are faithful representatives of visual elements composing the visual object. However, they do not represent, item for item, those elements which have *names;* there is not one blotch for the nose, one for the mouth, etc.; their shapes, in quite indescribable combinations, convey a total picture in which nameable features may be pointed out. The gradations of light and shade cannot be enumerated. They cannot be correlated, one by one, with parts or characteristics by means of which we might *describe* the person who posed for the portrait. The "elements" that the camera represents are not the "elements" that language represents. They are a thousand times more numerous. For this reason the correspondence between a word-picture and a visible object can never be as close as that between the object and its photograph. Given all at once to the intelligent eye, an incredible wealth and detail of information is conveyed by the portrait, where we do not have to stop to construe verbal meanings. That is why we use a photograph rather than a description on a passport or in the Rogues' Gallery.

Clearly, a symbolism with so many elements, such myriad relationships, cannot be broken up into basic units. It is impossible to find the smallest independent symbol, and recognize its identity when the same unit is met in other contexts. Photography, therefore, *has no vocabulary.* The same is obviously true of painting, drawing, etc. There is, of course, a technique of picturing objects, but the law governing this technique cannot properly be called a "syntax" since there are no items that might be called, metaphorically, the "words" of portraiture.

Since we have no words, there can be no dictionary of meanings for lines, shadings, or other elements of pictorial technique. We may well pick out some line, say a certain curve, in a picture, which serves to represent one nameable item; but in another place the same curve would have an entirely different meaning. It has no fixed meaning apart from its context. Also, there is no complex of other elements that is equivalent to it at all times, as "2+2" is equivalent to "4." Non-discursive symbols cannot be defined in terms of others, as discursive symbols can.

If there can be no defining dictionary, of course we have no translating dictionary, either. There are different media of graphic representation, but their respective elements cannot be brought into one-to-one correlation with each other, as in languages: "*chien*" = "dog," "*moi*" = "me," etc. There is no standard key for translating sculpture into painting, or drawing into ink-wash, because their equivalence rests on their common *total reference,* not on bit-for-bit equivalences of parts such as underlie a literal translation.

Furthermore, verbal symbolism, unlike the non-discursive kinds, has primarily a *general* reference. Only convention can assign a proper name— and then there is no way of preventing some other convention from assigning the same proper name to a different individual. We may name a child as oddly as we will, yet we cannot guarantee that no one else will ever bear that designation. A description may fit a scene ever so closely, but it takes some known proper name to refer it without possible doubt to one and only one place. Where the names of persons and places are withheld, we can never *prove* that a discourse refers—not merely applies—to a certain historic occasion. In the non-discursive mode that speaks directly to sense, however, there is no intrinsic generality. It is first and foremost a direct *presentation* of an individual object. A picture has to be schematized if it is to be capable of various meanings. In itself it represents just one object— real or imaginary, but still a unique object. The definition of a triangle fits triangles in general, but a drawing always presents a triangle of some specific kind and size. We have to abstract from the conveyed meaning in order to conceive triangularity in general. Without the help of words this generalization, if possible at all, is certainly incommunicable.

It appears, then, that although the different media of nonverbal representation are often referred to as distinct "languages," this is really a loose terminology. Language in the strict sense is essentially discursive; it has permanent units of meaning which are combinable into large units; it has fixed equivalences that make definition and translation possible; its connotations are general, so that it requires non-verbal acts, like pointing, looking, or emphatic voice-inflections, to assign specific denotations to its terms. In all these salient characters it differs from wordless symbolism, which is non-discursive and untranslatable, does not allow of definitions within its own system, and cannot directly convey generalities. The meanings given through language are successively understood, and gathered into a whole by the process called discourse; the meanings of all other symbolic elements that compose a larger, articulate symbol are understood only through the meaning of the whole, through their relations within the total structure. Their very functioning as symbols depends on the fact that they are involved in a simultaneous, integral presentation. This kind of semantic may be called "presentational symbolism," to characterize its essential distinction from discursive symbolism, or "language" proper.[15]

The recognition of presentational symbolism as a normal and prevalent vehicle of meaning widens our conception of rationality far beyond the traditional boundaries, yet never breaks faith with logic in the strictest sense. Wherever a symbol operates, there is a meaning; and conversely, different classes of experience—say, reason, intuition, appreciation—correspond to different types of symbolic mediation. No symbol is exempt from the office of logical formulation, of *conceptualizing* what it conveys; however simple its import, or however great, this import is a *meaning*, and therefore an element for understanding. Such reflection invites one to tackle anew, and

[15] It is relevant here to note that "picture language," which uses *separate pictures in place of words,* is a discursive symbolism, though each "word" is a presentational symbol; and that all codes, e.g. the conventional gestures of deaf-mutes or the drum communications of African tribes, are discursive systems.

with entirely different expectations, the whole problem of the limits of reason, the much-disputed life of feeling, and the great controversial topics of fact and truth, knowledge and wisdom, science and art. It brings within the compass of reason much that has been traditionally relegated to "emotion," or to that crepuscular depth of the mind where "intuitions" are supposed to be born, without any midwifery of symbols, without due process of thought, to fill the gaps in the edifice of discursive, or "rational," judgment.

John Hospers

MEANING*

When we state the meaning of a word or phrase, we are stating what the word refers to, what it has come by convention to stand for. This is doubtless the main sense in which the word "meaning" is used. There are other senses, however: for example, it can refer to causal consequences ("This means war"), logical entailment ("This means I have only $100 left"), general feeling of significance ("This old house means a great deal to me"), and intention ("I don't know what he means by acting that way"). Most of these meanings of "meaning" (Ogden and Richards list sixteen of them in *The Meaning of Meaning*) are fairly clear in actual usage from the contexts in which they occur. When we ask "What is the meaning of this word?" or "What is the meaning of his strange behavior?" or "You've found the footprints, but what do they mean?" people do not generally have trouble in understanding us, as is shown by the fact that they give the right kind of answers, the sort of thing we had in mind in asking the question.

The case is different with "What is the meaning of a work of art?" When this question is asked, I am not sure what the inquirer is asking for. We have already seen that a work of art is not a conventional symbol (or set of such symbols) that has meaning in the way a word does. Nor does it seem to indicate implication, intention, or any of the other usual meanings. A person may state what the structure of a given work of art is, what effects it has on him, what effects it has on others, and even what he thinks its effects on others should be; but if he has stated these things and is still asked, "What does the work *mean?*" then one may well wonder what the questioner is asking for, what he wants, what information he desires in answer to his question. Until this is known, there is no possibility of answering it. And, generally speaking, I suspect that most persons who ask this question have no clear idea what they are asking for. Perhaps the cardinal sin in philosophy is to demand answers (and be disappointed when none are forthcoming) when the whole fault is with the question—when the "question" is really no question at all but a set of words with a question mark at the end.

Under these circumstances it may not seem advisable at all to use the word "meaning" in speaking of works of art. And I am quite ready to agree with this sentiment; the term "meaning" when used in this context is vastly confusing. It derives its puzzling quality from the fact that it is meaningfully employed in other contexts and the person feels that it must mean something in this one, since "What is the meaning of this word?" and "What is the meaning of this composition?" *look* similar and seem like the same kind of question—not realizing that underneath the similarity of appearance, the meaning (reference) of the word "meaning" has changed, or vanished into nothing.

However, if one wants to retain the word in speaking of the arts, I suggest that it be defined somewhat as follows: a work of art means to us whatever effects (not necessarily emotions) it evokes in us; a work which has no effects on us means nothing to us, and whatever effects it does evoke constitute its meaning for us. As we become more acquainted with the work of art, the effects it evokes in us gradually change, but in that case its meaning for us (as I have defined it) gradually changes too. The work of art is one term in the relationship, the evoked reactions the other; and the gradual changing of the latter as we hear or see the work again constitutes a gradual change in its meaning for us. Its meaning may or may not be describable in words—in most cases it is not, since few if any states of mind (particularly affective states) are describable to the satisfaction of the person who experiences them.

This may seem to be an extremely arbitrary conception of artistic meaning. I grant that it is arbitrary, but I feel quite justified in making it so. My reason for this is simply the very elementary semantic principle that when a word has been given no meaning by convention when used in a certain context, one must (if he is to use it at all) arbitrarily confer a meaning upon it. This must be made clear beyond the slightest doubt:

No word has meaning (in the sense of reference) in itself; it has no meaning until it is *given* meaning by someone; lacking this, it is simply a row of marks on paper or uttered sounds. Most of the words in our language have been given meanings long ago, and this meaning has been agreed upon by the users of our language, so that the words have come by *convention* to stand for the things they now stand for, and all we have to do is learn them. Many words have several meanings (referents) and are called ambiguous words—in these cases we learn their multiple meanings; this is true of the word "meaning" along with thousands of other words. This word has a meaning when applied in such situations as "meaning of a word," "meaning of his behavior," etc. But just as words do not always have the same meaning in different contexts (as we have just seen in the case of the word "meaning" itself), there are contexts in which it has *no* meaning until it is *given* a meaning *for* that context. Thus, as we now use the word "on," the statement "The glass is on the table" has meaning but "The glass is on the universe" does not; the word "on" has been given meaning only within a certain physical context, and when it is not applied within that context it becomes simply a sound or mark on paper. The same is true for the word "meaning." It has a definite meaning (reference) in the ordinary situations referred to above, but when applied to a situation such as "What does this piece of music mean?" it does not, since the word "meaning" has been *given* no meaning in that context. At least it has no standard meaning (reference) in that context; different persons may mean (intend) different things by it, though for the most part I do not think they know what they really are after when they ask it. And in the absence of any standard meaning of the word "meaning" in this context, I have decided to give it one, i.e., arbitrarily to define the word when predicated of works of art. This would not be a justifiable procedure if the word (when used in this expression) already referred to something—just as it would not be justifiable for me to use the word "cat" to refer to any university building because the word already has a standard usage which is well understood; such a procedure would cause endless confusion. But this is not the case in situations where the word *has* (i.e., has been given) as yet no meaning. Where there is a common usage of the word, even when it is quite ambiguous, one should perform an *analysis* of it to try to discover which of several things people mean by it when they use it; but when this is not the case, it is rather pointless to attempt this procedure. So it is in the present case.

To a certain extent this is true of words we have discussed already. "Represent" and "express" are, as we have seen, certainly ambiguous enough. But they do possess a sufficient modicum of standard reference, even when applied to esthetics, to render useful an attempt to track down these different senses and find out which of a number of things people (especially artists and philosophers) really do mean when they say that a work of art represents or expresses. This is what I have tried to do in the last two chapters. But when we come to "meaning" this is no longer the case. Here, when a person asserts that a work of art means so-and-so, I really do not know what he means (intends) to say. And so, since the word "meaning" has no conventional meaning (reference) in locutions such as "What is the meaning of this piece of music?" I must, if I want to use the word at all, *stipulate* how I think the word might be usefully used here. And I submit the one just presented as one of those least likely to be ambiguous and misunderstood.

Moreover, it leads directly into a most interesting problem. Much of the controversy that is generally associated with the phrase "the meaning of a work of art" is not concerned with trying to answer the pseudo-question "What does the work mean?" but rather with the question of the relation of the formal element in art to the expressive or content-element—what has been described in Chapter I as "life-values." The disagreement concerns how much of the non-formal element should be predominant in the appreciation of the observer (listener, reader)—that is, which element should be foremost in artistic meaning in the sense I have defined. This is a most interesting controversy, and there are a number of clarifications that can be made in discussing it. It is this task which I shall now undertake, convinced that it is the most interesting and fruitful kind of issue that could be considered under the heading of "artistic meaning." I shall consider the arts of music, painting, and literature in turn.

SELECTED BIBLIOGRAPHY

1. Charles W. Morris, "Science, Art and Technology," *The Kenyon Review*, 1930. A semiotical analysis of language, meaning, and art.
2. Morris Weitz, "Art and Symbolism," *The Review of Metaphysics*, 1954. A critical review of Langer's theory that art is symbol and her general theory of language and meaning.
3. Gilbert Ryle, "The Theory of Meaning," in C. A. Mace (ed.), *British Philosophy in the Mid-Century*, George Allen and Unwin, 1957. An excellent survey and critique of traditional denotational, connotational, semiotic, and naming theories of meaning and language. Also a good summary and introduction to prevalent tendencies to recast the whole problem of language and meaning in philosophy, carried on by Wittgenstein, and others.
4. R. G. Collingwood. *The Principles of Art*, Ch. XI. An expressionist version of art as language.

THE MEDIUM

Every work of art has, as one of its ingredients, the material in which it is embodied. Without words, there would be no poems; without tones, no music; without paints and surfaces to put them on, no paintings; without bodily movements, no dance; and so on.

Aristotle was the first who, in a systematic way, referred to this material element in art as the *medium*, and he used this category as one basic principle for differentiation of the arts.

Since Aristotle, much has been written on the medium in art. In the main, these writings divide themselves into discussions of the nature of the different sorts of materials in the various arts, the importance of these materials in the separate arts, and the relations among the various media.

In regard to the first of these writings, there are many treatises on the nature of the different kinds of paints and surfaces, such as tempera as against oils, or linen as against fresco (wet plaster), in painting; on the intrinsic qualities of the various musical instruments; on the similarities and differences between stone, wood, bronze, etc., in sculpture.

It is the second and third problems, however, which have exercised philosophers and critics, since the first is primarily of concern to practitioners in the arts. The central issue, historically, is that of the "purity" of the medium: Can one art do what the others can; or are the arts distinct, according to their different media?

It was Gotthold Lessing who, in his *Laocoon*, on the famous Greek sculpture, gave the classic statement of the purist doctrine in regard to the medium. Our first selection, therefore, is from this great work. Lessing's main thesis is that the visual arts are spatial and the poetic arts temporal, and hence should not trespass on each other. His thesis has become one of the most important doctrines in the development of modern art: in all the arts his basic appeal to the principle of *Materialgerechtigkeit*—doing justice to the nature of the material—has been heeded.

The second selection, by Bernard Bosanquet, carries Lessing's argument further by a sensitive and penetrating account of the importance of the medium in the different arts.

Gotthold E. Lessing

THE PURITY OF THE MEDIUM*

II

Be it truth or fable that Love made the first attempt in the imitative arts, thus much is certain: that she never tired of guiding the hand of the great masters of antiquity. For although painting, as the art which reproduces objects upon flat surfaces, is now practised in the broadest sense of that definition, yet the wise Greek set much narrower bounds to it. He confined it strictly to the imitation of beauty. The Greek artist represented nothing that was not beautiful. Even the vulgarly beautiful, the beauty of inferior types, he copied only incidentally for practice or recreation. The perfection of the subject must charm in his work. He was too great to require the beholders to be satisfied with the mere barren pleasure arising from a successful likeness or from consideration of the artist's skill. Nothing in his art was dearer to him or seemed to him more noble than the ends of art.

"Who would want to paint you when no one wants to look at you?" says an old epigrammatist[1] to a misshapen man. Many a modern artist would say, "No matter how misshapen you are, I will paint you. Though people may not like to look at you, they will be glad to look at my picture; not as a portrait of you, but as a proof of my skill in making so close a copy of such a monster."

The fondness for making a display with mere manual dexterity, ennobled by no worth in the subject, is too natural not to have produced among

* From Gotthold Lessing's *Laocoon*. First published in 1766. Translated by E. Frothingham. Chapter II is here printed complete, and Chs. III and XVI printed in part.

Gotthold E. Lessing (1729–1781), famous German playwright, drama critic, and essayist, wrote this classic in aesthetics in reply to Johann Winckelmann's equally famous analysis of the sculpture, Laocoon, now in the Vatican Museum in Rome.

[1] Antiochus, Anthol. lib. ii, cap. 4.

the Greeks a Pauson and a Pyreicus. They had such painters, but meted out to them strict justice. Pauson, who confined himself to the beauties of ordinary nature, and whose depraved taste liked best to represent the imperfections and deformities of humanity, lived in the most abandoned poverty; and Pyreicus, who painted barbers' rooms, dirty workshops, donkeys, and kitchen herbs, with all the diligence of a Dutch painter, as if such things were rare or attractive in nature, acquired the surname of Rhyparographer,[2] the dirt-painter. The rich voluptuaries, indeed, paid for his works their weight in gold, as if by this fictitious valuation to atone for their insignificance.

Even the magistrates considered this subject a matter worthy their attention, and confined the artist by force within his proper sphere. The law of the Thebans commanding him to make his copies more beautiful than the originals, and never under pain of punishment less so, is well known. This was no law against bunglers, as has been supposed by critics generally, and even by Junius himself,[3] but was aimed against the Greek Ghezzi, and condemned the unworthy artifice of obtaining a likeness by exaggerating the deformities of the model. It was, in fact, a law against caricature.

From this same conception of the beautiful came the law of the Olympic judges. Every conqueror in the Olympic games received a statue, but a portrait-statue was erected only to him who had been thrice victor. Too many indifferent portraits were not allowed among works of art. For although a portrait admits of being idealized, yet the likeness should predominate. It is the ideal of a particular person, not the ideal of humanity.

We laugh when we read that the very arts among the ancients were subject to the control of civil law; but we have no right to laugh. Laws should unquestionably usurp no sway over science, for the object of science is truth. Truth is a necessity of the soul, and to put any restraint upon the gratification of this essential want is tyranny. The object of art, on the contrary, is pleasure, and pleasure is not indispensable. What kind and what degree of pleasure shall be permitted may justly depend on the law-giver.

The plastic arts especially, besides the inevitable influence which they exercise on the character of a nation, have power to work one effect which demands the careful attention of the law. Beautiful statues fashioned from beautiful men reacted upon their creators, and the state was indebted for its beautiful men to beautiful statues. With us the susceptible imagination of the mother seems to express itself only in monsters.

From this point of view I think I detect a truth in certain old stories which have been rejected as fables. The mothers of Aristomenes, of Aristo-

---

[2] Plinius, lib. xxx, sect. 37.
[3] De Pictura vet. lib. ii, cap. iv, sect. 1.

damas, of Alexander the Great, Scipio, Augustus, and Galerius, each dreamed during pregnancy that she was visited by a serpent. The serpent was an emblem of divinity. Without it Bacchus, Apollo, Mercury, and Hercules were seldom represented in their beautiful pictures and statues. These honorable women had been feasting their eyes upon the god during the day, and the bewildering dream suggested to them the image of the snake. Thus I vindicate the dream, and show up the explanation given by the pride of their sons and by unblushing flattery. For there must have been some reason for the adulterous fancy always taking the form of a serpent.

But I am wandering from my purpose, which was simply to prove that among the ancients beauty was the supreme law of the imitative arts. This being established, it follows necessarily that whatever else these arts may aim at must give way completely if incompatible with beauty, and, if compatible, must at least be secondary to it.

I will confine myself wholly to expression. There are passions and degrees of passion whose expression produces the most hideous contortions of the face, and throws the whole body into such unnatural positions as to destroy all the beautiful lines that mark it when in a state of greater repose. These passions the old artists either refrained altogether from representing, or softened into emotions which were capable of being expressed with some degree of beauty.

Rage and despair disfigured none of their works. I venture to maintain that they never represented a fury. Wrath they tempered into severity. In poetry we have the wrathful Jupiter, who hurls the thunderbolt; in art he is simply the austere.

Anguish was softened into sadness. Where that was impossible, and where the representation of intense grief would belittle as well as disfigure, how did Timanthes manage? There is a well-known picture by him of the sacrifice of Iphigenia, wherein he gives to the countenance of every spectator a fitting degree of sadness, but veils the face of the father, on which should have been depicted the most intense suffering. This has been the subject of many petty criticisms. "The artist," says one,[4] "had so exhausted himself in representations of sadness that he despaired of depicting the father's face worthily." "He hereby confessed," says another,[5] "that the bitterness of extreme grief cannot be expressed by art." I, for my part, see in this no proof of incapacity in the artist or his art. In proportion to the intensity of feeling, the expression of the features is intensified, and nothing is easier than to express extremes. But Timanthes knew the limits which

[4] Plinius, lib. xxxv, sect. 35.
[5] Valerius Maximus, lib. viii, cap. 2.

the graces have imposed upon his art. He knew that the grief befitting Agamemnon, as father, produces contortions which are essentially ugly. He carried expression as far as was consistent with beauty and dignity. Ugliness he would gladly have passed over, or have softened, but since his subject admitted of neither, there was nothing left him but to veil it. What he might not paint he left to be imagined. That concealment was in short a sacrifice to beauty; an example to show, not how expression can be carried beyond the limits of art, but how it should be subjected to the first law of art, the law of beauty.

Apply this to the Laocoon and we have the cause we were seeking. The master was striving to attain the greatest beauty under the given conditions of bodily pain. Pain, in its disfiguring extreme, was not compatible with beauty, and must therefore be softened. Screams must be reduced to sighs, not because screams would betray weakness, but because they would deform the countenance to a repulsive degree. Imagine Laocoon's mouth open, and judge. Let him scream, and see. It was, before, a figure to inspire compassion in its beauty and suffering. Now it is ugly, abhorrent, and we gladly avert our eyes from a painful spectacle, destitute of the beauty which alone could turn our pain into the sweet feeling of pity for the suffering object.

The simple opening of the mouth, apart from the violent and repulsive contortions it causes in the other parts of the face, is a blot on a painting and a cavity in a statue productive of the worst possible effect. Montfaucon showed little taste when he pronounced the bearded face of an old man with wide open mouth, to be a Jupiter delivering an oracle.[6] Cannot a god foretell the future without screaming? Would a more becoming posture of the lips cast suspicion upon his prophecies? Valerius cannot make me believe that Ajax was painted screaming in the above-mentioned picture of Timanthes. Far inferior masters, after the decline of art, do not in a single instance make the wildest barbarian open his mouth to scream, even though in mortal terror of his enemy's sword.[7]

This softening of the extremity of bodily suffering into a lesser degree of pain is apparent in the works of many of the old artists. Hercules, writhing in his poisoned robe, from the hand of an unknown master, was not the Hercules of Sophocles, who made the Locrian rocks and the Euboean promontory ring with his horrid cries. He was gloomy rather than wild. The Philoctetes of Pythagoras Leontinus seemed to communicate his pain to the beholder, an effect which would have been destroyed by the slightest disfigurement of the features. It may be asked how I know that this master

[6] Antiquit. expl. T. i, p. 50.
[7] Bellorii Admiranda, Tab. 11, 12.

made a statue of Philoctetes. From a passage in Pliny, which ought not to have waited for my emendation, so evident is the alteration or mutilation it has undergone.[8]

III

But, as already observed, the realm of art has in modern times been greatly enlarged. Its imitations are allowed to extend over all visible nature, of which beauty constitutes but a small part. Truth and expression are taken as its first law. As nature always sacrifices beauty to higher ends, so should the artist subordinate it to his general purpose, and not pursue it further than truth and expression allow. Enough that truth and expression convert what is unsightly in nature into a beauty of art.

Allowing this idea to pass unchallenged at present for whatever it is worth, are there not other independent considerations which should set bounds to expression, and prevent the artist from choosing for his imitation the culminating point of any action?

The single moment of time to which art must confine itself, will lead us, I think, to such considerations. Since the artist can use but a single moment of ever-changing nature, and the painter must further confine his study of this one moment to a single point of view, while their works are made not simply to be looked at, but to be contemplated long and often, evidently the most fruitful moment and the most fruitful aspect of that moment must be chosen. Now that only is fruitful which allows free play to the imagination. The more we see the more we must be able to imagine; and the more we imagine, the more we must think we see. But no moment in the whole course of an action is so disadvantageous in this respect as that of its culmination. There is nothing beyond, and to present the uttermost to the eye is to bind the wings of Fancy, and compel her, since she cannot soar beyond the impression made on the senses, to employ herself with feebler images, shunning as her limit the visible fulness already expressed. When, for instance, Laocoon sighs, imagination can hear him cry; but if he cry, imagination can neither mount a step higher, nor fall a step lower, without seeing him in a more endurable, and therefore less interesting, condition. We hear him merely groaning, or we see him already dead.

Again, since this single moment receives from art an unchanging duration, it should express nothing essentially transitory. All phenomena, whose nature it is suddenly to break out and as suddenly to disappear, which can remain as they are but for a moment; all such phenomena, whether agree-

[8] Pliny, lib. 34, sect. 19.

able or otherwise, acquire through the perpetuity conferred upon them by art such an unnatural appearance, that the impression they produce becomes weaker with every fresh observation, till the whole subject at last wearies or disgusts us. La Mettrie, who had himself painted and engraved as a second Democritus, laughs only the first time we look at him. Looked at again, the philosopher becomes a buffoon, and his laugh a grimace. So it is with a cry. Pain, which is so violent as to extort a scream, either soon abates or it must destroy the sufferer. Again, if a man of firmness and endurance cry, he does not do so unceasingly, and only this apparent continuity in art makes the cry degenerate into womanish weakness or childish impatience. This, at least, the sculptor of the Laocoon had to guard against, even had a cry not been an offence against beauty, and were suffering without beauty a legitimate subject of art. . . .

XVI

But I will try to prove my conclusions by starting from first principles.

I argue thus. If it be true that painting employs wholly different signs or means of imitation from poetry,—the one using forms and colors in space, the other articulate sounds in time,—and if signs must unquestionably stand in convenient relation with the thing signified, then signs arranged side by side can represent only objects existing side by side, or whose parts so exist, while consecutive signs can express only objects which succeed each other, or whose parts succeed each other, in time.

Objects which exist side by side, or whose parts so exist, are called bodies. Consequently bodies with their visible properties are the peculiar subjects of painting.

Objects which suceeed each other, or whose parts succeed each other in time, are actions. Consequently actions are the peculiar subjects of poetry.

All bodies, however, exist not only in space, but also in time. They continue, and, at any moment of their continuance, may assume a different appearance and stand in different relations. Every one of these momentary appearances and groupings was the result of a preceding, may become the cause of a following, and is therefore the centre of a present, action. Consequently painting can imitate actions also, but only as they are suggested through forms.

Actions, on the other hand, cannot exist independently, but must always be joined to certain agents. In so far as those agents are bodies or are regarded as such, poetry describes also bodies, but only indirectly through actions.

Painting, in its coexistent compositions, can use but a single moment of an action, and must therefore choose the most pregnant one, the one most suggestive of what has gone before and what is to follow.

Poetry, in its progressive imitations, can use but a single attribute of bodies, and must choose that one which gives the most vivid picture of the body as exercised in this particular action.

Hence the rule for the employment of a single descriptive epithet, and the cause of the rare occurrence of descriptions of physical objects.

I should place less confidence in this dry chain of conclusions, did I not find them fully confirmed by Homer, or, rather, had they not been first suggested to me by Homer's method. These principles alone furnish a key to the noble style of the Greek, and enable us to pass just judgment on the opposite method of many modern poets who insist upon emulating the artist in a point where they must of necessity remain inferior to him.

I find that Homer paints nothing but progressive actions. All bodies, all separate objects, are painted only as they take part in such actions, and generally with a single touch. No wonder, then, that artists find in Homer's pictures little or nothing to their purpose, and that their only harvest is where the narration brings together in a space favorable to art a number of beautiful shapes in graceful attitudes, however little the poet himself may have painted shapes, attitudes, or space. . . .

Bernard Bosanquet

THE IMPORTANCE OF THE MEDIUM*

Why are there different arts? The simple answer to this question takes us, I believe, to the precise root and source of the whole principle of esthetic expressiveness. . . .

We should begin, I am convinced, from the very simplest facts. Why do artists make different patterns, or treat the same pattern differently, in wood-carving, say, and clay-modeling, and wrought-iron work? If you can answer this question thoroughly, then, I am convinced, you have the secret of the classification of the arts and of the passage of feeling into its esthetic embodiment; that is, in a word, the secret of beauty.

* From Bernard Bosanquet's *Three Lectures on Aesthetic*, pp. 58–75. Copyright, 1915, by The Macmillan Company, Ltd. Reprinted by permission of Mrs. R. C. Bosanquet.

Bernard Bosanquet (1848–1923), Oxford Idealist, author of many books in philosophy, wrote on the history and some of the main problems of aesthetics.

Why, then, in general does a worker in clay make different decorative patterns from a worker in wrought-iron? I wish I could go into this question with illustrations and details, but I will admit at once that I am not really competent to do so, though I have taken very great interest in the problem. But in general there can surely be no doubt of the answer. You cannot make the same things in clay as you can in wrought-iron, except by a *tour de force.* The feeling of the work is, I suppose, altogether different. The metal challenges you, coaxes you, as William Morris said of the molten glass, to do a particular kind of thing with it, where its tenacity and ductility make themselves felt. The clay, again, is delightful, I take it, to handle, to those who have a talent for it; but it is delightful of course in quite different manipulations from those of the wrought-iron. I suppose its facility of surface, how it lends itself to modeling or to throwing on the wheel, must be its great charm. Now the decorative patterns which are carried out in one or the other may, of course, be suggested *ab extra* by a draughtsman, and have all sorts of properties and interests in themselves as mere lines on paper. But when you come to carry them out in the medium, then, if they are appropriate, or if you succeed in adapting them, they become each a special phase of the embodiment of your whole delight and interest of "body-and-mind" in handling the clay or metal or wood or molten glass. It is alive in your hands, and its life grows or rather magically springs into shapes which it, and you in it, seem to desire and feel inevitable. The feeling for the medium, the sense of what can rightly be done in it only or better than in anything else, and the charm and fascination of doing it so—these, I take it, are the real clue to the fundamental question of esthetics, which is "how feeling and its body are created adequate to one another." It is parallel to the question in general philosophy, "Why the soul has a body." It is the same sort of thing as the theory of the rising mountain, but it is much less open to caprice, being absolute fact all through, and it explains not merely the interpretation of lines and shapes, but the whole range and working of the esthetic imagination in the province of fine art, which is its special province.

To this doctrine belongs the very fruitful modern topic of the relation of beautiful handicraft with the workman's life as the outcome and expression of his body-and-mind, and amid all the disparagement which the most recent views of art are apt to throw upon Ruskin, we must remember that it was first and foremost to his inspired advocacy that this point of view owes its recognition to-day, and William Morris, for instance, recognized him, in this respect at least, as his master.

The differences of the great arts then are simply such differences as those between clay-modeling, wood-carving, and wrought-iron work, developed on an enormous scale, and with their inevitable consequences for whole provinces of esthetic imagination.

For this is a fact of the highest importance. Every craftsman, we saw, feels the peculiar delight and enjoys the peculiar capacity of his own medium. This delight and sense of capacity are of course not confined to the moments when he is actually manipulating his work. His fascinated imagination lives in the powers of his medium; he thinks and feels in terms of it; it is the peculiar body of which *his* esthetic imagination and no other is the peculiar soul.

Thus there grow up the distinct traditions, the whole distinctive worlds of imaginative thought and feeling, in which the great imaginative arts have their life and being. . . .

The ideal of every art must be revealed, I take it, in terms of the art itself; and it must be what underlies the whole series of efforts which the artist's imagination has made and is making, to create, in his own medium, an embodied feeling in which he can rest satisfied. It is the world as he has access to it through his art. It may seem to him more than any of his works; but it only has existence in them and in the effort which they imply when taken all together. The danger is to try and make a picture of this effort, apart from any of its achievements, which is really nothing. Then you get the enfeebled ideal, which means the omission of all character and individuality.

Now let us take a particular case. If our view of the distinction and connection of the arts is right, and it is simply a question of the medium adopted by each, and the capacities of that medium as proved by experience, what is to be said of the distinctive character of *poetry*? It seems in a sense to have almost no material element, to work directly with significant ideas in which the objects of the imagination are conveyed. Language is so transparent, that it disappears, so to speak, into its own meaning, and we are left with no characteristic medium at all.

I do not think there can be any doubt about the true attitude here. Poetry, like the other arts, has a physical or at least a sensuous medium, and this medium is sound. It is, however, significant sound, uniting inseparably in itself the factors of formal expression through an immediate pattern, and of representation through the meanings of language, exactly as sculpture and painting deal at once and in the same vision both with formal patterns and with significant shapes. That language is a physical fact with its own properties and qualities is easily seen by comparing different tongues, and noting the form which different patterns, such as sapphic or hexameter verse, necessarily receive in different languages, such as Greek and Latin.

To make poetry in different languages, *e.g.*, in French and German, is as different a task as to make decorative work in clay and iron. The sound meter and meaning are the same inseparable product in a poem as much as the color, form, and embodied feeling in a picture. And it is only an illusion to suppose that because you have significant sentences in poetry, therefore you are dealing with meanings which remain the same outside the poem, any more than a tree or a person whom you think you recognize in a picture, is, as you know them at home so to speak, *the* tree or *the* person *of* the picture. Poetry no more keeps its meaning when turned into corresponding prose, than a picture or a sonata keeps its meaning in the little analyses they print in the catalogues or programs.

Shelley, according to Professor Bradley, had a feeling of the kind referred to. Poetry seemed to him to deal with a perfectly apt and transparent medium, with no qualities of its own, and therefore approaching to being no medium at all, but created out of nothing by the imagination for the use of the imagination. While the media employed by the other arts, being gross and physical and having independent qualities of their own, seemed to him rather obstacles in the way of expression than apt instruments of it. The answer to such a view is what we have just given.

It is the qualities of the media which give them the capacity to serve as embodiments of feeling; and sonorous language, the medium of poetry, has its peculiarities and definite capacities precisely like the others.

Here, I cannot but think, we are obliged to part company, with some regret, from Benedetto Croce. He is possessed, as so often is the case with him, by a fundamental truth, so intensely that he seems incapable of apprehending what more is absolutely necessary to its realization. Beauty, he sees, is for the mind and in the mind. A physical thing, supposed unperceived and unfelt, cannot be said in the full sense to possess beauty. But he forgets throughout, I must think, that though feeling is necessary to its embodiment, yet also the embodiment is necessary to feeling. To say that because beauty implies a mind, therefore it is an internal state, and its physical embodiment is something secondary and incidental, and merely brought into being for the sake of permanence and communication—this seems to me a profound error of principle, a false idealism. It meets us, however, throughout Croce's system, according to which "intuition"—the inward vision of the artist—is the only true expression. External media, he holds, are, strictly speaking, superfluous, so that there is no meaning in distinguishing between one mode of expression and another (as between paint and musical sound and language). Therefore there can be no classification of the arts, and no fruitful discussion of what can better be done by one art than by another. And esthetic—the philosophy of expression—is set down as all one with linguistic—the philosophy of speech. For there is no meaning in distinguishing between language in the sense of speech, and other modes of expression. Of course, if he had said that speech is not the only form of language, but that every art speaks to us in a language of its own, that would have had much to be said for it. But I do not gather that that is his intention.

His notion is not a new one among theorists. It really is deeply rooted in a philosophical blunder. No doubt it seems obvious, when once pointed out, that things are not all there, not complete in all qualities, except when they are appreciated in a mind. And then, having rightly observed that this is so, we are apt to go on and say that you have them complete, and have all you want of them, if you have them before your mind and have not the things in bodily presence at all. But the blunder is, to think that you can have them completely before your mind without having their bodily presence at all. And because of this blunder, it seems fine and "ideal" to say that the artist operates in the bodiless medium of pure thought or fancy, and that the things of the bodily world are merely physical causes of sensation, which do not themselves enter into the effects he uses. It is rather a natural thing to say about poetry, because we discount the physical side of language. We glance at its words and do not sound them. And Shelley, as we saw, says something very like that.

But at the very beginning of all this notion, as we said, there is a blunder. Things, it is true, are not complete without minds, but minds, again, are not complete without things; not any more, we might say, than minds are complete without bodies. Our resources in the way of sensation, and our experiences in the way of satisfactory and unsatisfactory feeling, are all of them won out of our intercourse with things, and are thought and imagined by us as qualities and properties of the things. Especially we see this in music. Here we have an art entirely made up of a material— musical tone—which one may say does not exist at all in the natural world, and is altogether originated by our inventive and imaginative manipulation of physical things, pressing on in the line of creative discovery which something very like accident must at first have opened up to us.[1] Apart from this imaginative operation upon physical things, our fancy in the realm of music could have done as good as nothing.

And in principle it is the same with all the arts. All the material and the physical process which the artist uses—take our English language as

---

[1] This applies even to the development of song, so far as that involves a musical system.

used in poetry for an example—has been elaborated and refined, and, so to speak, consecrated by ages of adaptation and application in which it has been fused and blended with feeling—and it carries the life-blood of all this endeavor in its veins; and that is how, as we have said over and over again, feelings get their embodiment, and embodiments get their feeling. If you try to cut the thought and fancy loose from the body of the stuff in which it molds its pictures and poetic ideas and musical constructions, you impoverish your fancy, and arrest its growth, and reduce it to a bloodless shade. When I pronounce even a phrase so commonplace in itself as "Rule, Britannia!" the actual vibrations of the sound, the bodily experience I am aware of in saying it, is alive with the history of England which passed into the words in the usage and formation of the language. Up to a certain point, language is poetry ready-made for us.

And I suppose that a great painter, in his actual handling of his brush, has present with him a sense of meaning and fitness which is one with the joy of execution, both of which the experience of a lifetime has engrained in the coöperation of his hand and eye. I take it, there is a pleasure in the brush stroke, which *is also* a sense of success in the use of the medium, and of meaning in hitting the exact effect which he wants to get. We common people have something analogous to all this, when we enjoy the too-rare sensation of having found the right word. In such "finding" there is a creative element. A word is, quite strictly speaking, not used twice in the same sense.

Croce says, indeed, that the artist has every stroke of the brush in his mind as complete before he executes it as after. The suggestion is that using the brush adds nothing to his inward or mental work of art. I think that this is false idealism. The bodily thing adds immensely to the mere idea and fancy, in wealth of qualities and connections. If we try to cut out the bodily side of our world, we shall find that we have reduced the mental side to a mere nothing.

And so, when we said that you can carry away the soul of a thing and leave its body behind, we always added that you must in doing so confer its soul upon a new and spiritualized body. Your imagination must be an imagination of something, and if you refuse to give that something a definite structure, you pass from the esthetic semblance to the region of abstract thought. I have spoken of sound as physical; if this is a difficulty it is enough to call it sensuous, and sensuous in immediate connection with other physical properties and experiences. This applies both to music and to language.

All this later argument of ours, starting from the importance of medium and technique, has aimed at exhibiting in detail the double process of creation and contemplation which is implied in the esthetic attitude, and the impossiblity of separating one factor of it from another. And it is the same question as that stated in other words, how a feeling can be got into an object. This is the central problem of the esthetic attitude; and, as we have seen, the best material for solving it for us who are not great artists comes from any minor experience we may have at command in which we have been aware of the outgoing of feeling into expression. We must think not merely of the picture in the gallery or the statue in the museum, but of the song and the dance, the dramatic reading, the entering into music, or the feel of the material in the minor arts, or simply, of the creative discovery of the right word.

The festal or social view of art will help us here. Suppose a tribe or a nation has won a great victory; "they are feeling big, and they want to make something big," as I have heard an expert say. That, I take it, is the rough account of the beginning of the esthetic attitude. And according to their capacity and their stage of culture, they may make a pile of their enemies' skulls, or they may build the Parthenon. The point of the esthetic attitude lies in the adequate fusion of body and soul, where the soul is a feeling, and the body its expression, without residue on either side.

SELECTED BIBLIOGRAPHY

1. C. J. Ducasse, *Art, the Critics, and You,* Ch. II, Oskar Piest, 1944. This chapter contains one excellent criticism of the doctrine of purism, which is secured by a view about the different languages of the arts.
2. Bernhard Berenson, *Aesthetics and History,* Ch. I, (the section on materials especially), Pantheon Books, 1948. A brief counter to the thesis that materials are important in art. (Available as Anchor paperback.)
3. Ralph W. Church, *An Essay on Critical Appreciation,* Ch. III, Cornell University Press, 1938. A brief history of tempera and oils in painting and their relation to aesthetic analysis of the art of painting.

STYLE

The concept of style also is of fundamental importance in our understanding of art. All historical and comparative studies of art rely on it as a basic category of analysis. Terms such as "Classic," "Romantic," "Renaissance," "Baroque," "Byzantine," etc., are frequently style-terms. Meyer Shapiro, in his brilliant essay, "Style," (see bibliography) characterizes style as "the constant form—and sometimes the constant elements, qualities, and expression—in the art of an individual or a group" (*ibid.* p. 287); and, as such, style is an essential object of investigation for the art historian, critic, and aesthetician.

Among the many studies of style, that of André Malraux is one of the best. It is the very center of his tremendous work on the arts called, in its revised version, *The Voices of Silence*. Style is the essence of great art. Art, itself, for Malraux, is a revolt against man's fate, an age-long dialogue with destiny. Each of the great styles and movements in the history of art has conceived this revolt differently, and the diverse conceptions constitute the great styles. "Every true style is the scaling-down to our human perspective of that eternal flux on whose mysterious rhythms we are borne ineluctably, in a never-ceasing drift of stars." It is the artist who meets our destiny head-on and challenges it by creating his own universe of which he is the master. Each style is therefore a "new transformation of the meaning of the world." Style is an interpretation, in painting through the plastic materials of the artist, of the reality within the world of appearances, whether it be the Eternity of the Byzantine, the Serenity of the Chinese or the Drama of Christianity personalized in Christ.

The following selection from Malraux contains the heart of this brilliant

260

metaphysical excursus into art and style. It also includes a magnificent interpretation of Michelangelo's "Last Judgment," which serves as an example of Malraux's view of art and style as a new transformation of the significance of the world.

André Malraux

STYLE*

That is why every artist starts off with the pastiche. And this pastiche, into which sometimes genius furtively insinuates itself (like the humble figure at a garret window in some Flemish painting), is certainly an attempt at participation, but not participation in life itself. The fact that it is not the sight of a supremely beautiful woman, but the sight of a supremely beautiful painting that launches a painter on his career does not diminish the emotion behind his creative impulse; for, like all deep emotions, the emotion roused by art craves to make itself eternal. Practiced with ritual fervor, imitation is a familiar instrument of magic, and a painter needs but recall his first paintings, or a poet his first poems, to realize that they served him as a means of participating, not in the world of men, but in that of art, and what he asked of them was less a conquest of the world of reality, an escape from it, or even an expression of it, than a sense of fellowship with brother artists. It was Courbet, the realist, who entitled certain pictures in his first exhibition *Florentine Pastiche, Dutch Pastiche* and the like.

As most of us have realized, art is not a mere embellishment of life; nevertheless, having so long regarded it as such, the average European is still too apt to confuse the vocation of an artist with the activities of the jeweler. We all know that other worlds besides the real world exist, but nothing is gained by relegating them indiscriminately to a dream world, where the word "dream" expresses at once the vagaries of sleep and satisfaction of desire. The world of art is fantastic in the sense that its elements are not those of reality; but its fantasy is intrinsic and fundamental, quite other than the wayward imaginings of the daydream, and present no less in Velazquez and Titian than in Bosch or Goya; no less in Keats than in Shake-

* From André Malraux's *The Voices of Silence*, trans. by Stuart Gilbert, pp. 312–334. Copyright, 1953, by Doubleday & Company, Inc. Reprinted by permission of Doubleday & Company, Inc., and Martin Secker & Warburg, Ltd.

André Malraux (1901–   ) is one of the finest contemporary French novelists, and author of many books, including his masterpiece on the arts, the three volumes, *The Psychology of Art*, from which *The Voices of Silence* was rewritten.

speare. We need only recall the admiration and the other less definable emotions conjured up in us by the first great poem we encountered; they stemmed from a revelation, not from any reasoned judgment. It is significant that a young man, swept off his feet by a stage play, cannot decide if he wishes to become an actor or a poet. The world of art is not an idealized world but *another world*; thus every artist feels himself akin to the musical composer.

In his *Baalam* of 1626 Rembrandt did not set out to represent life but to speak the language of his master, Lastmann; for him the love of painting meant the possession, by painting it, of that plastic world which fascinated him, just as the young Greco sought to possess, by imitating it, the world of the Venetians. Every artist builds up his personality on these early imitations; the painter advances from one world of forms to another world of forms, as the writer from one world of words to another, and the composer from derivative music to his own. When Rouault mentioned certain influences in an early canvas, Degas replied: "And have you ever seen anyone born by his unaided efforts?"

The pastiche is not necessarily one of a single master; it sometimes combines a teacher with one or more masters (Rembrandt in his extreme youth combined Lastmann with Elsheimer); sometimes these masters are relatively different, sometimes akin (in his early Italian canvases El Greco owed more to Venetian art than to Bassano). Occasionally a style is imitated as a whole, and, it may be, something even less than a style—the prevailing taste of a period, the sparkling intricacies of Florentine composition, the tapestry effects of the Venetians, the Expressionism of German Gothic in its last phase, the limpid color of the Impressionists, the geometry of Cubism. The Munich exhibition which, after nearly twenty years of Hitlerian aesthetic, brought together self-taught artists under the style of "The Free Painters," gave the impression of being, as a whole, a pastiche of the School of Paris, though actually no individual French master was imitated by these painters.

Whether an artist begins to paint, write, or compose early or late in life, and however effective his first works may be, always behind them lies the studio, the cathedral, the museum, the library or the concert-hall. Inasmuch as painting, though representing or suggesting three dimensions, is limited to two, any painting of a landscape is bound to approximate more closely to any other painting of a landscape than to the actual scene depicted in it. Thus the young painter has not to make a choice between his personal "vision" and his master or masters, but between certain canvases and certain other canvases. Did he not derive his vision from some other painter or painters, he would have to invent the art of painting for himself.

One of the reasons why we fail to recognize the driving force of previous art behind each work of art is that for many centuries it has been assumed that there exists a styleless, photographic kind of drawing (though we know now that even a photograph has its share of style), which serves as the basis of works possessing style, that style being something added. This I call the fallacy of a "neutral style."

Its origin is the idea that a living model can be copied without interpretation or any self-expression; actually no such literal copy has ever been made. Even in drawing this notion can be applied only to a small range of subjects: to a standing horse seen in profile, for instance, but not to a galloping horse. This theory owes much to the silhouette, and underlying it is the assumption that the basic neutral style would be a bare outline. But any such method, if strictly followed, would not lead to any form of art, but would stand in the same relation to drawing as an art as the commercial or official style of writing stands to literature.

Expression through the medium of color was confused over a long period with the representation of color; told to paint a red curtain, an art student after blocking-in the outline covers the surface thus enclosed with any red he has to hand; just as in an industrial draftsman's office metal surfaces are shown in a symbolical blue. That red, too, is in no sense expressive; but, like the symbolical blue, *a sign*. Painting recognizes no neutral forms, though it recognizes signs—the forms that an artist discovers for himself and those already discovered by other artists. A neutral style no more exists than does a neutral language; styleless pictures no more exist than do wordless thoughts. Thus the teaching of the plastic arts (apart from mere training of the hand) is nothing more than the teaching of the significant elements in a style or several styles (thus, in our own, perspective is one of these elements). Academic drawing is a rationalized style—what theosophy is to religions or Esperanto to a living tongue. The art school does not teach students to copy "nature"; but only the work of masters. Though the life-stories of great painters show us pastiches as being the starting point of their art, none tells of a transition from the art school to genius without a conflict with some previous genius. Any more than the history of art can show us a style born directly from nature, and not from a conflict with another style.

Thus the artist is born prisoner of a style—which, however, ensures his freedom from the world of appearances. But even so, we are often told, he certainly chose his masters.

This is one of those "logical illusions" so frequent in the comedy of the human understanding. That word "choice" suggests a weighing-up of comparable significances and qualities: the attitude of a buyer at a shop-counter. But have we forgotten the first contacts of our early youth with genius? We never deliberately *chose* anything; we had successive, or simultaneous, enthusiasms, often quite incompatible with each other. What young poet ever *chose* between Baudelaire and Jean Aicard (or even Théophile Gautier)? What novelist between Dostoevski and Dumas (or even Dickens)? What painter between Delacroix and Cormon (or even Decamps)? What musician between Mozart and Donizetti (or even Mendelssohn)? Tristan did not choose between Isolde and the lady beside her. Every young man's heart is a graveyard in which are inscribed the names of a thousand dead artists but whose only actual denizens are a few mighty, often antagonistic, ghosts. Permanent survival is reserved to a few great immortal figures, and men do not "choose" them; for they do not allure, they exercise an irresistible fascination.

Love is not born of consecrated eminence; nor is our love of the great works of art. And, incidentally, we still are far from having discovered the sum total of these works; we are far from appreciating the music of other parts of the world, in all its richness, at a first hearing. True, we are quick to feel at home with a new Rembrandt, but a newly found Byzantine work is slow in extricating itself from the farrago whence it has emerged. And, lastly, one sees only what one looks at; in the twelfth century, men looked at the classical bas-reliefs very perfunctorily. The sensibility of a young artist is tempered by history, which made its choice before he came on the scene—primarily by its eliminations.

The relationship between the artist and art is of the order of a vocation. And the religious vocation, when authentic, is not felt as the result of a choice, but as an answer to God's call. The painter may spend his time choosing and preferring (as he thinks), but once his attitude to art takes a definitive form much of the freedom has gone out of it.

An artist's vocation almost always dates from adolescence and usually pivots on the art of his own time. Neither for Michelangelo nor for Raphael was the art of antiquity a starting-off point; nor even for David, who began as an eighteenth-century *petit maitre*. The artist needs "living" forbears though, in periods held by their painters to be decadent, these are not always his immediate predecessors, but the last great outstanding figures. For at a certain moment of history a picture or a statue speaks a language it will never speak again: the language of its birth. Varied as was the life-story of the Parcae from their Parthenon days to their journey's end in London, none has ever heard again the message they gave men on the Acropolis. The *Smiling Angel* of Rheims is a statue whose "stiffness" increased with every century; but at its birth it was a smile incarnate, a face that had suddenly come alive—like all faces sponsoring a discovery in the field of the lifelike. Only after we had seen color films did we become conscious of the monochrome of the early cinema; when they were a novelty, the hieratic photographs of our ancestors seemed the last possible word in realism. But the compelling effect of great works of art (though not always immediate) is not limited to innovations in the field of representation; it is inherent in all forms of true creation. It was not when they set eyes on Flemish art even at its most realistic, or on Italy's freest, airiest forms, that the crowd hailed the living figure and bore it aloft in triumph; it was when they set eyes on a certain Cimabue.

Since the visible world is never merely something to be reproduced, a painter can only copy another painter—or else blaze new trails. In the field of representation he seeks for what has not yet been portrayed (a new subject, movement, light); in the realm of creation, what has not yet been created. In either case he is bound to make discoveries, whether he be a Raphael or a Rembrandt, and the note he strikes is such that those who hear it for the first time often recognize in it (as did the creator) a proclamation of the artist's conquest of the world. It is exceptional that Cimabue's *Madonna* should have been borne in triumph *by the crowd,* but every artist of genius, so long as his discoveries retain their pungency, is secretly borne in triumph by artists. In the realm of modern art Cézanne is still a king. The reason why the great artist builds his genius up on the achievement of his immediate predecessors is doubtless that the leaven of discovery had not been exhausted in their art. From Cézanne's death to Renoir's, every true painter felt himself nearer to them than to Delacroix; the admiration they inspired in him had an immediacy that was lacking to their forerunners in the art museum; their art was *alive.* Though paintings and statues make Pheidias more present to us than Caesar, Rembrandt than Louis XIV—as Shakespeare means more to us than Elizabeth and Bach than Frederick II— there lies between a living art and the art museum something of the gulf that yawns between our lives today and history. As in music and literature, so in painting a living lesser art affects us more strongly than a great art, dead.

The previous work which gives the start to every artist's vocation has usually so violent an impact that we see not only the style that has fascinated him, but the subjects, too, incorporated in the pastiche. That a thirteenth-century sculptor should want to make a *Virgin* seems self-evident; but it is less of a foregone conclusion that we should discover in far-away Japan the landscapes of Aix and Cagnes, the Harlequins that Picasso inherited from Cézanne and the guitar he brought from Barcelona. And that *motif* of a lion savaging his prey which, from Mesopotamia down to the art of the Steppes, persisted through at least three cultures—how could it have owed its permanence to a religion it so long outlived? This continuance through so many centuries of a so small number of most-favored subjects is striking evidence of the blind infatuation of every painter in his early phase. In all the vast diversity of things young artists once seemed to see nothing except a comely youth, a Virgin, some mythological scenes or Venetian fêtes, just as today the young artist sees Harlequins and apples everywhere. For what he sees is not a diversity of objects asking to be painted, but those only which the style attached to them has segregated from reality.

The man whom painting affects solely as a form of representation is not the artist but the non-artist. But the man who is profoundly moved by Rembrandt's *Flayed Ox*, by Piero della Francesca's *Adoration of the Shepherds*, by Van Gogh's *Vincent's House*—does this man see merely scenes, however striking and well executed, in these paintings? Just as a certain sequence of chords can abruptly make one aware of the world of music, thus a certain compelling balance of colors and lines comes as a revelation to one who realizes that here is a magic casement opening on another world. Not necessarily a supernal world, or a glorified one; but a world different in kind from that of reality.

For thence it is that art is born: from the lure of the elusive, the inapprehensible, and a refusal to copy appearances; from a desire to wrest forms from the real world to which man is subject and to make them enter into a world of which he is the ruler. The artist knows that his domination is at best precarious, that its progress will be limited, yet he is conscious— passionately at first, then as the experience repeats itself, with diminishing intensity—of embarking on a vast adventure. The primordial impulse may have been no more than a craving to paint. Yet, whatever are the gifts revealed in his first attempts and whatever form his apprenticeship may take, he knows that he is starting a journey towards an unknown land, that this first stage of it has no importance, and that he is "bound to get somewhere."

Art has its impotents and its imposters—if fewer than in the field of love. As in the case of love its nature is often confused with the pleasure it may give; but, like love, it is not itself a pleasure but a passion, and involves a break-away from the world's values in favor of a value of its own, obsessive and all-powerful. The artist has need of others who share his passion and he can live fully only in their company. He is like Donatello who, as a legend tells us, struggled to prolong his death agony, so that his friends might have time to replace the tawdry crucifix on his breast with one of Brunelleschi's.

Like every conversion, the discovery of art is a rupture of an earlier relationship between man and the world, and it has the far-reaching intensity of what psychologists call "affects." Creators and connoisseurs, all those for whom art exists (in other words, who are as responsive to the forms it creates as to the most emotive mortal forms) share a faith in an immanent power peculiar to man. They devalorize reality, just as the Christian faith—and indeed every religious system—devalorizes it. Also, like the Christians, they devalorize it by their faith in a privileged estate, and a hope that man (and not chaos) contains within him the source of his eternity.

This immanent power of art can be equated to the fact that most works of the past usually affect us *through their styles*. The tenacious but mistaken belief that art is a means of representation and copies nature in nature's style and not in one of its own, and the equally mistaken belief that a "neutral" style exists—both of which beliefs were fostered by the long supremacy of the art of antiquity—gave rise to the view that styles are, as it were, successive varieties of ornament added to an immutable substratum, adjuncts and nothing more. Yet it is clear that the woman's body at Pergamum is prisoned within the Hellenistic arabesque, as was the Roman bust within the conventions of the Roman theater. After that great moment of art history when for the first time man arose, rejoicing in his strength, in the straight folds of the Auriga, then in the parallel lines of the Panathenaic frieze and the horsemen of the Acropolis, the "classical" sculptors replaced the hieratic line of Egyptian statuary by their broad shell-like curves and a facile majesty reminiscent of the trophy. Thus we see that what once ranked as absolute beauty now strikes us as the style, followed by the stylization, of the classical age. Both, like those of Byzantium, are the expression of a particular interpretation of the world—an interpretation calling for a special way of seeing before being enriched by it. When Claude Lorrain took sunset as his theme, what he saw in it was not so much the intrusion of the fleeting moment into the classical landscape as a perfect expression, in Time, of the embellished world he was aspiring to create; his sunset is not a fleeting moment but an ideal aspect of the universe like certain stormy skies of the Venetians, a transcendent hour standing to ordinary daylight as an idealized face stands to its ordinary aspect. For him it was not a model to be copied, but an accompaniment; as mist is to the lay-out of the Sung landscapists, and as is the schematic death's-head to so many Pre-Columbian figures. A style is not merely an idiom or mannerism; it becomes these only when, ceasing to be a conquest, it settles down into a convention. The tastes of a period are mannerisms which follow those of styles or may exist without them; but Romanesque was not a medieval "modern style," it illustrated a special attitude towards the cosmos; indeed every true style is the scaling-down to our human perspective of that eternal flux on whose mysterious rhythms we are borne ineluctably, in a never-ceasing drift of stars. Apollo, Prometheus—or Saturn; Aphrodite, or Ishtar; a resurrection of the flesh, or the Dance of Death. Once the Dance of Death becomes more than an allegory, it throws light on Northern Europe of the fifteenth century in the same way as the Panathenaic frieze throws light on the Acropolis. It has its own idiom, its own color. (Only imagine a Dance of Death treated in the style of Raphael, Fragonard or Renoir!) Its dancing throng points the way towards the *Christ in Prayer,* in the same sense that the processions of ancient Greece converged on the *Auriga* and the *"Apollo of the Tiber."*

Whatever the artist himself may say on the matter, never does he let himself be mastered by the outside world; always he subdues it to something he puts in its stead. Indeed this will to transform is inherent in his artistic personality. They are simpletons, those "theoreticians of the fruit-bowl" as we may call them, who refuse to see that the still life is a product not of primitive cultures but of advanced cultures; that our painters are not painters of fruit but of those modern still lifes, which follow each other like so many ikons, truculent or timid as the case may be. Thus, too, portraits, during those periods when the face was not yet treated as a still life, qualified as works of art in so far as they revealed or magnified what began where the mere reproduction of features ended. Our attitude towards an object varies according to the function we assign to it; wood can mean a tree, a fetish or a plank. The depiction of living forms begins not so much with the artist's submission to his model as with his domination of the model— with the expressive sign. Thus the sexual triangles imposed on the bodies of Cretan and Mesopotamian statuettes symbolize fecundity but do not represent it. For the visible world is not only a profusion of forms, it is a profusion of significances; yet as a whole it signifies nothing, for it signifies everything. Life is stronger than man by reason of its multiplicity and total independence of his will, and because what we regard both as chaos and as fatality are implicit in it; but, taken individually, each form of life is weaker than man, since no living form in itself *signifies* life. We may be sure that the ancient Egyptian's feeling of oneness with eternity was indicated less by his features and demeanor than by the statues that have come down to us. And though the world is stronger than man, the significance of the world is as strong as the world itself; a mason at work on Notre-Dame could, as a living, moving being, defy the sculptor's art—yet, though he was alive, he was not "Gothic."

Thus styles are *significations,* they impose a *meaning* on visual experience; though often we find them conflicting with each other, passing away and superseded, always we see them replacing the uncharted scheme of things by the coherence they enforce on all they "represent." However complex, however lawless an art may claim to be—even the art of a Van Gogh or a Rimbaud—it stands for unity as against the chaos of appearances; and when time has passed and it has borne fruit, this becomes apparent. Every style, in fact, creates its own universe by selecting and incorporating such elements of reality as enable the artist to focus the shape of things on some essential part of man.

The *Last Judgment* might be taken as a symbol of this significance implicit in all styles. In the Florentine "Christs" that Michelangelo had carved before this, there had not been a hint of that strange colossal figure whose maledictory gesture consigns to the outer darkness those wretched sinners wrested from the brief darkness of the tomb. When in one of his last works (in the Cathedral of Orvieto) Fra Angelico had portrayed that gesture, it was still charged with benediction and seemed to be directed towards the attendant angels. Its transformation is one of the most significant transformations in the whole history of art. In Michelangelo's fresco the Damned press forward towards that implacable Judge against whom crouches the Virgin of Pity; everything—even the light enveloping Christ's Herculean torso, twice as large as that accepted by the conventions of the day—conspires to make the surging throng of the Valley of Jehoshaphat resemble the triumphal progress of an *imperator*. If there be little of Jesus in the central figure, it is surely God incarnate.

How small a part, indeed, is played by Jesus in the Bible of the Sistine! The whole ceiling announced his coming, yet when at length He appears above the altar (almost thirty years later) a change has intervened. In this heroic threnody, unique in the world's art, there is no trace of the quivering movement Rembrandt's compassion imparts to the open hands of his Christ and even to the menacing hands of his prophets; for Rembrandt sponsors the whole Bible. Whereas in Michelangelo's vision of the last end of the human adventure what account is taken of the Incarnation? His all-conquering Messiah was not born in a stable, was never mocked and buffeted, succored no travelers on the Way to Emmaus, nor was He crucified between two thieves. Remote indeed is that divine humility which He shared with the saints who now escort Him, like a terrified bodyguard! The trumpets of Apocalypse have sounded, every wall has fallen, the immemorial lights twinkling on earth above the Christchild's crib have been put out, and with them the Star in the East—and Giotto's genius. Those friendly, understanding beasts beside the crib are now mere insensate animals. The incarnation has become an ordeal fraught with terrors and a time of humiliation.

Gothic Judgment Days—at Rheims and Bourges, for instance—had often been resurrections; Michelangelo's is a doomsday. His trembling saints are not the Blessed, and the composition of his fresco is not so much integrated around Christ (like Tintoretto's *Paradise*) as skilfully disintegrated by the great void down which are cataracting—without filling it—the Damned. The compelling influence exerted then and still exercised by Michelangelo's great work has been attributed to the nudes that figure in it; indeed the multitude of naked bodies caused offense and three popes gave orders for the destruction of *The Last Judgment*. This seems surprising when we remember that the Church tolerated the nude under certain circumstances: before the Fall and after death—Eve and the resuscitated bodies. This was the judicious answer given by the Inquisition of Venice when, summoned before them to justify his "profane" treatment of *The Last Supper*, Veronese fell back on the authority of Michelangelo to justify his harmless dogs. Surprising, too, is the fact that, during two centuries, charges of indecency were leveled against *The Last Judgment* (which had been bowdlerized into decorum a month before the artist's death); it was feared that this throng of burly Titans might evoke ribald comments from a populace that was being edified by Bernini's statues. Yet it is surely obvious that *The Last Judgment* is one of the world's least sensuous works of art. The truth is that Michelangelo's detractors, though unconscious of the true reasons for their antipathy, were not mistaken when they saw in this fresco a hostile work.

For these nudes are not idealized, they are magnified. Evil, for Michelangelo, is not a "deficiency," the negative of virtue, and his hell is not made of mud. The human dust that eddies in the whirlwind of the *Judgment* still forms part of the huge shadow cast by Lucifer; this is the Last Day, and also the last end of Satan, henceforth entombed forever in the kingdom of the dead. This Michelangelo expressed in terms of an art that foreshadowed Milton and Hugo in his last phase; and it was by way of man that he expressed it. But Michelangelo's "man" in this fresco (in which he no more says the last word of his art than Shakespeare does of his, in *Macbeth*) is quite other than Raphael's "man," who has made his peace with the universe; he is in the toils of a dilemma, a mystery without solution. Raphael's man is saved by the New Treatment, Michelangelo's aggrandized by the Old; his significance is heightened, he is forced into becoming the loftiest expression of his own tragedy, an echo of the drama of the universe. He is of heroic stature, not in so far as he dominates his situation, but in so far as he embodies in himself its harrowing grandeur. Art for Michelangelo is a means of revelation; he gives his own likeness to the hideous, ravaged visage St. Bartholomew displays, not to Christ, but to the spectator. Nothing brings out more clearly the new significance that genius can impose on a set theme than a comparison of the Gothic irony of Signorelli's skeletons with those deep organ-notes which in the lower portion of the fresco stress the polyphonic majesty of Michelangelo's vision: Death contemplated by Man, whose gaze neither the panic-stricken crowd nor the celestial Judge can avert from the fascination exercised by that inexorable face.

A Judge, nevertheless, such as had never before been seen, in whom not only the face but the significance of Christ was changed, and, as a result, the significance of the faces around Him. Though these nudes are so much like those on the Sistine ceiling and these faces like those of the Prophets, they acquire another meaning, because they follow the coming of Christ instead of announcing it. We can hardly conceive of this Judge in Israel figuring in *The Damned* of Signorelli with its devils with pointed wings and its knights borrowed from the Golden Legend; nor can we see how the nudes in the cathedrals or even the poor human herd of Orvieto could have been grouped around Him. Gothic nudes are men stripped of their garments—one can almost see them shivering with cold—and even in the Romanesque art of Autun the Damned have the look of punished children. Michelangelo's Damned are convulsed but not cowed by their terror, and that shattering gesture which casts them forth has come, by way of Angelico, from the remotest past; it is the same gesture as that which overwhelmed the revolting angels.

The fall of Satan and his host was to figure in front of *The Last Judgment*. But it was not needed; it was there already. Michelangelo expunged from Christendom a legendary lore that had held its ground for many centuries; his Christ is not a vanquisher of dragons but of men, men likewise of heroic stature by reason of their very damnation, a surging mass of Promethean rebels, suffering but unsubdued. What those who saw them were perturbed by in these nudes—petrified, like the woman in *The Deluge*, despite their writhings—was not their sensuality, for they had none (indeed Signorelli had gone further in this direction), but the epic note imparted to the doctrine of Augustine. "Man is so foully soiled by sin that his very love, were it not for grace, would befoul God Himself." Here in his estrangement from God, his reprobation, man attains sublimity; he is ennobled, not saved. When the fresco was unveiled the Pope, we are told, fell on his knees and prayed. At the same moment, very likely, Luther was thinking out his message. . . . Only one hope of salvation from the *Judgment* remained, and that was grace.

The effects of this new presentation of Christ were far-reaching; all subsequent portrayals of Him bear traces of it. Indeed these forms, under the name of Baroque, spread all over Europe. But though they involved a break-up of the forms on which, to begin with, Michelangelo had relied; though they ignored Donatello and Verrocchio no less than the lessons of Ghirlandaio's frescoes, and though the peremptory arm of Christ effaced the arm suavely portrayed by Fra Angelico—they kept the spacious settings of the earlier art. Although Michelangelo's genius had wholly transformed the Gothic treatment of the large-scale scene, Tintoretto's sumptuous vision retained not a little of it, but his color gave it a very different accent and transmuted Gothic emotivity into the chromatic splendors of the *Paradise* in the Doge's Palace. Then (after the dazzling but puerile *Last Judgment* of Rubens) there came a time when the Sistine *Dies Irae* confronted a Roman public so completely estranged from the voice of Augustine that they could not even hear it, and presently when the ruined Palace had come to mean no more than an obsolete *décor* to men who feasted their eyes on the luxuriance of Jesuit art, the Hebrew prophets, denizens of the Amsterdam ghetto, were to conjure up a new meaning of the world in the pregnant dusk of Rembrandt's studio.

Now that we are no longer blinded by that "lifelike" representation so tenaciously and successfully sought after during a few centuries of Mediterranean art, and now that our retrospect on art covers several thousand years, we are coming to perceive that while representation may be accessory to a style, style is never a means of representation. The impressionism of the Sung artists aimed at suggesting by a subtle use of the ephemeral that eternity in which man is swallowed up, as his gaze loses itself in the mist that blurs the landscape. It is an art of the moment, but of an eternal moment; whereas our modern Impressionists, in their concentration on the fleeting moment, aimed at giving individual man his maximum importance —and may not this have been a happy device of painting to enable Renoir to win his freedom and Matisse to fulfil himself? We see Christian art gathering all the dead branches it lays hands on into a single burning bush and Gandhara imprinting the cast of Buddhism on the faces of classical antiquity, just as Michelangelo sublimates them into his Christ, and Rembrandt illuminates with his vision of Christ even the faces of the beggar and the woman sweeping the floor. Every great style of the past impresses us as being a special interpretation of the world, but this collective conquest is obviously a sum total of the individual conquests that have gone to its making. Always these are victories over forms, achieved by means of forms, they are not the allegorical expression of some ideology. *The Last Judgment* was the outcome of a meditation on figures, and not a declaration of faith. Once we realize how all-important is the significance of styles, we understand why every artist of genius—whether like Gauguin and Cézanne he makes himself a recluse, or like Van Gogh a missionary, or like young Tintoretto exhibits his canvases in a booth on the Rialto—becomes a transformer of the meaning of the world, which he masters by reducing it to forms he has selected or invented, just as the philosopher reduces it to concepts and the physicist to laws. And he attains this mastery not through his visual experience of the world itself, but by a victory over one of the forms of an immediate predecessor that he has taken over and transmuted in the crucible of genius.

SELECTED BIBLIOGRAPHY

1. Meyer Shapiro, "Style" in A. Kroeber (ed.), *Anthropology Today*, University of Chicago Press, 1953. A superb summary of the meanings and history of style as an aesthetic concept.
2. Bernhard Berenson, *Aesthetics and History*, esp. pp. 160-165 of the Anchor paperback edition.
3. Erwin Panofsky, *Meaning in the Visual Arts*, Doubleday Anchor, 1955, Chaps. I-II.
4. Heinrich Wölfflin, *Principles of Art History*, Dover Publications, 1954. A classic in the area of style analysis.
5. Paul Zucker, *Styles in Painting*, The Viking Press, 1950, esp. Ch. I, on the meaning of style as a historical and aesthetic category.

INTENTION

In 1864, the great French philosopher-critic, Taine, wrote in his *Philosophy of Art* ". . . In order to comprehend a work of art, an artist, or a group of artists, we must clearly comprehend the general social and intellectual conditions of the times to which they belong."

Taine brought to a focus what have been variously called the intentional or extrinsic approaches to art. Since his time (but even before), theorists have asked whether historical, sociological, biographical, or ideational data are relevant to our understanding and evaluation of art. Freudians, Marxists, and others insist on the relevancy of such data. Many disagree: intentions, that is, what the artist intended, including *all* the causal influences on him, are never relevant; only the work itself is needed for a full comprehension of it. One extreme statement of the total repudiation of intentions is implied by Clive Bell in his famous injunction, "To appreciate a work of art we need bring with us nothing from life, no knowledge of its ideas and affairs, no familiarity with its emotions" (*Art*, p. 25). A more reasoned argument against the relevancy of intentions, at least in the evaluation of art, is that of our first selection, "The Intentional Fallacy," by W. K. Wimsatt and M. C. Beardsley. The second selection is one among many excellent counter-arguments, a brief but solid piece from an essay by Erwin Panofsky on the function of art history in the understanding and evaluation of art. The third essay, by Henry David Aiken, is an attempt to reveal the cluster of problems which "the problem of intention" really is.

William K. Wimsatt and Monroe C. Beardsley

THE INTENTIONAL FALLACY *

The claim of the author's "intention" upon the critic's judgment has been challenged in a number of recent discussions, notably in the debate entitled *The Personal Heresy*, between Professors Lewis and Tillyard. But it seems doubtful if this claim and most of its romantic corollaries are as yet subject to any widespread questioning. The present writers, in a short article entitled "Intention" for a *Dictionary*[1] of literary criticism, raised the issue but were unable to pursue its implications at any length. We argued that the design or intention of the author is neither available nor desirable as a standard for judging the success of a work of literary art, and it seems to us that this is a principle which goes deep into some differences in the history of critical attitudes. It is a principle which accepted or rejected points to the polar opposites of classical "imitation" and romantic expression. It entails many specific truths about inspiration, authenticity, biography, literary history and scholarship, and about some trends of contemporary poetry, especially its allusiveness. There is hardly a problem of literary criticism in which the critic's approach will not be qualified by his view of "intention."

"Intention," as we shall use the term, corresponds to *what he intended* in a formula which more or less explicitly has had wide acceptance. "In order to judge the poet's performance, we must know *what he intended.*" Intention is design or plan in the author's mind. Intention has obvious affinities for the author's attitude toward his work, the way he felt, what made him write.

We begin our discussion with a series of propositions summarized and abstracted to a degree where they seem to us axiomatic.

1) A poem does not come into existence by accident. The words of a poem, as Professor Stoll has remarked, come out of a head, not out of a hat. Yet to insist on the designing intellect as a *cause* of a poem is not to grant the design or intention as a *standard* by which the critic is to judge the worth of the poet's performance.

* From William Wimsatt's and Monroe Beardsley's "The Intentional Fallacy," in *The Verbal Icon*, Ch. I. Copyright, 1954, by The University of Kentucky Press. Reprinted by permission of The University of Kentucky Press and the authors.

William K. Wimsatt (1907–   ) is Professor of English at Yale University and author of many critical articles; Monroe C. Beardsley (1915–   ) is Professor of Philosophy at Swarthmore College and has written much on logic and aesthetics.

[1] *Dictionary of World Literature*, Joseph T. Shipley, ed. (New York, 1942), 326–29.

2) One must ask how a critic expects to get an answer to the question about intention. How is he to find out what the poet tried to do? If the poet succeeded in doing it, then the poem itself shows what he was trying to do. And if the poet did not succeed, then the poem is not adequate evidence, and the critic must go outside the poem—for evidence of an intention that did not become effective in the poem. "Only one *caveat* must be borne in mind," says an eminent intentionalist[2] in a moment when his theory repudiates itself; "the poet's aim must be judged at the moment of the creative act, that is to say, by the art of the poem itself."

3) Judging a poem is like judging a pudding or a machine. One demands that it work. It is only because an artifact works that we infer the intention of an artificer. "A poem should not mean but be." A poem can *be* only through its *meaning*—since its medium is words—yet it *is*, simply *is*, in the sense that we have no excuse for inquiring what part is intended or meant. Poetry is a feat of style by which a complex of meaning is handled all at once. Poetry succeeds because all or most of what is said or implied is relevant; what is irrevelant has been excluded, like lumps from pudding and "bugs" from machinery. In this respect poetry differs from practical messages, which are successful if and only if we correctly infer the intention. They are more abstract than poetry.

4) The meaning of a poem may certainly be a personal one, in the sense that a poem expresses a personality or state of soul rather than a physical object like an apple. But even a short lyric poem is dramatic, the response of a speaker (no matter how abstractly conceived) to a situation (no matter how universalized). We ought to impute the thoughts and attitudes of the poem immediately to the dramatic *speaker*, and if to the author at all, only by an act of biographical inference.

5) There is a sense in which an author, by revision, may better achieve his original intention. But it is a very abstract sense. He intended to write a better work, or a better work of a certain kind, and now has done it. But it follows that his former concrete intention was not his intention. "He's the man we were in search of, that's true," says Hardy's rustic constable, "and yet he's not the man we were in search of. For the man we were in search of was not the man we wanted."

"Is not a critic," asks Professor Stoll, "a judge, who does not explore his own consciousness, but determines the author's meaning or intention, as if the poem were a will, a contract, or the constitution? The poem is not the critic's own." He has accurately diagnosed two forms of irresponsibility, one

---

[2] J. E. Spingarn, "The New Criticism," in *Criticism in America* (New York, 1924), 24–25.

of which he prefers. Our view is yet different. The poem is not the critic's own and not the author's (it is detached from the author at birth and goes about the world beyond his power to intend about it or control it). The poem belongs to the public. It is embodied in language, the peculiar possession of the public, and it is about the human being, an object of public knowledge. What is said about the poem is subject to the same scrutiny as any statement in linguistics or in the general science of psychology.

A critic of our *Dictionary* article, Ananda K. Coomaraswamy, has argued[3] that there are two kinds of inquiry about a work of art: (1) whether the artist achieved his intentions; (2) whether the work of art "ought ever to have been undertaken at all" and so "whether it is worth preserving." Number (2), Coomaraswamy maintains, is not "criticism of any work of art *qua* work of art," but is rather moral criticism; number (1) is artistic criticism. But we maintain that (2) need not be moral criticism: that there is another way of deciding whether works of art are worth preserving and whether, in a sense, they "ought" to have been undertaken, and this is the way of objective criticism of works of art as such, the way which enables us to distinguish between a skillful murder and a skillful poem. A skillful murder is an example which Coomaraswamy uses, and in his system the difference between the murder and the poem is simply a "moral" one, not an "artistic" one, since each if carried out according to plan is "artistically" successful. We maintain that (2) is an inquiry of more worth than (1), and since (2) and not (1) is capable of distinguishing poetry from murder, the name "artistic criticism" is properly given to (2).

II

It is not so much a historical statement as a definition to say that the intentional fallacy is a romantic one. When a rhetorician of the first century A.D. writes: "Sublimity is the echo of a great soul," or when he tells us that "Homer enters into the sublime actions of his heroes" and "shares the full inspiration of the combat," we shall not be surprised to find this rhetorician considered as a distant harbinger of romanticism and greeted in the warmest terms by Saintsbury. One may wish to argue whether Longinus should be called romantic, but there can hardly be a doubt that in one important way he is.

Goethe's three questions for "constructive criticism" are "What did the author set out to do? Was his plan reasonable and sensible, and how far did he succeed in carrying it out?" If one leaves out the middle question, one

[3] Ananda K. Coomaraswamy, "Intention," in *American Bookman*, I (1944), 41–48.

has in effect the system of Croce—the culmination and crowning philosophic expression of romanticism. The beautiful is the successful intuition-expression, and the ugly is the unsuccessful; the intuition or private part of art is *the* aesthetic fact, and the medium or public part is not the subject of aesthetic at all. The Madonna of Cimabue is still in the Church of Santa Maria Novella; but does she speak to the visitor of to-day as to the Florentines of the thirteenth century?

> *Historical interpretation* labours . . . to reintegrate in us the psychological conditions which have changed in the course of history. It . . . enables us to see a work of art (a physical object) as its *author saw it* in the moment of production.[4]

The first italics are Croce's, the second ours. The upshot of Croce's system is an ambiguous emphasis on history. With such passages as a point of departure a critic may write a nice analysis of the meaning or "spirit" of a play by Shakespeare or Corneille—a process that involves close historical study but remains aesthetic criticism—or he may, with equal plausibility, produce an essay in sociology, biography, or other kinds of nonaesthetic history.

III

> I went to the poets; tragic, dithyrambic, and all sorts. . . . I took them some of the most elaborate passages in their own writings, and asked what was the meaning of them. . . . Will you believe me? . . . there is hardly a person present who would not have talked better about their poetry than they did themselves. Then I knew that not by wisdom do poets write poetry, but by a sort of genius and inspiration.

That reiterated mistrust of the poets which we hear from Socrates may have been part of a rigorously ascetic view in which we hardly wish to participate, yet Plato's Socrates saw a truth about the poetic mind which the world no longer commonly sees—so much criticism, and that the most inspirational and most affectionately remembered, has proceeded from the poets themselves.

Certainly the poets have had something to say that the critic and professor could not say; their message has been more exciting: that poetry

---

[4] It is true that Croce himself in his *Ariosto, Shakespeare and Corneille* (London, 1920), chap. VII, "The Practical Personality and the Poetical Personality," and in his *Defence of Poetry* (Oxford, 1933), 24, and elsewhere, early and late, has delivered telling attacks on emotive geneticism, but the main drive of the *Aesthetic* is surely toward a kind of cognitive intentionalism.

should come as naturally as leaves to a tree, that poetry is the lava of the imagination, or that it is emotion recollected in tranquillity. But it is necessary that we realize the character and authority of such testimony. There is only a fine shade of difference between such expressions and a kind of earnest advice that authors often give. Thus Edward Young, Carlyle, Walter Pater:

> I know two golden rules from *ethics,* which are no less golden in *Composition,* than in life. 1. *Know thyself;* 2dly, *Reverence thyself.*
> This is the grand secret for finding readers and retaining them: let him who would move and convince others, be first moved and convinced himself. Horace's rule, *si vis me flere,* is applicable in a wider sense than the literal one. To every poet, to every writer, we might say: Be true, if you would be believed.
> Truth! there can be no merit, no craft at all, without that. And further, all beauty is in the long run only *fineness* of truth, or what we call expression, the finer accommodation of speech to that vision within.

And Housman's little handbook to the poetic mind yields this illustration:

> Having drunk a pint of beer at luncheon—beer is a sedative to the brain, and my afternoons are the least intellectual portion of my life—I would go out for a walk of two or three hours. As I went along, thinking of nothing in particular, only looking at things around me and following the progress of the seasons, there would flow into my mind, with sudden and unaccountable emotion, sometimes a line or two of verse, sometimes a whole stanza at once.

This is the logical terminus of the series already quoted. Here is a confession of how poems were written which would do as a definition of poetry just as well as "emotion recollected in tranquillity"—and which the young poet might equally well take to heart as a practical rule. Drink a pint of beer, relax, go walking, think on nothing in particular, look at things, surrender yourself to yourself, search for the truth in your own soul, listen to the sound of your own inside voice, discover and express the *vraie vérité.*

It is probably true that all this is excellent advice for poets. The young imagination fired by Wordsworth and Carlyle is probably closer to the verge of producing a poem than the mind of the student who has been sobered by Aristotle or Richards. The art of inspiring poets, or at least of inciting something like poetry in young persons, has probably gone further in our day than ever before. Books of creative writing such as those issued

from the Lincoln School are interesting evidence of what a child can do.[5]
All this, however, would appear to belong to an art separate from criticism
—to a psychological discipline, a system of self-development, a yoga, which
the young poet perhaps does well to notice, but which is something different
from the public art of evaluating poems.

Coleridge and Arnold were better critics than most poets have been,
and if the critical tendency dried up the poetry in Arnold and perhaps in
Coleridge, it is not inconsistent with our argument, which is that judgment
of poems is different from the art of producing them. Coleridge has given us
the classic "anodyne" story, and tells what he can about the genesis of a
poem which he calls a "psychological curiosity," but his definitions of poetry
and of the poetic quality "imagination" are to be found elsewhere and in
quite other terms.

It would be convenient if the passwords of the intentional school,
"sincerity," "fidelity," "spontaneity," "authenticity," "genuineness," "originality," could be equated with terms such as "integrity," "relevance," "unity,"
"function," "maturity," "subtlety," "adequacy," and other more precise terms
of evaluation—in short, if "expression" always meant aesthetic achievement.
But this is not so.

"Aesthetic" art, says Professor Curt Ducasse, an ingenious theorist of
expression, is the conscious objectification of feelings, in which an intrinsic
part is the critical moment. The artist corrects the objectification when it
is not adequate. But this may mean that the earlier attempt was not successful
in objectifying the self, or "it may also mean that it was a successful objectification of a self which, when it confronted us clearly, we disowned and
repudiated in favor of another."[6] What is the standard by which we disown
or accept the self? Professor Ducasse does not say. Whatever it may be,
however, this standard is an element in the definition of art which will not
reduce to terms of objectification. The evaluation of the work of art remains
public; the work is measured against something outside the author.

IV

There is criticism of poetry and there is author psychology, which when
applied to the present or future takes the form of inspirational promotion;

---

[5] See Hughes Mearns, *Creative Youth* (Garden City, 1925), esp. 10, 27–29. The technique of inspiring poems has apparently been outdone more recently by the study of
inspiration in successful poets and other artists. See, for instance, Rosamond E. M.
Harding, *An Anatomy of Inspiration* (Cambridge, 1940); Julius Portnoy, *A Psychology
of Art Creation* (Philadelphia, 1942); Rudolf Arnheim and others, *Poets at Work* (New
York, 1947); Phyllis Bartlett, *Poems in Process* (New York, 1951); Brewster Ghiselin
(ed.), *The Creative Process: A Symposium* (Berkeley and Los Angeles, 1952).

[6] Curt Ducasse, *The Philosophy of Art* (New York, 1929), 116.

but author psychology can be historical too, and then we have literary biography, a legitimate and attractive study in itself, one approach, as Professor Tillyard would argue, to personality, the poem being only a parallel approach. Certainly it need not be with a derogatory purpose that one points out personal studies, as distinct from poetic studies, in the realm of literary scholarship. Yet there is danger of confusing personal and poetic studies; and there is the fault of writing the personal as if it were poetic.

There is a difference between internal and external evidence for the meaning of a poem. And the paradox is only verbal and superficial that what is (1) internal is also public: it is discovered through the semantics and syntax of a poem, through our habitual knowledge of the language, through grammars, dictionaries, and all the literature which is the source of dictionaries, in general through all that makes a language and culture; while what is (2) external is private or idiosyncratic; not a part of the work as a linguistic fact: it consists of revelations (in journals, for example, or letters or reported conversations) about how or why the poet wrote the poem—to what lady, while sitting on what lawn, or at the death of what friend or brother. There is (3) an intermediate kind of evidence about the character of the author or about private or semiprivate meanings attached to words or topics by an author or by a coterie of which he is a member. The meaning of words is the history of words, and the biography of an author, his use of a word, and the associations which the word had for *him*, are part of the word's history and meaning.[7] But the three types of evidence, especially (2) and (3), shade into one another so subtly that it is not always easy to draw a line between examples, and hence arises the difficulty for criticism. The use of biographical evidence need not involve intentionalism, because while it may be evidence of what the author intended, it may also be evidence of the meaning of his words and the dramatic character of his utterance. On the other hand, it may not be all this. And a critic who is concerned with evidence of type (1) and moderately with that of type (3) will in the long run produce a different sort of comment from that of the critic who is concerned with (2) and with (3) where it shades into (2).

The whole glittering parade of Professor Lowes' *Road to Xanadu*, for instance, runs along the border between types (2) and (3) or boldly traverses the romantic region of (2). " 'Kubla Khan,' " says Professor Lowes, "is the fabric of a vision, but every image that rose up in its weaving had passed that way before. And it would seem that there is nothing haphazard or fortuitous in their return." This is not quite clear—not even when Pro-

---

[7] And the history of words *after* a poem is written may contribute meanings which if relevant to the original pattern should not be ruled out by a scruple about intention.

fessor Lowes explains that there were clusters of associations, like hooked atoms, which were drawn into complex relation with other clusters in the deep well of Coleridge's memory, and which then coalesced and issued forth as poems. If there was nothing "haphazard or fortuitous" in the way the images returned to the surface, that may mean (1) that Coleridge could not produce what he did not have, that he was limited in his creation by what he had read or otherwise experienced, or (2) that having received certain clusters of associations, he was bound to return them in just the way he did, and that the value of the poem may be described in terms of the experiences on which he had to draw. The latter pair of propositions (a sort of Hartleyan associationism which Coleridge himself repudiated in the *Biographia*) may not be assented to. There were certainly other combinations, other poems, worse or better, that might have been written by men who had read Bartram and Purchas and Bruce and Milton. And this will be true no matter how many times we are able to add to the brilliant complex of Coleridge's reading. In certain flourishes (such as the sentence we have quoted) and in chapter headings like "The Shaping Spirit," "The Magical Synthesis," "Imagination Creatrix," it may be that Professor Lowes pretends to say more about the actual poems than he does. There is a certain deceptive variation in these fancy chapter titles; one expects to pass on to a new stage in the argument, and one finds—more and more sources, more and more about "the streamy nature of association."[8]

"Wohin der Weg?" quotes Professor Lowes for the motto of his book. "Kein Weg! Ins Unbetretene." Precisely because the way is *unbetreten*, we should say, it leads away from the poem. Bartram's *Travels* contains a good deal of the history of certain words and of certain romantic Floridian conceptions that appear in "Kubla Khan." And a good deal of that history has passed and was then passing into the very stuff of our language. Perhaps a peson who has read Bartram appreciates the poem more than one who has not. Or, by looking up the vocabulary of "Kubla Khan" in the *Oxford English Dictionary*, or by reading some of the other books there quoted, a person may know the poem better. But it would seem to pertain little to the poem to know that *Coleridge* had read Bartram. There is a gross body of life, of sensory and mental experience, which lies behind and in some sense causes every poem, but can never be and need not be known in the verbal and hence intellectual composition which is the poem. For all the objects of our manifold experience, for every unity, there is an action of

[8] Chaps. VIII, "The Pattern," and XVI, "The Known and Familiar Landscape," will be found of most help to the student of the poem.

the mind which cuts off roots, melts away context—or indeed we should never have objects or ideas or anything to talk about.

It is probable that there is nothing in Professor Lowes' vast book which could detract from anyone's appreciation of either *The Ancient Mariner* or "Kubla Khan." We next present a case where preoccupation with evidence of type (3) has gone so far as to distort a critic's view of a poem (yet a case not so obvious as those that abound in our critical journals).

In a well known poem by John Donne appears this quatrain:

> Moving of th' earth brings harmes and feares,
>   Men reckon what it did and meant,
> But trepidation of the spheares,
>   Though greater farre, is innocent.

A recent critic in an elaborate treatment of Donne's learning has written of this quatrain as follows:

> He touches the emotional pulse of the situation by a skillful allusion to the new and the old astronomy. . . . Of the new astronomy, the "moving of the earth" is the most radical principle; of the old, the "trepidation of the spheres" is the motion of the greatest complexity. . . . The poet must exhort his love to quietness and calm upon his departure; and for this purpose the figure based upon the latter motion (trepidation), long absorbed into the traditional astronomy, fittingly suggests the tension of the moment without arousing the "harmes and feares" implicit in the figure of the moving earth.[9]

The argument is plausible and rests on a well substantiated thesis that Donne was deeply interested in the new astronomy and its repercussions in the theological realm. In various works Donne shows his familiarity with Kepler's *De Stella Nova,* with Galileo's *Siderius Nuncius,* with William Gilbert's *De Magnete,* and with Clavius' commentary on the *De Sphaera* of Sacrobosco. He refers to the new science in his Sermon at Paul's Cross and in a letter to Sir Henry Goodyer. In *The First Anniversary* he says the "new philosophy calls all in doubt." In the *Elegy on Prince Henry* he says that the "least moving of the center" makes "the world to shake."

It is difficult to answer argument like this, and impossible to answer it with evidence of like nature. There is no reason why Donne might not have written a stanza in which the two kinds of celestial motion stood for two sorts of emotion at parting. And if we become full of astronomical ideas and see Donne only against the background of the new science, we may

[9] Charles M. Coffin, *John Donne and the New Philosophy* (New York, 1927), 97–98.

believe that he did. But the text itself remains to be dealt with, the analyzable vehicle of a complicated metaphor. And one may observe: (1) that the movement of the earth according to the Copernican theory is a celestial motion, smooth and regular, and while it might cause religious or philosophic fears, it could not be associated with the crudity and earthiness of the kind of commotion which the speaker in the poem wishes to discourage; (2) that there is another moving of the earth, an earthquake, which has just these qualities and is to be associated with the tear-floods and sigh-tempests of the second stanza of the poem; (3) that "trepidation" is an appropriate opposite of earthquake, because each is a shaking or vibratory motion; and "trepidation of the spheres" is "greater far" than an earthquake, but not much greater (if two such motions can be compared as to greatness) than the annual motion of the earth; (4) that reckoning what it "did and meant" shows that the event has passed, like an earthquake, not like the incessant celestial movement of the earth. Perhaps a knowledge of Donne's interest in the new science may add another shade of meaning, an overtone to the stanza in question, though to say even this runs against the words. To make the geocentric and heliocentric antithesis the core of the metaphor is to disregard the English language, to prefer private evidence to public, external to internal.

V

If the distinction between kinds of evidence has implications for the historical critic, it has them no less for the contemporary poet and his critic. Or, since every rule for a poet is but another side of a judgment by a critic, and since the past is the realm of the scholar and critic, and the future and present that of the poet and the critical leaders of taste, we may say that the problems arising in literary scholarship from the intentional fallacy are matched by others which arise in the world of progressive experiment.

The question of "allusiveness," for example, as acutely posed by the poetry of Eliot, is certainly one where a false judgment is likely to involve the intentional fallacy. The frequency and depth of literary allusion in the poetry of Eliot and others has driven so many in pursuit of full meanings to the *Golden Bough* and the Elizabethan drama that it has become a kind of commonplace to suppose that we do not know what a poet means unless we have traced him in his reading—a supposition redolent with intentional implications. The stand taken by F. O. Matthiessen is a sound one and partially forestalls the difficulty.

If one reads these lines with an attentive ear and is sensitive to their sudden shifts in movement, the contrast between the actual Thames and the idealized vision of it during an age before it flowed through a megalopolis is sharply conveyed by that movement itself, whether or not one recognizes the refrain to be from Spenser.

Eliot's allusions work when we know them—and to a great extent even when we do not know them, through their suggestive power.

But sometimes we find allusions supported by notes, and it is a nice question whether the notes function more as guides to send us where we may be educated, or more as indications in themselves about the character of the allusions. "Nearly everything of importance . . . that is apposite to an appreciation of 'The Waste Land,'" writes Matthiessen of Miss Weston's book, "has been incorporated into the structure of the poem itself, or into Eliot's Notes." And with such an admission it may begin to appear that it would not much matter if Eliot invented his sources (as Sir Walter Scott invented chapter epigraphs from "old plays" and "anonymous" authors, or as Coleridge wrote marginal glosses for The Ancient Mariner). Allusions to Dante, Webster, Marvell, or Baudelaire doubtless gain something because these writers existed, but it is doubtful whether the same can be said for an allusion to an obscure Elizabethan:

> The sound of horns and motors, which shall bring
> Sweeney to Mrs. Porter in the spring.

"Cf. Day, Parliament of Bees:" says Eliot,

> When of a sudden, listening, you shall hear,
> A noise of horns and hunting, which shall bring
> Actaeon to Diana in the spring,
> Where all shall see her naked skin.

The irony is completed by the quotation itself; had Eliot, as is quite conceivable, composed these lines to furnish his own background, there would be no loss of validity. The conviction may grow as one reads Eliot's next note: "I do not know the origin of the ballad from which these lines are taken: it was reported to me from Sydney, Australia." The important word in this note—on Mrs. Porter and her daughter who washed their feet in soda water—is "ballad." And if one should feel from the lines themselves their "ballad" quality, there would be little need for the note. Ultimately, the inquiry must focus on the integrity of such notes as parts of the poem, for where they constitute special information about the meaning of phrases in the poem, they ought to be subject to the same scrutiny as any of the other words in which it is written. Matthiessen believes the notes were the price Eliot "had to pay in order to avoid what he would have considered muffling the energy of his poem by extended connecting links in the text itself." But it may be questioned whether the notes and the need for them are not equally muffling. F. W. Bateson has plausibly argued that Tennyson's "The Sailor Boy" would be better if half the stanzas were omitted, and the best versions of ballads like "Sir Patrick Spens" owe their power to the very audacity with which the minstrel has taken for granted the story upon which he comments. What then if a poet finds he cannot take so much for granted in a more recondite context and rather than write informatively, supplies notes? It can be said in favor of this plan that at least the notes do not pretend to be dramatic, as they would if written in verse. On the other hand, the notes may look like unassimilated material lying loose beside the poem, necessary for the meaning of the verbal symbol, but not integrated, so that the symbol stands incomplete.

We mean to suggest by the above analysis that whereas notes tend to seem to justify themselves as external indexes to the author's *intention*, yet they ought to be judged like any other parts of a composition (verbal arrangement special to a particular context), and when so judged their reality as parts of the poem, or their imaginative integration with the rest of the poem, may come into question. Matthiessen, for instance, sees that Eliot's titles for poems and his epigraphs are informative apparatus, like the notes. But while he is worried by some of the notes and thinks that Eliot "appears to be mocking himself for writing the note at the same time that he wants to convey something by it," Matthiessen believes that the "device" of epigraphs "is not at all open to the objection of not being sufficiently structural." "The *intention*," he says, "is to enable the poet to secure a condensed expression in the poem itself." "In each case the epigraph is *designed* to form an integral part of the effect of the poem." And Eliot himself, in his notes, has justified his poetic practice in terms of intention.

> The Hanged Man, a member of the traditional pack, fits my purpose in two ways: because he is associated in my mind with the Hanged God of Frazer, and because I associate him with the hooded figure in the passage of the disciples to Emmaus in Part V. . . . The man with Three Staves (an authentic member of the Tarot pack) I associate, quite arbitrarily, with the Fisher King himself.

And perhaps he is to be taken more seriously here, when off guard in a note, than when in his Norton Lectures he comments on the difficulty of saying what a poem means and adds playfully that he thinks of prefixing to a second edition of *Ash Wednesday* some lines from *Don Juan:*

> I don't pretend that I quite understand
> My own meaning when I would be *very* fine;
> But the fact is that I have nothing planned
> Unless it were to be a moment merry.

If Eliot and other contemporary poets have any characteristic fault, it may be in *planning* too much.

Allusiveness in poetry is one of several critical issues by which we have illustrated the more abstract issue of intentionalism, but it may be for today the most important illustration. As a poetic practice allusiveness would appear to be in some recent poems an extreme corollary of the romantic intentionalist assumption, and as a critical issue it challenges and brings to light in a special way the basic premise of intentionalism. The following instance from the poetry of Eliot may serve to epitomize the practical implications of what we have been saying. In Eliot's "Love Song of J. Alfred Prufrock," toward the end, occurs the line: "I have heard the mermaids singing, each to each," and this bears a certain resemblance to a line in a Song by John Donne, "Teach me to heare Mermaides singing," so that for the reader acquainted to a certain degree with Donne's poetry, the critical question arises: Is Eliot's line an allusion to Donne's? Is Prufrock thinking about Donne? Is Eliot thinking about Donne? We suggest that there are two radically different ways of looking for an answer to this question. There is (1) the way of poetic analysis and exegesis, which inquires whether it makes any sense if Eliot-Prufrock *is* thinking about Donne. In an earlier part of the poem, when Prufrock asks, "Would it have been worth while, . . . To have squeezed the universe into a ball," his words take half their sadness and irony from certain energetic and passionate lines of Marvel "To His Coy Mistress." But the exegetical inquirer may wonder whether mermaids considered as "strange sights" (to hear them is in Donne's poem analogous to getting with child a mandrake root) have much to do with Prufrock's mermaids, which seem to be symbols of romance and dynamism, and which incidentally have literary authentication, if they need it, in a line of a sonnet by Gérard de Nerval. This method of inquiry may lead to the conclusion that the given resemblance between Eliot and Donne is without significance and is better not thought of, or the method may have the disadvantage of providing no certain conclusion. Nevertheless, we submit that this is the true and objective way of criticism, as contrasted to what the very uncertainty of exegesis might tempt a second kind of critic to undertake: (2) the way of biographical or genetic inquiry, in which, taking advantage of the fact that Eliot is still alive, and in the spirit of a man who would settle a bet, the critic writes to Eliot and asks what he meant, or if he had Donne in mind. We shall not here weigh the probabilities—whether Eliot would answer that he meant nothing at all, had nothing at all in mind—a sufficiently good answer to such a question—or in an unguarded moment might furnish a clear and, within its limit, irrefutable answer. Our point is that such an answer to such an inquiry would have nothing to do with the poem "Prufrock"; it would not be a critical inquiry. Critical inquiries, unlike bets, are not settled in this way. Critical inquiries are not settled by consulting the oracle.

Erwin Panofsky

ON INTENTIONS*

In defining a work of art as a "man-made object demanding to be experienced aesthetically" we encounter for the first time a basic difference between the humanities and natural science. The scientist, dealing as he does with natural phenomena, can at once proceed to analyze them. The humanist, dealing as he does with human actions and creations, has to engage in a mental process of a synthetic and subjective character: he has mentally to re-enact the actions and to re-create the creations. It is in fact by this process that the real objects of the humanities come into being. For it is obvious that historians of philosophy or sculpture are concerned with books and statues not in so far as these books and sculptures exist materially, but in so far as they have a meaning. And it is equally obvious that this meaning can only be apprehended by re-producing, and thereby, quite literally, "realizing," the thoughts that are expressed in the books and the artistic conceptions that manifest themselves in the statues.

Thus the art historian subjects his "material" to a rational archaeological analysis at times as meticulously exact, comprehensive and involved as any physical or astronomical research. But he constitutes his "material" by means

---

* From Erwin Panofsky's "The History of Art as a Humanistic Discipline," in T. M. Greene (ed.), *The Meaning of the Humanities,* Section IV. Copyright, 1940, by the Princeton University Press. Reprinted by permission of the Princeton University Press.

Erwin Panofsky (1892–   ), distinguished art historian, leading formulator of iconological studies in art, author of many brilliant works in art history, is now in residence at the Institute for Advanced Study, in Princeton.

of an intuitive aesthetic re-creation,[1] including the perception and appraisal of "quality," just as any "ordinary" person does when he or she looks at a picture or listens to a symphony.

How, then, is it possible to build up art history as a respectable scholarly discipline, if its very objects come into being by an irrational and subjective process?

This question cannot be answered, of course, by referring to the scientific methods which have been, or may be, introduced into art history. Devices such as chemical analysis of materials, X rays, ultraviolet rays, infrared rays and macrophotography are very helpful, but their use has nothing to do with the basic methodical problem. A statement to the effect that the pigments used in an allegedly mediaeval miniature were not invented before the nineteenth century may settle an art-historical question, but it is not an art-historical statement. Based as it is on chemical analysis plus the history of chemistry, it refers to the miniature not *qua* work of art but *qua* physical object, and may just as well refer to a forged will. The use of X rays, macrophotographs, etc., on the other hand, is methodically not different from the use of spectacles or of a magnifying glass. These devices enable the art historian to see more than he could see without them, but *what* he sees has to be interpreted "stylistically," like that which he perceives with the naked eye.

The real answer lies in the fact that intuitive aesthetic recreation and archaeological research are interconnected so as to form, again, what we have called an "organic situation." It is not true that the art historian first

[1] However, when speaking of "re-creation" it is important to emphasize the prefix "re." Works of art are both manifestations of artistic "intentions" and natural objects, sometimes difficult to isolate from their physical surroundings and always subject to the physical processes of aging. Thus, in experiencing a work of art aesthetically we perform two entirely different acts which, however, psychologically merge with each other into one *Erlebnis:* we build up our aesthetic object both by re-creating the work of art according to the "intention" of its maker, and by freely creating a set of aesthetic values comparable to those with which we endow a tree or a sunset. When abandoning ourselves to the impression of the weathered sculptures of Chartres, we cannot help enjoying their lovely mellowness and patina as an aesthetic value; but this value, which implies both the sensual pleasure in a peculiar play of light and color and the more sentimental delight in "age" and "genuineness," has nothing to do with the objective, or artistic, value with which the sculptures were invested by their makers. From the point of view of the Gothic stone carvers the processes of aging were not merely irrelevant but positively undesirable: they tried to protect their statues by a coat of color which, had it been preserved in its original freshness, would probably spoil a good deal of our aesthetic enjoyment. As a private person, the art historian is entirely justified in not destroying the psychological unity of *Alters-und-Echtheits-Erlebnis* and *Kunst-Erlebnis*. But as a "professional man" he has to separate, as far as possible, the recreative experience of the intentional values imparted to the statue by the artist from the creative experience of the accidental values imparted to a piece of aged stone by the action of nature. And this separation is often not as easy as it might seem.

constitutes his object by means of re-creative synthesis and then begins his archaeological investigation—as though first buying a ticket and then boarding a train. In reality the two processes do not succeed each other, they interpenetrate; not only does the re-creative synthesis serve as a basis for the archaeological investigation, the archaeological investigation in turn serves as a basis for the re-creative process; both mutually qualify and rectify one another.

Anyone confronted with a work of art, whether aesthetically re-creating or rationally investigating it, is affected by its three constituents: materialized form, idea (that is, in the plastic arts, subject matter) and content. The pseudo-impressionistic theory according to which "form and color tell us of form and color, that is all," is simply not true. It is the unity of those three elements which is realized in the aesthetic experience, and all of them enter into what is called aesthetic enjoyment of art.

The re-creative experience of a work of art depends, therefore, not only on the natural sensitivity and the visual training of the spectator, but also on his cultural equipment. There is no such thing as an entirely "naïve" beholder. The "naïve" beholder of the Middle Ages had a good deal to learn, and something to forget, before he could appreciate classical statuary and architecture, and the "naïve" beholder of the post-Renaissance period had a good deal to forget, and something to learn, before he could appreciate mediaeval, to say nothing of primitive, art. Thus the "naïve" beholder not only enjoys but also, unconsciously, appraises and interprets the work of art; and no one can blame him if he does this without caring whether his appraisal and interpretation are right or wrong, and without realizing that his own cultural equipment, such as it is, actually contributes to the object of his experience.

The "naïve" beholder differs from the art historian in that the latter is conscious of the situation. He *knows* that his cultural equipment, such as it is, would not be in harmony with that of people in another land and of a different period. He tries, therefore, to make adjustments by learning as much as he possibly can of the circumstances under which the objects of his studies were created. Not only will he collect and verify all the available factual information as to medium, condition, age, authorship, destina-ation, etc., but he will also compare the work with others of its class, and will examine such writings as reflect the aesthetic standards of its country and age, in order to achieve a more "objective" appraisal of its quality. He will read old books on theology or mythology in order to identify its subject matter, and he will further try to determine its historical locus, and to separate the individual contribution of its maker from that of forerunners and contemporaries. He will study the formal principles which control the rendering of the visible world, or, in architecture, the handling of what may be called the structural features, and thus build up a history of "motifs." He will observe the interplay between the influences of literary sources and the effect of self-dependent representational traditions, in order to establish a history of iconographic formulae or "types." And he will do his best to familiarize himself with the social, religious and philosophical attitudes of other periods and countries, in order to correct his own subjective feeling for content.[2] But when he does all this, his aesthetic perception as such will change accordingly, and will more and more adapt itself to the original "intention" of the works. Thus what the art historian, as opposed to the "naïve" art lover, does, is not to erect a rational superstructure on an irrational foundation, but to develop his re-creative experiences so as to conform with the results of his archaeological research, while continually checking the results of his archaeological research against the evidence of his re-creative experiences.[3]

[2] For the technical terms used in this paragraph, see The Introduction to E. Panofsky, *Studies in Iconology*.

[3] The same applies, of course, to the history of literature and of other forms of artistic expression. According to Dionysius Thrax (*Ars Grammatica*, ed. P. Uhlig, XXX, 1883, p. 5 ff.; quoted in Gilbert Murray, *Religio Grammatici, The Religion of a Man of Letters*, Boston and New York, 1918, p. 15), Γραμματική (history of literature, as we would say) is an ἐμπειρία (knowledge based on experience) of that which has been said by the poets and prose writers. He divides it into six parts, all of which can be paralleled in art history:

1) ἀνάγνωσις ἐντριβὴς κατὰ προσῳδίαν (expert reading aloud according to prosody): this is, in fact, the synthetic aesthetic recreation of a work of literature and is comparable to the visual "realization" of a work of art.

2) ἐξήλησις κατὰ τοὺς ἐνυπάρχοντας ποιητικοὺς τρόπους (explanation of such figures of speech as may occur): this would be comparable to the history of iconographic formulae or "types."

3) γλωσσῶν τε καὶ ἱστοριῶν πρόχειρος ἀπόδοσις (offhand rendering of obsolete words and themes): identification of iconographic subject matter.

4) ἐτυμολογίας εὕρησις (discovery of etymologies): derivation of "motifs."

5) ἀναλογίας ἐκλογισμός (explanation of grammatical forms): analysis of compositional structure.

6) κρίσις ποιημάτων, ὃ δὴ κάλλιστόν ἐστι πάντων τῶν ἐν τῇ τέχνῃ (literary criticism, which is the most beautiful part of that which is comprised by Γραμματική): critical appraisal of works of art.

The expression "critical appraisal of works of art" raises an interesting question. If the history of arts admits a scale of values, just as the history of literature or political history admits degrees of excellence or "greatness," how can we justify the fact that the methods here expounded do not seem to allow for a differentiation between first, second and third rate works of art? Now a scale of values is partly a matter of personal reactions and partly a matter of tradition. Both these standards, of which the second is the comparatively more objective one, have continually to be revised, and every investigation, however specialized, contributes to this process. But just for this reason the art historian cannot make an a priori distinction between his approach to a "masterpiece" and his approach to a "mediocre" or "inferior" work of art—just as a student of classical literature cannot investigate the tragedies by Sophocles in any other manner than the tragedies

Leonardo da Vinci has said: "Two weaknesses leaning against one another add up to one strength."[4] The halves of an arch cannot even stand upright; the whole arch supports a weight. Similarly, archaeological research is blind and empty without aesthetic re-creation, and aesthetic re-creation is irrational and often misguided without archaeological research. But, "leaning against one another," these two can support the "system that makes sense," that is, an historical synopsis.

As I have said before, no one can be blamed for enjoying works of art "naïvely"—for appraising and interpreting them according to his lights and not caring any further. But the humanist will look with suspicion upon what might be called "appreciationism." He who teaches innocent people to understand art without bothering about classical languages, boresome historical methods and dusty old documents, deprives naïveté of its charm without correcting its errors.

"Appreciationism" is not to be confused with "connoisseurship" and "art theory." The connoisseur is the collector, museum curator or expert who deliberately limits his contribution to scholarship to identifying works of art with respect to date, provenance and authorship, and to evaluating them with respect to quality and condition. The difference between him and the art historian is not so much a matter of principle as a matter of emphasis and explicitness, comparable to the difference between a diagnostician and a researcher in medicine. The connoisseur tends to emphasize the re-creative aspect of the complex process which I have tried to describe, and considers the building up of an historical conception as secondary; the art historian in the narrower, or academic, sense is inclined to reverse these accents. But the simple diagnosis "cancer," if correct, implies everything which the researcher could tell us about cancer, and therefore claims to be verifiable by subsequent scientific analysis; similarly the simple diagnosis "Rembrandt around 1650," if correct, implies everything which the historian of art could tell us about the formal values of the picture, about the interpretation of the subject, about the way it reflects the cultural attitude of seventeenth-century Holland, and about the way it expresses Rembrandt's

---

by Seneca. It is true that the methods of art history, *qua* methods, will prove as effective when applied to Dürer's *Melencolia* as when applied to an anonymous and rather unimportant woodcut. But when a "masterpiece" is compared and connected with as many "less important" works of art as turn out, in the course of the investigation, to be comparable and connectable with it, the originality of its invention, the superiority of its composition and technique, and whatever other features make it "great," will automatically become evident—not in spite but because of the fact that the whole group of materials has been subjected to one and the same method of analysis and interpretation.

[4] *Il codice atlantico di Leonardo da Vinci nella Biblioteca Ambrosiana di Milano*, ed. G. Piumati, Milan, 1894–1903, fol. 244 v.

personality; and this diagnosis, too, claims to live up to the criticism of the art historian in the narrower sense. The connoisseur might thus be defined as a laconic art historian, and the art historian as a loquacious connoisseur. In point of fact the best representatives of both types have enormously contributed to what they themselves do not consider their proper business.[5]

Art theory on, the other hand—as opposed to the philosophy of art or aesthetics—is to art history as poetics and rhetoric are to the history of literature.

Because of the fact that the objects of art history come into being by a process of re-creative aesthetic synthesis, the art historian finds himself in a peculiar difficulty when trying to characterize what might be called the stylistic structure of the works with which he is concerned. Since he has to describe these works, not as physical bodies or as substitutes for physical bodies, but as objects of an inward experience, it would be useless—even if it were possible—to express shapes, colors, and features of construction in terms of geometrical formulae, wave lengths and statical equations, or to describe the postures of a human figure by way of anatomical analysis. On the other hand, since the inward experience of the art historian is not a free and subjective one, but has been outlined for him by the purposeful activities of an artist, he must not limit himself to describing his personal impressions of the work of art as a poet might describe his impressions of a landscape or of the song of a nightingale.

The objects of art history, then, can only be characterized in a terminology which is as re-constructive as the experience of the art historian is re-creative: it must describe the stylistic peculiarities, neither as measurable or otherwise determinable data, nor as stimuli of subjective reactions, but as that which bears witness to artistic "intentions." Now "intentions" can only be formulated in terms of alternatives; a situation has to be supposed in which the maker of the work had more than one possibility of procedure, that is to say, in which he found himself confronted with a problem of choice between various modes of emphasis. Thus it appears that the terms used by the art historian interpret the stylistic peculiarities of the works as specific solutions of generic "artistic problems." This is not only the case with our modern terminology, but even with such expressions as *rilievo*, *sfumato*, etc., found in sixteenth-century writing.

When we call a figure in an Italian Renaissance picture "plastic," while describing a figure in a Chinese painting as "having volume but no mass"

---

[5] See M. I. Friedländer, *Der Kenner*, Berlin, 1919, and E. Wind, *Aesthetischer und kunstwissenschaftlicher Gegenstand, loc. cit.* Friedländer justly states that a good art historian is, or at least develops into, a *Kenner wider Willen*. Conversely, a good connoisseur might be called an art historian *malgré lui*.

(owing to the absence of "modeling"), we interpret these figures as two different solutions of a problem which might be formulated as "volumetric units (bodies) *vs.* illimited expanse (space)." When we distinguish between a use of line as "contour" and, to quote Balzac, a use of line as "le moyen par lequel l'homme se rend compte de l'effet de la lumière sur les objets," we refer to the same problem, while placing special emphasis upon another one: "line *vs.* areas of color." Upon reflection it will turn out that there is a limited number of such primary problems, interrelated with each other, which on the one hand beget an infinity of secondary and tertiary ones, and on the other hand can be ultimately derived from one basic antithesis: differentiation *vs.* continuity.[6]

To formulate and to systematize the "artistic problems"—which are of course not limited to the sphere of purely formal values, but include the "stylistic structure" of subject matter and content as well—and thus to build up a system of *"Kunstwissenschaftliche Grundbegriffe"* is the objective of art theory and not of art history. But here we encounter, for the third time, what we have called an "organic situation." The art historian, as we have seen, cannot describe the objects of his re-creative experience without re-constructing artistic intentions in terms which imply generic theoretical concepts. In doing this, he will, consciously or unconsciously, contribute to the development of art theory, which, without historical exemplification, would remain a meager scheme of abstract universals. The art theorist, on the other hand, whether he approaches the subject from the standpoint of Kant's *Critique,* of neo-scholastic epistemology, or of *Gestaltpsychologie,*[7] cannot build up a system of generic concepts without referring to works of art which have come into being under specific historical conditions; but in doing this he will, consciously or unconsciously, contribute to the development of art history, which, without theoretical orientation, would remain a congeries of unformulated particulars.

When we call the connoisseur a laconic art historian and the art historian a loquacious connoisseur, the relation between the art historian and the art theorist may be compared to that between two neighbors who have the right of shooting over the same district, while one of them owns the gun and the other all the ammunition. Both parties would be well advised if they realized this condition of their partnership. It has rightly been said that theory, if not received at the door of an empirical discipline, comes in through the chimney

[6] See E. Panofsky, "Ueber das Verhältnis der Kunstgeschichte zur Kunsttheorie," *Zeitschrift für Aesthetik und allgemeine Kunstwissenschaft,* XVIII, 1925, p. 129 ff., and E. Wind, "Zur Systematik der künstlerischen Probleme," *ibid.,* p. 438 ff.

[7] Cf. H. Sedlmayr, "Zu einer strengen Kunstwissenschaft," *Kunstwissenschaftliche Forschungen,* I, 1931, p. 7 ff.

like a ghost and upsets the furniture. But it is no less true that history, if not received at the door of a theoretical discipline dealing with the same set of phenomena, creeps into the cellar like a horde of mice and undermines the groundwork.

Henry David Aiken

THE AESTHETIC RELEVANCE OF ARTISTS' INTENTIONS*

Like most titles, this one is likely to prove misleading unless an initial disclaimer is made. In speaking of the aesthetic relevance of artists' intentions I want to come down rather lightly on the word "aesthetic." It is works of art that I want to discuss, and the cluster of questions concerning the relevance of intentions to their appraisal, appreciation, and interpretation.

There is one way of construing such questions which makes it very easy to dispose of them. If they are taken to concern the relevance of artists' intentions to appraisals and interpretations of *their* work, then it is apparent that such intentions are entirely relevant. What would it mean to speak of appraising your work, what it is that you have done or accomplished, apart from any consideration of what you are trying to do? The success or failure of your accomplishment depends upon the degree to which it fulfills your purpose; that is part of what is implied in calling it "your accomplishment." From such a standpoint, moreover, there is no important difference between appraising and appreciating. Both are estimates of your accomplishment, what it is that you have achieved. I cannot be said to appreciate your accomplishment if I totally ignore what you intended to do. The logic of appreciations of this sort leaves me no option in the matter. And for much the same reason I cannot ignore your intentions in trying to interpret what it is that you have accomplished. For the latter are part and parcel of the accomplishment, the thing achieved or done. You can't split off a man's intentions from what he has done in the way you can split off the branch from a tree. Change the intention and you change the act performed, the thing done or accomplished.

* Henry Aiken's "The Aesthetic Relevance of Artists' Intentions ," *The Journal of Philosophy*, Vol. LII, No. 24, November 24, 1955. Reprinted by permission of *The Journal of Philosophy* and the author.

Henry David Aiken (1912–   ), at present Professor of Philosophy at Harvard University, is the author of many essays on ethics and aesthetics and has also written *The Age of Ideology*.

Evidently, then, we have something else in mind, if we are serious, in raising questions about the relevance of artists' intentions to appraisals, appreciations, and interpretations of the works they have produced. What this may be begins to come out when we substitute for "the artist's work" the phrase "work of art." I can ask, with some show of a point, what the relevance of your intentions may be to the appraisal of the works of art you have happened to produce. It is here, therefore, that we must make our beginning: What is the role of the expression "work of art" in talking about the products of human ingenuity and imagination?

Notice, first of all, that questions concerning the relevance of an artist's intentions to the appraisal or interpretation of something he has produced *as a work of art* strongly suggest that the artist himself is not responsible for the fact that his production is a work of art. As an accomplishment, the artist's work is his own; but he alone does not and can not make it a work of art. This is not to say that in calling something a work of art we do not normally presuppose that it is a human artifact. But this is not what we are explicitly talking about when we refer to it as a work of art. Because of this, some aestheticians have supposed that the analysis of the expression "work of art" must be sought in the characteristics of the objects which we dignify by this title. And they have been mistaken. Like the term "happiness," the phrase "work of art" is not amenable to ordinary descriptive definitions, and the effects of so trying to define it are not what the definer may suppose: they do not clarify its use, but rather modify its range of application, and in so doing serve merely to redirect our attitudes toward the things to which the expression is subsequently applied. Moreover, the characteristics of the object to which we may point in giving reasons for calling it a work of art become reasons for so regarding it only because it is assumed that they help to make it worth contemplating in a certain way. Any feature of a work may provide a reason for speaking of it as a work of art, but only if that feature helps to make the whole of which it is a part something which is to be admired or appreciated for its own sake. It is for this reason that no particular symbolic form, no theme or subject-matter, no material or arrangement of materials, as such, can be definitive of what it is to be a work of art.

It is nevertheless possible to provide a characterization of the sort of thing that is being said when we call something a work of art. Works of art are so-called primarily because it is thought that when approached or handled in certain ways they tend to give satisfaction or pleasure to those who so handle them. But there is no one activity, no one way of approaching or handling works of art which is indispensable or which alone is appropriate to them all. Some aestheticians have tried to make such words as "contemplation" do the trick, and with disastrous results. Among other things, we contemplate pictures; but we read poetry, listen to music, witness plays, smell perfume, and taste fine wine or food. And when we do any of these things appreciatively and discriminatingly we are apt to call the things in question works of art. If we do not appreciate them, or if we find that our discriminations are not worth the candle, we resist any temptation to speak of them as works of art.

At this point it may be useful to compare the concept of a work of art with that of a tool. Both are what I sometimes call "functional concepts." By this I mean that they are used not to describe the physical attributes of things but rather to specify their roles in human life and the activities which are appropriate to them. A tool is an artifact that is used in certain characteristic ways to accomplish a certain kind of result, to get a certain sort of thing done. Tools, in short, have certain appropriate, conventional uses; they are also subject to misuse and have improper uses. Now works of art, like tools, are subject to improper uses; and, although in a somewhat different sense than that which we have in mind in speaking of the misuse of a tool, they may be misused. Unlike tools, however, works of art, as such, are not used to accomplish a certain result or to get something done. There are certain things which it is proper to do with works of art; but these are not done for the sake of a result, but, as we say, for the pleasure or satisfaction of the doing. The result of doing what is appropriate to a work of art may be anything under the sun from emotional catharsis to wish fulfillment. But such results are accidental; they have nothing to do with the function of a work of art as such.

Before concluding these remarks, it is necessary to bring out more emphatically an aspect of the concept of a work of art which affects the nature of any controversy as to the relevance of an artist's intentions to the appraisal, appreciation, or interpretation of his art. The point is that "work of art" is an expression of commendation. This becomes obvious when we think of what is being said when a rainbow or any other natural object is called a work of art. A work of art is something which is admirable, which is worthy of admiration, and which, perhaps, ought to be admired. This being so, any denial of the relevance of the artist's intentions to what he has accomplished as a work of art is bound to have the force of a prescription which enjoins us to disallow any consideration of such intentions in attempting to give reasons why it is worthy of admiration. Such denials, in short, do not so much state a fact as modify the ways in which we approach or handle the objects we are prepared to call works of art; they limit the scope of the considerations we may take into account in judging, appreciating, and interpreting, and in so doing profoundly affect our entire conception of what our artistic activities ought to be or become. This is why the debate over questions of the sort with which we have here to do is bound to be intense and acrimonious, and why any appeal to the "facts" concerning the character of the objects themselves or concerning our actual transactions with such objects is likely to be inconclusive. Nor do I deny that in trying to spell out some of the proprieties governing our discourse about works of art, I myself am at the same time protecting the activities of which such discourse is a part. Forms of words, it has been said, reflect forms of life. In characterizing, with approval, the logical amenities that govern the use of a form of words, I am doing something more than describing them; I am also reënforcing the modes of behavior to which the forms of words belong.

It is time, now, to turn to other matters. We cannot successfully understand the cluster of questions with which we are concerned without some preliminary discussion of the concepts of appraisal, appreciation, and interpretation as these are employed in talking about works of art.

To appraise a work of art, plainly, is to judge it, to estimate its worth. It must be borne in mind, however, that the things we call works of art are not merely such, that they often have other functions and interest us for other reasons. It is therefore essential to distinguish appraisals of pictures, musical compositions, or literary productions which judge them as works of art from those which estimate them from the standpoint of some other role or capacity. Our concern, here, is only with the former. It should be observed, also, that appraisals of works of art as such are properly and reasonably made only after the completion of other acts which are performed in dealing with works of art as such. Such acts, which would include reading, listening, witnessing, contemplating, and the like, may conveniently be called the "primary" or "aesthetic" activities required in dealing with works of art. Among such acts we would not include acts of judgment or appraisal; the latter are secondary, dependent acts which are performed subsequently to and in consequence of reading, listening, witnessing, and contemplating. You can't appreciate a piece of music as a work of art if you won't listen to it; but you can appreciate it without judging it; nor is it essential to the proper handling of any work of art that it be judged. But what we find when we perform the primary acts called for by a work of art provides the basis for a proper performance of such secondary acts as judging. How we appraise a work of art as such depends upon our appreciation of it and upon the performance of the primary acts upon which appreciation itself depends. Any reasons we may adduce for highly appraising a work of art which are not based upon what is found in performance of the primary activities are irrelevant to our appraisal or else, if we persist in them, transform the appraisal into a judgment which is not concerned with the object as a work of art.

The term "appreciate" is equivocal. In one sense, as we have seen, its meaning is like that of "appraise." But there is another important sense of the term which must be contrasted with this. When we speak of art appreciation or of appreciating a work of art as such, we are talking not about estimations and judgments, but rather about pleasurable or satisfying discrimination. In this sense, my capacity for appreciation is not my power to appraise but my sensitivity, my ability to discriminate and to be moved by the qualities of the work as a work of art. To appreciate a man's work, as we have seen, it is necessary to take into account his intentions; but it is not necessary, even though it may be desirable, to have regard to an artist's intentions in appreciating his product as a work of art. The question, here, concerns the fullness of our appreciation, not appreciation as such. In order to adequately appreciate a work of art, to discriminate and relate its qualities, to discern its full expressive content, one may have to consider the artist's intentions. But the latter, by the nature of the case, can have no authoritative claim upon us as appreciators or upon the subsequent judgments we may make as appreciators.

The term "interpretation" is used with abominable looseness by critics and philosophers of art. Sometimes, apparently, it is used in a way which seems to refer to the primary activities of reading, listening, and contemplating. I should regard this as a misuse of the expression. More properly it is employed to refer to the activities of a critic in paraphrasing, describing, explaining, explicating, analysing, and the like. In this sense, interpretation is clearly an ancillary activity, undertaken in order to accomplish something beyond itself. How great is the confusion latent in this equivocation becomes evident when we observe how different are the primary activities of looking or contemplating from those of explaining or explicating, and how different are their relations to the work of art itself. In effect, interpretations are tools for the use of an audience in readying itself for the activities involved in appreciation. But the appreciative reading of a poem is not a tool and is not undertaken to get something done; it does not ready us for something else and its adequacy is not judged by its effects.

The role of interpretation, then, is advisory. It serves to guide, direct, and in general to improve the facility with which the primary acts which are proper to works of art are performed. Interpretations of works of art are properly judged on this basis. But just as we frequently do other things,

often very well, without advice or counsel, so on occasion we may appreciate
a work of art very fully without the help of an interpretation, or without
interpreting it at all. Interpretations are useful or necessary precisely because not everything in most works of art is immediately perceivable, and
we resort to them, as a rule, because we fail to understand what we read
or see or because its relevance to other things in the work is not adequately
appreciated.

Interpretation and judgment obviously are not the same thing, any
more than interpretation and appreciation are the same thing. Judgment
presupposes appreciation; it does not presuppose interpretation. It is usually
assumed, however, and with some basis, that appraisals that are based upon
interpretation are sounder than those that are not. The reason for this is that
interpretations are presumed to enable the artist's audience to gain a more
adequate appreciation of the qualities of his art. But in speaking of appraisals as "based" upon interpretations it is possible to be misleading, precisely because of the equivocation mentioned above. In the sense here under
consideration, the appraisal of a work of art is only indirectly based upon
interpretation; it is directly based only upon what we find in performing
the primary acts proper to appreciation of a work of art. The relevance of
any interpretation of a work of art, in short, is always through appreciation.
It is only as it affects appreciation, through the modification of what we see,
hear, or feel, that any interpretation provides a basis for and is relevant to
the judgment of a work of art as such.

All interpretations of a work of art are bound to be selective and are
bound to be slanted toward a certain mode of appreciation. And because in
most cases alternative modes of appreciation are possible, there can be, as
a rule, no such thing as a definitive interpretation. The aesthetic relevance
of a particular interpretation, therefore, can be established only with respect to a certain mode of appreciation, a certain way of approaching and
handling the work of art. We cannot just say that the thing as interpreted
is "there" and have done. In speaking of a particular work of art, we are not
talking about something that has a certain single definitive shape or pattern.
Actually any particular work of art includes a considerable variety of such
patterns which cannot all be appreciated in a single reading or view of the
work. Each such pattern, moreover, answers to a particular mode of appreciation which is possible only if the work is approached and handled
in a certain way. Nor is any one of these patterns the only objective one,
the one that is constitutive of the work as it is "in reality." For this reason,
any prolonged debate over what is there in the work itself is bound to be
futile; and it will be so, in many cases, not just because our individual ex-

periences of a work are not the same, but because the work itself is capable of a number of modes of appreciation, one of which, in principle, may be as proper to it as another.

This inescapable and innocuous relativity of interpretations does not, however, preclude the possibility of saying that one interpretation is more adequate than another. The adequacy of any interpretation may be judged in at least two ways, according either to the adequacy with which it prepares us for a particular mode of appreciation or else to the comparative satisfactoriness of the mode of appreciation to which it leads. The question concerning the aesthetic relevance of an interpretation, therefore, is likely to be somewhat complicated. Nor can it be properly answered without regard to the complexities which unavoidably enter into our conception of a particular work of art.

A few words must now be said about the use of the word "intention." Here, also, much avoidable trouble has resulted from the failure to distinguish carefully among the several senses in which aestheticians and critics employ the word. In speaking of an artist's intentions, some writers appear to be thinking of the ends or goals for which the artist may undertake his work. Frequently, however, this is confused with what the artist intends to say or do in some part of the work. Manifestly, what I intend to accomplish in saying something is not the same thing as what I mean when I say it. And what answers to questions about the former does not at all answer to questions concerning the latter. Unfortunately, there are also other and different notions that are frequently introduced when questions concerning an artist's intentions are raised, which have to do neither with questions of ends nor with questions of what the artist intended to say or do in the work, but rather with the attitudes, conscious or otherwise, which cause him to choose his subject-matter or which condition his selection of themes, genres, or materials and determine the way in which he handles them. Such attitudes, so to say, affect the "personality" of the work of art as a whole, and our awareness of them is likely to affect our own view of it when we approach the work as appreciators and as interpreters.

It should be abundantly clear, by this time, that to raise questions as to the relevance of an artist's intentions to the appraisal, appreciation, and interpretation of works of art that he has produced is to raise a series of questions of very different sorts. In the remaining space I can merely indicate some of the considerations that are involved in trying to answer a few of them.

It is evident from what has already been said that in any of the above-mentioned senses, artists' intentions do not provide a standard for judging their productions as works of art. The only intrinsic standard afforded those who profess to judge the merits of works of art as such is the satisfaction that results when we engage in the primary activities that are proper to particular works. But it is too easily concluded from this that an artist's intentions are of no use to a potential judge. For by taking account of an artist's intentions we are frequently able to avoid the serious mistake of solemnly judging as works of art productions whose only interest, either to the artist or to ourselves, lies elsewhere. Properly regarded, artists' intentions are advisory: they help us to know what to expect and hence how to approach a particular artifact. They do not provide the criterion from which a work is to be judged as a work of art; but they are of help in deciding whether such a criterion is to be invoked in judging a work. This, I think, is their primary relevance, and no confusion of values or fallacy is involved in acknowledging the fact. Quite the contrary.

From the standpoint of appreciation, it is of the first importance not to confuse the various things which philosophers tend to lump together under the heading of "intentions." Consider, first, the artist's ulterior goals. Now as Hume long ago pointed out, one of the sources of our appreciation in contemplating a work of art is our awareness of the fitness of the work to the end for which it was produced. This functional beauty of a work of art can only be appreciated, however, if the artist's ulterior intentions are understood and borne in mind. Many works of art, of course, have no such interest; my only point in mentioning it is to show that you can't say out of hand that an artist's ulterior aims are irrelevant to the appreciation of his art. It depends upon the character of the individual work, upon the central focus of its artistic interest.

The same is true, although in another way, of the relevance of an artist's attitudes, the factors we lump together under the heading of his "personality." Now it is certainly possible to appreciate many works of art, some of them quite fully, without regard to the attitudes which, consciously or unconsciously, the artist may express in them. But works of art differ enormously with respect to the central focus of their interest. Some works are virtually anonymous; nothing is added to our interest from the knowledge of their authors' characters. Others are intensely personal. I have found, for example, that when I read the novels of Dickens or Dostoyevski with some awareness of their authors' personalities much becomes clear that I could not previously understand or appreciate. The very dramatic dimension of their art is measurably intensified thereby, and the whole takes on a new dimension of significance it did not have before. The result is not a distraction from what the author himself tells us, but rather an amplification of what he says or does, or, better, an amplification of what his work conveys to us as we read it. In short, a considerable part of our interest in many works of art arises from the fact that they express to us in a poignant and affecting way recurrent patterns of human behavior whose independent interest to us is funded into the artistic transaction which transpires as we read or look or listen.

It will doubtless be replied that when an artist's attitudes are relevant to the appreciation of his work as art they will be manifest to us in the act of appreciation so that it is unnecessary to go outside the work for additional information. And it will be urged that, if we have to go outside the work to discover what it may express, the work itself is *ipso facto* deficient as a work of art. I should reply, however, that just as no man is an island, so no work of art is an island, and that the integrity of a work of art, like the integrity of a person, is quite compatible with this fact. The phrase "going outside the work" is a treacherous one, responsible for no end of confusion and misconception as to the nature of works of art and the process whereby they are appreciated. For example, everyone knows that it is possible to go outside what one initially or immediately perceives in a work and yet not "read into" it something which is not there. Everyone knows also that it is frequently necessary to go outside the work as it immediately presents itself in order to gain access to its underlying meanings and depth values. The only serious question, therefore, is whether, having gone outside, what we find when we return is more meaningful, more satisfying, more moving. If so, then what we have "read into" the work as a consequence is "really" there in the only sense in which, in the present context, such a question has any interest.

We have still to consider the relevance of an artist's intentions in the more limited sense which has to do with what he means to say or do *in* the work of art. Now it will be argued, no doubt, that although such intentions may be relevant if our concern is to measure his achievement, they have no bearing upon the appreciation of the work of art as such. In one sense, I agree. I agree also that in the sense now being considered, an artist's intentions, unlike his motives or attitudes, do not comprise a distinguishable expressive or functional aspect of the work. If what the poet meant or intended to say does not finally coincide with what the work itself means it is irrelevant to the work and to our appreciation of it.

These banalities, however, have frequently misled aestheticians into the mistaken conclusion that consideration of an artist's intentions is irrelevant to the *interpretation* of his work. When I read a great work of art with full appreciation, the farthest thing from my mind is what he may have intended to say or what he means in a particular passage or by a particular allusion or figure of speech. The fact is, however, that full appreciation rarely occurs, and that with most complex works of art repeated study, with the aid of dictionaries, glossaries, mythologies, foot-notes, and God knows what else, is necessary in order to place oneself in a position to perform success-fully the primary acts required for the appreciation of a given work. In short, most works of art have to be interpreted, and it is because of this that consideration of what an artist intended to say or do in a work becomes relevant, although indirectly, to appreciation and to appraisal.

Just as we are all guilty, at one time or another, of the "one and only one meaning fallacy" so we are guilty of the fallacy of "fixed meaning." Words have meaning; they also acquire them. And for the purpose of under-standing the subtle nuance, overtone, or association which may explain a poet's use of a given word or figure we have to go outside what the dictionary is able to tell us. We must go somewhere. In ordinary discourse we make allowances for a person's intentions in construing what he has said. In the case of works of literary art we need not make allowances, but we are simply foolish not to accept any clue, however we may gain access to it, which will enable us to read a passage as intelligently as the work as a whole requires. Every interpretation, in one sense, goes outside the work as we immediately find it. This being so, it is of no importance whatever how an interpretation is come by, so long as the advice it gives us for the purpose of reading appreciatively actually serves that purpose. Whether the artist himself is in a privileged position to know what his work means I do not care. I care only that knowledge of his intentions sometimes enables me to construe a passage I could not otherwise adequately comprehend, and that when I follow such directions as he may give me for reading, looking, or listening, I commonly read, look, or listen in a way which is more satisfying.

There is nothing mysterious about the artists' intentions, as some theorists have argued. They are not private entities to which no one else can gain ac-cess. With artists as with less gifted folk, access to their intentions is gained in dozens of ways, from explicit, although by no means infallible, state-ments of intentions, from titles, stage directions, and other such parapher-nalia. We gain such knowledge, frequently, by examining other works of the artist himself or other works in the style, idiom, or tradition of the work under consideration. We gain it also from the internal evidence afforded by other parts of the particular work. All this we sift and fit together as best we can into the most coherent, most satisfactory interpretation of which we, with the artist's help, are capable.

The point is that we approach the interpretation of works of art not as omniscient observers who can always distinguish what an artist means from what he says, and who know in advance what is relevant or irrelevant. We consider an artist's intentions because we have questions about his work that we cannot always answer without his guidance, without knowledge of what he was trying to do or say. And we arrive at our interpretations not by gaping at the "work itself," but by a complex process of trial and error involving many things besides looking at the work. Anyone who has sought to interpret a work belonging to a culture other than his own knows how true this is.

As I have found from the examination of a great many pieces of criticism, references to the artist's intentions usually do not and are not meant to go outside the work. Nor do they in the least indicate that the critic who uses them is not interested in the work as a work of art or that he has been overcome by preoccupations with history or biography. On the contrary, in most cases, they are references to what, as the critic believes, is "really there," and are introduced only in order to provide us with the means to a fuller, more adequate appreciation. The function of critical references to an artist's intentions, nine times out of ten, is simply to go behind immediate appearances to underlying artistic realities that we otherwise stand no chance of appreciating. They do not take us away from the work, but, rather, bring us in the end closer to it. They do not divert attention from the "aesthetic object" but provide the opportunity to appreciate what is really there. And if, overwhelmed by the noisy cries of "fallacy" and "heresy" that surround us, we refuse to make use of them, the consequence will not be a purification of our aesthetic experience of art, but merely an impoverishment of our resources for having such experience—if there is any such thing.

SELECTED BIBLIOGRAPHY

1. Leslie Fiedler, "Archtype and Signature," *Sewanee Review,* 1952. A vigorous attack on "the intentional fallacy" and a defense of intentions as part of the work of art.
2. Lionel Trilling, "The Sense of the Past," in *The Liberal Imagination,* Viking Press, 1950. (Available as Anchor paperback.) A brilliant defense of the historicity of literature.
3. Edmund Wilson, "Dickens: The Two Scrooges," *Eight Essays,* Anchor paperback, 1954. An illuminating illustration of the biographical interpretation of literature.
4. Ernest Jones, *Hamlet and Oedipus,* W. W. Norton & Company, 1940. (Available as Anchor paperback.) A classic in the use of Freudian techniques in the exploration of art.
5. Ralph Fox, *The Novel and the People,* esp., Ch. I, International Publishers Company, 1937. A good statement of the Marxist intentional approach to art.

III

The Arts

III

The Arts

Introduction

Painting, music, poetry, architecture, sculpture, dance, and the motion picture each has its own combination of elements. The salient characteristics of these elements and their respective combinations can be enumerated and discussed without some total commitment to a general theory of art. If aesthetics is mainly concerned with a general theory of art, we may perhaps designate *poetics* to refer to the special theories of the different arts. This usage derives from Aristotle who, in the *Poetics,* presents a theory of the art of tragedy by setting forth and describing the fundamental elements of tragic drama—such as plot, character, thought, diction,—and their relations to each other. Since Aristotle, there have been many such specific theories of one or other of the various arts, about the nature of music, sculpture, dance, and so on. The most recent use of this sense of poetics as a specific theory of one art is that of Igor Stravinsky in his Norton Lectures, entitled the *Poetics of Music,* in which he discusses some of the fundamental elements of musical compositions and argues that melody is the most important element in music.

In this part there are presented some of the very best statements of the poetics of the various arts. In each case, the selections are from leading specialists, usually critics, in the fields of the various arts. This ensures an empirical, intimate, and viable description of the basic ingredients and problems of the different arts. In the case of painting, music and poetry, there are also included certain classic discussions concerning disputed elements in these arts, that is, selections on the legitimacy of representation in painting, or meaning in music, or truth in literature.

PAINTING

Note to the teacher: Throughout these selections there are references to many paintings. Reproductions of all of them are available as prints or slides. Many of these could be used profitably in conjunction with the reading materials. For reasons of cost and space only one reproduction, Dürer's engraving, "Melencolia I," has been included. It is an essential part of the page-by-page analysis given by Panofsky.

These readings—all from critics of paintings or from painters—deal with the fundamental elements of painting: line, color, texture, volume, space, composition, drawing, and the disputed ones of representation and symbolism. Albert Barnes discusses color, drawing and composition; Bernhard Berenson, tactile-values, movement, decoration and illustration; Henri Matisse, the organic nature of painting; Roger Fry, representation; and Panofsky, in his finest example of iconological analysis at work, the role of symbolism in painting. Taken together, these readings should provide a thorough introduction to painting.

Albert C. Barnes

COLOR, DRAWING AND COMPOSITION*

COLOR

As we have seen, color is the fundamental plastic means, and the other elements, line, light, and space may be regarded as modifications or aspects or results of it. Color has an effect which depends upon its intrinsic quality, independent of all relation to the other constituents of the picture. We all know, and the fact may be experimentally verified, that some colors produce quiet and restful effects, others are flamboyant and exciting to the sensibilities, so that the specific sensations of color with which a picture presents us have much to do with its appeal, both immediate and permanent. In Raphael, for example, the color, simply as sensuous material, is rarely good and when abstracted from the other plastic elements, it is usually like the colors in a cheap rug or fabric—either dull or overbrilliant. In Giorgione, Cézanne, or Renoir, on the contrary, immediate sensuous charm of color pervades and heightens all the more complicated effects. The result is not unlike that which simple physical charm gives to personality, in making moral and intellectual qualities more vivid and appealing, more intensely *felt,* as well as judged favorably or approved.

Variety or richness, and harmony, add greatly to "quality" in color, both in the picture as a whole and in the separate parts, elements, or units. In Giorgione, Titian, Rubens, Renoir, Cézanne, there seems to be no limit to the multiplicity of hues and tints introduced into the simplest object, an orange, a cup, a hand, a lock of hair; yet these color-chords are invariably units in themselves. The effect of unity in diversity is repeated again and again, with successively more comprehensive units, until we come to the picture as a whole, which seems a symphony of color, in which the direct sensuous appeal is enormously heightened by the sense of the relations between the colors employed, with each color setting off and being itself set off by all the others.

In order to appreciate the esthetic significance of color in the great modern painters, we must be acquainted with its use by the Venetians, above all by Giorgione, Titian, and Tintoretto. These painters employed colors which are intrinsically pleasing, and are diversified and harmonized to yield magnificent effects. Renoir advanced beyond the Venetian tradition by utilizing the contributions made by Rubens, the eighteenth century French painters, Delacroix, and by the impressionists, so that in the richly decorative aspects of his surfaces he is without a peer. On the other hand, the extreme richness, the voluptuousness of his color, detracts in some measure from his strength: there is in Cézanne a greater effect of power.

In contrast, Leonardo shows a relative barrenness of color. In both the London and the Paris version of his "Virgin of the Rocks," the color not only lacks obvious appeal, but in its variation throughout the picture there is a lack of inventiveness, of a sense of the possibilities of variation and harmony. It is mainly tone; when the tone is lighter in shade it seems to have an effect merely of shininess, when darker, of muddiness. Color itself, and color-relations, detract much from the value of his plastic form.

It must be remembered that sensuous charm or richness in color is not the same thing as brightness. Colors which are bright without being rich or deep give an effect of garishness or gaudiness, and the general effect is of superficiality. In Lorenzo Monaco and Baldung Grien among the early painters, and in Kisling, a modern artist, bright color gives no sense of glow or splendor, while in Daumier and Rembrandt, though the colors are very subdued, the effect is anything but drab or dingy.

Variety of color does not mean variety in the sense of employment of all the colors in the spectrum. Rembrandt's subtly modified dark tones suggest a great variety of color, and Piero della Francesca used chiefly a silvery blue so varied in shade, so tinged with light and shadow, that his repertoire of color seems extremely rich and the economy of his means appears only upon analysis. If Delacroix's colors were taken out of his canvases and arranged side by side, his vastly greater actual variety would be revealed, but a good Piero hung beside a Delacroix would show that Piero was the greater colorist.

We have hitherto used the word "richness" in a way that might be construed to mean "variety," as when we say that there is great richness of color in Renoir, and comparatively little in Perugino. But there is another sense of the word for which we may find a synonym, by a figure of speech, in "juiciness," as something opposed to "dryness." This is present nearly always in the greatest masters of color, in Titian, Constable, Delacroix, and Renoir. Its opposite, dryness, is not, however, a term of unqualified reproach. Poussin is a great artist and an important colorist, yet the color in his pictures is almost invariably dry. The distinction is thus not always one between good and bad, since there are esthetic effects to which dry color is a positive reënforcement; a painter may use very juicy color, like Monticelli, without thereby becoming an artist of the first rank. Again, if Puvis de Chavannes had emulated Renoir in the use of juicy color, his own distinctive form would have suffered rather than gained.

The most important difference in color-quality appears when we consider the relation of color to light, composition, modeling, etc. Color combines with light to form what may be called atmosphere, and this may be a most important element in esthetic effect, as in the Venetians, in Rembrandt, and in the impressionists. Furthermore, light has a direct influence upon color, enriching it by an internal luminosity, and the incapacity to take advantage of this influence is a serious defect in plastic form. In the world of real things, color changes in quality under different degrees of illumination, and the ability to utilize the alteration so effected is an important part of the painter's command over his materials. When light is not properly used in connection with color, plastic reality suffers because of the absence of the modification and enrichment that light works upon color. Instead of bringing out and revealing new harmonies within color, the light seems to efface color and act merely as a substitute for it. In Leonardo and Raphael, too much light overemphasizes the contrast between light and shadow, and, in addition, the light fails to make the color function vigorously. The contrast between light and shadow is even more striking in Rembrandt, but his handling of color-indications is so skilful that the chiaroscuro is utilized as an enhancement of color and not as camouflage for lack of it.

The use of light in connection with color as atmosphere is to be seen conspicuously in the Venetians, in the painters of the Barbizon school, and in the impressionists. It appears earlier in the work of the fourteenth century Florentine, Masaccio. In the real world, atmosphere blurs the outlines of objects at a distance from the eye. This naturalistic effect is in Masaccio's painting enlarged in esthetic value by an addition of color to the simple haze of nature. Except among the primitives, almost all painters reproduce the blurred outlines of distant objects, but the effect of atmosphere as a luminous color in which all things float is not universal in painting. Sometimes, as in Whistler, it is an obvious imitation of mist; sometimes it is a source of melodramatic pseudo-romance, as in Turner; but when employed with discrimination, as in Claude and the Venetians, it is a powerful reënforcement having its own esthetic effect. It is usually golden in Claude, in the Venetians it is golden with an admixture of brown, and in Corot it is silvery. As a translucent atmosphere, a circumambient glow, it supplements or blends with the local colors, augments decorative quality, aids in knitting the composition together, and thus functions as an important element in the plastic form.

The rôle of color in drawing and composition is as important as its joint function with light in creating atmosphere, but it may be more conveniently discussed in the chapters dealing with those topics. There remains one other important distinction in the use of color to be discussed at this point. Color may or may not seem to be a part of the actual structure or mass of an object. As we have seen, the usual manner of rendering solidity is to show a graduated increase in light or shadow. Such modeling was developed to a very high degree of perfection in Leonardo and Michelangelo, and since their time it has been the usual method of giving the impression of solidity. But modeling has a richer plastic value when the artist is able to make color an integral part of the solid structure. The Venetians were the first to realize this structural use of color and it became an important plastic resource in subsequent great painters, notably, Constable, Delacroix, Velásquez, El Greco, Renoir, and Cézanne. In Giorgione, Titian, and Tintoretto, a solid body does not appear as something which has substance in itself independent of color. The substance seems to be built up out of color, that is, the color seems to go down into the solid substance and permeate it. In every detail in Titian's "Man with Glove," for example, color seems to be the actual material out of which the form is wrought. In contrast, Leonardo's effects of solidity are largely independent of color: there is not a great deal of color at best, and what there is is usually superficial. In Ingres's paintings, we usually get the impression that the form was completely fashioned or modeled before any thought of color entered the painter's mind; the result is a lack of the solidity which accrues when color is used structurally. The color is often quite pleasing, but it tends to be a mere decorative adjunct, without organic plastic function.

Another kind of pervasive color-effect is best illustrated in Giotto. His color is not structural in the Venetian sense, though it is an integral part of the general form of the picture. The atmosphere is usually as clear as crystal, and the colors stand out like jewels, in contrast to the Venetian glow in which there is a suggestion of translucency amounting at times to a haze. In spite of this crystalline transparency of Giotto, the pervasive color, into which reddish, yellowish, and bluish tints merge, is extremely marked, and adds much to the elevated and mysterious effect. The religious character imparted may be expressed if we say that in Giotto the world is *transfigured*, and that the limpid, sparkling color-glow is the main agent in the transfiguration. In Rembrandt, though the actual color is very different, we find the same mystical effect, the same sense of reality without any approach to photographic representation, and here too the effect is due to the same extreme sensitiveness to color-values and ability to render them by subtle yet unmistakable means. Indeed, the mysticism which art at its best conveys seems to attach itself in a peculiar degree to the masterful handling of color, and points to the fact that color is *the* source, *par excellence,* of the highest "quality" in painting.

Another form of color-effect is that in Piero della Francesca. In him we have neither the solid structural use of color, nor the juiciness which is so often a sign of great ability in color-handling. His color is unmistakably dry. His total effect, of an all-embracing coolness, requires exactly the colors which he uses. The basis of this effect is blue; but it is a blue so infinitely diversified by light that it becomes a whole series of blues with only the most subtle distinctions between them. They are so juxtaposed and blended with other harmonious colors, cool greens, grays, reds, as to provide a complete set of new and distinctive color-forms. This dominant note of coolness is Piero's characteristic form, and is perfectly blended with the drawing, composition, expression, etc., to create a distinctive note of the highest esthetic excellence.

Fra Angelico used a pleasing bright blue but with less sense of harmony with other colors. Instead of the pervasive charm of Piero or the brilliance and power of Giotto, we have a staccato effect as one color follows another across the canvas, and this, though it constitutes a color-form of a kind, is not esthetically very moving. The color-relations are too reminiscent of those of other painters, and this deficiency is made more serious by the fact that they are usually superficial.

The foregoing illustrations embody effects perceptible when we isolate color from all other plastic elements and consider it as a thing in itself. But there are types of definite color-designs other than the glows or suffusions of which we have been speaking. The use of color to make a design is well illustrated in Soutine, a contemporary painter. Soutine's characteristic form is that of intense movement, of passion, and his choice and combination of colors is peculiarly adjusted to this effect. His hot, juicy, vivid, and varied color is the antithesis of Piero's, yet both men achieve color-design of a high order. In Tintoretto's "Paradise" and in Renoir's "Bathing Group," the rhythmic flow of color is an essential part of the general effect of fluid, graceful, swirling movement, and forms a rich color-design which plays its own part.

A somewhat similar effect is to be found in Poussin, whose color is rather dry, and though it cannot be called superficial, is not deeply structural in its function. But its flow and rhythm extend to every part of the canvas

and make up a design well in harmony with Poussin's general form of delicacy and "choiceness." The color-design reënforces his linear and compositional rhythms, and appears as a distinguishable but perfectly merged element in his plastic form.

Leonardo rarely makes color function successfully in the design; in
"Mona Lisa" he approaches the goal, but in his "Bacchus" the color adds but
little to the design. Indeed, one of the chief reasons for denying to Leonardo
a place among the greatest artists is his inability to merge light with color,
as they are merged whenever either appears at its best, as in Giotto, Giorgione, Titian, Tintoretto, Dürer, van Eyck, Rembrandt, Cézanne, and
Renoir.

In Perugino, although the color is not deeply felt or organically used
and lacks juiciness and richness, it is occasionally, as in his "Combat of Love
and Chastity," in keeping with the design, which is, on the whole, light and
delicate, tasteful rather than moving. In Raphael, there is almost no real
color-sense. If we abstract the other elements and look for a color-design, we
usually find nothing of great esthetic significance. Everything else, light,
line, placing of masses, modeling, pattern, is practically complete without
color. Usually his color is taken from other painters and used with little or
no individuality though occasionally, as in "Virgin with Blue Diadem" and
"Woman with Veil," it does contribute to the ensemble effect. In his famous
"Madonna: *la Belle Jardinière*," one must be able to ignore the color to enjoy
the fine linear effects and feeling for space. The color is garish and drab, in
spite of the bright red of the dress. The good modeling with light loses its
force because of the absence of color, which is called for to make the figure
live. The effect is doughy and pasty, as of a statue in soft plaster. Raphael's
inferiority as a colorist appears again in the contrast between his "Count
Baldassare Castiglione," in which there is lack of harmony in color relations,
and Titian's "Man with Glove." In both pictures the color is present mainly
as tone, but in the Raphael it is superficial, dry, monotonous, and it has little
or no value as a design; in the Titian, subtle but rich color-chords are present
and enhance the ensemble.

In "Ascent to Calvary," by Simone Martini, the bright colors make a
pattern lending vivacity to a picture which is essentially illustration, rather
than a complete plastic form. Their brightness does not make them really
moving; nevertheless their ensemble effect fits in well with the general form
of the picture. In Mantegna, the lack of quality in color-relations and their
failure to form a unity are sometimes positive drawbacks. That this is not
due to the specific colors used is apparent from the fact that the dark greens
which appear in the Louvre pictures by him are used by many other

painters, and with no effect of dullness or muddiness. In "Agony in the Garden," he appears to better advantage, for there color does function successfully in unifying the design and enriching plastic form.

In the use of color, academicism is very common. Raphael is an instance of this at a comparatively high level of skill; in his imitators, Guido Reni and Giulio Romano, the imitation of Raphael is doubly academic and is not merely indifferent but offensive. The Venetian glow becomes an academic device in the lesser painters of the school, Palma Vecchio and Sebastiano del Piombo: an overaccentuation, a melodrama, with imitative character testified to by overemphasis, in practically every detail. In the Barbizon painter, Rousseau, Claude's color is academicized, with resulting artificiality and feebleness; the same is true of van Dyck, in relation to Rubens. The Poussin tradition becomes academic, cheap, and tawdry in Le Sueur, whose color is hopelessly gaudy and trivial. His plagiarism is obvious and is unredeemed by any plastic force or reality.

The foregoing discussion, brief and incomplete as it is, shows how superficial is the view of nearly all the critics that color is a relatively unimportant element in painting. This view is definitely stated by Roger Fry; it is stated and then retracted by Berenson, but the judgments on pictures to which he gives expression in his books on the Italian painters, show how little he really appreciates the rôle played by color in plastic art. In esthetic criticism of lower order, such as Mather's, there is no evidence of any intelligent conception of the function of color in painting. The importance of Giotto as a colorist, for example, is entirely overlooked, and so is the function of color throughout the whole Florentine school, which is said to be preoccupied with "tactile values," that is modeling—really a very secondary matter. Again, in the Venetians, though the rôle of color is emphasized, its significance is never explained even in general principles, and the organic and structural functions of color are totally ignored. These critics fail to see that by far the most important aspect of color is not its sensuous quality but the part which its relations play in organizing a picture. That color-relations are all-important in plastic form, that composition at its best is effected by means of color, is one of the most weighty facts in esthetics, and it is one to which the great majority of writers on plastic art seem to be totally oblivious.

DRAWING

Drawing is often understood as a function of the line which defines contour and marks off adjacent objects from one another. The only conception of drawing, however, which does justice to the plastic function here in question is that which includes in its meaning the whole process of *drawing out* whatever aspects are significant for the painter's design. We have already seen that all art is selective, concerned only with certain phases of its subject-matter, and that even these phases are never literally reproduced. They are emphasized or even distorted in various degree, and set in a new context by which their esthetic significance is enhanced. This selection and interpretation is the essence of the expressive act; in it all the artist's powers are called into play and put on trial; it is what really constitutes drawing. In terms of plastic art, drawing is a fusion of all the plastic means, an interrelation of line with light, color, and space, the esthetic value of which is proportionate to the degree of union achieved. In drawing of the very first order, line is not a sharp demarcation between adjacent areas of color, but is color itself, either as an actual narrow colored band, as often in Cézanne and Matisse, or as an area into which the color overflows from the objects on either side. The latter form of drawing, which originated with the Venetians, attained in Renoir its supreme degree of perfection. Even when there is no overflow of color, as in such early painters as Giotto, van Eyck, and Dürer, clean-cut line may be so well harmonized with the other plastic means that perfect integration is achieved. Unreality appears only when line stands in isolation, when there is no organic relation between contours and what they enclose.

The relation of line to drawing is, however, very close. We speak of a summary or digest of essential features in anything as an "outline"; to portray is to "delineate"; and the features which make any one what he is are his "lineaments." A pen-and-ink drawing may be an excellent illustration, in the esthetically expressive as well as the illustrative sense. Hence the use of line is the natural point of departure for a discussion of drawing, provided the fact is kept in mind that line is *plastically* significant only in so far as it is related to the other elements in the form as a whole.

Painting developed out of mosaics. In them, the definition of contour was of necessity absolutely distinct and this distinctness remained for a long time characteristic of painting. In Cimabue, the line of demarcation between one object and another is very clear-cut, so that the surface of the canvas is divided into what might be called color-tight compartments, and the line between them seems to belong to neither compartment. Line so used produces a rigid fixity in the movement and expression of all the figures so that the impression of actual movement is lacking. Also, there is comparatively little integration of the lines of separate objects in a linear design in the picture as a whole. After Cimabue, line became more integrated with light, with color, and with composition, so that these elements are recognizable only upon abstraction and analysis. At the start, the pictures seem like line-drawings to which color, light, etc., were applied after the design was essentially complete; subsequently, the drawing was conceived in terms of all the plastic elements, with the result of a great increase in unity, reality, and moving force. In Giotto, line is no longer literal or isolated but a simple, terse, and forceful factor the significance of which can be fully grasped only with the aid of the imagination. The line is still clear-cut, but the color and light on each side are merged with it to give an ensemble effect of more convincing reality than is possible from line alone; in other words, the line gets its force from the relations it assumes, and thus becomes plastic. In the drawing of individual objects, and of the picture as a whole, the sequence of line and mass is fluid, rhythmic, and harmonized to make up the total design.

In Masaccio, we have the first important step toward naturalistic effects in drawing, in the employment of blurred outline. In Andrea del Castagno, the sharpness of line is diminished through the use of a swirl, and this necessitates further simplification and abandonment of mere literalism, with the result that the expressiveness of the line, and its use in abstract design, is further heightened. In Fra Filippo Lippi, line is less expressive and powerful than in Masaccio and Andrea del Castagno, but there is an increase of grace and decorative quality, which adds a fresh enrichment to design. In Uccello, the line is stiffer, less fluid, and more varied in direction; by reason of these qualities it has a quite peculiar effect in achieving individual patterns. Line is still very sharp in both these men, and has little or no effect of movement, even when the subject-matter is ostensibly dynamic.

In Piero della Francesca, line is more reënforced by color, and the general design is much more elaborate, varied, and powerful esthetically. He gets many of the effects of drawing by means of color, without abandoning the clearly separate character of the two elements. The absence of movement or drama in his drawing is required by his generally quiet and detached style.

In Botticelli, line gives the effect of active movement, but it is so isolated, elaborated, and overworked that plastic unity is largely lost. The line forms an intricate series of arabesques, so feebly supported by the other plastic means that the drawing is not really an element in structural form, but is rather decoration. The result is an effect of facile virtuosity which is superficially attractive but has little moving force. The line forms a pattern but is rarely an integral part of the design, and is used without consideration of the appropriateness to subject-matter: in his religious pictures, for example, it produces a tendency to an incongruous swirl.

Leonardo's sharp line also stands out clearly, but, since it is merged with the modeling and plays a more integral part in the design, it is much less of an overaccentuation than Botticelli's. In "Mona Lisa," for example, the lines in the sleeves and in the background really give an impression of solidity and depth, as compared with the merely decorative quality of the more elaborate linear pattern in Botticelli's "Birth of Venus." Leonardo's line was taken over by Raphael and made more incisive, more dramatic, more rhythmically varied, and on the whole a more interesting feature of the design. In both men, it often tended toward literal expression and over-sweetness, and this is not entirely counterbalanced in Leonardo by the three-dimensionality of his masses, or in Raphael by the impression of vigorous movement. Raphael's line is prodigal rather than terse, and consequently lacks the high degree of expressive power which comes with economy of means. His line is very sharp, is quite independent of color, and the light, by which it is complemented, heightens the sense of overdramatization.

In Michelangelo, line and color are distinct but are so well related that the drawing has a quality of great strength. His drawing was a modification of that of Signorelli and Cosimo Tura, but he merged it in a special way in the form as a whole, and used it to give more melodramatic expression to subject-matter.

The drawing of the Venetians was an advance over that of their prede-cessors in that they made a systematic use of color and of blurred contour. Because of their structural color and atmospheric glow, the definition of areas by sharp lines was neither necessary nor desirable for the general design. The earlier Venetians, Bellini and Carpaccio, retained the use of sharp line and merged it well with color and light, though not sufficiently to attain the convincing reality found in Giorgione and Titian. In Giorgione the contours are comparatively little blurred but they do not stand out and cause the attention to be centered on themselves. Titian often uses a broad line of contour which is sometimes relatively isolated from the form and, while it adds to decoration, very frequently weakens expression. Sometimes Titian's line is so loose that the objects seem to melt into surrounding space, and this represents the expressive function of drawing achieved with the minimum of means. Here line, color, and light are fully synthesized, and drawing reaches the highest estate as yet attained.

In Tintoretto, linear contour is often accentuated as a narrow band of color, but the line, light, and color are all completely merged in the form of a swirl which is the most effective means of representing powerful move-ment and drama, and may also be adapted to other purposes. When the swirl is toned down and used to depict the hard, clear quality of textures, the organic use of the color prevents the clear demarcations from seeming like isolated lines, and the effect is one of greater solidity and reality. In Paolo Veronese, the line is also sometimes accentuated as a band of color as in Titian and Tintoretto, but on the whole contour is sharper than in the other important Venetians. In his "Burning of Sodom," line pervades the whole picture, flows from object to object, and gives the effect of motion in a particular direction by its general disposition through the canvas. This pervasively unifying line is characteristic of all the best Venetian painters.

Poussin's line is more Florentine than Venetian. It is extremely graceful, elegant, delicate, charming, but it has not the power of that of the best of the Venetians and is less firmly supported by structural color. It is less incisive than Raphael's or Leonardo's; but both of these modifications are well adapted to Poussin's designs, and they function very effectively in both decorative and expressive rôles.

In Rubens, contour is sharper than in Titian but less sharp than in Raphael. His swirl necessarily gives the effect of broken line, so that within the confines of a surface there is less of the broad, unbroken area of color which throws hard contours into sharp relief. His line is repeated rhythmically over and over, and contributes strongly to the effect of animation and movement, but is less convincing and powerful than Tintoretto's, in which color is more deeply fused with all the other plastic elements.

Rembrandt's drawing is accomplished with extreme subtlety and economy of means. The merging of light, line, and color is so perfect that minute analysis is required to differentiate between them; in addition, the effects are more restrained and so more powerful esthetically, than those of Rubens. There is perfect differentiation of masses, and yet the actual marks on the canvas by which this is done are scarcely perceptible. His subtle line is infinitely more expressive than Botticelli's or Raphael's in conveying feeling and characteristic movement or gesture with the utmost sensitiveness. There is a similar subtlety in Velásquez but of a lesser degree. El Greco's line is so distorted and so varied in direction, length, and proportions as to give an impression of emotional frenzy carried to the highest intensity. But the effect is not melodramatic—the activity of the line is perfectly matched by similar activity in the light, color, and all other plastic factors.

Upon close inspection, Claude's drawing of individual units seems inferior to that of the greatest painters in that his line lacks terseness, individuality, expressiveness. But if we examine the drawing of the picture as a whole, we find linear effects formed by the sequence of masses instead of by the definition of one mass against another, and that larger line is fluid, varied, rhythmic, and distinctive. Claude's design required the rendering of the lineaments of a total scene, which he was able to do better by slighting the drawing of the details of individual objects. In Boucher the line is quite hard and partakes of Botticelli's qualities of grace and sensuous charm, with much decorative and little real expressive power. Its sharpness imparts a delicate cameo-quality. Watteau and Fragonard show softer contours, with a general tendency to diffuseness; the imperfect fusion of line with color results in rather weak drawing. In Chardin the contour is sharper, but the drawing is so sensitive, expressive, and tempered with light and color, that it seems subdued and makes a strong but unobtrusive element in the plastic form.

David's drawing, skilful but hard and cold, is fundamentally academic; Ingres's is far more varied, rhythmic, and sensitive, and is more original. The classic feeling of coldness is present and the line is very tight; but there is a sense in which it is more effective than in any other painter. Although Ingres's pictures may almost be said to be made out of line, the line does much more than define the meeting-place of two distinct objects. It renders the basic feeling of the surfaces depicted without much aid from color and light, so that the line is the groundwork of the painting. In a measure, it does for Ingres what chiaroscuro does for Rembrandt, that is, gives an equivalent for the other plastic means. Of course, line cannot give the full equivalent; but it does function organically, and so is far less of an over-accentuation than it is in Botticelli, in whom it is little more than a pattern. Ingres's use of line is really art and not mere virtuosity, but it is not the greatest art, partly because this particular means is inadequate to bear the full weight of plastic form, partly because Ingres lacked the freshness and depth of insight of the really great masters: he did not have a great deal to say.

Daumier was another master of drawing, though of quite a different sort. His line is often broad at the contour, as in Titian and Tintoretto, but is more broken in continuity. It is highly vigorous, concentrated, expressive, and it coöperates with light and modeling to give an effect of great weight and solidity combined with activity. In some paintings his drawing is comparable in power and expressiveness with that of Rembrandt, and is executed by a coalition of line, light, and color.

Delacroix's drawing is relatively negligible from the standpoint of original plastic expressiveness. In line, light, and color it derives from Rubens, and is too often perverted to noisy purposes that are obviously narrative and psychological. This psychological motif was rendered with much more effect by Degas, who added the flexibility, variety, and skill of Ingres, and made a form in which the psychological expressiveness of line is given an adequate plastic embodiment. In Degas' paintings, as distinguished from his work in pastel, there is a tendency to rely too much on line without sufficient support from the other plastic means, so that in spite of the genuineness of his effects his paintings do not reach the highest level of achievement.

Courbet's line is comparatively hard, but his total drawing is firm and has distinction and power in conveying his particular realistic effects. In Manet, line is merged well with the other plastic elements and his drawing successfully avoids imitation and achieves a very distinctive design. In Claude Monet, line is often almost dissolved in an excess of light and color, and the result is a loss of vigor, expressiveness, and strength of design. There is not the firm structure beneath the veil of color and light that there is in Renoir and Cézanne.

In these later men, the contributions of all previous painters are in large measure summed up and revised to make new forms. In Renoir, drawing is derived fundamentally from the Venetians, but it is extended in range of expressiveness by an infinitely better fusion of line and light with color, and by his own modification of the brushwork of the impressionists. Color flows over contour more freely in Renoir than in any previous painter; line, as an independent entity, practically disappears in his latest work, without in the least compromising the masses outlined against one another. Objects are thus enriched by the wealth of color-relations which enter into them, and at the same time the broader, more fluid drawing eliminates non-essentials and reveals inherent quality as the Venetian drawing, even at its best, never does. In Cézanne, the tradition of Michelangelo, Tintoretto, and El Greco, who employed distortions to get strength, is passed through the channels of impressionism, and emerges with a new note of significance and reality, heightened by planes intersecting in perspective. In a still later painter, Glackens, we have a general style similar to Renoir's, modified by the psychological expressiveness of Daumier and Degas, but even more simplified and especially illustrative of posture, gesture, and movement.

Drawing, in brief, is good art when it is free from confusing elements, like isolated literal contour or overdecorative quality; when it is so condensed, so simplified that it carries in itself sufficient revelation of objective fact to enable us to grasp the essence, significance, conviction of objective reality in the things portrayed. In short, drawing consists not in the literal reproduction of linear contours or shapes; it is a mark of the artist's ability to resolve the lines of demarcation into separate parts, select certain parts for emphasis, and recombine them into a new ensemble that is a form in itself, not merely a duplication of the shape of an object. Line gets power by what it does to what is contained between the lines; that is, as with all other forms, its essential characteristic resides in the relations it assumes and creates. A line in isolation is rarely to be considered in a painting; it gets form from its relation to other lines; its value in the hierarchy of art is determined by its significant use in connection with the other elements—color, light, space, mass, shadow—which make up drawing.

A man's drawing is as distinctive of himself, of his personality—his candor, reality, freedom from affectation—as is his face, his writing, or his psychological make-up as revealed by analysis.

COMPOSITION

As drawing constitutes the way in which significant aspects of things are selected, drawn out, and molded in accordance with the painter's design, so composition is the whole process of ordering, organizing, and unifying the plastic elements in the form of a picture. Conventionally, the term "composition" has been applied to the distribution of masses, but this is an unjustifiable limitation of its meaning. The compositional units of a picture may, but need not, be masses; they may also be areas of color, islands of light, linear arabesques, or any means whatever by which balance and unity are secured. The Venetian glow, Rembrandt's chiaroscuro, Renoir's color-suffusion, and Matisse's pattern of color-compartments, all serve to unite every part of a picture in a rhythmic, organic unity. In modern painting especially, in which the use of relatively abstract design is very extensive, all the parts of the picture are more nearly on an equal footing compositionally than in the primitive and Renaissance pictures, the organization of which is usually focused about individual volumes or groups of volumes. In tracing the development of composition, therefore, we shall begin with the distribution of masses, which may most conveniently be designated "mass-composition," and observe the way in which, as time goes on, composition becomes more fluid and more organically related to the use of color. Composition by means of color represents the supreme form of plastic integration.

There are a number of general types of mass-composition which are constantly encountered and which require examination. The simplest form is that of a central mass with balancing figures to right and left by which bilateral symmetry is attained; this form is usually that of a pyramid, and achieves the sense of stability and rhythm in an obvious form. It is illustrated in most of Raphael's Madonnas, but with him it is so stereotyped as to indicate a poverty of imagination. However, this form, although in itself trite, may be combined with other qualities, color, light, line, of such personal and distinctive character, as in the Castelfranco Giorgione, that it is redeemed from banality. Greater personal expressiveness is achieved in the distribution of masses when instead of a complete bilateral symmetry we have volumes different in kind but similar in function, which surprise and yet fulfil the normal desire for balance. In Titian's "Disciples at Emmaus," the number of figures on the left of the central figure is greater than on the right, but there is in addition on the right a window opening out on a landscape, which adds to the interest of the design; thus unity is not disturbed and variety is increased.

In the foregoing, it is their relation to a central mass that ties together the separate masses. The central figure is usually in these cases the one of greatest interest, so that there is an obvious parallel between plastic and narrative or human values of the several units. But the object that ties up the parts of a picture may be in itself trivial from the illustrative point of view as, for example, the Cupid in Titian's "Jupiter and Antiope," or the tree in Cosimo Rosselli's "Pharaoh's Destruction in the Red Sea." A radically different type of composition is achieved when the central mass is not the main focus of interest as in Giorgione's "Concert in the Open Air," or is discarded, as in some of the Assisi Giottos. In these pictures the elements are kept from falling apart by subtle relationships, by which the artist's feeling for grouping is expressed. This "feeling for grouping" means a feeling for harmonious relationships, and in plastic art it may vary independently of the other factors: in Raphael, for example, it is much better than his color.

In a good painting all the factors are integrated, and disposition of masses is one of these factors. Paintings of the highest value are composed with color, so that the two factors, composition and color, are blended. In Piero della Francesca and Giotto, firm integration makes their pictures highly personal and individual. In Giorgione's "Concert in the Open Air," the color-rhythms bind the picture together, along with the sequence of line and mass. In Titian's "Entombment," the color, rich, varied, and deep, permeates the entire canvas and ties the units together. The color in the cloaks of the bending figures, at the right and left of the central group, functions as a frame to enclose and unify it. In Tintoretto's "Paradise," the rhythmic succession of color unites with the rhythm of line to give the effect of swirling movement which is the keynote of the picture's design. Here, as always, the greater the fusion of means the more living, convincing, real, individual, is the effect, and the farther removed from mechanism or academicism.

Another adjunct to composition is the distribution of light. Here, as with color, the light represented in various parts of the canvas often forms a pattern in itself. A figure or object functions quite differently according to its place in the pattern of light, which is a distinguishable but inseparable part of the plastic form. The pattern of light in Titian's "Man with Glove" is vital to the composition. In other words, the manner in which a picture is composed is an essential part of the total design, and must be judged as subsidiary to it; and this is the reason for the futility of all academic rules for judging composition in isolation.

The lines which define the contours of objects have an important function in composition. In Courbet's "Painter's Studio" and in Poussin's "Blindmen of Jericho," the figures are held together not only by their placing with reference to a central point, but by linear effects carried over from one mass to another. The whole composition flows, it is never static. When abstracted the line is seen to form a pattern in itself which is made up of a series of subsidiary patterns all merged with one another. This interweaving of line in combination with a central figure is very important in all closely-knit compositions. In Leonardo's "Virgin, St. Anne, and the Infant Jesus," or Raphael's "Holy Family, of François I," the figures, both as wholes and with reference to their parts, are focal points in a network of lines in three dimensions. The way in which linear patterns contrast with each other, reënforce each other, may be infinitely varied according to the feeling of the painter for space-effects. In Uccello's "Rout of San Romano," linear effects constitute the chief compositional factor in the plastic form, which is clearly separable from and independent of the subject-matter. This again illustrates the necessity of judging all plastic elements in relation to design. Judged by academic standards, the Uccello would be uncomposed, but with the design in mind the relation of the parts to one another at once becomes apparent. In its abstractness, Uccello's form resembles that of the cubists, and cannot be judged by any criterion of representative accuracy.

Individual figures or masses do not always operate singly as compositional units: they may be perceived as part of a whole group which functions as a unit, as in powerful compositions on a large scale. In that case there is a subsidiary composition within the group, just as in a symphony we find several movements each one a composition in itself. In Francesco di Giorgio's "Rape of Europa," for example, the entire group of trees and foliage plays the part of a single mass, within which the individual trees, branches, and leaves make up a subordinate composition. Similarly in Rembrandt's "Unmerciful Servant," the three figures at the right are a single mass balancing the single figure at the left; within that mass the individual elements are clearly distinguished and make up an interesting composition in themselves. This subordinate composition will in a great painting fit into and enhance the general design; in an inferior painting it may be good in itself, but it may fail to integrate with the total design. In Botticelli's "Incidents in the Life of Moses," there are two separate pictures which do not unify into a single composition; in Cosimo Rosselli's "Pharaoh's Destruction in the Red Sea," a similar double theme does unify. In Titian's "Assumption," this integration of different groups is present in a very high degree, the rhythms of line and mass being reënforced by light, color, and space, all binding the picture together in a harmonious unity, with human values and plastic values perfectly merged. A similar compositional problem in Raphael's "Transfiguration" is treated by superficial and specious means.

Transition to space-composition may be made if we consider relation of figures and masses to background. In work of the greatest esthetic power many features of composition depend upon representation of the third dimension. Even in painting which tends to be flat, such as Matisse's or Manet's, not everything depicted is shown as on the same plane, and though spatial depth is not emphasized, it is by no means eliminated. The relation of a single head, as in a portrait, to what is back of it, should be considered a part of the composition of the picture. This relation is partly determined by color, partly by compositional means in the narrower sense. The pattern of lines in a portrait may be carried into the background, or there may be superficially no relation, as in the Pisanello "Princess of the Este Family." Here the background of foliage and flowers may seem plastically unrelated to the girl's head; really, however, the relation is an organic one established by duplication of rhythmic patterns. In Fra Filippo Lippi's "Virgin Adoring the Child," the relation between the central figures and the background is exceedingly important, though the objects in the background are felt like the pattern on a screen. On the other hand the background may be extremely simple, as in Rembrandt's "Hendrickje Stoffels," or Titian's "Man with Glove," in both of which, by means that are very subtle, the figure is distinguished, set out from what is back of it. The effect of infinite depth achieved in both these pictures is an extraordinary triumph of space-composition. In Rubens' "Baron Henri de Vicq," though the placing of the head against the background is effective, the means employed, that is, sharply contrasting colors, are obvious and more facile, and the lesser economy of means reduces the esthetic value in comparison with the Titian and Rembrandt.

Space-composition is achieved largely through use of perspective and is at its best when color is the chief constructive factor in it. But skilful perspective is not the same thing as effective space-composition. The difference is that in effective space-composition not only is the illusion of depth rendered, but the intervals, the relations of distance, are intrinsically pleasing and represent personal feeling instead of literal imitation. The mere representation of distance has no closer relation to art than the work of the surveyor or civil engineer. Objects well composed in space are not huddled or crowded: each object is in its own space, each has elbow-room, no matter how small the space may be. The ordering of these relationships constitutes the space-composition of the picture as a whole and is an important source of esthetic pleasure.

In architecture and sculpture, where space is actually present, there is the same distinction between a vital, personal arrangement of spaces which gives the *feeling* of depth or extensity, and the inability really to conceive the object in three-dimensional terms. Primitive Negro art shows this power of conception in three dimensions, while in much of Greek sculpture it is comparatively lacking.

In composition in three dimensions, all the effects of two-dimensional composition are amplified. Thrust and counterthrust, balance, rhythm, the effects of light and shadow, are heightened in variety and power. The sense of real space, harmoniously subdivided, appears in Claude, in Poussin, in Perugino, in Raphael, in all the great Venetians. In regard to space alone Raphael is a really important artist. He and Perugino were doubtless influenced to achieve it by the clear air and mountainous country of Central Italy, in which striking relations of masses in obvious deep space are almost forced upon the attention.

In practically all of Poussin's pictures we find not only a clear indication of distance everywhere, but great appeal in the intervals themselves. The masses are related backward and forward as well as on the surface of the canvas, and these relationships form an integral part of the general plastic design. This design in space is reënforced by color, both in its appealing sensuous quality and in the relations of the colors to each other, and by line and light and shadow; all these elements combine to give a distinctively clear, light, airy, and charming design. In Giorgione's "Concert in the Open Air," the relation of all parts of the landscape to the blue and golden distance contributes greatly to the impression of mystery, romance, and glamor. Claude's effects are more romantic, more majestic, and they would be impossible but for the unlimited spaciousness of his pictures, which gives reality to the vast patterns of light. In addition, the ways in which the intervals are proportioned and related to one another are also immediately pleasing in themselves. A final example of space-composition is Giotto's: his perspective, from the acadamic standpoint, is very faulty, but he had the utmost genius for placing objects, in deep space, in relations which are varied, powerful, absolutely unstereotyped, but always appropriate and in harmony with the general design.

Space-composition, like the other plastic functions, reaches its greatest

height when color takes the most active part in it. Cézanne's dynamic organization of volumes in deep space is a partial illustration of this compositional
rôle of color, since color is the material and organizing force in all his painting; but an even better example is to be found in Renoir's work, especially
that done after 1900. Color extends over contours so freely that spatial intervals are felt primarily as color-relations, and in many of his paintings a suffu-
sion of color floods every part of the picture, uniting each compositional
element with all the others in an indissoluble entity.

Space-composition shares with the other plastic factors the possibility
of becoming academic, usually through overaccentuation. An example of
this is found in Perugino's fresco, "Christ Giving the Keys to Peter," in
which the grouping of the figures and the linear patterns on the pavement
cheapen the effect by their extreme obviousness. In Turner's "Dido Building
Carthage," there is the same overdramatization of space, but in this case
the theft from Claude is so obvious that the picture is plagiaristic rather
than academic.

Bernhard Berenson

DECORATION AND ILLUSTRATION*

TACTILE VALUES

The first of the great personalities in Florentine painting was Giotto.
Although he affords no exception to the rule that the great Florentines exploited all the arts in the endeavor to express themselves, he, Giotto, renowned as architect and sculptor, reputed as wit and versifier, differed from
most of his Tuscan successors in having peculiar aptitude for the essential
in painting *as an art*.

Before we can appreciate his real value, we must come to an agreement
as to what in the art of figure-painting—the craft has its own altogether
diverse laws—*is* the essential; for figure-painting, we may say at once, was
not only the one pre-occupation of Giotto, but the dominant interest of the
entire Florentine school.

* From Bernhard Berenson's *The Italian Painters of the Renaissance*, pp. 62–69; 131–
141; 197–201; 304–306. Copyright, 1930, by The Clarendon Press. Reprinted by permission of The Clarendon Press.

Bernhard Berenson, (1865–   ), art collector and art historian extraordinare, has
devoted a lifetime of love and scholarship to paintings, especially to Italian Renaissance
ones. He has written much, but his general aesthetics of painting was already worked out
with great power in his first major work, from which we here reprint.

Psychology has ascertained that sight alone gives us no accurate sense of the third dimension. In our infancy long before we are conscious of the process, the sense of touch, helped on by muscular sensations of movement, teaches us to appreciate depth, the third dimension, both in objects and in space.

In the same unconscious years we learn to make of touch, of the third dimension, the test of reality. The child is still dimly aware of the intimate connection between touch and the third dimension. He cannot persuade himself of the unreality of Looking-Glass Land until he has touched the back of the mirror. Later, we entirely forget the connection, although it remains true, that every time our eyes recognize reality, we are, as a matter of fact, giving tactile values to retinal impressions.

Now, painting is an art which aims at giving an abiding impression of artistic reality with only two dimensions. The painter must, therefore, do consciously what we all do unconsciously—construct his third dimension. And he can accomplish his task only as we accomplish ours, by giving tactile values to retinal impressions. His first business, therefore, is to rouse the tactile sense, for I must have the illusion of being able to touch a figure, I must have the illusion of varying muscular sensations inside my palm and fingers corresponding to the various projections of this figure, before I shall take it for granted as real, and let it affect me lastingly.

It follows that the essential in the art of painting—as distinguished from the art of coloring, I beg the reader to observe—is somehow to stimulate our consciousness of tactile values, so that the picture shall have at least as much power as the object represented, to appeal to our tactile imagination.

Well, it was of the power to stimulate the tactile consciousness—of the essential, as I have ventured to call it, in the art of painting—that Giotto was supreme master. This is his everlasting claim to greatness, and it is this which will make him a source of highest aesthetic delight for a period at least as long as decipherable traces of his handiwork remain on moldering panel or crumbling wall. For great though he was as a poet, enthralling as a story-teller, splendid and majestic as a composer, he was in these qualities superior in degree only, to many of the masters who painted in various parts of Europe during the thousand years that intervened between the decline of antique, and the birth, in his own person, of modern painting. But none of these masters had the power to stimulate the tactile imagination, and, consequently, they never painted a figure which has artistic existence. Their works have value, if at all, as highly elaborate, very intelligible symbols, capable, indeed, of communicating something, but losing all higher value the moment the message is delivered.

Giotto's paintings, on the contrary, have not only as much power of appealing to the tactile imagination as is possessed by the objects represented—human figures in particular—but actually more; with the necessary result that to his contemporaries they conveyed a *keener* sense of reality, of life-likeness than the objects themselves! We whose current knowledge of anatomy is greater, who expect more articulation and suppleness in the human figure, who, in short, see much less naïvely now than Giotto's contemporaries, no longer find his paintings more than life-like; but we still feel them to be intensely real in the sense that they powerfully appeal to our tactile imagination, thereby compelling us, as do all things that stimulate our sense of touch while they present themselves to our eyes, to take their existence for granted. And it is only when we can take for granted the existence of the object painted that it can begin to give us pleasure that is genuinely artistic, as separated from the interest we feel in symbols.

At the risk of seeming to wander off into the boundless domain of aesthetics, we must stop at this point for a moment to make sure that we are of one mind regarding the meaning of the phrase 'artistic pleasure', in so far at least as it is used in connection with painting.

What is the point at which ordinary pleasures pass over into the specific pleasures derived from each one of the arts? Our judgement about the merits of any given work of art depends to a large extent upon our answer to this question. Those who have not yet differentiated the specific pleasures of the art of painting from the pleasures they derive from the art of literature, will be likely to fall into the error of judging a picture by its dramatic presentation of a situation or its rendering of character; will, in short, demand of a painting that it shall be in the first place a good *illustration*. Others who seek in painting what is usually sought in music, the communication of a pleasurable state of emotion, will prefer pictures which suggest pleasant associations, nice people, refined amusements, agreeable landscapes. In many cases this lack of clearness is of comparatively slight importance, the given picture containing all these pleasure-giving elements in addition to the qualities peculiar to the art of painting. But in the case of the Florentines, the distinction is of vital consequence, for they have been the artists in Europe who have most resolutely set themselves to work upon the specific problems of the art of figure-painting, and have neglected, more than any other school, to call to their aid the secondary pleasures of association. With them the issue is clear. If we wish to appreciate their merit, we are forced to disregard the desire for pretty or agreeable types, dramatically interpreted situations, and, in fact, 'suggestiveness' of any kind. Worse still, we must even forgo our pleasure in color, often a genuinely artistic pleasure, for they never systematically exploited this element, and in some of their best works the color is actually harsh and unpleasant. It was in fact upon form, and form alone, that the great Florentine masters concentrated their efforts, and we are consequently forced to the belief that, in their pictures at least, form is the principal source of our aesthetic enjoyment.

Now in what way, we ask, can form in painting give me a sensation of pleasure which differs from the ordinary sensations I receive from form? How is it that an object whose recognition in nature may have given me no pleasure, becomes, when recognized in a picture, a source of aesthetic enjoyment, or that recognition pleasurable in nature becomes an enhanced pleasure the moment it is transferred to art? The answer, I believe, depends upon the fact that art stimulates to an unwanted activity psychical processes which are in themselves the source of most (if not all) of our pleasures, and which here, free from disturbing physical sensations, never tend to pass over into pain. For instance: I am in the habit of realizing a given object with an intensity that we shall value as 2. If I suddenly realize this familiar object with an intensity of 4, I receive the immediate pleasure which accompanies a doubling of my mental activity. But the pleasure rarely stops here. Those who are capable of receiving direct pleasure from a work of art, are generally led on to the further pleasures of self-consciousness. The fact that the psychical process of recognition goes forward with the unusual intensity of 4 to 2 overwhelms them with the sense of having twice the capacity they had credited themselves with: their whole personality is enhanced, and, being aware that this enhancement is connected with the object in question, they for some time after take not only an increased interest in it, but continue to realize it with the new intensity. Precisely this is what form does in painting: it lends a higher coefficient of reality to the object represented, with the consequent enjoyment of accelerated psychical processes, and the exhilarating sense of increased capacity in the observer. (Hence, by the way, the greater pleasure we take in the object painted than in itself.)

And it happens thus. We remember that to realize form we must give tactile values to retinal sensations. Ordinarily we have considerable difficulty in skimming off these tactile values, and by the time they have reached our consciousness, they have lost much of their strength. Obviously, the artist who gives us these values more rapidly than the object itself gives them, gives us the pleasures consequent upon a more vivid realization of the object, and the further pleasures that come from the sense of greater psychical capacity.

Furthermore, the stimulation of our tactile imagination awakens our consciousness of the importance of the tactile sense in our physical and mental functioning, and thus, again, by making us feel better provided for life than we were aware of being, gives us a heightened sense of capacity. And this brings us back once more to the statement that the chief business of the figure painter, as an artist, is to stimulate the tactile imagination.

The proportions of this book forbid me to develop further a theme, the adequate treatment of which would require more than the entire space at my command. I must be satisfied with the crude and unillumined exposition given already, allowing myself this further word only, that I do not mean to imply that we get no pleasure from a picture except the tactile satisfaction. On the contrary, we get much pleasure from composition, more from color, and perhaps more still from movement, to say nothing of all the possible associative pleasures for which every work of art is the occasion. What I do wish to say is that *unless* it satisfies our tactile imagination, a picture will not exert the fascination of an ever-heightened reality; first we shall exhaust its ideas, and then its power of appealing to our emotions, and its 'beauty' will not seem more significant at the thousandth look than at the first.

My need of dwelling upon this subject at all, I must repeat, arises from the fact that although this principle is important indeed in other schools, it is all-important in the Florentine school. Without its due appreciation it would be impossible to do justice to Florentine painting. We should lose ourselves in admiration of its 'teaching', or perchance of its historical importance—as if historical importance were synonymous with artistic significance!—but we should never realize what artistic idea haunted the minds of its great men, and never understand why at a date so early it became academic.

ILLUSTRATION AND DECORATION

The consistent pursuit of the Florentine painters was form and movement; of the Venetians, splendor and harmony of color: what did the Central Italians contribute to the magic of Renaissance art? Rarely does color penetrate the senses and warm the heart more quickly than in certain frescoes or panels of Simone Martini or Gentile da Fabriano, of Perugino or Raphael. Yet even these great masters could be at times indifferent, or, indeed, harsh, while their inferiors have slight merit as colorists. Seldom have problems of form and movement been better solved than by Signorelli; but he had few, if any, followers. It is not with the magicians in color and the creators in form that the Central Italian Painters, as a school, hold high rank. What is it, then, that gives them their place not only with the greatest, but with

the most popular names in art? Our present quest, if successful, will yield
an answer.

I

Every time we see an object we carry away in our memory some shadow
of its shape and color. This ghost of animate or inanimate things, passing
under the name of 'visual image', haunts different minds in different degrees.
Some people scarcely recognize its presence, although they know it exists;
others can at will conjure up shadows so defined that they, in their turn,
evoke emotions after their kind, and tinged with the poignancy of the feelings aroused by the objects themselves; still others need only shut their
eyes to see absent shapes with the vividness and warmth of direct retinal
impressions. Strictly speaking, each person varies from every other in the
richness of his visual images, but for our purpose it suffices to distribute all
people into the three classes we have just defined. Of the first, we say that
they visualize badly, or not at all; of the second, that they visualize fairly;
of the third, that they visualize perfectly.

The course of art would probably have been a very different one if
people had never visualized at all, or had always visualized perfectly. Had
we no faculty whatever for calling up the shapes of things, it might never
have given us pleasure to see mere reproductions of them. Why should it?
Nor should we be any more likely to care for mere reproductions if we had
within ourselves the faculty of calling up at will perfect visual images. But
most of us belong to the second class—those who have a moderate power of
visualizing. When objects are named, some image of them looms up in our
minds. It is, however, apt to be so vague, so elusive, that it tantalizes rather
than satisfies. After a vain effort to fix the image of an absent friend, the
crudest manual reproduction may be pounced upon with pleasure, and a
photograph seem the friend himself; for almost anything may be more complete and more vivid than our indwelling picture of him.

All this would be different if we visualized perfectly. At the mention of
a friend's name we should see him almost as if he were present—nay, more—
as we have seen him at a hundred significant moments. Not one, but a
thousand sweet shades of himself hover past, each greeting us as our friend;
and at will, as mood inspires, we fix upon this or that as his best and faith-
fullest lieutenant in our affection. Should we still care for the mere reproduction of his likeness? Granting that the reproduction, as such, were perfect,
it would be one, and only one, moment in the flux of his life. Any other
instant would represent him perhaps equally well. But does the single

moment represent him at all? Even the single images we have of him each take color and warmth from the others. The mere reproduction of our friend would hardly please us, because it could convey one only of his manifold aspects, an aspect which, even then, would be inferior to any one single image of him in our own minds. The pleasure in mere likeness is, in fact, the outcome of a feeble power of visualizing, and but for this might never have been known.

Now conceive of an art that could have had no purpose in helping out our actual visualizing, each one of our images being perfect. What could such an art have done to please us through the channel of our eyes? It still would have had two broad domains, one of which we shall call Illustration, and the other Decoration. Both terms need explanation, if not apology. By Decoration I mean all those elements in a work of art which appeal directly to the senses, such as Color and Tone; or directly stimulate ideated sensations, such as, for instance, Form and Movement. The word has never deliberately been used in quite so wide a sense; indeed, it is one of the vaguest and least hedged-in terms of our language; but as the tendency for some time past has been to make it designate all in a work of art that is not merely expressive, or academic, or dexterous, we shall not be imposing upon it too hard a burden if we make it convey the full meaning I have given it.

A definition of Illustration now follows as a matter of course: it is all that which, in a work of art, is not Decorative. But this definition is too negative, too verbal, to satisfy. We must make it more concrete. The current use of the word is at once too comprehensive, and, as I shall try to show, too narrow. Raphael's illustrations to the Bible in the *loggia* of the Vatican cannot be illustrations in the same sense as are the photographic views which commonly embellish magazine articles on travel. We all feel the difference; but in what does it really consist? The answer will appear if we stop to consider what each does for us. The view being a mere reproduction, we regard it as a fact, and not as art at all. It may give pleasure, but only to such as crave either for knowledge, or for greater precision of visual imagery. Raphael's frescoes reproduce nothing which was ever seen in that precise form in the world about us, either by himself or by any one else. They convey no information. But do they also do nothing for our visualizing? On the contrary, they stock our minds with images. Images of what—of scenes that never took place? Just so. But surely these are not the visual images we spoke of a little while ago, which we agreed were but shadows in the mind of things actually seen? What, then, are they?

Ultimately they also are shadows of things actually seen, but combined, blended, and composed in the artist's mind under the spell of the Bible narrative. The process which went on in Raphael's brain takes place in all of us who visualize with any ease. Every word tends to evoke an image, and as we read we are accompanied by an ever unfolding scroll of vague and evanescent shapes—blendings and fusings of the shadows dwelling within— which correspond to the sense of the phrases. Even if this panorama in our own minds lacked nothing in distinctness, we still should get a certain pleasure from the images conjured up by the same words in another mind; not, as in the case of very poor visualizers, because we longed for greater precision of imagery, but simply for the reason that the imaginary picture can never be quite the same in any two minds. And what if another mind is stocked with shadows of shapes in themselves superior to those of our individual world; what if that mind also possesses a more effective power of fusing and blending these images, already more attractive than ours? Let that person read the Old Testament, or contemplate anything that can possibly have its graphic counterpart, and pictures will troop past his mental vision which, could we but see them, would reveal higher conceptions and deeper meanings than we ourselves had found, would thrill us with the contagious presence of an imagination—here and at the moment, at least— richer, warmer, and completer than our own.

But how does a mental picture like this become a work of art? The answer would seem simple enough: before the mental image becomes a work of art it must be copied exactly in marble or on canvas. But *is* that really all? Most people would unhesitatingly say yes. They would define art as the faithful reproduction of things in themselves beautiful, or of the fused and blended images of such things. The old talk of the ideal, the new talk of the temperament, Aristotle and Zola, nestle comfortably in this basket. And the common difficulty, the difference between a photograph and such a work of art as, for example, a portrait by Watts, most people would explain by saying that the one reproduces a single image of a person, the other reproduces a composite formed by a mind of exceptional power. And thus great art would be defined not as the blind imitation of nature, but as the reproduction of the visual images haunting great minds.

There are some people, however, who would not rest happy in this definition. Mere reproduction, they would say, is not art, no matter how beautiful and exalted the object reproduced. The pleasure this gives, they would add, is not artistic, but aesthetic in a more general sense, or perhaps only intellectual; and they would insist on making a difference between a thing in itself beautiful (or a beautiful mental picture) on the one hand, and a work of art on the other. They would insist also on distinguishing between the terms 'aesthetic' and 'artistic', allowing the meaning of the first to include the second, but confining 'artistic' to designate that pleasure only which is derived from a conscious appreciation of the equality that makes the difference between objects, or mental images—in themselves beautiful —and works of art having the qualities which I have called Decorative. They would not deny that a work of art might gain from the character of the object, or of the mental image reproduced, but they would uphold that its specific value as Art was perfectly distinct from, and but slightly dependent upon, the value of the original. They would go even farther and say that the work of art, as such, had comparatively little to gain from the attractiveness of the object represented, but that the artist could enhance and glorify almost any object that lent itself to his treatment. Mere reproducions of things, no matter how exalted in themselves, no matter whether of objects in actual existence, or of the sublimest visions of the sublimest imaginations, they would speak of as 'Literature'—and I, disagreeing with them only in phrase, as Illustration.

At last we have seen the definition we have been seeking. Illustration is everything which in a work of art appeals to us, not for any intrinsic quality, as of color or form or composition, contained in the work of art itself, but for the value the thing represented has elsewhere, whether in the world outside, or in the mind within. If a work of art have no intrinsic value whatever, or if we fail to perceive it, for us it is nothing but an Illustration, and it does not matter whether it be drawn, engraved, or colored on sheets of paper, or painted on a panel or wall. Raphael and Michelangelo, Leonardo and Giorgione, if we perceive in them no qualities except such as, in the realms of actual or ideal things, belong to the images set down in their paintings, are as much mere Illustrators as the hacks who furnish designs for the popular press. In the domain of Illustration, there are, it is true, whole universes of difference between the illustrations of the great men just named and the illustrations of the nameless folk of to-day, but from this point of view they are all mere Illustrators.

'Illustration', as I shall employ the word, is, then, somewhat narrower, and, at the same time, considerably wider a term than the current use, which confines it to art as subordinated to letterpress. It will exclude mere reproduction of single perceptions of objects, too formless to give pleasure to any but the quite uncultivated, for whom simple recognition is already a delight. It will comprise, on the other hand, the mere reproduction of all those visual images, no matter how elaborate and significant, and no matter in what shapes they are cast, of which the form has no intrinsic merit of its own that we more or less consciously perceive.

II

Now it is no academic reason which has led me, at the opening of a small book on the Central Italian Painters, to speak of visual images, and to distinguish clearly in the work of art between Decoration and Illustration. It is a steep short-cut—would we had had the leisure to build a broad, gently climbing highway!—which, once bravely over, places us where we shall understand a great deal that otherwise would have for ever puzzled and perplexed us.

What more perplexing, for example, than the veerings of fashion, or even of taste? It makes scornful sceptics of most, and forces upon the few who still believe, the alternative of silence or paradox. *De gustibus non est disputandum* is a maxim no less maintained now than in more barbarous ages. It is true, politeness forbids pushing too far a discussion on matters of taste; but if such questions were of enough consequence to compel attention, and if we could communicate our views without fear of offending, is it so certain that we should arrive at no conclusions? I think not. Fortunately it is not our business here and now to make the perilous attempt. But one thing, at least, must be made clear at once. It is this. The question of preference in art is not at all the same that it is in life. Life makes different demands from generation to generation, from decade to decade, from year to year, nay, from day to day, and hour to hour. Our attention is stretched with the utmost interest toward those things that will help us to satisfy these de- mands, and with admiration toward those of our fellows who, without crowd- ing or hindering us, have perfectly satisfied them. As the demands, so the objects of our desire and our admiration vary. And as the objects of desire and admiration are altered, so will the subject-matter of the arts change. It cannot be otherwise. But depth of conception and attractiveness of ideal are, as we have seen, all that the greater number of even cultivated people care for in the arts; and, this being so, art must either present the current conceptions and ideals, or fail of a result in which even a restricted public will take an interest. Now the fluctuation of the ideal can affect those elements only in the work of art in which the ideal can be obviously mani- fest—in the Illustrative part. But this, as we have agreed, is far from being the whole, or even the more essential factor in art. There remain all the Decorative elements which mere change in the ideal cannot touch, for the good reason that the ideal can be adequately presented without them. All, therefore, in the work of art which distinguishes it from the mere mental image, all the Decorative elements, the more essential elements, as I believe, are above the revolutions of fashion and taste. Ages may arise which lack even the few who in better periods have a feeling for Art as distinct from Illustration or dexterity, and they are ages of bad taste—not of different taste. Some may prefer Guido Reni to Botticelli, the Caracci to Giorgione, and Bouguereau to Puvis de Chavannes, but let them not fancy that their preference rests on artistic grounds. The truth is that the elements essential to a painting as a work of art are beyond their perception, and that they look in a picture for nothing but a representation of something that would please them in actual life, or perhaps for the exhibition of a kind of skill that they happen to appreciate. (There are a thousand standards whereby one's tastes in matters of actual life may be judged, but as none of them are purely artistic, they are not my concern just here.)

Thus our rough division of the elements that constitute the work of art and divide it into two classes, the one Illustrative and the other Decorative, has already been of service. It has enabled us to distinguish what is subject to change and fashion from what is permanent in the work of art. The Decorative elements, the intrinsic values, are as perdurable as the psychic processes themselves, which, as we have reason to believe, vary only in degree from age to age, but in kind remain the same through all time. But Illustration changes from epoch to epoch with the contents of the mind, the visual part of which it reproduces, and it is as varied as are races and individuals.

It follows, then, as a clear conclusion that a phase of art which contains few if any except Illustrative elements will tend to pass away with the ideals it reproduces; also, that if we do not perceive the Decorative factors in the work of art (which yet may exist there in spite of our incapacity) we shall cease caring for it the moment we are tired of the phase of life or feeling or thought which it embodies.

SPACE-COMPOSITION

And if space-composition could do so much for Pintoricchio, how much more could it accomplish for Perugino or Raphael, who possessed far greater dominion over it! In them it was all clear gain, for, slight though their mastery over the most essential qualities in the figure arts, they took good care not to advertise their failings, and seldom do they offend by attempts too ambitious for their powers. Yet, apart from their greatness, particularly Raphael's, as Illustrators, their only conspicuous merit as artists was in space-composition, in which art Perugino surpassed all who ever came before him, and indeed all who came after him, excepting, however, his own pupil, Raphael, by whom even he was left far behind.

But what is this unheard-of art of space-composition? To begin with, it is not at all a synonym for 'composition' as ordinarily used, a word by which, I take it, we mean such an arrangement of objects within a given area as will satisfy our feelings for symmetry, harmony, compactness, and clearness. But all this arrangement is with reference to a flat surface, and extensions up and down, to right and left of an ideal centre—not inwards, —and we already have met with a perfect example of this art in Duccio's 'Incredulity of Thomas'. Now space-composition differs from ordinary composition in the first place most obviously in that it is not an arrangement to be judged as extending only laterally, or up and down on a flat surface, but as extending inwards in depth as well. It is composition in three dimensions, and not in two, in the cube, not merely on the surface. And, though less obviously, space-composition differs even more widely from ordinary composition in its effect. The latter, reduced to its elements, plays only on our feeling for pattern—itself a compound of direct optical sensations and their mental consequences, of faint impressions of balance, and fainter ideated movements. Space-composition is much more potent. Producing as it does immediate effects—how and why cannot here be discussed—on the vaso-motor system, with every change of space we suffer on the instant a change in our circulation and our breathing—a change which we become aware of as a feeling of heightened or lowered vitality. The direct effect, then, of space-composition is not only almost as powerful as that of music, but is brought about in much the same way; for, although many other factors enter in to produce the impression made by music, the body of its force grows out of the revolutions it produces in the vaso-motor system. Hence the likeness so often felt, but, to my knowledge at least, never explained, between music and architecture,—the latter, in so far as it is not merely superior carpentry, being essentially a manifestation, the most specific and the most powerful, of the art of space-composition.

With this last statement many will agree who then will wonder how in painting space-composition can have a place, unless, indeed, it reproduce architecture. But a painting that represents architecture is intrinsically no more of a space-composition than any other picture. This art comes into existence only when we get a sense of space not as a void, as something merely negative, such as we customarily have, but, on the contrary, as something very positive and definite, able to confirm our consciousness of being, to heighten our feeling of vitality. Space-composition is the art which humanizes the void, making of it an enclosed Eden, a domed mansion wherein our higher selves find at last an abode, not only as comforting, as measured to our every-day needs, as the homes of the happier among us, but as transporting, as exalting as are those things only which build up the ideal life. Near as it is to music in the form of great architecture, space-composition is even more musical in painting; for here there is less of the tyranny of mere masses of material, and their inexorable suggestions of weight and support; here there is more freedom, less is determined for one, although nothing is left to wayward fancy; and here, with this seeming greater freedom, many more instruments are playing to woo us away from our tight, painfully limited selves, and to dissolve us into the space presented, until at last we seem to become its indwelling, permeating spirit.

Space-composition in painting, then, is not the upstart rival of architecture, but its lovelier sister, an art capable of effects finer, more enchanting, more surely winning. And it produces its effects by totally different means. Architecture closes in and imprisons space, is largely an affair of interiors. Painted space-composition opens out the space it frames in, puts boundaries only ideal to the roof of heaven. All that it uses, whether the forms of the natural landscape, or of grand architecture, or even of the human figure, it reduces to be its ministrants in conveying a sense of untrammelled, but not chaotic spaciousness. In such pictures how freely one breathes—as if a load had just been lifted from one's breast; how refreshed, how noble, how potent one feels; again, how soothed; and still again, how wafted forth to abodes of far-away bliss!

The feeling just described is one that, at happy moments, many of us have had in the presence of nature, and it is one that we expect, but too seldom get, from landscape-painting. Yet space-composition is as distinct from the art of landscape as it is from architecture. It can produce its effects with a grand city square (as indeed we have it in paintings by Piero della Francesca) no less, if not better, than with the lines of the hills; its triumphs do not depend on subtle modelling of the atmosphere, nor on elaborate study of light and shade. Nay, so little mere dexterity, skill, and science are required to succeed in this art, that, provided the artist have the feeling for it, and be brought up in a good tradition, even the poorest can attain to some success: and there scarcely can be found an Umbrian picture, wretched though it may be in all other respects, which does not win us by its pleasant sweep of space. And if our interest be really in the work of art—not in the artist, and his madness, triumph, or despair—we shall not despise space-composition because it requires less dexterity and skill than landscape-painting as now practised. Believe me, if you have no native feeling for space, not all the science, not all the labor in the world will give it you. And yet without this feeling there can be no perfect landscape. In spite of the exquisite modelling of Cézanne, who gives the sky its tactile values as perfectly as Michelangelo has given them to the human figure, in spite of all Monet's communication of the very pulse-beat of the sun's warmth over fields and trees, we are still waiting for a real art of landscape. And this will come only when some artist, modelling skies like Cézanne's, able to communicate light and heat as Monet does, will have a feeling for space rivalling Perugino's or even Raphael's. And because Poussin, Claude, and Turner have had much of this feeling, despite their inferiority in other respects to some of the artists of our own generation, they remain the greatest European landscape painters—for space-composition is the bone and marrow of the art of landscape.

PRETTINESS AND EXPRESSION

But why, one may ask, are prettiness and expression not sources of artistic enjoyment? The answer is that mere prettiness appeals, not to those ideated sensations which are art's real province, but directly to the head, to the heart, and to less noble parts of us; and appeals as actuality, not as art. The admirers of a pretty woman in a picture regard her with Stendhal's eyes as the promise of the same face in real life—it cannot be otherwise, since living prettiness is so overwhelmingly attractive. Prettiness is thus little more than a pictograph, and is scarcely an art quality at all, seeing that the figure arts have for their materials the only elements that in vision can cause direct life enhancement—form, movement, space, and color—and of these prettiness is practically independent.

Expression is the twin sister of prettiness. Of course I do not refer to the unconscious mirroring in the face of the entire body's action. That is permissible, and may have independent quality as Illustration, although the greater the art the more careful is it not to let this quality get out of hand. But I mean the expression which in actual life we connect with the emotions, and which is reproduced for the value it has there. In art it can have little or no intrinsic merit, for all such merit accrues from tactile values and from action and their harmonies, while the muscles concerned with the subtle facial transformations required for emotional expression have little if any systemic effect upon us, and the ideation of their play can have but the faintest direct life-communicating power.

Besides these specifically artistic reasons, there is at least one other, of a more general but important order, against emotional expression in art. It is this. Directly expression surpasses its visible cause—the action manifested by the figures—we are inevitably led to seek for the cause of it in sources beyond and outside the work of art. The aesthetic moment—that too brief but most exquisite ecstasy when we and the work of art are one—

is prevented from arriving; for the object of vision, instead of absorbing our entire attention as if it were a complete universe, and permitting us to enjoy the feeling of oneness with it, drives us back on curiosity and afield for information, setting up within us a host of mental activities hostile to the pure enjoyment of art.

And if all this be true of figures and whole compositions, it is much more true of single heads. In the best art the head alone is but a limited vehicle for expression, and great art has always been perfectly aware of these limitations, making a point, it would seem, of giving the face, when presented alone, its most permanent aspect. But such treatment requires genius on the part of the producer, and natural as well as cultivated appreciation on the part of his public. The ordinary craftsman must exercise such functions as he has, and, standing at the level of the masses, he produces what they crave for, pictures that communicate information and promises, instead of life and beatitude.

Henri Matisse

NOTES OF A PAINTER*

A painter who addresses the public not in order to present his work but to reveal some of his ideas on the art of painting exposes himself to several dangers. In the first place, I know that some people like to think of painting as dependent upon literature and therefore like to see in it not general ideas suited to pictorial art, but rather specifically literary ideas. I fear, therefore, that the painter who risks himself in the field of the literary man may be regarded with disapproval; in any case, I myself am fully convinced that the best explanation an artist can give of his aims and ability is afforded by his work.

However, such painters as Signac, Desvallières, Denis, Blanche, Guérin, Bernard, etc. have written on such matters in various periodicals. In my turn I shall endeavor to make clear my pictorial intentions and aspirations without worrying about the writing.

One of the dangers which appears to me immediately is that of con-

* From Alfred Barr, Jr.'s *Matisse: His Art and His Public*, pp. 119–123. Matisse's "Notes d'un Peintre" was translated by Margaret Scolari. Copyright, 1951, The Museum of Modern Art. Reprinted by permission of The Museum of Modern Art.

Henri Matisse (1869–1954) was one of the giants of modern art. His "Notes" was one of the few essays he did on the aesthetics of painting.

tradicting myself. I feel very strongly the bond between my old works and my recent ones. But I do not think the way I thought yesterday. My fundamental thoughts have not changed but have evolved and my modes of expression have followed my thoughts. I do not repudiate any of my paintings but I would not paint one of them in the same way had I to do it again. My destination is always the same but I work out a different route to get there.

If I mention the name of this or that artist it will be to point out how our manners differ so that it may seem that I do not appreciate his work. Thus I may be accused of injustice towards painters whose efforts and aims I best understand, or whose accomplishments I most appreciate. I shall use them as examples not to establish my superiority over them but to show clearly through what they have done, what I am attempting to do.

What I am after, above all, is expression. Sometimes it has been conceded that I have a certain technical ability but that, my ambition being limited, I am unable to proceed beyond a purely visual satisfaction such as can be procured from the mere sight of a picture. But the purpose of a painter must not be conceived as separate from his pictorial means, and these pictorial means must be the more complete (I do not mean complicated) the deeper is his thought. I am unable to distinguish between the feeling I have for life and my way of expressing it.

Expression to my way of thinking does not consist of the passion mirrored upon a human face or betrayed by a violent gesture. The whole arrangement of my picture is expressive. The place occupied by figures or objects, the empty spaces around them, the proportions, everything plays a part. Composition is the art of arranging in a decorative manner the various elements at the painter's disposal for the expression of his feelings. In a picture every part will be visible and will play the rôle conferred upon it, be it principal or secondary. All that is not useful in the picture is detrimental. A work of art must be harmonious in its entirety; for superfluous details would, in the mind of the beholder, encroach upon the essential elements.

Composition, the aim of which is expression, alters itself according to the surface to be covered. If I take a sheet of paper of given dimensions I will jot down a drawing which will have a necessary relation to its format —I would not repeat this drawing on another sheet of different dimensions, for instance on a rectangular sheet if the first one happened to be square. And if I had to repeat it on a sheet of the same shape but ten times larger I would not limit myself to enlarging it: a drawing must have a power of expansion which can bring to life the space which surrounds it. An artist who wants to transpose a composition onto a larger canvas must conceive it over again in order to preserve its expression; he must alter its character and not just fill in the squares into which he has divided his canvas.

Both harmonies and dissonances of color can produce very pleasurable effects. Often when I settle down to work I begin by noting my immediate and superficial color sensations. Some years ago this first was often enough for me—but today if I were satisfied with this my picture would remain incomplete. I would have put down the passing sensations of a moment; they would not completely define my feelings and the next day I might not recognize what they meant. I want to reach that state of condensation of sensations which constitutes a picture. Perhaps I might be satisfied momentarily with a work finished at one sitting but I would soon get bored looking at it; therefore, I prefer to continue working on it so that later I may recognize it as a work of my mind. There was a time when I never left my paintings hanging on the wall because they reminded me of moments of nervous excitement and I did not like to see them again when I was quiet. Nowadays I try to put serenity into my pictures and work at them until I feel that I have succeeded.

Supposing I want to paint the body of a woman: First of all I endow it with grace and charm but I know that something more than that is necessary. I try to condense the meaning of this body by drawing its essential lines. The charm will then become less apparent at first glance but in the long run it will begin to emanate from the new image. This image at the same time will be enriched by a wider meaning, a more comprehensively human one, while the charm, being less apparent, will not be its only characteristic. It will be merely one element in the general conception of the figure.

Charm, lightness, crispness—all these are passing sensations. I have a canvas on which the colors are still fresh and I begin work on it again. The colors will probably grow heavier—the freshness of the original tones will give way to greater solidity, an improvement to my mind, but less seductive to the eye.

The impressionist painters, Monet, Sisley especially, had delicate, vibrating sensations; as a result their canvases are all alike. The word "impressionism" perfectly characterizes their intentions for they register fleeting impressions. This term, however, cannot be used with reference to more recent painters who avoid the first impression and consider it deceptive. A rapid rendering of a landscape represents only one moment of its appearance. I prefer, by insisting upon its essentials, to discover its more enduring character and content even at the risk of sacrificing some of its pleasing qualities.

Underneath this succession of moments which constitutes the superficial existence of things animate and inanimate and which is continually obscuring and transforming them, it is yet possible to search for a truer, more essential character which the artist will seize so that he may give to reality a more lasting interpretation. When we go into the XVII and XVIII century sculpture rooms in the Louvre and look for instance at a Puget, we realize that the expression is forced and exaggerated in a very disquieting way. Then, again, if we go to the Luxembourg the attitude in which the painters seize their models is always the one in which the muscular development will be shown to greatest advantage. But movement thus interpreted corresponds to nothing in nature and if we catch a motion of this kind by a snapshot the image thus captured will remind us of nothing that we have seen. Indication of motion has meaning for us only if we do not isolate any one sensation of movement from the preceding and from the following one.

There are two ways of expressing things; one is to show them crudely, the other is to evoke them artistically. In abandoning the literal representation of movement it is possible to reach towards a higher ideal of beauty. Look at an Egyptian statue: it looks rigid to us; however, we feel in it the image of a body capable of movement and which despite its stiffness is animated. The Greeks too are calm; a man hurling a discus will be shown in the moment in which he gathers his strength before the effort or else, if he is shown in the most violent and precarious position implied by his action, the sculptor will have abridged and condensed it so that balance is re-established, thereby suggesting a feeling of duration. Movement in itself is unstable and is not suited to something durable like a statue unless the artist had consciously realized the entire action of which he represents only a moment.

It is necessary for me to define the character of the object or of the body that I wish to paint. In order to do this I study certain salient points very carefully: if I put a black dot on a sheet of white paper the dot will be visible no matter how far I stand away from it—it is a clear notation; but beside this dot I place another one, and then a third. Already there is confusion. In order that the first dot may maintain its value I must enlarge it as I proceed putting other marks on the paper.

If upon a white canvas I jot down some sensations of blue, of green, of red—every new brushstroke diminishes the importance of the preceding ones. Suppose I set out to paint an interior: I have before me a cupboard; it gives me a sensation of bright red—and I put down a red which satisfies me; immediately a relation is established between this red and the white of the canvas. If I put a green near the red, if I paint a yellow floor, there must still be between this green, this yellow and the white of the canvas a relation that will be satisfactory to me. But these several tones mutually weaken one another. It is necessary, therefore, that the various elements that I use be so balanced that they do not destroy one another. To do this I must organize my ideas; the relation between tones must be so established that they will sustain one another. A new combination of colors will succeed the first one and will give more completely my interpretation. I am forced to transpose until finally my picture may seem completely changed when, after successive modifications, the red has succeeded the green as the dominant color. I cannot copy nature in a servile way, I must interpret nature and submit it to the spirit of the picture—when I have found the relationship of all the tones the result must be a living harmony of tones, a harmony not unlike that of a musical composition.

For me all is in the conception—I must have a clear vision of the whole composition from the very beginning. I could mention the name of a great sculptor who produces some admirable pieces but for him a composition is nothing but the grouping of fragments and the result is a confusion of expression. Look instead at one of Cézanne's pictures: all is so well arranged in them that no matter how many figures are represented and no matter at what distance you stand, you will be able always to distinguish each figure clearly and you will always know which limb belongs to which body. If in the picture there is order and clarity it means that this same order and clarity existed in the mind of the painter and that the painter was conscious of their necessity. Limbs may cross, may mingle, but still in the eyes of the beholder they will remain attached to the right body. All confusion will have disappeared.

The chief aim of color should be to serve expression as well as possible. I put down my colors without a preconceived plan. If at the first step and perhaps without my being conscious of it one tone has particularly pleased me, more often than not when the picture is finished I will notice that I have respected this tone while I have progressively altered and transformed the others. I discover the quality of colors in a purely instinctive way. To paint an autumn landscape I will not try to remember what colors suit this season, I will only be inspired by the sensation that the season gives me; the icy clearness of the sour blue sky will express the season just as well as the tonalities of the leaves. My sensation itself may vary, the autumn may be soft and warm like a protracted summer or quite cool with a cold sky and lemon yellow trees that give a chilly impression and announce winter.

My choice of colors does not rest on any scientific theory; it is based on observation, on feeling, on the very nature of each experience. Inspired by certain pages of Delacroix, Signac is preoccupied by complementary colors and the theoretical knowledge of them will lead him to use a certain tone in a certain place. I, on the other hand, merely try to find a color that will fit my sensation. There is an impelling proportion of tones that can induce me to change the shape of a figure or to transform my composition. Until I have achieved this proportion in all the parts of the composition I strive towards it and keep on working. Then a moment comes when every part has found its definite relationship and from then on it would be impossible for me to add a stroke to my picture without having to paint it all over again. As a matter of fact, I think that the theory of complementary colors is not absolute. In studying the paintings of artists whose knowledge of colors depends only upon instinct and sensibility and on a consistency of their sensations, it would be possible to define certain laws of color and so repudiate the limitations of the accepted color theory.

What interests me most is neither still life nor landscape but the human figure. It is through it that I best succeed in expressing the nearly religious feeling that I have towards life. I do not insist upon the details of the face. I do not care to repeat them with anatomical exactness. Though I happen to have an Italian model whose appearance at first suggests nothing but a purely animal existence yet I succeed in picking out among the lines of his face those which suggest that deep gravity which persists in every human being. A work of art must carry in itself its complete significance and impose it upon the beholder even before he can identify the subject matter. When I see the Giotto frescoes at Padua I do not trouble to recognize which scene of the life of Christ I have before me but I perceive instantly the sentiment which radiates from it and which is instinct in the composition in every line and color. The title will only serve to confirm my impression.

What I dream of is an art of balance, of purity and serenity devoid of troubling or depressing subject matter, an art which might be for every mental worker, be he business man or writer, like an appeasing influence, like a mental soother, something like a good armchair in which to rest from physical fatigue.

Often a discussion arises upon the value of different processes, and their relation to different temperaments. A distinction is made between artists who work directly from nature and those who work purely from their imagination. I think neither of these methods should be preferred to the exclusion of the other. Often both are used in turn by the same man; sometimes he needs tangible objects to provide him with sensations and thus excite his creative power; at other times when his pictorial sensations are already present in his mind he needs contact with reality before he can organize them into a picture. However, I think that one can judge of the vitality and power of an artist when after having received impressions from nature he is able to organize his sensations to return in the same mood on different days, voluntarily to continue receiving these impressions (whether nature appears the same or not); this power proves he is sufficiently master of himself to subject himself to discipline.

The simplest means are those which enable an artist to express himself best. If he fears the obvious he cannot avoid it by strange representations, bizarre drawing, eccentric color. His expression must derive inevitably from his temperament. He must sincerely believe that he has only painted what he has seen. I like Chardin's way of expressing it: "I put on color until it resembles (is a good likeness)," or Cézanne: "I want to secure a likeness," or Rodin: "Copy nature!" or Leonardo, "He who can copy can do (create)." Those who work in an affected style, deliberately turning their backs on nature, are in error—an artist must recognize that when he uses his reason his picture is an artifice and that when he paints he must feel that he is copying nature—and even when he consciously departs from nature he must do it with the conviction that it is only the better to interpret her.

Some will object perhaps that a painter should have some other outlook upon painting and that I have only uttered platitudes. To this I shall answer that there are no new truths. The rôle of the artist, like that of the scholar, consists in penetrating truths as well known to him as to others but which will take on for him a new aspect and so enable him to master them in their deepest significance. Thus if the aviators were to explain to us the researches which led to their leaving earth and rising in the air they would be merely confirming very elementary principles of physics neglected by less successful inventors.

An artist has always something to learn when he is given information about himself—and I am glad now to have learned which is my weak point. M. Peladon in the "Revue Hébdomadaire" reproaches a certain number of painters, amongst whom I think I should place myself, for calling themselves *"Fauves"* (wild beasts) and yet dressing like everyone else so that they are no more noticeable than the floor walkers in a department store. Does genius count for so little? In the same article this excellent writer pretends that I do not paint honestly and I feel that I should perhaps be annoyed though I admit that he restricts his statement by adding, "I mean honestly with respect to the Ideal and the Rules." The trouble is that he does not mention where these rules are—I am willing to admit that they exist but were it possible to learn them what sublime artists we would have!

Rules have no existence outside of individuals: otherwise Racine would be no greater genius than a good professor. Any of us can repeat a fine sentence but few can also penetrate the meaning. I have no doubt that from a study of the works of Raphael or Titian a more complete set of rules can be drawn than from the works of Manet or Renoir but the rules followed by Manet and Renoir were suited to their artistic temperaments and I happen to prefer the smallest of their paintings to all the work of those who have merely imitated the "Venus of Urbino" or the "Madonna of the Goldfinch." Such painters are of no value to anyone because, whether we want to or not, we belong to our time and we share in its opinions, preferences and delusions. All artists bear the imprint of their time but the great artists are those in which this stamp is most deeply impressed. Our epoch for instance is better represented by Courbet than by Flandrin, by Rodin better than by Fremiet. Whether we want to or not between our period and ourselves an indissoluble bond is established and M. Peladon himself cannot escape it. The aestheticians of the future may perhaps use his books as evidence if they get it in their heads to prove that no one of our time understood a thing about the art of Leonardo da Vinci.

Roger Fry

THE PROBLEM OF REPRESENTATION *

This appears to be the view indicated by Mr. Richards. He says: "There are great pictures . . . in which the contribution to the whole response made through representation is trivial and may be disregarded. It is equally certain that there are great pictures in which the contribution to the whole response made through representation is not less than that made more directly through form and color. To those who can accept the general psychological standpoint already outlined, or indeed any modern account of the working of the mind, the assertion that there is no reason why representative and formal factors in an experience should conflict, but much reason why they should co-operate, will need no discussion. The psychology of 'unique esthetic emotions' and 'pure art values' upon which the contrary view relies is merely a caprice of the fancy."

Let us take this passage as the text for a further inquiry into this interesting and intricate problem. It is a problem also that is of too vital im-

* From Roger Fry's "Some Questions in Esthetics," in *Transformations*, pp. 18–31, Doubleday Anchor Edition. Copyright, 1926, by Chatto & Windus, Ltd. Reprinted by permission of Chatto & Windus, Ltd.

portance to the critic of pictorial art for me to be altogether satisfied by such a summary and theoretical conclusion as Mr. Richards' last two sentences supply. I prefer in this, as in other matters, a more experimental method. Instead of deciding on *a priori* grounds that these two elements should always co-operate, let us take various instances and see what happens.

Let us take first a picture in which the representational element is obviously of great importance, for instance, Pieter Brueghel's "Carrying of the Cross" in the museum at Vienna. Here we look out upon a large stretch of country filled with crowds of figures which are inevitably so small in scale that they can hardly be related plastically with the picture space. Nor is any attempt made to do this. Rather we are invited by the whole method of treatment to come close and peer at each figure in turn, and read from it those details which express its particular state of mind so that we may gradually, almost as we might in a novel, bring them together to build up a highly complex psychological structure. We are able thus to distinguish the figure of Christ bearing the Cross, and, with the knowledge of the Gospel story which is presupposed, we get the central motive of the dramatic theme which is pursued throughout the picture with that leisurely accumulation of separate psychological elements which is characteristic of some dramatic literature. In the distance we recognize the hill of Calvary and on it what looks like a black ring, too small indeed to have any significance in a plastic sense, but when we look close and realize that it represents the crowds who have long been struggling for a favorable point of view for the forth-coming spectacle of the Crucifixion, we get a peculiar thrill of dramatic terror and pity. We recognize at once that this is a great psychological invention, setting up profound vibrations of feeling within us by its poignant condensation of expression. It is such an invention as Shakespeare will at times throw in in a couple of lines of description. But it is, I repeat, purely literary, and throughout this picture it is clear that Brueghel has subordinated plastic to psychological considerations. It is indeed to my mind entirely trivial and inexpressive when judged as a plastic and spatial creation. In short, it is almost pure illustration, for we may as well use that as a convenient term for the visual arts employed on psychological material. And we must regard illustration as more closely akin in its essence to literature than it is to plastic art, although in its merely external and material aspect it belongs to the latter. It is indeed this, from a fundamental point of view, accidental association which has been the source of so much difficulty and confusion about the nature and purpose of pictorial and glyptic art.

The next case I propose to examine is Daumier's "Gare St. Lazare."

Speaking for myself, the first impression derived from this is of the imposing effect of the square supports of the arcade, the striking and complicated silhouette of the man to the right, the salience of the centre figure so firmly planted on his feet, and the contrast of all this with the gloomy space which retires to the left, and finally the suggestion of wide aerial spaces given by the houses glimpsed to the right. The first effect, then, is mainly of feelings aroused by plastic relations. But I am almost immediately seized by curiosity about the striking silhouette to the right. Not only the strong contrast of light and shade, but the intricate and accented contours and the agitated movement help to attract attention. The interpretation of these forms as representing an extremely fussy, egoistic, well-to-do, middle-aged, professional gentleman of the '50's sets my imagination going down quite other paths, and so vivid is the notation and appropriateness of every detail that vague adumbrations of his whole domestic life with his pretty, timid, conventional wife, flit across the consciousness. In a similar but less acute way we almost instantly "place" the stout, self-possessed, retired colonel or country gentleman with the muffler. In between these we note the two poor people waiting patiently and uncomplainingly against the column, and share for an instant Daumier's slightly sentimental attitude about the poor which helps to excite, by its adroit contrast, our critical feelings towards the professional gentleman, and we come back to note the avaricious grasp with which he clutches his umbrella.

Then the incident of the sportsman turning round to whistle his dog gives another suggestion of human life and a hint at quite another type of character. We note the extreme aptness to the type of the florid features and the alert gesture, not without a thrill of admiration at the economy with which all this is given, since the imagination is always most satisfied when it is forced into activity by having to complete the suggestions given to it. Then we turn to the groups to the left—less emphatic because enveloped in the penumbra of the arcade—to the soldier and the priest who merely contribute vague suggestions of the variety of human types without adding anything very pointed; and then to the rather too noble old man invoking the protection of heaven on his daughter leaving him for service in a distant place, and here, speaking personally, I feel that for the first time in this picture a slightly false note is struck, a note that mars though ever so slightly the perfection of the psychological structure.

So all this time we have been entirely forgetting plastic and spatial values we have, through vision, plunged into that spaceless, moral world which belongs characteristically to the novel, and we can hardly help noting, by the way, how distinct this state of mind is from that with which we began. If, however, having for the moment exhausted the rich illustrational matter we return to the contemplation of plastic relations we shall find, I think, that it is not possible to push them much further. We find, no doubt, a generally coherent and intelligible disposition of the volumes in the space. The ample block made by the colonel's figure creates the chief salience and divides the space left to right satisfactorily—or nearly so, for I find myself always wondering whether it should not be a little further to the left for perfect balance; nor is it after all quite big enough as volume to fulfil the function it has to perform. For this it should be fused more closely with some other mass to the left instead of being, as it is, rather sharply cut off from the light on the pious father, whose forms, thus cut into, are rather meagre and insignificant. And this failure in plastic completeness seems actually due to Daumier's desire to bring out more clearly this particular dramatic incident. Nor can we be much interested in the solid rectangle of figures to the left from which four, too equally spaced, upright volumes detach themselves; no interesting plastic sequences here invite us to further contemplation. We see at once that one of the hardest plastic problems of such a scene is due to the fact that human beings are all of about the same height and that a crowd produces a rectangular mass which it is very difficult to relate significantly with the architectural setting. Daumier was clearly conscious of this, for it would be absurd to suppose that his illustrational preoccupations blinded him to plastic considerations, and the seated peasants are an excellent device to break this monotony, as is also the space left between them and the colonel which invites the eye to break into the too monotonous mass by a diagonal receding movement. This may have suggested the excellent pose of the sportsman which is all-effective in enforcing this movement, though its value is somewhat lessened by an uncertainty as to his position in the space. If we regard his head and shoulders he appears to be, like the child beside him, some way back; the light appears to fall on him through the second opening in the arcade; but when we see, none too clearly, his feet, we find that he is far nearer to us and is, in fact, lit by the first arcade. In addition to this the dog is so placed that, although his pose is rightly conceived for assisting the diagonal movement, he blocks the space and hinders the spatial organization. Had the man been definitely situated in the second opening and the dog had been moving towards him through the shadow we should have been more able to articulate this part of the composition intelligibly. The group to the right is the most plastically satisfactory of all, and the device of the box being lowered from the cab roof and carrying on the diagonal of the man's top-hat breaks for the first time the monotony of the horizontal line of heads.

We have to admit, then, that impressive as the general setting is, the design is not so organized plastically as to unfold to our contemplative gaze new interrelations and correspondences. Nor do I think we have ever been able, except perhaps in the case of the sportsman, definitely to relate plastic with psychological considerations, or find any marked co-operation between the two experiences.

A third case shall be Poussin's "Ulysses discovering Achilles among the daughters of Lycomedon," in the Louvre. I do not consider this as by any means one of Poussin's masterpieces. I have chosen it because it bears a sufficient likeness to the Daumier, so far as the problem of a group of people related to architecture is concerned. Proceeding in the same manner as before, let us note our impressions as nearly as possible in the order in which they arise. First the curious impression of the receding rectangular hollow of the hall seen in perspective and the lateral spread, in contrast to that, of the chamber in which the scene takes place. This we see to be almost continuously occupied by the volumes of the figures disposed around the circular table, and these volumes are all ample and clearly distinguished but bound together by contrasted movements of the whole body and also by the flowing rhythm set up by the arms, a rhythm which, as it were, plays over and across the main volumes. Next, I find, the four dark rectangular openings at the end of the hall impose themselves and are instantly and agreeably related to the two dark masses of the chamber wall to right and left, as well as to various darker masses in the dresses. We note, too, almost at once, that the excessive symmetry of these four openings is broken by the figure of one of the girls, and that this also somehow fits in with the slight asymmetry of the dark masses of the chamber walls. So far all our interests have been purely plastic. What the picture is about has not even suggested itself. Perhaps in taking my own experience I am not quite typical: others may at an earlier stage have felt the need of inquiring a little more curiously into this. But at whatever stage we do turn to this we are not likely to get much for our pains. The delight of the daughters in the trinkets which they are examining is expressed in gestures of such dull conventional elegance that they remind me of the desolating effect of some early Victorian children's stories, nor is Ulysses a more convincing psychological entity, and the eager pose of his assistant is too palpably made up because the artist wanted to break the rectangle behind and introduce a diagonal leading away from the upright of Ulysses. Finally, Achilles acts very ill the part of a man suddenly betrayed by an overwhelming instinct into an unintentional gesture. Decidedly the psychological complex is of the meagrest, least satisfactory, kind, and the imagination turns from it, if not with disgust, at least with relief at having done with so boring a performance. We return to the contemplation of the plasticity with the conviction that our temporary excursion into the realm of psychology has led us nowhere. But on the other hand our contemplation of plastic and spatial relations is continually rewarded. We can dwell with delight on every interval, we accept the exact situation of every single thing with a thrilling sense of surprise that it should so exactly satisfy the demands which the rest of the composition sets up. How unexpectedly, how deliciously right! is our inner ejaculation as we turn from one detail to another or as we contemplate the mutual relations of the main volumes to the whole space. And this contemplation arouses in us a very definite mood, a mood which, if I speak for myself, has nothing whatever to do with psychological entities, which is as remote from any emotions suggested by the subject, as it would be if I listened to one of Bach's fugues. Nor does the story of Ulysses enter into this mood any more than it would into the music if I were told that Bach had composed the fugue after reading that story. As far as I can discover, whatever Poussin may have thought of the matter—and I suspect he would have been speechless with indignation at my analysis—the story of Achilles was merely a pretext for a purely plastic construction. Nor can I, in this case at least, discover any trace of co-operation between the psychological and the plastic experiences which we derive from this work of art, though we have seen, in the pose of Ulysses' attendant, at least one instance of plastic needs making the psychological complex even more insignificant than it would have been otherwise.

Are we not almost forced by these considerations to conclude that our experiments fail to confirm those theoretical and *a priori* conclusions laid down by Mr. Richards? I think in these matters it is safer to base ourselves on exact observation of our own reactions than on results predicted from a theoretical consideration of how our sensibilities ought to function. There are, indeed, in the long sequence of European art a good many cases which must make us pause before accepting as a fact the co-operation between the illustrational and plastic elements in a picture so confidently predicted by Mr. Richards. We may omit the innumerable cases where, as in Poussin, the illustrational element may be entirely neglected and look at one or two where it is undoubtedly effective. In the case of Raphael, we find a psychological realization which, whatever we may think of it ourselves, has proved its crudely popular but effective appeal on each succeeding generation for centuries; and, in astonishing divergence from that, a plastic realization of so rare and subtle a perfection that those who are capable of responding to its appeal can generally disregard, more or less completely, the distracting impertinences of Raphael's psychology.

El Greco affords another interesting case. I suspect that for his own generation his psychological appeal was strong. His contemporaries knew intimately, or at least admired profoundly, those moods of extravagant pietistic ecstasy which he depicts. Those abandoned poses, those upturned eyes brimming with penitential tears, were the familiar indications of such states of mind. To us they seem strangely forced and hint a suspicion of insincerity which forbids our acquiescence, and we almost instinctively turn aside to invitations to a quite different mood which his intense and peculiar plasticity holds out. No less does the colour, with its entrancing sublimation of Venetian opulence, draw us in a direction which, to us at all events, is utterly distinct from that given by his illustration which, to tell the truth, clamours for a quite other method, for something more akin to the penitential gloom of Ribera.

Co-operation, then, between the two experiences derived from the psychological and plastic aspects of a picture does not appear to be inevitable. I have not sought to prove that it is impossible or that it never occurs.

Indeed, one case at once suggests itself of possibly finding that fortunate correspondence, namely Rembrandt. Rembrandt is certainly rare, if not unique, among artists in having possessed two separate gifts in the highest degree. His psychological imagination was so sublime that, had he expressed himself in words, he would, one cannot help believing, have been one of the greatest dramatists or novelists that has ever been, whilst his plactic constructions are equally supreme. To what extent he could control these two methods of expression, when using illustration instead of words for his psychological constructions, so that they should always reinforce one another would require a detailed examination of his whole work. I suspect that there was often a tension between the two. In the early work illustration tends to predominate, often to the evident diminution of plastic completeness. Of this one may take the "Philosopher" in the National Gallery, and the "Last Supper" of the Jacquemart-André collection as examples. Throughout his life there was a gradual shift of emphasis from psychological to plastic expression, as though, after all, the medium of paint was more nicely suited to that than to the other. In short, I do not know whether the world would not have gained had Rembrandt frankly divided his immoderate genius into a writer's and a painter's portion and kept them separate.

I find it hard in looking through his work to find examples where either one or the other element does not clearly predominate or where the mutual accommodation of the two does not entail some sacrifice. Perhaps one of the best examples will be that of the "Christ before Pilate," in the National Gallery. This is surely a masterpiece of illustration. As Rembrandt has seen it, Christ Himself falls into the background. This in itself is a striking indication of how fresh and original Rembrandt's dramatic imagination was. As he reconstructed from the Gospel text the whole scene before his inner vision he saw that such a moment as he has chosen must have arisen. It is the moment of greatest dramatic tension, where the protagonists are no longer Pilate and Christ, but Pilate and the Rabbis. And he has given this moment with astonishing perception of exactly the kind of characters involved and the inevitable effect of their clash. Pilate is an elderly, cultured, civil servant, a diplomat who has always moved in polite society and has found how to shelter his essentially feeble character behind an entrenchment of decorum and precedent. The shock to his feelings produced by this sudden onrush of elderly churchmen maddened with theological prejudice and hatred is admirably given in the fussy indignation of his gesture. No less perfect are the various types of the Rabbis, one, hardly moved from his self-satisfied, self-important grossness, one so abandoned to the passion of hate that he shakes the prætorial wand of office in his frenzy, one screaming out his vindictive fury, one turning back to restrain for a moment the crowd that they have hypnotized into madness. Behind, and hardly more than indicated, since at this moment it falls dramatically into the second place, the group of soldiers who out of sheer indifference and habit continue to buffet and maltreat the tortured figure of Christ, which too is given with that unmitigated psychological truth that Rembrandt was bound to follow. Certainly as drama this seems to me a supreme example of what the art of illustration can accomplish. And as a plastic construction it is also full of interest and strange unexpected inventions. The main group piles up into a richly varied but closely knit plastic whole which leads on by the long upward curve of Pilate's robe and turban to the less clearly modelled volume of the soldiers around Christ. Around these Rembrandt has created first of all the concavity of shade beneath the overhanging baldachin of the judge's seat, and this opens out into the vaster concavity of the public place through which a diagonal movement, hinted at by the inpouring crowds, leads us away under the arched entrance.

Personally I feel that the great, uprising pillar surmounted by the bust of Cæsar, admirable as it is in its dramatic suggestiveness, is a little detrimental to the spatial harmony. Still, one cannot deny the plastic beauty of the whole conception, although it is somewhat too crowded and overlaid with detail to be considered one of Rembrandt's great discoveries. This may, perhaps, be placed to the psychological account, since the general agitation and bustle of every detail increases the idea of the whole mad turbulence of the scene.

Here, then, is perhaps as good an instance as one can get of that co-operation of the dramatic and plastic experiences in a single picture. But I think that we cannot help noticing that even here we are compelled to focus the two elements separately. Indeed, I cannot see how one is to avoid this. How can we keep the attention equally fixed on the spaceless world of psychological entities and relations and upon the apprehension of spatial relations? What, in fact, happens is that we constantly shift our attention backwards and forwards from one to the other. Does the exaltation which gratification in one domain gives increase our vigilance and receptiveness when we turn to the other, as would be implied by true co-operation? In this case I incline to think it does, although I doubt whether this more than compensates for a certain discomfort which the perpetual shifting of focus inevitably involves.

We may get a little further light on our question by examining another example of Rembrandt's art, and this time we will take one of those innumerable drawings in which the point of departure was a dramatic event or situation.

In the "Parable of the Hidden Talent" the psychological complex formed by the clash of these two characters seems to me to be vividly realized. The types which give this its significance are chosen with Rembrandt's unfailing psychological insight. The dignified, grave and austere man of business one guesses to be a man of conscious rectitude, just but inflexible, and the other exactly such a type of slovenly incapacity as would not be able to restrain his ready, pot-house eloquence even at the risk of still further outraging his master by his self-justification. It will be noticed that the full value of the representational element almost always depends on a reference to something outside the actual work of art, to what is brought in by the title and such knowledge as the title implies to the spectator, whereas plastic values inhere in the work itself.

Now in this drawing the plastic and spatial elements are also such as to give us a keen satisfaction. The volumes of the two figures are made vivid to the imagination by the amazing evocative power of Rembrandt's few hasty indications; we accept with delight the interplay of their movements. No less clear and significant is the relation of these volumes to the enclosing space, though this too is given rather by a few vivid suggestions than with any full realization. So that here, far more definitely, I think, than in any picture, that co-operation which we have been seeking for seems realized. This may, perhaps, give us a hint as to the nature of such combinations of two arts, namely, that co-operation is most possible where neither of them are pushed to the fullest possibilities of expression, where in both a certain freedom is left to the imagination, where we are moved rather by suggestion than statement.

Erwin Panofsky

SYMBOLISM AND DÜRER'S 'MELENCOLIA I.'*

The St. Jerome differs from the Knight, Death and Devil in that it opposes the idea of the "vita contemplativa" to that of the "vita activa." But it differs much more emphatically from the Melencolia I in that it opposes a life in the service of God to what may be called a life in competition with God—the peaceful bliss of divine wisdom to the tragic unrest of human creation. While the St. Jerome and the Knight, Death and Devil illustrate two opposite methods of reaching a common objective, the St. Jerome and Melencolia I express two antithetical ideals. That Dürer conceived of these two prints as spiritual "counterparts" within the triad of the "Meisterstiche" can be concluded from the fact that he was in the habit of giving them away together and that collectors looked at and discussed them side by side. No less than six copies were disposed of as pairs while only one copy of the Melencolia I was given away singly and no impression of the Knight, Death and Devil changed hands together with either of the two other prints.

The two compositions offer, indeed, a contrast too perfect to be accidental. While the St. Jerome is comfortably installed at his writing desk, the winged Melancholia sits in a crouching position, not unlike that of the Job in the "Jabach altarpiece," on a low slab of stone by an unfinished building. While he is secluded in his warm, sunlit study she is placed in a chilly and lonely spot not far from the sea, dimly illuminated by the light of the moon—as can be inferred from the cast-shadow of the hourglass on the wall—and by the lurid gleam of a comet which is encircled by a lunar rainbow. While he shares his cell with his contented, well-fed animals, she is accompanied by a morose little *putto* who, perched on a disused grindstone, scribbles something on a slate, and by a half-starved, shivering hound. And while he is serenely absorbed in his theological work, she has lapsed

* From Erwin Panofsky's *The Life and Art of Albrecht Dürer*, one-volume edition, pp. 156–171. Copyright, 1955, by Princeton University Press. Reprinted by permission of the Princeton University Press.

into a state of gloomy inaction. Neglectful of her attire, with dishevelled hair, she rests her head on her hand and with the other mechanically holds a compass, her forearm resting on a closed book. Her eyes are raised in a lowering stare.

The state of mind of this unhappy genius is reflected by her paraphernalia whose bewildering disorder offers, again, an eloquent contrast to the neat and efficient arrangement of St. Jerome's belongings. Attached to the unfinished building are a pair of scales, an hourglass, and a bell under which a so-called magic square is let into the wall; leaning against the masonry is a wooden ladder which seems to emphasize the incompleteness of the edifice. The ground is littered with tools and objects mostly pertaining to the crafts of architecture and carpentry. In addition to the grindstone already mentioned, we find: a plane, a saw, a ruler, a pair of pincers, some crooked nails, a molder's form, a hammer, a small melting pot (perhaps for melting lead) with a pair of tongs to hold the burning coals, an inkpot with a penbox; and, half hidden beneath the skirt of the Melancholia, an instrument which can be identified—on the basis of a woodcut by Hans Döring—as the mouth of a pair of bellows. Two objects seem to be not so much tools as symbols or emblems of the scientific principle which underlies the arts of architecture and carpentry: a turned sphere of wood and a truncated rhombo-hedron of stone. Like the hourglass, the pair of scales, the magic square, and the compass, these symbols or emblems bear witness to the fact that the terrestrial craftsman, like the "Architect of the Universe," applies in his work the rules of mathematics, that is, in the language of Plato and the *Book of Wisdom*, of "measure, number and weight."

In modern usage, melancholy means, to quote from the Oxford Dictionary, "mental depression, lack of cheerfulness; tendency to low spirits and brooding; depressing influence of a place, etc." However, when Dürer composed his engraving the expression could not yet have been used as of a transient mood, much less of the gloomy emanation of a locality. In order to understand the title "Melencolia I"—inscribed on the wings of a squeaking bat—we must, instead, recall to mind that theory of the "four humors" which has already been touched upon in connection with Dürer's interpretations of the Fall of Man. This theory, fully developed by the end of classical Antiquity, was based on the assumption that both the body and the mind of man were conditioned by four basic fluids which in turn were supposed to be coessential with the four elements, the four winds (or directions of space), the four seasons, the four times of day, and the four phases of life. Choler, or yellow gall, was associated with the element of fire and was believed to share the latter's qualities of heat and dryness. It was thus held to correspond to the hot and dry Eurus, to summer, to midday, and to the age of manly maturity. Phlegm, on the other hand, was supposed to be moist and cold like water and was connected with the wind Austere, with winter, with night, and with old age. The blood, moist and warm, was equated with air and was likened to the pleasant Zephyr, to spring, to morning, and to youth. The melancholy humor, finally—the name deriving from Greek μέλαινα χόλος, black gall—was supposed to be coessential with earth and to be dry and cold; it was related to the rough Boreas, to autumn, evening, and an age of about sixty. Dürer himself has illustrated this cosmological scheme in one of his woodcuts for Conrad Celtes which differs from the original tradition only in that the melancholy humor is identified with winter instead of with autumn, and the phlegmatic with autumn instead of with winter—an understandable concession to the climatic difference between Germany and ancient Greece.

In an ideal or absolutely healthy human being these four humors would be perfectly balanced so that none would predominate over the others. But such a human being would be immortal and free from sin, and we know that both these advantages were irretrievably forfeited by the Fall of Man. In practice, therefore, one of the four humors prevails over the others in every individual, and this determines his or her entire personality. Apart from the fact that each of the humors asserts itself, quite generally, according to the course of the year, the day and the human life—we still speak of "sanguine youth" or "the melancholy of autumn"—every man, woman and child is constitutionally either a sanguine, or a choleric, or a melancholic, or a phlegmatic. These four types differ from one another in every possible respect. Each of them is marked by a peculiar physical habitus—slender or stout, tender or tough, robust or delicate; by the color of hair, eyes and skin (the word "complexion" derives, in fact, from the Latin word for "humoral mixture" or "temperament"); by a susceptibility to specific diseases; and, above all, by characteristic moral and intellectual qualities. The phlegmatic is inclined to other vices—and, conversely, is capable of other virtues—than the choleric; he behaves differently toward his fellow-men, he is suited to a different set of professions, and he has a different philosophy of life.

As long as the predominance of any one humor keeps within reasonable bounds the mind and body of the individual is merely qualified in this peculiar way. But if his humor gets out of control—either by an excessive increase in quantity which may occur for a variety of reasons, or by a deterioration in quality which may be caused by inflammation, chill or "adustion"—he ceases to be a normal or "natural" phlegmatic, melancholic, etc. He falls sick and may ultimately die; we still speak of "melancholy" and "cholera" as mental or physical diseases.

Obviously the four humors or temperaments could not be considered as equally desirable. The sanguine temperament, associated with air, spring, morning and youth, was, and in some measure still is, regarded as the most auspicious one. Favored with a well-knit body and a ruddy complexion, the sanguine seemed to surpass all other types in natural cheerfulness, sociability, generosity and talents of all description; even his faults, a certain weakness for wine, good food and love, were of the amiable and pardonable kind. Blood is, after all, a nobler and healthier fluid than the two kinds of gall or phlegm. We remember that certain theorists considered the sanguine temperament as the original, or perfectly balanced, condition of man; and even after this ideal equilibrium had been destroyed by the sin of Adam the predominance of the blood was much preferred to any of the other alternatives.

As the sanguine condition was greeted as the most fortunate, so the melancholic was hated and feared as the worst. When excessively augmented, inflamed, or otherwise disturbed, the black gall causes the most dreaded of all diseases, insanity; this disease can befall anybody, but the melancholics by nature are its most likely prey. And even without a downright pathological disturbance the natural or constitutional melancholics—generally considered as *pessime complexionati* ("the most ill-mixtured")—are both unfortunate and disagreeable. Thin and swarthy, the melancholic is "awkward, miserly, spiteful, greedy, malicious, cowardly, faithless, irreverent and drowsy." He is "surly, sad, forgetful, lazy and sluggish"; he shuns the company of his fellow-men and despises the opposite sex; and his only redeeming feature—and even this is frequently omitted from the texts—is a certain inclination for solitary study.

Before Dürer, pictorial representations of melancholy were chiefly found, first, in technical treatises on medicine; second, in popular books or broadsheets which dealt with the theory of the four humors, especially in manuscript or printed Calendars. In the medical books melancholy was discussed as a disease, and the main purpose of the illustrations was to show different methods of treatment—how melancholy derangement could be cured by music, or by flogging, or by cauterization. In the popular broad-sheets, Calendars and "Complexbüchlein," on the other hand, the Melancholic was depicted not as a pathological case but as a type of human nature. He appeared within a series of four figures or scenes intended to bring out the more or less desirable but, each in its way, perfectly "normal" features of the Four Temperaments.

We have said "four figures or scenes" because the representations of the Four Temperaments fall, roughly speaking, into two classes, one of a purely descriptive, the other of a scenic or dramatic character.

In illustrations of the descriptive type (which ultimately derive from Hellenistic cycles representing the Four Ages of Man) each temperament is typified by one figure only. These four figures—usually on foot, but occasionally on horseback—are differentiated according to age, social status, and profession. In the woodcut illustrated in *fig.* 214,[1] for instance, the sanguine temperament is represented by a youthful, fashionable falconer who walks on a band of clouds and stars which indicates his congeniality with the element of air. The Phlegmatic—always hard to characterize because, as was already observed by Galen, his humor does not make for "characteristic" qualities— appears as a fattish burgher who stands in a pool of water, holding a rosary. The Choleric is a warlike man of about forty briskly walking through fire; to show his irascible temper he brandishes a sword and a stool. The Melancholic, finally, is depicted as an elderly, cheerless miser standing on the solid ground. Leaning against a locked desk the top of which is all but covered with coins, he gloomily rests his head on his right hand while with his left he grasps the purse hanging from his belt.

In illustrations of the scenic or dramatic type the four temperaments are typified by couples. As a rule, there is some indication of the elements, but the figures themselves are not differentiated as to age, social standing and occupation. They reveal their temperament only by their behavior, and it is interesting to note that they do this by reenacting scenes originally used for the characterization of vices. During the high Middle Ages the types of human behavior had been studied and depicted not for their own sake but with reference to the system of moral theology. They were not illustrated in secular monographs but, under the guise of Vices, in the reliefs of such Cathedrals as Chartres, Paris, and Amiens, or in the miniatures of such moral treatises as the *Somme le Roi.* Toward the end of the Middle Ages these moralistic patterns were gradually converted into characterological specimens, the accent on good and evil being lessened and ultimately abolished. Many a trait in Chaucer's "Canterbury Tales" derives from the negative examples adduced in sermons of the twelfth and thirteenth centuries, and many a "Fool" in Sebastian Brant's *Narrenschyff* has originally been—and to the surly author's mind still was—a reprehensible sinner. Thus, when a fifteenth century artist sought models which he might use for a dramatic instead of a merely descriptive representation of the Four Temperaments he had nothing to turn to except the traditional types of the Vices.

In this way the dramatic interpretation of the sanguine temperament, as found in several illuminated manuscripts and printed Calendars, reverts to the high medieval picture of Luxury. As in the *Luxuria* relief at Amiens

---

[1] Not reproduced here (ed.).

Cathedral, the Sanguines are depicted as a couple clasped in a fervent embrace. Similarly the choleric temperament is exemplified by a man striking and kicking a woman, which is merely a transformation of what at Amiens Cathedral had been a representation of Discord. Now, as the main characteristic of the melancholy man in popular medieval writing was glumness and drowsiness, his type was modelled upon the pattern of Sloth or "Acedia." This pattern—freely employed, as we remember, in Dürer's *"Dream of the Doctor"*—is based on the idea of the sinful sleep, the pictures showing a farmer asleep by his plow, a burgher asleep by a crucifix to which he ought to pray, a woman asleep by her distaff; the last of these three types was so popular that Sebastian Brant adopted it for his "Fulheit" (Laziness)— with the kind-hearted amendment that the lazy spinner burns her leg in her sleep.

Consequently the dramatic representations of Melancholy show a woman asleep by her distaff combined with a man asleep at a table or even in bed, at times the man has a book over which he has dozed off, and in some later instances the slothful couple is joined by a hermit, a humble representative of study and solitude.

Blasphemous toward Dürer as it may sound—these homespun images must be counted among the ancestry of his famous engraving. Primitive though they are, they supplied its basic compositional formula, as well as the general idea of gloomy inertia. In both cases a woman, prominently placed in the foreground, is accompanied in a diagonal grouping by a less important representative of the opposite sex, and in both cases the essential characteristic of the main figure is her inaction. Needless to say, however, the differences outweight the similarities. In the miniatures and woodcuts of the fifteenth century the secondary figure is as sleepy and slothful as the principal one, while Dürer's engraving shows a deliberate contrast between the inaction of the Melancholia and the strenuous efforts of the scribbling *putto*. And, more important, the Melancholia is idle and the women in the earlier illustrations have abandoned their distaffs for entirely opposite reasons. These lowly creatures have gone to sleep out of sheer laziness. The Melancholia, on the contrary, is what may be called super-awake; her fixed stare is one of intent though fruitless searching. She is inactive not because she is too lazy to work but because work has become meaningless to her; her energy is paralyzed not by sleep but by thought.

In Dürer's engraving the whole conception of melancholy is thus shifted to a plane wholly beyond the compass of his predecessors. Instead of a sluggish housewife we have a superior being—superior, not only by virtue of her wings but also by virtue of her intelligence and imagination—sur-

rounded by the tools and symbols of creative endeavor and scientific research. And here we perceive a second and more delicate thread of tradition
which went into the fabric of Dürer's composition.

From the middle of the twelfth century, with the "Portail Royal" of
Chartres as the first known example, we find, in ever increasing numbers,
personifications of the Arts. Their circle was originally limited to the aristocratic Seven Liberal Arts enumerated by Martianus Capella, but it was soon
enlarged by a less definite number of "Mechanical Arts" so as to illustrate the
Aristotelianizing definition of art as "every productive effort based on a
rational principle." The composition of these images followed a constant
formula. A female figure, typifying one of the arts—or, on occasion, art in
general—and at times accompanied by assistants or subsidiary personifications, is surrounded by the attributes of her activity, holding the most
characteristic ones herself. A fourteenth century miniature—one of the rare
examples of "Art in General"—fairly bristles with all kinds of scientific and
technical implements, and when these implements came to be scattered
in three-dimensional space instead of being displayed on a plane surface the
general effect began to approach that of Dürer's *Melencolia I.*

In one specific instance a definite iconographic connection can be established. In the 1504 and 1508 editions of Gregor Reisch's *Margarita Philo-
sophica,* one of the most widely read encyclopedic treatises of the period, we
find a woodcut entitled "Typus Geometriae" which includes nearly all the
devices appearing in Dürer's *Melencolia I.* It synthesizes, so to speak,
the type of the Liberal Arts with that of the Technical, for it is intended to
show that almost all the crafts and many branches of "natural philosophy"
depend on geometrical operations.

Geometry, depicted as a richly attired lady, is engaged in measuring a
sphere with her compass. She sits at a table on which are drafting instruments, an inkpot and models of stereometrical bodies. An unfinished building, with an ashlar still in the prongs of a crane, is checked over by an
assistant while two others work at a drafting board and make a topographical
survey. Scattered about the ground are a hammer, a ruler and two molder's
forms; and clouds, the moon and stars, announcing the celestial phenomena in Dürer's engraving, are observed by means of quadrants and
astrolabes. Not only meteorology and astronomy—a further allusion to the
latter, by the way, is the peacock's feather on the hat of Geometry, the
peacock's plumage being an ancient symbol of the starry firmament—but
also all the technical arts are thus interpreted as applications of geometry;
and to this Dürer's conception conforms. His *Underweysung der Messung* is
dedicated, "not only to painters but also to goldsmiths, sculptors, stone-

masons, carpenters and all those who make use of geometry"; and in a draft probably written just about 1513-15 the "plane and the turning lathe"—the operation of both being based on a geometrical principle—are mentioned together just as the plane and the turned sphere are juxtaposed in the *Melencolia I*. In fact, the whole array of implements in the engraving can be summed up under the heading "Typus Geometriae," the book, the inkpot and the compass standing for pure geometry; the magic square, the hour-glass with the bell, and the pair of scales for measurement in space and time ("Geo ponderat," "geometry weighs," to quote from an old mnemonic verse); the technical instruments for applied geometry; and the truncated rhomboid for descriptive geometry, particularly stereography and perspective.

Thus Dürer's engraving represents a fusion of two iconographic formulae hitherto distinct: the "Melancholici" of popular Calendars and "Complexbüchlein," and the "Typus Geometriae" of philosophical treatises and encyclopedic decorations. The result was an intellectualization of melancholy on the one hand, and a humanization of geometry on the other. The former Melancholics had been unfortunate misers and sluggards, despised for their unsociability and general incompetence. The former Geometries had been abstract personifications of a noble science, devoid of human emotions and quite incapable of suffering. Dürer imagined a being endowed with the intellectual power and technical accomplishments of an "Art," yet despairing under the cloud of a "black humor." He depicted a Geometry gone melancholy or, to put it the other way, a Melancholy gifted with all that is implied in the word geometry—in short, a "Melancholia artificialis" or Artist's Melancholy.

Thus almost all the motifs employed in Dürer's engraving can be accounted for by well-established textual and representational traditions pertaining to "melancholy" on the one hand, and to "geometry" on the other. But Dürer, while fully aware of their emblematic significance, also invested them with an expressive, or psychological, meaning.

That the conventional tools and symbols of the "geometrical" professions are arranged, or rather disarranged, so as to convey a feeling of discomfort and stagnation has already been mentioned. The comet and the rainbow, causing the scenery to phosphoresce in an uneasy twilight, not only serve to signify astronomy but also have a weird, ill-boding emanation of their own. Both the bat and the dog were traditionally associated with melancholy, the former (*vespertilio* in Latin) because he emerges at dusk and lives in lonely, dark and decaying places; the latter because he, more than other animals, is subject to spells of dejection and even to madness, and because he looks the more woebegone the more intelligent he is ("the most sagacious dogs are those who carry a melancholy face before themselves," to quote an author of the early sixteenth century who obviously thought of what we call bloodhounds). But in Dürer's engraving the bat and the dog are not merely emblems but, even more, living creatures, one squeaking with evident ill-will, the other shrivelled up with general misery.

What is true of the accessories is no less true of the main figure. Her book and compass belong, of course, to the typical attributes of Geometry; but that she does not make use of either reveals her torpid dejection. That she rests her head on her hand is in keeping with a tradition which can be traced back to ancient Egyptian art. As an expression of brooding thought, fatigue or sorrow this attitude is found in hundreds and thousands of figures and had become a standing attribute of melancholy and "Acedia," and even that her hand is clenched to a fist is not as unusual as it may seem. The *pugillum clausum* was a typical symbol of avarice—we still speak of "tight-fistedness," and Dante says that misers will be resurrected "col pugno chiuso" —and it was supposed that if this melancholy vice assumed the proportions of real insanity the patients would never unclench their fingers because they imagined themselves holding a treasure or even the whole world in their fist. But in Dürer's engraving the motif has a totally different meaning. In medieval miniatures the Melancholic displays his clenched fist as a symptomatic attribute, much as St. Bartholomew displays his knife, or the Magdalen her ointment jar. Dürer, in making the fist support the head, the center of thought and imagination, transforms a characterological or even medical symptom into an expressive gesture. His Melancholic is neither a miser nor a mental case, but a thinking being in perplexity. She does not hold on to an object which does not exist, but to a problem which cannot be solved.

One of the chief characteristics of the traditional melancholic is his swarthy, "earthlike" complexion which under certain circumstances can deepen to actual blackness. This *facies nigra* was still in Milton's mind when he described his "divinest Melancholy" as one

> *"Whose saintly visage is too bright*
> *To hit the sense of human sight,*
> *And therefore to our weaker view*
> *O'erlaid with black, staid wisdom's hue."*

Dürer, almost as subtle as Milton, substituted a luminary effect for the material discoloration of the skin. The face of his Melancholia—like that of Michelangelo's "Pensieroso"—is overcast by a deep shadow. It is not so much a dark as a darkened face, made all the more impressive by its contrast with the startling white of the eyes.

The wreath which she wears on her head is primarily a palliative against the dangers of the *humor melancholicus*. To counteract the bad effects of "dryness" it was recommended to put on one's head "the leaves of plants having a watery nature," and it is precisely of such plants that the wreath is composed; it consists of water-ranunculus—which also occurs in the "Aqua" section of Dürer's cosmological woodcut for Celtes—and watercress. But the very idea of a wreath—normally a symbol of joy or superiority, as in many portraits of humanists or in Dürer's own representations of the Emperor Sigismund, a Wise Virgin, Hercules and the poet Terence—is here belied by the gloom of the general atmosphere. Again a mere emblem is used as a vehicle of psychological expression.

Perhaps we have no right to assume that practically every detail in the *Melencolia I* has a special "meaning." But the selection of two inconspicuous plants which have nothing in common except their "watery" nature— Copernicus still believed that the seeds of watercress caused "unhealthy humidity" because the plant grows in humid places—can hardly be an accident. Moreover, we know by Dürer's own testimony that in the context of this engraving even the most conventional and commonplace accessories of a "Hausfrau's" costume are meant to have an emblematical significance. Attached to the belt of the Melancholia are a purse and a bunch of keys. Compared with the neat and orderly appearance of these objects in an engraving like the *Virgin by the Wall*, they, too, express the distraught condition of their owner, for the keys are disarranged and the purse trails on the ground with its leather strips twisted and partly unfastened. But in addition to revealing that "careless desolation" which still marks the "melancholic" of the Elizabethan stage, they signify two definite concepts. On one of Dürer's sketches for the *Melencolia I* we find the following note: "Schlüssel betewt gewalt, pewtell betewt reichtum" ("Key denotes power, purse denotes wealth").

The purse is still a common symbol of wealth, particularly in its less enjoyable aspects of parsimony and avarice, and the papal "power of the keys" is still as proverbial in English as the matrimonial "Schlüsselgewalt"— already mentioned in connection with Dürer's *Glorification of the Virgin*—is in German. The purse is therefore a frequent attribute of the miserly Melancholic, and the keys, too, can be connected with the concept of melancholy. As we shall shortly see, the melancholy humor was associated with the planet Saturn who, as the oldest and highest of the planetary divinities, was held to wield as well as to bestow "power," and was in fact occasionally represented with a key or bunch of keys.

However, since Dürer's Melancholia is no ordinary Melancholy, but, as we expressed it, the "Melancholia Artificialis" or Artist's Melancholy, we may well ask whether there might not be a special connection between the qualities of power and wealth and professional artistic activity. This seems indeed to be the case. In his theoretical writings Dürer not only insists that wealth is, or at least should be, the well-deserved reward of the artist (his earliest draft, composed about 1512, emphatically closes with the sentence: "If you were poor, you may achieve great prosperity through such art"), he also uses the German word for power, "Gewalt," as a specific term denoting that consummate mastery which is the final goal of every artist and can be attained only by passionate study and the grace of God: "And the true artists recognize at once whether or not a work is powerful [*gewaltsam*], and a great love will grow in those who understand"; or: "God gives much power [*viel Gewalts*] to ingenious men."

Now this consummate mastery results, according to Dürer—and to all other thinkers of the Renaissance—from a perfect coordination of two accomplishments: theoretical insight, particularly a thorough command of geometry ("Kunst" in the original sense of "knowledge"), and practical skill ("Brauch"). "These two must be together," Dürer says, "for the one without the other is of no avail."

This explains not only the deranged and neglected condition of the Melancholia's keys and purse, which indicates a temporary absence of wealth and power rather than their presence, but also the significant contrast between her torpid inaction and the bustling activity of the *putto*. The mature and learned Melancholia typifies Theoretical Insight which thinks but cannot act. The ignorant infant, making meaningless scrawls on his slate and almost conveying the impression of blindness, typifies Practical Skill which acts but cannot think (whereby it should be noted that Dürer's expression for theoretical insight, "Kunst," is of the feminine gender whereas his term for practical skill, "Brauch," is masculine). Theory and practice are thus not "together," as Dürer demands, but thoroughly disunited; and the result is impotence and gloom.

Three questions remain to be answered. First, with what right could Dürer substitute a spiritual tragedy for what had been the sluggishness and obtuseness of an inferior temperament? Second, on what grounds could he associate, or even identify, the idea of melancholy with that of geometry? Third, what is the meaning of the number "I" which follows the word "Melencolia"?

The answer to the first question lies in the fact that the whole concept of melancholy had been revised, or rather reversed, by Marsilio Ficino, the leading spirit of the Neo-Platonic "Academy" at Florence, and that this new doctrine, developed in Ficino's "Letters" and conclusively formulated in his treatise *De Vita Triplici,* had met with great success in Germany as well as in Italy. The "Letters" had been published by Koberger, and the first two Books of the three "Libri de Vita" had even been translated into German. Of these developments Dürer was certainly aware, for he quotes the "Platonic ideas" as early as 1512.

Marsilio Ficino, himself a man of delicate health and melancholy disposition, tried to alleviate the real and imaginary tribulations of his humor by the time-honored devices of exercise, regular hours, a careful diet and music (Dürer, by the way, also recommends the "cheerful tunes of the lute" in case "a young painter should overwork, from which his melancholy might exceed"). But he found greater consolation in an Aristotelian discourse which, though occasionally quoted by scholastic philosophers, had thus far failed to change the general dislike and fear of melancholy. According to this brilliant analysis of what may be called the psycho-physiology of human greatness (*Problemata,* xxx, 1), the "melancholics by nature"—as opposed to the downright insane—are marked by a peculiar excitability which either over-stimulates or cripples their thoughts and emotions and may, if not controlled, cause raving madness or imbecility; they walk, as it were, on a narrow ridge between two abysses. But they walk, just for this reason, way above the level of ordinary mortals. If they succeed in keeping their equilibrium so that "their very anomaly behaves somehow in a well-balanced and beautiful way," as Aristotle admirably puts it, they may still be subject to depression and overexcitement, but they outrank all other men: "All truly outstanding men, whether distinguished in philosophy, in statecraft, in poetry or in the arts, are melancholics—some of them even to such an extent that they suffer from ailments induced by the black gall."

The Florentine Neo-Platonists were quick to perceive that this Aristotelian doctrine supplied a scientific basis for Plato's theory of "divine frenzy." The action of the melancholy humor, which Aristotle had likened to that of strong wine, seemed to explain, or at least to concur with, those mysterious ecstasies which "petrify and almost kill the body while they enrapture the soul." Thus the expression *furor melancholicus* came to be synonymous with *furor divinus.* What had been a calamity and, in its mildest form, a handicap became a privilege still dangerous but all the more exalted: the privilege of genius. Once this idea—utterly foreign to the Middle Ages where men could become saints but not "divine" philosophers or poets—had been reborn under the joint auspices of Aristotle and Plato, the hitherto disparaged melancholy became surrounded with the halo of the sublime. Outstanding achievements automatically included the reputation of melancholy—even of Raphael it was said that he was "malinconico come tutti gli huomini di questa eccelenze"—and soon the Aristotelian tenet that all great men were melancholics was twisted into the assertion that all melancholics were great men: "Malencolia significa ingegno" ("Melancholy signifies genius"), to quote from a treatise which tries to demonstrate the excellence of painting by the fact that the better class of painters were just as melancholy as poets or philosophers. Small wonder that persons with social ambitions were as anxious to "learn how to be melancholy," as Ben Jonson's Stephen puts it, as they are today to learn tennis or bridge. A climax of refinement is reached in Shakespeare's Jaques who uses the mask of a melancholic by fashion and snobbery to hide the fact that he is a genuine one.

This humanistic glorification of melancholy entailed, and even implied, another phenomenon: the humanistic ennoblement of the planet Saturn. As physical bodies, the seven planets were held to be determined by the same four combinations of qualities as the terrestrial elements; as sidereal personalities, on the other hand, they had retained the characters and powers of the classical gods after whom they were named. They, too, could thus be correlated with the four temperaments, and a complete system of coordination is already found in Arabic sources of the ninth century. The sanguine temperament was associated with friendly Venus, who was considered as moist and warm like air, or, even more frequently, with the equally well-tempered and benevolent Jupiter; the choleric with the fiery Mars; the phlegmatic with the Moon whom Shakespeare still calls the "watery star"; and the melancholic—as has already been mentioned in passing—with Saturn, the ancient god of the earth. We still use the expression "saturnine" almost as a synonym of "melancholy"—much as we do with the expressions "jovial" and "sanguine"—and in the German woodcut previously mentioned as a specimen of "descriptive" illustrations of the Four Temperaments the unflattering characterization of the Melancholic concludes with the line: "Saturnus und herbst habent die schulde" ("Saturn and autumn are guilty of this").

Once established, this "consonance" between melancholy and Saturn was never questioned. Every human being, mineral, plant or animal supposed to have a melancholy nature—among them, for instance, the dog and the bat—*ipso facto* "belonged" to Saturn, too. The very posture of sadness, with the head resting on the hand, is melancholy as well as Saturnian; and as the black gall was considered the most ignoble of humors, so the "Saturnus impius" was held to be the most unfortunate of celestial influences. As the highest of the planets, as the oldest of the Olympians, and as the former ruler of the Golden Age, he could give power and riches. But as a dry and icy star, and as a cruel father-god dethroned, castrated and imprisoned in the bowels of the earth, he was associated with old age, disablement, sorrow, all kinds of misery, and death. Even under favorable circumstances those born under him could be wealthy and mighty only at the cost of generosity and goodness of heart, and wise only at the cost of happiness. Normally, they were hard-working peasants or laborers in stone and wood—for Saturn had been a god of the earth—privy-cleaners, grave-diggers, cripples, beggars, and criminals.

The Florentine Neo-Platonists, however, discovered that Plotinus and his followers had thought as highly of Saturn as Aristotle had thought of melancholy. Since that which is higher is more "exalted" than that which is lower, and since that which begets is closer to the source of all things than that which is begotten, Saturn was thought superior to Jupiter, let alone the rest of the planets. He symbolized the "Mind" of the world where Jupiter merely symbolized its "Soul"; he had thought out what Jupiter had merely learned to govern; he stood, in short, for profound contemplation as opposed to mere practical action. Thus interpreted, the domination of Saturn was willingly accepted by those "whose minds are bent to contemplate and to investigate the highest and most secret things." They hailed him as their celestial patron just as they reconciled themselves to melancholy as their terrestrial condition. The most illustrious members of the Florentine circle—among them, besides Ficino, Pico della Mirandola and Lorenzo the Magnificent—referred to themselves, only half playfully, as "Saturnians," and they discovered to their immense satisfaction that Plato, too, had been born under the sign of Saturn.

This philosophical rehabilitation of Saturn could not weaken the popular belief that he was the most malignant of planets; and Ficino himself, whose horoscope showed "Saturnum in Aquario ascendentem," lived under a permanent cloud of anxiety. He took, and advised his fellow-scholars to take, all possible precautions. He even used and recommended astrological talismans which might counteract the influence of Saturn by invoking the power of Jupiter, and this, by the way, explains the magic square in Dürer's *Melencolia I.* It can be identified as the sixteen-celled *Mensula Jovis;* engraved upon a slab of tin, it will "turn evil into good" and "dispel all worries and fear." However, all said and done, Ficino bravely submitted to his Saturnian destiny: "Not only those who take refuge to Jupiter, but also those who wholeheartedly and sincerely concentrate on that divine contemplation which is signified by Saturn, will escape from the latter's pernicious influences and only enjoy his benefits. . . . To the spirits that dwell in the spheres of the sublime Saturn himself is a benevolent father [*juvans pater,* that is, Jupiter]."

It is this new and most humanistic conception of the melancholy and "saturnine" genius that found expression in Dürer's engraving. But what, to turn to the second of our questions, is the specific connection between the ideas of melancholy and Saturn on the one hand, and of geometry and the geometrical arts on the other?

It has been mentioned that Saturn, as god of the earth, was associated with work in stone and wood; in one of the earliest pictorial surveys of what may be called the Saturnian professions, the murals in the "Salone" at Padua, we already encounter the stonemason and the carpenter, here still conceived as lowly manual laborers. But as god of agriculture Saturn had also to supervise the "measurements and quantities of things" and particularly the "partition of land." This is precisely the original meaning of the Greek word Γεωμετρία, and it is not surprising to come upon several manuscripts of the fifteenth century where the rustic attributes of Saturn are supplemented by a compass. Jacob de Gheyn was to monumentalize this concept of a Saturn-Geometrician in one of his most impressive engravings. One or two of those fifteenth century manuscripts add the explanation: "Saturn the planet sends us the spirits that teach us geometry"; and in a Calendar published in Nuremburg exactly one year after the *Melencolia I* we read the phrase: "Saturnus . . . bezaichet aus den Künsten die Geometrei" ("Of the arts, Saturn denotes geometry").

In addition to this astrological connection between geometry and Saturn there existed, however, a much subtler psychological connection between geometry and melancholy—a connection brilliantly expounded by the great scholastic philosopher Henry of Ghent who had been greeted as a kindred spirit by Pico della Mirandola, and whose analysis of melancholy was extensively quoted and endorsed in the latter's *Apologia de Descensu Christi ad Inferos*. There exist, to summarize this argument, two kinds of thinkers. On the one hand, there are the philosophical minds which find no difficulty in understanding such purely metaphysical notions as the ideas of an angel or of extramundane nothingness. On the other hand, there are those "in whom the imaginative power predominates over the cognitive one." They "will accept a demonstration only to that extent as their imagination can keep step with it. . . . Their intellect cannot transcend the limits of imagination . . . and can only get hold of space [*magnitudo*] or of that which has a location and position in space. . . . Whatever they think is a quantity, or is located in quantity as is the case with the point. Therefore such men are melancholy, and become excellent mathematicians but very bad metaphysicians, for they cannot extend their thought beyond location and space which are the foundations of mathematics."

Melancholics, then, are gifted for geometry—for, Henry's own definition

Melencolia I BY DÜRER

restricts the field of "mathematics" to a science of *situs et magnitudo*—because they think in terms of concrete mental images and not of abstract philosophical concepts; conversely, people gifted for geometry are bound to be melancholy because the consciousness of a sphere beyond their reach makes them suffer from a feeling of spiritual confinement and insufficiency.

This is precisely what Dürer's Melancholia seems to experience. Winged, yet cowering on the ground—wreathed, yet beclouded by shadows— equipped with the tools of art and science, yet brooding in idleness, she gives the impression of a creative being reduced to despair by an awareness of insurmountable barriers which separate her from a higher realm of thought. Was it perhaps in order to emphasize this idea of a first, or lowest, degree of achievement that Dürer added the number "I" to the inscription? This numeral can hardly refer to the other temperaments, for it is difficult to imagine that Dürer should have planned three more engravings of a similar kind, and no less difficult to find a series of the Four Humors which would begin with Melancholy. The number "I" may thus imply an ideal scale of values, rather than an actual sequence of prints, and this conjecture can be corroborated, if not proved, by what seems to be the most important literary source of Dürer's composition: Cornelius Agrippa of Nettesheim's *De Occulta Philosophia*.

As published in 1531, this famous book appears to be an item from the study of Dr. Faustus, fairly confused in plan and full of cabalistic charms, astrological and geomantic tables and other magical devices. The orginal version of 1509/10, however, which had been dedicated to a friend of Pirck- heimer's, the Abbot Trithemius of Würzburg, and was circulated among the German humanists in manuscript form, was a much shorter and more "rea- sonable" book. It is only about one-third as long as the printed version, and the already noticeable emphasis on magic does not yet obscure a clear and, in its way, consistent system of natural philosophy. The author, largely basing himself on Marsilio Ficino, sets forth the Neo-Platonic doctrine of cosmic forces whose flux and reflux unifies and enlivens the universe, and he tries to show how the operation of these forces enables man not only to practice legitimate magic—as opposed to necromancy and commerce with the Devil—but also to achieve his greatest spiritual and intellectual triumphs. Of these man is capable through direct "inspiration" from above (it is worth noting that Dürer, too, refers to "öbere Eingiessungen"); and this inspiration can come to him in three forms—through prophetic dreams, through intense contemplation, and through the *furor melancholicus* induced by Saturn.

In the original version of Agrippa's *De Occulta Philosophia* this theory of melancholy genius—later arbitrarily tucked away in the First Book of the printed edition—is expounded near the end of the last Book and thus marks the climax of his whole work. That it is derived from Ficino's *Libri de Vita Triplici* goes without saying; whole sentences are taken over almost verbatim. But Agrippa differs from Ficino in one important point, and in so doing reveals himself as the intermediary between Ficino and Dürer.

Ficino had little interest in politics and no interest whatever in art. He conceived of geniuses primarily in terms of "studiosi" and "literati," and according to him the creative, Saturnian melancholy is a prerogative of theologians, poets and philosophers. It is only the purely metaphysical and therefore highest of our faculties, the intuitive "mind" (*mens*), which is susceptible to the inspiring influences of Saturn. Discursive "reason" (*ratio*), which controls the sphere of moral and political action, belongs to Jupiter; and "imagination" (*imaginatio*), which guides the hands of artists and craftsmen, to Mars or to Sol. According to Agrippa of Nettesheim, however, the *furor melancholicus*, that is, the Saturnian inspiration, can stimulate each of these three faculties to an extraordinary or even "superhuman" activity.

Agrippa thus distinguishes among three kinds of geniuses, all of whom act under the impulse of Saturn and his *furor melancholicus*. Those in whom "imagination" is stronger than the "mind" or "reason" will turn out to be wonderful artists and craftsmen such as painters or architects; and if they should be blessed with the gift of prophecy their predictions will be restricted to physical phenomena ("elementorum turbationes temporumque vicissitudines") such as "storms, earthquakes or floods, epidemics, famines, and other catastrophes of this kind." He in whom discursive "reason" predominates will become an ingenious scientist, physician or statesman, and his predictions, if any, will refer to political events. Those finally in whom the intuitive "mind" outweighs the other faculties will know the secrets of the realm divine and excel in all that is implied in the word theology; if prophetic, they will foresee religious crises such as the appearance of a new prophet or a new creed.

In the light of this system Dürer's Melancholia, the "Artist's Melancholy," can in fact be classified as "Melencolia I." Moving as she does in the sphere of "imagination"—which is, by definition, the sphere of spatial quantities—she typifies the first, or least exalted, form of human ingenuity. She can invent and build, and she can think, to quote Henry Ghent, "as long as her imagination keeps step with her thought"; but she has no access to the metaphysical world. Even if she were to venture into the realm of prophecy she would be limited to the domain of physical phenomena; the ominous apparitions in the firmament, in addition to denoting the science of astronomy, may also allude to Agrippa's "elementorum turbationes tem-

porumque vicissitudines," and the fact that some of the trees in the background are surrounded by water may suggest those "floods" which he
explicitly mentions among the natural catastrophes foreseen by the "imaginative" melancholic—and which, incidentally, were believed to be caused
by Saturn or Saturnian comets. Thus Dürer's Melancholia belongs in fact
to those who "cannot extend their thought beyond the limits of space." Hers
is the inertia of a being which renounces what it could reach because it
cannot reach for what it longs.

The influence of Dürer's *Melencolia I*—the first representation in which
the concept of melancholy was transplanted from the plane of scientific and
pseudo-scientific folklore to the level of art—extended all over the European
continent and lasted for more than three centuries. Its composition was
simplified or made even more complicated, and its content was either reconciled with earlier traditions—as is the case with most of the variations
produced by Northern artists of the sixteenth century—or reinterpreted according to the taste and mental habits of the day. It was mythologized by
Vasari and emblematically transformed by Cesare Ripa; it was emotionalized
by such Baroque artists as Guercino, Domenico Feti, Benedetto Castiglione
or Nicolas Chaperon who frequently fused it with the then fashionable
allegories of Transience and tried to gratify the popular enthusiasm for
ruins; it was sentimentalized in English eighteenth century art; it was ro-
manticized by J. E. Steinle and Caspar David Friedrich; and it inspired
poetic and literary paraphrases—such as the famous one in James Thomson's
City of Dreadful Night—as well as paintings, drawings and prints.

In spite of this universal appeal, it has always been felt that Dürer's
engraving has an eminently personal connotation. It has been suggested
that its somber mood might reflect Dürer's sorrow at the death of his mother
who had passed away on May 17, 1514; and it has even been supposed that
the numerical elements of this date—17, 5, 15, 14—are in some way referred
to in the magic square which consists of 16 cells, and where (therefore)
each row of four figures adds up to 34. However, even if the numerological
treatment of the date were less arbitrary than it is, even if the *Mensula Jovis*,
like all the other "Seals of the Planets," could not be traced back to Arabic
sources of the ninth or tenth century, and even if its presence in Dürer's
engraving could not be accounted for by good internal reasons; even then
this hypothesis would be hard to believe. Dürer respected his "poor and
pious mother"; as a dutiful son, he felt sorry for her hard life, and he admired her patience in "many a painful illness, great poverty, derision, contempt, sneering words, anxieties and other troubles on end." But his real love
belonged to his father, and no personal grief would have occasioned an

engraving so esoteric and, at the same time, so programmatic in character. Instead of saying that the death of Dürer's mother caused him to create the *Melencolia I*, one might rather contend that only an artist pregnant with the *Melencolia I* could have interpreted the face of an old woman—her squint bringing to mind Shakespeare's Paulina, "one eye declined for the loss of her husband, another elevated that the oracle was fulfilled"—in such a manner as Dürer did when he portrayed his mother two months before her death.

In fact the *Melencolia I* reflects the whole of Dürer's personality rather than a single experience, however moving. In a drawing of about 1512/13, apparently made for the purpose of consulting a doctor, Dürer represented himself in the nude, his finger pointing to a mark on the left side of his abdomen. The inscription reads: "Where the yellow spot is, to which I point with my finger, there it hurts"; and the sore spot is obviously the spleen, supposedly the very kernel of melancholy disease. Melanchthon, on the other hand, extols the "melancholia generosissima Düreri" ("Dürer's most noble melancholy"), thus classifying him as a melancholic in the sense of the new doctrine of genius.

Dürer himself, then, was, or at least thought he was, a melancholic in every possible sense of the word. He knew the "inspirations from above," and he knew the feeling of "powerlessness" and dejection. But, more important still, he was also an artist-geometrician, and one who suffered from the very limitations of the discipline he loved. In his younger days, when he prepared the engraving "Adam and Eve," he had hoped to capture absolute beauty by means of a ruler and a compass. Shortly before he composed the *Melencolia I* he was forced to admit: "But what absolute beauty is, I know not. Nobody knows it except God." Some years later, he wrote: "As for geometry, it may prove the truth of some things; but with respect to others we must resign ourselves to the opinion and judgment of men." And: "The lie is in our understanding, and darkness is so firmly entrenched in our mind that even our groping will fail"—a phrase which might well serve as a motto for the *Melencolia I.*

Thus Dürer's most perplexing engraving is, at the same time, the objective statement of a general philosophy and the subjective confession of an individual man. It fuses, and transforms, two great representational and literary traditions, that of Melancholy as one of the four humors and that of Geometry as one of the Seven Liberal Arts. It typifies the artist of the Renaissance who respects practical skill, but longs all the more fervently for mathematical theory—who feels "inspired" by celestial influences and eternal ideas, but suffers all the more deeply from his human frailty and intellectual finiteness. It epitomizes the Neo-Platonic theory of Saturnian genius as revised by Agrippa of Nettesheim. But in doing all this it is in a sense a spiritual self-portrait of Albrecht Dürer.

SELECTED BIBLIOGRAPHY

1. DeWitt Parker, *The Analysis of Art*, Ch. III, Yale University Press, 1926. A good supplementary example of a philosophically committed theory applied with range and sensitivity to painting.
2. Susanne Langer, *Feeling and Form*, Chaps. 5–6, Scribner's Sons, 1953. An interpretation of painting as presentational symbol.
3. Erwin Panofsky, *Studies in Iconology*, Oxford University Press, 1939. A classic in the relation between symbolism and painting.
4. Rudolf Arnheim, *Art and Visual Perception*, University of California Press, 1954. A remarkable survey of recent psychological results in the general area of the aesthetics of painting.

MUSIC

Music is tones, conveyed by instruments, including the human voice, in certain rhythmic and harmonic relations. Everyone agrees on this. The aesthetic problem begins when the question arises, "does music contain other elements as well, specifically, ideas, emotions, representations?" Traditionally, there are two disputing schools, the *autonomy* and the *heteronomy*. The first maintains that music is primarily sounds in motion, with no (possible) reference to anything outside of music; the second holds that music is more than mere sounds in motion, that it can and frequently does include ideas, emotions, stories and even philosophies of life. Sometimes the issue is stated in terms of whether music is a language or means anything.

Critics, composers, psychologists, and philosophers have written much and with vehemence on this problem. Two contrasting versions of the dispute as to what music is are presented here. The longer one is by Eduard Hanslick, from his *The Beautiful in Music,* in which he characterizes music as pure sounds in motion and goes on to criticize the popular view that music represents or is a language of anything. The second selection, in opposition to Hanslick, is from J. W. N. Sullivan's *Beethoven: His Spiritual Development,* in which Sullivan argues that, at least in the case of Beethoven, music can include spiritual values.

Eduard Hanslick

MUSIC, REPRESENTATION AND MEANING*

THE BEAUTIFUL IN MUSIC

We must now . . . endeavour to determine of what nature the beautiful in music is.

Its nature is specifically musical. By this we mean that the beautiful is not contingent upon, or in need of any subject introduced from without, but that it consists wholly of sounds artistically combined. The ingenious co–ordination of intrinsically pleasing sounds, their consonance and contrast, their flight and re–approach, their increasing and diminishing strength —this it is, which in free and unimpeded forms, presents itself to our mental vision.

The primordial element of music is *euphony,* and *rhythm* is its soul. Rhythm in general, or the harmony of a symmetrical structure; and rhythm in particular, or the systematically reciprocal motion of its several parts within a given measure. The crude material which the composer has to fashion, the vast profusion of which it is impossible fully to estimate, is the entire scale of *musical notes* and their inherent adaptability to an endless variety of melodies, harmonies, and rhythms. *Melody,* unexhausted, nay, inexhaustible, is pre–eminently the source of musical beauty. *Harmony* with its countless modes of transforming, inverting, and intensifying, offers the material for constantly new developments; while rhythm, the main artery of the musical organism, is the regulator of both, and enhances the charms of the "timbre" in its rich varieties.

To the question—what is to be expressed with all this material? the answer will be: *musical ideas.* Now, a musical idea, reproduced in its entirety, is not only an object of intrinsic beauty, but also an end in itself, and not a means for representing feelings and thoughts.

The essence of music is *sound and motion.*

---

* From Eduard Hanslick's *The Beautiful in Music,* trans. Gustav Cohen. First published in 1854. I reproduce here Chapters III and II, almost in their entirety, with minor grammatical changes; the order is changed to III and II because III discusses the nature of music; II, what music is not.

Eduard Hanslick (1825–1904), world-renowned music critic of the *Wiener Zeitung,* opponent of Richard Wagner, champion of Johannes Brahms, wrote *The Beautiful in Music* as a defense of a non-emotionalist theory of music. Its lucidity, brilliance and devastatingly good sense earned for it an enormous reputation throughout Europe which it retains.

The arabesque, a branch of the art of ornamentation, dimly betokens in what manner music may exhibit *forms of beauty*, though no definite emotion be involved. We see a plexus of flourishes, now bending into graceful curves, now rising in bold sweeps; moving now towards, and now away from each other; correspondingly matched in small and large arcs; apparently incommensurable, yet duly proportioned throughout; with a duplicate or counterpart to every segment; in fine, a compound of oddments, and yet a perfect whole. Imagine now an arabesque, not still and motionless, but rising before our eyes in constantly changing forms. Behold the broad and delicate lines, how they pursue one another; how from a gentle curve they rise up into lofty heights, presently to descend again; how they widen and contract; surprising the eye with a marvellous alternation of quiescence and mobility. The image thus becomes nobler and more exalted. If, moreover, we conceive this living arabesque as the active emanation of inventive genius, the artistic fulness of whose imagination is incessantly flowing into the heart of these moving forms, the effect, we think, will be not unlike that of *music*.

When young, we have probably all been delighted with the ever–changing tints and forms of a *kaleidoscope*. Now, music is a kind of kaleidoscope, though its forms can be appreciated only by an infinitely higher ideation. It brings forth a profuseness of beautiful tints and forms, now sharply contrasted and now almost imperceptibly graduated; all logically connected with each other, yet all novel in their effect, forming, as it were, a complete and self–subsistent whole, free from any alien admixture. The main difference consists in the fact that the *musical kaleidoscope* is the direct product of a creative mind, whereas the optic one is but a cleverly constructed mechanical toy. If, however, we stepped beyond the bounds of analogy, and in real earnest attempted to raise mere color to the rank of music by foisting on one art the means of another, we should be landed in the region of such puerile contrivances as the "Color Piano" or the "Ocular Organ," though these contrivances significantly prove both phenomena to have, morphologically, a common root.

If any sentimental lover of music thinks that analogies, such as the one mentioned, are degrading to the art, we reply that the only question is whether they are *relevant* or not. A subject is not degraded by being studied. If we wish to disregard the attributes of motion and successive formation, which render a comparison with the kaleidoscope particularly applicable, we may, forsooth, find a more dignified parallel for beautiful music in architecture, the human body, or a landscape, because these all possess original beauty of outline and color, quite irrespective of the intellectual substratum, the soul.

The reason why people have failed to discover the beauties in which pure music abounds, is, in great measure, to be found in the *underrating*, by the older systems of aesthetics, of the *sensuous element*, and in its subordination to morality and feeling—in Hegel to the "idea." Every art sets out from the sensuous and operates within its limits. The theory relating to the expression of feelings ignores this fact, and disdainfully pushing aside the act of *hearing*, it passes on immediately to the *feelings*. Music, say they, is food for the soul, and the organ of hearing is beneath their notice.

True, it is not for the organ of hearing as such, for the "labyrinth" or the "tympanum" that a Beethoven composes. But our *imagination*, which is so constituted as to be affected by auditory impressions (and in relation to which the term *organ* means something very different from a channel directed towards the world of physical phenomena), delights in the sounding forms and musical structures, and, conscious of their sensuous nature, lives in the immediate and free contemplation of the beautiful.

It is extremely difficult to define this self–subsistent and specifically musical beauty. As music has no prototype in nature, and expresses no definite conceptions, we are compelled to speak of it either in dry, technical terms, or in the language of poetic fiction. Its kingdom is, indeed, "not of this world." All the fantastic descriptions, characterizations, and periphrases are either metaphorical or false. What in any other art is still descriptive, is in music already figurative. Of music it is impossible to form any but a musical conception, and it can be comprehended and enjoyed only in and for itself.

The "specifically musical" must not, however, be understood only in the sense of acoustic beauty or symmetry of parts—both of which elements it embraces as of secondary importance—and still less can we speak of "a display of sounds to tickle the ear," or use similar phraseology, which is generally intended to emphasize the absence of an intellectual principle. But, by laying stress on musical beauty, we do not exclude the intellectual principle; on the contrary, we imply it as essential; for we would not apply the term "beautiful" to anything wanting in intellectual beauty; and in tracing the essential nature of beauty to a morphological source, we wish it to be understood that the intellectual element is most intimately connected with these sonorific forms. The term "form" in musical language is peculiarly significant. The forms created by *sound* are not empty; not the envelope enclosing a vacuum, but a well, replete with the living creation of inventive genius. Music, then, as compared with the arabesque, is a *picture*, yet a picture the subject of which we cannot define in words, or include in any category of thought. In music there is both meaning and logical sequence, but in a *musical* sense; it is a language we speak and understand, but which we are unable to *translate*. It is a highly suggestive fact that, in speaking of musical compositions, we likewise employ the term "thought," and a critical mind easily distinguishes real thoughts from hollow phrases, precisely as in speech. The Germans significantly use the term "Satz" (sentence) for the logical consummation of a part of a composition, for we know exactly when it is finished, just as in the case of a written or spoken sentence, though each has a logic of its own.

The logic in music, which produces in us a feeling of satisfaction, rests on certain elementary laws of nature, which govern both the human organism and the phenomena of sound. It is, above all, the primordial law of "harmonic progression" which, similarly to the curve-lines in painting and sculpture, contains the germ of development in its main forms, and the—unfortunately almost unexplained—cause of the link which connects the various musical phenomena.

All musical elements are in some occult manner connected with each other by certain natural affinities, and since rhythm, melody, and harmony are under their invisible sway, the music created by man must conform to them—any combinations conflicting with them bearing the impress of caprice and ugliness. Though not demonstrable with scientific precision, these affinities are instinctively felt by every experienced ear, and the organic completeness and logic, or the absurdity and unnaturalness of a group of sounds, are intuitively known, without the intervention of a definite conception as the standard of measure, the *tertium comparationis*.

From this negative rationalness, inherent in music and founded on laws of nature, springs the possibility of its becoming invested also with *positive* forms of beauty.

The act of composing is a mental working on material capable of receiving the forms which the mind intends to give. The musical material in the hands of creative genius is as plastic and pliable as it is profuse. Unlike the architect, who has to mould the coarse and unwieldy rock, the composer reckons with the ulterior effect of past sounds. More ethereal and subtle than the material of any other art, sound adapts itself with great facility to any idea the composer may have in his mind. Now, as the union of sounds (from the interdependence of which the beautiful in music flows) is not effected by mechanically stringing them together, but by acts of a free imagination, the intellectual force and idiosyncrasy of the particular mind will give to every composition its individual character. A musical composition, as the creation of a thinking and feeling mind, may, therefore, itself possess intellectuality and pathos in a high degree. Every musical work ought to bear this stamp of intellectuality, but the *music itself* must furnish evidence of its existence. Our opinion regarding the seat of the intellectual and emotional elements of a musical composition stands in the same relation to the popular way of thinking as the idea of *immanence* does to that of *transcendence*. The object of every art is to clothe in some material form an idea which has originated in the artist's imagination. In music this idea is an *acoustic* one; it cannot be expressed in words and subsequently translated into sounds. The initial force of a composition is the invention of some definite theme, and not the desire to describe a given emotion by musical means. Thanks to that primitive and mysterious power, whose mode of action will for ever be hidden from us, a theme, a melody flashes on the composer's mind. The origin of this *first* germ cannot be explained, but must simply be accepted as a fact. When once it has taken root in the composer's imagination, it forthwith begins to grow and develop; the principal theme being the centre round which the branches group themselves in all conceivable ways, though always unmistakably related to it. The beauty of an independent and simple theme appeals to our aesthetic feeling with that directness, which tolerates no explanation, except, perhaps, that of its inherent fitness and the harmony of parts, to the exclusion of any alien factor. It pleases for its own sake, like an arabesque, a column, or some spontaneous product of nature—a leaf or a flower.

There is no greater and more frequent error than to distinguish between "beautiful music," *with* and *without* a definite subject. The error is due to the extremely narrow conception of the beautiful in music, leading people to regard the artistically constructed form and the soul infused into it, as two independent and unrelated existences. All compositions are accordingly divided into full and empty "champagne bottles"; musical "champagne," however, has the peculiarity of developing *with* the bottle.

One musical thought is refined in and through itself and for no further reason; another is vulgar; this final cadence is imposing, while by the alteration of but two notes it becomes commonplace. We are perfectly justified in calling a musical theme grand, graceful, warm, hollow, vulgar; but all these terms are exclusively suggestive of the *musical* character of the particular passage. To define the musical complexion of a given theme, we often speak in terms used to describe *emotions*, such as "proud, gloomy, tender, ardent, longing." But we may with equal justice select them from a different order of phenomena, and call a piece of music, "sweet, fresh, cloudy, cold." Our feelings, to be descriptive of the character of a musical composition, must be regarded in the light of mere *phenomena*, just as any other phenomenon which happens to present certain analogies. Epithets, such as we have mentioned, may be used so long as we remain fully conscious of their figurative sense—nay, we may even be unable to avoid them; but let us never say, this piece of music *expresses* pride, &c.

A close examination of the musical definiteness of a theme convinces us however—the inscrutability of the ultimate ontological causes notwithstanding—that there are various proximate causes with which the intellectual element in a composition is intimately associated. Every musical factor (such as an interval, the "timbre," a chord, the rhythm, &c.) has a distinctive feature of its own and its individual mode of action. Though the composer's mind be a mystery, its product is quite within the grasp of our understanding.

A theme harmonized with the common chord, sounds differently if harmonized with the chord of the sixth; a melody progressing by an interval of the seventh produces quite a distinct effect from one progressing by an interval of the sixth. The rhythm, the volume of sound, or the "timbre"—each alters the specific character of a theme entirely—in fine, every single musical factor necessarily contributes to a certain passage assuming just *this* particular aspect, and affecting the listener in *this* particular way. What it is that makes Halévy's music appear fantastic, that of Auber graceful—what enables us immediately to recognize Mendelssohn or Spohr—all this may be traced to purely *musical* causes, without having recourse to the mysterious element of the *feelings*.

On the other hand, *why* the frequent chords of $\frac{6}{4}$ and the concise, diatonic themes of Mendelssohn, the chromatic and enharmonic music of Spohr, the short two-bar rhythm of Auber, &c., invariably produce this specific impression and none other—this enigma, it is true, neither psychology nor physiology can solve.

If, however, we enquire into the *proximate* cause—and that is, after all, what concerns us most in any art—we shall find that the thrilling effect of a theme is owing, not to the supposed extreme grief of the composer, but to the extreme intervals; not to the beating of his heart, but to the beating of the drums; not to the craving of his soul, but to the chromatic progression of the music. The *link* connecting the two we would by no means ignore; on the contrary, we shall presently subject it to a careful analysis. Meanwhile, we must remember that a scientific enquiry into the effect of a theme can deal only with such *musical* factors as have an enduring and objective existence, and not with the presumable state of mind in which the composer happened to be. The conclusion reached by arguing from the composer's state of mind directly to the effect of the music *might*, perchance, be correct; but the most important part of the syllogism, the middle term—i.e., *the music isefl,* would thus be ignored.

A good composer always has, perhaps more by intuition than by rote, a *practical* knowledge of the character of every musical element; but in order to give a rationale of the various musical sensations and impressions, we require a *theoretical* knowledge of those characters from the most intricate combinations down to scarcely distinguishable gradations. The specific effect of a melody must not be taken as "a marvel mysterious and unaccountable," which we can only "feel" or "divine"; but it is the inevitable result of the musical factors united in this particular manner. A short or long rhythm, a diatonic or chromatic progression—each has its individual physiognomy and an effect of its own. An intelligent musician will, therefore, get a much clearer notion of the character of a composition which he has not heard himself, by being told that it contains for instance, too many diminished sevenths, or too many tremolos, than by the most poetic description of the emotional crises through which the listener passed.

To ascertain the nature of each musical factor, its connection with a specific effect—its proximate, not its ultimate cause—and finally, to explain these particular observations by more general laws would be to establish that "philosophic foundation of music" to which so many writers aspire, though none has ever told us in which sense he understands this phrase. The psychical or physical effect of a chord, a rhythm, or an interval is not accounted for by saying that *this* is the expression of hope, *that* the expression of disappointment, as we should say, this is red, that green, but only by placing specifically musical attributes in general aesthetic categories, and the latter under one supreme principle. After having explained the isolated action of each single element, it would be incumbent upon us to show in what manner they govern and modify one another in all their various combinations. Most musical critics have ascribed the intellectual merit of a composition more particularly to the *harmony* and the *contrapuntal* accompaniment. The arguments, however, are both superficial and desultory. *Melody,* the alleged vehicle of sensuousness and emotion, was attributed to the inspiration of genius—the Italian school accordingly receiving a gracious word of praise; while *harmony,* the supposed vehicle of sterling thought, in contradistinction to melody, was deemed to be simply the result of study and reflection. It is strange how long people were satisfied with so unscientific a view of the subject. Both propositions contain a grain of truth, but they are neither universally applicable nor are the two factors in question, in reality, ever so strictly isolated. The soul and the talent for musical construction are bound up in one inseparable whole. Melody and harmony issue simultaneously in *one and the same armor* from the composer's mind. Neither the principle of subordination nor that of contrast affect the nature of the relation of harmony to melody. Both may display now an equal force of independent development, and now an equally strong tendency to voluntary subordination—yet, in either case, supreme intellectual beauty may be attained. Is it, perchance, the (altogether absent) *harmony* in the principal themes of Beethoven's Overture to "Coriolanus," or of Mendelssohn's Overture to "The Hebrides," which gives them the character of profound thought? Is the intellectual merit of Rossini's theme "Oh, Matilda!" or of some Neapolitan song, likely to be enhanced by substituting for the original meagre harmony a *basso continuo,* or some complicated succession of chords? The theme was conceived with *that* harmony, *that* rhythm, and *that* instrumentation. The intellectual merit lies in the union of *all* these factors; hence the mutilation of one entails that of the others. The *prominence* of the melody, the rhythm, or the harmony, as the case may be, improves the effect of the whole, and it is sheer pedantry to say that the excellence or the triviality is owing here to the presence of certain chords, and there to their absence. The camellia is destitute of odor, and the lily of color; the rose is rich both in odor and color; each is beautiful, and yet their respective attributes cannot be interchanged.

A "philosophic foundation of music" would first of all require us, then, to determine the definite conceptions which are invariably connected with each musical element and the nature of this connection. The double requirement of a strictly scientific framework, and an extremely comprehensive casuistry, renders it a most arduous though not an impossible task, unless, indeed, our ideal is that of a science of music in the sense in which chemistry and physiology are sciences!

The manner in which the creative act takes place in the mind of a composer of instrumental music gives us a very clear insight into the peculiar nature of musical beauty. A *musical* idea originates in the composer's imagination; he develops it—more and more crystals coalesce with it, until by imperceptible degrees the whole structure in its main features appears before him. Nothing then remains to be done but to examine the composition, to regulate its rhythm and modify it according to the canons of the art. The composer of instrumental music never thinks of representing a definite subject; otherwise he would be placed in a false position, rather outside than within the domain of music. His composition in such a case would be *programme music,* unintelligible without the programme. If this brings the name of Berlioz to our mind, we do not hereby call into question or underrate his brilliant talent. In his step followed Liszt, with his much weaker "Symphonic Poems."

As the same block of marble is converted by one sculptor into the most exquisite forms, by another into a clumsy botch, so the musical scale, by different manipulation, becomes now an Overture of Beethoven, and now one of Verdi. In what respect do they differ? Is it that one of them expresses more exalted feelings, or the same feelings more accurately? No, but simply because its musical structure is more beautiful. One piece of music is good, another bad, because one composer invents a theme full of life, another a commonplace one; because the former elaborates his music with ingenious originality, whereas with the latter it becomes, if anything, worse and worse; because the harmony in one case is varied and novel, whereas in the other it drags on miserably in its poverty; because in one the rhythm is like a pulse, full of strength and vitality, whereas in the other it is not unlike a tattoo.

There is no art which, like music, uses up so quickly such a variety of forms. Modulations, cadences, intervals and harmonious progressions become so hackneyed within fifty nay, thirty years, that a truly original composer cannot well employ them any longer, and is thus compelled to think of a new musical phraseology. Of a great number of compositions which rose far above the trivialities of their day, it would be quite correct to say that there was a time when they were beautiful. Among the occult and primitive affinities of the musical elements and the myriads of possible combinations, a great composer will discover the most subtle and unapparent ones. He will call into being forms of music which seemingly are conceived at the composer's pure caprice, and yet, for some mysterious and unaccountable reason, stand to each other in the relation of cause and effect. such compositions in their entirety, or fragments of them, may, without hesitation, he said to contain the "spark of genius." This shows how mistaken Oulibicheff is, when he asserts, that instrumental music cannot possibly be "*spirituel*," because the "*esprit*" of the composer consists solely in *adapting* his music in "a certain manner to a direct or indirect programme." In our opinion we are quite warranted in saying, that the celebrated D sharp in the *Allegro,* or the descending "unisono" passage in the Overture to "Don Giovanni," is imbued with the spirit of genius. The former, however, as little represents (as Oulibicheff imagines) "*Don Giovanni's* hostile attitude to the human race," as the latter does "the parents, the husbands, the brothers and the lovers of the women whom *Don Giovanni* seduced." Such interpretations are not only questionable in themselves, but are particularly so in respect of Mozart, who—the greatest musical genius the world has ever seen—transformed into music all he touched. Oulibicheff also thinks that Mozart's G minor Symphony accurately describes the history of a passionate amour in four different phases. But the G minor Symphony is music, neither more nor less; and that is quite enough. If instead of looking for the expression of definite states of mind, or certain events in musical works, we seek *music* only, we shall then, free from other associations, enjoy the perfections it so abundantly affords. Wherever musical beauty is wanting, no meaning, however profound, which sophistical subtlety may read into the work can ever compensate for it; and where it exists, the meaning is a matter of indifference. It directs our musical judgment, at all events, into a wrong channel. The same people who regard music as a mode in which the human intellect finds expression—which it neither is nor ever can be, on account of its inability to impart *convictions*—these very people have also brought the word "intention" into vogue. But in music there is no "intention" that can make up for "invention." Whatever is not clearly contained in the music, is to all intents and purposes non-existent, and what it does contain has passed the stage of mere intention. The saying: "He intends something" is generally used in a eulogistic sense. To us it seems rather to imply an unfavorable criticism which, translated into plain language would run thus: the composer would like to produce something, but he cannot. Now, an art is to do something, and he who cannot do anything takes refuge in—"intentions."

As the musical elements of a composition are the source of its beauty, so are they likewise the source of the laws of its construction. A great number of false and confused notions are entertained on this subject, but we will only single out one.

We mean the commonly accepted theory of the *Sonata* and *Symphony*, grounded on the assumption that feelings are expressible by musical means. In accordance with this theory, the task of the composer is to represent in the several parts of the Sonata four *states of mind*, all differing among themselves, and yet related to one another. (How?) In order to account for the connection which undoubtedly exists between the various parts, and to explain the difference in their effect, it is naively taken for granted that a definite feeling underlies each of them. The construction put upon them sometimes fits, but more frequently it does not, and it never follows as a necessary consequence. It will always, however, be a matter of course, that the four different parts are bound up in a harmonious whole, and that each should set off and heighten the effect of the others, according to the aesthetic laws of *music*. We are indebted to the inventive genius of M. v. Schwindt for a very interesting illustration of Beethoven's "Fantasia for the Pianoforte" (Op. 80), the several parts of which the artist interprets as representing connected incidents in the lives of the principal actors, and then gives a pictorial description of them. Now, just as the painter transforms the sounds into scenes and shapes, so does the listener transform them into feelings and occurrences. Both stand in a certain relation to the music, but neither of them in a *necessary* one, and it is only with *necessary* relations that science is concerned.

It is often alleged that Beethoven, when making the rough sketch of a composition, had before him certain incidents or states of mind. Whenever Beethoven (or any other composer) adopted this method, he did so to smooth his task; to render the achievement of musical unity easier by keeping in view the connecting links of certain objective phenomena. If Berlioz, Liszt, and others fancied that a poem, a title, or an event yielded them something *more* than that, they were laboring under a delusion. It is the *frame of mind* bent on *musical* unity which gives to the four parts of a sonata the character of an organically-related whole, and not their connection with an *object* which the composer may have in view. Where the latter denied himself the luxury of these poetic leading-strings, and followed purely musical inspiration, we shall find no other than a musical unity of parts. Aesthetically speaking, it is utterly indifferent whether Beethoven really did associate all his works with certain ideas. We do not know them, and as far as the composition is concerned, they do not exist. It is the composition itself, apart from all comment, which has to be judged; and as the lawyer completely ignores whatever is not in his brief, so aesthetic criticism must disregard whatever lies outside the work of art. If the several parts of a composition bear the stamp of unity, their correlation must have its root in musical principles.

To avoid even the possibility of misapprehension, we will now define our conception of the "beautiful in music" from three points of view. The "beautiful in music," in the specific sense in which we understand it is neither confined to the "classical style," nor does it imply a preference for this over the "romantic style." It may exist in one style no less than the other, and may occur in Bach as well as in Beethoven; in Mozart as well as in Schumann. Our proposition is thus above all suspicion of partisanship. The whole course of the present enquiry never approaches the question of what *ought to be,* but simply of what *is.* We can deduce from it no definite ideal of the truly beautiful in music, but it enables us to show what is equally beautiful even in the most opposite styles.

Not long since the fashion began to regard works of art in connection with the ideas and events of the time which gave them birth. This connection is undeniable and exists probably also in music. Being a product of the human mind, it must naturally bear some relation to the other products of mind; to contemporaneous works of poetry and the fine arts; to the state of society, literature, and the sciences of the period; and finally, to the individual experiences and convictions of the author. To observe and demonstrate the existence of this connection in the case of certain composers and works is not only a justifiable proceeding, but also a true gain to knowledge. We should, nevertheless, always remember, that parallelisms between specific works of art and the events of certain epochs belong to the *history* of art rather than to the *science of aesthetics.* Though methodological considerations may render it necessary to connect the history of art with the science of aesthetics, it is yet of the utmost importance that the proper domain of each of these sciences be rigorously guarded from encroachment on either side. The historian viewing a work of art in all its bearings may discover in Spontini "the expression of French imperialism," in Rossini "the political restoration"; but the student of aesthetics must restrict himself to the examination of the works themselves, in order to determine what is beautiful in them and why it is so. The aesthetic enquirer knows nothing (nor can he be expected to know anything) about the personal circumstances or the political surroundings of the composer—he hears and believes nothing, but what the music itself contains. He will, therefore, without knowing the name or the biography of the author, detect in Beethoven's Symphonies impetuousness and struggling, an unsatisfied longing and a defiance, supported by a consciousness of strength. But he could never glean from his works that he favored republicanism, that he was a bachelor and deaf, or any of the numerous circumstances on which the art-historian is wont to dilate; nor could such facts enhance the merit of the music. It may be very interesting and praiseworthy to compare the various schools of philosophy to which Bach, Mozart, and Haydn belonged, and to draw a parallel between them and the works of these composers. It is, however, a most arduous undertaking, and one which can but open the door to fallacies in proportion as it attempts to establish causal relations. The danger of exaggeration is exceedingly great, when once this principle is accepted. The slender influence of contemporariness may easily be construed as an inherent necessity, and the ever-untranslatable language of music be interpreted in the way which best fits the particular theory: all depends on the reasoning abilities; the same paradox which in the mouth of an accomplished dialectician appears a truism, seems the greatest nonsense in the mouth of an unskilled speaker.

Hegel, too, by his dissertation on music, has been the cause of misconceptions, for he quite unconsciously confounded the point of view of *art–history,* which was pre–eminently his own, with that of pure aesthetics, and attributed an explicitness to music which, as such, it never possessed. The character of a piece of music undoubtedly stands in some relation to the character of its author; but for the student of aesthetics the relation is non–existent. The abstract notion of a necessary interdependence of all phenomena whatsoever may in its concrete application be distorted into a caricature of the reality. It requires, now–a–days, great moral courage to militate against a doctrine which is advocated with such skill and eloquence, and openly to affirm that "the grasp of historical relations" is one thing, and "aesthetic judgment" another. Objectively speaking, it is beyond doubt, *firstly,* that the different styles of expression of distinct works and schools are due to a completely different collocation of the *musical* elements; and *secondly,* that what rightly gives pleasure in a composition, be it a severely classical Fugue of Bach, or the dreamiest Nocturne of Chopin, is the beautiful in a *musical* sense only.

Even less than with the classical does the beautiful in music coincide with one of its branches, the *architectonic.* The rigid sublimity of super–incumbent harmonies, and the artistic blending of the many different parts (of which no isolated segment is ever free and self–dependent, because the complete work alone is so) have their imprescriptible justification; yet those imposing and sombre pyramids of sound of the old Italian and Dutch schools, and the finely–chased salt–cellars and silver candlesticks, so to speak, of venerable Sebastian Bach, are but small provinces within the kingdom of musical beauty.

Many schools of aesthetics think musical enjoyment is fully accounted for by the pleasure derived from mere *regularity* and *symmetry;* but these never were the sole attributes of beauty in the abstract, and much less so of beauty in music. The most insipid theme may be symmetrical. "Symmetry" connotes proportion only, and leaves unanswered the question: *what* is it that impresses us as being symmetrical? A systematic distribution of parts, both uninteresting and commonplace, often exists in the most pitiable compositions, but the musical sense wants symmetry combined with *originality.*

Oerstedt, to crown all, carried this Platonic doctrine so far as to cite the circle, for which he claims positive beauty, as a parallel case. Should he, himself, never have experienced the horror of a completely round composition? . . .

Between *language* and music, parallels have also been frequently drawn and an attempt made to lay down for the latter laws governing only the former. The relation between *song* and language is patent enough, no matter whether we found it on the identity of the physiological conditions, or on the character which both have in common—namely, that of expressing thoughts and feelings by means of the human voice. The analogy, indeed, is so obvious as to render unnecessary further discussion. We admit at once that wherever music is merely the subjective manifestation of a state of mind, the laws of *speech* are, in a measure, applicable also to *singing*. That under the influence of passion the pitch of the voice is raised, while the propitiating orator lowers it; that sentences of great force are spoken slowly, and unimportant ones quickly; these and kindred facts the composer of songs, and the *musical dramatist* especially, will ever bear in mind. People, however, did not rest satisfied with these limited analogies; but conceiving *music* proper to be a *kind of speech* (though more indefinite and subtle), they forthwith deduced its aesthetic laws from the properties of language. Every attribute and every effect of music was believed to have its analogy in speech. We ourselves are of opinion, that where the question turns on the specific nature of an art, the points in which it differs from cognate subjects are more important than its points of resemblance. An aesthetic enquiry, unswayed by such analogies which, though often tempting, do not affect the essence of music, must ever advance towards the point where speech and music irreconcilably part. Only from beyond this point may we hope to discover truly useful facts in respect of music. The fundamental difference consists in this: while *sound* in *speech* is but a sign, that is, *a means* for the purpose of expressing something which is quite distinct from its medium; *sound* in *music* is the *end*, that is, the ultimate and absolute object in view. The intrinsic beauty of the musical forms in the latter case, and the exclusive dominion of thought over sound as a mere medium of expression, in the former, are so utterly distinct as to render the union of these two elements a logical impossibility.

Speech and music, therefore, have their centres of gravity at different points, around which the characteristics of each are grouped; and while all specific *laws of music* will centre in its independent forms of beauty, all *laws of speech* will turn upon the correct use of sound as a medium of expressing ideas.

The most baneful and confused notions have sprung from the attempt to define music as a kind of speech, and we may observe their practical consequences every day. Composers of feeble genius, in particular, were only too ready to denounce as false and sensual the ideal of intrinsic musical beauty, because it was beyond their reach, and to parade in its place the characteristic significance of music. Quite irrespective of Richard Wagner's operas, we often find in the most trivial instrumental compositions disconnected cadences, recitatives, &c., which interrupt the flow of the melody, and which, while startling the listener, affect to have some *deep meaning*, though in reality they only display want of beauty. Modern pieces, in which the principal rhythm is constantly upset in order to bring into prominence certain mysterious appendages and a super–abundance of glaring contrasts, are praised for striving to pass the "narrow limits" of music, and to elevate it to the rank of *speech*. Such praise has always appeared to us somewhat ambiguous. The limits of music are by no means narrow, but they are clearly defined. Music can never be "elevated to the rank of speech"— musically speaking "lowered" would be a more appropriate term—for music to be speech at all would, of course, be a *superlative degree* of speech.

Our singers always forget this, when in moments of intense emotion they ejaculate sentences as though they were *speaking,* and think they thus attain to the highest degree of musical expression. It does not strike them that the transition from song to speech is always a descent, so that the highest pitch of normal speech sounds deeper than the low notes in singing, though both proceed from the same organ. As mischievous in their practical consequences (if not more so, because of the impossibility of disproving them by actual experiment) are those *theories* which try to impose on music the laws of development and construction peculiar to speech, as in former days Rameau and Rousseau, and in modern times the disciples of Richard Wagner have endeavored to do. In this attempt the life of the music is destroyed; the innate beauty of form annihilated in pursuit of the phantom "meaning." One of the most important tasks of the aesthetics of music would, therefore, be that of demonstrating with inexorable logic the fundamental difference between music and language, and of never departing from the principle that, wherever the question is a specifically musical one, all parallelisms with language are wholly irrelevant.

THE REPRESENTATION OF FEELINGS IS NOT THE SUBJECT OF MUSIC

The proposition that the *feelings* are the *subject* which music has to represent is due partly to the theory according to which the *ultimate aim* of music is to excite feelings, and partly to an amended form of this theory.

A philosophical disquisition into an art demands a clear definition of its *subject–matter*. The diversity of the subject–matter of the various arts and the fundamental difference in the mode of treatment, are a natural sequence of the dissimilarity of the *senses* to which they severally appeal. Every art comprises a range of ideas, which it expresses after its own fashion, in sound, language, color, stone, &c. A work of art, therefore, endows a definite conception with a material form of beauty. This definite conception, its embodiment, and the union of both, are the conditions of an aesthetic ideal, with which a critical examination into every art is indissolubly connected.

The subject of a poem, a painting, or statue may be expressed in words and reduced to ideas. We say, for instance, this picture represents a flower–girl, this statue a gladiator, this poem one of Roland's exploits. Upon the more or less perfect embodiment of the particular subject in the artist's production depends our verdict respecting the beauty of the work of art.

The whole gamut of human *feelings* has with almost complete unanimity been proclaimed to be *the subject of music,* since the emotions were thought to be in antithesis to the definiteness of intellectual conceptions. This was supposed to be the feature by which the musical ideal is distinguished from the ideal of the other fine arts and poetry. According to this theory, therefore, sound and its ingenious combinations are but the material and the medium of expression, by which the composer represents love, courage, piety, and delight. The innumerable varieties of emotion constitute the idea which, on being translated into sound, assumes the form of a musical composition. The beautiful melody and the skilful harmony as such, do not harm us, but only what they imply: The whispering of love, or the clamor of ardent combatants.

In order to escape from such vague notions, we must, first of all, sever from their habitual associations metaphors of the above description. The *whispering* may be expressed, true; but not the whispering of "love"; the *clamor* may be reproduced, undoubtedly; but not the clamor of "ardent combatants." Music may reproduce phenomena such as whispering, storming, roaring, but the feelings of love or anger have only a subjective existence.

Definite feelings and emotions are unsusceptible of being embodied in music.

Our emotions have no isolated existence in the mind, and cannot, therefore, be evoked by an art which is incapable of representing the remaining series of mental states. They are, on the contrary, dependent on physiological and pathological conditions, on notions and judgments; in fact, on all the processes of human reasoning which so many conceive as antithetical to the emotions.

What then transforms an indefinite feeling into a *definite* one—into the feeling of longing, hope, or love? Is it the mere degree of intensity; the fluctuating rate of inner motion? Assuredly not. The latter may be the same in the case of dissimilar feelings or may, in the case of the same feeling, vary with the time and the person. Only by virtue of ideas and judgments—unconscious though we may be of them when our feelings run high—can an indefinite state of mind pass into a definite feeling. The feeling of hope is inseparable from the conception of a happier state that is to come, and which we compare with the actual state. The feeling of sadness involves the notion of a past state of happiness. These are perfectly definite ideas or conceptions, and in default of them—*the apparatus of thought,* as it were— no feeling can be called "hope" or "sadness," for through them alone can a feeling assume a definite character. On excluding these conceptions from consciousness, nothing remains but a vague sense of motion which at best could not rise above a general feeling of satisfaction or discomfort. The feeling of love cannot be conceived apart from the image of the beloved being, or apart from the desire and the longing for the possession of the object of our affections. It is not the kind of psychical activity, but the intellectual substratum, the subject underlying it, which constitutes it *love.* Dynamically speaking, love may be gentle or impetuous, buoyant or de- pressed, and yet it remains love. This reflection alone ought to make it clear that music can express only those qualifying adjectives, and not the substantive, love, itself. A determinate feeling (a passion, an emotion) as such, never exists without a definable meaning, which can, of course, only be comunicated through the medium of definite ideas. Now, since music as an "indefinite form of speech" is admittedly incapable of expressing definite ideas, is it not a psychologically unavoidable conclusion, that it is likewise incapable of expressing definite emotions? For the *definite character* of an emotion rests entirely on the meaning involved in it.

How it is that music may, nevertheless, awaken feelings (though not necessarily so) such as sadness, joy, &c., we shall try to explain hereafter, when we come to examine music from a subjective point of view. At this stage of our enquiry it is enough to determine whether music is capable of *representing* any definite emotion whatever. To this question only a negative answer can be given, the definiteness of an emotion being inseparably con- nected with concrete notions and conceptions, and to reduce these to a material form is altogether beyond the power of music. A certain class of *ideas,* however, is quite susceptible of being adequately expressed by means which unquestionably belong to the sphere of music proper. This class com- prises all ideas which, consistently with the organ to which they appeal, are associated with audible changes of strength, motion, and ratio: the ideas of intensity waxing and diminishing; of motion hastening and lingering; of in- geniously complex and simple progression, &c. The aesthetic expression of music may be described by terms such as graceful, gentle, violent, vigorous, elegant, fresh; all these ideas being expressible by corresponding modifica- tions of sound. We may, therefore, use those adjectives as directly describing musical phenomena, without thinking of the ethical meanings attaching to them in a psychological sense, and which, from the habit of associating ideas, we readily ascribe to the effect of the music, or mistake even for purely musical properties.

The ideas which a composer expresses are mainly and primarily of a *purely musical* nature. His imagination conceives a definite and graceful melody aiming at nothing beyond itself. Every concrete phenomenon suggests the class to which it belongs, or some still wider conception in which the latter is included, and by continuing this process, the idea of the absolute is reached at last. This is true also of musical phenomena. This melodious Adagio, for instance, softly dying away, suggests the ideas of gentleness, and concord *in the abstract.* Our imaginative faculty, ever ready to establish relations between the conceptions of art and our sentiments, may construe these softly-ebbing strains of music in a still loftier sense—e.g., as the placid resignation of a mind at peace with itself, and they may rouse even a vague sense of everlasting rest.

The primary aim of Poetry, Sculpture, and Painting is likewise to produce some concrete image. Only by way of inference can the picture of a flower–girl call up the wider notion of maidenly content and modesty; the picture of a snow-covered churchyard the transitoriness of earthly existence. In like manner, but far more vaguely and capriciously, may the listener discover in a piece of music the idea of youthful contentedness or that of transitoriness. These abstract notions, however, are by no means the subject–matter of the pictures or the musical compositions, and it is still more absurd to talk as if the *feelings* of "transitoriness" or of "youthful contentedness" could be represented by them.

There are *ideas* which, though not occurring as *feelings,* are yet capable of being fully expressed by music; and conversely, there are *feelings* which affect our minds, but which are so constituted as to defy their adequate expression by any *ideas* which music can represent.

What part of the feelings, then, can music represent, if not the subject involved in them?

Only their *dynamic* properties. It may reproduce the motion accompanying psychical action, according to its momentum: speed, slowness, strength, weakness, increasing and decreasing intensity. But motion is only one of the concomitants of feeling, not the feeling itself. It is a popular fallacy to suppose that the descriptive power of music is sufficiently qualified by saying that, although incapable of representing the *subject* of a feeling, it may represent the feeling itself—not the object of love, but the "feeling of love." In reality, however, music can do neither. It cannot reproduce the feeling of love, but only the element of motion, and this may occur in any other feeling just as well as in love, and in no case is it the distinctive feature. The term "love" is as abstract as "virtue" or immortality," and it is quite superfluous to assure us that music is unable to express abstract notions. No art can do this, for it is a matter of course that only definite and concrete ideas (those that have assumed a living form, as it were) can be incorporated by an art. But no instrumental composition can describe the ideas of love, wrath, or fear, since there is no *causal nexus* between these ideas and certain combinations of sound. Which of the elements inherent in these ideas, then, does music turn to account so effectually? Only the element of *motion*—in the wider sense, of course, according to which the increasing and decreasing force of a single note or chord is "motion" also. This is the element which music has in common with our emotions, and which, with creative power, it contrives to exhibit in an endless variety of forms and contrasts.

Though the idea of *motion* appears to us a most far–reaching and important one, it has hitherto been conspicuously disregarded in all enquiries into the nature and action of music.

Whatever else there is in music that apparently pictures states of feeling, is *symbolical*.

Sounds, like colors, are originally associated in our minds with certain symbolical meanings, which produce their effects independently of, and antecedently to any design of art. Every color has a character of its own; it is not a mere cipher into which the artist blows the breath of life, but a force. Between it and certain states of mind Nature herself has established a sympathetic connection. Are we not all acquainted with the unsophisticated meanings of colors, so dear to the popular imagination, and which cultured minds have exalted into poetic refinement? Green is associated with a feeling of hope, blue with fidelity. Rosenkranz recognizes "graceful dignity" in orange, "philistine politeness" in violet, &c. ("Psychologie," 2nd edition, page 102.)

In like manner, the first elements of music, such as the various keys, chords, and "timbres," have severally a character of their own. There exists, in fact, a but too ready art of interpreting the meanings of musical elements. Schubart's symbolism of the keys in music forms a counterpart, as it were, to Goethe's interpretation of colors. Such elements (sounds, colors,) however, when employed for the purposes of art, are subject to laws quite distinct from those upon which the effect of their isolated action depends. When looking at a historical painting we should never think of construing the red appearing in it as always meaning joy, or the white as always meaning innocence. Just as little in a symphony would the key of A flat major

always awaken romantic feelings, or the key of B minor always misanthropic
ones, every triad a feeling of satisfaction, and every diminished seventh
a feeling of despair. Aesthetically speaking, such primordially distinctive traits are non-existent when viewed by the light of those wider
laws to which they are subordinate. The relation in question cannot,
for a moment, be assumed to *express* or *represent* anything definite whatsoever. We called it "symbolical" because the subject is exhibited not directly,
but in a form essentially different from it. If yellow is the emblem of
jealousy, the key of G major that of gaiety, the cypress that of mourning,
such interpretations, and the definite character of our emotions, imply a
psycho–physiological relation. The color, the sound, or the plant as such, are
not related to our emotions, but only the meanings we ourselves attach to
them. We cannot, therefore, speak of an isolated chord as representing a
determinate feeling, and much less can we do so when it occurs in a connected piece of music.

Beyond the analogy of motion, and the symbolism of sounds, music
possesses no means for fulfilling its alleged mission.

Seeing then how easy it is to deduce from the inherent nature of sound
the inability of music to represent definite emotions, it seems almost incredible that our every-day experience should, nevertheless, have failed
firmly to establish this fact. Let those who, when listening to some instrumental composition, imagine the strings to quiver with a profusion of feeling, clearly show what feeling is the subject of the music. The experiment is
indispensable. If, for instance, we were to listen to Beethoven's Overture to
"Prometheus," an attentive and musical ear would successively discover
more or less the following: the notes of the first bar, after a fall into the
lower fourth, rise gently and in rapid succession; a movement repeated in
the second bar. The third and fourth bars continue it in wider limits. The
jet propelled by the fountain comes trickling down in drops, but rises once
more, only to repeat in the following four bars the figure of the preceding
four. The listener thus perceives that the first and second bars of the *melody*
are symmetrical; that these two bars and the succeeding two are likewise so,
and that the same is true of the wider arc of the first four bars and the
corresponding arc of the following four. The bass which indicates the *rhythm*
marks the beginning of each of the first three bars with one single beat, the
fourth with two beats, while the same rotation is observed in the next four
bars. The fourth bar, therefore, is different from the first three, and this
point of difference becoming symmetrical, through being repeated in the
following four bars, agreeably impresses the ear, as an unexpected development within the former limits. The *harmony* of the theme exhibits the same

correspondence of one large and two small arcs: the common chord of C of the first four bars corresponds to the chord of $\frac{6}{4}$ of the fifth and sixth, and to the chord of $\frac{6}{5}$ of the seventh and eighth bars. This systematic correspondence of melody, rhythm, and harmony results in a structure composed of parts at once symmetrical and dissimilar, into which further gradations of light and shade are introduced through the "timbre" peculiar to each instrument and the varying volume of sound. . . .

Any other *subject* than the one alluded to we absolutely fail to find in the theme, and still less could we mention a *feeling* it represents, or necessarily arouses in the listener. An analysis of this kind reduces, it is true, to a skeleton, a body glowing with life; it destroys the beauty, but at the same time it destroys all false constructions.

No other theme of instrumental music will fare any better than the one which we have selected at random. A numerous class of lovers of music think that it is a characteristic feature of the older "classical" music only, to disregard the representation of feelings, and it is at once admitted that no feeling can be shown to form the subject of the forty-eight Preludes and Fugues of J. S. Bach's "well-tempered clavichord." However glaringly unscientific and arbitrary such a distinction may be—a distinction, by the way, which has its explanation in the fact that the older music affords still more unmistakable proof that it aims at nothing beyond itself, and that interpretations of the kind mentioned would, in this case present more obstacles than attractions—this alone is enough to prove that music need not *necessarily* awaken feelings, or that it must *necessarily* be the object of music to represent them. The whole domain of florid counterpoint would then have to be ignored. But if large departments of art, which can be defended both on historical and aesthetic grounds, have to be passed over for the sake of a theory, it may be concluded that such a theory is false. Though a single leak will sink a ship, those who are not content with that, are at liberty to knock out the whole bottom. Let them play the theme of a Symphony by Mozart or Haydn, an Adagio by Beethoven, a Scherzo by Mendelssohn, one of Schumann's or Chopin's compositions for the piano, anything, in short, from the stock of our standard music, or again, the most popular themes from Overtures of Auber, Donizetti, and Flotow. Who would be bold enough to point out a definite feeling as the subject of any of these themes? One will say "love." He may be right. Another thinks it is "longing." Perhaps so. A third feels it to be "religious fervour." Who can contradict him? Now, how can we talk of definite feeling being *represented*, when nobody really knows *what* is represented? Probably all will agree about the beauty or beauties of the composition, whereas all will differ regarding its subject. To *represent* something is clearly to exhibit it; distinctly to set it before us. But how can we call *that* the subject represented by an art, which is really its vaguest and most indefinite element, and which must, therefore, for ever remain highly debatable ground?

We have intentionally selected examples from *instrumental music,* for only what is true of the latter is true also of music as such. If we wish to decide the question whether music possesses the character of definiteness, what its nature and properties are, and what its limits and tendencies, no other than instrumental music can be taken into consideration. What *instrumental music* is unable to achieve, lies also beyond the pale of *music proper;* for it alone is pure and self-subsistent music. No matter whether we regard vocal music as superior to, or more effective than instrumental music—an unscientific proceeding, by the way, which is generally the upshot of one-sided dilettantism—we cannot help admitting that the term "music," in its true meaning, must exclude compositions in which words are set to music. In vocal or operatic music it is impossible to draw so nice a distinction between the effect of the music, and that of the words, that an exact definition of the share which each has had in the production of the whole becomes practicable. An enquiry into the subject of music must leave out even compositions with inscriptions, or so-called programme-music. Its union with poetry, though enhancing the power of music, does not widen its limits.

Vocal music is an undecomposable compound, and it is impossible to gauge the relative importance of each of its constituents. In discussing the effect of *poetry,* nobody, surely, will quote the *opera* as an example. Now, it requires a greater effort, but no deeper insight, to follow the same line of thought when the fundamental principles of musical aesthetics are in question.

Vocal music colors, as it were, the poetic drawing. In the musical elements we were able to discover the most brilliant and delicate hues, and an abundance of symbolic meanings. Though by their aid it might be possible to transform a second-rate poem into a passionate effusion of the soul, it is not the music, but the words which *determine* the subject of a vocal composition. Not the coloring, but the drawing renders the represented subject intelligible. We appeal to the listener's faculty of abstraction, and beg him to think, in a purely musical sense, of some dramatically effective melody, *apart* from the context. A melody, for instance, which impresses us as highly dramatic, and which is intended to represent the feeling of *rage,* can express this state of mind in no other way than by quick and impetuous motion. Words expressing passionate *love,* though diametrically opposed in meaning, might, therefore, be suitably rendered by the same melody.

At a time when thousands (among whom there were men like Jean Jacques Rousseau) were moved to tears by the air from "Orpheus"

> J'ai perdu mon Eurydice,
> Rien n'égale mon malheur,

Boye, a contemporary of Gluck, observed that precisely the same melody would accord equally well, if not better, with words conveying exactly the reverse, thus

> J'ai trouvé mon Eurydice,
> Rien n'égale mon bonheur. . . .

What is true of isolated passages is true also in a wider application. There are many cases where an entirely new text has been employed for a complete musical work. If Meyerbeer's "Huguenots," after changing the scene of action, the time, the characters, and the plot, were to be performed as "The Ghibellines of Pisa," though so clumsy an adaptation would, undoubtedly, produce a disagreeable impression, the purely musical part would in no way suffer. And yet the religious feeling and fanaticism which are entirely wanting in "The Ghibellines" are supposed to be the motive power in "The Huguenots." Luther's hymn must not be cited as counter-evidence, as it is merely a *quotation*. From a musical point of view it is consistent with any profession of faith whatever. Has the reader ever heard the *Allegro fugato* from the Overture to "The Magic Flute" changed into a vocal quartet of quarrelling Jewish pedlars? Mozart's music, though not altered in the smallest degree, fits the low text appallingly well, and the enjoyment we derive from the gravity of the music in the opera can be no heartier than our laugh at the farcical humor of the parody. We might quote numberless instances of the plastic character of every musical theme and every human emotion. The feeling of religious fervor is rightly considered to be the least liable to musical misconstruction. Yet there are countless village and country churches in Germany in which at Eucharist pieces like Proch's "Alpine Horn," or the *Finale* from the "Sonnambula" (with the coquettish leap to the tenth) are performed on the organ. Foreigners who visit churches in Italy hear, to their amazement, the most popular themes from operas by Rossini, Bellini, Donizetti, and Verdi. Pieces like these and of a still more secular character, provided they do not lose the quality of sobriety altogether, are far from interfering with the devotions of the congregation, who on the contrary, appear to be greatly edified. If music, as such, were capable of representing the feeling of piety, a *quid pro quo* of this kind would be as unlikely as the contingency of a preacher reciting from the pulpit a novel by Tieck or an Act of Parliament. The greatest masters of sacred music afford abundant examples in proof of our proposition. Handel, in particular, set to work with the greatest nonchalance in this respect. Winterfield has shown that many of the most celebrated airs from "The Messiah," including those most of all admired as being especially suggestive of piety, have been taken from secular duets (mostly erotic) composed in the years 1711–1712, when Handel set to music certain *Madrigals by Mauro Ortensio* for the Electoral Princess Caroline of Hanover. The music of the second duet:

> No, di voi non vo' fidarmi,
> Cieco amor, crudel beltà;
> Troppo siete menzognere
> Lusinghiere deità!

Handel employed unaltered both in key and melody for the chorus in the first part of "The Messiah," "For unto us a Child is born." The third part of the same duet. "Sò per prova i vostri inganni," contains the same themes which occur in the chorus of the second part of "The Messiah," "All we like sheep." The music of the Madrigal, No. 16 (duet for soprano and alto), is essentially the same as the duet from the third part of "The Messiah," "Oh death, where is thy sting?" But the words of the madrigal are as follows:

> Se tu non lasci amore
> Mio cor, ti pentirai
> Lo sò ben io!

There is a vast number of similar instances, but we need here only refer to the entire series of pastoral pieces from the "Christmas" Oratorio, which, as is well known, were naively taken from secular contatas composed for special occasions. And Gluck, whose music, we are taught, attained the sublime height of dramatic accuracy, only by every note being scrupulously adapted to each special case, nay, by the melodies being extracted from the very rhythm of the syllables—Gluck has transferred to his "Armida" no fewer than five airs from his earlier Italian operas (compare with the author's "Moderne Oper," page 16). It is obvious, therefore, that *vocal music,* which in theory can never determine the principles of music proper, is likewise, in practice, powerless to call in question the canons which experience has established for instrumental music.

The proposition which we are endeavoring to disprove has become, as it were, part and parcel of current musical aesthetics, so that all derivative and collateral theories enjoy the same reputation of invulnerability. To the latter belongs the theory that music is able to reproduce visual and auditory impressions of a non-musical nature. Whenever the question of the representation of objects by musical means (Tonmalerei) is under debate, we are, with an air of wisdom, assured over and over again that though music is unable to portray *phenomena* which are foreign to its province, it, nevertheless, may picture the *feeling* which they excite. The very reverse is the case. Music can undertake to imitate objective phenomena only, and never the specific feeling they arouse. The falling of snow, the fluttering of birds, and the rising of the sun can be painted musically only, by producing auditory impressions which are dynamically related to those phenomena. In point of strength, pitch, velocity, and rhythm, sounds present to the ear a *figure*, bearing that degree of analogy to certain visual impressions which sensations of various kinds bear to one another. As there is, physiologically speaking, such a thing as a vicarious function (up to a certain point), so may sense–impressions, aesthetically speaking, become vicarious also. There is a well–founded analogy between motion in space and motion in time, between the color, texture, and size of an object and the pitch, "timbre," and strength of a tone, and it is for this reason quite practicable to paint an object musically. The pretension, however, to describe by musical means the "feeling" which the falling snow, the crowing cock, or a flash of lightning excites in us, is simply ludicrous.

Although, as far as we remember, all musical theorists tacitly accept, and base their arguments on the postulate, that music has the power of representing definite emotions—yet, their better judgment has kept them from openly avowing it. The conspicuous absence of *definite ideas* in music troubled their minds and induced them to lay down the somewhat modified principle that the object of music was to awaken and represent "indefinite," not definite emotions. Rationally understood, this can only mean that music ought to deal with the *motion* accompanying a feeling, regardless of its essential part, with what is felt; in other words, that its function is restricted to the reproduction of what we termed the *dynamic* element of an emotion, a function which we unhesitatingly conceded to music. But this property does not enable music "to represent indefinite feelings" for to "represent" something "indefinite" is a contradiction in terms. Psychical motion, considered as motion apart from the state of mind it involves, can never become the object of an art, because without an answer to the query: what is moving, or what is being moved, an art has nothing tangible to work upon. That which is implied in the proposition—namely, that music is not intended to represent a *definite* feeling (which is undoubtedly true) is only a negative aspect of the question. But what is the positive, the creative factor, in a musical composition? An indefinite feeling as such, cannot supply a *subject:* to utilize it, an art would, first of all, have to solve the problem: What *form* can be given to it? The function of art consists in *individualizing*, in evolving the definite out of the indefinite, the particular out of the general. The theory respecting "indefinite feelings" would reverse this process. It lands us in even greater difficulties than the theory that music represents something, though it is impossible to define what. This position is but a step removed from the clear recognition that music represents *no feelings,* either definite or indefinite. Yet, where is the musician who would deprive his art of that domain which from time immemorial has been claimed as belonging to it?

This conclusion might give rise to the view that the representation of definite feelings by music, though impracticable, may yet be adopted as an ideal, never wholly realizable, but which it is possible, and even necessary, to approach more and more closely. The many high–sounding phrases respecting the tendency of music to cast off its vagueness and to become concrete speech, no less than the fulsome praises bestowed on compositions aiming, or supposed to be aiming at this, are a proof of the popularity of the theory in question.

Having absolutely denied that possibility of representing emotions by musical means, we must be still more emphatic in refuting the fallacy which consider it the *aesthetic touchstone* of music.

The *beautiful* in music would not depend on the accurate representation of feelings even if such a representation were *possible.* Let us, for argument's sake, assume the possibility and examine it from a practical point of view.

It is manifestly out of the question to test this fallacy by *instrumental music,* as the latter could be shown to represent definite feelings only by arguing in a circle. We must, therefore, make the experiment with vocal music, as being that music whose office it is to emphasize clearly defined states of mind.

Here the *words* determine the subject to be described; music may give it life and breath, and impart to it a more or less distinct individuality. This is done by utilizing as far as possible the characteristics peculiar to motion and the symbols associated with sounds. If greater attention is bestowed on the words than on the production of purely musical beauty, a high degree of individuality may be secured—nay, the delusion may even arise that the music alone expresses the emotion which, though susceptible of intensification, was already immutably contained in the words. Such a tendency is in its consequences on a par with the alleged practicability of *representing* a certain feeling as the subject of a given "piece of music." Suppose there did exist perfect congruity between the real and the assumed power of music; that it was possible to represent feelings by musical means, and that these feelings were the subject of musical compositions. If this assumption be granted, we should be logically compelled to call *such* compositions the best as perform the task in the most *perfect manner*. Yet do we not all know compositions of exquisite beauty without any definite subject? We need but instance Bach's Preludes and Fugues. On the other hand, there are vocal compositions which aim at the most accurate expression of certain emotions, within the limits referred to, and in which the supreme goal is *truthfulness* in this descriptive process. On close examination we find that the rigor with which music is subordinated to words is generally in an inverse ratio to the independent beauty of the former; otherwise expressed, that *rhetorico-dramatical* precision and *musical perfection* go together but half-way, and then proceed in different directions.

The *recitative* affords a good illustration of this truth, since it is that form of music which best accommodates itself to rhetorical requirements, down to the very accent of each individual word; never even attempting to be more than a faithful copy of rapidly–changing states of mind. This, there-fore, in strict accordance with the theory before us, should be the highest and most perfect music. But in the Recitative music degenerates into a mere shadow and relinquishes its individual sphere of action altogether. Is not this a proof that the representing of definite states of mind is contrary to the nature of music, and that in their ultimate bearings they are antagonistic to one another? Let anyone play a long Recitative, leaving out the words, and enquire into its musical merit and subject. *Any kind of music* claiming to be the sole factor in producing a given effect should be able to stand this test.

This is true, by no means, of the Recitative alone; the most elevated and excellent forms of music equally bear out the assertion that the *beautiful* tends to disappear in proportion as the *expression of some specific feeling* is aimed at; for the former can expand only if untrammeled by alien factors, whereas the latter relegates music to a subservient place.

We will now ascend from the declamatory principle in the Recitative to the dramatic principle in the Opera. In Mozart's operas there is perfect congruity between the music and the words. Even the most intricate parts, the *Finales,* are beautiful if judged as a whole, quite apart from the words, although certain portions in the middle might without them become some-what obscure. To do justice in a like degree, both to the musical and the dramatic requirements, is rightly considered to be the ideal of the Opera. But that for this reason there should be perpetual *warfare* between the principles of dramatic nicety and musical beauty, entailing never-ending concessions on both sides, has, to my knowledge, never been conclusively demonstrated. The principle involved in the Opera is not undermined or weakened by the fact that all the parts are *sung*—our imagination being easily reconciled to an illusion of this kind—but it is the constraint imposed alike upon music and words that leads to continual acts of trespass or concession, and reduces the opera, as it were, to a constitutional government, whose very existence depends upon an incessant struggle between two parties, equally entitled to power. It is from this conflict, in which the composer allows now one principle and now the other to prevail, whence arise all the imperfections of the opera, and whence, at the same time, all rules important for *operatic* works are deduced. The principles in which music and the drama are grounded, if pushed to their logical consequences, are mutually destructive; but they point in so similar a direction that they appear almost *parallel*. . . .

The opera can never be *quite* on a level with a recited drama, or with purely instrumental music. A good opera composer will, therefore, constantly endeavor to combine and reconcile the two factors, instead of automatically emphasizing now one and now the other. When in doubt, however, he will always allow the claim of *music* to prevail, the chief element in the Opera being not dramatic, but musical beauty. This is evident from the different attitudes of mind in which we listen to a play or an opera in which the same subject is treated. The neglect of the musical part will always be far more keenly felt.

To us it appears that the importance, as regards the history of the art of music, of the celebrated controversy between the disciples of *Gluck* and those of *Piccini* lies in the fact that the question of the internal conflict in the *Opera*, caused by the incompatibility of the musical and the dramatic principles, was then, for the first time, thoroughly discussed. The controversy, it is true, was carried on without a clear perception of the immense influence which the issue would have on the whole mode of thinking. He who does not shrink from the labor—a very profitable labor, by the way—of tracing this musical controversy to its sources, will notice in the vast range from adulation down to ill-breeding all the wit and smartness of French polemics, but likewise so childish a treatment of the abstract part of the question, and such want of deeper knowledge, that the science of musical aesthetics could gain *nothing* from the endless disputation. The most gifted controversialists: Suard and the Abbe Arnaud on Gluck's side, and Marmontel and La Harpe of the opposite camp, though going repeatedly beyond the limits of Gluck's critique, and into a more minute examination of the *dramatic* principle of the Opera, and its relation to *music*, treated this relation, nevertheless, as one of the many properties of the Opera, but by no means as one of the most vital importance. It never struck them that the very life of the Opera depended on the nature of this relationship. It is certainly remarkable how very near some of Gluck's opponents, in particular, were at times to the position from which the fallacy of the dramatic principle can be clearly seen and confuted. Thus La Harpe, in the *Journal de Politique et de Littérature* of the 5th October, 1777, says:

> "On objecte qu'il n'est pas naturel de chanter un air de cette nature dans une situation passionée, que c'est un moyen d'arrêter la scène et de nuir à l'effet. Je trouve ces objections absolument illusoires. D'abord, dès qu'on admet le chant, il faut l'admettre le plus beau possible et il n'est pas plus naturel de chanter mal, que de chanter bien. Tous les arts sont fondes sur des conventions, sur des données. Quand je viens a l'opera, c'est pour entendre la musique. Je n'ignore pas, qu' Alceste ne faisait ses Adieux a Admète en chantant un air; mais comme Alceste est sur le Théatre pour chanter, si je retrouve sa douleur et son amour dans un air bien mélodieux, je jouirai de son chant en m'intéressant à son infortune."

Is it credible that La Harpe should have failed to recognize the security and unassailableness of his position? For, after a while, it occurs to him to object to the duet of *Agamemnon* and *Achilles* in "Iphigenia" because "it is inconsistent with the dignity of the two heroes to talk simultaneously." With this remark he quits the vantage–ground of the principle of purely musical beauty and tacitly—nay, unconsciously accepts the theory of his adversaries.

The more scrupulous we are in keeping pure the *dramatic* element of the opera, by withholding from it the vivifying breath of musical beauty, the more quickly it faints away like a bird in the exhausted receiver of an air pump. We have, therefore, no course open but to fall back upon the pure, *spoken* drama which, at all events, is a proof of the *impossibility* of the opera, unless, though fully aware of the unreality involved, we assign to the *musical* element the foremost rank. In the true exercise of the art, this fact has, indeed, never been questioned. Even Gluck, the most orthodox dramaturgist, although he originated the fallacy that opera-music should be nothing but exalted declamation, has, in practice, often allowed his musical *genius* to get the better of him, and this invariably to the great advantage of the work. The same holds good of Richard Wagner. For the object of these pages, it is enough to denounce emphatically as false Wagner's principal theorem, as stated in the first volume of "Oper und Drama." "The misconception respecting the Opera, viewed as a work of art, consists in the fact that the means (the music) is regarded as the end, and the end (the drama) as the means." An Opera, however, in which the music is really and truly employed *solely as a medium* for dramatic expression is a musical monstrosity.

One of the inferences to be drawn from Wagner's proposition (respecting the means and the end) is, that all composers who have set indifferent librettos to anything better than indifferent music, were guilty of a great impropriety, as we ourselves are in admiring such music.

The connection of poetry with music and with the opera is a sort of morganatic union, and the more closely we examine this morganatic union of musical beauty and definite thoughts, the more sceptical do we become as regards its indissolubility.

How is it that in every song slight alterations may be introduced, which, without in the least detracting from the accuracy of expression, immediately destroy the beauty of the theme? This would be impossible, if the latter were inseparably connected with the former. How, again, is it, that many a song, though adequately expressing the drift of the poem, is nevertheless quite intolerable? The theory that music is capable of expressing emotions, furnishes us with no explanation. . . .

J. W. N. Sullivan

MUSIC AS EXPRESSION*

We have seen that there is no reason to believe that uniqueness implies isolation. Poetic experiences are quite as unique as musical experiences, but nobody imagines that they form a closed world of their own, that they are wholly dissociated from the rest of the poet's nature and from his experience of life. It is true that, for the appreciation of a work of art in any medium, special sensibilities are required, and such sensibilities can be pleasurably exercised in almost complete independence of any other interests. Thus much of Spenser's poetry may perhaps be regarded as existing in a moral and spiritual vacuum; it has, so to say, almost no discoverable context. Here the specific poetic sensibilities are being exercised "for their own sakes." Music, much more than poetry, affords specimens of works which lead this curiously independent existence, but it need be no more true of music than of poetry that it must be essentially meaningless. If, therefore, we find that some compositions irresistibly suggest to us some spiritual context we need not resist this impulse on theoretical grounds. We need not suppose that we are the victims of a literary culture and an imperfectly developed musical faculty. As a matter of fact, all the greatest music in the world, and some of the worst, does suggest a spiritual context. It does more than suggest; its whole being

* From J. W. N. Sullivan's *Beethoven: His Spiritual Development*, Bk. One, Ch. III. Copyright, 1927, by J. W. N. Sullivan. Reprinted by permission of Alfred A. Knopf, Inc., and Navin Sullivan.

J. W. N. Sullivan (1886–1937), mathematician and writer, wrote numerous books on science and philosophy. His book on Beethoven is an attempt to relate music and certain life values which he thought some music could embody.

is conditioned by this context, and it lives to express it. This context is directly perceived even by those who, for theoretical reasons, do not explicitly admit its existence. The most ardent advocate of the isolation theory will, for example, describe one composition as more "profound" than another, will describe one melody as "noble" and another as "sentimental." Such judgments are incompatible with the isolation theory, for on that theory nothing could be said except that a piece of music afforded a greater or less degree of a unique and incommunicable pleasure. A composition could be no more profound or noble or sentimental than a wine. Yet such judgments, in the case of many compositions, are quite unavoidable.

If this be admitted we may, for our present purposes, divide musical compositions into three classes. We may admit that, so far as our present analysis penetrates, there are compositions which exist in isolation. Secondly, there are compositions which spring from a spiritual context and express spiritual experiences. And, thirdly, there is the class of music ordinarily called programme music. Of these classes the second is the most important.

In our reactions to compositions belonging to the first group we find that nothing is involved but our perceptions of musical quality and the delight those perceptions afford. An analysis of these perceptions could only be undertaken on the basis of a theory of musical aesthetics, and no satisfactory theory exists. No theory that has yet been proposed, such as Darwin's theory that music is a highly developed form of the sexual calls of animals, or Spencer's theory that it is an elaboration of emotional speech, gives any explanation of why one musical phrase is pleasing and another not nor, more important still, why one sequence of phrases seems satisfactory, stimulating and "logical," while another sequence appears arbitrary and boring. It is possible that, in the remote future, the physiology of the nervous system will throw some light on the matter, but at present it is impossible to give any recipes for writing good melodies or for developing a musical theme in a satisfactory manner. The rules which have from time to time been propounded, based on the examination of large numbers of examples, are as faithfully obeyed by bad music as by good. What is quite certain is that musical phrases differ in quality and that successions of phrases differ in the degree of their musical fitness and coherence. Whether any music really exists which involves *only* these perceptions we are not here concerned to argue. We are prepared to admit that, so far as our analysis extends, there are compositions which appeal only to our musical perceptions of quality and coherence, variety, invention, and so on, leaving it to the science of the future to say what connection these musical perceptions may have with the rest of our perceptions.

Our response to music of the second kind involves more factors than does our response to music of the first kind. Music which impresses us as expressing spiritual experiences and as springing from a spiritual context is still music. It must satisfy the musical faculty; it must obey all the criteria that "pure" music obeys. But the musical experiences it communicates are less isolated than those of pure music; a greater extent, as it were, of the artist's nature has been concerned in their creation; more comprehensive and, probably, deeper needs are satisfied by them. Amongst musical phrases are some which do more than please our musical faculty. They stir other elements in us; they reverberate throughout a larger part of our being. Certain emotions and expectations are aroused beside those that accompany our reactions to pure music. And the sequences of such phrases, besides satisfying our musical faculty's criteria of coherence and fitness, also satisfy these other expectations, give a natural development to these other emotions, continue, by a process of organic growth, this wilder life that has been awakened in us. But the poverty of language in names for subjective states has tempted many writers to describe these experiences, communicated to us by music, by describing some situation or event which would, they think, arouse a similar response. And because such situations are very largely conditioned by the critic's sensibility and imagination the same composition may be given a great apparent variety of interpretations. But, in any case, the bare statement of a situation of the composition is supposed to be about tells us nothing of any value. Even if the composer had a definite situation in mind, and one knew precisely what that situation was, a description of the situation tells us nothing of the quality of the response awakened by the music.

Beethoven's imaginative realization of the death of a hero, in the slow movement of the Eroica symphony, for instance, is utterly different in quality from Wagner's realization of the same situation in the Siegfried funeral march. What these compositions mean to us is precisely their communication, in each case, of the personal and individual conception of the situation. And it is this personal conception which reveals to us directly the depth and subtlety of the composer's feelings and perceptions. Such communications inform us directly of the spiritual context from which they spring, and they do this even if we are completely ignorant of any situation that may be involved. On the other hand, knowledge of the situation tells us nothing that we want to know. If we use the word "heroic" to describe the music of the Eroica symphony, that is not because the symphony is "about" Napoleon or Abercrombie, but because Heroism, as a state of being, was realized by Beethoven to the extent that he has expressed it, and it is the quality of his realization that is important. It is *his* conception of the heroic that matters to us, and which is a clue to the greatness of the soul which is expressing itself. The comparative tawdriness of Wagner's music is not due to any difference there might be in the imagined situation, but to the comparative poverty of his inner resources.

A knowledge of the situation that a musical composition is "about," therefore, can tell us little of value. And in practice we almost always know nothing of the situation, if any, that was in the mind of the composer. Nevertheless, a great deal of writing on music consists in presentations of imagined situations, and this is one reason why writing on music is properly classed as one of the dreariest branches of literature. It is possible that a great literary artist could so select and present a situation that experiences similar to those evoked by a given composition would be experienced by the reader. Beethoven, for instance, when asked for the "meaning" of the Appassionata sonata told his questioner to read Shakespeare's *Tempest*. No two compositions could be more unlike, and Beethoven was either joking or knew nothing of the play but its title. But he could, with more point, have referred a questioner to *Macbeth* as an illustration of the first movement of the C minor symphony. Even such vague correspondences are rare, however, and the usual "programme" presented by the writer on music seems to have little more relation to the composition than would a newspaper report of a street accident. But just as the journalist may have had emotions justifying his use of the word "Tragedy," so these programmes may represent something to their authors. These strange landscapes and violent variations in the weather conditions that so many compositions seem to suggest are, we may suppose, the symbols for experiences that are less trivial than they seem. They are merely unsuccessful devices of communication. We cannot know, for instance, what significance dancing elves, murmuring brooks and thunderstorms may have in the imagination of the descriptive writer. Such programmes are merely unintelligible. A man thinks of what symbols he can, and the symbols he invents are conditioned not only by his sensibility and imagination, but by his experience. To this is due the great variety of interpretations of the same composition. It is possbile that the different interpreters had similar spiritual experiences evoked by the composition, but it requires a great artist to express such experiences unambiguously. We may conclude then, that it is very doubtful whether any compositions of the kind we are discussing are "about" any of the programmes that have been suggested for them. And as we have said, if we did know the programme we should know nothing of importance about the composition. The "meaning" of these compositions is to be found in the spiritual experiences they evoke. The musical critic who wishes to describe these experiences is faced with precisely the same task as the literary critic who wishes to describe the significance of a poem and, like the literary critic, he is likely to achieve but a stammering success. But his task is no harder. Both critics should eschew "programmes" as irrelevant, although as the situation is explicit in a poem it is much easier to regard it as vital. But it is really no more illuminating to be told that Wordsworth wrote a sonnet about the view of London from Westminster Bridge than it is to be told that Chopin wrote a waltz about a puppy chasing its tail. The difference is that the poet himself cannot express his reaction to the situation without mentioning the situation, whereas the musician can do so. Music, compared with the other arts, is a kind of disembodied ghost, and has all the advantages and disadvantages of that state.

The reluctance of many musicians to admit that music of the kind we are discussing (which includes almost the whole of Beethoven's music) is in any sense programme music is due to their feeling that any proposed "situation" is not only inadequate but even irrelevant. In denying the adequacy of any proposed situation to the musical effect they have been led to the strained position that music has no extra-musical content whatever, that it witnesses to nothing in the composer except his possession of an isolated faculty called musical imagination. This view, as we have said, is not compatible with our direct reactions to music, and even the exponents of this view seem to find it almost impossible, as their writings prove, to hold it consistently. It is also in direct contradiction to the expressed views of some of the great composers themselves. Beethoven most certainly regarded his music as expressing states of consciousness which might conceivably have been expressed by some other art. Indeed, he seems to have regarded music not only as a medium for the presentation of "beauty," but as a language with which he was more familiar than any other. The evidence of his letters and reported remarks is quite clear on this point. Thus, in describing his method of composition to Louis Schlosser he refers to himself as "incited by moods, which are translated by the poet into words, by me into tones that sound, and roar and storm about me until I have set them down in notes." And in conversation with Neate he said: "I always have a picture in my mind when composing, and follow its lines." That we are not to take the word "picture" in this remark too literally is shown by his letter of July 15, 1817, to Wilhelm Gerhard where he says: "The description of a picture belongs to the field of painting; in this the poet can count himself more fortunate than my muse for his territory is not so restricted as mine in this respect, though mine, on the other hand, extends into other regions, and my dominion is not easily reached." And Schindler reports that Beethoven, in his later years, complained that people were less able to grasp the meaning of music than they were in his young days, and he even thought of giving poetic titles to his earlier works to supply this deficiency in his hearers' imaginations. It is certain, therefore, that Beethoven, at any rate, considered that his music had an extra-musical content, that is to say, a content that could conceivably be expressed in some other medium. But we may be quite certain that whatever poetic titles Beethoven or anybody else had given to his compositions would not have assisted his hearers in grasping this content. For the content, as we have said, is the composer's reaction to the situation, not the situation. And this reaction is conditioned by the spiritual nature of the man and is a revelation of it. In his capacity to express this content Beethoven reveals himself as a great musical genius, and the content itself reveals him as a great spirit.

Music, as an expressive art, evokes states of consciousness in the hearer which are analogous to states that may be produced by extra-musical means. It is usual to describe these states as "emotions" but this word, unless carefully used, is misleading. Psychologists have tabulated human emotions, that is, they have given a list of those emotions for which names exist. But it is difficult to find a musical composition whose effect is adequately described as evoking one or more of these emotions. No composition, for instance, can be adequately described as "melancholy" or "joyful." Such emotions, if they enter at all into the total effect, never enter as isolated elements. Gurney has proposed the term "fused emotion" to describe the musical experience, but the term is not very illuminating. We are again in presence of the mystery that attends our reaction to any work of art. There are as few melancholy or joyful poems as there are musical compositions. It may be that our reaction to a work of art is a synthesis of relatively simple emotions, but the analysis would probably teach us little. For the effect exists as a whole and not as an assemblage of its elements, just as a living creature is more than an assemblage of its constituent molecules. Such synthetic wholes are doubtless the highest experiences of which we are capable, but they are probably too rare and of too little practical importance to have received names. There is no harm in calling them emotions, provided it is realized that we are only rarely referring to named emotions. Some fairly complex emotions, such as "awe," have received names and have been more or less plausibly analyzed into a number of simpler constituent emotions. But our reactions to a work of art have hitherto resisted analysis into these simple terms, and for that reason many people have supposed that some unique "æsthetic emotion" is involved. But we have already objected to that theory that it does not account for the differences in our reactions to different works of art.

The most valuable states or "emotions" that music arouses are those that spring from the richest and deepest spiritual context. We are immediately aware, with great compositions of this kind, that the state of consciousness expressed by the composer is the result of certain perceptions and experiences. So far as we can recognize the emotion communicated to us we can say something of the conditions it, as it were, presupposes. If there is nothing in our experience akin to that of the composer his composition can be for us nothing but an example of "pure music." But the experiences we attribute to the composer tell us nothing, of course, about the causes of those experiences. To suppose that they do is to fall into the error of the programme writer. Thus when Marx describes the A minor quartet as inspired by Beethoven's progress from a sick bed to health we feel that the description is both inadequate and arbitrary. He has failed to do justice to the quality of the experience from which the work sprang, and he has quite arbitrarily invented a cause of the experience. But the critic who should deny any spiritual content whatever to the A minor quartet, who should fail to see that it could only germinate in the soil of some profound experience, would fail even more signally than Marx.

The function of the kind of music we have been discussing is to communicate valuable spiritual states, and these states testify to the depth of the artist's nature and to the quality of his experience of life. Such states cannot usually be correlated with definite situations, and for that reason no programme for them can be given. They are the fruits of countless experiences as realized and coordinated by the artist, and they enter into the very texture of his spiritual being. But there are certain classes of experiences, not perhaps of the highest order, for which situations can be assigned. Music expressing such experiences, deliberately relating them to the situation, is the highest form of what is ordinarily called programme music. We may take Beethoven's Pastoral symphony as being, on the whole, a composition of this class. It is concerned, for the most part, to depict its composer's reactions to various pastoral scenes. But, together with this, it contains a good deal of programme music of a different order whose purpose it is to give a musical representation of certain physical perceptions. The notorious cuckoo notes, the effect of flowing water in the Beside the Brook movement, the storm, are specimens of music of this class. It would not be sufficient to say of such music that its purpose is to represent physical perceptions. The representation must be musical, and only as realistic as is compatible with that condition. This means that the representation can never be completely realistic except when the physical perceptions concerned are musical sounds. Thus a tolling bell can be represented very realistically by tolling a bell. But it is only the most stupid modern composers who give equally realistic representations of trains and motor-horns. In any case, the actual physical perceptions that can be communicated by music are very few, although there is evidence that music can, for some people, suggest other than auditory perceptions. Thus there can be no doubt that, for some minds, sounds and colours are associated. Many lists have been given of the colour equivalents of the different orchestral instruments. The lists do not agree, but that does nothing to invalidate the existence of the correspondences. Even keys have their characteristic colours for some minds. It is possible, therefore, that by correct choice of key and instrumentation compositions could be designed which would powerfully suggest to such minds certain landscape effects. We also find that some music irresistibly reminds certain musical critics of food. Or it may arouse olfactory images. Writings on music abound in which colours, wines, peaches and perfumes are suggested to the authors by musical compositions. But such powers of evocation belong to the more freakish resources of music. No compositions worth talking about are designed to arouse such images, and probably those who experience them would regard them as amongst the least valuable of their reactions to the music. Such by-products of auditory stimuli do not help us to understand the peculiar character of programme music. That character does not consist in any correspondences that may exist between auditory and other physical perceptions, but in the analogy between the musical emotions communicated and the emotions aroused by the external situation that forms the programme of the composition. If it be said, for instance, that Debussy's L'Après-midi d'un Faune makes the impression of "a vegetable world alive in quivering hot sunshine . . . the life of trees, streams and lakes, the play of light upon water and on clouds, the murmur of plants drinking and feeding in the sunlight," it is not because musical sounds can evoke images of heat and light and vegetables, but because a man in such surroundings may typically experience emotions analogous to those communicated by the music. Programme music, in the strict sense, may be defined as music that communicates musical experiences analogous to extra-musical experiences that may be associated with some definite external situation. It does not, any more than any other music, depict any part of the external world.

SELECTED BIBLIOGRAPHY

1. D. F. Tovey, *Musical Articles from the Encyclopaedia Britannica*, Oxford University Press, 1944. Tovey is uniformly excellent. His essays on the elements of music, historically unfolded, are second to none. (Available as Meridian paperback entitled, *The Forms of Music.*)
2. Aaron Copland, *What to Listen for in Music*, McGraw-Hill Company, 1939. Very good on the elements of music, especially in chapters 4–9. (Available as Mentor paperback.)
3. Arthur Schopenhauer, *The World as Will and Idea*, Part III on "music as embodiment of the will." A classic version of the heteronomy doctrine.
4. Susanne Langer, *Feeling and Form*, Chaps. 7–8, Scribner's Sons, 1953. Music as the symbol of time.
5. John Hospers, *Meaning and Truth in the Arts*, esp. Part IV, section I, University of North Carolina Press, 1946. A good exposition of the conflict between the autonomy and heteronomy views along with a reconciliation by the author.
6. Leonard Meyer, *Emotion and Meaning in Music*, esp. Chaps. I–II, University of Chicago Press, 1956. An important attempt to dissolve old versions of the problem of meaning in music, but vitiated by questionable theories of meaning.

POETRY

In this section, we study one of the literary arts, poetry, and one of its central problems, its relation to truth and belief.

For the first, the description of the various ingredients of poetry, there are selections from a recent, excellent text-anthology, *Exploring Poetry*, by M. L. Rosenthal and A. J. M. Smith. These selections, taken as one piece, cover and illustrate all the elements of poetry: words, sound, meaning, metrics, images, rhythm, metaphor, symbols, truth-claims, and the organic relationship of these elements.

On the problem of truth in poetry (and literature generally), the famous piece on "Poetry and Beliefs" by I. A. Richards is included. It remains the clearest argument against the popular view that poetry is a use of language which makes true or false statements about the world.

M. L. Rosenthal and A. J. M. Smith

THE ELEMENTS OF POETRY*

THE CRAFTSMAN'S WORK

The original meaning of the word "poet" as it comes to us from the Greek is *maker*. A poem is something made, a thing shaped and constructed

* From M. L. Rosenthal and A. J. M. Smith's *Exploring Poetry*, pp. 33–36; 47–51; 66–71; 89–93; 179–183; 185–187; 476–483; 497–502; 509–511; 693–695; and 703–704, Copyright, 1955, by The Macmillan Company. Reprinted by permission of The Macmillan Company.

M. L. Rosenthal (1917–   ) and A. J. M. Smith (1902–   ), are both Professors of literature, the first at New York University, the second at Michigan State University. Both have written on various aspects of literature.

by conscious craftsmanship. Skill has gone into its making, and it is important for the student of poetry to understand something of the technical problems which the poet has met and solved. The analysis of poems into their several elements of conception and technique helps us to discover the secret of their power to illuminate our world. The careful reader will find one of the most remarkable things about a good poem is that its significance is not diminished but increased by analysis and study.

This does not mean that analysis and study are ends in themselves or that such preliminary and essential critical activity can account for all the effects of poetry (though it can, however, save us from the sentimental illusion of finding pleasure in what is not in a poem at all but is misread into it by carelessness, ignorance, or haste). Formulas and explanations cannot account for its emotional power. There are certain memorable lines whose appeal can perhaps never be fully explained by even the most accomplished critic:

Brightness falls from the air. . . .
THOMAS NASHE

In the gloom the gold
Gathers the light about it.
EZRA POUND

To cut across the reflex of a star. . . .
WILLIAM WORDSWORTH

Breaking the silence of the seas
Among the farthest Hebrides. . . .
WILLIAM WORDSWORTH

Keep up your bright swords, for the dew will rust them.
WILLIAM SHAKESPEARE

In such magical lines as these there is a fusion of music, imagery, and thought which calls forth more than an intellectual response. But the more than rational power to respond to poetry, called "sensibility," must—although it exists potentially in everyone—be stimulated by contact with life and with poems, and if possible by much reading aloud and listening to others read aloud. Owing to a changed emphasis in education and public taste, modern readers often miss this once fairly common experience with verse. Shakespeare's audience, though not very sophisticated in reading, was accustomed to hearing poetry whenever it attended the theater; there was no problem of getting used to it such as faces an audience today. When, at the end of *Hamlet,* the dying hero wants his friend Horatio to let other people know what has happened, he does not turn to him and say,

> Horatio, we've been friends a long time. Don't—don't—bad as the world is— commit suicide yet. Tell the public the real story of what happened, as a final favor to me—won't you?

Hamlet's audience would have had none of such talk. They expected *poetry,* and here is what Shakespeare actually gave them:

> If thou didst ever hold me in thy heart,
> Absént thee from felicity a while
> And in this harsh world draw thy breath in pain
> To tell my story.

These lines follow a scene of great violence. Their calmer, yet sad, earnest, and affectionate music remained in the audience's ears long after most of them had forgotten Hamlet's specific words. The effect was in part derived from the dramatic situation, but mainly it came from the arrangement of images and sounds within the context of that situation.

If we pause for a moment to consider this observation, we may be able to see a few of the reasons why these lines strike us as "pure" poetry. For as Herbert Read tells us, although "we have no rational explanation of the process of imagination"—that is, the power of conceiving the sound-effects, the ideas, and the suggestive implications of a poem and combining them so effectively that they "render emotion exactly" or very nearly so—yet we are able to analyze these several elements created and used by the poet's imagination.[1]

Thus, the special effect of Hamlet's speech can be, in some degree, "accounted for." The passage contains hardly a single literal statement, hardly a phrase in fact that means just what it says—though each phrase, by straining the truth to just the right extent, contributes to the feeling created by the whole speech. No one can literally hold another person in his heart; even if we overlook the irony of the second line, to die by suicide is not at all, in Christian thinking, automatically to achieve "felicity"—perfect happiness; and no physically healthy person, however "harsh" the world may seem to him, can be said to feel pain at every breath. Each of these phrasings exaggerates just a little, and each serves to stress the emotional state it evokes—a friend's love first, then unwilling self-denial, and finally deep misery. Hamlet recognizes these states of feeling in his friend and,

[1] Herbert Read, *Phases of English Poetry.*

through revealing his sensitiveness to them, makes his appeal a remarkably consoling gesture of sympathy. Simultaneously, our appreciation of Hamlet's own gentleness and nobility is enhanced by this concern for his friend at the moment before his own death.

Meanwhile, the mood, tone, spirit of the situation is communicated also in the music of the verse. The *sounds* are echoing and re-echoing one another. Notice the *h*'s, short *e*'s, *l*'s, and *r*'s in the important words *ever, hold, absént, harsh, world, breath,* and *story;* the long *e*'s of the second syllables that provide a constant background of sound—*me, thee,* feli*city,* sto*ry;* and the *th*'s and long *i*'s in *thou, thy, thee, while, this, my*. But the word that echoes longest is *pain,* though it is linked in sound with the other important words only through the consonant *n* which is also found in *absént. Pain* therefore stands out against the flow of patterned sound like a rock against a current, and *pain* is the one word which gives the passage its deepest emotional coloration.

Observe that the third line, which ends in the word *pain,* actually sounds like what the speaker is talking about, like the speech of a man gasping out strongly felt ideas with great difficulty. Whereas the previous line was lilting and fluent, this one makes us pause over almost every one of its ten monosyllabic words—and especially the fourth, fifth, sixth, eighth, and tenth. Tremendous emphasis is gained by this damming-up effect. All speed is gone from the line by the time we have passed *harsh world draw,* and after the added barrier of *breath* there is almost a full stop at *pain.* The halting effect continues to the very end of the sentence.

A word of caution is necessary here: Sounds do not in themselves convey a meaning. Liquid sounds are lighter and more graceful than gutturals, and there are many other differences among sound-effects, but this does not mean that every *l* or *r* carries a definite idea or feeling with it, or every *k* a harsher idea or feeling. However, in a passage with an unusual number of *l*'s and *k*'s we may find an underlying pattern of pure sound effects balanced against one another—an actual music of sounds. If we want to know the connection between this pure sound-pattern and the feeling and thought of the poem, we must note where the most important words fall. In a good poem, there will be a definite relationship between the points of emphasized thought and emotion and the pattern of sound. Unless we are dealing with nonsense rhymes or pure sound-effects, it is the thought and the emotion that give the sounds their meaning. The words in the *Hamlet* passage which we must emphasize because of their meaning are also the words in which the most important sound-effects are found. The *h*'s, *l*'s, and so on become associated with these words and take their emotional effect from their meaning. Thus, since *hold* and *heart* are strongly stressed, the vowels and consonants in them, when repeated in later words, recall them again. Without these important words, the alliteration alone—the musical effect gained by the repetition of sounds, particularly in stressed syllables—could not ordinarily stir us deeply.

We see, therefore, that although its character and origin have some irrational aspects poetry can certainly be understood and analyzed. To try to *write* poems out of calculation alone would be fruitless, but that is another thing altogether from trying with all our sympathies and intelligence to gain the most accurate perception and the fullest appreciation of them after they are written. Though they may be conceived through "inspiration," they are constructed by craftsmanship. Even the simplest of poems is a gathering and compression of elements, including many assumptions normally shared by writer and reader, which are neither indefinable nor irrelevant to the poem's achievement.

POETIC FIGURES AND POETIC MEANING

Here, near the beginning of our study of poetry, it will be helpful to try to put out of our minds any *preconceived* opinions about its nature, purposes, or methods. Let us forget any such arbitrary laws as that poetry is or ought to be emotional, that it must be "elevated" and "beautiful," or that it must deal with "poetic" subjects. Where these assertions are not too hopelessly vague, they have some validity; but their main tendency is to limit and dilute our appreciation of the poet's art. The subject-matter of poetry is much wider in scope, more immediate and less selective in its sources, and more intense and less respectable in its responses and expression than many people have been taught. "Fair and foul are near of kin" cries the speaker in one of Yeats's poems; there may be deep significance and even beauty in what seemed only loathsome.

We do, however, need some test of the genuineness and value of a poem. One such test, though it cannot be applied indiscriminately and will vary in usefulness according to the knowledge and the developed sensibility of the reader, is the intensity with which the poet has entered into an experience and recognized and communicated its implications. *The nature of his original experience, whether it be physical, emotional, or intellectual, does not determine the genuineness or goodness of the poem. What counts is the pressure of the feeling and of the thinking generated by the experience.* There are no "poetic" subjects as such; any subject, no matter how apparently unpromising, can be made poetic when shaped by the poetic imagination.

Accuracy of perception and clarity of expression—what might, in its finest manifestation, be called "nakedness of vision"—can make of the humblest and even the vilest object a source of poetry, just as it can, also, bring home to us the purest spiritual truths.

Even in disillusioned and bitter poetry, however, it is delight and love that are at the heart of a poet's vision. The vividness of his writing is a direct result of the delight and love. It comes from a sort of visual thirst that drinks eagerly whatever it lights upon:

> Eye, gazelle, delicate wanderer,
> Drinker of horizon's fluid line—

as Stephen Spender has expressed it. In the finest poetry the pictures presented to our senses and imagination are not contrived merely as ornament or illustration, but they themselves generate the meaning of the poem. Over three hundred years ago the Elizabethan poet Samuel Daniel spoke of the way this creation of a meaning through the senses takes place:

> Glory is most bright and gay
> In a flash, and so away.
> Feed apace then, greedy eyes,
> On the wonder you behold.
> Take it sudden as it flies
> Though you take it not to hold;
> When your eyes have done their part,
> Thought must length it in the heart.

But thought cannot ponder fruitfully what our senses have perceived, unless the perceptions are accurate and sharply defined. Accuracy and clarity are marks both of the poet's sincerity and of his craftsmanship. Consider Browning's

> The wild tulip, at end of its tube, blows out its great red bell
> Like a thin clear bubble of blood

or Whitman's

> Earth of the vitreous pour of the full moon just tinged with blue!
> Earth of shine and dark mottling the tide of the river!

These sense-impressions appeal to the eye. The following lines by Herrick add movement, touch, and sound in their presentation of the rippling glitter and swish of a lady's silks as she walks:

> Whenas in silks my Julia goes,
> Then, then (methinks), how sweetly flows
> The liquefaction of her clothes.
>
> Next, when I cast mine eyes and see
> That brave vibration each way free,
> O how that glittering taketh me!
>
> ROBERT HERRICK *Upon Julia's Clothes*

And Milton, to suggest the beauty of a woman's singing, and the loveliness and virtue of the singer herself, actually presents one sensation in terms of another:

> At last a soft and solemn breathing sound
> Rose like a steam of rich distilled perfumes,
> And stole upon the air. . . .

In these passages we find direct sense-impressions and pictured comparisons. Such impressions and comparisons are called *images*. It is through images that the threefold nature of poetic experience and expression reveals itself as the accurate and intense perception of objects, the stimulation of feeling, and the operation of the mind. Poetic imagery has a sensuous, an emotional, and an intellectual source, and it communicates on all three of these levels.

Imagery is sometimes the direct concrete expression of vivid sense perceptions, but often—as almost all the foregoing instances reveal—it is figurative rather than literal. Figures of speech are not, of course, confined to poetry; they are a part of all linguistic activity except the most rigorously factual, and are familiar to most of us in slang and other popular, inventive, and indeed poetic adventures with language.

In poetry itself the commonest and most useful figures of speech— *simile, metaphor, personification,* and *conceit*—involve comparison, not a comparison between things that are actually very much alike but a comparison between things which have one often unexpected quality in common. The function of the figure is to direct our attention with special vividness to this particular quality. There is no figure involved in comparing a rose to a carnation, but when a poet compares his girl to a rose (in order to suggest her sweetness, freshness, loveliness, and perhaps also the frailty and impermanence of that loveliness) he is not making a literal factual statement; he is appealing to the imagination. Such poetic statements as Burns' "O my luve is like a red, red rose" or Shakespeare's "My Mistress' eyes are nothing like the sun" or the more concentrated "her diamond eyes" (i.e.—her diamond-like eyes) or Campion's "Her brows like bended bows"—statements in which always the comparison is explicitly expressed by the use of some such words as *like, as,* and *similar to*—are called similes.

When a figure is presented not as a directly stated comparison but as an identity, then we have not a simile but a metaphor: "My love is a red, red rose," "Her eyes are diamonds," and Tennyson's "The black bat Night" are metaphors. One of the most frequently encountered types of metaphor is personification, well illustrated in such a characteristic image as this from Shelley's *To Night:*

> Blind with thine hair the eyes of Day;
> Kiss her until she be wearied out. . . .

or in Milton's address to the spirit of Melancholy:

> Come, pensive nun, devout and pure,
> Sober, steadfast, and demure. . . .

Sometimes personification is combined with simile, as in the exciting virtuosity of T. S. Eliot's

> . . . the evening is spread out against the sky
> Like a patient etherised upon a table. . . .

The boldness and originality of this image is characteristic of the conceit—a favorite device of the seventeenth-century Metaphysical poets and their modern followers. The principle behind the conceit is that the greater the gap between the two things compared in a simile or identified in a metaphor—the greater, that is, the imaginative leap the poet's mind achieves —the greater the satisfaction and the sharper the conviction. Many successful images, therefore, are paradoxical; they seem fanciful or out-of-kilter until the reader's own mind makes the leap.

From both the esthetic and the psychological points of view the metaphysical poet's aim is to achieve the *widest* possible gap between the arms of his comparison. If the gap is too narrow, that is, if the things or qualities compared are too much alike, the result is flat and dull. If on the other hand, the comparison is, literally, too far-fetched, the failure is of a different sort, and the result is unconvincing or ridiculous.

Any bold far-fetched figure of comparison, whether successful or not, is called a conceit. (The word is related to *concept,* a mental image.) The description of the evening as an etherised patient is a conceit; so is John Donne's famous comparison of absent lovers to a pair of compasses:

If they be two, they are two so
    As stiff twin compasses are two;
Thy soul, the fix'd foot, makes no show
    To move, but doth, if th' other do.

And though it in the centre sit,
    Yet, when the other far doth roam,
It leans, and hearkens after it,
    And grows erect, as that comes home.

So, too, though a less adventurous one, is Thomas Campion's elaboration of images in *Cherry-ripe*. The poet is telling how the lovely virtuous maiden guards the cherries of her lips:

Her eyes like angels watch them still;
    Her brows like bended bows do stand,
Threat'ning with piercing frowns to kill
    All that attempt with eye or hand
        Those sacred cherries to come nigh,
        Till "Cherry-ripe" themselves do cry.

From these brief illustrations it should be clear that an effective figure of speech is both a perception of reality and a projection of the imagination. It is a sudden insight into a meaningful relationship between things not often thought to be like.

RHYTHM AND MOVEMENT

Through its rhythmic movement, poetry that is alive creates a heightened sense of mood and tone. Rhythmic movement has the power to subordinate our conscious thought to the emotional pulsations of the moment. The skilful poet can simulate the gay turn of the waltz, the beat of the war-drum, the running excitement of a mob, the stately monotony of official ceremony. And he applies Alexander Pope's "rule" that "the sound must seem an echo to the sense" to much more than the imitation of such rhythmic events in the real world. The sense of inner harmony, and of its right relation to the feeling behind what is being said, is basic to good poetry. Consequently, there is purposeful rhythmic technique in almost any effective poem, even the simplest.

A favorite children's poem, William Allingham's *The Fairies*, begins in a burst of movement that carries over into an awestruck whisper and then a vivid picture:

> Up the airy mountain,
>> Down the rushy glen,
> We daren't go a-hunting
>> For fear of little men;
> Wee folk, good folk,
>> Trooping all together;
> Green jacket, red cap,
>> And white owl's feather.

The buoyant words "airy" and "rushy" help the first two lines build up their speed. There are only three stop-sounds in them—sounds which cannot be indefinitely continued. Two of them, the *p* and the *d*, come at the beginnings of their lines and help push them off to a fast start; the third, the *t*, is buried in an unstressed syllable.

Every sound, every syllable contributes to a poem's movement. Sounds and syllables therefore are more than the elements of particular words; they are also elements of the basic rhythmic units called *feet*, units generally made up of two or three syllables. When most of the feet begin as the first two lines of *The Fairies* do—with a stressed syllable followed by one or more unaccented ones—we have a *falling* meter: emphatic, and immediately suggesting a chant of some kind. When the unaccented syllable precedes the accented one, as in the third and fourth lines, we have a *rising* meter—the type usually considered most natural for English verse. (The accented syllable usually bringing such lines to conclusion is called a *masculine* ending.) When, as in the fifth line, an accented syllable is followed by another of the same kind, the accent is said to be a *hovering* one—it does not rise or fall but slows up or arrests the movement for a moment. And when, as at the close of the third line, there is an extra unaccented syllable speeding up the movement momentarily, we have a *feminine ending*. If we break up the foregoing stanza into feet and indicate their accentual pattern, we can see that the movement "falls" swiftly, "rises" more waveringly, focuses attention emphatically in the fifth line, rides out swiftly again with the "wee folk" as it did at first, pulls up hoveringly again, and at last lets go rapidly in a line which actually combines all three kinds of meter.

> UP the/ AIRy/ MOUNtain,/
>> DOWN the/ RUSHy/ GLEN,/
> We DAR/en't GO/ a-HUNT/ing/
>> For FEAR/ of LIT/tle MEN;/
> WEE FOLK,/ GOOD FOLK,/
>> TROOPing/ ALL to/GETHer;/
> GREEN JACKet,/ RED CAP,/
>> And WHITE/ OWL'S/ FEATHer./

We may, if we wish, imagine musical rests after "glen" and before "owl's," or tuck the left-over "ing" of the third line into the preceding foot as has been done with the final syllable of "jacket." Such details, however, are of no real importance in themselves. The usefulness of metrical information does not lie in the diagrams it can produce, but in the way it can help us see the relation of rhythmic effects to meaning and feeling. The informed reader of poetry is likely to know enough about it to be able to describe the general movement of a poem or to follow the comments of most critics on it.

The most commonly used types of feet are the iamb, found in the fourth line of Allingham's poem, and the trochee, found in the first line. Since iambic feet are closest to the rhythm of natural speech, any other kind of foot seems to create a special effect. Lines that are predominantly iambic often begin with a trochaic foot for initial emphasis:

Season of mists and mellow fruitfulness

KEATS

Often, too, one finds anapestic feet—consisting of two unaccented syllables followed by an accented one—substituted for iambic ones, to gain variety and speed. In the following line, the first two feet are iambs, the second two anapests:

The world is charged with the grandeur of God

HOPKINS

In the same way, the dactyl—one stressed syllable followed by two unstressed ones—is often substituted for a trochaic foot, with a similar effect of heightened speed. Here is a line in which the two kinds of feet alternate in a truly "rocking" movement:

Out of the cradle endlessly rocking

WHITMAN

Hovering accents, when the accented syllables that come together are in the same foot, are called spondees. The spondaic foot is used for unusually strong emphasis:

Black town, beige woods, green frozen creek

WILLIAM GIBSON

In most lines, not every accented syllable is as heavily stressed as every other, nor is every unstressed one as light as every other. Note, for instance, in the lines just quoted, the difference in emphasis of the first and the third syllable of "fruitfulness," and the special force of the word "charged." Such shadings of stress or lightness make for a richer, more complicated sound-effect than rough scansion will indicate. Sometimes, therefore, it is convenient to speak of secondary stresses, as in the final syllable of

Season of mists and mellow fruitfulness

KEATS

And on the other hand, it is often sufficient for descriptive purposes simply to indicate the number of heavily stressed syllables without regard to such differences. Thus, we may speak of Shakespeare's characteristic five-stress line. In general, however, we can describe a line with some degree at least of precision by referring to the type of foot predominating in it, and to the number of feet and the kind of substitute feet it contains. A one-foot line is called monometer, a two-foot line dimeter, and so on through trimeter, tetrameter, pentameter, hexameter (or Alexandrine, if predominantly iambic), and heptameter. In using this technical terminology, of course, we must remain aware of its true end: to aid our appreciation of the chiming together of the varied elements in any given poem.

How important *are* such considerations? If we now examine briefly a complete poem by A. E. Housman . . . we shall see even more readily how metrical technique contributes to poetic meaning and effect.

> He stood, and heard the steeple
>   Sprinkle the quarters on the morning town.
> One, two, three, four, to market-place and people
>   It tossed them down.
>
> Strapped, noosed, nighing his hour,
>   He stood and counted them and cursed his luck;
> And then the clock collected in the tower
>   Its strength, and struck.
>
>   A. E. HOUSMAN *Eight O'Clock*

The impact of this poem is truly terrific. Its force is intensified by the sharpest possible contrast in rhythm between the scattered tinkling diversity of the second line and the slow forceful beat of the first half of the third line. This contrast is intensified in the second stanza and is brought to a climax in the deliberate, wavelike build-up of weight in the last two lines.

The effect is redoubled by the suspenseful pause after "strength," followed by the final heavy blow at the very end.

The voice we hear speaking in *Eight O'Clock* is that of a narrator who is very closely in sympathy with the psychological state of the doomed man. He feels the pressure of time weighing on him, and is aware of the irony in the fact that the clock itself seems to the doomed man to be the agent of his death. The impact would not be so great were it not that the beat, or rhythm, of the poem goes on in two ways at once. There is the effect of the contrasts, the suspense and gathering, and the final blow built up by the individual, dramatic manner of presentation; and there is also the basic, conventional pattern of the form the poet has chosen—the four-line stanza with alternating rhymes, and with a basic iambic pattern of alternating light and heavy stresses: "He stóod, and héard the stéeple. . . ." Not all the syllables alternate so regularly, but this is the predominant pattern; and when, as in the second, third, and fifth lines, we find other variations, we can feel them pulling against this pattern to create a special emphasis. So also, each stanza begins with a line of three feet; the second and third lines have five feet, and the fourth, after this effect of expansion, contracts sharply to two. Meaningful variation within a pattern, and the use of skilfully contrived forms to suggest the sound of real speech, are signs of poetic craftsmanship.

This poem shows how important to poetic rhythm are its pauses. If a line makes a complete unit of meaning in itself, coming to a halt of some kind at its end, we say it is end-stopped. If its meaning and movement carry over to the succeeding line we call it a run-on line (enjambment). A good poet can control his effects to a high degree by his skill in handling longer and shorter units. He therefore knows how to manage the caesura, a definite pause, usually near the middle of a line, which marks a break both in meaning and metrical pattern.

> He stood, // and heard the steeple. . . .

Notice how, in the first first stanza of *Eight O'Clock*, Housman achieves great variety by placing the caesura early in the first line, then using a long breathsweep without another break until the end of the second line, then giving us three sharp pauses and a long fourth one in his third line, and at last sweeping on again without a pause to the end of the stanza. In the second stanza, he begins with two heavy stresses, each followed by a caesura, brings the first line up short, and then continues without a break until the middle of the last line. Here he pauses weightily, coming down with all the force he can in the concluding foot. Thus, the placing of the pauses has a great deal to do with the pacing and final force of the poem.

A good deal of the music, emotional subtlety, and tempo of a poem derives from such interplay between its "natural" and its "artificial" rhythms. Though the poet may seem to be concentrating all his energies on the ideas, images, and general content of his poem, he organizes and displays them through the underlying conventional pattern of rhythm and stanza-form. The situation is analogous to the working of the human body. We act as though we were perfectly free agents, yet all the time we are profoundly disciplined by mechanical controls of innumerable physiological processes.

THE POEM AS A WHOLE

It is the interrelationship of many elements that counts—elements that make for a poem's sense of reality, its intellectual and moral realizations, and its level of emotional intensity. If we may here venture a summarizing definition, we might say: A poem is a form of expression in which an unusual number of the resources of language are concentrated into a patterned, organic unit of significant experience. . . .

It is perhaps easiest to see the emergence of an organic structure in successful poems written in some conventional, simple, and familiar form such as the sonnet. A sonnet is a fourteen-line reflective poem which almost always falls into one of two fairly strictly defined patterns, one known as the English (or sometimes Shakespearean, or Elizabethan) sonnet and the other as the Italian (or Petrarchan) sonnet. The English sonnet is made up of three four-line stanzas, called quatrains, and a final couplet. In each of the quatrains, the first and third lines rhyme with one another, and the second and fourth rhyme with each other also, while the closing couplet adds yet another rhyming unit. (We describe this rhyme-scheme as *abab, cdcd, efef, gg.*) Finally, the sonnet line is ordinarily an iambic pentameter; that is, each line contains five stressed syllables, and if the meter were perfectly regular these stressed syllables would each be preceded by an unstressed syllable. However, we shall almost always find some variations from the pattern, for mere regularity makes for monotonous and slavish rhythm.

It is interesting to observe how, in the following sonnet by Shakespeare, these quite arbitrary conventional limitations are so used as to make the form of the poem seem both natural and especially suitable for its unique thought and feeling. A simple thought grows into a complex meaning intensely experienced because of the way in which all its formal elements support and affect one another.

> That time of year thou mayst in me behold
> When yellow leaves, or none, or few, do hang
> Upon those boughs which shake against the cold,
> Bare ruin'd choirs, where late the sweet birds sang,
> In me thou seest the twilight of such day
> As after sunset fadeth in the West,
> Which by and by black night doth take away,
> Death's second self that seals up all in rest.
> In me thou seest the glowing of such fire,
> That on the ashes of his youth doth lie,
> As the death-bed, whereon it must expire
> Consum'd with that which it was nourish'd by.
> This thou perceiv'st, which makes thy love more strong
> To love that well, which thou must leave ere long.

WILLIAM SHAKESPEARE *Sonnet LXXIII*

The logical structure of this poem is quite clear: the same thing is said three times (in a different way each time), and then a consequence of it is stated in the concluding couplet. Reduced to its essence, the argument runs as follows: I am growing old and my youth must die. You, beloved, see the signs of this, yet it makes you love me all the more.

But a poem is much more than a mere summary of its argument. Each of the three quatrains making up the main part of the sonnet presents the idea of age and the approach of an ending in terms of a different image: autumn, the ending of the year, in the first; twilight and sunset, the ending of a day, in the second; and the dying of a fire in the third. These images are not, on the surface, original. What strikes us first in them is their appropriateness, their universality, and especially the rich emotional overtones with which the poet's musical language endows them.

The line

Bare ruin'd choirs, where late the sweet birds sang

is particularly rich in its evocations, even though some of the implications it would leave in the mind of an Elizabethan Englishman may need to be pointed out in a note. (The reference, though indirect, is clear: it is to the many cathedrals and churches which with the coming of the Protestant monarchs were stripped of their rich and often beautiful ornaments and hangings.)

The reference to "black night" as "Death's second self," though a commonplace of medieval poetry, serves to suggest, without stating it directly, that it is not only youth which will soon be gone, but life itself, and this is reinforced by the image of the dying fire and the reference to the "death-bed."

The line

Consum'd with that which it was nourish'd by,

is a good instance of Shakespeare's concentrated accuracy. The key idea is that, as it slowly burns out, an aging man's life must feed on its own accumulated richness. This idea emerges perfectly in the image of a fire choked with ashes because of the very abundance of the fuel—a thought which gains in intensity and clarity because it is presented thus in terms of a concrete image.

The organic growth, as though it were a living thing, of this poem may be seen in this sequence of images. All suggest aging and dying, but each provides a different shade of feeling or thought. Each image, indeed, has a second image lurking within it, and it is this second image that makes each stage of the poem significantly different from the others. The speaker compares himself to trees in late autumn; but almost at once our attention is turned to a second image, of the trees as abandoned choirs where sweet music was once heard. The painful loss of a beautiful, vital youth is what age is shown to mean here, at the beginning of the poem. At the next phase of its growth, the poem gives us another image of the coming of old age— the twilight of the day—but now shifts our attention to the future rather than to the past: Death, of which night is the "second self" or twin, is not far in the offing. And in the third stage, the image of the dying fire, at first apparently so simple, is seen as the most complex of all. An aging man is a dying fire, but that fire's own ashes, once its source of nourishment, are also its deathbed. And to this paradoxical picture still another paradox is added: the ashes are actually "consuming" the fire which once fed on *them*.

The third image, it is clear, brings together the connotations of the first (the sense of lost beauty and richness) and of the second (the unavoidable coming on of death). But it also, because of its intricacy and clever suggestion of the ironic and surprising nature of life, prepares us for the speaker's own admiration and delight, at the close of the sonnet, in the character of the beloved person he is addressing.

The poem, therefore, grows into paradox as well as surprise. It has an unexpected, and therefore forceful, happy ending which is nevertheless an integral part of the body of the poem. The strangely intense love granted the poet grows, increases, and does not die. This love becomes an image of glowing life and permanence, and throws back a new, unforeseen, and cheering ray on all that has gone before—all the dark, gloomy images of change and decay. It is as if the birds, the daylight, and the fire were not to be lost forever after all. All this is embodied in the neat concluding couplet, which serves to convey the poet's sense of his own lucky uniqueness. Because of his beloved's devotion, he has been singled out by fortune to triumph over age and death.

POETIC INTEGRITY

We have noted that the basic poetic device—basic because it comes closest to the essential character of poetry as naked vision and intense realization—is the metaphor. The metaphor gives us a flash of perception of relationships that has the kick of experience in it. The price the poet pays for this power of perception is that he must always tell the truth as he sees it. Poetic statement and imagery are often likely to expose unsuspected or hitherto unaccepted realities, perhaps even distasteful realities, through the media of our senses and emotions; and the poet runs the risk of becoming especially concerned with the troublesome matters most of us, most of the time, would like to keep ourselves from thinking about—the meaning of death, for example, or the great cruelties human beings can often inflict upon one another, or the hypocrisies and weaknesses of our own society.

Let us turn, for illustration, to Matthew Arnold's *Dover Beach*, a poem which, like many other poems of the later nineteenth century, sketches a bleak picture of the universe of modern man. Our universe, Arnold argues, is one in which the old faith in a life securely and eternally guided by a benevolent God has begun to disappear, leaving many people with the feeling that they have nothing to depend on but the affection of beloved individuals.

> The sea is calm tonight.
> The tide is full, the moon lies fair
> Upon the straits;—on the French coast the light
> Gleams and is gone; the cliffs of England stand,
> Glimmering and vast, out in the tranquil bay.
> Come to the window, sweet is the night-air!
> Only, from the long line of spray
> Where the sea meets the moon-blanched land,
> Listen! you hear the grating roar
> Of pebbles which the waves draw back, and fling,
> At their return, up the high strand,
> Begin, and cease, and then again begin,
> With tremulous cadence slow, and bring
> The eternal note of sadness in.

Sophocles long ago
Heard it on the Ægæan, and it brought
Into his mind the turbid ebb and flow
Of human misery; we
Find also in the sound a thought,
Hearing it by this distant northern sea.

The Sea of Faith
Was once, too, at the full, and round earth's shore
Lay like the folds of a bright girdle furled.
But now I only hear
Its melancholy, long, withdrawing roar,
Retreating, to the breath
Of the night-wind, down the vast edges drear
And naked shingles of the world.

Ah, love, let us be true
To one another! for the world, which seems
To lie before us like a land of dreams,
So various, so beautiful, so new,
Hath really neither joy, nor love, nor light,
Nor certitude, nor peace, nor help for pain;
And we are here as on a darkling plain
Swept with confused alarms of struggle and flight,
Where ignorant armies clash by night.

MATTHEW ARNOLD *Dover Beach*

In this poem the effect of calm beauty in the opening picture of Dover
Beach and the sea at night is soon submerged in the melancholy impression
of the first stanza's closing lines. The sound of the waves reminds the speaker
of the "eternal" recurrence of this impression, for there have always been
men who lived near the sea and heard the same melancholy note—the great
Greek writer of tragedy, Sophocles, for example. Having struck this philosophical note, the poem can then go on to the allegorical third stanza, which
is not about geographical places or historical personalities but about an
abstraction—a state of mind which has changed the meaning of life for most
people.[2] And finally there is the appeal to a beloved woman that she and
the speaker keep their faith in one another, since the calm, beautiful scene
outside is mere deception, while in reality terror and confusion lurk everywhere.

Dover Beach is not "against" delight in the world's beauty and in religious
faith. On the contrary, the images applied to them make it clear that they
have a strong hold on the poet's affections. But he fears life too, because of

[2] The "Sea of Faith" is a typically allegorical figure of speech.

the challenge to old beliefs that has come from the new scientific developments of the nineteenth century; and between fear and loss of faith, much of
the delight seems to have been spoiled for him.

By now we have moved a great distance from the popular conception
of poetry as something flowery, vague, and conventional in a "nice" and
undisturbing way. If this widespread conception were true, poetry would
be without passion, originality, or intelligent direction. Not such easy things
to achieve as vagueness and "niceness," but things difficult to achieve—
frankness, precision, intensity—are the marks of the genuine in poetry. . . .

Poetry often expresses ideas and emotions felt by all mankind to be
true in the long run to the common experience of humanity. Such poetry
is affirmative, traditional, and genuinely popular. It does not make its appeal
by its originality or its unexpectedness, or even by its profundity (though
it does not necessarily lack these qualities), but by its convincing rightness,
by the *felt* truth with which it confirms people in what they have come to feel
and believe without ever having been able to put it into memorable words.
This is the idea of Pope's Horatian conception of poetry as "What oft was
thought but ne'er so well expressed," and of Keats's psychological phrasing
of the same idea:

> I think poetry should surprise by a fine excess, and not by singularity. It should
> strike the reader as a wording of his own highest thoughts, and appear almost
> a remembrance.[3]

Poems and images fitting these descriptions are immediately satisfying;
they are accepted at once and never forgotten. Lines whose impressiveness
are of this order are the easiest to call to mind:

> She walks in beauty like the night
> GEORGE GORDON, LORD BYRON

> The day is done and the darkness
> Falls from the wings of night
> As a feather is wafted downward
> From an eagle in his flight.
> HENRY WADSWORTH LONGFELLOW

> O my luve is like a red, red rose,
> That's newly sprung in June
> ROBERT BURNS

[3] Letter to John Taylor, February 27, 1818.

The uncertain glory of an April day
WILLIAM SHAKESPEARE

If we place alongside these beautiful images parallel ones of a more complex kind, we shall discover that the greater complexity is due to the distance between the arms of the comparison—between, for instance, the brightness of God and the depth of darkness in the first quotation below. The things compared or identified are not so easily seen to be alike. The effect is not so much to reassure us of what we already feel as to startle us awake, so that we experience something not experienced before:

There is in God (some say)
A deep but dazzling darkness.
HENRY VAUGHAN

I should have been a pair of ragged claws
Scuttling across the floors of silent seas.
T. S. ELIOT

April is the cruelest month. . . .
T. S. ELIOT

The two types of images differ in a more fundamental way than in their relative complexity. The second type peers below the surface of life to its ever-present but often dark and confusing realities. It does not confirm what is established; it affirms new and sometimes terrifying perceptions. As the discoverer of "underground secrets" of the human consciousness, the poet is indeed often, as Louis MacNeice has said, an "informer"—and in the derogatory sense of the word. He "tells on" us, not caring what the telling may do to our self-esteem. . . .

Human affirmation can sometimes be made even more powerfully in works of pure imagination. Blake's strange poem *The Tyger* is a case in point. In this poem, the problem of evil—the existence of terrible, uncontrolled forces and their relation to the nature of God—is dynamically symbolized with naked directness.

Tyger! Tyger! burning bright
In the forests of the night,
What immortal hand or eye
Could frame thy fearful symmetry?

In what distant deeps or skies
Burnt the fire of thine eyes?

On what wings dare he aspire?
What the hand dare seize the fire?

And what shoulder, and what art
Could twist the sinews of thy heart?
And when thy heart began to beat,
What dread hand? and what dread feet?

What the hammer? what the chain?
In what furnace was thy brain?
What the anvil? what dread grasp
Dare its deadly terrors clasp?

When the stars threw down their spears,
And water'd heaven with their tears,
Did he smile his work to see?
Did he who made the Lamb make thee?

Tyger! Tyger! burning bright
In the forests of the night,
What immortal hand or eye,
Dare frame thy fearful symmetry?

WILLIAM BLAKE The Tyger

The very thought of the tiger, as he is presented in these six stanzas, excites the speaker here in a curious way. It is possible to look upon tigers as things in the zoo—fierce, striped animals that are worth staring at as they pace about inside their cages. And it is possible, with only slightly superior scientific knowledge, to see them as interesting examples of certain species. But the speaker in the poem can hardly be said to be *amused* by the tiger, nor does he seem to care much about the zoological facts as such. His reaction, rather, resembles the primordial terror of a child, an almost instinctive terror with which we can all sympathize, and he sees in the tiger a mysterious, sinister vision of supernatural power.

In this vision, the tiger looms as a freely moving force in the dark forests of, not Asia or Africa, but "the night." So we are led to think of him as ever-present, ever-dangerous, a "burning bright" symbol of the savagery in every human soul and in all existence; a satanic beast. As we follow the poem through its images of the strength, the dreadfulness, and the wonder of the tiger, we become more and more aware of the speaker's chilled sense of awe when he thinks of the inscrutable purposes and unimaginable power of the creator of such a being. This awe reaches a shocked climax in the fifth stanza, when the speaker, remembering the miraculous events on the night Christ was born, asks the natural but startling question, "Did he who made the Lamb make thee?" Without rationalizing away this frightening fact, that all we see as gentlest and all that we see as most violently and perilously dynamic proceed from the same vital, daring source, the speaker faces the double nature of the universe with a full awareness of its awful dangers and endless possibilities.

As the poem develops, we can see clearly how its form helps create and sustain the religious-emotional pitch of feeling. The first outcry, together with the simple rhyme, fixes a dynamic picture profoundly in our minds:

> Tyger! Tyger! burning bright
> In the forests of the night. . . .

Immediately afterwards we are drawn into a ceremonial dance of questions. Each question leads to the same answer as to the nature of the Creator, and each associates God with his untamable creation, so that the repeated questions beat their meaning at us like savage drums. God, we are being told, is not to be understood in human terms. There is something about him that matches the tiger: He is "dread"; he responds to the challenge of the "distant deeps or skies" whose dangerous fires he must seize to create this terrible symbol. The rhymes come very fast in an obsessive chant of fascinated horror at the concentrated vision of the meaning of experience which has seized upon the speaker.

At the end the tiger still ranges supreme in his own domain, and we feel that he is "real" in a sense not felt by the zoologist or the casual visitor to the zoo. He has the kind of reality that forces men to examine the meaning of their own lives because they have found a symbol with a truly compelling moral force. The profound questions raised in this poem, together with the stark pictures and the piled-up short phrases, may startle us into a kind of humility rare in our day. What we would ordinarily think of as evil has been shockingly related to what we think of as absolute good. We are sure of the compelling importance of the questions and of the image around which they are gathered. An emotional assertion of meaning has been made so vividly in these questions that it has brought into the open our sense of the terrible reality of evil.

METAPHYSICAL POETRY

Intellect and wit are not the exclusive property of the Metaphysical poet, but they are inseparable from his work. Successful Metaphysical verse, indeed, so interweaves these qualities with its emotional effects as to make clearer than any other mode of poetry the tremendous importance of *thought* in poetic achievement. Two poems by John Donne—*The Sun Rising* and *Good Friday, 1613. Riding Westward*—will illustrate the "development by rapid association of thought"[4] and the mature, analytical, and complex personality that characterize this poetry at its best. Donne is its classic representative—a man whose instinct compelled him to bring the whole of experience into his verse and to choose the most direct and what, for his learned and fantastic mind, was the most natural form of expression. (Donne was roughly of the same generation as Shakespeare, Ben Jonson, and the dramatists of the Mermaid Tavern, but he was not, like them, a man of the people, the son of a yeoman or a brirklayer, but a representative of the gentry. He was Catholic by birth, educated at the university, trained for the law and the Church, and closely attached to the Court.) He is colloquial, elevated, slangy, rhetorical, erudite, familiar—all in the same brief poem; and he takes his language from the court and the camp, from the jargon of the law, from the study, and from the market place.

This curious combination of qualities, it is interesting to note, can be found alike in his youthful "profane" love poems and in the passionate religious poems of his later life. This can be made clear by a detailed examination of a characteristic example of each group. Here is one of the early poems.

> Busy old fool, unruly Sun,
>   Why dost thou thus,
> Through windows, and through curtains, call on us?
> Must to thy motions lovers' seasons run?
>   Saucy pedantic wretch, go chide
>   Late school-boys and sour prentices,
>   Go tell court-huntsmen that the king will ride,
>   Call country ants to harvest offices;
> Love, all alike, no season knows nor clime,
> Nor hours, days, months, which are the rags of time.
>
>   Thy beams so reverend and strong
>   Why shouldst thou think?
> I could eclipse and cloud them with a wink,
> But that I would not lose her sight so long.
>   If her eyes have not blinded thine,
>   Look, and to-morrow late tell me,
>   Whether both th' Indias of spice and mine
>   Be where thou left'st them, or lie here with me.
> Ask for those kings whom thou saw'st yesterday,
> And thou shalt hear, "All here in one bed lay."

[4] T. S. Eliot, "The Metaphysical Poets." (*Selected Essays*)

> She's all states, and all princes I;
>   Nothing else is;
> Princes do but play us; compared to this,
> All honour's mimic, all wealth alchemy.
>   Thou, Sun, art half as happy as we,
>   In that the world's contracted thus;
>   Thine age asks ease, and since thy duties be
>   To warm the world, that's done in warming us.
> Shine here to us, and thou art everywhere;
> This bed thy centre is, these walls thy sphere.   30
>
> JOHN DONNE *The Sun Rising*

The Sun Rising is, in the first place, intended to be an amusing, witty, "clever" poem. It is light verse, but it is also, as we shall see, intensely serious —a good demonstration of the fact that seriousness has nothing to do with solemnity and can be accompanied by a good deal of levity. The poem, of course, is addressed to a somewhat sophisticated audience—sophisticated not so much with respect to manners and morals as with respect to literary convention. The poet is reacting against the artificiality and absurdity of the fashionable love poetry of courtly chivalry in which the conceit of the beloved's eyes outshining the sun had long become a tedious cliché.[5] Donne laughs as the hyperboles (the fantastic exaggerations) of the courtly poetry by pretending to accept them. He piles hyperbole on hyperbole and praises his mistress in the most extravagant manner.

But the poem is not intended to be merely literary satire or criticism. It is a genuine and deeply felt expression of the poet's sense of the beauty and perfection of his loved one. Its final purpose is to express the poet's sense of happiness and completeness in the possession of his mistress. *She* is so all-perfect, all-lovely, all-complete that she, and she alone, makes the fantastic hyperboles of the courtly poets sober truth.

From the first line we must be aware that the *tone* of the poem and the changes and developments of the tone are of the first importance. The poem begins with a ranting, swashbuckling, arrogant address to the sun. Like many of Donne's poems this one begins suddenly, with a sharp, surprising colloquial exclamation:

> Busy old fool, unruly Sun. . . .

Why this tone? And why the contempt so harshly expressed all through this first stanza—"saucy pedantic wretch," "court-huntsmen," "country ants"?

The reason is that in the happy and complete possession of his mistress the poet feels that he possesses, rules, and controls the whole world, and

[5] Cf. Shakespeare's sonnet *My mistress' eyes are nothing like the sun.*

therefore is superior to the sun itself. The lover complaining against the sun at morning for ending a night of happiness was, of course, one of the traditional themes of courtly love poetry, but Donne treats it familiarly, colloquially, irreverently. One of the most concentrated paradoxes of the poem is the application in the first line of the epithet "unruly" to the sun. The sun is actually the standard of order, regulation, and law; but order, rule, and law in the field of nature, of society, of business, and of the court threaten the interests and pleasures of love. So the poet-lover rails against them all. Love transcends time, and the lovers cannot help regarding the sun, which makes time, as a wretch and a busybody to be scorned and triumphed over.

In the second stanza the poet, still ranting and swaggering, proceeds to develop the thought of the present good fortune that makes him superior to the world-dominating sun. And he does so in terms that also manage to pay exquisite compliments to his mistress. The girl sums up in herself all the riches and perfume of the Orient and the West; she is the glory of the whole world, concentrated and epitomized. Also, the setting of the scene, only implied in the first stanza, is now made more specific.

One of the strangest and most powerful effects of the poem is the progressive softening of the tone until the outrageous and amusing hyperboles of the opening stanza and the air of extravagant enthusiasm with which they are delivered modulate, in the final stanza, into a hushed and serious (though still fantastic and half-playful) expression of the happiness and trust of a completely satisfied devotion.

The Sun Rising is characteristic of Donne's youthful secular love poetry. It is lighter in texture but not essentially different in method from the deeply felt and sometime terror-stricken religious poems of his maturity and old age. In fact, if we compare it with *Good Friday, 1613*, a poem of greater complexity and scope written after Donne was forty, we find some startling parallels. The earlier poem proudly mocks the sun and the principle of universal order it represents. It argues satirically against the imperious demands of time and the powers that be upon the happy, self-contained world of the two lovers. *Good Friday, 1613*, on the other hand, is a humble and pious if even more passionate statement. In it the image of the sun is approached with absolute awe and respect. Christ, the *son* of God, is pictured as the *sun* (the pun is deliberate on Donne's part) around which the poet's soul, in the figure of a heavenly "sphere," should properly revolve. A deeply serious though wittily imaginative argument, ending in a prayer, reverses the relation between the speaker and the sun that we remember in *The Sun Rising*. The poems are indeed unlike in their literal themes and in their feeling toward the central images of universal authority, but the similarity in technique should be apparent:

Let man's soul be a sphere, and then in this
The intelligence that moves, devotion is;
And as the other spheres, by being grown
Subject to foreign motion, lose their own,
And being by others hurried every day,
Scarce in a year their natural form obey:
Pleasure or business so, our souls admit
For their first mover, and are whirled by it.
Hence is 't that I am carried towards the west
This day, when my soul's form bends towards the east.
There I should see a sun, by rising set,
And by that setting, endless day beget;
But that Christ on this cross did rise and fall,
Sin had eternally benighted all.
Yet dare I'almost be glad I do not see
That spectacle of too much weight for me.
Who sees God's face, that is self life, must die;
What a death were it then to see God die!
It made his own lieutenant, nature, shrink;
It made his footstool crack, and the sun wink.
Could I behold those hands which span the poles
And tune all spheres at once, pierced with those holes?
Could I behold that endless height, which is
Zenith to us and our antipodes,
Humbled below us? or that blood which is
The seat of all our souls, if not of his,
Made dirt of dust, or that flesh which was worn
By God for his apparel, ragg'd and torn?
If on these things I durst not look, durst I
Upon his miserable mother cast mine eye,
Who was God's partner here, and furnished thus
Half of that sacrifice which ransomed us?
Though these things, as I ride, be from mine eye,
They are present yet unto my memory,
For that looks towards them; and thou look'st towards me,
O Savior, as thou hang'st upon the tree;
I turn my back to thee but to receive
Corrections, till thy mercies bid thee leave.
Oh, think me worth thine anger, punish me,
Burn off my rusts, and my deformity;
Restore thine image, so much, by thy grace,
That thou mayst know me, and I'll turn my face.

JOHN DONNE *Good Friday, 1613*

A brief summary of the ideas and progress of thought in this poem
should be useful. Good Friday is part of Holy Week, the week preceding
Easter Sunday. On Good Friday the Crucifixion of Christ is commemorated,

and on Easter His Resurrection is celebrated. The poet is therefore thinking in a vein appropriate to the observation of the day that makes the most
solemn religious symbol of the Christian faith: the sacrifice of Jesus. At the
same time, he very strikingly applies the language of traditional science
and philosophy to this contemplation. Hence the special terms and concepts
used in this poem: the medieval concept of an "intelligence," for instance—a
guiding spirit or angel who directs and governs the laws by which heavenly
bodies move; the Aristotelian terms "form" (the essential nature of a thing)
and "first mover" (a philosophical, secular phrase for denoting the creative
aspect of God); or the notion, from medieval physiology, of blood as the
vehicle uniting the soul to the body—hence, in line 26, "the seat of all our
souls." Donne's beginning is at once "scientific" and religious: Imagine, he
says, that man's soul is a sphere, like one of the heavenly bodies, and that
its guiding spirit is pious devotion.

But the heavenly bodies, he reminds us, all have distorted orbits because
of the influence of the motions of other spheres; and so it is with the soul,
which is often "whirled" from its true course by business or pleasure instead of holding to it through piety. On Good Friday, the soul's whole attention should be bent eastward—that is, toward the place where the Crucifixion
occurred. Instead, the less essential concerns that take up most of our time
are bearing it away from contemplation of divine sacrifice—"westward."
Besides, the poet admits, he is afraid of such contemplation. It would be a
terrible thing to see the living God directly, and therefore even more terrible
to gaze upon Him dying, humbled, and tortured, and upon the suffering of
Mary, His mother. (The truly devout soul would envisage these events so
vividly that they would take place, literally, before it.) The poet does,
however, even as he is being borne away from direct contact with these
tragic events, remember them and pray for Christ's grace, so that he may
learn how to be more devoted and be purged of his sins and hence be
enabled to hope for final salvation. Thus, he implies, the influence of divine
mercy may prove stronger than that of the secular world and help his weak
soul to find its proper orbit once more.

Now it is clear that Donne is not here offering *proof* of the soul's
existence and nature, or of the rightness of his religious faith. These are
assumptions his poem takes for granted with intense sincerity. Rather, the
argument of the poem has to do with the *relation* between the speaker and
these unchallenged truths of faith. First we see him *separated* from Christ,
who *came toward* man in dying for him, though the poet expresses his overwhelming fear of coming into the divine presence. And finally we see
envisioned a way by which God and the speaker (that is, God and man)

can come together after all. The sense of *movement,* apart and together, is brought out by the image of the sphere traveling through space and falsely curving away from its true center of attraction and from its own true orbit. Donne's witty puns and paradoxes, with their "double meanings," are minia- ture replicas of this double movement in the poem's central image.

The movement of thought in *Good Friday,* then, has been projected by a series of images: the image of the moving of spheres around a magnetic center, and of contrary forces at work on them; the image of Jesus on the cross—first pictured as a rising and setting sun, and later as a vast paradox containing infinite space and yet subject to infinite humbling and reduction; the image of Mary; and finally, the image of the speaker in his own person appealing directly to Christ. Paralleling this movement, the tone of the language develops from that of intellectual and scientific reasoning (lines 1-10) to one of earnest prayer at the end. In between, the subtle reasoner of the opening lines has become the factual observer (11-14), the humble and awestruck apologist for himself (15-32), the object of God's attention (35-36) and the humble penitent (37-38). The statement has grown increasingly personal, as though with the development of his poetic theme the author had actually come closer to God and God become more particularly attentive to him, until he is emboldened to make the final appeal of the closing couplet.

Donne's poems, we have noted, are classic examples of Metaphysical verse. The chief characteristic of Metaphysical writing that we are in- terested in here is its *emotional intellectuality.* The speaker is always a complex personality, always aware of the involved nature of moral choice and of the ideas current among educated people of his time; and he has too much respect for his intellectual training and integrity to sacrifice his knowledge for the sake of the excitement of being carried away by his feelings. So, what he knows about science, about his own weaknesses and needs, about actual human nature keeps cropping up in his verse, lending it wryness, subtlety, irony and humor. Wit is essential to writing of this kind, which balances so many diverse elements. Metaphysical poetry is an amalgam of the "pure" poetry of emotional incantation and the analytical poetry of men like Pope and Rochester; or rather, it represents the attempt of a highly civilized personality to remain true to his basic, instinctive humanity while applying the lessons of science, philosophy, and sophisticated religion to the central problems of his life.

SYMBOL AND EVOCATION

"Man," says the philosopher Ernst Cassirer, "lives in a symbolic universe. Language, myth, art, and religion are parts of this universe. They are the varied threads which weave the symbolic net, the tangled web of human experience."[6]

Even our most prosaic thinking is dominated by symbols—coins, trademarks, directional signals on cars, for example. And our emotional lives are full of such symbols as engagement rings, gifts, meaningful looks and gestures, diplomas and prizes. Insofar as one thing is used to represent something else, we may call it a symbol. A symbol may be quite without emotional connotation—witness the numbers and signs used in mathematics to denote relationships and quantities. But it may also be charged with feeling: the Flag, the Cross, the Statue of Liberty. The latter kind of symbol not only denotes an idea, but also connotes, and evokes, an attitude toward it and an emotion that surrounds it. The symbols of poetry fall in this second class.

In the most general sense—too general to be very useful in practice—all poetry is symbolic, since it has the power to control our imaginations by suggesting new associations for familiar ideas and experiences. From this point of view, Shakespeare's metaphor beginning his *Sonnet LXXIII* is symbolic:

> That time of year thou mayst in me behold
> When yellow leaves, or none, or few do hang
> Upon those boughs which shake against the cold. . . .

The association of the barren, abandoned, chilled look of trees in late autumn with old age is a visible and generally sensuous representation of something not itself directly present to the senses.

But more precisely, we do not use the word "symbol" merely as a synonym for "figure of speech." An image is a symbol, first, when it comes already fraught with literary, historical, or popular associations; its emotional power will be most strongly felt, of course, when it is placed in the right context and so phrased as to be unusually startling and significant. Three lines by the Elizabethan poet Thomas Nashe will illustrate this principle:

> Brightness falls from the air,
> Queens have died young and fair,
> Dust both closed Helen's eye. . . .

Nowhere in these lines does the poet explicitly state his melancholy underlying theme that death must come to all things, even the most beautiful. It is the unusual, brilliant effect of the beginning that especially takes the imagination. The notion is so unexpected that at first we may get the *wrong* impression, an impression of heavenly brightness descending and illuminating us—a happy and blessed picture. Then the true picture takes shape, of

[6] Ernst Cassirer, *An Essay on Man*.

bright daylight that disappears and leaves the air dark, dull, and cold. The shock of this belated realization adds to its power and intensity, to the effect of irredeemable loss. And finally therefore, aided by the lines that follow "Brightness falls from the air," we will think of the universal fact of death, applicable to all things however glorious and lovely.

Supporting this striking image that so takes us unawares, we have first the simple pathos—half folk-wisdom and half a "truth" of fairy-tale lore—of "Queens have died young and fair." The fresh, naïve directness of the statement saves it from triteness and provides an emotional frame for the preceding line. And afterward, the full elegiac note of sadness is struck in the reminder of the death of Helen of Troy, the great popularly accepted symbol of erotic feminine beauty in all ages since Homer. It is hard to think of Helen dead, and the somewhat surprising use of her name with all its evocative power in this way helps give the passage its reverberating richness. The second and third lines lend to the extraordinary image they follow the quality of a traditional symbol, for they bring to it their own connotations of fallen brightness from mythology and popular legendry.

Images become symbols in yet other ways. If a poet lays emphasis on an image by pointing out that it has a special meaning and perhaps even defining that meaning for us, it then becomes a symbol almost by main force. The following passage from Wordsworth's *The Prelude* contains two examples of this second, more obvious, and often more static type of poetic symbolism. Notice how explicitly the poet makes clear what his symbolic clues are, and how we are to interpret them. Wordsworth, in this passage, tells how he would gaze at the faces on London's crowded streets, trying to fathom the mysterious meaning behind each of them. The blind beggar he once saw there, wearing his pathetic "written paper" that told his life story, signifies the futile superficiality of all men's supposed knowledge. Similarly, the poet's vision of a "second-sight procession" is a sign of the vagueness with which, at best, essential truth presents itself to our limited human understanding. It should be clear from these lines that even such interpreted symbols vary greatly in their intensity of evocation.

> How oft, amid those overflowing streets,
> Have I gone forward with the crowd, and said
> Unto myself, "The face of every one
> That passes by me is a mystery!"
> Thus have I looked, nor ceased to look, oppressed
> By thoughts of what and whither, when and how,
> Until the shapes before my eyes became
> A second-sight procession, such as glides
> Over still mountains, or appears in dreams;

> And once, far-travelled in such mood, beyond
> The reach of common indication, lost
> Amid the moving pageant, I was smitten
> Abruptly, with the view (a sight not rare)
> Of a blind Beggar, who, with upright face,
> Stood, propped against a wall, upon his chest
> Wearing a written paper, to explain
> His story, whence he came, and who he was.
> Caught by the spectacle my mind turned round
> As with the might of waters; an apt type
> This label seemed of the utmost we can know,
> Both of ourselves and of the universe;
> And, on the shape of that unmoving man,
> His steadfast face and sightless eyes, I gazed,
> As if admonished from another world.

Wordsworth's symbolism here is effective, both in clarifying his conception and in suggesting the feeling with which he associated it. But one of his symbols, the blind beggar with his piece of paper, is far inferior in emotional power to the symbol that precedes it—the dim, visionary procession gliding in the distance, elusive and significant as a dream. One reason is that the poet comments on the obvious meaning of the beggar-symbol so quickly and explicitly that it is hard for us to catch its special evocation peculiar to itself. Unlike the purer symbol it follows, it is overly dominated by its intended didactic function. Were it not for the grave and compelling seriousness of "steadfast face and sightless eyes," it would serve this function very poorly; it would merely illustrate an idea, mechanically and without being itself the embodiment of a living meaning. . . .

One of the important considerations of which a poet who falls into such mechanical didacticism loses sight is the essential technical difference between a symbol and an ordinary figure of speech: the greater magnetic power in the former to evoke many psychological associations. This magnetic power is most completely felt in the purest poetic symbols, in which a figure of speech is *implied but not stated.* In this kind of image, the poet does not, for example, say that his love is like a rose; he does not say, even, that she *is* a rose. Rather, perhaps, he will treat the rose itself as his subject, but in a special way. Omitting any reference to the woman who would ordinarily be his main topic, he may yet attribute to the rose qualities he feels belong both to it and to her, and other qualities arising from the association itself. The result, if successful, will produce not only the effect an ordinary metaphor would have produced, but also the transcendent, subtle, and vital connotations which William Butler Yeats has called "perfectly symbolical." Once again we may turn to Blake for an example:

> O Rose, thou art sick!
> The invisible worm,
> That flies in the night,
> In the howling storm,
>
> Has found out thy bed
> Of crimson joy;
> And his dark secret love
> Does thy life destroy.

WILLIAM BLAKE *The Sick Rose*

In this poem we have the purest sort of symbolism, in which we feel a precise, concentrated, terrifyingly significant meaning. The atmosphere is tragic; the imagery suggests the corruption of life and joy by death or by some force hostile to them yet needing them for its own nourishment. The "worm" suggests both the snake that corrupted Eden and the worms of the grave; darkness and terror attend it. The rose suggests full-blown womanliness, beautiful and vulnerable. Something in the world has infected and blighted this joyous presence in life, and is destroying it. We may read a number of possible interpretations, all actually present, into this symbolism; however, its power will be explained not by any one interpretation, nor yet by the flash of perception in the implied metaphors, but by the violent, self-contained life of the symbol itself: the flower possessed and being killed by the worm.

Why should "natural" symbols like the rose and the "brightness" that "falls from the air" strike us as purer in their evocative power than most traditional symbols? Logically, it would seem that symbols of the latter type, trailing their inherited associations behind them as they enter a poem, carry a greater suggestiveness from the start than those the poet himself has brought into significant focus for the first time. We remember the aura about the name of Helen of Troy, in Nashe's lines. And when Spenser writes of a knight that

> .... on his breast a bloody Cross he bore,
> The dear remembrance of his dying Lord,

we respond at once to the knight's character and to the virtues he represents. . . .

A typical example of the transmuting of a traditional symbol by a modern poet may be found in T. S. Eliot's vision, in *The Waste Land*, of London as a hellish place, the abode of the living dead. His method is to describe the crowds on the street as though they were passing through the mysteriously "unreal" landscape of Hell, in an atmosphere of murk and filth, with an unwilled, pointless, flowing movement. Eliot's picture is based on the oldest traditions of European literature and mythology, and especially on Dante's *Inferno*. It is the unexpected literalness with which he describes the actual city, London, in terms of Hell that turns his symbolism into something completely new:

> Unreal City,
> Under the brown fog of a winter dawn,
> A crowd flowed over London Bridge, so many,
> I had not thought death had undone so many.
> Sighs, short and infrequent, were exhaled,
> And each man fixed his eyes before his feet.

The final three lines of this quotation closely echo lines in Canto III of the *Inferno,* in which Dante describes his entrance into Hell. Here, near the very gates, he sees the horde of souls who "lived without blame, and without praise," who never committed themselves to good or evil causes but were only "for themselves," who never made a decision nor entered into life and consequently have no being or personality that can know either salvation or damnation. They are the hollow men, the vast multitudes of the mediocre and the timidly selfish. Dante is overwhelmed by their number: "I had not thought death had undone so many." Death has "undone" them in the elementary sense that they have died. But the word itself has a certain rich ambiguity, for it also suggests, as part of this ruin that death has brought them, the unwrapping of flesh and bones from the bodiless spirits. And more than this, it suggests the special misery of their present indefinite status. We are told that they have passed into utter oblivion; even "deep Hell receives them not, for the wicked would have some glory over them," and "they are envious of every other lot."

The shock of Eliot's lines echoing Dante lies in the sudden apparition of the big-city multitudes as misery-driven creatures, so uninspired and characterless that they are like these forgotten shades, excluded from further damnation as well as from glory, envisioned in the *Inferno*. Of course, Eliot does not say they are "like" the shades, or that they are suffering spirits wavering on the edge of Hell. Rather, he creates his own symbol in which all the suggestions of unreality, suffering, and pity converge: Here is the Unreal City, and here are its inhabitants. The reader should compare this brief passage with that by Wordsworth (*The Prelude*). He will see that they share the essential evocativeness of all symbolism, but that the Eliot passage omits explanation, transition, everything that will not contribute to the purest evocative effect.

In reviewing these various forms the symbol may take—simple and complex, natural and traditional, static and pure and poet-transmuted—we must always remember the special evocative character of the poetic symbol. It is the kind of image which directs our sensibilities, magnetically, toward a deep emotional awareness that includes but goes beyond intellectual concepts. It may appear in a single line or group of lines only. It may, by itself or in relation to other symbols, dominate the structure of a whole poem. Or it may, in the purest and most concentrated poetry, actually be inseparable from the poem as a whole. . . .

Most symbols derive their rich suggestiveness from their gradual accumulation of associations in the speech and thought of mankind at large. Others are developed in the history of literature itself, and still others in the work of a single writer. (The more we study the work of any serious, accomplished poet, the more we shall understand the special meaning he habitually gives to certain images. He thus makes them symbols uniquely his own—symbols that are at once the clues to the deepest meanings of his work and to values intensely significant to mankind at large.) But there is a constant cross-fertilization going on among these symbols despite their apparently varied sources. Fletcher's youthful Christ is a traditional symbol personally re-created. Eliot's London is a personal symbol tremendously reinforced by traditional and literary evocations. So are the surprising angels of Blake, which become an important symbol in his work because of their compelling nature and recurrent appearance, and—for similar reasons—the music and wine in the poetry of Keats, the towers of Shelley and Yeats, and the mountains and rivers of Wordsworth.

QUEST AND RECONCILIATION

> *Even through the hollow eyes of death*
> *I spy life peering.*
>
> SHAKESPEARE

. . . We return to the largest frame of reference of poetry—the extent of the poet's awareness of the discrepancies between what *is* and what *seems*, and between what *is* and what *ought to be*. All the resources of the great poet, all his powers of description, image-making, story-telling, dramatization, intellectual suppleness, and imaginative conception are put to the test in his ultimate effort to deal with these discrepancies. He needs both technical proficiency and tough integrity of character, and must not be satisfied with glib or easy solutions. He must recognize, as John Donne's *Third Satyre* has it, that truth "stands on a huge hill," "craggy and steep,"

... and he that will
Reach her, about must, and about must go;
And what the hill's suddenness resists, win so. . . .

In solving the moral and esthetic problem of how to tell the truth, the
poet seems often to be hostile to the world around him. In truth, however
bitter its savor, there is nevertheless always an implied affirmation of the
essential value of honesty. One does not find a powerful poem of rejection
without also finding a possibility implied of accepting life as a whole and
in a better way. Though such poetry is often necessarily complex and
ambiguous, it may also brilliantly simplify in order to strike to the heart of
a situation and squeeze the real and the ideal as close together as possible.
Blake's *London* is one of the brilliantly simple poems, presenting its
criticism of life and its affirmations of value in the very same images.

I wander thro' each charter'd street,
Near where the charter'd Thames does flow,
And mark in every face I meet
Marks of weakness, marks of woe.

In every cry of every Man,
In every Infant's cry of fear,
In every voice, in every ban,
The mind-forg'd manacles I hear.

How the Chimney-sweeper's cry
Every blackening Church appalls;
And the hapless Soldier's sigh
Runs in blood down Palace walls.

But most, thro' midnight streets I hear
How the youthful Harlot's curse
Blasts the new-born Infant's tear,
And blights with plagues the Marriage hearse.

WILLIAM BLAKE *London*

London, at first, seems an expression of outright rejection. Blake sees
not merely unrealized potentialities but deathly pain—"weakness" and
"woe"—everywhere. Each face, each voice, reminds him of the frustrations,
lies, and cruelty of the city's life in the early years of the Industrial Revolution. The pathetic little chimney-sweeps make religion and morality seem
arrant hypocrisy; the suffering of soldiers belies the benevolence of govern-
ments and rulers; the cursing street-harlots force him to think of the per-

version of marital happiness which their existence means. (The final lines compress references to illegitimate birth, syphilis, and the ugliness which seems to the speaker to have blighted love in all its aspects; the compression is achieved by a series of related outbursts of sound and image, culminating in the paradoxical "Marriage hearse" which brings the poem to its tragic close.)

Yet to feel so strongly on the subject of the "chartering"—the parceling out for hire and profit—of the city while the potentialities for joy and love are thwarted is to have a humane vision of the right relations between man and man, man and woman, and man and God. The corruption of society, the failure of Church and State, the perversion of love can arouse savage condemnation only in someone with a blazing concern for those right relations. Thus, *London*, in the very vehemence of its description and its rejection of all that has blighted human life and affection, gives us a pure affirmation of their intrinsic beauty. Blake views evil and suffering in the light of his concept of *love* as the great creative force. His *London* exemplifies the way in which many poems of stature imply critical and affirmative attitudes at one and the same time. The importance of such "opposite implication" must be recognized if we are to understand the real functions of much of the paradoxical, ironic, ambiguous, and mystical language of poetry. Blake's method here is to give us images that paint the harsh truth as tragically and nakedly as possible, and yet are also unmistakable emblems of what is valued most (freedom, health, joy, enlightenment, the happiness of children, peace, and innocent sexual love). . . .

Great poetry has this kind of growth into affirmation of its own kind. The affirmation may be made with the sharpest cutting blade, as in Blake's *London*, or it may rise through a subtler poetic logic of associations. But it will be present, though the difficulties in its way will generally also be present. And when it is, the triumph is of the candid, passionate, and resurgent poetic imagination rather than of any particular creed or ideology. In fact, the very construction of an integrated and living poem is symbolically an affirmation of the value of human will and imagination.

Ivor A. Richards

POETRY AND BELIEFS*

The business of the poet, as we have seen, is to give order and coherence, and so freedom, to a body of experience. To do so through words which act as its skeleton, as a structure by which the impulses which make up the experience are adjusted to one another and act together. The means by which words do this are many and varied. To work them out is a problem for linguistic psychology, that embarrassed young heir to philosophy. What little can be done shows already that most critical dogmas of the past are either false or nonsense. A little knowledge is not here a danger, but clears the air in a remarkable way.

Roughly and inadequately, even in the dim light of present knowledge, we can say that words work in the poem in two main fashions. As sensory stimuli and as (in the *widest* sense) symbols. We must refrain from considering the sensory side of the poem, remarking only that it is *not* in the least independent of the other side, and that it has for definite reasons prior importance in most poetry. We must confine ourselves to the other function of words in the poem, or rather, omitting much that is of secondary relevance, to one form of that function, let me call it *pseudo-statement*.

It will be admitted—by those who distinguish between scientific statement, where truth is ultimately a matter of verification as this is understood in the laboratory, and emotive utterance, where "truth" is primarily acceptability *by* some attitude, and more remotely is the acceptability *of* this attitude itself—that it is *not* the poet's business to make scientific statements. Yet poetry has constantly the air of making statements, and important ones; which is one reason why some mathematicians cannot read it. They find the alleged statements to be *false*. It will be agreed that their approach to poetry and their expectations from it are mistaken. But what exactly is the other, the right, the poetic, approach and how does it differ from the mathematical?

The poetic approach evidently limits the framework of possible consequences into which the pseudo-statement is taken. For the scientific ap-

---

* From I. A. Richards' *Science and Poetry*, 2nd ed., revised and enlarged, pp. 61–74 and 92–94. Copyright, 1935, by Kegan Paul, Trench, Trubner & Co., Ltd. Reprinted by permission of Routledge & Kegan Paul, Ltd.

Ivor A. Richards (1893–   ), English critic and semanticist, is author of many books on language, meaning, aesthetics, and especially on the principles of literary criticism.

proach this framework is unlimited. Any and every consequence is relevant. If any of the consequences of a statement conflicts with acknowledged fact then so much the worse for the statement. Not so with the pseudo-statement when poetically approached. The problem is—just how does the limitation work? One tempting account is in terms of a supposed universe of discourse, a world of make-believe, of imagination, of recognized fictions common to the poet and his readers. A pseudo-statement which fits into this system of assumptions would be regarded as "poetically true"; one which does not, as "poetically false." This attempt to treat "poetic truth" on the model of general "coherence theories" is very natural for certain schools of logicians but is inadequate, on the wrong lines from the outset. To mention two objections, out of many; there is no means of discovering what the "universe of discourse" is on any occasion, and the kind of coherence which must hold within it, supposing it to be discoverable, is not an affair of logical relations. Attempt to define the system of propositions into which

"O Rose, thou art sick!"

must fit, and the logical relations which most hold between them if it is to be "poetically true"; the absurdity of the theory becomes evident.

We must look further. In the poetic approach the relevant consequences are not logical or to be arrived at by a partial relaxation of logic. Except occasionally and by accident logic does not enter at all. They are the consequences which arise through our emotional organization. The acceptance which a pseudo-statement receives is entirely governed by its effects upon our feelings and attitudes. Logic only comes in, if at all, in subordination, as a servant to our emotional response. It is an unruly servant, however, as poets and readers are constantly discovering. A pseudo-statement is "true" if it suits and serves some attitude or links together attitudes which on other grounds are desirable. This kind of "truth" is so opposed to scientific "truth" that it is a pity to use so similar a word, but at present it is difficult to avoid the malpractice.[1]

This brief analysis may be sufficient to indicate the fundamental disparity and opposition between pseudo-statements as they occur in poetry and statements as they occur in science. A pseudo-statement is a form of words which is justified entirely by its effect in releasing or organizing our impulses and attitudes (due regard being had for the better or worse organi-

[1] A pseudo-statement, as I use the term, is not necessarily false in any sense. It is merely a form of words whose scientific truth or falsity is irrelevant to the purpose in hand.

"Logic" in this paragraph is, of course, being used in a limited and conventional, or popular, sense.

zations of these *inter se*); a statement, on the other hand, is justified by its truth, *i.e.*, its correspondence, in a highly technical sense, with the fact to which it points.

Statements true and false alike do, of course, constantly touch off attitudes and action. Our daily practical existence is largely guided by them. On the whole true statements are of more service to us than false ones. None the less we do not and, at present, cannot order our emotions and attitudes by true statements alone. Nor is there any probability that we ever shall contrive to do so. This is one of the great new dangers to which civilization is exposed. Countless pseudo-statements—about God, about the universe, about human nature, the relations of mind to mind, about the soul, its rank and destiny—pseudo-statements which are pivotal points in the organization of the mind, vital to its well-being, have suddenly become, for sincere, honest and informed minds, impossible to believe as for centuries they have been believed.[2] The accustomed incidences of the modes of believing are changed irrecoverably; and the knowledge which has displaced them is not of a kind upon which an equally fine organization of the mind can be based.

This is the contemporary situation. The remedy, since there is no prospect of our gaining adequate knowledge, and since indeed it is fairly clear that scientific knowledge cannot meet this need, is to cut our pseudo-statements free from that kind of belief which is appropriate to verified statements. So released they will be changed, of course, but they can still be the main instruments by which we order our attitudes to one another and to the world. This is not a desperate remedy, for, as poetry conclusively shows, even the most important among our attitudes can be aroused and maintained without any believing of a factual or verifiable order entering in at all. We need no such beliefs, and indeed we must have none, if we are to read *King Lear*. Pseudo-statements to which we attach no belief and statements proper, such as science provides, cannot conflict. It is only when we introduce inappropriate kinds of believing into poetry that danger arises. To do so is from this point of view a profanation of poetry.

Yet an important branch of criticism which has attracted the best talents from prehistoric times until to-day consists of the endeavour to

[2] See Appendix. For the mind I am considering here the question "Do I believe x?" is no longer the same. Not only the "What" that is to be believed but the "How" of the believing has changed—through the segregation of science and its clarification of the techniques of proof. This is the danger; and the remedy suggested is a further differentiation of the "Hows." To these differences correspond differences in the senses of "is so" and "being" where, as is commonly the case, "is so" and "being" assert believings. As we admit this, the world that "is" divides into worlds incommensurable in respect of so called "degrees of reality." Yet, and this is all-important, these worlds have an order, with regard to one another, which is the order of the mind; and interference between them imperils sanity.

persuade men that the functions of science and poetry are identical, or that the one is a "higher form" of the other, or that they conflict and we must choose between them.

The root of this persistent endeavour has still to be mentioned; it is the same as that from which the Magical View of the world arose. If we give to a pseudo-statement the kind of unqualified acceptance which belongs by right only to certified scientific statements—and those judgments of the routine of perception and action from which science derives—, if we can contrive to do this, the impulses and attitudes with which we respond to it gain a notable stability and vigour. Briefly, if we can contrive to believe poetry, then the world *seems*, while we do so, to be transfigured. It used to be comparatively easy to do this, and the habit has become well established. With the extension of science and the neutralization of nature it has become difficult as well as dangerous. Yet it is still alluring; it has many analogies with drug-taking. Hence the endeavours of the critics referred to. Various subterfuges have been devised along the lines of regarding Poetic Truth as figurative, symbolic; or as more immediate, as a truth of Intuition transcending common knowledge; or as a higher form of the same truth that science yields. Such attempts to use poetry as a denial or as a corrective of science are very common. One point can be made against them all: they are never worked out in detail. There is no equivalent of Mill's *Logic* expounding any of them. The language in which they are framed is usually a blend of obsolete psychology and emotive exclamations.

The long-established and much-encouraged habit of giving to emotive utterances—whether pseudo-statements simple, or looser and larger wholes taken as saying something figuratively—the kind of assent which we give to unescapable facts, has for most people debilitated a wide range of their responses. A few scientists, caught young and brought up in the laboratory, are free from it; but then, as a rule, they pay no *serious* attention to poetry. For most men the recognition of the neutrality of nature brings about—through this habit—a divorce from poetry. They are so used to having their responses propped up by beliefs, however vague, that when these shadowy supports are removed they are no longer able to respond. Their attitudes to so many things have been forced in the past, over-encouraged. And when the world-picture ceases to assist there is a collapse. Over whole tracts of natural emotional response we are to-day like a bed of dahlias whose sticks have been removed. And this effect of the neutralization of nature is perhaps only in its beginnings. However, human nature has a prodigious resilience. Love poetry seems able to out-play psychoanalysis.

A sense of desolation, of uncertainty, of futility, of the groundlessness of aspirations, of the vanity of endeavour, and a thirst for a life-giving water which seems suddenly to have failed, are the signs in consciousness of this necessary reorganization of our lives.[3] Our attitudes and impulses are being compelled to become self-supporting; they are being driven back upon their biological justification, made once again sufficient to themselves. And the only impulses which seem strong enough to continue unflagging are commonly so crude that, to more finely developed individuals, they hardly seem worth having. Such people cannot live by warmth, food, fighting, drink, and sex alone. Those who are least affected by the change are those who are emotionally least removed from the animals. As we shall see at the close of this essay, even a considerable poet may attempt to find relief by a reversion to primitive mentality.

It is important to diagnose the disease correctly and to put the blame in the right quarter. Usually it is some alleged "materialism" of science which is denounced. This mistake is due partly to clumsy thinking, but chiefly to relics of the Magical View. For even if the Universe were "spiritual" all through (whatever that assertion might mean; all such assertions are probably nonsense), that would not make it any more accordant to human attitudes. It is not what the universe is made of but how it works, the law it follows, which makes verifiable knowledge of it incapable of spurring on our emotional responses, and further, the nature of knowledge itself makes it inadequate. The contact with things which we therein establish is too sketchy and indirect to help us. We are beginning to know too much about the bond which unites the mind to its object in knowledge[4] for that old dream of a perfect knowledge which would guarantee perfect life to retain its sanction. What was thought to be pure knowledge, we see now to have been

[3] My debt to *The Waste Land* here will be evident. The original footnote seems to have puzzled Mr. Eliot and some other readers. Well it might! In saying, though, that he "had effected a complete severance between his poetry and all beliefs" I was referring not to the poet's own history, but to the technical detachment of the poetry. And the way in which he then seemed to me to have "realized what might otherwise have remained a speculative possibility" was by finding a new order through the contemplation and exhibition of disorder.

"Yes! Very funny this terrible thing is. A man that is born falls into a dream like a man who falls into the sea. If he tries to climb out into the air as inexperienced people endeavour to do, he drowns—*nicht wahr?* . . . No! I tell you! The way is to the destructive element submit yourself, and with the exertions of your hands and feet in the water make the deep, deep sea keep you up. So if you ask me how to be? In the destructive element immerse . . . that was the way." *Lord Jim*, p. 216. Mr. Eliot's later verse has sometimes shown still less "dread of the unknown depths." That, at least, seems in part to explain to me why *Ash Wednesday* is better poetry than even the best sections of *The Waste Land*.

[4] Verifiable scientific knowledge, of course. Shift the sense of "knowledge" to include hope and desire and fear as well as reference, and what I am saying would no longer be true. But then the relevant sense of "true" would have changed too. Its sanction would no longer be verifiability.

shot through with hope and desire, with fear and wonder; and these intrusive elements indeed gave it all its power to support our lives. In knowledge, in the "How?" of events, we can find hints by which to take advantage of circumstances in our favour and avoid mischances. But we cannot get from it a *raison d'être* or a justification of more than a relatively lowly kind of life.

The justification, on the reverse, of any attitude lies, not in the object, but in itself, in its serviceableness to the whole personality. Upon its place in the whole system of attitudes, which is the personality, all its worth depends. This is as true for the subtle, finely compounded attitudes of the civilized individual as for the simpler attitudes of the child.

In brief, the imaginative life is its own justification; and this fact must be faced, although sometimes—by a lover, for example—it may be very difficult to accept. When it is faced, it is apparent that all the attitudes to other human beings and to the world in all its aspects, which have been serviceable to humanity, remain as they were, as valuable as ever. Hesitation felt in admitting this is a measure of the strength of the evil habit I have been describing. But many of these attitudes, valuable as ever, are, now that they are being set free, more difficult to maintain, because we still hunger after a basis in belief.

APPENDIX

Two chief words seem likely occasions of misunderstanding in the above; and they have in fact misled some readers. One is *Nature,* the other is *Belief.*

Nature is evidently as variable a word as can be used. It senses range from the mere inclusive THAT, in which we live and of which we are a part, to whatever would correspond to the most detailed and interconnected account we could attain of this. Or we omit ourselves (and other minds) and make Nature *either* what influences us (in which case we should not forget our metabolism), *or* an object we apprehend (in which case there are as many Natures as there are types of apprehension we care to distinguish). And what is "natural" to one culture is strange and artificial to another. (See *Mencius on the Mind,* chap. III.) More deceptively, the view here being inseparable from the eye, and this being a matter of habitual speculation, we may talk, as we think, the same language and yet put very different things into Nature; and what we then find will not be unconnected with what we have put in. I have attempted some further discussion of these questions in Chapters VI and VII of *Coleridge on Imagination.*

Belief. Two "beliefs" may differ from one another: (1) In their objects (2) In their statements or expressions (3) In their modes (4) In their grounds (5) In their occasions (6) In their connections with other "beliefs" (7) In their links with possible action (8) And in other ways. Our chief evidence usually for the beliefs of other people (and often for our own) must be some statement or other expression. But very different beliefs may fittingly receive the same expression. Most words used in stating any speculative opinion are as ambiguous as "Belief"; and yet by such words belief-objects must be distinguished.

But in the case of "belief" there is an additional difficulty. Neither it nor its partial synonyms suggest the great variety of the attitudes (3) that are commonly covered (and confused) by the term. They are often treated as though they were mere variations in degree. Of what? Of belief, it would be said. But this is no better than the parallel trick of treating all varieties of love as a mere more or less only further differentiated by their objects. Such crude over-simplifications distort the structure of the mind and, although favourite suasive devices with some well-intentioned preachers, are disastrous.

There is an ample field here awaiting a type of dispassionate inquiry which it has seldom received. A world threatened with ever more and more leisure should not be too impatient of important and explorable subtleties.

Meanwhile, as with "Nature," misunderstandings should neither provoke nor surprise. I should not be much less at my reader's mercy if I were to add notes doubling the length of this little book. On so vast a matter, even the largest book could contain no more than a sketch of how things have seemed to be sometimes to the writer.

SELECTED BIBLIOGRAPHY

1. R. Wellek and Austin Warren, *Theory of Literature*, Harcourt, Brace and Company, 1942. Excellent bibliographies on all phases of literature and the aesthetic problems involved in its studies. (Available as Harvest paperback.)
2. Harold Osborne, *Aesthetics and Criticism*, Philosophical Library, 1955. Chapter X is on the anatomy of literature and contains many valuable references which the interested student can follow up.
3. Susanne Langer, *Feeling and Form*, Chaps. 13–19, Charles Scribner's Sons, 1953. A good example of a philosophically committed interpretation of literature.
4. Philip Wheelright, "On the Semantics of Poetry," *The Kenyon Review*, 1940. A reply to Richards on poetry, belief and truth.
5. Morris Weitz, "Truth in Literature," *Revue Internationale de Philosophie*, 1955.

Another reply to Richards and an attempt to work out the problem along lines of a new conception of the language of fiction.

6. John Hospers, *Meaning and Truth in the Arts*, Part II, University of North Carolina Press, 1946. A good treatment of the distinction between "truth-about" and "truth-to" as applied to the problem of truth and art.

Note: There are, of course, literally, thousands of items which could be listed here on the aesthetics of literature. The knowledgeable student can make his own way into the areas of discussions of metaphor, imagery, paradox, etc. The listings given above are mainly for students from the arts other than literature who wish to explore further some of the problems in the aesthetics of literature.

ARCHITECTURE

There are many fine discussions of the nature and principles of architecture. Here two selections are offered, both of which characterize the basic elements of architecture and also dissociate these from other elements sometimes theoretically attributed to architecture. The first is by Geoffrey Scott and is a statement of the relations among space, mass, and line in classical architecture. The second, by J. M. Richards, is a summary of recent trends in architecture, with particular stress on the contemporary emphasis on materials in buildings.

Geoffrey Scott

THE ELEMENTS OF ARCHITECTURE[*]

THE ARCHITECTURE OF HUMANISM

"Well-building hath three conditions: Commodity, Firmness, and Delight." From this phrase of an English humanist[1] a theory of architecture might take its start. Architecture is a focus where three separate purposes

---

[*] From Geoffrey Scott's *The Architecture of Humanism,* "Introduction," Pt. I, and Ch. 8. Copyright, 1914, by Constable and Company, Ltd. Reprinted by permission of Constable and Company, Ltd.; and Charles Scribner's Sons.

Geoffrey Scott (1885–1929), essayist, world authority on Boswell and Dr. Johnson, was also a student of architecture, and especially an advocate of Italian Renaissance styles. His major work, *The Architecture of Humanism,* is one of those rare books on aesthetics which combine theory and application, in this case to Renaissance architecture.

[1] Sir Henry Wotton, *Elements of Architecture.* He is adapting Vitruvius, Bk. 1, chap. iii.

have converged. They are blended in a single method; they are fulfilled in a single result; yet in their own nature they are distinguished from each other by a deep and permanent disparity. The criticism of architecture has been confused in its process; it has built up strangely diverse theories of the art, and the verdicts it has pronounced have been contradictory in the extreme. Of the causes which have contributed to its failure, this is the chief: that it has sought to force on architecture an unreal unity of aim. "Commodity, firmness, and delight"; between these three values the criticism of architecture has insecurely wavered, not always distinguishing very clearly between them, seldom attempting any statement of the relation they bear to one another, never pursuing to their conclusion the consequences which they involve. It has leaned now this way and now that, and struck, between these incommensurable virtues, at different points, its arbitrary balance.

Architecture, the most complex of the arts, offers to its critics many paths of approach, and as many opportunities for avoiding their goal. At the outset of a fresh study in this field, it is well, at the risk of pedantry, to define where these paths lead.

Architecture requires "firmness." By this necessity it stands related to science, and to the standards of science. The mechanical bondage of construction has closely circumscribed its growth. Thrust and balance, pressure and its support, are at the root of the language which architecture employs. The inherent characters of marble, brick, wood and iron have moulded its forms, set limits to its achievement, and governed, in a measure, even its decorative detail. On every hand the study of architecture encounters physics, statics, and dynamics, suggesting, controlling, justifying its design. It is open to us, therefore, to look in buildings for the logical expression of material properties and material laws. Without these, architecture is impossible, its history unintelligible. And if, finding these everywhere paramount, we seek, in terms of material properties and material laws, not merely to account for the history of architecture, but to assess its value, then architecture will be judged by the exactness and sincerity with which it expresses constructive facts, and conforms to constructive laws. That will be the scientific standard for architecture: a logical standard so far as architecture is related to science, and no further.

But architecture requires "commodity." It is not enough that it should possess its own internal coherence, its abstract logic of construction. It has come into existence to satisfy an external need. That, also, is a fact of its history. Architecture is subservient to the general uses of mankind. And, immediately, politics and society, religion and liturgy, the large movements of races and their common occupations, become factors in the study. These determine what shall be built, and, up to a point, in what way. The history of civilization thus leaves in architecture its truest, because its most unconscious record. If, then, it is legitimate to consider architecture as an expression of mechanical laws, it is legitimate, no less, to see in it an expression of human life. This furnishes a standard of value totally distinct from the scientific. Buildings may be judged by the success with which they supply the practical ends they are designed to meet. Or, by a natural extension, we may judge them by the value of those ends themselves; that is to say, by the external purposes which they reflect. These, indeed, are two very different questions. The last makes a moral reference which the first avoids, but both spring, and spring inevitably, from the link which architecture has with life—from that "condition of well-building" which Wotton calls commodity.

And architecture requires "delight." For this reason, interwoven with practical ends and their mechanical solutions, we may trace in architecture a third and different factor—the disinterested desire for beauty. This desire does not, it is true, culminate here in a purely aesthetic *result,* for it has to deal with a concrete basis which is utilitarian. It is, none the less, a purely aesthetic *impulse,* an impulse distinct from all the others which architecture may simultaneously satisfy, an impulse by virtue of which architecture becomes art. It is a separate instinct. Sometimes it will borrow a suggestion from the laws of firmness or commodity; sometimes it will run counter to them, or be offended by the forms they would dictate. It has its own standard, and claims its own authority. It is possible, therefore, to ask how far, and how successfully, in any architectural style, this aesthetic impulse has been embodied; how far, that is to say, the instincts which, in the other arts, exert an obvious and unhampered activity, have succeeded in realizing themselves also through this more complicated and more restricted instrument. And we can ask, still further, whether there may not be aesthetic instincts, for which this instrument, restricted as it is, may furnish the sole and peculiar expression. This is to study architecture, in the strict sense, as an art.

Here, then, are three "conditions of well-building," and corresponding to them three modes of criticism, and three provinces of thought.

Now what, in fact, is the result? The material data of our study we certainly possess in abundance: the statistics of architecture, the history of existing works, their shape and size and authorship, have long been investigated with the highest scholarship. But when we ask to be given not history but criticism, when we seek to know what is the value of these works of art, viewed in themselves or by comparison with one another, and why they are to be considered worthy of this exact attention, and whether one is to be considered more deserving of it than another, and on what grounds, the answers we obtain may be ready and numerous, but they are certainly neither consistent nor clear.

The criticism of architecture has been of two kinds. The first of these remains essentially historical. It is content to describe the conditions under which the styles of the past arose. It accepts the confused and partly fortuitous phenomenon which architecture actually is, and estimates the phenomenon by a method as confused and fortuitous as itself. It passes in and out of the three provinces of thought, and relates its subject now to science, now to art, and now to life. It treats of these upon a single plane, judging one building by standards of constructive skill, another by standards of rhythm and proportion, and a third by standards of practical use or by the moral impulse of its builders. This medley of elements, diverse and uncommensurated as they are, can furnish no general estimate or true comparison of style.

Doubtless, *as a matter of history*, architecture has not come into existence in obedience to any *a priori* aesthetic. It has grown up around the practical needs of the race, and in satisfying these it has been deflected, now by the obstinate claims of mechanical laws, now by a wayward search for beauty. But the problem of the architect and that of the critic are here essentially different. The work of the architect is synthetic. He must take into simultaneous account our three "conditions of well-building," and find some compromise which keeps a decent peace between their claims. The task of the critic, on the contrary, is one of analysis. He has to discover, define, and maintain the ideal standards of value in each province. Thus the three standards of architecture, united in practice, are separable, and must be separated, in thought. Criticism of the historical type fails to apply an ideal and consistent analysis, for the insufficient reason that the *practice* of architecture has, of necessity, been neither consistent nor ideal. Such criticism is not necessarily misleading. Its fault is more often that it leads nowhere. Its judgments may be individually accurate, but it affords us no general view, for it adopts no fixed position. It is neither simple, nor comprehensive, nor consistent. It cannot, therefore, furnish a theory of style.

The second type of criticism is more dangerous. For the sake of simplicity it lays down some "law" of architectural taste. Good design in architecture, it will say, should "express the uses the building is intended to serve"; "it should faithfully state the facts of its construction," or again it should "reflect the life of a noble civilization." Then, having made these plausible assumptions, it drives its theory to a conclusion, dwells on the examples that support its case, and is willing, for the sake of consistency, to condemn all architecture in which the theory is not confirmed. Such general anathemas are flattering alike to the author and his reader. They greatly simplify the subject. They have a show of logic. But they fail to explain why the styles of architecture which they find it necessary to condemn have in fact been created and admired. Fashion consequently betrays these faultless arguments; for whatever has once genuinely pleased is likely to be again found pleasing; art and the enjoyment of art continue in the condemned paths undismayed; and criticism is left to discover a sanction for them, if it can, in some new theory, as simple, as logical, and as insufficient as the first.

The true task of criticism is to understand such aesthetic pleasures as have in fact been felt, and then to draw whatever laws and conclusions it may from that understanding. But no amount of reasoning will create, or can annul, an aesthetic experience; for the aim of the arts has not been logic, but delight. The theory of architecture, then, requires logic; but it requires, not less, an independent sense of beauty. Nature, unfortunately, would seem to unite these qualities with extreme reluctance.

Obviously, there is room for confusion. The "condition of delight" in architecture—its value as an art—may conceivably be found to *consist in* its firmness, or in its commodity, or in both; or it may consist in something else different from, yet dependent upon these; or it may be independent of them altogether. In any case, these elements are, at first sight, distinct. There is no reason, *prima facie*, to suppose that there exists between them a pre-established harmony, and that in consequence a perfect principle of building can be laid down which should, in full measure, satisfy them all. And, in the absence of such a principle, it is quite arbitrary to pronounce dogmatically on the concessions which art should make to science or utility. Unless it can be proved that these apparently different values are in reality commensurable, there ought to be three separate schemes of criticism: the first based on construction, the second on convenience, the third on aesthetics. Each could be rational, complete, and, within its own province, valid. Thus by degrees might be obtained what at present is certainly lacking—the data for a theory of architecture which should not be contradicted at once by the history of taste.

The present study seeks to explain one chapter of that history. It deals with a limited period of architecture, from a single point of view.

HUMANIST VALUES

I

Architecture, simply and immedaitely perceived, is a combination, revealed through light and shade, of spaces, of masses, and of lines. These few elements make the core of architectural experience: an experience which the literary fancy, the historical imagination, the casuistry of conscience and the calculations of science, cannot constitute or determine, though they may encircle and enrich. How great a chaos must ensue when our judgments of architecture are based upon these secondary and encircling interests the previous chapters have suggested, and the present state of architecture might confirm. It remains to be seen how far these central elements—these spaces, masses and lines—can provide a ground for our critcism that is adequate or secure.

The spaces, masses and lines of architecture, as perceived, are appearances. We may infer from them further facts about a building which are not perceived; facts about construction, facts about history or society. But the art of architecture is concerned with their immediate aspect; it is concerned with them as appearances.

And these appearances are related to human functions. Through these spaces we can conceive ourselves to move; these masses are capable, like ourselves, of pressure and resistance; these lines, should we follow or describe them, might be our path and our gesture.

Conceive for a moment a "top-heavy" building or an "ill-proportioned" space. No doubt the degree to which these qualities will be found offensive will vary with the spectator's sensibility to architecture; but sooner or later, if the top-heaviness or the disproportion is sufficiently pronounced, every spectator will judge that the building or the space is ugly, and experience a certain discomfort from their presence. So much will be conceded.

Now what is the cause of this discomfort? It is often suggested that the top-heavy building and the cramped space are ugly because they suggest the idea of instability, the idea of collapse, the idea of restriction, and so forth. But these *ideas* are not in themselves disagreeable. We read the definition of such words in a dictionary with equanimity, yet the definition, if it a true one, will have conveyed the idea of restriction or collapse. Poetry will convey the ideas with vividness. Yet we experience from it no shadow of discomfort. On the contrary, Hamlet's "cabined, cribbed, confined" delights us, for the very reason that the idea is vividly conveyed. Nor does Samson painfully trouble *our* peace, when

> Those two massie Pillars
> With horrible convulsions to and fro
> He tugged, he shook, till down they came and drew
> The whole roof after them with burst of thunder
> Upon the head of all who sate beneath.

Clearly, then, our discomfort in the presence of such architecture cannot spring merely from the idea of restriction or instability.

But neither does it derive from an actual weakness or restriction in our immediate experience. It is disagreeable to have our movements thwarted, to lose strength or to collapse; but a room fifty feet square and seven feet high does not restrict our actual movements, and the sight of a granite building raised (apparently) on a glass shop-front does not cause us to collapse.

There is instability—or the appearance of it; but it is in the building. There is discomfort, but it is in ourselves. What then has occurred? The conclusion seems evident. The concrete spectacle has done what the mere idea could not: it has stirred our physical memory. It has awakened in us, not indeed an actual state of instability or of being overloaded, but that condition of spirit which in the past has belonged to our actual experiences of weakness, of thwarted effort or incipient collapse. We have looked at the building and identified ourselves with its apparent state. *We have transcribed ourselves into terms of architecture.*

But the "states" in architecture with which we thus identify ourselves need not be actual. The actual pressures of a spire are downward; yet no one speaks of a "sinking" spire. A spire, when well designed, appears—as common language testifies—to soar. We identify ourselves, not with its actual downward pressure, but its apparent upward impulse. So, too, by the same excellent—because unconscious—testimony of speech, arches "spring," vistas "stretch," domes "swell," Greek temples are "calm," and baroque façades "restless." The whole of architecture is, in fact, unconsciously invested by us with human movement and human moods. Here, then, is a principle complementary to the one just stated. *We transcribe architecture into terms of ourselves.*

This is the humanism of architecture. The tendency to project the image of our functions into concrete forms is the basis, for architecture, of creative design. The tendency to recognize, in concrete forms, the image of those functions is the true basis, in its turn, of critical appreciation.[2]

[2] The theory of aesthetic here implied, is, needless to say, not new. It was first developed by Lipps twenty years ago, and since then has been constantly discussed and frequently misunderstood.

In what follows I owe a debt to many suggestive points in Mr. Berenson's studies of Italian painting, where this view of aesthetics found its most fruitful concrete application. With this exception the present chapter has been derived wholly from the author's own immediate experience in the study and practice of architecture, and is intended to satisfy rather an architectural than a philosophical curiosity. Time-honoured as Lipp's theory now is, and valid as it appears to me to be, its influence upon purely architectural criticism has been negligible. In English architectural writing it is totally ignored; even Mr. Blomfield, the most philosophical of our critics, gives it but a frigid welcome.

II

To this statement several objections may be expected. This "rising" of towers and "springing" of arches, it will be said—these different movements which animate architecture—are mere metaphors of speech. No valid inference can be drawn from them. Again, the enjoyment of fine building is a simple and immediate experience, while this dual "transcription," by which we interpret the beauty of architecture, is a complicated process. And not only—it will again be objected—is the theory too complicated; it is also too physical. The body, it will be said, plays no part—or a small and infrequent part—in our conscious enjoyment of architecture, which commonly yields us rather an intellectual and spiritual satisfaction than a conscious physical delight. And it will be further said that such a theory is too "farfetched"; we cannot readily imagine that the great architects of the past were guided by so sophisticated a principle of design. And, if some such process has indeed a place in architecture, it may be doubted finally how far it can account for all the varied pleasures we obtain. It will be convenient to consider these objections at the outset.

The springing of arches, the swelling of domes, and the soaring of spires are "mere metaphors of speech." Certainly they are metaphors. But a metaphor, when it is so obvious as to be universally employed and immediately understood, presupposes a true and reliable experience to which it can refer. Such metaphors are wholly different from literary conceits. A merely literary metaphor lays stress on its own ingenuity or felicity. When we read

> Awake, for Morning in the bowl of Night
> Has flung the Stone which puts the stars to flight,

we are first arrested by the obvious disparity between the thing and its description; we then perceive the point of likeness. But when we speak of a tower as "standing" or "leaning" or "rising," or say of a curve that it is "cramped" or "flowing," the words are the simplest and most direct description we can give of our impression. We do not argue to the point of likeness, but, on the contrary, we are first conscious of the fitness of the phrase

---

(*The Mistress Art*, p. 118). Yet its architectural importance, both for theory and practice, is immense; and it is for lack of its recognition that the Fallacies of Criticism still flourish so abundantly. For some theory criticism must have, and in the absence of the true, it makes shift with the palpably false.

I have avoided, as far as clearness seems to permit, all purely psychological discussion. Those interested in this aspect of the matter will find in the recent writings of Vernon Lee the most extensive survey of the question which has appear in English, together with all necessary references to the foreign literature of the subject.

and only subsequently perceive the element of metaphor. But art addresses us through immediate impressions rather than through the process of reflection, and this universal metaphor of the body, a language profoundly felt and universally understood, is its largest opportunity. A metaphor is, by definition, the transcription of one thing into terms of another, and this in fact is what the theory under discussion claims. It claims that architectural art is the transcription of the body's states into forms of building.

The next point is more likely to cause difficulty. The process of our theory is complex; the process of our felt enjoyment is the simplest thing we know. Yet here, too, it should be obvious that a process simple in consciousness need not be simple in analysis. It is not suggested that we *think* of ourselves as columns, or of columns as ourselves. No doubt when keen aesthetic sensibility is combined with introspective habit, the processes of transcription will tend to enter the field of consciousness. But there is no reason why even the acutest sensibility to a resultant pleasure should be conscious of the processes that go to make it. Yet some cause and some process there must be. The processes of which we are least conscious are precisely the most deep-seated and universal and continuous, as, for example, the process of breathing. And this habit of projecting the image of our own functions upon the outside world, of reading the outside world in our own terms, is certainly ancient, common, and profound. It is, in fact, the *natural* way of perceiving and interpreting what we see. It is the way of the child in whom perpetual pretence and "endless imitation" are a spontaneous method of envisaging the world. It is the way of the savage, who believes in "animism," and conceives every object to be invested with powers like his own.[3] It is the way of the primitive peoples, who in the elaborate business of the dance give a bodily rendering to their beliefs and desires long before thought has accurately expressed them. It is the way of a superbly gifted race like the Greeks, whose mythology is one vast monument to just this instinct. It is the way of the poetic mind at all times and places, which humanizes the external world, not in a series of artificial conceits, but simply so perceiving it. To perceive and interpret the world scientifically, as it actually is, is a later, a less "natural," a more sophisticated process, and one

[3] Thus it has of late been more fully realized that children and primitive races are often capable of very remarkable achievement in expressive art, while the scientific perception of the world for the most part undermines the gift. If the child or the savage is incapable of appreciating great architecture, it is not because they lack the aesthetic sense (for a child the general forms, for instance, of a piece of furniture are often charged with significance and impressiveness), but because the scope and continuity of their attention is too limited to organize these perceptions into an aesthetic whole, still more to give them concrete realization. None the less, it is on this half-conscious or subconscious, yet not quite undiscoverable world in which, more than ourselves, they live, that architecture, like all the arts, depends for its effect.

from which we still relapse even when we say the sun is rising. The scientific
perception of the world is forced upon us; the humanist perception of it is
ours by right. The scientific method is intellectually and practically useful,
but the naïve, the anthropomorphic way which humanizes the world and
interprets it by analogy with our own bodies and our own wills, is still
the aesthetic way; it is the basis of poetry, and it is the foundation of architecture.

A similar confusion between what is conscious in architectural pleasure,
and what is merely implied, seems to underlie the objection that our theory
lays too great a stress on physical states. Our pleasure in architecture, it is
true, is primarily one of the mind and the spirit. Yet the link between physical
states and states of the mind and the emotions needs no emphasis. Our
theory does not say that physical states enter largely into the spectator's
consciousness; it says that they, or the suggestion of them, are a necessary
precondition of his pleasure. Their absence from consciousness is indeed a
point of real importance. Large modifications in our physical condition,
when they occur, alter our mental and emotional tone; but, also, they absorb
our consciousness. A person, for example, who is taking part in an exciting
game, will feel exhilaration and may enjoy it; but the overtones of gaiety,
the full intellectual and emotional interest of the state, are drowned in the
physical experience. The mind is not free to attend to them. It is precisely
because the *conscious* physical element in architectural pleasure is so slight,
our imitative self-adjustment to architectural form so subtle, that we are
enabled to attend wholly to the intellectual and emotional value which
belongs to the physical state. If we look at some spirited eighteenth-century
design, all life and flicker and full of vigorous and dancing curves, the
physical echo of movement which they awaken is enough to recall the
appropriate mental and emotional penumbra; it is not sufficient to overwhelm it. No one has suggested that the experiences of art are as violent
or exciting as the experiences of physical activity; but it is claimed for them
that they are subtler, more profound, more lasting, and, as it were, possessed of greater resonance. And this difference the theory we are considering assists us to understand.

Any explanation of the workings of the aesthetic instinct, however
accurate, must inevitably have a modern ring. It must seem incongruous
when applied to the artists of the past, for the need and the language of such
explanations are essentially of our own day. It would not therefore—to pass
to the next objection—be a serious obstacle to our theory if the conception
of architecture, as an art of design based on the human body and its states,
had been wholly alien to the architects of the past. But this is not altogether
the case. The Renaissance architects were, in fact, frequently curious to

found their design upon the human body, or, rather, to understand how the human body entered into the current traditions of design. Among their sketches may be found some where the proportions of the male form are woven into those of an architectural drawing and made to correspond with its divisions. An elaborate, though uninspired, rendering of the Tuscan, Ionic, and Corinthian Orders into human forms was published by John Shute in the earliest printed work on architecture in England. And in this connection the ancient, though seldom felicitous, habit of actually substituting caryatides and giants for the column itself is not without significance. It was realized that the human body in some way entered into the question of design. But habits of thought were at that time too objective to allow men any clear understanding of a question which is, after all, one of pure psychology. What they instinctively apprehended they had no means intellectually to state; and that correspondence of architecture to the body, which was true in abstract principle, they sometimes vainly sought to prove in concrete detail. Thus they looked in architecture for an actual reproduction of the proportion and symmetries of the body, with results that were necessarily sometimes trivial and childish. Vasari was nearer the truth when he said in praise of a building that it seemed "not built, but born"—*non murato ma veramente nato*. Architecture, to communicate the vital values of the spirit, must appear organic like the body. And a greater critic than Vasari, Michael Angelo himself, touched on a truth more profound, it may be, than he realized, when he wrote of architecture: "He that hath not mastered, or doth not master the human figure, and in especial its anatomy, may never comprehend it."

III

But, how far, it is natural to ask, can such an explanation be carried? Granting its truth, can we establish its sufficiency? Our pleasure in architectural form seems manifold. Can one such principle explain it? A full answer to this question is perhaps only to be earned in the long process of experiment and verification which the actual practice of architecture entails. How minutely Humanism can enter into the detail of architecture, how singularly it may govern its main design, could not, in any case, be demonstrated without a mass of instances and a free use of illustration. A study of these, drawn from Renaissance architecture, could form the matter of another volume. But the main divisions of the subject—space, mass, line and coherence, with their more obvious applications—may here be singled out.

The principle is perhaps most clearly to be recognized in *line*. Lines of one sort or another always form a large part of what is visually presented to us in architecture. Now in most cases, when we bring our attention to bear on one of these lines, its whole extent is not seen with absolute simultaneity; we "follow" it with our eye. The mind passes successively over points in space, and that gives us movement. But when we have got movement we have got expression. For our own movements are the simplest, the most instinctive, and the most universal forms of expression that we know. Identified with ourselves, movement has meaning; and line, through movement, becomes a gesture, an expressive act. Thus, for example, the curves of a volute are recognized as bold or weak, tense or lax, powerful, flowing, and so forth. It is by such terms as these, in fact, that we praise or condemn them. But we must recognize them as having these qualities by unconscious analogy with our own movements, since it is only in our own bodies that we know the relation of the line—or movement—to the feeling it denotes.

Movement is most obviously communicated by curved lines; but it is conveyed also by lines which are straight. No doubt the straight lines which bound the rectangular forms of architecture, its doors and its windows, are chiefly realized, not as sensations in themselves, but as definitions of the shapes they enclose. Their chief use is to determine the position of a patch upon a given surface; and the aesthetic value of this will be considered in a moment. But any emphasis upon vertical lines immediately awakens in us a sense of upward direction, and lines which are spread—horizontal lines— convey suggestions of rest. Thus the architect has already, in the lines of a design, a considerable opportunity. He controls the path of the eye; the path we follow is our movement; movement determines our mood.

But line is not the sole means of affecting our sense of movement. Space, also, controls it. Spaces may be in two dimensions or in three. We may consider the simpler case first. A large part of architectural design consists in the arrangement of forms upon surfaces, that is to say, within spaces. The part which movement here plays will be clear from a common instance. A man who is arranging pictures on a wall will say that one is "crowded" or "lost" in the space it occupies, that it "wants to come" up or down. That is to say, the position of forms upon a surface is realized in terms of our physical consciousness. If a certain patch "wants to come" down, we ourselves, by our unconscious imitation of it, have the sense of a perpetually thwarted instinct of movement. The arrangement of the scheme is imperfectly *humanized*. It may be picturesque, it may be useful, it may be mechanically superior; but it is at variance with our ideal movement. And beauty of disposition in architecture, like beauty of line, arises from our own physical experience of easy movement in space.

But not all movements are pleasant or unpleasant in themselves; the majority of them are indifferent. Nevertheless, a *series* of suggested movements, in themselves indifferent, may awaken in us an expectancy and consequent desire of some further movement; and if the spaces of architecture are so arranged as first to awaken and then falsify this expectation, we have ugliness. For example, if a design be obviously based on symmetry and accustoms us to a rhythm of equal movements—as in the case of a typical eighteenth-century house—and one of the windows were placed out of line and lower than the rest, we should feel discomfort. The offense would lie against our sense of a movement, which, when it reaches that point of a design, is compelled to drop out of step and to dip against its will. Yet the relation of the window to its immediately surrounding forms might not in itself be necessarily ugly.

A converse instance may here be given. Classic design—the style which in Italy culminated in Bramante—aims at authority, dignity, and peace. It does this by conveying at every point a sense of equipoise. The forms are so adjusted amid the surrounding contours as to *cancel all suggested movement:* they are placed, as it were, each at the centre of gravity within the space, and our consciousness is thus sustained at a point of rest. But the baroque architects rejected this arrangement. They employed space adjustments which, *taken in isolation,* would be inharmonious. In their church façades, as Wölfflin has pointed out, they quite deliberately congested their forms. The lower windows are jammed between the pilasters on either side; they are placed above the centre of gravity; they give the sense of lateral pressure and upward movement. This, taken alone, would leave us perpetually in suspense. But in the upper part of the design our expectancy is satisfied; the upward movement is allowed to disperse itself in greater areas of lateral space, and makes its escape in a final flourish of decorative sculpture; or it is laid to rest by an exaggerated emphasis upon the downward movement of the crowning pediment and on the horizontals of the cornice. Here, therefore, a movement, which in the midst of a Bramantesque design would be destructive and repugnant, is turned to account and made the basis of a more dramatic, but not less satisfying treatment, the motive of which is not peace, but energy.

IV

But besides spaces which have merely length and breadth—surfaces, that is to say, at which we look—architecture gives us spaces of three dimensions in which we stand. And here is the very centre of architectural art. The functions of the arts, at many points, overlap; architecture has much that it holds in common with sculpture, and more that it shares with music. But it has also its peculiar province and a pleasure which is typically its own. It has the monopoly of space. Architecture alone of the Arts can give space its full value. It can surround us with a void of three dimensions; and whatever delight may be derived from that is the gift of architecture alone. Painting can depict space; poetry, like Shelley's, can recall its image; music can give us its analogy; but architecture deals with space directly; it uses space as a material and sets us in the midst.

Criticism has singularly failed to recognize this supremacy in architecture of spatial values. The tradition of criticism is practical. The habits of our mind are fixed on matter. We talk of what occupies our tools and arrests our eyes. Matter is fashioned; space comes. Space is "nothing"—a mere negation of the solid. And thus we come to overlook it.

But though we may overlook it, space affects us and can control our spirit; and a large part of the pleasure we obtain from architecture—pleasure which seems unaccountable, or for which we do not trouble to account— springs in reality from space. Even from a utilitarian point of view, space is logically our end. To enclose a space is the object of building; when we build we do but detach a convenient quantity of space, seclude it and protect it, and all architecture springs from that necessity. But aesthetically space is even more supreme. The architect models in space as a sculptor in clay. He designs his space as a work of art; that is, he attempts through it means to excite a certain mood in those who enter it.

What is his method? Once again his appeal is to Movement. Space, in fact, is liberty of movement. That is its value to us, and as such it enters our physical consciousness. We adapt ourselves instinctively to the spaces in which we stand, project ourselves into them, fill them ideally with our movements. Let us take the simplest of instances. When we enter the end of a nave and find ourselves in a long vista of columns, we begin, almost under compulsion, to walk forward: the character of the space demands it. Even if we stand still, the eye is drawn down the perspective, and we, in imagination, follow it. The space has suggested a movement. Once this suggestion has been set up, everything which accords with it will seem to assist us; everything which thwarts it will appear impertinent and ugly. We shall, moreover, require something to close and satisfy the movement—a window, for example, or an altar; and a blank wall, which would be inoffensive as the termination of a symmetrical space, becomes ugly at the end of an emphasized axis, simply because movement without motive and without climax contradicts our physical instincts: it is not humanized.

A symmetrical space, on the other hand, duly proportioned to the body —(for not *all* symmetrical spaces will be beautiful)—invites no movement in any one direction more than another. This gives us equipoise and control; our consciousness returns constantly to the centre, and again is drawn from the centre equally in all directions. But we possess in ourselves a physical memory of just the movement. For we make it every time we draw breath. Spaces of such a character, therefore, obtain an additional entry to our sense of beauty through this elementary sensation of expansion. Unconscious though the process of breathing habitually is, its vital value is so emphatic that any restriction of the normal function is accompanied by pain, and— beyond a certain point—by a peculiar horror; and the slightest assistance to it—as, for example, is noticed in high air—by delight. The need to expand, felt in all our bodily movements, and most crucially in breathing, is not only profound in every individual, but obviously of infinite antiquity in the race. It is not surprising, then, that it should have become the body's veritable symbol of well-being, and that spaces which satisfy it should appear beautiful, those which offend it ugly.

We cannot, however, lay down fixed proportions of space as architecturally right. Space value in architecture is affected first and foremost, no doubt, by actual dimensions; but it is affected by a hundred considerations besides. It is affected by lighting and the position of shadows: the source of light attracts the eye and sets up an independent suggested movement of its own. It is affected by color: a dark floor and a light roof give a totally different space sensation to that created by a dark roof and a light floor. It is affected by our own expectancy: by the space we have immediately left. It is affected by the character of the predominating lines: an emphasis on verticals, as is well known, gives an illusion of greater height; an emphasis on horizontals gives a sense of greater breadth. It is affected by projections— both in elevation and in plan—which may cut the space and cause us to feel it, not as one, but several. Thus, in a symmetrical domed church it will depend on the relation of the depth of the transepts to their own width, and to that of the span of the dome, whether we experience it as one space or as five; and a boldly projecting cornice may set the upward limit of space-sensation instead of the actually enclosing roof.

Nothing, therefore, will serve the architect but the fullest power to *imagine* the space-value resulting from the complex conditions of each particular case; there are no liberties which he may not sometimes take, and no "fixed ratios" which may not fail him. Architecture is not a machinery but an art; and those theories of architecture which provide ready-made tests for the creation or criticism of design are self-condemned. None the less, in the beauty of every building, space-value, addressing itself to our sense of movement, will play a principal part.

V

If voids are the necessary medium of movement, solids are the essential instrument of support; and a dependence upon physical firmness and security is not less fundamental to our nature than that instinctive need for expansion which gives value to architectural space. Any unlooked-for failure of *resistance* in tangible objects defeats the vital confidence of the body; and if this were not already obvious, the pervasive physical disquiet which the mildest tremor of earthquake is sufficient to excite, might show how deeply organized in our nature is our reliance upon the elementary stability of mass. Weight, pressure and resistance are part of our habitual body experience, and our unconscious mimetic instinct impels us to identify ourselves with apparent weight, pressure, and resistance exhibited in the forms we see. Every object, by the disposition of the bulk within its contours, carries with it suggestions of weight easily or awkwardly distributed, of pressures within itself and upon the ground, which have found—or failed to find—secure and powerful adjustment. This is true of any block of matter, and the art of sculpture is built upon this fact. But when such blocks are structurally combined, complex suggestions of physical function are involved—greater in number, larger and more obvious in scale. Architecture selects for emphasis those suggestions of pressure and resistance which most clearly answer to, and can most vividly awaken, our own remembrance of physical security and strength. In the unhumanized world of natural forms, this standard of our body is on all hands contradicted. Not only are we surrounded by objects often weak and uncompacted, but also by objects which, being strong, are yet not strong in our own way, and thus incapable of raising in ourselves an echo of their strength. Nature, like the science of the engineer, requires from objects such security and power as shall in fact be necessary to each; but art requires from them a security and power which shall resemble and confirm our own. Architecture, by the value of mass, gives to solid forms this human adequacy, and satisfies a vital instinct in ourselves. It exacts this adequacy in the detail of its decoration, in the separate elements that go to make its structure, in the structure itself, and in the total composition. The Salute at Venice—to take a single instance—possesses the value of mass in all these particulars. The sweeping movement suggested by the continuous horizontal curve of the Grand Canal is brought to rest by the static mass of the church that stands like its gate upon the sea. The lines of the dome create a sense of massive bulk at rest; of weight that loads, yet does not seem to crush, the church beneath; as the lantern, in its turn, loads yet does not crush the dome. The impression of mass immovably at rest is strengthened by the treatment of the sixteen great volutes. These, by disguising the abrupt division between the dome and church, give to the whole that unity of bulk which mass requires. Their ingenious pairing makes a perfect transition from the circular plan to the octagonal. Their heaped and rolling form is like that of a heavy substance that has slidden to its final and true adjustment. The great statues and pedestals which they support appear to arrest the outward movement of the volutes, and to pin them down upon the church. In silhouette the statues serve (like the obelisks of the lantern) to give a pyramidal contour to the composition, a line which more than any other gives mass its unity and strength. Save for a few faults of design in the lower bays, there is hardly an element in the church which does not proclaim the beauty of mass, and the power of mass to give essential simplicity and dignity even to the richest and most fantastic dreams of the baroque.

In architecture, then, the principal conditions of mass are these. In the first place the effect of the whole must predominate over that of the parts; the parts must enforce the general character of the whole and help us to realize its bulk; they must not detach themselves from the mass in such a way as to detract from its apparent unity. This, for example, is the ground of the Renaissance insistence upon crowning cornices and other devices for tying the elements of a building, and forcing it as a single impression on the eye.

Secondly, the disposition of the whole must conform to our sense of powerfully adjusted weight. Hence the careful study which the baroque architects gave to the effect of receding planes, and the influence of upward perspective upon mass. Hence also, obviously, the use of rusticated bases, battered plinths, pyramidal composition and the subordination of the Doric to the lighter Ionic and Corinthian Orders.

Finally, it is necessary that the several parts of a building should be kept in proper "scale." Scale, in any design, is that relation of ornament (or minor features) to the larger elements, which controls our impression of its size. In any building three things may be distinguished: the bigness which it actually has, the bigness which it appears to have, and the feeling of bigness which it gives. The two last have often been confused, but it is the feeling of bigness which alone has aesthetic value. It is no demerit in a building that it should fail (as St. Peter's is said to fail) to "look its size." For big things are not, as such, more beautiful than small, and the smallest object—a mere gem for example—if it satisfies the three conditions just stated, may

convey a feeling of dignity, mass, and largeness. On the other hand, a building which looks big may fail to convey a *feeling* of bigness. No one, for
instance, looking at the new Museum at South Kensington, could fail to
realize that its dimensions are vast; it looks its size. But the whole does not
predominate over the parts, the parts are many and the scale is small. Hence,
while we perceive this building to be large, it conveys a feeling not of largeness, but of smallness multiplied.

Small scale, no less than large, may be employed to emphasize effects
of mass, as, for example, when fine mouldings are used in combination with
large, unbroken surfaces. In transcribing ourselves into such a building we
instinctively take its detail as our unit of measurement, and this gives us an
increased sense of the grandeur and simplicity of the unbroken mass. Broadly
speaking the *quattrocento* architects employed this method, while the baroque architects sought to emphasize mass by the magnitude of the parts
themselves. But in both cases the conditions of success were the same: the
whole must predominate over the parts, the weight seem powerfully adjusted,
the scale be consistently maintained.

VI

The humanist instinct looks in the world for physical conditions that
are related to our own, for movements which are like those we enjoy, for
resistances that resemble those that can support us, for a setting where we
should be neither lost nor thwarted. It looks, therefore, for certain masses,
lines, and spaces, tends to create them and recognize their fitness when
created. And, by our instinctive imitation of what we see, their seeming fitness becomes our real delight.

But besides these favorable physical states, our instinct craves for order,
since order is the pattern of the human mind. And the pattern of the mind,
no less than the body's humor, may be reflected in the concrete world. Order
in architecture means the presence of fixed relations in the position, the
character and the magnitude of its parts. It enables us to interpret what we
see with greater readiness; it renders form intelligible by making it coherent;
it satisfies the desire of the mind; it humanizes architecture.

Nevertheless order, or coherence, in architecture stands on a different
plane to the values of mass, space, and line; for these, of themselves, give
beauty, while order (as was shown in the last chapter) is compatible with
ugliness. Yet it is clear that in all the architecture which descends from
Greece and Rome, order plays a principal part. What then is its place and
function?

Order—a presence of fixed ratios—will not give beauty, nor will a mixture of order and variety, but so much order, merely, and of such a kind, as is necessary for the effects which humanized mass and space and line are at any point intended to convey. Thus, in making the masses, spaces, and lines of architecture respond to our ideal movement and ideal stability, a measure of symmetry and balance are constantly entailed. Not perfect symmetry, necessarily. We in our bodies have a sense of right and left, and instinctively require that architecture should conform to this duality. Without it we could not so smoothly read or interpret architecture in our own terms. Dissymmetry in an object involves an emphasis or inclination to one side or the other in the movement it suggests, and this sometimes may be appropriate to the mood of the design. But, whenever architecture seeks to communicate the pleasure of equipoise and calm, or to impart a sense of forward, unimpeded movement, symmetrical composition and axial planning must result. Symmetry and Balance are forms of Order; but they are beautiful, not because they are orderly, but because they carry with them a movement and stability which are our natural delight. Then, since architecture is a monumental art, surrounding us with an influence never relaxed and not to be escaped, calm and unthwarted movement will here most often be desired. Thus Order, though it cannot ensure beauty, may follow in its wake.

Yet Coherence in architecture, distinct though it is from beauty, has a function of its own. Humanized mass, space, and line are the basis of beauty, but coherence is the basis of style. Mass, space, and line afford the material of individual aesthetic pleasures, of beauty isolated and detached. But architecture aims at more than isolated pleasures. It is above all else an art of synthesis. It controls and disciplines the beauty of painting, sculpture, and the minor arts; it austerely orders even the beauty which is its own. It seeks, through style, to give it clarity and scope, and that coherence which the beauty of Nature lacks. Nature, it is true, is for science an intelligible system. But the *groups* which the eye, at any one glance, discovers in Nature are not intelligible. They are understood only by successive acts of attention and elimination; and, even then, we have to supplement what our vision gives us by the memory or imagination of things not actually seen. Thus, Order in Nature bears no relation to *our* act of vision. It is not humanized. It exists, but it continually eludes us. This Order, which in Nature is hidden and implicit, architecture makes patent to the eye. It supplies the perfect correspondence between the act of vision and the act of comprehension. Hence results the law of coherence in architecture; what is simultaneously seen must be simultaneously understood. The eye and the mind must travel together; thought and vision move at one pace and in step. Any breach in continuity, whether of mood or scale, breaks in upon this easy unison and throws us back from the humanized world to the chaotic. The values of mass, space, and line are as infinite as the moods of the spirit, but they are not to be simultaneously achieved, for they are mutually conflicting. Style, through coherence, subordinates beauty to the pattern of the mind, and so selects what it presents that all, at one sole act of thought, is found intelligible, and every part re-echoes, explains, and reinforces the beauty of the whole.

Of all the styles of building that yet have been created, the forms of Greece and Rome, with those of the Renaissance after them, were in this point the most exact and strict. They are by consequence the fittest instruments for giving clarity to sharp ideas, however varied, of function and of scale. Other instruments, doubtless, there will be in the future. For if the scope of classical design could be perpetually enlarged until the eighteenth century, it is not probable that its history is closed. But first we must discard a century of misplaced logic. Architecture must be perceived sensitively but simply; the "theories" of the art have blunted sensitive perception without achieving intellectual force. Architecture that is spacious, massive and coherent, and whose rhythm corresponds to our delight, has flourished most, and most appropriately, at two periods, antiquity and the period of which antiquity became the base—two periods when thought itself was humanistic. The center of that architecture was the human body; its method, to transcribe in stone the body's favorable states; and the moods of the spirit took visible shape along its borders, power and laughter, strength and terror and calm. To have chosen these nobly, and defined them clearly, are the two marks of classic style. Ancient architecture excels in perfect definition; Renaissance architecture in the width and courage of its choice.

J. M. Richards

MODERN ARCHITECTURE*

THE GROWTH OF THE IDEA

Having indicated in the preceding chapters some of the ideas the modern architect has in his mind and some of the materials and methods he has

* From J. M. Richards' *An Introduction to Modern Architecture*, pp. 61–84. Copyright, 1953, by Penguin Books, Ltd. Reprinted by permission of Penguin Books Limited, Harmondsworth, Middlesex, England.

J. M. Richards (1907–   ), trained as an architect, became a critic and editor of various architectural journals. He has written extensively on modern architecture.

at his disposal, these being jointly responsible for the different appearance of modern architecture from that of earlier generations, we can leave it to the illustrations and the comments accompanying them to show what happens when the ideas and methods are put into practice. For the performance of architecture is infinitely more informative than any amount of theory. But before we look at some examples of recent buildings it may be interesting to see by what stages the ideas behind them gradually established themselves. The early history of modern architecture makes a revealing story, and one that throws considerable light on the present phase of its development.

Modern architecture did not spring into being all at once. It evolved gradually as it became more and more apparent that a new architecture, based on scientific progress, would satisfy modern needs, both practical and spiritual, in a way that the connoisseur's architecture of the late nineteenth and early twentieth centuries showed no capability of doing. And it did not evolve continuously. During the hundred or so years of its history, signs of its advent appeared in many forms: sometimes as new aesthetic theories, sometimes in an attempt to produce a non-period style of ornament, sometimes simply in the shape of strange new buildings belonging to no familiar school, the product of original genius that may or may not have realized the nature of the trail it was blazing. It is only in comparatively recent years that these assorted experiments and ideas have coalesced to form a recognizable movement.

We saw in Chapter II how, with the break-up of the eighteenth-century social order, a romantic movement that had started as a dilettante interest in antique and exotic motifs developed into a general revival of all historic styles; how the skilful application of these styles became the whole of architecture, the important jobs that society needed architects to perform (and hence the real architecture of the period) being done by engineers and builders. In the case of the fundamental jobs of planning, in many instances they simply were not done at all. The nineteenth century watched industry become the dominating activity in the national life of most countries without planning for its advent, and we are still suffering from that inertia to-day.

Various English architects of the early nineteenth century realized that there was something wrong, notably Augustus Welby Pugin, an architect of French descent who worked in England during the thirties and forties. His particular contribution was to realize and expound the importance of structure as the basis of architecture, and he published a book which had great influence, called *Contrasts*, comparing the spirited architecture of the mediaeval period with the hidebound academic rigidity which was all he saw in the Classic. His enthusiasm for Gothic architecture was bound up with a contemporary religious revival. He advocated a "re-Christianizing" of church architecture. Unfortunately his appreciation of Gothic architecture's structural logic ended in a devotion to the Gothic style as one on which modern buildings might be based. His own designs were something more than mere imitations, but the Gothic revival of which he was the leading exponent ended only in antiquarianism. John Ruskin, the famous critic, was another enthusiastic advocate of Gothic design, its naturalness and spiritual honesty. His writings are full of serious disquisitions on the philosophy of architecture; but his influence, too, did little more than set a fashion for particular mediaeval styles. These prophets of the Gothic Revival, however, together with Viollet-le-Duc, a French student of mediaeval life and buildings, and William Morris, whom I have already mentioned, did at least make later progress easier, as they helped to break away from the existing academic tendency to codify architectural design into a system of increasingly rigid formulae. Their limitation was that they could not visualize a new architecture that was not a return to that of some past age.

William Morris's struggle to restore the spirit of handcraftsmanship in the face of the advancing power of machinery has already been referred to. But in spite of this struggle being doomed to failure he has a very important place in the early history of modern architecture. This place is symbolized by the house at Bexley Heath in Kent, which he had built for himself in 1859. It is known as Red House, being in red brick and tile. The architect was Philip Webb, but the house probably embodies its owner's ideas just as much as it architect's. It was inspired by Morris's enthusiasm for the craftsmanship and character of humble local building, as distinct from the grandiose designs of sophisticated architects. It had many original personal touches, since Webb was an inventive artist, but in general character it might be taken for a slightly unusual farmhouse: and in its time was something quite revolutionary. Its rustic materials—local bricks, tiles, and timber—produced a sensational contrast with the prevalent Italian-style stucco villa and the fashionable architectural ornament imported from mediaeval Venice or from French chateaux.

By building in so simple a fashion Morris let a new light into the practice of architecture. He was followed by others: notably by Norman Shaw, an architect of great inventiveness, who introduced many new motifs, adapted from past styles, into nineteenth-century English architecture, but who also designed country houses in a romantic rustic manner that carried Philip Webb's experiments in local building methods and materials one stage further; and by C. F. A. Voysey, the most original yet most unassuming of all the new school of domestic architects. Voysey built a number of houses

in a purely vernacular fashion. . . . It is difficult to realize how revolutionary
such a house as the top one was in 1890. It is only a common type now
because of the influence that Voysey and his contemporaries had. Voysey
was not trying to devise a modern architecture, nor have the vernacular
buildings of this type much in common with modern architecture as we
see it to-day, but he was one of the people who made modern architecture
possible because he discarded "styles" and allowed the job to be done to be
the source of style, instead of a historical precedent or accumulation of
precedents selected by the architect. He designed in brick, stone, and white-
wash, tiles and slates and timber; directly, as a local builder might who had
also the eye of an artist to enable him to make something satisfying out of
combining his simple walls, roofs, and gables.

Voysey's style was much purer than Norman Shaw's, who, although
designing with great freedom and originality, was eclectic; that is, he used
any combination of borrowed materials and motifs that he thought helped
the effect. Though a healthy influence, his was a sophisticated architecture,
like the romantic Swedish architecture exemplified in Stockholm Town Hall
which so strongly influenced the eclectic architects of the 1930s.

Coinciding with this new domestic architecture of the 1880s and 1890s
was another sign of interest in rural simplicity: the first Garden Suburb. In
1877–80 Norman Shaw designed Bedford Park in west London, a colony
of houses placed in gardens amongst trees, and the prototype of all modern
suburbs. It is also, alas, the prototype of the endless spread-out of later
suburbs which, especially in the period between the two world wars,
strangled our towns by cutting them off from the country and nearly killed
the idea of the town as a compact aggregation of people living *together,* at
the same time killing the art of street design. But at that time it was another
breath of nature let into the artificiality of architectural fancy dress. And,
together with Ebenezer Howard's later Garden City ideals, it became even
more important as an aspect of English domestic architecture that had remarkable influence abroad.

The new English domestic style went from strength to strength. It is
only possible to mention the names of some of its leading members, who
continued the good work started by Morris, Shaw, and Voysey into the
present century: C. R. Ashbee, Baillie Scott, C. R. Mackintosh, George Walton, Ernest Newton, W. R. Lethaby, C. H. Townsend, Guy Dawber, Edwin
Lutyens. They built houses for living in, first and foremost. That is their contribution to architectural awakening. Technically of course they still used
traditional methods. This revolution in architecture, moreover, important
though it was, was confined to domestic buildings. England had to wait a

long time before a similar breath of fresh air was let into architecture generally.

Independently, throughout the nineteenth century, the engineers were also experimenting with work that in another way was to help clear the path for modern architecture itself. We have seen how in the early nineteenth century the great English railway and other engineers made the only creative use of the new materials that industry was producing. We have also seen how later in the century French engineers, particularly in the buildings they designed for the great Paris exhibitions of 1867, 1878, and 1889, showed what steel could do. In these years many notable experiments were made, especially in France, in the use of steel and concrete, but they too had little immediate effect on the design of buildings generally.

It is significant that the earliest of all these great exhibition halls was an English one, that designed to contain the Great Exhibition in Hyde Park of 1851, and christened the "Crystal Palace." It was in cast iron, not in steel, but had all the inspiring qualities of these great envelopes, which served their purpose of enclosing a huge amount of space beautifully and economically. It was designed by a gardener turned engineer, Sir Joseph Paxton, and historically is more accurately described as the last of the great engineering feats of the early nineteenth century, than as the first monument of a new era. For it set no fashion and caused no immediate revolution. It was only rediscovered as a thing of architectural significance by modern architects in later years. The exhibits it housed included perhaps the most eccentric collection of ornate but tasteless objects in the way of furniture and manufactured articles ever assembled together, and contemporary critics (with the exception of a few whom no one listened to) were blind to the building's beauty. Ruskin hated it, though it embodied a more genuine return to pure and lively structure after the Gothic spirit than anything Pugin or the Gothic Revival produced. It founded no school, yet it is important to us not only because of the simple architectural virtues it and the other great engineering works of the time can now be seen to possess, but because it was an early example of the right use of mass-production. Its whole secret as a building was that it was designed in standard parts: standard sections of cast iron and standard-size sheets of glass; and the speed and ease with which it was erected was a triumph of industrial organization—a greater triumph indeed than its design. Being the perfect prefabricated building it was equally easily taken down when the Exhibition was over and re-erected on Sydenham Hill to stand for many years as a reproach to architects who would not learn what modern industry could achieve for them.

The rustic or vernacular domestic architecture of Philip Webb, Shaw, and Voysey and the engineering triumphs fifty years earlier of Telford, Brunel, Robert Stephenson, and Paxton are the two English contributions to the growth of the modern architectural idea. After this for many years our story is set elsewhere. For in the same way that Paxton's Crystal Palace had no influence in its time, the revolutionary work of Morris and Voysey, that reached its height at the end of last century, had no influence in the country of its origin beyond its own sphere of small country and suburban houses. The development of modern architecture, though freed from stylistic routine by these pioneers, went no further in England.

On the continent of Europe, as in England, signs of a coming change in architecture appeared independently in different forms. One was a much more conscious attempt than any I have described in England to produce a style that owed nothing to the past. It started in Belgium in the eighties, in a movement led by Henri van de Velde, which began as discussion among a group of artists about structure and form being the true basis of architecture, much as Ruskin and William Morris had discussed things thirty and forty years earlier. In fact, this movement, which was known as the *Art Nouveau* movement—*Jugendstil* when it spread to Germany—was indirectly inspired by William Morris. It never got further, however, than the invention of a new kind of ornament. This consisted of an expressive and forceful use of flowing lines, generally based on plant forms, in striking contrast to the rigid geometrical forms of conventional architectural decoration. In this country the movement is best known by the drawings of Aubrey Beardsley, whose decorative style is a close equivalent to that of *Art Nouveau* decoration, though of course linear where the latter is plastic. But the *Art Nouveau* movement could never form the basis of a new architecture, as it was only concerned with *applied* ornament. Before long it degenerated into fantasy, forgot about the logic of structure—and, lacking any kind of root, died as a result of its own freedom; but it, too, introduced fresh thought of another kind into the academic sterility of most nineteenth-century architecture.

Art Nouveau had a fashionable success at the Paris Exhibition of 1900. In England it never took strong root, probably because it was not compatible with the already well established Arts and Crafts movement, the latter being based on tradition and the former on novelty. There was one exponent in England, however, of considerable importance. This was Charles Rennie Mackintosh, who worked in Glasgow during the last twenty years of the nineteenth century. He has already been mentioned as one of the pioneers of the new vernacular domestic architecture. He is still very little known in his own country, but in Scottish isolation he designed buildings of remarkable originality and having many qualities in common with modern architecture. His most famous work, the School of Art in Glasgow, began in 1898. . . . Its interior belongs to the school of *Art Nouveau*, as do the interiors he (in collaboration with George Walton) designed and furnished about the same time for a number of Glasgow teashops.

Macintosh had considerable influence all over Europe, where several exhibitions of his work were held; in fact, at this time all the English experiments already described were bearing fruit on the Continent. Von Hermann Muthesius, a German for some while resident in England, made the domestic achievements of the English architects known by publishing a book about their work, *Das Englische Haus*, in 1904, which created a sensation in Germany. The casualness and freedom of the work it illustrated, although in many ways an incidental attribute of the rural vernacular ideal, appeared as a quite inspired new architectural philosophy. For on the Continent academic architecture, tight-laced within symmetrical façades, was even more rigidly formal than in England. The Continent had not even had the benefit of the upheaval produced in England by the Gothic Revival. But the *Art Nouveau* movement, even if as a self-contained style it developed only into a rather futile ornamentalism, had prepared the ground for a freer outlook, and the influence of English domestic architecture widened its scope and put it on a more realistic basis. Germany became the center of much new architectural experiment. In 1907 Henri van de Velde had been appointed director of the Weimar School of Art. From being concerned with *Art Nouveau* furniture and decoration he turned his attention to the purification of the practical arts (including architecture) and the establishment of new values based on, among other things, the disciplines imposed by new techniques. He and his followers also produced a number of small houses that translated the still rather romantic English ideal into a more rational type. His position gave him considerable influence, and from this time the positive building up of a new architectural style may be said to date, the earlier efforts that I have described being more concerned with breaking down the false academic tradition that had driven architecture away from contemporary life.

Similar efforts were being made at the same time in America, although here the break with academic traditions was confined at first to one type of building, the multi-storey office-block, and one city, Chicago, and made no impression on architecture generally. There had, however, been one earlier pioneer who must not be left out: Henry Hobson Richardson, whole role in America lies somewhere between that of Norman Shaw in England and that of H. P. Berlage (who will be mentioned shortly) on the continent of

Europe. Richardson designed in a style reminiscent of the Romanesque, but not in a directly imitative way. He used massively modeled stone walling and semi-circular arcading to produce vigorous geometrical compositions whose sincerity did much to free American building from the trivialities of current antiquarian fashions, and he was responsible for one building, the Marshall Field store in Chicago, completed in 1887, which served more than any other single building of its time as a reminder that good architecture springs directly from honest construction.

The Marshall Field store was of solid stone, but at the time it was built the architect-engineers of Chicago were already venturing into metal-frame construction, which had previously been the subject of but tentative experiments in Britain and France. Most of the pioneer work was done by William Le Baron Jenney, whose ten-storey Home Insurance building was completed in 1885. This was followed by a number of other office buildings, nearly all likewise in Chicago, by various architects, which showed the same appreciation of the regular all-over rhythm that properly belonged to frame buildings, expressed their construction in forthright style and filled the spaces between the structural framework with large windows to let plenty of light into the offices within. The most notable of these early Chicago skyscrapers were the Leiter and Manhattan buildings (also by Jenney), the Tacoma building (by Holabird and Roche), and the Carson-Pirie-Scott department store (by Louis Sullivan).

Sullivan's work (mostly done in partnership with Dankmar Adler) was by far the greatest of any produced by the Chicago school of architects. He translated their logical practicality into an architecture of mature artistic rhythms, and his skyscrapers of the 1890s, which included also the Wainwright building at St. Louis, the Gage building at Chicago and the Bayard building at New York, were more truly modern than any other American commercial architecture until the 1930s. Sullivan was also a far-sighted architectural philosopher, who saw the architecture of the New World as something itself new in inspiration. There was indeed one moment when, through him, American architecture might have come to lead the modern world: the planning of the great Chicago Exhibition of 1893. It only needed the right kind of impetus to bring a new school of architecture into being, and Sullivan was anxious that this exhibition should provide the architectural occasion America needed. The question was debated, but the exhibition authorities decided to play safe, and selected a grandiose Roman Renaissance architectural scheme for the exhibition buildings. In Sullivan's own words spoken at the time: "thus architecture died in the land of the free and the home of the brave—in a land declaring its democracy, inventiveness, unique daring, enterprise, and progress. Thus ever works the pallid academic mind, denying the real, exalting the fictitious and false. The damage wrought by the World's Fair will last for half a century from its date, if not longer." His words came true. A pompous Classic became America's national style, coupled with that horrible invention, Collegiate Gothic, which was devised when her great educational establishments demanded a style distinct from that adopted by big business. America relapsed into the nineteenth century.

The skyscraper, the disappointing child of four grandparents: steel-frame building construction, the electric lift, high city land-values, and American belief in competitive advertisting, became for many years no more than a structural skeleton covered with stone designed in some period style —fundamentally there was no difference except one of feet and inches between the Woolworth Building and the Ritz Hotel, and sheer size, from which the skyscraper derived its impressiveness, is not an architectural virtue in itself. The achievements of American architects lay elsewhere. Surprisingly, they competed most successfully with European architects in the skill with which they used period detail for ornamental purposes. Trained in many cases, for reasons of American cultural snobbery, at the *Beaux Arts* school in Paris, American architects eclipsed their own masters in the inventiveness with which banks, libraries, and business houses were decked out with Florentine Renaissance detail, or the magnificance with which a railway terminus was furnished with the costume of an ancient Roman Bath. In the hands of such remarkable men as McKim, Mead, and White this sort of thing was done with astonishing facility; but this too, as we realize to-day, has little to do with architecture.

One man, however, stood out as an exception: Frank Lloyd Wright, the only native American architect of world significance, and a pupil of Louis Sullivan. Working in the early years of the twentieth century, at the same time as Mackintosh in Scotland, Berlage and van de Velde in northern Europe, and Otto Wagner in Vienna, he worked out quite independently an original architectural philosophy of his own, going only to the Japanese for foreign inspiration. His houses, which are mostly in or around Chicago, and of which the first was built in 1889, are most striking in being freely planned internally and lit by long horizontal windows beneath widely overhanging eaves. They bear a remarkable contrast to the rigid formal planning of most houses of the period. In other ways his actual building technique and the way he uses natural materials such as wood and stone show many ideas similar to those of William Morris's Arts and Crafts movement, yet he accepted the arrival of the machine as they had never done. Taking his inspiration from the nature of his materials, whether fashioned by hand or machine, he evolved many new and dramatic forms from them. Mistrusting academic rules and sophisticated fashions, he retained his roots in the American soil and the American pioneering tradition, always stressing the importance of a close relationship between buildings and landscape.

Arising from this was his insistence on horizontal lines. He believed that buildings whose main lines lay along the surface of the earth would preserve a proper sense of belonging to it: an idea often justified by the results, yet also typical of the mystical outlook that has coloured much of Wright's life and philosophy. His sympathetic approach to nature did not, however, make him a traditionalist; on the contrary, he showed himself a bold innovator at times. Several of his early houses, like that at Woodlawn Avenue, Chicago (1908), were directly inspired by the new potentalities of reinforced concrete; in other houses and at Midway Gardens, Chicago (1914), he based new decorative effects on the use of mass-produced concrete blocks with patterns cast in reief, and his Imperial Hotel, Tokyo (completed 1922), which had floor-slabs balanced over central supports to minimize the effect of earthquake shocks, proved a structural triumph as it was one of the few large buildings in Tokyo to survive the great earthquake of 1923.

But this is taking us ahead of our story. We shall return to Frank Lloyd Wright again. Meanwhile it must be noted that at first his work was largely ignored in his own country, though his influence on modern European architects was, and has since been, profound, the chief intermediary in the first place being the Dutch architect Berlage.

However impersonal much of it is in character, the history of the new architecture is inevitably one of personalities. The pioneer work of individuals comes first, just as the anonymous universal English style of the eighteenth century began with Sir Christopher Wren, Gibbs, Hawksmoor, and William Kent. Our story now returns to central Europe where, in the early years of the twentieth century, a number of great men were independently working their way towards the same goal. Simultaneously with van de Velde at Weimar in Germany, Otto Wagner and Joseph Hoffmann in Austria, H. P. Berlage in Holland, Hans Poelzig and Peter Behrens also in Germany, were among the most notable pioneers. In some cases the advance their work shows was only a new consciousness of the architect's freedom to design rather than imitate, or a new appreciation of simplicity and geometrical form. In others it was a more complete synthesis of means and ends that is recognizable as belonging to the same category as the modern architecture we know. A new architecture was growing up with the new century. What is more, it was at last being applied to other than domestic buildings: to factories, hospitals, schools, the very buildings that belong most typically to modern times.

The next concerted architectural movement was one of the utmost importance for similar reasons. It gave an opportunity for the new ideas to be realistically applied. This was the foundation of the *Deutscher Werkbund* in 1907. It was in a sense a development of the *Art Nouveau* movement of twenty years earlier; but instead of being a movement with all the limitations of art practiced for art's sake it was a practical attempt—the first one in history—to get modern artists used by the new industry. The *Deutscher Werkbund* was an association of craftsmen, who arranged exhibitions and studied the problems of applied design. It was therefore also related to the English Arts and Crafts movement fostered by Ruskin and William Morris, the ideals of which had been widely appreciated on the Continent, but is was also fundamentally different in accepting modern industry—that is, machine production—instead of turning its back on it.

It really established the success of the ideas it stood for when Peter Behrens, the most important of the new Continental architects, was appointed, as a result of the *Werkbund* movement, by one of the leading electrical firms in Germany, the A. E. G., both as architect *and as designer of their products,* and even their advertisements. His appointment is a landmark: once more the architect was in his rightful position as the expert on design and master of the machine.

Nevertheless, many of the most notable examples of modern design applied strictly to buildings during this period are private houses, probably because they represented the only architectural type available for free experiment. Adolf Loos, an Austrian, who lived from 1870 to 1933, may be said to be the designer of the first "modern" house, built round about 1910. . . . We have seen how the *Art Nouveau* movement, though succeeding in breaking free from the imitation of period styles, only finished by becoming another period style: architecture under its influence was as much a matter of applied ornament as ever. Loos realized this danger, that lies in all new movements, that they become only an end in themselves, and set himself against all ornament, believing that architecture sufficiently well thought-out and designed with sufficient imagination had no need to hide its form under any system of ornament. This creed, again, was not exactly new, but Loos taught it and wrote about it in terms of the conditions that prevailed in his day. The houses he built look somewhat crude to us, but they show remarkable logic and grasp of essentials. Loos, even more than van de Velde, can claim to be the link between the break-away from the old architecture and the building up of a new, without whom the latent good in the *Art*

Nouveau movement (which he himself despised) and the conscientious design revival of the *Deutscher Werkbund,* might never have been turned to architectural account. The danger against which Adolf Loos crusaded, of "modern" design becoming only another applied style, is, as I remarked in the Introduction, an even more real one to-day. The very confusion that his clear mind sought to avoid has become one of our own greatest handicaps.

Hitherto we have been discussing symptoms and trends, but in the work of Peter Behrens we find modern architecture itself. . . . The Turbo factory in Berlin, built in 1909, has been called the first piece of modern architecture. It provides a rational solution to a typically modern industrial problem; it makes logical use of modern materials such as steel and glass; it displays with a quite monumental impressiveness the power latent in the simple geometrical shapes that the return to elementary principles of form and technique produced. And it was built in the same year as Selfridge's building in Oxford Street, London. Behrens, incidentally, designed the first modern building in England: a house near Northampton which he was commissioned to design by a Mr. Bassett-Lowke in 1926.

Modern architecture had now become more conscious of itself. Instead of individuals working out ideas in isolation or in local groups as in the case of the *Deutscher Werkbund* or Joseph Hoffmann's Viennese *Sezession,* it was finding its feet as an international movement, its practitioners in different countries and in different circumstances becoming aware of each other's experiments and being influenced and stimulated by them. But it was not till after the war of 1914–18 that the new architecture attained real status. The special conditions prevalent in 1919 gave it just the stimulus it needed: a new order to be set up in accordance with a new idealism that grew out of the disillusion of the war years; a new housing problem; complete economic and industrial reconstruction, especially in Central Europe, and, again especially in Central Europe, a condition of financial stringency that encouraged strict regard for what was necessary and practical.

Before we come to this period one other contribution to history needs to be recorded. So far we have said nothing about France, except to refer to the great engineering feats that distinguished the Paris Exhibitions of 1867, 1878, and 1889, and Hennébique's experiments in reinforced concrete. France has always been remarkable for engineers of genius, at least since the great Vauban, designer of fortresses for Louis XIV; in fact most engineering and similar inventions of modern times can be traced back to French inventive genius: the motor-car largely to De Dion and Levassor, the photograph partially to Daguerre, and so on. And France can claim that she not only gave modern architecture its favorite structural material, re-inforced concrete, but showed how it should be used. It is possible that it was France's very strong academic tradition that prevented her playing an earlier part in the development of modern architecture, a tradition that remained so lively and flexible that it did not give birth to a generation of architectural revolutionaries plotting release from its fetters, as did the sterile academies elsewhere during the latter part of the nineteenth century.

It is during the first two decades of the twentieth century that modern French architects come on the scene, translating the inventions of their own earlier engineers into architectural form. Auguste Perret, in particular, designed a number of reinforced concrete buildings that have been an inspiration to the whole of Europe. His apartment house in the Rue Frank-lin, Paris, built in 1903, was the first example of reinforced concrete frame construction in architecture. His most epoch-making buildings, all in rein-forced concrete, are a garage in the Rue Ponthieu, Paris (1905), a series of dock buildings at Casablanca (1916), and a remarkable church at Le Raincy, near Paris (1925). Tony Garnier should also be mentioned, espe-cially his *Cité Industrielle,* a model town for 35,000 people designed in 1907 for construction wholly in concrete. Many of the ideas contained in it Garnier was able to realize some years later in his native city of Lille.

Thus at the end of the war of 1914–18, when new social and economic conditions were present to give a new architecture its chance, architects were already equipped with new building techniques from France, a new freedom of planning long ago established in England and America and im-ported and preserved in Germany and Austria, and in these two latter coun-tries they were even equipped with by no means tentative examples of what a new architecture might actually look like. One further influence should be mentioned, although the whole relationship between the aes-thetic ideals of architecture and the development of the other arts is too complicated to be discussed here. This is the influence of Cubism, an im-mediately pre-war movement in which painters and sculptors concerned themselves with laying bare the geometrical form and structure behind the superficial appearance of things. It is natural that architects should become involved with the ideas on which the Cubist movement was based; indeed Cubism may be said to aim at bringing out the architectural beauty, as distinct from other sources of beauty, in the forms of everything seen; but strangely, except for the single instance of Le Corbusier, whom we shall come back to later, Cubist painting was chiefly allowed to influence modern architecture by way of Holland. A group of Dutch artists, who put forward their ideas in a magazine they designed and published called *De Stijl,* was formed in 1917 under the leadership of the architect Doesberg. It included the painter Piet Mondrian and the architect Oud, and throughout the nineteen-twenties its studies of Cubism and later of abstract art did much to establish the standards of pure geometrical refinement that modern architecture could later claim to have in common with the architecture of ancient Greece and that of England in the late eighteenth century.

AFTER 1918

The last chapter outlined the growth of modern architecture until immediately after the war of 1914–18. The subsequent period has been one of increasingly rapid architectural change and development, and these are now continuing all round us. At first the most exciting developments took place in Europe, especially in France, Germany, Austria, Holland, and Switzerland. Then the Scandinavian countries joined in, and then Great Britain, the U.S.A., the South American countries, and Italy, roughly in that order.

To represent the developments characteristic of the nineteen-twenties and early nineteen-thirties—a most important formative period—it should be sufficient to say something about the work of two architects, not only because they are the two greatest that modern European architecture has produced, but because they personify two tendencies in which the trend of modern architecture between the wars can be summed up.

These two are Walter Gropius and Le Corbusier. Gropius may be said to be the senior of the two as his earliest works date from about 1911, whereas Le Corbusier is entirely a post-1918 figure. Gropius's earlier works were industrial; they carried on directly the pioneer tradition of Behrens; but his great opportunity came soon after 1919 when Germany, his native country, was undergoing internal reconstruction on a scale that needed the services of architects with far-seeing ideas and the ability to plan for actual social needs, not architects who regarded buildings merely as isolated occasions for putting into practice their personal talent for invention. In the early twenties under the German Republic many enormous housing schemes were planned, following the example of those erected by the socialist municipality of Vienna. They consisted of huge colonies, known as *Siedlungen,* usually complete with schools and shopping centres, the residential part consisting of blocks of flats well spaced apart—quite differently from the old-fashioned dark courtyard plan which has given such a bad name to large-scale official housing in many countries—and carefully aligned to make the most of the sun. The gardens between the blocks were for the common use of the tenants, though sometimes small private plots were provided as well, and each flat had a spacious balcony of the kind that is now provided for all modern flats. The numerous *Siedlungen,* notably those round the outskirts of Berlin and at Frankfurt and elsewhere, constitute one of the greatest building schemes in history, and provided wonderful experience for the modern architects to whom they were entrusted.

Gropius himself designed several of these housing schemes, but his fame chiefly rests on another achievement: the celebrated *Bauhaus* at Dessau, which was a sort of university of design. Henri van de Velde's influence as director of the Weimar Art School has already been mentioned. In 1919 Gropius was appointed to succeed van de Velde and was given the opportunity of remodeling the school according to plans of his own. In 1925 the school was moved to Dessau, where Gropius was invited by the Town Council to design a great group of buildings, including the school itself with all necessary living accommodation, a labour exchange and a housing colony. Here it flourished until the advent of the Nazi regime in 1933, when it was closed down. At the same time Gropius, who had resigned from the *Bauhaus* in 1928 to concentrate on his own housing work, left the country.

The idea on which the *Bauhaus* School was based was partly the importance of unity between all the arts and partly the importance of industrial production as the biggest factor in modern design. Gropius's aim was, in his own words, that of "realizing a modern architectural art which, like human nature, should be all-embracing in its scope. Within that sovereign federative union all the different 'arts' (with the various manifestations and tendencies of each)—every branch of design, every form of technique—could be co-ordinated and find their appointed place. Our ultimate goal, therefore, was the complete and inseparable work of art, the great building, in which the old dividing-line between monumental and decorative elements would have disappeared for ever."[1]

One means of achieving this aim was to produce in the various departments of the school a high quality of standard designs for mass production: units for prefabricated building as well as furniture, textiles, and so on, that would meet all the technical, aesthetic, and commercial demands of contemporary conditions. With this last point in view, that is, in order to keep the students of design working in relation to the machines that would have to make their products, manual instruction was the basis of tuition, "not", to use Gropius's own words again, "as an end in itself, or

---

[1] Quoted from *The New Architecture and the Bauhaus,* by Walter Gropius (translated by P. Morton Shand). London; Faber & Faber, 1935.

with an idea of turning it to incidental account by actually producing handicrafts" (this, of course, is the fundamental difference between the *Bauhaus* movement and William Morris's Arts and Crafts movement), "but as providing a good all-round training for hand and eye, and being a practical first step in mastering industrial processes. The *Bauhaus* workshops were really laboratories for working out practical new designs for present-day articles and improving models for mass production." The actual building of the new school at Dessau, in which students and teachers co-operated, was also a valuable practical experience.

The *Bauhaus* rapidly acquired wide influence, not only because designs which it produced were adopted for mass production by industrial concerns, but because it became the intellectual centre and fount of inspiration for the whole new architectural movement that was spreading fast through Central Europe. The unanswerable logic of Gropius's own ideas was supplemented by the actual work of students and teaching staff, who included some of the best artists and designers in Germany, many of whom the reputation of the *Bauhaus* had brought from other countries.

Gropius's own architecture, as exemplified in the *Bauhaus* buildings, is rational to the point of extreme—almost forbidding—severity; but so thoroughly and rhythmically planned, with every part in perfect co-ordination, as to give the whole a sort of nobility that a more fanciful style seldom achieves.

This quality of rectitude is in striking contrast to the romantic, poetic quality we find in the work of Le Corbusier. Le Corbusier is Swiss by origin and his real name is Charles Edouard Jeanneret; but he has lived so long in Paris and such a large part of his work has been done in France that he may reasonably be regarded as a French architect. The real nature of his work is the subject of much confusion, as his character as a propagandist so often seems to differ from his character as an architect. His name, because of his writings, became closely associated with the idea of "functionalism," yet his buildings are much less functionalist than those of Gropius. Similarly, his writings are full of social philosophy and of plans for a new architectural Utopia, yet Gropius's buildings did much more to relate architecture to immediate social needs, Le Corbusier's being more personal and impulsive. Although he is always true to his enthusiasm for modern technique, it has been aptly said that he designs rather than builds. His best work shows a poetic and imaginative use of geometrical forms, inspired originally by Cubism.

Another contrast that illustrates still further the conflicting yet complementary tendencies which emerged as modern architecture established itself simultaneously in different parts of the world, is the contrast between the work of Le Corbusier and that of Frank Lloyd Wright, the American architect who, as already described in the last chapter, had long been fighting a solitary battle in his own country. Wright builds consciously in sympathy with nature; Le Corbusier in defiance of it. He exploits the surprising, and at first sight unnatural, things modern construction will do. Unlike Wright, whose buildings lie close to the ground, Le Corbusier's often stand up on pillars as near as possible floating in the air, dissociated from the earth. Further, the contrasting nature of their work illustrates the two dangers that modern architecture tends to be led into. Le Corbusier's romantic geometry, disciplined by Cubism, tends to exhaust itself in sterile abstraction of form, or in a renewal of academic formulae. It has this tendency in common with the more doctrinaire modernism of the *Bauhaus* School. In contrast, Wright's more "natural" architecture tends to escape from technical and social problems into art-and-crafty idealism. The ideal of course is a fusion of these two tendencies: an architecture that is free and natural without being unworldly and in tune with the mechanical world without being inhumanly exclusive.

SELECTED BIBLIOGRAPHY

1. Sigfried Giedion, *Space, Time and Architecture*, Harvard University Press, 1941. Difficult but well worth the effort, especially as an integration of the two readings of Scott and Richards, since Giedion's book is an interpretation of architecture since the Renaissance.
2. Walter Gropius, *The New Architecture and the Bauhaus*, Faber and Faber, 1935. A presentation of the ideals and program of one of the influential schools of modern architecture.
3. Le Corbusier (C. E. Jeanneret-Gris), *Towards A New Architecture*, Payson and Clarke, 1927. A modern classic, setting forth with conviction the principles of an architecture in an age of machines.
4. Frank Lloyd Wright, *Modern Architecture*, Princeton University Press, 1931. Wright's most important statement of his organic philosophy of architecture.
5. DeWitt Parker, *The Analysis of Art*, Ch. V, Yale University Press, 1926. A fine philosophical statement of the "paradox" of architecture and utility.

SCULPTURE

The principles of sculpture have been traditionally assimilated to those of painting or architecture. Since Rodin, sculpture has effected its its independence from the other arts and has formulated its own capacities and limitations. Fundamentally, sculptors have rejected the theory that their art represents three-dimensional objects in a three-dimensional space whereas painting represents these objects in a two-dimensional space.

To illustrate this insistence upon the autonomy of sculpture, part of an essay by Herbert Read on the work of the great contemporary English sculptor, Henry Moore, is reproduced here. In this selection, Read traces the history of sculpture from its dependence on painting to its complete break from all the other arts. Sculpture, he argues, is not representation-in-space but creations of solid shapes with their inherent values of bulk, volume, and ponderability. It was Rodin, Read points out, who first stated this sculptural search for forms in his remark that a woman, a mountain, or a horse are formed according to the same principles. For Read, this search for spatial forms, conceived in terms of their corresponding materials, dominates the whole of the development of contemporary sculpture from Maillol to Gabo.

Henry Moore's own essay, "The Sculptor's Aims," which is a powerful exposition of Moore's sculpture and sculptural ideals, is included as a companion piece to Read's selection.

Herbert Read

THE ART OF SCULPTURE*

I

The art of sculpture is notoriously difficult to appreciate. To the Greeks
it was the supreme art, the one which called for the highest talent in the
artist and the subtlest sensibility in the spectator. The Renaissance, for
reasons which I shall discuss presently, depreciated sculpture and gave
the highest place to painting. Leonardo, who practiced both arts, stated
bluntly that sculpture is "less intellectual" than painting, in that it calls for
less skill in the artist. Certainly, to the Renaissance artist (and that means
to all artists for about five centuries) sculpture seemed a clumsy and inferior method *of arriving at an identical result:* the representation of natural appearances. But it was precisely the restriction of sculpture to this
aim which brought about first its supersession by the art of painting, and
then its complete degeneracy.

Painting, essentially a two-dimensional art, was for centuries dominated
by the effort to achieve tri-dimensionality—or, more strictly, an "aerial" or
spatial perspective within which tri-dimensional objects can be given a
position. Since the painter can thus within his frame control and "fix" his
conditions of lighting and atmosphere; and since he has, moreover, the
whole range of colours at his service, he can achieve an infinite number of
natural "effects" beyond the capacity of the sculptor, who is limited to a
few materials like stone, wood and metal, and has then to abandon his
completed work to a lighting and environment which he can no longer
control. It is true that a painting may equally suffer by being badly hung;
but when it is properly seen a painting, in the Renaissance conception of
art, is an extension of nature, a world into which we completely enter and
by which we are imaginatively "enclosed"; whereas a piece of sculpture is
objectively external to us, an object sharing our realistic environment. So
conscious were Renaissance artists of this supposed limitation of the art
of sculpture that they made what must be regarded as grotesque efforts to

* From Herbert Read's "Henry Moore," in *The Philosophy of Modern Art,* pp. 195–
207. Copyright, 1952, by Herbert Read. Reprinted by permission from *The Philosophy
of Modern Art* by Sir Herbert Read, Horizon Press, New York.

   Sir Herbert Read (1893–   ), English critic, poet, and essayist, is author of many
books on all phases of art, including his recent *The Art of Sculpture.*

overcome it, compelling sculpture to imitate the effects of painting as in the bronze reliefs of Ghiberti and Brunelleschi.[1]

Sculpture begins as a three-dimensional art; that is the "specialty" it shares with architecture, the art most nearly related to it. But sculpture is solid, whereas architecture is hollow. Architecture becomes more sculptural as it tends to neglect its inner spatial functions, as Greek and Egyptian architecture did. Sculpture, on the other hand, is never in any true sense architectural. That is one of the misunderstandings which has led to its undoing. Architecture must have a base—a bed or plinth from which it rises, and to which it is inevitably bound. Sculpture suffers no such necessity; it can be free, and perfectly free. The earliest known piece of sculpture, the prehistoric ivory statuette from the Grotte de Lespugue, has no base; is valid from any angle, from any point of view. Sculpture can be something to hold in the hand, or carry in the pocket, like a Japanese *netsuke*. It can hover in the air, like Barlach's war memorial at Güstrow, or rest on a pivotal point, like Brancusi's *Le Commencement du Monde*. The American sculptor Alexander Calder has perfected a form of sculpture which *moves;* proving that even in the contemporary craze for "animation" sculpture is not to be outdone by the cartoon.

The "basic" prejudice is easy to understand. The earliest types of sculpture were probably votive: symbolic figures associated with religious cults and preceding, in evolution, religious temples and monuments. But when the temple had been evolved, it was natural to associate symbolic sculpture with it, and eventually to combine the symbolic with the structural. Thus arose the caryatides or columnar figures of the Erectheion and of Chartres. But even apart from such an evolutionary explanation, it is a natural instinct to give an object a base; even a painter generally seeks his horizon line, or some reference to solid ground. The sculptor has the very practical consideration of stability; that is to say, if he is a naturalistic sculptor, and wants his figure to stand, he must replace the muscular tensions which keep the living model on its feet by a solid block of some sort to which the figure's feet are securely attached. This may seem a trivial observation, but it is a fact which has distorted the whole development of sculpture in its naturalistic phase. For the base has inevitably shifted the centre of gravity of the sculptured object; indeed, the object has in itself

---

[1] This aim is revealed very clearly in Ghiberti's own "Commentaries" which have survived in a multilated condition (see Julius von Schlosser: *Lorenzo Ghibertis Denkwurdigkeiten*, 2 vols., Berlin, 1912). The third commentary is a collection of texts on optics and perspective interspersed with Ghiberti's own observations, and the whole document, which is of outstanding importance for the early history of Renaissance sculpture, shows Ghiberti's preoccupation with securing, in sculpture, those same illusions of natural appearance which were being achieved by the painters of the time.

lost its true centre of gravity and in the physical sense becomes merely a protuberance from a substantial mound of some sort.

The art of sculpture was for centuries enslaved by this naturalism, this pinning-down to a base, to a single line of ponderation. There is no intrinsic reason for such a limitation. Sculpture is the creation of solid forms which give aesthetic pleasure. There is an infinite variety of such forms, and they arise, and are proliferated, by laws which are formal and not representational. As an art, sculpture has nothing in common with painting, and Leonardo, in comparing the two arts, was guilty of a paralogism. Nothing, in the history of art, is so fatal as the representational fallacy; nowhere, in the history of art, is that fatality so inevitable as in the evolution of sculpture. Repeatedly the art dies of this disease. It has never, hitherto, been in the power of a civilization to recover the art. An attempt is now being made.

II

That attempt began with Auguste Rodin. We do not today sufficiently appreciate the greatness of this artist. The task accomplished by his contemporaries, the great Impressionists and Cézanne, was immense; but they at least had immediate precursors, like Constable and Turner, who pointed the way. Rodin, as a sculptor, inherited a piece of waste land, and in the half-century of his active life he literally rediscovered a lost art. "I have invented nothing," he once said, "I only rediscover and it seems to be new because the aim and the methods of my art have in a general way been lost sight of. People mistake for innovation what is only a return to the laws of the great statuary of antiquity. It is true that I like certain symbols. I look at things from a symbolic point of view, but it is nature that gives me all that. I do not imitate the Greeks, but I try to put myself in the state of mind of the men who have left us the statues of antiquity. The schools copy their works, but what is of importance, is to rediscover their methods."

By rediscovering the methods of the Greek sculptors, Rodin did not mean the technical methods by which they achieved their sculptural effects; as a matter of fact, he was comparatively indifferent to these. He meant rather the attitude which the Greek sculptor had adopted to his subject. It did not seem to him that European sculpture had degenerated for lack of technical capacity or craftsmanship—there were no secrets of this kind to be rediscovered. Methods are always subordinate to aims, and it was the aims of the Greek artist which had remained such a mystery. Since the

Renaissance the aim of the artist, expressed in one word, had been *beauty;* and few people, even today, would question that aim. But Rodin saw that nothing is so fatal as to strive too directly or too officiously for an abstract quality like beauty. Beauty, he said in one of his best-known aphorisms, is not a starting-point, but a point of arrival, and that expressed the tragedy of five centuries of misdirected effort. "A thing can only be beautiful if it be true"—a fact which gives us a starting-point, not in academic rules and aesthetic abstractions, but in nature. "By following Nature one obtains everything. When I have a beautiful woman's body as a model, the drawings I make of it also give me pictures of insects, birds and fishes. That seems incredible and I did not know it myself until I found out. . . . There is no need to create. To create, to improvise, are words that mean nothing. Genius only comes to those who know how to use their eyes and their intelligence. A woman, a mountain, or a horse are formed according to the same principles."

The reader should memorize these sentences, for they are an epitome of the modern movement in sculpture, and all that one can do, by way of patient exegesis, is to show their implications, or rather, the implications of this return to a true naturalism—a naturalism of realities instead of appearances; of physics rather than of optics. On the same occasion Rodin also wrote: "I am not a dreamer, but a mathematician, and my sculpture is good because it is geometrical." He also said: "I find the cubic factor (*la raison cubique*) everywhere, so that plane and volume seem to me to be the laws of all life and all beauty." All these, and many other statements one could quote, show that Rodin had an understanding of the art of sculpture comprehensive enough to include all the developments that have taken place since his time. If his art does not satisfy us fully today, it is because he did not completely realize his own ideals. I think it would be possible to show that as a matter of fact Rodin's work somewhere or other does foreshadow all the subsequent phases of modern sculpture, but as a whole it is undoubtedly too idealistic, too symbolic, too "psychological," for the modern taste. This reaction was first represented in sculpture by Aristide Maillol, who, with specific reference to Rodin, expressed his desire for *formes plus stables et plus fermés.* The diversity of the human personality cannot, of course, be reduced to a single artistic formula, and the distinctions between "open" and "closed" form, impressionism and realism, romanticism and classicism, etc., etc., reduce in the end to differences of psychological type. All psychological types, all phenomenal variations whatsoever, are equally "natural," and the realities of art, as they must be expressed in any criticism which pretends to be more than the expression of personal prejudices, must relate to the normal, the fundamental, what Rodin called *le vrai,* rather than to the "accidentality" or "incidentality" of the formulation of such principles. The cabbage is just as natural as the crystal, and the natural laws underlying these phenomena are essentially identical. For this reason we should not make too much of the different modes of expression represented by Rodin and Maillol, or the different *methods* of expression represented by the techniques of modelling and carving.

In the too limited consideration which I gave to this problem in an earlier introduction to Henry Moore's work,[2] I hinted that the quarrel between the carvers and the modellers belonged to the sphere of ethics rather than to that of aesthetics. "Truth to material" is, of course, as much an aesthetic injunction as "truth to nature"; it is the preference for stone, as against clay, or for the chisel as against the naked fingers, which is an emotional prejudice. "The complete sculptor," I said in my first essay, "will be prepared to use every degree in the scale of solids, from clay to obsidian, from wood to steel," and that, I still think, expressed the simple truth of the matter. You might with equal justice limit the musician to an instrument like the piano-forte as the sculptor to a material like stone, or to tools like the hammer and chisel. What is important is that the effects of one set of tools on one kind of material should not be imitated in another material by another set of tools.

The modern sculptor, from Rodin onwards, was to be increasingly involved in a dilemma, but in so far as it was posed in the form of modelling versus direct cutting, it was a false dilemma. The real dilemma is illustrated clearly enough in various types of contemporary sculpture, but it was already present in Rodin's consciousness of the geometrical basis of natural forms. If we carry the analysis of nature to the limits, we are left with an antithesis which can be formulated as mind/matter, but equally as intuitive apprehension (idea) /rational measure (number), and scores of other antinomies which only represent the binomial aspects of a fundamentally isomorphic reality. The artist, in his search for a starting-point in the chaos of natural appearances, will tend to select one or the other term of the antithesis. The finishing-point is to be beauty—something not given in nature; it is a romantic prejudice to imagine that nature itself is beautiful. Beauty is a human creation. Animals have no sense of beauty; the nightingale's song is the automatic repetition of an instinctive cry. Beauty begins with intelligence. It is man's sensuous apprehension of the godlike; the result of his assumption of a *constructive* function. In nature (which is what is given to man) the artist finds measure, which is a reality he has learned

[2] London (A. Zwemmer), 1934.

to express in number. One form of art, one point of arrival in beauty, consists in the manipulation of measure, the constructive expression of numerical relationships. This point of arrival, known to the Greeks since it is obvious in their architecture and was made explicit in Plato's aesthetics, has been rediscovered in our own time; it was rediscovered by Cézanne and Seurat in painting, and by Rodin and Maillol in sculpture; it has reached its logical conclusion in that phase of modern art known as constructivism.

Another form of art, equally natural and fundamental, has its point of departure in idea, in the intuitive apprehension of the object. It does not reject measure (any more than the first mentioned point of departure ignored idea), but it prefers to follow the path indicated by organic or biological evolution. Nature has been selective in its manipulation of geometrical data; growth is not amorphous, but restricted by a limited number of physical laws. These might be called environmental laws; the laws which determine the inter-relations of chemical substances. The egg is not an arbitrary shape; it is determined, as we say, by physical laws.

The second type of artist follows a path determined by these same physical laws. His matter is moulded like the egg or the apple *in an organic fashion.*[3] The organism and the construction are two derivations from the same source; elaborations of distinct aspects of the same reality.

To prefer the organic to the constructive (the usual reaction) is merely to express a prejudice. The constructive principle, whether in architecture or in sculpture, or in any other art, is a perfectly legitimate derivation from natural premises; so is the organic principle. The most one can say is that for purely practical or functional reasons, one principle may be preferred to the other in a particular art. The constructive principle has generally seemed more appropriate to architecture, though even here the organic principle has its relevance—a fact upon which Frank Lloyd Wright has always insisted. Where a functional purpose is not in question, the choice becomes a personal one, determined by personal predilections or *tastes.* The story of modern sculpture between Rodin and Henry Moore is the story of a wholly unin-

---

[3] To be quite specific: The form of the envelope of an egg (see D'Arcy Thompson, *On Growth and Form*, p. 941, 1942 edn.) can be expressed in an equation as follows: $p_n + T (1/r + 1/r) = P$, where p_n is the normal component of external pressure at a point where r and r are the radii of curvature. T is the tension of the envelope, and P the internal fluid pressure. The artist can imagine variations in T and P and produce an object which is egg-like to the extent that represents the same equation with different 'values'. This is the 'organic' type of art. But the artist might also accept the given values of this equation in a particular egg and use the numerical proportions he thus derives from nature in the construction of entirely different forms—the body of an aeroplane, for example or a purely imaginary or non-functional object. It is really a choice between applying the values of a particular formula, or varying the values of a general formula. It is only necessary to add that the artist, even if he is a constructivist, proceeds by intuitive rather than calculative methods.

telligent strife between these two principles—a strife which sometimes takes place within the conscience of the artist. Brancusi,[4] Archipenko, Lipchitz, Laurens, Duchamp-Villon, Giacometti, Arp, Schlemmer, Tatlin, Pevsner, Gabo and Barbara Hepworth are the names of some of the participants in this confused movement, from which, however, the antithesis of organic and constructive does finally emerge in all its clarity and inevitability.

I have explained the scientific justification for both terms of the antithesis, but in the appreciation of art we tend to dispense with theory, and rely on the obvious and apparent differences. No one is likely to confuse the "constructive" with the "organic" if faced with typical examples of both types of art; and however much we may insist that the constructive work is no less justified in nature than the organic work, there will always be a tendency to associate the organic with the vital and therefore with the human. We have seen that constructive elements underlie all natural phenomena; that organic growth follows laws, and involves structures, which are as geometrical, or mathematical, as anything created by a constructive artist. Everything, in the world of human thought and invention, is in some sense "organic"—everything, in human physique and natural organisms, is in some sense "constructive." The division which used to be made between the organic and the inorganic in science has been abandoned by science itself, but nevertheless a distinction which is popularly associated with the phenomenon of "life" does exist, and Henry Moore himself has suggested that *vital* rather than "organic" might therefore be a better word to describe the art which is the antithesis of constructivism. But vital is also an ambiguous word, for we are apt to call anything vital which forcibly impresses our senses. Our whole language is riddled with analogies and metaphors drawn from the organic world, and it is almost impossible to speak and make one's self understood about motor cars, for example, and machines generally, without drawing on such a vitalistic vocabulary. Constructive art is often associated with the machine; nevertheless, in describing its qualities of

[4] Brancusi has a special place in the movement, a position of relatively serene detachment. Henry Moore has paid his own tribute to this sculptor: "Since Gothic, European sculpture had become overgrown with moss, weeds—all sorts of surface excrescences which completely concealed shape. It has been Brancusi's special mission to get rid of this overgrowth, and to make us once more shape-conscious. To do this he has had to concentrate on very simple direct shapes, to keep sculpture, as it were, one-cylindered, to refine and polish a single shape to a degree almost too precious. Brancusi's work, apart from its individual value, has been of great historical importance in the development of contemporary sculpture. But it may now be no longer necessary to close down and restrict sculpture to the single (static) form unit. We can now begin to open out. To relate and combine together several forms of varied sizes, sections and direction, into one organic whole" (*The Painter's Object*, p. 23). These last two sentences define precisely enough the difference between the stages of historical development represented by Brancusi and Moore.

movement and rhythm, we are compelled in just the same way to rely on a vitalistic vocabulary. The constructive artist himself, seeking for a word to describe his creation, will often choose a word from the vocabulary of the organic world.

What still remains to be explained is why the artist who frankly resorts to vital or organic forms, does not literally reproduce them, but recombines them or distorts them in an apparently wilful manner.

I think the answer to this important question (which refers directly to the work of Henry Moore) involves something more than aesthetics. It involves a certain philosophy of life. Modern civilized man regards that faculty which attributes spiritual or vital qualities to inanimate objects as the mark of a primitive stage in human development; and it would be a mistake to identify modern art with any revival of such "animism." But modern man at his most "civilized" (the modern scientist) has restored a degree of animation to matter, which a short time ago was regarded as merely inert. Common sense still maintains a strict division between the quick and the dead, even between things which wax and wane and things which merely accrete and erode. But if we require monuments, stable symbols, to represent our religious or emotional ideas, it no longer seems either necessary or appropriate to choose anthropomorphic forms. The mystery of life is too ubiquitous, too diffused, too cosmic to be subordinate to such human vanity and egocentricity. Some part of our life is superpersonal, even if it is not transcendental, and this collective unconscious, as the psychoanalysts have called it, is best represented by images from the same region of our mental personality. How these images arise in the consciousness of the artist is a problem perhaps unsolvable, and certainly outside the scope of this essay.

Henry Moore, in common with artists of his type throughout the ages, believes that behind the appearance of things there is some kind of spiritual essence, a force or immanent being which is only partially revealed in actual living forms. Those actual forms are, as it were, clumsy expedients determined by the haphazard circumstances of time and place. The end of organic evolution is functional or utilitarian, and, spiritually speaking, a blind end. It is the business of art, therefore, to strip forms of their casual excrescences, to reveal the forms which the spirit might evolve if its aims were disinterested.

But there is still a choice before such an artist. He may, for example, imagine that all forms should strive towards one canon of form, which he will call beauty, and all his efforts will be directed towards reducing the forms of nature to this one type. Such was the classical ideal of art, and we must remember that this ideal also represents a distortion of actual appearances. It is only because we have become so habituated to such types as late Greek sculptors evolved that we do not realize how far they actually depart from the casual forms of nature. The acanthus motive, for example, is so stylized that scholars actually cannot agree as to which particular plant it was based on. In the decadent period of Greek sculpture (by which I mean anything later than about 500 B.C.) there seems to have been an attempt to reduce the canon of beauty to rigid laws of geometric proportion, and these laws were revived in the Renaissance period. But an artist like Henry Moore regards such a procedure as merely escaping from one kind of false imprisonment (truth to appearance) to another kind of false imprisonment (truth to type). The kind of fidelity he seeks is of an altogether different kind.

It is a kind of fidelity represented by Greek sculpture before 500 B.C. by certain kinds of Egyptian sculpture and very definitely by Mexican sculpture of the Aztec period, but perhaps originally and with the greatest sureness by early Chinese sculpture and by the long tradition which spread from the East and permeated the North and West known to art historians as the Animal Style. It is so called because it finds its most characteristic expression in the representation of animal forms. In such representations there is no attempt to conform with the exact but casual appearances of animals; and no desire to evolve an ideal type of animal. Rather from an intense awareness of the nature of the animal, its movements and its habits, the artist is able to select just those features which best denote its vitality, and by exaggerating these and distorting them until they cohere in some significant rhythms and shape, he produces a representation which conveys to us the very essence of the animal. The same significant vitality is developed, perhaps from the same origins, by the Romanesque and Gothic sculptors of Northern Europe.

It is from such a point of view that we must approach the sculpture of Henry Moore. But since we live in a much more complicated age than, say, that of the nomad tribes of Central Asia, we must expect in a modern sculptor reactions more complicated than any found in the sculpture of the Animal Style. In modern Europe we cannot avoid certain humanitarian preoccupations. We live in cities, and even in the country animals no longer play a predominant part in our economy. The modern sculptor, therefore, more naturally seeks to interpret the human form; at least, this has been the normal tendency of sculptors for many centuries, and in this respect Henry Moore is normal. In his case the tendency has been modified by a desire to relate the human form to certain universal forms which may be found in nature—an aspect of his work which I will deal with presently. But first I wish to emphasize the fact that Henry Moore's sculpture, like that of his great predecessors, is based primarily on the close observation and study of the human form. As a student he drew and modelled from life for many years, and he still periodically returns to life drawing. It is so important to stress this fact, that I would like to quote his own words to me:

"Every few months I stop carving for two or three weeks and do life drawing. At one time I used to mix the two, perhaps carving during the day and drawing from a model during the evening. But I found this unsatisfactory—the two activities interfered with each other, for the mental approach to each is different, one being objective and the other subjective. Stone as a medium is so different from flesh and blood that one cannot carve directly from life without almost the certainty of ill-treating the material. Drawing and carving are so different that a shape or size or conception which ought to be satisfying in a drawing will be totally wrong realized as stone. Nevertheless there is a connection between my drawings and my sculpture. Drawing keeps one fit, like physical exercises—perhaps acts like water to a plant—and it lessens the danger of repeating oneself and getting into a formula. It enlarges one's form repertoire, one's form experience. But in my sculpture I do not draw directly upon the memory or observations of a particular object, but rather use whatever comes up from my general fund of knowledge of natural forms."

That is to say, the artist makes himself so familiar with the ways of nature—particularly the ways of growth— that he can out of the depth and sureness of that knowledge create ideal forms which have all the vital rhythm and structure of natural forms. He can escape from what is incidental in nature and create what is spiritually necessary and eternal.

But there is just this difficulty; most of the forms of natural growth are evolved in labile materials—flesh and blood, tender wood and sap—and these cannot be translated directly into hard and brittle materials like stone and metal. Henry Moore has therefore sought among the forms of nature for harder and slower types of growth, realizing that in these he would find the forms *natural* to his carving materials. He has gone beneath the flesh to the hard structure of bone; he has studied pebbles and rock formations. Pebbles and rocks show nature's way of treating stone—smooth sea-worn pebbles reveal the contours inherent in stones, contours determined by variations in the structural cohesion of stone. Stone is not an even mass, and symmetry is foreign to its nature; worn pebbles show the principles of its asymmetrical structure. Rocks show stone torn and hacked by cataclysmic forces, or eroded and polished by wind and rain. They show the jagged rhythms into which a laminated structure breaks; the outlines of hills and mountains are the nervous calligraphy of nature. More significant still are the forms built up out of hard materials, the actual growth in nature of crystals, shells and bones. Crystals are a key to geometrical proportions assumed naturally by minerals, whilst shells are nature's way of evolving hard hollow forms, and are exact epitomes of harmony and proportion. Bones combine great structural strength with extreme lightness; the result is a natural tenseness of form. In their joints they exhibit the perfect transition of rigid structures from one variety of direction to another. They show the ideal torsions which a rigid structure undergoes in such transitional movements.

Having made these studies of natural form (and always continuing to make them) the sculptor's problem is then to apply them in the interpretation of his mental conceptions. He wishes to express in stone his emotional apprehension of, say, the human figure. To reproduce such a figure directly in stone seems to him a monstrous perversion of stone, and in any case a misrepresentation of the qualities of flesh and blood. Representational figure sculpture can never be anything but a travesty of one material in another—and actually, in most periods, sculptors have tried to disguise the stony nature of their representations by painting or otherwise colouring their statues. It is only in decadent periods that the aim has persisted of trying to represent the qualities of flesh in natural stone. *The aim of the sculptor like Henry Moore is to represent his conceptions in the forms natural to the material he is working in.* I have explained how by intensive research he discovers the forms natural to his materials. His whole art consists in effecting a credible compromise between these forms and the concepts of his imagination. A similar aim has characterized all the great periods of art; a confusion arises when we seek to identify this aim with a particular ideal of beauty. Henry Moore has dared to say that beauty, in the usually accepted sense of the term, is not the aim of his sculpture. As already noted, he substitutes the word *vitality*. The distinction is so important for an understanding of his work, and, indeed, for an understanding of many phases of modern art, that his words should be carefully pondered:

> For me a work must first have a vitality of its own. I do not mean a reflection of the vitality of life, of movement, physical action, frisking, dancing figures and so on, but that a work can have in it a pent-up energy, an intense life of its own, independent of the object it may represent. When work has this powerful vitality we do not connect the word beauty with it.
>
> Beauty, in the later Greek or Renaissance sense, is not the aim of my sculpture.
>
> Between beauty of expression and power of expression there is a difference of function. The first aims at pleasing the senses, the second has a spiritual vitality which for me is more moving and goes deeper than the senses.

Because a work does not aim at reproducing natural appearances it is not, therefore, an escape from life—but may be a penetration into reality, not a sedative or drug, not just the exercise of good taste, the provision of pleasant shapes and colours in a pleasing combination, not a decoration to life, but an expression of the significance of life, a stimulation to greater effort of living.[5]

These are the words of an artist—an artist who has had no truck with metaphysics or aesthetics, an artist who speaks directly out of experience. But they point with precision to the crux of a great debate which extends far beyond our immediate subject. The terms of the debate need careful definition, but obviously the whole scope of art is altered if you make it, instead of the more or less sensuous symbolization of intellectual ideals, the direct expression of an organic vitalism. No doubt intellectual elements will enter into the choice and elaboration of the images which the intellect selects to represent its ideals; but the difference is about as wide as is humanly possible.

Henry Moore

THE SCULPTOR'S AIMS*

Each sculptor through his past experience, through observation of natural laws, through criticism of his own work and other sculpture, through his character and psychological make-up, and according to his stage of development, finds that certain qualities in sculpture become of fundamental importance to him. For me these qualities are:

Truth to material. Every material has its own individual qualities. It is only when the sculptor works direct, when there is an active relationship with his material, that the material can take its part in the shaping of an idea. Stone, for example, is hard and concentrated and should not be falsified to look like soft flesh—it should not be forced beyond its constructive build to a point of weakness. It should keep its hard tense stoniness.

Full three-dimensional realization. Complete sculptural expression is form in its full spatial reality.

Only to make relief shapes on the surface of the block is to forgo the full power of expression of sculpture. When the sculptor understands his

[5] *Unit One,* p. 30 (1934).

* From Henry Moore's "The Sculptor's Aims," from Herbert Read (ed.), *Unit One.* Copyright, 1934, by Henry Moore. Reprinted by permission of the author.

Henry Moore (1898-   ) is the great contemporary English sculptor.

material, has a knowledge of its possibilities and its constructive build, it is possible to keep within its limitations and yet turn an inert block into a composition which has a full form-existence, with masses of varied size and section conceived in their air-surrounded entirety, stressing and straining, thrusting and opposing each other in spatial relationship—being static, in the sense that the center of gravity lies within the base (and does not seem to be falling over or moving off its base)—and yet having an alert dynamic tension between its parts.

Sculpture fully in the round has no two points of view alike. The desire for form completely realized is connected with asymmetry. For a symmetrical mass being the same from both sides cannot have more than half the number of different points of view possessed by a non–symmetrical mass.

Asymmetry is connected also with the desire for the organic (which I have) rather than the geometric.

Organic forms, though they may be symmetrical in their main disposition, in their reaction to environment, growth and gravity, lose their perfect symmetry.

Observation of natural objects. The observation of nature is part of an artist's life, it enlarges his form-knowledge, keeps him fresh and from working only by formula, and feeds inspiration.

The human figure is what interests me most deeply, but I have found principles of form and rhythm from the study of natural objects such as pebbles, rocks, bones, trees, plants, etc.

Pebbles and rocks show nature's way of working stone. Smooth, sea-worn pebbles show the wearing away, rubbed treatment of stone and principles of asymmetry.

Rocks show the hacked, hewn treatment of stone, and have a jagged nervous block rhythm.

Bones have marvellous structural strength and hard tenseness of form, subtle transition of one shape into the next and great variety in section.

Trees (tree trunks) show principles of growth and strength of joints, with easy passing of one section into the next. They give the ideal for wood sculpture, upward twisting movement.

Shells show nature's hard but hollow form (metal sculpture) and have a wonderful completeness of single shape.

There is in nature a limitless variety of shapes and rhythms (and the telescope and microscope have enlarged the field) from which the sculptor can enlarge his form-knowledge experience.

But besides formal qualities there are qualities of vision and expression:

Vision and expression. My aim in work is to combine as intensely as possible the abstract principles of sculpture along with the realization of my idea.

All art is an abstraction to some degree: (in sculpture a material alone forces one away from pure representation and towards abstraction).

Abstract qualities of design are essential to the value of a work, but to me of equal importance is the psychological, human element. If both abstract and human elements are welded together in a work, it must have a fuller, deeper meaning.

Vitality and power of expression. For me a work must first have a vitality of its own. I do not mean a reflection of the vitality of life, of movement, physical action, frisking, dancing figures and so on, but that a work can have in it a pent-up energy, an intense life of its own, independent of the object it may represent. When a work has this powerful vitality we do not connect the word Beauty with it.

Beauty, in the later Greek or Renaissance sense, is not the aim in my sculpture.

Between beauty of expression and power of expression there is a difference of function. The first aims at pleasing the senses, the second has a spiritual vitality which for me is more moving and goes deeper than the senses.

Because a work does not aim at reproducing natural appearances it is not, therefore, an escape from life—but may be a penetration into reality, not a sedative or drug, not just the exercise of good taste, the provision of pleasant shapes and colours in a pleasing combination, not a decoration to life, but an expression of the significance of life, a stimulation to greater effort in living.

SELECTED BIBLIOGRAPHY

1. Auguste Rodin, *Art.* (Any edition.) Still an excellent statement of the aims and principles of sculpture by the French master.
2. Bruno Adriani, *Problems of the Sculptor,* Nierendorf Gallery, 1943.
3. Agnes Rindge, *Sculpture,* Payson and Clarke, 1929. A standard work in the field.
4. Herbert Read, *The Art of Sculpture,* Pantheon Books, 1955. Read's National Gallery Lectures on sculpture as an art of "touch-space."

DANCE

The "poetics" of the dance is stated clearly and fully in a number of recent books. Here two selections from one of these books, John Martin's *An Introduction to the Dance,* are reprinted.

As dance critic of *The New York Times* for many years, Martin has been very much concerned with the principles of the modern dance. In his first selection, he elucidates the view that dance is basically an art of space, time, and dynamics, worked out through organized bodily movements with their own implications of mood, purpose, function, and emotion. In the second selection he illustrates these principles in a sensitive analysis of and tribute to the dance of Mary Wigman, a genius of the modern movement.

John J. Martin

THE ELEMENTS OF THE DANCE*

THE CHARACTER OF MATERIALS

As in any other art or craft, the nature and behavior of materials in the dance amount to inherent laws. Though the dancer makes some use of music, costume, architecture, acting, the painter's sense of color in decor and lighting, and in a small way even poetry where his titles are concerned, the actual stuff in which he works is movement.

* From Martin: *An Introduction to the Dance,* pp. 61–71; 230–236. Copyright, 1939, by W. W. Norton & Company, Inc. Reprinted by permission of W. W. Norton & Company, Inc.

John J. Martin (1893–   ) is the famous dance critic of *The New York Times.*

All motion exists in the three dimensions of space, time and dynamics, and these must be considered not alone in their separate characters but also in the fusions and overlappings which give rise to such secondary phenomena as rhythm and phrasing, sequence and counterpoint. First, however, it is necessary to realize that dance employs a particular type of motion which affects all calculations. An inanimate object may be in motion if it is dropped or hurled or pushed, but the dance deals with the animate human body, not merely tossed about through the application of outside force, but in motion through its own volition. In other words, the body *moves,* whereas inanimate objects *are moved.* This obviously puts a definite color of motivation upon every phase of activity in any of the three dimensions of motion— upon direction, for example, and speed, and gradations of energy. Ultimately, it is true, all the other arts have similar demands to meet, and none of them can permit unmotivated and arbitrary lines, sounds, colors, masses. The dance, however, works in the most personal of all mediums, and the body that is seen making arbitrary and unmotivated movements is more than likely either to be unintelligible or to present a picture of insanity, since the normally co–ordinated human being does not make functionless movements in life. "Pure" form and "pure" line become therefore manifestly impossible in the dance, for in any movement or posture, however based merely on laws of design, there is bound to be an implication either of motivation or else of the inco-ordinations of mental unbalance.

This is perhaps the cardinal consideration in the approach to dance composition, namely, that movement of whatever kind carries within itself the implications of mood, purpose, function, emotion. The dancer does not work with an objective instrument like a piano or a palette of colors; he is himself the instrument. This makes it impossible for him to escape from connotations of the realism of human behavior, even though as a dancer he necessarily departs from representationalism and all possible suggestion of pantomime. Thus, if he extends his leg so that his foot is higher than his head and sustains the position long enough (certainly an attitude without representational implications) he will most probably evoke applause from an audience; not because he has awakened any sense of abstract beauty by the obtuse angle he has formed, but because the muscular strain (a recognizable part of human behavior) which he has been able to withstand has surpassed normal endurance and his feat has been admired. The same thing will happen if he makes a great many turns at a great rate of speed, or performs any other series of extraordinarily rapid or manifestly difficult movements which in themselves are not expressive and might be counted on to function simply as elements of pure decoration or geometrics of motion. A succession of movements of this sort can become extremely exciting to an audience, by the evocation of sympathetic muscular experience, and it will sooner or later have to find a vent for its synthetically stirred–up state by shouting and beating its hands together. The niceties of pure aesthetic design, however, will have counted for little or nothing if, indeed, they have chanced to be present; the link exists in the connotations, however remote, of human behavior. The body is totally incapable of becoming an abstraction itself or of producing movement that is abstract in the sense of divorced from behavior.

It is easy to see how this situation affects the dance composer's dimensions of space, time and dynamics. His use of them is dictated first of all by the character of what he has to say and not by any extraneous principles of design. That there is another factor that tends to exert pressure upon him in the opposite direction we shall see in a moment, but it can safely be stated that the content of a work of art is the primary determinant of its form, just as water, sand, coal, milk and the uses to which they are put, determine the shape and texture of vessels suitable to contain them.

The dance is the only art that makes equal use of space, time and dynamics, but it is, of course, impossible to consider it as consisting of elements of space plus elements of time plus elements of dynamics, for they are not separable. It is possible, however, for the sake of analysis to consider the whole from the point of view of one of these aspects at a time.

Spatial problems have been treated most cavalierly by composers in general; it has frequently been thought quite enough to keep the face toward the audience and to balance a sortie to the right with a sortie to the left. Instinctively the better composers have discovered other and more respectable devices from time to time, but not until the advent of Rudolf von Laban with his theory, and more particularly Mary Wigman with her incomparable practice, was the subject of space given the attention it deserves.

By the dancer's prevailing awareness of the space in which and through which he moves, he relates himself consciously and visibly to his environment, and not only to the physical aspects of that environment but also to its emotional overtones. He places himself, as it were, in his universe, recognizing the existence of outside forces, benign and hostile. The dancer, on the other hand, who lacks this consciousness of the immediate world that surrounds him must necessarily concentrate on the exploitation of his person and his skills.

On this basis a wholly spectacular department of the dance has been built up, ranging from the bald exhibition of an ego in a vacuum to the development in the academic ballet of an exquisitely classic art. Following the line of classic practice in general, this departs by intention from the main stream of the dance as a biological phenomenon, so to speak, and sets up a self-contained existence upon the premise of an invented code of laws, quite unrelated to natural impulse and subjective experience and in no wise concerned with the illumination of man's relation to man or to his universe. Being thus cut off from the parent body of the dance, it is affected only in part by the operation of its laws. There is perhaps no more crucial point of division than that arising out of the spatial issue.

The pervasive presence of space, nevertheless, is the dancer's native realm, in much the same sense that air is the bird's or water the fish's, and it makes imperious demands upon both the performer and the composer. For the latter there is first of all the question of the amount of space to be employed and its character. Some compositions involve the extensive traversing of ground up to the utilization of the whole area available, while others unfold without change of base, that is, with the dancer remaining virtually in one spot. Because of the spatial values in the dance, stage setting and lighting assume a closer integrality with the composition itself than in other types of theatrical production. Here they do not serve merely as decoration or as descriptive place backgrounds, but take on the functional responsibilities of defining and delimiting the dancer's working area. Platforms, steps, ramps, pedestals and other structural forms are made to serve variously to break up a perhaps too monotonous expanse of merely empty stage with points of orientation, to afford areas where sheer height is available, to provide levels of contrasting elevation and different modes of access to them. Light can be used to restrict area and to increase it at will, to establish localized areas of different quality and accent, to cut off or to accentuate height, to blot out all tangible background and suggest limitless range.

These synthetic controls of space must, of course, be completely under the direction of the composer, who knows when he needs artificial elevation, points of orientation and constriction of expansion of working area. In the hands of stage designers working independently, they can become ruinous examples of mere visual ingenuity, impeding movement and throwing their own formal intentions athwart the dancer's design. The first important developments in this auxiliary branch of dance production were made in the years just before the World War by Appia, Salzman and Dalcroze in Hellerau, but little was done afterwards until Arch Lauterer turned his attention to the subject at the Bennington Festivals and produced for Hanya Holm's "Trend" in 1937 the first truly collaborative and functional stage setting for the dance to be seen in America.

But to return to the specific concern of the composer. Once the working area has been determined, there arise considerations of the possible disposition of the figure in the space available. It will achieve varying degrees of emphasis by being placed in the center of the area or at one side, forward or back; by clinging to the perimeter or by using the free body of the stage. In the matter of direction of movement, the forward and backward, the sideward, the diagonal, the curvilinear path, the broken line of progress, the turn in place, the shift of direction, all have definite values of their own.

Then there are the manifest differences of implication in the vertical aspects of the body—when it is seated or kneeling or lying on the ground, when it is crouching or stooped, when it is upright, when it is elevated upon the toes, when it is leaping into the air, and when it is falling. None of these things is a matter of free choice or pure invention for the creative choreographer, but will evolve for him in the main out of inner impulsion.

Also touching in a measure upon the category of space problems is the consideration of whether the movement of the individual is simple, as when the entire body unites in the performance of a single action, or complex, as when parts of the body move in opposition to each other. When this essential problem is increased in dimensions, with different dancers, instead of different parts of the same body, working in opposition to each other, there can be no question that space problems are involved, for here we have a definite instance of spatial counterpoint. With a composition involving more than one dancer, all space relations are intensified. Aside from the subtleties and the selective aspects of composition, it becomes necessary at once to guard against such major dangers as simple confusion in which some figures interfere with the activity of others and nothing emerges with clarity. It is manifestly impossible to move a stageful of dancers always in uniform mass, and the evolving of simultaneous patterns in space necessitates the careful maintenance of relationships so that emphasis falls only where it should for the adequate development of the central plan. The cardinal issue here is how much the spectator can be counted upon to perceive; and of that, more later.

All these problems of space involve elements of time as well, for manifestly it is impossible to move through space without occupying time. Thus the number and variety of impressions made by spatial conduct are increased in geometrical proportion by the added consideration of their time aspects.

With such elementary matters as speed and slowness, gradual accelerations and retardations, or sudden shifts in the rate of movement there are no bewilderments. It is when we approach more complicated involve-

ments in which time and dynamics are concerned together that difficulties
appear. This is the category in which the vexed subject of rhythm exists,
with its corollaries, phrasing and sequential development. Indeed, as soon
as rhythm is mentioned, we are likely to find ourselves enveloped in as
dense a fog of mysticism and vagueness as that which beclouds the subject of
form itself.

It is wise when considering rhythm in the dance to put aside all
preconceptions deriving from musical rhythm. The latter, it is true, originates
at the same source, namely, the natural movement of the body, but as
music has been developed as an absolute art, its relation to bodily experience has become increasingly attenuated until in many instances it approaches the point of disappearance.

All rhythms are products of dynamics, concerned only incidentally
with time. They consist basically of the alternations of accent and unaccent;
the time element enters only with the periodicity of the alternations.

Bodily rhythms are made up of the successive contractions and relaxations of muscles. The most persuasive of them, because they are continuous,
organic, generally regular, and above all, because we are aware of them,
are the pulse of the blood and the process of breathing. Against these as a
background, we are inclined subconsciously to measure all other rhythms,
phrasings and tempos.

Walking, hammering and similar repetitive activities are readily seen
to be rhythmic successions of contractions and relaxations, fairly simple in
character. Any movement is rhythmic, however, even though there is not
such a marked contrast between its strong and weak elements, if it maintains
a comfortable alternation of contractions and relaxations. It is not necessary for the two elements to be of equal duration, for this is frequently not
the case even in movements that appear to be regular, like breathing.

Rhythm in the dance, being merely a concentrated adaptation of the
rhythms of the body, is similarly based on alternation and recurrence, but
it need not therefore be the monotonous succession of single units like the
action of hammering. Once the presence of a periodic dynamic alternation
has been established, almost limitless variations may be played upon it. The
pattern of each variation may then be set up as a larger rhythmic unit in
itself, namely, the phrase, to be subjected in turn to alternation and recurrence. Variations, to be sure, cannot be arbitrary, for it is perhaps necessary
to repeat that the dancer cannot dodge the responsibility for setting up
implications of function and intention by whatever he does. The larger
rhythmic unit, the motor phrase, must therefore have some organic logic
about its development. If the motor phrase were subjected to definition it

would probably be described as a succession of movements from a common impulse, not necessarily sufficient to constitute a complete statement of action but containing either the introduction of a theme or a response to such a theme already introduced.

To illustrate, it might consist, let us say, of some such elements as a sequence of steps to the front ending with one foot raised, while the arms complete a wide circle upwards. Or perhaps in a more clearly functional manifestation, it might be made up of an initial movement which tends to throw the body out of equilibrium and those succeeding movements in the course of which equilibrium is restored. In any case, the series of movements would necessarily have a characteristic pulse, though they need not inevitably be evenly spaced or timed, and would possess a unity that set them apart from what had been done previously or what was to follow. This unity would be the natural outcome of the fact that the phrase was the result of a single impulse, a single motor idea, so to speak.

There is no prescribed length for a motor phrase nor any fixed regulation as to how much material it must contain. A complete statement of action comparable to a sentence in rhetoric or a period in music may demand several phrases, consisting not only of a subject and a response but perhaps also of the introduction of new subjects before the first has been resolved. The content of the projected work is the sole arbiter. Thus we are led at once into the matter of sequential development, and a composition is seen to be built up by the juxtaposition of motor phrases.

In dance rhythms and phrases, time will play the smallest conscious part, and the spectator will be aware of them chiefly in terms of recurrent spatial patterns with dynamic variations. Dynamism, indeed, is the heart and soul of rhythm and the vitalizer of the whole art. All movements exist between the extremes of complete tension and complete relaxation, and dance composition concerns itself accordingly not only with the distribution of movement through space and time, but also with the amount of movement to be utilized. As music consists of a continuous stream of sound—punctuated by brief pauses and modified in pitch, speed and intensity, but still a continuous stream—so dance consists of a continuous stream of movement, similarly modified. Spasmodic bursts of movement scattered through space no more constitute a dance than separate bits of marble scattered through space constitute a sculpture. A unity of substance, a continuum, so to speak, is required, which in the dance consists of a sustained muscular tone, a heightened dynamic state, which is never allowed to lapse, though it is constantly varied, until the dance is over.

This dynamic continuum is primarily a matter of quantity determining whether dance movement exists at all and in what degree, but its variations constitute that aspect of movement which we call quality. In the field of comparative intensities lie all increases and diminutions of force, all degrees of sharpness of attack, rigidity and fluidity, gradations of accent and un-accent, flexions, extensions, and rotations, leaps and falls, devitalization and rest.

MARY WIGMAN

It is not until after the war that the expressional dance enters a new phase and finds itself labeled as "modern." Just as an earlier day prepared the ground for Isadora [Duncan], with a return to fundamentals as its drive, now Mary Wigman was the product of a time when these newly revealed fundamentals were being whipped into form. "Without ecstasy," she has written, "there is no dance." But with the economical, organic, functional attitude which modernism takes toward the subject of form, what was demanded for the dance was not merely something to contain its ecstasy, but something to embody it. The materials of which it was made, in other words, must be allowed to externalize its subjective concepts accord-ing to the laws inherent in their own natures.

Rudolf von Laban had already formulated an analytical approach to dance in which the body's relations to the space about it were exhaustively examined. It was seen that the structure of the various members and the resultant types, directions and extents of movement possible for them, set up the immediate sphere of a dancer's movement in an imaginary ico-sahedron, with its various lines and planes. These dimensions and directions, however, were not ends to be sought, in any way comparable to the prescrip-tions of the academic ballet, but constituted only a summing up of all pos-sible spatial and directional possibilities. The dancer's movement was predicated entirely upon an inward will to move, which determined all the aspects of his motor performance.

For Wigman, however, such unexceptionable reasoning dramatized itself emotionally, and space assumed definite entity, almost as a tangible presence in every manifestation of movement. As man and his environment interact upon each other, shaping and altering each other's character and destiny, so movement and its environment, space, interact, and the resultant is dance. The dancer, therefore, is no longer an ego in a Vacuum, so to speak, but an epitome of the individual in his universe. He is consciously engaging the forces within him with those forces which press upon him from without, sometimes yielding to them, sometimes opposing them, but ever aware of them, and finding his identity only in this dynamic process.

Now for the first time the creative dance was brought within the range of form, for it was able at last to create something with an existence of its own. Heretofore it had been at best simply an emanation from a person, as when Isadora by her irresistible power to awaken sympathetic experience was able to project an emotional concept directly into the minds of her audience. Now it assumed the dimensions of an objective work of art, for it had entered into the full-bodied world of relationships. Instead of being lyric—that is, consisting of a simple outpouring of feeling of whatever depth and intensity—it became dramatic, presenting the conflict between two forces.

As has already been pointed out, it is not the artist's purpose merely to work his audience up into a state about a particular experience or set of circumstances, conveying to him thus a specific revelation that will not leave him where he was before, but will change his feeling toward some aspect of life. Emotion is not enough; it must be emotion in relation to something, and part of the artist's responsibility is to establish this something with sufficient clarity to give direction to his emotion. With Wigman's sense of space as a tangible symbol of universal forces, the dancer is supplied with something outside himself, which he may shape to his purposes, and toward which he may direct his emotional reactions so that even his most subjective experiences become visibly externalized.

Here we find the dance recapturing the essential element from which the theater grew in the days of the dithyramb, and which is the heart and soul of the theater at all times. In that Bacchic religion from which the dithyramb stemmed, the god himself, as Jane Harrison has said, is the projection of group emotion. Thus drama was born in that prehistoric moment when the mass emotion of a group of frenzied dancers became so powerful that it seemed to be a force outside themselves and was personalized under the name of Dionysos; he was a symbolized presence of their awareness of external forces toward which to direct their emotional outpourings, hitherto only a focusless discharge. What we are held by in a dramatic performance is not beautiful words beautifully spoken, not an actor's exhibition of his personal charms, his voice, his enunciation, his emotional gamut, his technical skill; it is the relationships that are created in action before us between the human beings and the forces of life about him, and between human beings and human beings, under the influence of these forces. These constitute the substance that the true theater art creates, the thing that was not there before, its entity.

With Wigman, dance creates a similar entity, and touches for the first time in many centuries its common ground with theater. Isadora knew that dance was not of the theater, but Wigman's has acquired an extra dimension which allows it to stand alone, so to speak, upon a stage. As must be evident, this did not come about through trying to force it into the patterns which the theater has taken in its generations of development away from the dance. Certainly it has nothing to do with that degeneration of the conception of the theater which makes it a place for spectacle and exhibition, a show business in far more than the colloquial sense of that phrase. In the nature of the dance itself, movement in relation to space, she touched quite as a matter of course the elements in which the theater exists, man in relation to his universe.

To grasp the full meaning of Wigman's use of space, however, it is essential to remember that it is not confined to the area and cubic content of the stage on which she is working, but accepts these only as a kind of gateway through which to enter the symbolic sphere of space as universe. In just such a way the great actor uses his immediate environment of wood and canvas and paint as a channel through which to bring into experience his larger and more significant universe. This has been, beyond question, her greatest contribution to the discovery of the dance and its unfoldment, and it is so great a one, indeed, that all future development must ultimately accept it and build upon it, as she accepted and built upon the revelation of Isadora. It by no means comprises her total achievement, however. The whole spirit of modernism compelled her to go farther than this. If she knew that the dance consisted of two elements, subjectively created movement and symbolically materialized space, it became immediately incumbent upon her to learn the nature and character of these materials in order that the inherent, self-determined forms of the dance might be realized.

In her approach to movement, the physical training of the body as such is a thorough one, based on a natural gymnastic that will produce not a vocabulary or a style of movement or a self-existent virtuosity, but a perfectly functioning instrument able to respond to the demands made upon it. To a great extent these demands are themselves a part of the training, for it is fundamental to the Wigman theory that emotion is not put upon the outside of movements already evolved, but that the emotion actually evolves the movements. Thus there is as much stress laid upon emotional training as upon physical, and more, perhaps, upon the production of movement from subjective impulses than upon either element separately. The full possibilities of the body have been explored and a range of movement has resulted that is extraordinary both in its eloquence and in its freedom from stereotype. The emotional aspects of dynamics have been sensed so fully that the dancer works consciously in various keys of tension, and becomes deeply aware of both extremes of the scale and of the basis of rhythm that lies in their alternation. The study of space in its significant aspects is in large measure inseparable from these studies of movement, for the one cannot exist without the other.

In her treatment of music, Wigman has again been completely radical. With such a clear vision of the creative sources of the dance and of the medium in which it exists, it is not surprising to find the domination both of musical formalism and of its emotional suggestion completely destroyed. Her very first dance was, as a matter of interest, without music of any sort, and frequently since then she has omitted all sound from the accompaniment of some of her compositions and of particular sections of others. In her theory of this much misunderstood relationship, she has once more uncovered principles which can never be denied as such, however differently they may be applied in practice.

With a realization of the fact that the dancer's music is essentially his own song with the percussive accents of his bodily rhythms, she has evolved the ideal type of dance accompaniment. Her music, composed either along with the creation of her dance or after the dance has been completed, is of greatest simplicity and frequently has no independent musical validity whatever apart from the dance. It employs almost exclusively nonorchestral instruments, matching the quality of the dance's tone with melodies on unsophisticated flutes, gongs, drums. The employment at times of the inappropriate and unadaptable piano, which practical necessity makes apparently unavoidable for the dancer, is the only exception to her complete musical logic.

With Wigman the dance stands for the first time fully revealed in its own stature; it is not storytelling or pantomime or moving sculpture or design in space or acrobatic virtuosity or musical illustration, but dance alone, an autonomous art exemplifying fully the ideals of modernism in its attainment of abstraction and in its utilization of the resources of its materials efficiently and with authority. This brings it, however, to no state of finality, no crystallization, but only to a complete statement of its selfhood, to a revelation of the principles upon which it may enlarge its borders and deepen its awareness of itself. New vistas are continually opening up, demanding that new elements be considered and new principles evolved for them, but this necessitates no invalidation of the old ones which have proved themselves basic.

These principles are entirely impersonal and of universal application. That Wigman, their first advocate and exemplar, has applied them in a manner purely personal, colored both by national cultural influences and by her striking individuality as person and artist, does not imply that they are thus wedded to her style and point of view, but indicates on the contrary, that they are amenable to the subtlest variations of temperament and artistic manipulation.

In her own dances, Wigman has reflected the general philosophical tendency of the German mind; they are dances of introspection rather than of action, concerned with revealing inward states of being. Because of the intensity of her own passions, the states of being she has visualized have been by no means static or remote, but vital, vibrant, stirring. From the tenderest of lyrical moods she has jumped to extremes of grotesque and demonic obsessions and back again to the restraints and nobility of tragedy. The magnificent aliveness and eloquence of her body, her profundity of emotional penetration, and her ability to communicate her perceptions in the unintellectualized realm of experience make her dancing a thing of constant evocation, and mark her as certainly one of the greatest figures in the modern arts.

That there are superficial aspects of her performances that do not translate easily is necessarily true, for all art takes on the colors of its immediate environment, and the more sensitively it is conceived, the more in need of translation it becomes. Such things as these, however, have to do wholly with national taste and background and do not in the least affect the substance of her art itself.

The theories that underlie her dance could not have been determined in advance by sitting down and taking thought; they are too patently subjective and subjectively arrived at. Nevertheless, with that devotion to analyzing and ordering principles into a consistent philosophy which is so typical of the German mentality, they got themselves somehow objectified and integrated so as to be systematically teachable. The genius of Wigman, to be sure, cannot be thus pinned down, but the laws which are seen to function beneath the surface of her dance can be and have been, and in that orderly methodology and its results lies a basis of continuity such as no amount of personal genius can guarantee.

SELECTED BIBLIOGRAPHY

1. Margaret N. H'Doubler, *Dance: A Creative Art Experience,* F. S. Crofts and Company, 1940. A standard work.
2. Curt Sachs, *World History of the Dance,* W. W. Norton and Company, 1937. A fine historical treatment of the dance.
3. E. S. Selden, *The Dancer's Quest,* University of California Press, 1935. Another good introduction.
4. Susanne Langer, *Feeling and Form,* Chaps. 11–12, Scribner's Sons, 1953. The dance as virtual powers.

MOTION PICTURE

Erwin Panofsky's "Style and Medium in the Motion Picture," remains the best short essay on the art of the film. Around the twin concepts of the 'dynamization of space,' and the 'spatialization of time,' he explains the nature and uniqueness of the motion picture as an art, and the radical differences between it and stage drama. It is reproduced here in its entirety.

Erwin Panofsky

STYLE AND MEDIUM IN THE MOTION PICTURE*

Film art is the only art the development of which men now living, have witnessed from the very beginnings; and this development is all the more interesting as it took place under conditions contrary to precedent. It was not an artistic urge that gave rise to the discovery and gradual perfection of a new technique; it was a technical invention that gave rise to the discovery and gradual perfection of a new art.

From this we understand two fundamental facts. First, that the primordial basis of the enjoyment of moving pictures was not an objective interest in a specific subject matter, much less an aesthetic interest in the

* From Erwin Panofsky's "Style and Medium in the Motion Picture," *Critique*, I, No. 3, 1947. Reprinted by permission of the author. In granting permission, the author has asked that one change be made, which I have done and indicated in the appropriate footnote.

formal presentation of subject matter, but the sheer delight in the fact that things seemed to move, no matter what things they were. Second, that films—first exhibited in "kinetoscopes," viz., cinematographic peep-shows, but projectable to a screen since as early as 1894—are, originally, a product of genuine folk art (whereas, as a rule, folk art derives from what is known as "higher art"). At the very beginning of things we find the simple recording of movements: galloping horses, railroad trains, fire engines, sporting events, street scenes. And when it had come to the making of narrative films these were produced by photographers who were anything but "producers" or "directors," performed by people who were anything but actors, and enjoyed by people who would have been much offended had anyone called them "art lovers."

The casts of these archaic films were usually collected in a "café" where unemployed supers or ordinary citizens possessed of a suitable exterior were wont to assemble at a given hour. An enterprising photographer would walk in, hire four or five convenient characters and make the picture while carefully instructing them what to do: "Now, you pretend to hit this lady over the head"; and (to the lady): "And you pretend to fall down in a heap." Productions like these were shown, together with those purely factual recordings of "movement for movement's sake," in a few small and dingy cinemas most frequented by the "lower classes" and a sprinkling of youngsters in quest of adventure (about 1905, I happen to remember there was only one obscure and faintly disreputable *kino* in the whole city of Berlin, bearing, for some unfathomable reason, the English name of "The Meeting Room"). Small wonder that the "better classes," when they slowly began to venture into these early picture theaters, did so, not by way of seeking normal and possibly serious entertainment, but with that characteristic sensation of self-conscious condescension with which we may plunge, in gay company, into the folkloristic depths of Coney Island or a European Kermis; even a few years ago it was the regulation attitude of the socially or intellectually prominent that one could confess to enjoying such austerely educational films as "The Sex Life of the Starfish" or films with "beautiful scenery," but never to a serious liking for narratives.

Today there is no denying that narrative films are not only "art"—not often good art, to be sure, but this applies to other media as well—but also, besides architecture, cartooning, and "commercial design," the only visual art entirely alive. The "movies" have re-established that dynamic contact between art production and art consumption which, for reasons too complex to be considered here, is sorely attentuated, if not entirely interrupted, in many other fields of artistic endeavor. Whether we like it or not, it is the movies that mold, more than any other single force, the opinions, the taste, the language, the dress, the behavior, and even the physical appearance of a public comprising more than 60% of the population of the earth. If all the serious lyrical poets, composers, painters and sculptors were forced by law to stop their activities, a rather small fraction of the general public would become aware of the fact and a still smaller fraction would seriously regret it. If the same thing were to happen with the movies the social consequences would be catastrophic.

· · ·

In the beginning, then, there were the straight recordings of movement no matter what moved, viz., the prehistoric ancestors of our "documentaries"; and, soon after, the early narratives, viz., the prehistoric ancestors of our "feature films." The craving for a narrative element could be satisfied only by borrowing from older arts, and one should expect that the natural thing would have been to borrow from the theater, a theater play being apparently the *genus proximum* to a narrative film in that it consists of a narrative enacted by persons that move. But in reality the imitation of stage performances was a comparatively late and thoroughly frustrated development. What happened at the start was a very different thing: instead of imitating a theatrical performance already endowed with a certain amount of motion, the earliest films added movement to works of art originally stationary, so that the dazzling technical invention might achieve a triumph of its own without intruding upon the sphere of higher culture. The living language, which is always right, has endorsed this sensible choice when it still speaks of a "moving picture" or, simply, a "picture," instead of accepting the pretentious and fundamentally erroneous "screen play."

The stationary works enlivened in the earliest movies were indeed pictures: bad nineteenth-century paintings and postcards (or wax works *à la* Madame Tussaud's), supplemented by the comic strips—a most important root of cinematic art—and the subject matter of popular songs, pulp magazines and dime novels; and the films descending from this ancestry appealed directly and very intensely to a folk art mentality. They gratified—often simultaneously—first: a primitive sense of justice and decorum when virtue and industry were rewarded while vice and laziness were punished; second, plain sentimentality when "the thin trickle of a fictive love interest" took its course "through somewhat serpentine channels," or when, father, dear father, returned from the saloon to find his child dying of diphtheria; third, a primordial instinct for bloodshed and cruelty when Andreas Hofer faced the firing squad, or when (in a film of 1893/94) the head of Mary Queen of Scots actually came off; fourth, a taste for mild pornography (I remember with great pleasure a French film of *ca.* 1900 wherein a seemingly but not really well-rounded lady as well as a seemingly but not really slender one were shown changing to bathing suits—an honest, straightforward *porcheria* much less objectionable than the now extinct Betty Boop films and, I am sorry to say, some of the more recent Walt Disney productions); and, finally, that crude sense of humor, graphically described as "slap-stick," which feeds upon the sadistic and the pornographic instinct, either singly or in combination.

Not until as late as *ca.* 1905 was a film adaptation of "Faust" ventured upon (cast still "unknown," characteristically enough), and not until 1911 did Sarah Bernhardt lend her prestige to an unbelievably funny film tragedy *Queen Elizabeth of England.* These films represent the first conscious attempt at transplanting the movies from the folk art level to that of "real art"; but they also bear witness to the fact that this commendable goal could not be reached in so simple a manner. It was soon realized that the imitation of a theater performance with a set stage, fixed entries and exits, and distinctly literary ambitions is the one thing the film must avoid.

The legitimate paths of evolution were opened, not by running away from the folk art character of the primitive film but by developing it within the limits of its own possibilities. Those primordial archetypes of film productions on the folk art level—success or retribution, sentiment, sensation, pornography, and crude humor—could blossom forth into genuine history, tragedy and romance, crime and adventure, and comedy, as soon as it was realized that they could be transfigured: not by an artificial injection of literary values but by the exploitation of the unique and specific possibilities of the new medium. Significantly, the beginnings of this legitimate development antedate the attempts at endowing the film with higher values of a foreign order (the crucial period being the years from 1902 to *ca.* 1905), and the decisive steps were taken by people who were laymen or outsiders from the view-point of the serious stage.

These unique and specific possibilities can be defined as *dynamization of space* and, accordingly, *spatialization of time*. This statment is self-evident to the point of triviality but it belongs to that kind of truths which, just because of their triviality, are easily forgotten or neglected: all that which exists in space, even the walls of a room or the Rock of Gibraltar, can and should be invested with a semblance of movement, while all that which happens in time, even the thoughts and feelings in the souls of men, can and should be made visible.

In a theater, space is static, that is, the space represented on the stage, as well as the spatial relation of the beholder to the spectacle, are unalterably fixed. The spectator cannot leave his seat, and the setting of the stage cannot change, during one act (except for such incidentals as rising moons or gathering clouds and such illegitimate re-borrowings from the film as turning wings or gliding backdrops). But, in return for this restriction, the theater has the advantage that time, the medium of emotion and thought conveyable by speech, is free and independent of anything that may happen in visible space. Hamlet may deliver his famous monologue lying on a couch in the middle distance, doing nothing and only dimly discernible to the spectator and listener, and yet by his mere words enthrall him with a feeling of intensest emotional action.

With the movies the situation is reversed. Here, too, the spectator occupies a fixed seat, but only physically, not as the subject of an aesthetic experience. Aesthetically, he is in permanent motion as his eye identifies itself with the lens of the camera which permanently shifts in distance and direction. And as movable as the spectator is, as movable is, for the same reason, the space presented to him. Not only bodies move in space, but space itself does, approaching, receding, turning, dissolving and recrystallizing as it appears through the controlled locomotion and focusing of the camera and through the cutting and editing of the various shots—not to mention such special effects as visions, transformations, disappearances, slow-motion and fast-motion shots, reversals and trick films. This opens up a world of possibilities of which the stage can never dream. Quite apart from such photographic tricks as the participation of disembodied spirits in the action of the *Topper* series, or the more effective wonders wrought by Roland Young in *The Man Who Could Work Miracles*, there is, on the purely factual level, an untold wealth of themes as inaccessible to the "legitimate" stage as a fog or a snowstorm is to the sculptor; all sorts of violent elemental phenomena and, conversely, events too microscopic to be visible under normal conditions (such as the life-saving injection with the serum flown in at the very last moment, or the fatal bite of the yellow fever mosquito); full-scale battle scenes: all kinds of operations, not only in the surgical sense but also in the sense of any actual construction, destruction or experimentation, as in *Louis Pasteur* or *Madame Curie;* a really grand party, moving through many rooms of a mansion or palace. Features like these, even the mere shifting of the scene from one place to another by means of a car perilously negotiating heavy traffic or a motor-boat steered through a nocturnal harbour, will not only always retain their primitive cinematic appeal but also remain enormously effective as a means of stirring the emotions and creating suspense.

In addition, the movies have the power, entirely denied to the theater, to convey psychological experiences by directly projecting their content to the screen, substituting, as it were, the eye of the beholder for the consciousness of the character (as when the imaginings and hallucinations of the drunkard in the otherwise overrated *Lost Weekend* appear as stark realities instead of being described by mere words. But any attempt to convey thought and feelings exclusively, or even primarily, by speech leaves us with a feeling of embarrassment, boredom, or both.

What I mean by thoughts and feelings "conveyed exclusively, or even primarily, by speech" is simply this: contrary to naïve expectation, the invention of the sound track in 1928 has been unable to change the basic fact that a moving picture, even when it has learned to talk, remains a picture that moves, and does not convert itself into a piece of writing that is enacted. Its substance remains a series of visual sequences held together by an uninterrupted flow of movement in space (except, of course, for such checks and pauses as have the same compositional value as a rest in music), and not a sustained study in human character and destiny transmitted by effective, let alone "beautiful," diction. I cannot remember a more misleading statement about the movies than Mr. Eric Bentley's in *The Playwright as Thinker*, p. 289: "[The potentialities of the talking screen] differ from those of the silent screen in adding the dimension of dialogue—which, potentially, is poetry." I would suggest: "The potentialities of the talking screen differ from those of the silent screen in integrating visible movement with dialogue which, therefore, had better not be poetry."

All of us, if we are old enough to remember the period prior to 1928, recall the old-time pianist who, with his eyes glued on the screen, would accompany the events with music adapted to their mood and rhythm; and we also recall the weird and spectral feeling overtaking us when this pianist left his post for a few minutes and the film was allowed to run by itself, the darkness haunted by the monotonous rattle of the machinery. Even the silent film, then, was never mute. The visible spectacle always required, and received, an audible accompaniment which, from the very beginning, distinguished the film from simple pantomime and rather classed it—*mutatis mutandis*—with the ballet. The advent of the talkie meant, not so much an "addition" as a transformation: the transformation of musical sound into articulate speech and, therefore, of quasipantomime into an entirely new species of spectacle which differs from the ballet, and agrees with the stage play, in that its acoustic component consists of intelligible words, but differs from the stage play and agrees with the ballet in that this acoustic component is not detachable from the visual. In a film, that which we hear remains, for good or worse, inextricably fused with that which we see; the sound, articulate or not, cannot express any more than is expressed, at the same time, by visible movement; and in a good film it does not even attempt to do so. To put it briefly: the play—or, as it is very properly called, the "script"—of a moving picture is subject to what might be termed the *principle of coexpressibility.*

Empirical proof of this principle is furnished by the fact that, wherever the dialogical or monological element gains temporary prominence there appears, with the inevitability of a natural law, the "close-up." What does the close-up achieve? In showing us, in magnification, either the face of the speaker or the face of the listeners or both in alternation, the camera transforms the human physiognomy into a huge field of action where—given the qualification of the performers—every subtle movement of the features, almost imperceptible from a natural distance, becomes an expressive event in visible space and thereby completely integrates itself with the expressive content of the spoken word; whereas on the stage, the spoken word makes a stronger rather than a weaker impression if we are not permitted to count the hairs in Romeo's mustache.

This does not mean that the scenario is a negligible factor in the making of a moving picture. It only means that its artistic intention differs in kind from that of a stage play, and much more from that of a novel or a piece of poetry. As the success of a Gothic jamb figure depends, not only upon its quality as a piece of sculpture but also, or even more so, upon its integrability with the architecture of the portal, so does the success of a movie script—not unlike that of an opera libretto—depend, not only upon its quality as a piece of literature but also, or even more so, upon its integrability with the events on the screen.

As a result—another empirical proof of the coexpressibility principle— good movie scripts are unlikely to make good reading and have seldom been published in book form: whereas, conversely, good stage plays have to be severely altered, cut, and, on the other hand, enriched by interpolations to make good movie scripts. In Shaw's *Pygmalion,* for instance, the actual process of Eliza's phonetic education and, still more important, her final triumph at the grand party, are wisely omitted; we see—or, rather, hear— some samples of her gradual linguistic improvement and finally encounter her, upon her return from the reception, victorious and splendidly arrayed but deeply hurt for want of recognition and sympathy. In the film adaptation, precisely these two scenes are not only supplied but also strongly emphasized; we witness the fascinating activities in the laboratory with its array of spinning disks and mirrors, organ pipes and dancing flames, and we participate in the ambassadorial party, with many moments of impending catastrophe and a little counter-intrigue thrown in for suspense. Unquestionably these two scenes, entirely absent from the play, and indeed unachievable upon the stage, were the highlights of the film; whereas the Shavian dialogue, however severely cut, turned out to fall a little flat in certain moments. And wherever, as in so many other films, a poetic emotion, a musical outburst, or a literary conceit (even, I am grieved to say, some of the wisecracks of Groucho Marx) entirely lose contact with visible movement, they strike the sensitive spectators as, literally, out of place. It is certainly terrible when a soft-boiled He-Man, after the suicide of his mistress, casts a twelve-foot glance upon her photograph and says something less-than-coexpressible to the effect that he would never forget her. But when he recites, instead, a piece of poetry as sublimely more-than-coexpressible as Romeo's monologue at the bier of Juliet, it is still worse. Reinhardt's *Midsummer Night's Dream* is probably the most unfortunate major film ever produced; and Olivier's *Henry V* owes its comparative success, apart from the all but providential adaptability of this particular play, to so many *tours de force* that it will remain, God willing, an exception rather than set a pattern. It combines "judicious pruning" with the interpolation of pageantry, non-verbal comedy and melodrama; it uses a device perhaps best designated as "oblique close-up" (Mr. Olivier's beautiful face inwardly listening to but not pronouncing the great soliloquy); and, most notably, it shifts between three levels of archaeological reality: a reconstruction of Elizabethan London, a reconstruction of the events of 1415 as laid down in Shakespeare's play, and the reconstruction of a performance of this play on Shakespeare's own stage. All this is perfectly legitimate; but, even so, the highest praise of the film will always come from those who, like the critics of the *New Yorker*, are not quite in sympathy with either the movies *au naturel* or Shakespeare *au naturel*.

•   •   •

As the writings of Conan Doyle potentially contain all modern mystery stories (except for the tough specimens of the Dashiell Hammett school), so do the films produced between 1900 and 1910 pre-establish the subject matter and methods of the moving picture as we know it. This period produced the incunabula of the Western and the crime film (Edwin S. Porter's amazing *Great Train Robbery* of 1903) from which developed the modern Gangster, Adventure, and Mystery pictures (the latter, if well done, is still one of the most honest and genuine forms of film entertainment, space being doubly charged with time as the beholder asks himself, not only "what is going to happen?" but also "what has happened before?"). The same period saw the emergence of the fantastically imaginative film (Méliès) which was to lead to the expressionist and surrealist experiments (*The Cabinet of Dr. Caligari, Sang d'un Poète*, etc.), on the one hand, and to the more superficial and spectator fairy tales *à la* Arabian Nights, on the other. Comedy, later to triumph in Charlie Chaplin, the still insufficiently appreciated Buster Keaton, the Marx Brothers, and the pre-Hollywood creations of René Clair, reached a respectable level in Max Linder and others. In historical and melodramatic films the foundations were laid for movie iconography and movie symbolism, and in the early work of D. W. Griffith we find, not only remarkable attempts at psychological analysis (*Edgar Allen Poe*) and social criticism (*A Corner in Wheat*) but also such basic technical innovations as the long-shot, the flash-back and the close-up. And modest trick-films and cartoons paved the way to Felix the Cat, Pop-Eye the Sailor, and Felix's prodigious offspring, Mickey Mouse.

Within their self-imposed limitations the earlier Disney films, and certain sequences in the later ones,[1] represent, as it were, a chemically pure distillation of cinematic possibilities. They retain the most important folk-loristic elements—sadism, pornography, the humor engendered by both, and moral justice—almost without dilution and often fuse these elements into a variation on the primitive and inexhaustible David-and-Goliath motif, the

[1] I make this distinction because it was, in my opinion, a fall from grace when *Snow-White* introduced the human figure and when *Fantasia* attempted to picturalize The World's Great Music. The very virtue of the animated cartoon is to animate, that is to say, endow lifeless things with life, or living things with a different kind of life. It effects a metamorphosis, and such a metamorphosis is wonderfully present in Disney's animals, plants, thunderclouds and railroad trains. Whereas his dwarfs, glamorized princesses, hillbillies, baseball players, rouged centaurs and *amigos* from South America are not transformations but caricatures at best, and fakes or vulgarities at worst. Concerning music, however, it should be borne in mind that its cinematic use is no less predicated upon the principle of co-expressibility than is the cinematic use of the spoken word. There is music permitting or even requiring the accompaniment of visible action (such as dances, ballet music and any kind of operatic compositions) and music of which the opposite is true; and this is, again, not a question of quality (most of us rightly prefer a waltz by Johann Strauss to a symphony by Sibelius) but one of intention. In *Fantasia* the hippopotamus ballet was wonderful, and the Pastoral Symphony and Ave Maria sequences were deplorable, not because the cartooning in the first case was infinitely better than in the two others (*cf. above*), and certainly not because Beethoven and Schubert are too sacred for picturalization, but simply because Ponchielli's Dance of the Hours is coexpressible while the Pastoral Symphony and the Ave Maria are not. In cases like these even the best imaginable music and the best imaginable cartoon will impair rather than enhance each other's effectiveness.

Experimental proof of all this was furnished by Disney's more recent *Make Mine Music* where The World's Great Music was fortunately restricted to Prokofieff. Even among the other sequences the most successful ones were those in which the human element was either absent or reduced to a minimum; Willie the Whale, the Ballad of Johnny Fedora and Alice Blue-Bonnet, and, above all, the truly magnificent Goodman Quartet.

triumph of the seemingly weak over the seemingly strong; and their fantastic independence of the natural laws gives them the power to integrate
space with time to such perfection that the spatial and temporal experiences
of sight and hearing come to be almost interconvertible. A series of soap
bubbles, successively punctured, emits a series of sounds exactly corresponding in pitch and volume to the size of the bubbles; the three uvulae of Willie
the Whale—small, large and medium—vibrate in consonance with tenor,
bass and baritone notes; and the very concept of stationary existence is
completely abolished. No object in creation, whether it be a house, a piano,
a tree, or an alarm clock, lacks the faculties of organic, in fact anthropomorphic, movement, facial expression and phonetic articulation. Incidentally,
even in normal, "realistic" films the inanimate object, provided that it is
dynamizable, can play the role of a leading character as do the ancient
railroad engines in Buster Keaton's *General* and *Niagara Falls.* How the
earlier Russian films exploited the possibility of heroizing all sorts of machinery lives in everybody's memory; and it is perhaps more than an accident
that the two films which will go down in history as the great comical and
the great serious masterpiece of the silent period bear the names and im-
mortalize the personalities of two big ships: Keaton's *Navigator* (1924) and
Eisenstein's *Potemkin* (1925).

.   .   .

The evolution from the jerky beginnings to this grand climax offers the
fascinating spectacle of a new artistic medium gradually becoming conscious
of its legitimate, that is, exclusive, possibilities and limitations—a spectacle
not unlike the development of the mosaic, which started out with transposing
illusionistic genre pictures into a more durable material and culminated in
the hieratic supernaturalism of Ravenna; or the development of line engraving, which started out as a cheap and handy substitute for book illumination and culminated in the purely "graphic" style of Dürer.

Just so the silent movies developed a definite style of their own, adapted
to the specific conditions of the medium. A hitherto unknown language was
forced upon a public not yet capable of reading it, and the more proficient
the public became the more refinement could develop in the language. For
a Saxon peasant of around 800 it was not easy to understand the meaning
of a picture showing a man as he pours water over the head of another man,
and even later many people found it difficult to grasp the significance of
two ladies standing behind the throne of an emperor. For the public of
around 1910 it was no less difficult to understand the meaning of the speechless action in a moving picture, and the producers employed means of

clarification similar to those we find in medieval art. One of these were printed titles or letters, striking equivalents of the medieval *tituli* and scrolls (at a still earlier date there even used to be explainers who would say, *viva voce:* "Now he thinks his wife is dead but she isn't" or: "I don't wish to offend the ladies in the audience but I doubt that any of them would have done that much for her child"). Another, less obtrusive method of explanation was the introduction of a fixed iconography which from the outset informed the spectator about the basic facts and characters, much as the two ladies behind the emperor, when carrying a sword and a cross, respectively, were uniquely determined as Fortitude and Faith. There arose, identifiable by standardized appearance, behavior, and attributes, the well-remembered types of the Vamp and the Straight Girl (perhaps the most convincing modern equivalents of the medieval personifications of the Vices and Virtues), the Family Man, and the Villain, the latter marked by a black mustache and walking stick. Nocturnal scenes were printed on blue or green film. A checkered table cloth meant, once for all, a "poor but honest" milieu; a happy marriage, soon to be endangered by the shadows from the past, was symbolized by the young wife's pouring the breakfast coffee for her husband; the first kiss was invariably announced by the lady's gently playing with her partner's necktie and was invariably accompanied by her kicking out with her left foot. The conduct of the characters was predetermined accordingly. The poor but honest laborer who, after leaving his little house with the checkered table cloth, came upon an abandoned baby could not but take it to his home and bring it up as best he could; the Family Man could not but yield, however temporarily, to the temptations of the Vamp. As a result these early melodramas had a highly gratifying and soothing quality in that events took shape, without the complications of individual psychology, according to a pure Aristotelian logic so badly missed in real life.

Devices like these became gradually less necessary as the public grew accustomed to interpret the action by itself and were virtually abolished by the invention of the talking film. But even now there survive—quite legitimately, I think—the remnants of a "fixed attitude and attribute" principle and, more basic, a primitive or folkloristic concept of plot construction. Even today we take it for granted that the diphtheria of a baby tends to occur when the parents are out, and, having occurred, solves all their matrimonial problems. Even today we demand of a decent mystery film that the butler, though he may be anything from an agent of the British Secret Service to the real father of the daughter of the house, must not turn out to be the murderer. Even today we love to see Pasteur, Zola, or Ehrlich win out against stupidity and wickedness, with their respective wives trusting and trusting all the time. Even today we much prefer a happy finale to a gloomy one, and insist, at the very least, on the observance of the Aristotelian rule that the story have a beginning, a middle, and an ending—a rule the abrogation of which has done so much to estrange the general public from the more elevated spheres of modern writing. Primitive symbolism, too, survives in such amusing details as the last sequence of *Casablanca* where the delightfully crooked and right-minded *Préfet de Police* casts an empty bottle of Vichy water into the wastepaper basket; and in such telling symbols of the supernatural as Sir Cedric Hardwicke's Death in the guise of a "gentleman in a dustcoat trying" (*On Borrowed Time*) or Claude Rains' Hermes Psychopompos in the striped trousers of an airline manager (*Here Comes Mister Jordan*).

The most conspicuous advances were made in directing, lighting, camera work, cutting, and acting proper. But while in most of these fields the evolution proceeded continuously—though, of course, not without detours, breakdowns and archaic relapses—the development of acting suffered a sudden interruption by the invention of the talking film; so that the style of acting in the silents can already be evaluated in retrospect, as a lost art not unlike the painting technique of Jan van Eyck or, to take up our previous simile, the burin technique of Dürer. It was soon realized that acting in a silent film neither meant a pantomimic exaggeration of stage acting (as was generally and erroneously assumed by professional stage actors who more and more frequently condescended to perform in the movies), nor could dispense with stylization altogether; a man photographed while walking down a gangway in ordinary, every-day-life fashion looked like anything but a man walking down a gangway when the result appeared on the screen. If the picture was to look both natural and meaningful the acting had to be done in a manner equally different from the style of the stage and the reality of ordinary life; speech had to be made dispensable by establishing an organic relation between the acting and the technical procedure of cine-photography—much as in Dürer's prints color had been made dispensable by establishing an organic relation between the design and the technical procedure of line engraving.

This was precisely what the great actors of the silent period accomplished, and it is a significant fact that the best of them did not come from the stage, whose crystallized tradition prevented Duse's only film, *Cenere*, from being more than a priceless record of Duse. They came instead from the circus or the variety, as was the case of Chaplin, Keaton and Will Rogers; from nothing in particular, as was the case of Theda Bara, of her greater European parallel, the Danish actress Asta Nielsen, and of Garbo; or from everything under the sun, as was the case of Douglas Fairbanks. The style of these "old masters" was indeed comparable to the style of line engraving in that it was, and had to be, exaggerated in comparison with stage acting (just as the sharply incised and vigorously curved *tailles* of the burin are exaggerated in comparison with pencil strokes or brush-work), but richer, subtler and infinitely more precise. The advent of the talkies, reducing if not abolishing this difference between movie[2] acting and stage acting, thus confronted the actors and actresses of the silent screen with a serious problem. Buster Keaton yielded to temptation and fell. Chaplin first tried to stand his ground and to remain an exquisite archaist but finally gave in, with only moderate success (*The Dictator*). Only the glorious Harpo has thus far successfully refused to utter a single articulate sound; and only Greta Garbo succeeded, in a measure, in transforming her style in principle. But even in her case one cannot help feeling that her first talking picture, *Anna Christie*, where she could ensconce herself, most of the time, in mute or monosyllabic sullenness, was better than her later per-formances; and in the second, talking version of *Anna Karenina*, the weak-est moment is certainly when she delivers a big Ibsenian speech to her hus-band, and the strongest when she silently moves along the platform of the railroad station while her despair takes shape in the consonance of her move-ment (and expression) with the movement of the nocturnal space around her, filled with the real noises of the trains and the imaginary sound of the "little men with the iron hammers" that drives her, relentlessly and almost without her realizing it, under the wheels.

Small wonder that there is sometimes felt a kind of nostalgia for the silent period and that devices have been worked out to combine the virtues of sound and speech with those of silent acting, such as the "oblique close-up" already mentioned in connection with *Henry V;* the dance behind glass doors in *Sous les Toits de Paris;* or, in the *Histoire d'un Tricheur*, Sacha Guitry's recital of the events of his youth while the events themselves are "silently" enacted on the screen. However, this nostalgic feeling is no argu-ment against the talkies as such. Their evolution has shown that, in art, every gain entails a certain loss on the other side of the ledger; but that the gain remains a gain, provided that the basic nature of the medium is realized and respected. One can imagine that, when the cave-men of Alta-mira began to paint their buffaloes in natural colors instead of merely incising the contours, the more conservative cave-men foretold the end of palaeolithic art. But palaeolithic art went on, and so will the movies. New technical in-ventions always tend to dwarf the values already attained, especially in a

[2] Professor Panofsky asks that "movie" be inserted here, (ed.).

medium that owes its very existence to technical experimentation. The earliest talkies were infinitely inferior to the then mature silents, and most of the present technicolor films are still inferior to the now mature talkies in black and white. But even if Aldous Huxley's nightmare should come true and the experiences of taste, smell and touch should be added to those of sight and hearing, even then we may say with the Apostle, as we have said when first confronted with the sound track and the technicolor film: "We are troubled on every side, yet not distressed; we are perplexed, but not in despair."

.   •   •   •

From the law of time-charged space and space-bound time, there follows the fact that the *"screen play,"* in contrast to the theater play, *has no aesthetic existence independent of its performance, and that its characters have no aesthetic existence outside the actors.*

The playwright writes in the fond hope that his work will be an imperishable jewel in the treasure house of civilization and will be presented in hundreds of performances that are but transient variations on a "work" that is constant. The script writer, on the other hand, writes for one producer, one director and one cast. Their work achieves the same degree of permanence as does his; and should the same or a similar scenario ever be filmed by a different director and a different cast there will result an altogether different "play."

Othello and Nora are definite, substantial figures created by the playwright. They can be played well or badly, and they can be "interpreted" in one way or another; but they most definitely exist, no matter who plays them or even whether they are played at all. The character in a film, however, lives and dies with the actor. It is not the entity "Othello" interpreted by Robeson or the entity "Nora" interpreted by Duse; it is the entity "Greta Garbo" incarnate in a figure called Anna Christie or the entity "Robert Montgomery" incarnate in a murderer who, for all we know or care to know, may forever remain anonymous but will never cease to haunt our memories. Even when the names of the characters happen to be Henry VIII or Anna Karenina, the King who ruled England from 1509 to 1547 and the woman created by Tolstoi do not exist outside the being of Garbo and Laughton. They are but empty and incorporeal outlines like the shadows in Homer's Hades, assuming the character of reality only when filled with the life blood of an actor. Conversely, if a movie role is badly played there remains literally nothing of it, no matter how interesting the character's psychology or how elaborate the words.

What applies to the actor applies, *mutatis mutandis,* to most of the other artists, or artisans, who contribute to the making of a film: the director, the sound man, the enormously important camera man, even the make-up man. A stage production is rehearsed until everything is ready, and then it is repeatedly performed in three consecutive hours. At each performance everybody has to be on hand and does his work; and afterwards he goes home and to bed. The work of the stage actor may thus be likened to that of a musician, and that of the stage director to that of a conductor. Like these, they have a certain répertoire which they have studied and present in a number of complete but transitory performances, be it "Hamlet" today and "Ghosts" tomorrow, or "Life with Father" *per saecula saeculorum.* The activities of the film actor and the film director, however, are comparable, respectively, to those of the plastic artist and the architect, rather than to those of the musician and conductor. Stage work is continuous but transitory; film work is discontinuous but permanent. Individual sequences are done piecemeal and out of order according to the most efficient use of sets and personnel. Each bit is done over and over again until it stands; and when the whole has been cut and composed everyone is through with it forever. Needless to say that this very procedure cannot but emphasize the curious consubstantiality that exists between the person of the movie actor and his role. Coming into existence piece by piece, regardless of the natural sequence of events, the "character" can grow into a unified whole only if the actor manages to be, not merely to play, Henry VIII or Anna Karenina throughout the entire wearisome period of shooting. I have it on the best of authorities that Laughton was really difficult to live with in the particular six or eight weeks during which he was doing—or rather being—Captain Bligh.

It might be said that a film, called into being by a cooperative effort in which all contributions have the same degree of permanence, is the nearest modern equivalent of a medieval cathedral; the role of the producer corresponding, more or less, to that of the bishop or archbishop; that of the director to that of the architect-in-chief; that of the scenario writers to that of the scholastic advisers, establishing the iconographical program; and that of the actors, camera men, cutters, sound men, make-up men and the divers technicians to that of those whose work provided the physical entity of the finished product, from the sculptors, glass painters, bronze casters, carpenters and skilled masons down to the quarry men and woodsmen. And if you speak to any one of these collaborators he will tell you, with perfect *bona fides,* that his is really the most important job—which is quite true to the extent that it is indispensable.

This comparison may seem sacrilegious, not only because there are, proportionally, fewer good films than there are good cathedrals, but also because the movies are commercial. However, if commercial art be defined as all art not primarily produced in order to gratify the creative urge of its maker but primarily intended to meet the requirements of a patron or a buying public, it must be said that non-commercial art is the exception rather than the rule, and a fairly recent and not always felicitous exception at that. While it is true that commercial art is always in danger of ending up as a prostitute, it is equally true that non-commercial art is always in danger of ending up as an old maid. Non-commercial art has given us Seurat's *Grande Jatte* and Shakespeare's Sonnets, but also much that is esoteric to the point of incommunicability. Conversely, commercial art has given us much that is vulgar or snobbish (two aspects of the same thing) to the point of loathsomeness, but also Dürer's prints and Shakespeare's plays. For, we must not forget that Dürer's prints were partly made on commission and partly intended to be sold in the open market; and that Shakespeare's plays—in contrast to the earlier masques and *intermezzi* which were produced at court by aristocratic amateurs and could afford to be so incomprehensible that even those who described them in printed monographs occasionally failed to grasp their intended significance—were meant to appeal, and did appeal, not only to the select few but also to everyone who was prepared to pay a shilling for admission.

It is this requirement of communicability that makes commercial art more vital than non-commercial, and therefore potentially much more effective for better or for worse. The commercial producer can both educate and pervert the general public, and can allow the general public—or rather his idea of the general public—both to educate and to pervert himself. As is demonstrated by a number of excellent films that proved to be great box office successes, the public does not refuse to accept good products if it gets them. That it does not get them very often is caused, not so much by commercialism as such as by too little discernment and, paradoxical though it may seem, too much timidity in its application. Hollywood believes that it must produce "what the public wants" while the public would take whatever Hollywood produces. If Hollywood were to decide for itself what it wants it would get away with it—even if it should decide to "depart from evil and do good." For, to revert to whence we started: in modern life the movies are what most other forms of art have ceased to be, not an adornment but a necessity.

That this should be so is understandable, not only from a sociological but also from an art-historical point of view. The processes of all the earlier representational arts conform, in a higher or lesser degree, to an idealistic conception of the world. These arts operate from top to bottom, so to speak, and not from bottom to top; they start with an idea to be projected into shapeless matter and not with the objects that constitute the physical world. The painter works on a blank wall or canvas which he organizes into a likeness of things and persons according to his idea (however much this idea may have been nourished by reality); he does not work with the things and persons themselves even if he works "from the model." The same is true of the sculptor with his shapeless mass of clay or his untooled block of stone or wood; of the writer with his sheet of paper or his dictaphone; and even of the stage designer with his empty and sorely limited section of space. It is the movies, and only the movies, that do justice to that materialistic interpretation of the universe which, whether we like it or not, pervades contemporary civilization. Excepting the very special case of the animated cartoon, the movies organize material things and persons, not a neutral medium, into a composition that receives its style, and may even become fantastic or pretervoluntarily symbolic,[3] not so much by an interpretation in the artist's mind as by the actual manipulation of physical objects and recording machinery. The medium of the movies is physical reality as such: the physical reality of eighteenth-century Versailles—no matter whether it be the original or a Hollywood facsimile indistinguishable therefrom for all aesthetic intents and purposes—or of a suburban home in Westchester; the physical reality of the Rue de Lappe in Paris or of the Gobi Desert, of Paul Ehrlich's apartment in Frankfurt or of the streets of New York in the rain; the physical reality of engines and animals, of Edward G. Robinson and Jimmy Cagney. All these objects and persons must be organized into a work of art. They can be arranged in all sorts of ways ("arrangement" comprising, of course, such things as make-up, lighting and camera work); but there is no running away from them. From this point of view it becomes evident that an attempt at subjecting the world to artistic pre-stylization, as in the expressionist settings of *The Cabinet of Doctor Caligari* (1919), could be no more than an exciting experiment that could exert but little influence upon the general course of events. To pre-stylize reality prior to tackling it amounts to dodging the problem. The problem is to manipulate and shoot unstylized reality in such a way that the result has style. This is a proposition no less legitimate and no less difficult than any proposition in the older arts.

[3] I cannot help feeling that the final sequence of the Marx Brothers film *Night in Casablanca*—where Harpo unaccountably usurps the pilot's seat of a big airplane, causes incalculable havoc by flicking one tiny little control after another, and waxes the more insane with joy the greater the disproportion between the smallness of his effort and the magnitude of the disaster—is a magnificent and terrifying symbol of man's behavior in the "atomic age." No doubt the Marx Brothers would vigorously reject this interpretation; but so would Dürer have done had anyone told him that his Apocalypse foreshadowed the cataclysm of the Reformation.

SELECTED BIBLIOGRAPHY

1. S. M. Eisenstein, *The Film Sense,* Harcourt, Brace and Company, 1942. A standard work by the Russian master film producer, with full explanations of montage and other elements of the motion picture as an art.
2. Roger Manvell, *Film,* Penguin Books, 1946. An excellent introduction to the art and history of the film.
3. Parker Tyler, *Magic and Myth of the Movies,* Henry Holt and Company, 1947. An interesting iconological analysis of film and society.

IV

Tragedy and the Problem of Genres

Introduction

The problem of the nature of the different kinds or types of art has long exercised aesthetic theorists. What is comedy, satire, tragedy? What is landscape, epic, lyric, novel, concerto?—these are questions that tax all of us.

One simple solution, offered by Croce, is that there is no problem, that these questions are all logical perversions of the aesthetic approach to art. Every work of art is individual and unique; hence to conceive it as a member of any class is to destroy its aesthetic intuitive character, to convert it into a non-artistic conceptualized datum.

But most critics and philosophers do not accept Croce's verdict. Of course, they insist, some works of art have more in common with each other than they do with many other works. Genres are as real as any other classes; and classes exist in virtue of some set of shared properties.

Nothing illustrates better or longer this conviction that there are artistic genres than the history of theories concerning tragic dramas. From Aristotle to the present day, there has been agreement that all tragedies do have something in common in virtue of which they are tragic. The primary function of theory here has been and still is to discover what that tragic essence is.

In this part, the problem of genres is illustrated by five sets of readings from Aristotle to J. W. Krutch—all on the nature of tragedy. Aristotle, Hume, Nietzsche, Bradley, and Krutch agree that there is a genre of tragedy in art; and each purports to state its defining property. These five views, I think, represent adequately the major theories of tragedy.

Aristotle, in his famous definition—perhaps the most influential one in the entire history of aesthetics—says: "Tragedy, then, is an imitation of an action that is serious, complete, and of a certain magnitude; in language embellished with each kind of ornament, the several kinds being found in separate parts of the play; in the form of action, not of narrative; through pity and fear effecting the proper purgation of these emotions." Almost the whole of the *Poetics* is an explication of this definition.

David Hume shifts the problem to the psychological query: "Why should the depiction of suffering please?" and answers in terms of a notion of tragedy as imitation of suffering which, because it is fictitious and eloquently expressed, does please.

For Nietzsche, tragedy is essentially human affirmation of life against the inevitability of suffering. It does not depict defeat or invite despair but proclaims that life is ". . . at bottom, in spite of all the alternations of appearances, indestructible, powerful, and joyous." Tragedy unites the Apollian (or ordered) and the Dionysian (or frenzied) forces in existence into a dramatic, ritualistic assertion of life. It is through sharing in this act of affirmation that we (as spectators) derive our "metaphysical comfort" from tragedy in a total world which is basically brutal and absurd.

A. C. Bradley expounds Hegel's theory of tragedy as the conflict between limited goods, and not between good and evil, in a world governed by the unfolding of the "ethical substance"; and also adds his own definition (brilliantly developed in his *Shakespearean Tragedy*), that tragedy is a self-division and self-waste of spirit.

In the final selection, J. W. Krutch, in his jeremiad on the "modern temper," denies the possibility of tragedy except in those ages when man accepts as real his own nobility and importance in the universe. Tragedy, he holds, is not representation of noble actions, but of actions *considered* to be noble. It is this projection of nobility, without which there is no tragedy, that constitutes the "tragic fallacy."

Aristotle

THE DEFINITION OF TRAGEDY*

6

Of the poetry which imitates in hexameter verse, and of Comedy, we will speak hereafter. Let us now discuss Tragedy, resuming its formal definition, as resulting from what has been already said.

* From Aristotle's *Poetics*, trans., S. H. Butcher (1895; rev. ed., 1911), Chs. VI-XIX. Copyright, 1911, by The Macmillan Company, Ltd. Reprinted by permission of The Macmillan Company, Ltd.

2. Tragedy, then, is an imitation of an action that is serious, complete, and of a certain magnitude; in language embellished with each kind of artistic ornament, the several kinds being found in separate parts of the play; in the form of action, not of narrative; through pity and fear effecting the proper purgation of these emotions. 3. By "language embellished," I mean language into which rhythm, "harmony," and song enter. By "the several kinds in separate parts," I mean, that some parts are rendered through the medium of verse alone, others again with the aid of song.

4. Now as tragic imitation implies persons acting, it necessarily follows, in the first place, that Spectacular equipment will be a part of Tragedy. Next, Song and Diction, for these are the medium of imitation. By "Diction" I mean the mere metrical arrangement of the words: as for "Song," it is a term whose sense every one understands.

5. Again, Tragedy is the imitation of an action; and an action implies personal agents, who necessarily possess certain distinctive qualities both of character and thought; for it is by these that we qualify actions themselves, and these—thought and character—are the two natural causes from which actions spring, and on actions again all success or failure depends. 6. Hence, the Plot is the imitation of the action:—for by plot I here mean the arrangement of the incidents. By Character I mean that in virtue of which we ascribe certain qualities to the agents. Thought is required wherever a statement is proved, or, it may be, a general truth enunciated. 7. Every Tragedy, therefore, must have six parts, which parts determine its quality —namely, Plot, Character, Diction, Thought, Spectacle, Song. Two of the parts constitute the medium of imitation, one the manner, and three the objects of imitation. And these complete the list. 8. These elements have been employed, we may say, by the poets to a man; in fact, every play contains Spectacular elements as well as Character, Plot, Diction, Song, and Thought.

9. But most important of all is the structure of the incidents. For Tragedy is an imitation, not of men, but of an action and of life, and life consists in action, and its end is a mode of action, not a quality. 10. Now character determines men's qualities, but it is by their actions that they are happy or the reverse. Dramatic action, therefore, is not with a view to the representation of character: character comes in as subsidiary to the actions. Hence the incidents and the plot are the end of a tragedy; and the end is the chief thing of all. 11. Again, without action there cannot be a tragedy; there may be without character. The tragedies of most of our modern poets fail in the rendering of character; and of poets in general this is often true. It is the same in painting; and here lies the difference between Zeuxis and Polygnotus. Polygnotus delineates character well: the style of Zeuxis is

devoid of ethical quality. 12. Again, if you string together a set of speeches expressive of character, and well finished in point of diction and thought, you will not produce the essential tragic effect nearly so well as with a play which, however deficient in these respects, yet has a plot and artistically constructed incidents. 13. Besides which, the most powerful elements of emotional interest in Tragedy—Peripeteia or Reversal of the situation, and Recognition scenes—are parts of the plot. 14. A further proof is, that novices in the art attain to finish of diction and precision of portraiture before they can construct the plot. It is the same with almost all the early poets.

The Plot, then, is the first principle, and, as it were, the soul of a tragedy: Character holds the second place. 15. A similar fact is seen in painting. The most beautiful colors, laid on confusedly, will not give as much pleasure as the chalk outline of a portrait. Thus Tragedy is the imitation of an action, and of the agents mainly with a view to the action.

16. Third in order is Thought,—that is, the faculty of saying what is possible and pertinent in given circumstances. In the case of oratory, this is the function of the political art and of the art of rhetoric: and so indeed the older poets make their characters speak the language of civic life; the poets of our time, the language of the rhetoricians.

17. Character is that which reveals moral purpose, showing what kind of things a man chooses or avoids. Speeches, therefore, which do not make this manifest, or in which the speaker does not choose or avoid anything whatever, are not expressive of character. Thought, on the other hand, is found where something is proved to be or not to be, or a general maxim is enunciated.

18. Fourth among the elements enumerated comes Diction; by which I mean, as has been already said, the expression of the meaning in words; and its essence is the same both in verse and prose.

19. Of the remaining elements Song holds the chief place among the embellishments.

The Spectacle has, indeed, an emotional attraction of its own, but, of all the parts, it is the least artistic, and connected least with the art of poetry. For the power of Tragedy, we may be sure, is felt even apart from representation and actors. Besides, the production of spectacular effects depends more on the art of the stage machinist than on that of the poet.

7

These principles being established, let us now discuss the proper structure of the Plot, since this is the first and most important thing in Tragedy.

2. Now, according to our definition, Tragedy is an imitation of an action that is complete, and whole, and of a certain magnitude; for there may be a whole that is wanting in magnitude. 3. A whole is that which has a beginning, a middle, and an end. A beginning is that which does not itself follow anything by causal necessity, but after which something naturally is or comes to be. An end, on the contrary, is that which itself naturally follows some other thing, either by necessity, or as a rule, but has nothing following it. A middle is that which follows something as some other thing follows it. A well constructed plot, therefore, must neither begin nor end at haphazard, but conform to these principles.

4. Again, a beautiful object, whether it be a picture of a living organism or any whole composed of parts, must not only have an orderly arrangement of parts, but must also be of a certain magnitude; for beauty depends on magnitude and order. Hence an exceedingly small picture cannot be beautiful; for the view of it is confused, the object being seen in an almost imperceptible moment of time. Nor, again, can one of vast size be beautiful; for as the eye cannot take it all in at once, the unity and sense of the whole is lost for the spectator; as for instance if there were one a thousand miles long. 5. As, therefore, in the case of animate bodies and organisms a certain magnitude is necessary, and a magnitude which may be easily embraced in one view; so in the plot, a certain length is necessary, and a length which can be easily embraced by the memory. 6. The limit of length in relation to dramatic competition and sensuous presentment, is no part of artistic theory. For had it been the rule for a hundred tragedies to compete together, the performance would have been regulated by the water-clock,— as indeed we are told was formerly done. 7. But the limit as fixed by the nature of the drama itself is this:—the greater the length, the more beautiful will the piece be by reason of its size, provided that the whole be perspicuous. And to define the matter roughly, we may say that the proper magnitude is comprised within such limits, that the sequence of events, according to the law of probability or necessity, will admit of a change from bad fortune to good, or from good fortune to bad.

8

Unity of plot does not, as some persons think, consist in the unity of the hero. For infinitely various are the incidents in one man's life, which cannot be reduced to unity; and so, too, there are many actions of one man out of which we cannot make one action. 2. Hence the error, as it appears, of all poets who have composed a Heracleid, a Theseid, or other poems of the kind. They imagine that as Heracles was one man, the story of Heracles must also be a unity. 3. But Homer, as in all else he is of surpassing merit, here too —whether from art or natural genius—seems to have happily discerned the truth. In composing the Odyssey he did not include all the adventures of Odysseus—such as his wound on Parnassus, or his feigned madness at the mustering of the host—incidents between which there was no necessary or probable connexion: but he made the Odyssey, and likewise the Iliad, to center round an action that in our sense of the word is one. 4. As therefore, in the other imitative arts, the imitation is one when the object imitated is one, so the plot, being an imitation of an action, must imitate one action and that a whole, the structural union of the parts being such that, if any one of them is displaced or removed, the whole will be disjointed and disturbed. For a thing whose presence or absence makes no visible difference, is not an organic part of the whole.

9

It is, moreover, evident from what has been said, that it is not the function of the poet to relate what has happened, but what may happen,—what is possible according to the law of probability or necessity. 2. The poet and the historian differ not by writing in verse or in prose. The work of Herodotus might be put into verse, and it would still be a species of history, with metre no less than without it. The true difference is that one relates what has happened, the other what may happen. 3 Poetry, therefore, is a more philosophical and a higher thing than history: for poetry tends to express the universal, history the particular. 4. By the universal I mean how a person of a certain type will on occasion speak or act, according to the law of probability or necessity; and it is this universality at which poetry aims in the names she attaches to the personages. The particular is—for example— what Alcibiades did or suffered. 5. In Comedy this is already apparent: for here the poet first constructs the plot on the lines of probability, and then inserts characteristic names;—unlike the lampooners who write about particular individuals. 6. But tragedians still keep to real names, the reason being that what is possible is credible: what has not happened we do not at once feel sure to be possible: but what has happened is manifestly possible: otherwise it would not have happened. 7. Still there are some tragedies in which there are only one or two well known names, the rest being fictitious. In others, none are well known,—as in Agathon's Antheus, where incidents and names alike are fictitious, and yet they give none the less pleasure. 8. We must not, therefore, at all costs keep to the received legends, which are the usual subjects of Tragedy. Indeed, it would be absurd to attempt it; for even subjects that are known are known only to a few, and yet give pleasure to all. 9. It clearly follows that the poet or "maker" should be the maker of plots rather than of verses; since he is a poet because he imitates, and what he imitates are actions. And even if he chances to take an historical subject, he is none the less a poet; for there is no reason why some events that have actually happened should not conform to the law of the probable and possible, and in virtue of that quality in them he is their poet or maker.

10. Of all plots and actions the epeisodic are the worst. I call a plot "epeisodic" in which the episodes or acts succeed one another without probable or necessary sequence. Bad poets compose such pieces by their own fault, good poets, to please the players; for, as they write show pieces for competition, they stretch the plot beyond its capacity, and are often forced to break the natural continuity.

11. But again, Tragedy is an imitation not only of a complete action, but of events inspiring fear or pity. Such an effect is best produced when the events come on us by surprise; and the effect is heightened when, at the same time, they follow as cause and effect. 12. The tragic wonder will then be greater than if they happened of themselves or by accident; for even coincidences are most striking when they have an air of design. We may instance the statue of Mitys at Argos, which fell upon his murderer while he was a spectator at a festival, and killed him. Such events seem not to be due to mere chance. Plots, therefore, constructed on these principles are necessarily the best.

10

Plots are either Simple or Complex, for the actions in real life, of which the plots are an imitation, obviously show a similar distinction. 2. An action which is one and continuous in the sense above defined, I call Simple, when the change of fortune takes place without Reversal of the Situation and without Recognition.

A Complex action is one in which the change is accompanied by such Reversal, or by Recognition, or by both. 3. These last should arise from the internal structure of the plot, so that what follows should be the necessary or probable result of the preceding action. It makes all the difference whether any given event is a case of *propter hoc* or *post hoc*.

11

Reversal of the Situation is a change by which the action veers round to its opposite, subject always to our rule of probability or necessity. Thus in

the Oedipus, the messenger comes to cheer Oedipus and free him from
his alarms about his mother, but by revealing who he is, he produces the
opposite effect. Again in the Lynceus, Lynceus is being led away to his
death, and Danaus goes with him, meaning to slay him; but the outcome of
the action is, that Danaus is killed and Lynceus saved.

2. Recognition, as the name indicates, is a change from ignorance to
knowledge, producing love or hate between the persons destined by the
poet for good or bad fortune. The best form of recognition is coincident
with a Reversal of the Situation, as in the Oedipus. 3. There are indeed other
forms. Even inanimate things of the most trivial kind may sometimes be
objects of recognition. Again, we may recognize or discover whether a
person has done a thing or not. But the recognition which is most intimately
connected with the plot and action is, as we have said, the recognition of
persons. 4. This recognition, combined with Reversal, will produce either
pity or fear; and actions producing these effects are those which, by our
definition, Tragedy represents. Moreover, it is upon such situations that
the issues of good or bad fortune will depend. 5. Recognition, then, being
between persons, it may happen that one person only is recognized by the
other—when the latter is already known—or it may be necessary that the
recognition should be on both sides. Thus Iphigenia is revealed to Orestes by
the sending of the letter; but another act of recognition is required to make
Orestes known to Iphigenia.

6. Two parts, then, of the Plot—Reversal of the Situation and Recognition—turn upon surprises. A third part is the Scene of Suffering. The Scene
of Suffering is a destructive or painful action, such as death on the stage,
bodily agony, wounds, and the like.

12

[The parts of Tragedy which must be treated as elements of the whole,
have been already mentioned. We now come to the quantitative parts—
the separate parts into which Tragedy is divided—namely, Prologue, Episode,
Exode, Choric song; this last being divided into Parode and Stasimon. These
are common to all plays: peculiar to some are the songs of actors from the
stage and the Commoi.

2. The Prologue is that entire part of a tragedy which precedes the
Parode of the Chorus. The Episode is that entire part of a tragedy which is
between complete choric songs. The Exode is that entire part of a tragedy
which has no choric song after it. Of the Choric part the Parode is the first
undivided utterance of the Chorus: the Stasimon is a Choric ode without

anapaests or trochaic tetrameters: the Commos is a joint lamentation of Chorus and actors. 3. The parts of Tragedy which must be treated as elements of the whole have been already mentioned. The quantitative parts—the separate parts into which it is divided—are here enumerated.]

13

As the sequel to what has already been said, we must proceed to consider what the poet should aim at, and what he should avoid, in constructing his plots; and by what means the specific effect of Tragedy will be produced.

2. A perfect tragedy should, as we have seen, be arranged not on the simple but on the complex plan. It should, moreover, imitate actions which excite pity and fear, this being the distinctive mark of tragic imitation. It follows plainly, in the first place, that the change of fortune presented must not be the spectacle of a virtuous man brought from prosperity to adversity: for this moves neither pity nor fear; it merely shocks us. Nor, again, that of a bad man passing from adversity to prosperity: for nothing can be more alien to the spirit of Tragedy; it possesses no single tragic quality; it neither satisfies the moral sense, nor calls forth pity or fear. Nor, again, should the downfall of the utter villain be exhibited. A plot of this kind would, doubtless, satisfy the moral sense, but it would inspire neither pity nor fear; for pity is aroused by unmerited misfortune, fear by the misfortune of a man like ourselves. Such an event, therefore, will be neither pitiful nor terrible. 3. There remains, then, the character between these two extremes,—that of a man who is not eminently good and just, yet whose misfortune is brought about not by vice or depravity, but by some error or frailty. He must be one who is highly renowned and prosperous,—a personage like Oedipus, Thyestes, or other illustrious men of such families.

4. A well constructed plot should, therefore, be single in its issue, rather than double as some maintain. The change of fortune should be not from bad to good, but, reversely, from good to bad. It should come about as the result not of vice, but of some great error or frailty, in a character either such as we have described, or better rather than worse. 5. The practice of the stage bears out our view. At first the poets recounted any legend that came in their way. Now, the best tragedies are founded on the story of a few houses,—on the fortunes of Alcmaeon, Oedipus, Orestes, Meleager, Thyestes, Telephus, and those others who have done or suffered something terrible. A tragedy, then, to be perfect according to the rules of art should be of this construction. 6. Hence they are in error who censure Euripides just because he follows this principle in his plays, many of which end un-

happily. It is, as we have said, the right ending. The best proof is that on the stage and in dramatic competition, such plays, if well worked out, are the most tragic in effect; and Euripides, faulty though he may be in the general management of his subject, yet is felt to be the most tragic of the poets.

7. In the second rank comes the kind of tragedy which some place first. Like the Odyssey, it has a double thread of plot, and also an opposite catastrophe for the good and for the bad. It is accounted the best because of the weakness of the spectators; for the poet is guided in what he writes by the wishes of his audience. 8. The pleasure, however, thence derived is not the true tragic pleasure. It is proper rather to Comedy, where those who, in the piece, are the deadliest enemies—like Orestes and Aegisthus— quit the stage as friends at the close, and no one slays or is slain.

14

Fear and pity may be aroused by spectacular means; but they may also result from the inner structure of the piece, which is the better way, and indicates a superior poet. For the plot ought to be so constructed that, even without the aid of the eye, he who hears the tale told will thrill with horror and melt to pity at what takes place. This is the impression we should receive from hearing the story of the Oedipus. 2. But to produce this effect by the mere spectacle is a less artistic method, and dependent on extraneous aids. Those who employ spectacular means to create a sense not of the terrible but only of the monstrous, are strangers to the purpose of Tragedy; for we must not demand of Tragedy any and every kind of pleasure, but only that which is proper to it. 3. And since the pleasure which the poet should afford is that which comes from pity and fear through imitation, it is evident that this quality must be impressed upon the incidents.

Let us then determine what are the circumstances which strike us as terrible or pitiful.

4. Actions capable of this effect must happen between persons who are either friends or enemies or indifferent to one another. If an enemy kills an enemy, there is nothing to excite pity either in the act or the intention,— except so far as the suffering in itself is pitiful. So again with indifferent persons. But when the tragic incident occurs between those who are near or dear to one another—if, for example, a brother kills, or intends to kill, a brother, a son his father, a mother her son, a son his mother, or any other deed of the kind is done—these are the situations to be looked for by the poet. 5. He may not indeed destroy the framework of the received legends —the fact, for instance, that Clytemnestra was slain by Orestes and Eriphyle

by Alcmaeon—but he ought to show invention of his own, and skilfully handle the traditional material. Let us explain more clearly what is meant by skilful handling.

6. The action may be done consciously and with knowledge of the persons, in the manner of the older poets. It is thus too that Euripides makes Medea slay her children. Or, again, the deed of horror may be done, but done in ignorance, and the tie of kinship or friendship be discovered afterwards. The Oedipus of Sophocles is an example. Here, indeed, the incident is outside the drama proper; but cases occur where it falls within the action of the play: one may cite the Alcmaeon of Astydamas, or Telegonus in the Wounded Odysseus. 7. Again, there is a third case,—<to be about to act with knowledge of the persons and then not to act. The fourth case is> when some one is about to do an irreparable deed through ignorance, and makes the discovery before it is done. These are the only possible ways. For the deed must either be done or not done,—and that wittingly or unwittingly. But of all these ways, to be about to act knowing the persons, and then not to act, is the worst. It is shocking without being tragic, for no disaster follows. It is, therefore, never, or very rarely, found in poetry. One instance, however, is in the Antigone, where Haemon threatens to kill Creon. 8. The next and better way is that the deed should be perpetrated. Still better, that it should be perpetrated in ignorance, and the discovery made afterwards. There is then nothing to shock us, while the discovery produces a startling effect. 9. The last case is the best, as when in the Cresphontes Merope is about to slay her son, but recognizing who he is, spares his life. So in the Iphigenia, the sister recognizes the brother just in time. Again in the Helle, the son recognizes the mother when on the point of giving her up. This, then, is why a few families only, as has been already observed, furnish the subjects of tragedy. It was not art, but happy chance, that led poets to look for such situations and so impress the tragic quality upon their plots. They are compelled, therefore, to have recourse to those houses whose history contains moving incidents like these.

Enough has now been said concerning the structure of the incidents, and the proper constitution of the plot.

15

In respect of Character there are four things to be aimed at. First, and most important, it must be good. Now any speech or action that manifests moral purpose of any kind will be expressive of character: the character will be good if the purpose is good. This rule is relative to each class. Even a woman may be good, and also a slave; though the woman may be said to be an inferior being, and the slave quite worthless. 2. The second thing to aim at is propriety. There is a type of manly valour; but valour in a woman, or unscrupulous cleverness, is inappropriate. 3. Thirdly, character must be true to life: for this is a distinct thing from goodness and propriety, as here described. 4. The fourth point is consistency: for though the subject of the imitation, who suggested the type, be inconsistent, still he must be consistently inconsistent. 5. As an example of motiveless degradation of character, we have Menelaus in the Orestes: of character indecorous and inappropriate, the lament of Odysseus in the Scylla, and the speech of Melanippe: of inconsistency, the Iphigenia at Aulis,—for Iphigenia the suppliant in no way resembles her later self.

6. As in the structure of the plot, so too in the portraiture of character, the poet should always aim either at the necessary or the probable. Thus a person of a given character should speak or act in a given way, by the rule either of necessity or of probability; just as this event should follow that by necessity or probable sequence. 7. It is therefore evident that the unravelling of the plot, no less than the complication, must arise out of the plot itself, it must not be brought about by the *Deus ex Machina*—as in the Medea, or in the Return of the Greeks in the Iliad. The *Deus ex Machina* should be employed only for events external to the drama,—for antecedent or subsequent events, which lie beyond the range of human knowledge, and which require to be reported or foretold; for to the gods we ascribe the power of seeing all things. Within the action there must be nothing irrational. If the irrational cannot be excluded, it should be outside the scope of the tragedy. Such is the irrational element in the Oedipus of Sophocles.

8. Again, since Tragedy is an imitation of persons who are above the common level, the example of good portrait-painters should be followed. They, while reproducing the distinctive form of the original, make a likeness which is true to life and yet more beautiful. So too the poet, in representing men who are irascible or indolent, or have other defects of character, should preserve the type and yet ennoble it. In this way Achilles is portrayed by Agathon and Homer.

9. These then are rules the poet should observe. Nor should he neglect those appeals to the senses, which, though not among the essentials, are the concomitants of poetry; for here too there is much room for error. But of this enough has been said in our published treatises.

16

What Recognition is has been already explained. We will now enumerate its kinds.

First, the least artistic form, which, from poverty of wit, is most commonly employed—recognition by signs. 2. Of these some are congenital,—such as "the spear which the earth-born race bear on their bodies," or the stars introduced by Carcinus in his Thyestes. Others are acquired after birth; and of these some are bodily marks, as scars; some external tokens, as necklaces, or the little ark in the Tyro by which the discovery is effected. 3. Even these admit of more or less skilful treatment. Thus in the recognition of Odysseus by his scar, the discovery is made in one way by the nurse, in another by the swineherds. The use of tokens for the express purpose of proof—and, indeed, any formal proof with or without tokens—is a less artistic mode of recognition. A better kind is that which comes about by a turn of incident, as in the Bath Scene in the Odyssey.

4. Next come the recognitions invented at will by the poet, and on that account wanting in art. For example, Orestes in the Iphigenia reveals the fact that he is Orestes. She, indeed, makes herself known by the letter; but he, by speaking himself, and saying what the poet, not what the plot requires. This, therefore, is nearly allied to the fault above mentioned:—for Orestes might as well have brought tokens with him. Another similar instance is the "voice of the shuttle" in the Tereus of Sophocles.

5. The third kind depends on memory when the sight of some object awakens a feeling: as in the Cyprians of Dicaeogenes, where the hero breaks into tears on seeing the picture; or again in the "Lay of Alcinous," where Odysseus, hearing the minstrel play the lyre, recalls the past and weeps; and hence the recognition.

6. The fourth kind is by process of reasoning. Thus in the Choëphori:—"Some one resembling me has come: no one resembles me but Orestes: therefore Orestes has come." Such too is the discovery made by Iphigenia in the play of Polyidus the Sophist. It was a natural reflection for Orestes to make, "So I too must die at the altar like my sister." So, again, in the Tydeus of Theodectes, the father says, "I came to find my son, and I lose my own life." So too in the Phineidae: the women, on seeing the place, inferred their fate:—"Here we are doomed to die, for here we were cast forth." 7. Again, there is a composite kind of recognition involving false inference on the part of one of the characters, as in the Odysseus Disguised as a Messenger. A said <that no one else was able to bend the bow; . . . hence B (the disguised Odysseus) imagined that A would> recognize the bow which, in fact, he had not seen; and to bring about a recognition by this means—the expectation that A would recognize the bow—is false inference.

8. But, of all recognitions, the best is that which arises from the incidents themselves, where the startling discovery is made by natural means. Such is that in the Oedipus of Sophocles, and in the Iphigenia; for it was

natural that Iphigenia should wish to dispatch a letter. These recognitions alone dispense with the artificial aid of tokens ar amulets. Next came the recognitions by process of reasoning.

17

In constructing the plot and working it out with the proper diction, the poet should place the scene, as far as possible, before his eyes. In this way, seeing everything with the utmost vividness, as if he were a spectator of the action, he will discover what is in keeping with it, and be most unlikely to overlook inconsistencies. The need of such a rule is shown by the fault found in Carcinus. Amphiaraus was on his way from the temple. This fact escaped the observation of one who did not see the situation. On the stage, however, the piece failed, the audience being offended at the oversight.

2. Again, the poet should work out his play, to the best of his power, with appropriate gestures; for those who feel emotion are most convincing through natural sympathy with the characters they represent; and one who is agitated storms, one who is angry rages, with the most life-like reality. Hence poetry implies either a happy gift of nature or a strain of madness. In the one case a man can take the mold of any character; in the other, he is lifted out of his proper self.

3. As for the story, whether the poet takes it ready made or constructs it for himself, he should first sketch its general outline, and then fill in the episodes and amplify in detail. The general plan may be illustrated by the Iphigenia. A young girl is sacrificed; she disappears mysteriously from the eyes of those who sacrificed her; she is transported to another country, where the custom is to offer up all strangers to the goddess. To this ministry she is appointed. Some time later her own brother chances to arrive. The fact that the oracle for some reason ordered him to go there, is outside the general plan of the play. The purpose, again, of his coming is outside the action proper. However, he comes, he is seized, and, when on the point of being sacrificed, reveals who he is. The mode of recognition may be either that of Euripides or of Polyidus, in whose play he exclaims very naturally:—"So it was not my sister only, but I too, who was doomed to be sacrificed"; and by that remark he is saved.

4. After this, the names being once given, it remains to fill in the episodes. We must see that they are relevant to the action. In the case of Orestes, for example, there is the madness which led to his capture, and his deliverance by means of the purificatory rite. 5. In the drama, the episodes are short, but it is these that give extension to Epic poetry. Thus the story

of the Odyssey can be stated briefly. A certain man is absent from home for many years; he is jealously watched by Poseidon, and left desolate. Meanwhile his home is in a wretched plight—suitors are wasting his substance and plotting against his son. At length, tempest-tost, he himself arrives; he makes certain persons acquainted with him; he attacks the suitors with his own hand, and is himself preserved while he destroys them. This is the essence of the plot; the rest is episode.

18

Every tragedy falls into two parts.—Complication and Unravelling or *Dénouement.* Incidents extraneous to the action are frequently combined with a portion of the action proper, to form the Complication; the rest is the Unravelling. By the Complication I mean all that extends from the beginning of the action to the part which marks the turning-point to good or bad fortune. The Unravelling is that which extends from the beginning of the change to the end. Thus, in the Lynceus of Theodectes, the Complication consists of the incidents presupposed in the drama, the seizure of the child, and then again * * <The Unravelling> extends from the accusation of murder to the end.

2. There are four kinds of Tragedy, the Complex, depending entirely on Reversal of the Situation and Recognition; the Pathetic (where the motive is passion),—such as the tragedies on Ajax and Ixion; the Ethical (where the motives are ethical),—such as the Phthiotides and the Peleus. The fourth kind is the Simple. <We here exclude the purely spectacular element>, exemplified by the Phorcides, the Prometheus, and scenes laid in Hades. 3. The poet should endeavour, if possible, to combine all poetic elements; or failing that, the greatest number and those the most important; the more so, in face of the cavilling criticism of the day. For whereas there have hitherto been good poets, each in his own branch, the critics now expect one man to surpass all others in their several lines of excellence.

In speaking of a tragedy as the same or different, the best test to take is the plot. Identity exists where the Complication and Unravelling are the same. Many poets tie the knot well, but unravel it ill. Both arts, however, should always be mastered.

4. Again, the poet should remember what has been often said, and not make an Epic structure into a Tragedy—by an Epic structure I mean one with a multiplicity of plots—as if, for instance, you were to make a tragedy out of the entire story of the Iliad. In the Epic poem, owing to its length, each part assumes its proper magnitude. In the drama the result is far from

answering to the poet's expectation. 5. The proof is that the poets who have dramatised the whole story of the Fall of Troy, instead of selecting portions, like Euripides; or who have taken the whole tale of Niobe, and not a part of her story, like Aeschylus, either fail utterly or meet with poor success on the stage. Even Agathon has been known to fail from this one defect. In his Reversals of the Situation, however, he shows a marvellous skill in the effort to hit the popular taste,—to produce a tragic effect that satisfies the moral sense. 6. This effect is produced when the clever rogue, like Sisyphus, is outwitted, or the brave villain defeated. Such an event is probable in Agathon's sense of the word: "it is probable," he says, "that many things should happen contrary to probability."

7. The Chorus too should be regarded as one of the actors; it should be an integral part of the whole, and share in the action, in the manner not of Euripides but of Sophocles. As for the later poets, their choral songs pertain as little to the subject of the piece as to that of any other tragedy. They are, therefore, sung as mere interludes,—a practice first begun by Agathon. Yet what difference is there between introducing such choral interludes, and transferring a speech, or even a whole act, from one play to another?

19

It remains to speak of Diction and Thought, the other parts of Tragedy having been already discussed. Concerning Thought, we may assume what is said in the Rhetoric, to which inquiry the subject more strictly belongs. 2. Under Thought is included every effect which has to be produced by speech, the subdivisions being,—proof and refutation; the excitation of the feelings, such as pity, fear, anger, and the like; the suggestion of importance or its opposite. 3. Now, it is evident that the dramatic incidents must be treated from the same points of view as the dramatic speeches, when the object is to evoke the sense of pity, fear, importance, or probability. The only difference is, that the incidents should speak for themselves without verbal exposition; while the effects aimed at in speech should be produced by the speaker, and as a result of the speech. For what were the business of a speaker, if the Thought were revealed quite apart from what he says?

4. Next, as regards Diction. One branch of the inquiry treats of the Modes of Utterance. But this province of knowledge belongs to the art of Delivery and to the masters of that science. It includes, for instance,—what is a command, a prayer, a statement, a threat, a question, an answer, and so forth. 5. To know or not to know these things involves no serious censure upon the poet's art. For who can admit the fault imputed to Homer by

Protagoras,—that in the words, "Sing, goddess, of the wrath," he gives a command under the idea that he utters a prayer? For to tell some one to do a thing or not to do it is, he says, a command. We may, therefore, pass this over as an inquiry that belongs to another art, not to poetry.

David Hume

OF TRAGEDY*

It seems an unaccountable pleasure which the spectators of a well-written tragedy receive from sorrow, terror, anxiety, and other passions that are in themselves disagreeable and uneasy. The more they are touched and affected, the more are they delighted with the spectacle; and as soon as the uneasy passions cease to operate, the piece is at an end. One scene of full joy and contentment and security is the utmost that any composition of this kind can bear; and it is sure always to be the concluding one. If in the texture of the piece there be interwoven any scenes of satisfaction, they afford only faint gleams of pleasure, which are thrown in by way of variety, and in order to plunge the actors into deeper distress by means of that contrast and disappointment. The whole art of the poet is employed in rousing and supporting the compassion and indignation, the anxiety and resentment, of his audience. They are pleased in proportion as they are afflicted, and never are so happy as when they employ tears, sobs, and cries, to give vent to their sorrow, and relieve their heart, swollen with the tenderest sympathy and compassion.

The few critics who have had some tincture of philosophy have remarked this singular phenomenon, and have endeavoured to account for it.

L'Abbé Dubos, in his Reflections on Poetry and Painting, asserts, that nothing is in general so disagreeable to the mind as the languid, listless state of indolence into which it falls upon the removal of all passion and occupation. To get rid of this painful situation, it seeks every amusement and pursuit: business, gaming, shows, executions; whatever will rouse the passions and take its attention from itself. No matter what the passion is: let it be disagreeable, afflicting, melancholy, disordered; it is still better than that insipid languor which arises from perfect tranquillity and repose.

---

* From David Hume's "Of Tragedy", first published in Hume's *Four Dissertations,* 1757.

David Hume (1711–1776), renowned English empiricist philosopher, was also a writer of assorted essays, including some on aesthetic matters.

It is impossible not to admit this account as being, at least in part, satisfactory. You may observe, when there are several tables of gaming, that all the company run to those where the deepest play is, even though they find not there the best players. The view, or, at least, imagination of high passions, arising from great loss or gain, affects the spectator by sympathy, gives him some touches of the same passions, and serves him for a momentary entertainment. It makes the time pass the easier with him, and is some relief to that oppression under which men commonly labor when left entirely to their own thoughts and meditations.

We find that common liars always magnify, in their narrations, all kinds of danger, pain, distress, sickness, deaths, murders, and cruelties, as well as joy, beauty, mirth, and magnificence. It is an absurd secret which they have for pleasing their company, fixing their attention, and attaching them to such marvellous relations by the passions and emotions which they excite.

There is, however, a difficulty in applying to the present subject, in its full extent, this solution, however ingenious and satisfactory it may appear. It is certain that the same object of distress which pleases in a tragedy, were it really set before us, would give the most unfeigned uneasiness; though it be then the most effectual cure to languor and indolence. Monsieur Fontenelle seems to have been sensible of this difficulty, and accordingly attempts another solution of the phenomenon, at least makes some addition to the theory above mentioned.

"Pleasure and pain," says he, "which are two sentiments so different in themselves, differ not so much in their cause. From the instance of tickling it appears, that the movement of pleasure pushed a little too far, becomes pain, and that the movement of pain, a little moderated, becomes pleasure. Hence it proceeds, that there is such a thing as a sorrow, soft and agreeable: It is a pain weakened and diminished. The heart likes naturally to be moved and affected. Melancholy objects suit it, and even disastrous and sorrowful, provided they are softened by some circumstance. It is certain, that, on the theatre, the representation has almost the effect of reality; yet it has not altogether that effect. However we may be hurried away by the spectacle, whatever dominion the senses and imagination may usurp over the reason, there still lurks at the bottom a certain idea of falsehood in the whole of what we see. This idea, though weak and disguised, suffices to diminish the pain which we suffer from the misfortunes of those whom we love, and to reduce that affliction to such a pitch as converts it into a pleasure. We weep for the misfortune of a hero to whom we are attached. In the same instant we comfort ourselves by reflecting, that it is nothing but a fiction: And it is precisely that mixture of sentiments which composes an agreeable sorrow, and tears that delight us. But as that affliction which is caused by exterior and sensible objects is stronger than the consolation which arises from an internal reflection, they are the effects and symptoms of sorrow that ought to predominate in the composition."

This solution seems just and convincing; but perhaps it wants still some new addition, in order to make it answer fully the phenomenon which we here examine. All the passions, excited by eloquence, are agreeable in the highest degree, as well as those which are moved by painting and the theatre. The epilogues of Cicero are, on this account chiefly, the delight of every reader of taste; and it is difficult to read some of them without the deepest sympathy and sorrow. His merit as an orator, no doubt, depends much on his success in this particular. When he had raised tears in his judges and all his audience, they were then the most highly delighted, and expressed the greatest satisfaction with the pleader. The pathetic description of the butchery made by Verres of the Sicilian captains, is a masterpiece of this kind. But I believe none will affirm, that the being present at a melancholy scene of that nature would afford any entertainment. Neither is the sorrow here softened by fiction. For the audience were convinced of the reality of every circumstance. What is it then which in this case raises a pleasure from the bosom of uneasiness, so to speak, and a pleasure which still retains all the features and outward symptoms of distress and sorrow?

I answer: this extraordinary effect proceeds from that very eloquence with which the melancholy scene is represented. The genius required to paint objects in a lively manner, the art employed in collecting all the pathetic circumstances, the judgment displayed in disposing them; the exercise, I say, of these noble talents, together with the force of expression, and beauty of oratorial numbers, diffuse the highest satisfaction on the audience, and excite the most delightful movements. By this means, the uneasiness of the melancholy passions is not only overpowered and effaced by something stronger of an opposite kind, but the whole impulse of those passions is converted into pleasure and swells the delight which the eloquence raises in us. The same force of oratory, employed on an uninteresting subject, would not please half so much, or rather would appear altogether ridiculous; and the mind, being left in absolute calmness and indifference, would relish none of those beauties of imagination or expression, which, if joined to passion, give it such exquisite entertainment. The impulse or vehemence arising from sorrow, compassion, indignation, receives a new direction from the sentiments of beauty.[1] The latter, being the predominant emotion, seize the whole

[1] Painters make no scruple of representing distress and sorrow, as well as any other passion: But they seem not to dwell so much on these melancholy affections as the poets, who, though they copy every motion of the human breast, yet pass quickly over the

mind, and convert the former into themselves, at least tincture them so strongly as totally to alter their nature. And the soul being at the same time roused by passion and charmed by eloquence, feels on the whole a strong movement, which is altogether delightful.

The same principle takes place in tragedy; with this addition, that tragedy is an imitation, and imitation is always of itself agreeable. This circumstance serves still further to smooth the motions of passion, and convert the whole feeling into one uniform and strong enjoyment. Objects of the greatest terror and distress please in painting, and please more than the most beautiful objects that appear calm and indifferent. The affection, rousing the mind, excites a large stock of spirit and vehemence; which is all transformed into pleasure by the force of the prevailing movement. It is thus the fiction of tragedy softens the passion, by an infusion of a new feeling, not merely by weakening or diminishing the sorrow. You may by degrees weaken a real sorrow, till it totally disappears; yet in none of its gradations will it ever give pleasure; except, perhaps, by accident, to a man sunk under lethargic indolence, whom it rouses from that languid state.

To confirm this theory, it will be sufficient to produce other instances, where the subordinate movement is converted into the predominant, and gives force to it, though of a different, and even sometimes though of a contrary nature.

Novelty naturally rouses the mind, and attracts our attention; and the movements which it causes are always converted into any passion belonging to the object, and join their force to it. Whether an event excites joy or sorrow, pride or shame, anger or good-will, it is sure to produce a stronger affection, when new or unusual. And though novelty of itself be agreeable, it fortifies the painful, as well as agreeable passions.

Had you any intention to move a person extremely by the narration of any event, the best method of increasing its effect would be artfully to delay informing him of it, and first excite his curiosity and impatience before you let him into the secret. This is the artifice practiced by Iago in the famous scene of Shakespeare; and every spectator is sensible that Othello's jealousy acquires additional force from his preceding impatience, and that the subordinate passion is here readily transformed into the predominant one.

Difficulties increase passions of every kind; and by rousing our attention, and exciting our active powers, they produce an emotion which nourishes the prevailing affection.

---

agreeable sentiments. A painter represents only one instant; and if that be passionate enough, it is sure to affect and delight the spectator: But nothing can furnish to the poet a variety of scenes, and incidents, and sentiments, except distress, terror, or anxiety. Complete joy and satisfaction is attended with security and leaves no further room for action.

Parents commonly love that child most whose sickly infirm frame of body has occasioned them the greatest pains, trouble, and anxiety, in rearing him. The agreeable sentiment of affection here acquires force from sentiments of uneasiness.

Nothing endears so much a friend as sorrow for his death. The pleasure of his company has not so powerful an influence.

Jealousy is a painful passion; yet without some share of it, the agreeable affection of love has difficulty to subsist in its full force and violence. Absence is also a great source of complaint among lovers, and gives them the greatest uneasiness: yet nothing is more favourable to their mutual passion than short intervals of that kind. And if long intervals often prove fatal, it is only because, through time, men are accustomed to them, and they cease to give uneasiness. Jealousy and absence in love compose the *dolce peccante* of the Italians, which they suppose so essential to all pleasure.

There is a fine observation of the elder Pliny, which illustrates the principle here insisted on. "It is very remarkable," says he, "that the last works of celebrated artists, which they left imperfect, are always the most prized, such as the *Iris* of Aristides, the *Tyndarides* of Nicomachus, the *Medea* of Timomachus, and the *Venus* of Apelles. These are valued even above their finished productions. The broken lineaments of the piece, and the half-formed idea of the painter, are carefully studied; and our very grief for that curious hand, which had been stopped by death, is an additional increase to our pleasure."

These instances (and many more might be collected) are sufficient to afford us some insight into the analogy of nature, and to show us, that the pleasure which poets, orators, and musicians give us, by exciting grief, sorrow, indignation, compassion, is not so extraordinary or paradoxical as it may at first sight appear. The force of imagination, the energy of expression, the power of numbers, the charms of imitation; all these are naturally, of themselves delightful to the mind. And when the object presented lays hold also of some affection, the pleasure still rises upon us, by the conversion of this subordinate movement into that which is predominant. The passion, though perhaps naturally, and when excited by the simple appearance of a real object, it may be painful; yet is so smoothed, and softened, and mollified, when raised by the finer arts, that it affords the highest entertainment.

To confirm this reasoning, we may observe, that if the movements of the imagination be not predominant above those of the passion, a contrary effect follows; and the former, being now subordinate, is converted into the latter, and still further increases the pain and affliction of the sufferer.

Who could ever think of it as a good expedient for comforting an afflicted parent, to exaggerate, with all the force of elocution, the irreparable loss which he has met with by the death of a favourite child? The more power of imagination and expression you here employ, the more you increase his despair and affliction.

The shame, confusion, and terror of Verres, no doubt, rose in proportion to the noble eloquence and vehemence of Cicero: So also did his pain and uneasiness. These former passions were too strong for the pleasure arising from the beauties of elocution; and operated, though from the same principle, yet in a contrary manner, to the sympathy, compassion, and indignation of the audience.

Lord Clarendon, when he approaches towards the catastrophe of the royal party, supposes that his narration must then become infinitely disagreeable; and he hurries over the king's death without giving us one circumstance of it. He considers it as too horrid a scene to be contemplated with any satisfaction, or even without the utmost pain and aversion. He himself, as well as the readers of that age, were too deeply concerned in the events, and felt a pain from subjects which an historian and a reader of another age would regard as the most pathetic and most interesting, and, by consequence, the most agreeable.

An action, represented in tragedy, may be too bloody and atrocious. It may excite such movements of horror as will not soften into pleasure; and the greatest energy of expression, bestowed on descriptions of that nature, serves only to augment our uneasiness. Such is that action represented in the *Ambitious Step-mother,* where a venerable old man, raised to the height of fury and despair, rushes against a pillar, and, striking his head upon it, besmears it all over with mingled brains and gore. The English theatre abounds too much with such shocking images.

Even the common sentiments of compassion require to be softened by some agreeable affection, in order to give a thorough satisfaction to the audience. The mere suffering of plaintive virtue, under the triumphant tyranny and oppression of vice, forms a disagreeable spectacle, and is carefully avoided by all masters of the drama. In order to dismiss the audience with entire satisfaction and contentment, the virtue must either convert itself into a noble courageous despair, or the vice receive its proper punishment.

Most painters appear in this light to have been very unhappy in their subjects. As they wrought much for churches and convents, they have chiefly represented such horrible subjects as crucifixions and martyrdoms, where nothing appears but tortures, wounds, executions, and passive suffering, without any action or affection. When they turned their pencil from this ghastly mythology, they had commonly recourse to Ovid, whose fictions, though passionate and agreeable, are scarcely natural or probable enough for painting.

The same inversion of that principle which is here insisted on, displays itself in common life, as in the effects of oratory and poetry. Raise so the subordinate passion that it becomes the predominant, it swallows up that affection which it before nourished and increased. Too much jealousy extinguishes love; too much difficulty renders us indifferent; too much sickness and infirmity disgusts a selfish and unkind parent.

What so disagreeable as the dismal, gloomy, disastrous stories, with which melancholy people entertain their companions? The uneasy passion being there raised alone, unaccompanied with any spirit, genius, or eloquence, conveys a pure uneasiness, and is attended with nothing that can soften it into pleasure or satisfaction.

Friedrich Nietzsche

DIONYSOS AND APOLLO*

I

Much will have been gained for esthetics once we have succeeded in apprehending directly—rather than merely *ascertaining*—that art owes its continuous evolution to the Apollonian-Dionysiac duality, even as the propagation of the species depends on the duality of the sexes, their constant conflicts and periodic acts of reconciliation. I have borowed my adjectives from the Greeks, who developed their mystical doctrines of art through plausible *embodiments,* not through purely conceptual means. It is by those two art-sponsoring deities, Apollo and Dionysos, that we are made to recognize the tremendous split, as regards both origins and objectives, between the plastic, Apollonian arts and the non-visual art of music inspired by Dionysos. The two creative tendencies developed alongside one another, usually in fierce opposition, each by its taunts forcing the other to more energetic production, both perpetuating in a discordant concord that agon which the

* From Friedrich Nietzsche's *The Birth of Tragedy*, trans., Francis Golffing, Sections I, VII. Copyright © 1956, by Doubleday & Company. Reprinted by permission of Doubleday & Company, Inc.

Friedrich Nietzsche (1844–1900), famous German philosopher, wrote many books which have influenced the world. His *Birth of Tragedy* (1872) was his first; and his suggestions about the origin of Greek tragedy led to fruitful researches by many others, including Jane Harrison, Gilbert Murray and followers of the Cambridge School of Classical Anthropology.

term *art* but feebly denominates: until at last, by the thaumaturgy of an Hellenic act of will, the pair accepted the yoke of marriage and, in this condition, begot Attic tragedy, which exhibits the salient features of both parents.

To reach a closer understanding of both these tendencies, let us begin by viewing them as the separate art realms of *dream* and *intoxication,* two physiological phenomena standing toward one another in much the same relationship as the Apollonian and Dionysiac. It was in a dream, according to Lucretius, that the marvelous gods and goddesses first presented themselves to the minds of men. That great sculptor, Phidias, beheld in a dream the entrancing bodies of more-than-human beings, and likewise, if anyone had asked the Greek poets about the mystery of poetic creation, they too would have referred him to dreams and instructed him much as Hans Sachs instructs us in *Die Meistersinger:*

> My friend, it is the poet's work
> Dreams to interpret and to mark.
> Believe me that man's true conceit
> In a dream becomes complete:
> All poetry we ever read
> Is but true dreams interpreted.

The fair illusion of the dream sphere, in the production of which every man proves himself an accomplished artist, is a precondition not only of all plastic art, but even, as we shall see presently, of a wide range of poetry. Here we enjoy an immediate apprehension of form, all shapes speak to us directly, nothing seems indifferent or redundant. Despite the high intensity with which these dream realities exist for us, we still have a residual sensation that they are illusions; at least such has been my experience—and the frequency, not to say normality, of the experience is borne out in many passages of the poets. Men of philosophical disposition are known for their constant premonition that our everyday reality, too, is an illusion, hiding another, totally different kind of reality. It was Schopenhauer who considered the ability to view at certain times all men and things as mere phantoms or dream images to be the true mark of philosophic talent. The person who is responsive to the stimuli of art behaves toward the reality of dream much the way the philosopher behaves toward the reality of existence: he observes exactly and enjoys his observations, for it is by these images that he interprets life, by these processes that he rehearses it. Nor is it by pleasant images only that such plausible connections are made: the whole divine comedy of life, including its somber aspects, its sudden balkings, impish accidents, anxious expectations, moves past him, not quite like a shadow play—for it is he himself, after all, who lives and suffers through these scenes—yet never without giving a fleeting sense of illusion; and I imagine that many persons have reassured themselves amidst the perils of dream by calling out, "It is a dream! I want it to go on." I have even heard of people spinning out the causality of one and the same dream over three or more successive nights. All these facts clearly bear witness that our innermost being, the common substratum of humanity, experiences dreams with deep delight and a sense of real necessity. This deep and happy sense of the necessity of dream experiences was expressed by the Greeks in the image of Apollo. Apollo is at once the god of all plastic powers and the soothsaying god. He who is etymologically the "lucent" one, the god of light, reigns also over the fair illusion of our inner world of fantasy. The perfection of these conditions in contrast to our imperfectly understood waking reality, as well as our profound awareness of nature's healing powers during the interval of sleep and dream, furnishes a symbolic analogue to the soothsaying faculty and quite generally to the arts, which make life possible and worth living. But the image of Apollo must incorporate that thin line which the dream image may not cross, under penalty of becoming pathological, of imposing itself on us as crass reality: a discreet limitation, a freedom from all extravagant urges, the sapient tranquillity of the plastic god. His eye must be sun-like, in keeping with his origin. Even at those moments when he is angry and ill-tempered there lies upon him the consecration of fair illusion. In an eccentric way one might say of Apollo what Schopenhauer says, in the first part of *The World as Will and Idea,* of man caught in the veil of Maya: "Even as on an immense, raging sea, assailed by huge wave crests, a man sits in a little rowboat trusting his frail craft, so, amidst the furious torments of this world, the individual sits tranquilly, supported by the *principium individuationis* and relying on it." One might say that the unshakable confidence in that principle has received its most magnificent expression in Apollo, and that Apollo himself may be regarded as the marvelous divine image of the *principium individuationis,* whose looks and gestures radiate the full delight, wisdom, and beauty of "illusion."

In the same context Schopenhauer has described for us the tremendous awe which seizes man when he suddenly begins to doubt the cognitive modes of experience, in other words, when in a given instance the law of causation seems to suspend itself. If we add to this awe the glorious transport which arises in man, even from the very depths of nature, at the shattering of the *principium individuationis,* then we are in a position to apprehend the essence of Dionysiac rapture, whose closest analogy is furnished by physical intoxication. Dionysiac stirrings arise either through the influence of those narcotic potions of which all primitive races speak in their hymns, or through the powerful approach of spring, which penetrates with joy the whole frame of nature. So stirred, the individual forgets himself completely. It is the same Dionysiac power which in medieval Germany drove ever increasing crowds of people singing and dancing from place to place; we recognize in these St. John's and St. Vitus' dancers the bacchic choruses of the Greeks, who had their precursors in Asia Minor and as far back as Babylon and the orgiastic Sacaea. There are people who, either from lack of experience or out of sheer stupidity, turn away from such phenomena, and, strong in the sense of their own sanity, label them either mockingly or pityingly "endemic diseases." These benighted souls have no idea how cadaverous and ghostly their "sanity" appears as the intense throng of Dionysiac revelers sweeps past them.

Not only does the bond between man and man come to be forged once more by the magic of the Dionysiac rite, but nature itself, long alienated or subjugated, rises again to celebrate the reconciliation with her prodigal son, man. The earth offers its gifts voluntarily, and the savage beasts of mountain and desert approach in peace. The chariot of Dionysos is bedecked with flowers and garlands; panthers and tigers stride beneath his yoke. If one were to convert Beethoven's "Paean to Joy" into a painting, and refuse to curb the imagination when that multitude prostrates itself reverently in the dust, one might form some apprehension of Dionysiac ritual. Now the slave emerges as a freeman; all the rigid, hostile walls which either necessity or despotism has erected between men are shattered. Now that the gospel of universal harmony is sounded, each individual becomes not only reconciled to his fellow but actually at one with him—as though the veil of Maya had been torn apart and there remained only shreds floating before the vision of mystical Oneness. Man now expresses himself through song and dance as the member of a higher community; he has forgotten how to walk, how to speak, and is on the brink of taking wing as he dances. Each of his gestures betokens enchantment; through him sounds a supernatural power, the same power which makes the animals speak and the earth render up milk and honey. He feels himself to be godlike and strides with the same elation and ecstasy as the gods he has seen in his dreams. No longer the *artist,* he has himself become a *work of art:* the productive power of the whole universe is now manifest in his transport, to the glorious satisfaction of the primordial One. The finest clay, the most precious marble—man—is here kneaded and hewn, and the chisel blows of the Dionysiac world artist are accompanied by the cry of the Eleusinian mystagogues: "Do you fall on your knees, multitudes, do you divine your creator?"

VII

At this point we need to call upon every esthetic principle so far discussed, in order to find our way through the labyrinthine origins of Greek tragedy. I believe I am saying nothing extravagant when I claim that the problem of these origins has never even been posed, much less solved, no matter how often the elusive rags of ancient tradition have been speculatively sewn together and ripped apart. That tradition tells us in no uncertain terms that tragedy arose out of the tragic chorus and was, to begin with, nothing but chorus. We are thus bound to scan the chorus closely as the archetypal drama, disregarding the current explanations of it as the idealized spectator, or as representing the populace over against the noble realm of the set. The latter interpretation, which sounds so grandly edifying to certain politicians (as though the democratic Athenians had represented in the popular chorus the invariable moral law, always right in face of the passionate misdeeds and extravagances of kings) may have been suggested by a phrase in Aristotle, but this lofty notion can have had no influence whatever on the original formation of tragedy, whose purely religious origins would exclude not only the opposition between the people and their rulers but any kind of political or social context. Likewise we would consider it blasphemous, in the light of the classical form of the chorus as we know it from Aeschylus and Sophocles, to speak of a "foreshadowing" of constitutional democracy, though others have not stuck at such blasphemy. No ancient polity ever embodied constitutional democracy, and one dares to hope that ancient tragedy did not even foreshadow it.

Much more famous than this political explanation of the chorus is the notion of A. W. Schlegel, who advises us to regard the chorus as the quintessence of the audience, as the "ideal spectator." If we hold this view against the historical tradition according to which tragedy was, in the beginning, nothing but chorus, it turns out to be a crude, unscholarly, though dazzling hypothesis—dazzling because of the effective formulation, the typically German bias for anything called "ideal," and our momentary wonder at the notion. For we are indeed amazed when we compare our familiar theater audience with the tragic chorus and ask ourselves whether the former could conceivably be construed into something analogous to the latter. We tacitly deny the possibility, and then are brought to wonder both at the boldness of Schlegel's assertion and at what must have been the totally different complexion of the Greek audience. We had supposed all along that the spectator, whoever he might be, would always have to remain conscious of the fact that he had before him a work of art, not empiric reality, whereas the tragic chorus of the Greeks is constrained to view the characters enacted on the stage as veritably existing. The chorus of the Oceanides think that they behold the actual Titan Prometheus, and believe themselves every bit as real as the god. Are we seriously to assume that the highest and purest type of spectator is he who, like the Oceanides, regards the god as physically present and real? That it is characteristic of the ideal spectator to rush on stage and deliver the god from his fetters? We had put our faith in an artistic audience, believing that the more intelligent the individual spectator was, the more capable he was of viewing the work of art as art; and now Schlegel's theory suggests to us that the perfect spectator viewed the world of the stage not at all as art but as reality. "Oh these Greeks!" we moan. "They upset our entire esthetic!" But once we have grown accustomed to it, we repeat Schlegel's pronouncement whenever the question of the chorus comes up.

The emphatic tradition I spoke of militates against Schlegel: chorus as such, without stage—the primitive form of tragedy—is incompatible with that chorus of ideal spectators. What sort of artistic genre would it be that derived from the idea of the spectator and crystallized itself in the mode of the "pure" spectator? A spectator without drama is an absurdity. We suspect that the birth of tragedy can be explained neither by any reverence for the moral intelligence of the multitude nor by the notion of a spectator without drama, and, altogether, we consider the problem much too complex to be touched by such facile interpretations.

An infinitely more valuable insight into the significance of the chorus was furnished by Schiller in the famous preface to his *Bride of Messina,* where the chorus is seen as a living wall which tragedy draws about itself in order to achieve insulation from the actual world, to preserve its ideal ground and its poetic freedom.

Schiller used this view as his main weapon against commonplace naturalism, against the illusionistic demand made upon dramatic poetry. While the day of the stage was conceded to be artificial, the architecture of the set symbolic, the metrical discourse stylized, a larger misconception still prevailed. Schiller was not content to have what constitutes the very essence of poetry merely tolerated as poetic license. He insisted that the introduction of the chorus was the decisive step by which any naturalism in art was openly challenged. This way of looking at art seems to me the one which our present age, thinking itself so superior, has labeled pseudo-idealism. But I very much fear that we, with our idolatry of verisimilitude, have arrived at the opposite pole of all idealism, the realm of the waxworks. This too betrays a kind of art, as do certain popular novels of today. All I ask is that we not be importuned by the pretense that such art has left Goethe's and Schiller's "pseudo-idealism" behind.

It is certainly true, as Schiller saw, that the Greek chorus of satyrs, the chorus of primitive tragedy, moved on ideal ground, a ground raised high above the common path of mortals. The Greek has built for his chorus the scaffolding of a fictive chthonic realm and placed thereon fictive nature spirits. Tragedy developed on this foundation, and so has been exempt since its beginning from the embarrassing task of copying actuality. All the same, the world of tragedy is by no means a world arbitrarily projected between heaven and earth; rather it is a world having the same reality and credibility as Olympus possessed for the devout Greek. The satyr, as the Dionysiac chorist, dwells in a reality sanctioned by myth and ritual. That tragedy should begin with him, that the Dionysiac wisdom of tragedy should speak through him, is as puzzling a phenomenon as, more generally, the origin of tragedy from the chorus. Perhaps we can gain a starting point for this inquiry by claiming that the satyr, that fictive nature sprite, stands to cultured man in the same relation as Dionysiac music does to civilization. Richard Wagner has said of the latter that it is absorbed by music as lamplight by daylight. In the same manner, I believe, the cultured Greek felt himself absorbed into the satyr chorus, and in the next development of Greek tragedy state and society, in fact all that separated man from man, gave way before an overwhelming sense of unity which led back into the heart of nature. The metaphysical solace (with which, I wish to say at once, all true tragedy sends us away) that, despite every phenomenal change, life is at bottom indestructibly joyful and powerful, was expressed most concretely in the chorus of satyrs, nature beings who dwell behind all civilization and preserve their identity through every change of generations and historical movement.

With this chorus the profound Greek, so uniquely susceptible to the subtlest and deepest suffering, who had penetrated the destructive agencies of both nature and history, solaced himself. Though he had been in danger of craving a Buddhistic denial of the will, he was saved by art, and through art life reclaimed him.

While the transport of the Dionysiac state, with its suspension of all the ordinary barriers of existence, lasts, it carries with it a Lethean element in which everything that has been experienced by the individual is drowned. This chasm of oblivion separates the quotidian reality from the Dionysiac. But as soon as that quotidian reality enters consciousness once more it is viewed with loathing, and the consequence is an ascetic, abulic state of mind. In this sense Dionysiac man might be said to resemble Hamlet: both have looked deeply into the true nature of things, they have *understood* and are now loath to act. They realize that no action of theirs can work any change in the eternal condition of things, and they regard the imputation as ludicrous or debasing that they should set right the time which is out of joint. Understanding kills action, for in order to act we require the veil of illusion; such is Hamlet's doctrine, not to be confounded with the cheap wisdom of John-a-Dreams, who through too much reflection, as it were a surplus of possibilities, never arrives at action. What, both in the case of Hamlet and of Dionysiac man, overbalances any motive leading to action, is not reflection but understanding, the apprehension of truth and its terror. Now no comfort any longer avails, desire reaches beyond the transcendental world, beyond the gods themselves, and existence, together with its gulling reflection in the gods and an immortal Beyond, is denied. The truth once seen, man is aware everywhere of the ghastly absurdity of existence, comprehends the symbolism of Ophelia's fate and the wisdom of the wood sprite Silenus: nausea invades him.

Then, in this supreme jeopardy of the will, art that sorceress expert in healing, approaches him; only she can turn his fits of nausea into imaginations with which it is possible to live. These are on the one hand the spirit of the *sublime*, which subjugates terror by means of art; on the other hand the *comic* spirit, which releases us, through art, from the tedium of absurdity. The satyr chorus of the dithyramb was the salvation of Greek art; the threatening paroxysms I have mentioned were contained by the intermediary of those Dionysiac attendants.

Andrew C. Bradley

HEGEL'S THEORY OF TRAGEDY*

Since Aristotle dealt with tragedy, and, as usual drew the main features of his subject with those sure and simple strokes which no later hand has rivalled, the only philosopher who has treated it in a manner both original and searching is Hegel.[1] I propose here to give a sketch of Hegel's theory,

* From Andrew Bradley's *Oxford Lectures on Poetry*, Lecture Three, Copyright, 1909, The Macmillan Company, Ltd. Reprinted by permission of The Macmillan Company, Ltd.

Andrew Cecil Bradley (1851–1935), distinguished Oxford Professor, wrote many essays on literature and general aesthetic problems, including his famous *Shakespearean Tragedy*.

[1] See, primarily, *Aesthetik*, iii. 479-581, and especially 525-581. There is much in *Aesthetik*, i. 219-306, and a good deal in ii. 1-243, that bears on the subject. See also the section on Greek religion in *Religionsphilosophie*, ii. 96-156, especially 131-6, 152-6; and the references to the death of Socrates in *Geschichte der Philosophie*, ii. 81 ff., especially 102-5. The works so far cited all consist of posthumous redactions of lecture-notes. Among

and to add some remarks upon it. But I cannot possibly do justice in a sketch to a theory which fills many pages of the *Aesthetik;* which I must tear from its connections with the author's general view of poetry, and with the rest of his philosophy;[2] and which I must try to exhibit as far as possible in the language of ordinary literature. To estimate this theory, therefore, from my sketch would be neither safe nor just—all the more because, in the interest of immediate clearness, I have not scrupled to insert without warning various remarks and illustrations for which Hegel is not responsible.

On certain characteristics of tragedy the briefest reminder will suffice. A large part of the nature of this form of drama is common to the drama in all its forms; and of this nothing need be said. It will be agreed, further, that in all tragedy there is some sort of collision or conflict—conflict of feelings, modes of thought, desires, wills, purposes; conflict of persons with one another, or with circumstances, or with themselves; one, several, or all of these kinds of conflict, as the case may be. Again, it may be taken for granted that a tragedy is a story of unhappiness or suffering, and excites such feelings as pity and fear. To this, if we followed the present usage of the term, we should add that the story of unhappiness must have an unhappy end; by which we mean in effect that the conflict must close with the death of one or more of the principal characters. But this usage of the word "tragedy" is comparatively recent; it leaves us without a name for many plays, in many languages, which deal with unhappines without ending unhappily; and Hegel takes the word in its older and wiser sense.

Passing on from these admitted characteristics of tragedy, we may best approach Hegel's peculiar view by observing that he lays particular stress on one of them. That a tragedy is a story of suffering is probably to many people the most obvious fact about it. Hegel says very little of this; partly, perhaps, because it is obvious, but more because the essential point to him is not the suffering but its cause, namely, the action or conflict. Mere suffering, he would say, is not tragic, but only the suffering that comes of a special kind of action. Pity for mere misfortune, like fear of it, is not tragic pity or fear. These are due to the spectacle of the conflict and its attendant suffering, which do not appeal simply to our sensibilities or our instinct of self-preservation, but also to our deeper mind or spirit (*Geist,*

works published by Hegel himself, the early essay on "Naturrecht" (*Werke,* i. 386 ff.), and *Phaenomenologie d. Geistes,* 320-348, 527-542, deal with or bear on Greek tragedy. See also *Rechtsphilosophie,* 196, note. There is a note on *Wallenstein* in *Werke,* xvii. 411-4. These references are to the second edition of the works cited, where there are two editions.

[2] His theory of tragedy is connected with his view of the function of negation in the universe. No statement therefore which ignores his metaphysics and his philosophy of religion can be more than a fragmentary account of that theory.

a word which, with its adjective, I shall translate "spirit," "spiritual," because our words "mind" and "mental" suggest something merely intellectual).

The reason why the tragic conflict thus appeals to the spirit is that it is itself a conflict of the spirit. It is a conflict, that is to say, between powers that rule the world of man's will and action—his "ethical substance." The family and the state, the bond of parent and child, of brother and sister, of husband and wife, of citizen and ruler, or citizen and citizen, with the obligations and feelings appropriate to these bonds; and again the powers of personal love and honour, or of devotion to a great cause or an ideal interest like religion or science or some kind of social welfare—such are the forces exhibited in tragic action; not indeed alone, not without others less affirmative and perhaps even evil, but still in preponderating mass. And as they form the substance of man, are common to all civilized men, and are acknowledged as powers rightfully claiming human allegiance, their exhibition in tragedy has that interest, at once deep and universal, which is essential to a great work of art.

In many a work of art, in many a statue, picture, tale, or song, such powers are shown in solitary peace or harmonious co-operation. Tragedy shows them in collision. Their nature is divine, and in religion they appear as gods; but, as seen in the world of tragic action, they have left the repose of Olympus, have entered into human wills, and now meet as foes. And this spectacle, if sublime, is also terrible. The essentially tragic fact is the self-division and intestinal warfare of the ethical substance, not so much the war of good with evil as the war of good with good. Two of these isolated powers face each other, making incompatible demands. The family claims what the state refuses, love requires what honour forbids. The competing forces are both in themselves rightful, and so far the claim of each is equally justified; but the right of each is pushed into a wrong, because it ignores the right of the other, and demands that absolute sway which belongs to neither alone, but to the whole of which each is but a part.

And one reason why this happens lies in the nature of the characters through whom these claims are made. It is the nature of the tragic hero, at once his greatness and his doom, that he knows no shrinking or half-heartedness, but identifies himself wholly with the power that moves him, and will admit the justification of no other power. However varied and rich his inner life and character may be, in the conflict it is all concentrated in one point. Antigone *is* determination to do her duty to her dead brother; Romeo is not a son or a citizen as well as a lover, he is lover pure and simple, and his love is the whole of him.

The end of the tragic conflict is the denial of both the exclusive claims. It is not the work of chance or blank fate; it is the act of the ethical substance itself, asserting its absoluteness against the excessive pretensions of its particular powers. In that sense, as proceeding from an absolute right which cancels claims based on right but pushed into wrong, it may be called the act of "eternal justice." Sometimes it can end the conflict peacefully, and the tragedy closes with a solution. Appearing as a divine being, the spiritual unity reconciles by some adjustment the claims of the contending powers (*Eumenides*); or at its bidding one of them softens its demand (*Philoctetes*); or again, as in the more beautiful solution of the *Oedipus Coloneus*, the hero by his own self-condemnation and inward purification reconciles himself with the supreme justice, and is accepted by it. But sometimes the quarrel is pressed to extremes; the denial of the one-sided claims involves the death of one or more of the persons concerned; and we have a catastrophe. The ultimate power thus appears as a destructive force. Yet even here, as Hegel insists, the end is not without an aspect of reconciliation. For that which is denied is not the rightful powers with which the combatants have identified themselves. On the contrary, those powers, and with them the only thing for which the combatants cared, are affirmed. What is denied is the exclusive and therefore wrongful assertion of their right.

Such in outline is Hegel's main view. It may be illustrated more fully by two examples, favourites of his, taken from Aeschylus and Sophocles. Clytemnestra has murdered Agamemnon, her husband and king. Orestes, their son, is impelled by filial piety to avenge his father, and is ordered by Apollo to do so. But to kill a mother is to sin against filial piety. The spiritual substance is divided against itself. The sacred bond of father and son demands what the equally sacred bond of son and mother forbids. When, therefore, Orestes has done the deed, the Furies of his murdered mother claim him for their prey. He appeals to Apollo, who resists their claim. A solution is arrived at without a catastrophe. The cause is referred to Athene, who institutes at Athens a court of sworn judges. The votes of this court being equally divided, Athene gives her casting-vote for Orestes; while the Furies are at last appeased by a promise of everlasting honour at Athens.

In the *Antigone*, on the other hand, to Hegel the "perfect exemplar of tragedy," the solution is negative. The brother of Antigone has brought against his native city an army of foreigners bent on destroying it. He has been killed in the battle, and Creon, the ruler of the city, has issued an edict forbidding anyone on pain of death to bury the corpse. In so doing he not only dishonours the dead man, but violates the rights of the gods of the dead. Antigone without hesitation disobeys the edict, and Creon, despite the remonstrance of his son, who is affianced to her, persists in exacting the penalty. Warned by the prophet Teiresias, he gives way, but too late. Antigone, immured in a rocky chamber to starve, has anticipated her death. Her lover follows her example, and his mother refuses to survive him. Thus Antigone has lost her life through her absolute assertion of the family against the state; Creon has violated the sanctity of the family, and in return sees his own home laid in ruins. But in this catastrophe neither the right of the family nor that of the state is denied; what is denied is the absoluteness of the claim of each.

The danger of illustrations like these is that they divert attention from the principle illustrated to questions about the interpretation of particular works. So it will be here. I cannot stay to discuss these questions, which do not affect Hegel's principle; but it will be well, before going further, to remove a misunderstanding of it which is generally to be found in criticisms of his treatment of the *Eumenides* and the *Antigone*. The main objection may be put thus: "Hegel talks of equally justified powers or claims. But Aeschylus never meant that Orestes and the Furies were equally justified; for Orestes was acquitted. Nor did Sophocles mean that Antigone and Creon were equally right. And how can it have been equally the duty of Orestes to kill his mother and not to kill her?" But, in the first place, it is most important to observe that Hegel is not discussing at all what we should generally call the moral quality of the acts and persons concerned, or, in the ordinary sense, what it was their duty to do. And, in the second place, when he speaks of "equally justified" powers, what he means, and, indeed, sometimes says, is that these powers are *in themselves* justified. The family and the state, the bond of father and son, the bond of mother and son, the bond of citizenship, these are each and all, one as much as another, powers rightfully claiming human allegiance. It is tragic that observance of one should involve the violation of another. These are Hegel's propositions, and surely they are true. Their truth is quite unaffected by the fact (assuming it is one) that in the circumstances the act combining this observance of one and violation of another was morally right, or by the fact (if so it is) that one such act (say Antigone's) was morally right, and another (say Creon's) was morally wrong. It is sufficient for Hegel's principle that the violation should take place, and that we should feel its weight. We do feel it. We may approve the act of Antigone or Orestes, but in approving it we still feel that it is no light matter to disobey the law or to murder a mother, that (as we might say) there is much justice in the pleas of the Furies and of Creon, and that the *tragic* effect depends upon these facts. If, again, it is objected that the underlying conflict in

the *Antigone* is not between the family and the state, but between divine
and human law, that objection, if sound, might touch Hegel's interpretation,[3] but it would not affect his principle, except for those who recognize
no obligation in human law; and it will scarcely be contended that Sophocles is to be numbered among them. On the other hand, it is, I think, a
matter for regret that Hegel employed such words as "right," "justified,"
and "justice." They do not mislead readers familiar with his writings, but
to others they suggest associations with criminal law, or our everyday
moral judgments, or perhaps the theory of "poetic justice"; and these are
all out of place in a discussion on tragedy.

Having determined in outline the idea or principle of tragedy, Hegel
proceeds to give an account of some differences between ancient and modern works. In the limited time at our disposal we shall do best to confine
ourselves to a selection from his remarks on the latter. For in speaking of
ancient tragedy Hegel, who finds something modern in Euripides, makes
accordingly but little use of him for purposes of contrast, while his main
point of view as to Aeschylus and Sophocles has already appeared in the
illustrations we have given of the general principle. I will only add, by
way of preface, that the pages about to be summarized leave on one, rightly
or wrongly, the impression that to his mind the principle is more adequately
realized in the best classical tragedies than in modern works. But the question whether this really was his deliberate opinion would detain us too long
from weightier matters.[4]

Hegel considers first the cases where modern tragedy resembles ancient
in dealing with conflicts arising from the pursuit of ends which may be
called substantial or objective and not merely personal. And he points out
that modern tragedy here shows a much greater variety. Subjects are taken,
for example, from the quarrels of dynasties, of rivals for the throne, of kings
and nobles, of state and church. Calderon shows the conflict of love and
honour regarded as powers imposing obligations. Schiller in his early works
makes his characters defend the rights of nature against convention, or of
freedom of thought against prescription—rights in their essence universal.
Wallenstein aims at the unity and peace of Germany; Karl Moor attacks
the whole arrangement of society; Faust seeks to attain in thought and
action union with the Absolute. In such cases the end is more than personal;
it represents a power claiming the allegiance of the individual; but, on
the other hand, it does not always or generally represent a great *ethical*

[3] I say "might," because Hegel himself in the *Phaenomenologie* uses those very terms
"divine" and "human law" in reference to the *Antigone*.
[4] See Note at end of lecture.

institution or bond like the family or the state. We have passed into a wider world.

But secondly, he observes, in regard to modern tragedy, that in a larger number of instances such public or universal interests either do not appear at all, or, if they appear, are scarcely more than a background for the real subject. The real subject, the impelling end or passion, and the ensuing conflict, is personal,—these particular characters with their struggle and their fate. The importance given to subjectivity—this is the distinctive mark of modern sentiment, and so of modern art; and such tragedies bear its impress. A part at least of Hegel's meaning may be illustrated thus. We are interested in the personality of Orestes or Antigone, but chiefly as it shows itself in one aspect, as identifying itself with a certain ethical relation; and our interest in the personality is inseparable and indistinguishable from our interest in the power it represents. This is not so with Hamlet, whose position so closely resembles that of Orestes. What engrosses our attention is the whole personality of Hamlet in his conflict, not with an opposing spiritual power, but with circumstances and, still more, with difficulties in his own nature. No one could think of describing Othello as the representative of an ethical family relation. His passion, however much nobility he may show in it, is personal. So is Romeo's love. It is not pursued, like Posa's freedom of thought, as something universal, a right of man. Its right, if it could occur to us to use the term at all, is Romeo's right.

On this main characteristic of modern tragedy others depend. For instance, that variety of subject to which reference has just been made depends on it. For when so much weight is attached to personality, almost any fatal collision in which a sufficiently striking character is involved may yield material for tragedy. Naturally, again, characterisation has become fuller and more subtle, except in dramas which are more or less an imitation of the antique. The characters in Greek tragedy are far from being types or personified abstractions, as those of classical French tragedy tend to be: they are genuine individuals. But still they are comparatively simple and easy to understand, and have not the intricacy of the characters in Shakespeare. These, for the most part, represent simply themselves; and the loss of that interest which attached to the Greek characters from their identification with an ethical power, is compensated by an extraordinary subtlety in their portrayal, and also by their possession of some peculiar charm or some commanding superiority. Finally, the interest in personality explains the freedom with which characters more or less definitely evil are introduced in modern tragedy. Mephistopheles is as essentially modern as Faust. The passion of Richard or Macbeth is not only personal, like that of Othello; it is egoistic and anarchic, and leads to crimes done with a full knowledge of their wickedness; but to the modern mind the greatness of the personality justifies its appearance in the position of hero. Such beings as Iago and Goneril, almost portents of evil, are not indeed made the heroes of tragedies; but, according to Hegel, they would not have been admitted in Greek tragedy at all. If Clytemnestra had been cited in objection as a parallel to Lady Macbeth, he would have replied that Lady Macbeth had not the faintest ground of complaint against Duncan, while in reading the *Agamemnon* we are frequently reminded that Clytemnestra's husband was the sacrificer of their child. He might have added that Clytemnestra is herself an example of the necessity, where one of the principal characters inspires hatred or horror, of increasing the subtlety of the drawing or adding grandeur to the evil will.

It remains to compare ancient and modern tragedy in regard to the issue of the conflict. We have seen that Hegel attributes this issue in the former to the ethical substance or eternal justice, and so accounts for such reconciliation as we feel to be present even where the end is a catastrophe. Now, in the catastrophe of modern tragedy, he says, a certain justice is sometimes felt to be present; but even then it differs from the antique justice. It is in some cases more "abstract": the end pursued by the hero, though it is not egoistic, is still presented rather as his particular end than as something rightful though partial; and hence the catastrophe appears as the reaction, not of an undivided ethical totality, but merely of the universal turning against a too assertive particular.[5] In cases, again, where the hero (Richard or Macbeth) openly attacks an ethical power and plunges into evil, we feel that he meets with justice, and only gets what he deserves; but then this justice is colder and more "criminalistic" than that of ancient tragedy. Thus even when the modern work seems to resemble the ancient in its issue, the sense of reconciliation is imperfect. And partly for this reason, partly from the concentration of our interest on individuality as such, we desire to see in the individual himself some sort of reconciliation with his fate. What shape this will take depends, of course, on the story and the character of the hero. It may appear in a religious form, as his feeling that he is exchanging his earthly being for an indestructible happiness; or again, in his recognition of the justice of his fall; or at least he may show us that, in face of the forces that crush him to death, he maintains untouched the freedom and strength of his own will.

But there remain, says Hegel, many modern tragedies where we have

[5] This interpretation of Hegel's "abstract" is more or less conjectural and doubtful.

to attribute the catastrophe not to any kind of justice, but to unhappy circumstances and outward accidents. And then we can only feel that the individual whose merely personal ends are thwarted by mere particular circumstances and chances, pays the penalty that awaits existence in a scene of contingency and finitude. Such a feeling cannot rise above sadness, and, if the hero is a noble soul, it may become the impression of a dreadful external necessity. This impression can be avoided only when circumstance and accident are so depicted that they are felt to coincide with something in the hero himself, so that he is not simply destroyed by an outward force. So it is with Hamlet. "This bank and shoal of time" is too narrow for his soul, and the death that seems to fall on him by chance is also within him. And so in *Romeo and Juliet* we feel that the rose of a love so beautiful is too tender to bloom in the stormswept valley of its birth. But such a feeling of reconciliation is still one of pain, an unhappy blessedness.[6] And if the situation displayed in a drama is of such a kind that we feel the issue to depend *simply* on the turn the dramatist may choose to give to the course of events, we are fully justified in our preference for a happy ending.

In this last remark (or rather in the pages misrepresented by it) Hegel, of course, is not criticizing Shakespeare. He is objecting to the destiny-dramas of his own time, and to the fashionable indulgence in sentimental melancholy. Strongly as he asserted the essential function of negation throughout the universe, the affirmative power of the spirit, even in its profoundest divisions, was for him the deepest truth and the most inspiring theme. And one may see this even in his references to Shakespeare. He appreciated Shakespeare's representation of extreme forms of evil, but, even if he was fully satisfied of its justification, his personal preference lay in another direction, and while I do not doubt that he thought *Hamlet* a greater work than *Iphigenie,* I suspect he loved Goethe's play the best.

Most of those who have thought about this subject will agree that the ideas I have tried to sketch are interesting and valuable; but they suggest scores of questions. Alike in the account of tragedy in general, and in that of the differences between ancient and modern tragedy, everyone will find statements to doubt and omissions to regret; and scarcely one of Hegel's interpretations of particular plays will escape objection. It is impossible for me to touch on more than a few points; and to the main ideas I owe so much that I am more inclined to dwell on their truth than to criticize what seem to be defects. But perhaps after all an attempt to supplement

---

[6] Hegel's meaning does not fully appear in the sentences here condensed. The "blessedness" comes from the sense of the greatness or beauty in the characters.

and amend may be the best way of throwing some part of Hegel's meaning more into relief. And I will begin with the attempt to supplement.

He seems to be right in laying emphasis on the action and conflict in tragedy rather than on the suffering and misfortune. No mere suffering or misfortune, no suffering that does not spring in great part from human agency, and in some degree from the agency of the sufferer, is tragic, however pitiful or dreadful it may be. But, sufficient connection with these agencies being present, misfortune, the fall from prosperity to adversity, with the suffering attending it, at once becomes tragic; and in many tragedies it forms a large ingredient, as does the pity for it in the tragic feeling. Hegel, I think, certainly takes too little notice of it; and by this omission he also withdraws attention from something the importance of which he would have admitted at once; I mean the way in which suffering is borne. Physical pain, to take an extreme instance, is one thing: Philoctetes, bearing it, is another. And the noble endurance of pain that rends the heart is the source of much that is best worth having in tragedy.

Again, there is one particular kind of misfortune *not* obviously due to human agency, which undoubtedly may affect us in a tragic way. I mean that kind which suggests the idea of fate. Tragedies which represent man as the mere plaything of chance or a blank fate or a malicious fate, are never really deep: it is satisfactory to see that Maeterlinck, a man of true genius, has now risen above these ideas. But, where those factors of tragedy are present which Hegel emphasizes, the impression of something fateful in what we call accident, the impression that the hero not only invites misfortune by his exceptional stature and exceptional daring, but is also, if I may so put it, strangely and terribly unlucky, is in many plays a genuine ingredient in tragic effect. It is so, for example, in the *Oedipus Tyrannus*. It is so even in dramas like Shakespeare's, which exemplify the saying that character is destiny. Hegel's own reference to the prominence of accident in the plot of *Hamlet* proves it. Othello would not have become Iago's victim if his own character had been different; but still, as we say, it is an extraordinary fatality which makes him the companion of the one man in the world who is at once able enough, brave enough, and vile enough to ensnare him. In the *Antigone* itself, and in the very catastrophe of it, accident plays its part; we can hardly say that it depends solely on the characters of Creon and Antigone that the one yields just too late to save the life of the other. Now, it may be said with truth that Hegel's whole account of the ultimate power in tragedy is a rationalization of the idea of fate, but his remarks on this particular aspect of fate are neither sufficient nor satisfactory.

His insistence on the need for some element of reconciliation in a tragic catastrophe, and his remarks on the various forms it assumes, have the greatest value; but one result of the omissions just noticed is that he sometimes exaggerates it, and at other times rates it too low. When he is speaking of the kind of tragedy he most approves, his language almost suggests that our feeling at the close of the conflict is, or should be, one of complete reconciliation. This it surely neither is nor can be. Not to mention the suffering and death we have witnessed, the very existence of the conflict, even if a supreme ethical power is felt to be asserted in its close, remains a painful fact, and, in large measure, a fact not understood. For, though we may be said to see, in one sense, how the opposition of spiritual powers arises, something in us, and that the best, still cries out against it. And even the perception or belief that it must needs be that offenses come would not abolish our feeling that the necessity is terrible, or our pain in the woe of the guilty and the innocent. Nay, one may conjecture, the feeling and the pain would not vanish if we fully understood that the conflict and catastrophe were by a rational necessity involved in the divine and eternally accomplished purpose of the world. But this exaggeration in Hegel's language, if partly due to his enthusiasm for the affirmative, may be mainly, like some other defects, an accident of lecturing. In the *Philosophy of Religion,* I may add, he plainly states that in the solution even of tragedies like the *Antigone* something remains unresolved (ii. 135).

On the other hand, his treatment of the aspect of reconciliation in modern tragedy is in several respects insufficient. I will mention only one. He does not notice that in the conclusion of not a few tragedies pain is mingled not merely with acquiescence, but with something like exultation. Is there not such a feeling at the close of *Hamlet, Othello,* and *King Lear;* and that although the end in the last two cases touches the limit of legitimate pathos? This exultation appears to be connected with our sense that the hero has never shown himself so great or noble as in the death which seals his failure. A rush of passionate admiration, and a glory in the greatness of the soul, mingle with our grief; and the coming of death, so far from destroying these feelings, appears to leave them untouched, or even to be entirely in harmony with them. If in such dramas we may be said to feel that the ultimate power is no mere fate, but a spiritual power, then we also feel that the hero was never so near to this power as in the moment when it required his life.

The last omission I would notice in Hegel's theory is that he underrates the action in tragedy of what may be called by a rough distinction moral evil rather than defect. Certainly the part played by evil differs greatly in different cases, but it is never absent, not even from tragedies of Hegel's favourite type. If it does not appear in the main conflict, it appears in its occasion. You may say that, while Iago and Macbeth have evil purposes, neither the act of Orestes nor the vengeance of the Furies, neither Antigone's breach of the edict nor even Creon's insistence on her punishment, springs from evil in them; but the situation with which Orestes or Antigone has to deal, and so in a sense the whole tragedy, arises from evil, the murder of Agamemnon, and the attempt of Polyneices to bring ruin on his native city. In fact, if we confine the title "tragedy" to plays ending with a catastrophe, it will be found difficult to name great tragedies, ancient or modern, in which evil has not directly or indirectly a prominent part. And its presence has an important bearing on the effect produced by the catastrophe. On the one hand, it deepens the sense of painful awe. The question why affirmative spiritual forces should collide is hard enough; but the question why, together with them, there should be generated violent evil and extreme depravity is harder and more painful still. But, on the other hand, the element of reconciliation in the catastrophe is strengthened by recognition of the part played by evil in bringing it about; because our sense that the ultimate power cannot endure the presence of such evil is implicitly the sense that this power is at least more closely allied with good. If it rejects the exaggerated claims of its own isolated powers, that which provokes from it a much more vehement reaction must be still more alien to its nature. This feeling is forcibly evoked by Shakespeare's tragedies, and in many Greek dramas it is directly appealed to by repeated reminders that what is at work in the disasters is the unsleeping Ate which follows an ancestral sin. If Aristotle did not in some lost part of the *Poetics* discuss ideas like this, he failed to give a complete rationale of Greek tragedy.

I come lastly to the matter I have most at heart. What I take to be the central idea in Hegel's theory seems to me to touch the essence of tragedy. And I will not assert that his own statement of it fails to cover the whole field of instances. For he does not teach, as he is often said to do, that tragedy portrays only the conflict of such ethical powers as the family and the state. He adds to these, as we have seen, others, such as love and honour, together with various universal ends; and it may even be maintained that he has provided in his general statement for those numerous cases where, according to himself, no substantial or universal ends collide, but the interest is centered on "personalities." Nevertheless, when these cases come to be considered more fully—and, in Hegel's view they are the most characteristically modern cases—we are not satisfied. They naturally tend to appear as declensions from the more ideal ancient form; for how can a personality which represents only itself claim the interest of one which represents something universal? And further, they are sometimes described in a manner which strikes the reader, let us say, of Shakespeare, as both insufficient and misleading. Without raising, then, unprofitable questions about the comparative merits of ancient and modern tragedy, I should like to propose a restatement of Hegel's general principle which would make it more obviously apply to both.

If we omit all reference to ethical or substantial powers and interests, what have we left? We have the more general idea—to use again a formula not Hegel's own—that tragedy portrays a self-division and self-waste of spirit, or a division of spirit involving conflict and waste. It is implied in this that on *both* sides in the conflict there is a spiritual value. The same idea may be expressed (again, I think, not in Hegel's own words) by saying that the tragic conflict is one not merely of good with evil, but also, and more essentially, of good with good. Only in saying this, we must be careful to observe that "good" here means anything that has spiritual value, not moral goodness alone,[7] and that "evil" has a similarly wide sense.

Now this idea of a division of spirit involving conflict and waste covers the tragedies of ethical and other universal powers, and it covers much besides. According to it the collision of such powers would be one kind of tragic collision, but only one. Why are we tragically moved by the conflict of family and state? Because we set a high value on family and state. Why then should not the conflict of anything else that has sufficient value affect us tragically? It does. The value must be sufficient—a moderate value will not serve; and other characteristics must be present which need not be considered here. But, granted these conditions, *any* spiritual conflict involving spiritual waste is tragic. And it is just one greatness of modern art that it has shown the tragic fact in situations of so many and such diverse kinds. These situations have not the peculiar effectiveness of the conflicts preferred by Hegel, but they may have an equal effectiveness peculiar to themselves.

Let me attempt to test these ideas by choosing a most unfavourable instance—unfavourable because the play seems at first to represent a conflict simply of good and evil, and so, according both to Hegel's statement and the proposed restatement, to be no tragedy at all: I mean *Macbeth*. What is the conflict here? It will be agreed that it does not lie between two ethical powers or universal ends, and that, as Hegel says, the main interest is in personalities. Let us take it first, then, to lie between Macbeth and the persons opposing him, and let us ask whether there is not spiritual value

[7] Hegel himself expressly guards against this misconception.

or good on both sides—not an equal amount of good (that is not necessary), but enough good on each to give the impression of spiritual waste.
Is there not such good in Macbeth? It is not a question merely of moral
goodness, but of good. It is not a question of the use made of good, but
of its presence. And such bravery and skill in war as win the enthusiasm
of everyone about him; such an imagination as few but poets possess; a
conscience so vivid that his deed is to him beforehand a thing of terror,
and, once done, condemns him to that torture of the mind on which he
lies in restless ecstasy; a determination so tremendous and a courage so
appalling that, for all this torment, he never dreams of turning back, but,
even when he has found that life is a tale full of sound and fury, signifying
nothing, will tell it out to the end though earth and heaven and hell are
leagued against him; are not these things, in themselves, good, and glori-
ously good? Do they not make you, for all your horror, admire Macbeth,
sympathize with his agony, pity him, and see in him the waste of forces on
which you place a spiritual value? It is simply on this account that he is
for you, not the abstraction called a criminal who merely "gets what he
deserves" (art, like religion, knows no such thing), but a tragic hero, and
that his war with other forces of indubitable spiritual worth is a tragic
war.[8]

It is required by the restatement of Hegel's principle to show that in
the external conflict of persons there is good on both sides. It is not required that this should be true, secondly, of both sides in the conflict within
the hero's soul; for the hero is only a part of the tragedy. Nevertheless in
almost all cases, if not in all, it is true. It is obviously so where, as in the
hero and also the heroine of the *Cid*, the contending powers in this internal
struggle are love and honour. Even when love is of a quality less pure and
has a destructive force, as in Shakespeare's Antony, it is clearly true. And
it remains true even where, as in Hamlet and Macbeth, the contest seems
to lie, and for most purposes might conveniently be said to lie, between
forces simply good and simply the reverse. This is not really so, and the
tragic effect depends upon the fact. It depends on our feeling that the
elements in the man's nature are so inextricably blended that the good in
him, that which we admire, instead of simply opposing the evil, reinforces
it. Macbeth's imagination deters him from murder, but it also makes the

---

[8] The same point may be put thus, in view of that dangerous word "personality." Our
interest in Macbeth may be called interest in a personality; but it is not an interest
in some bare form of self-consciousness, nor yet in a person in the legal sense, but in
a personality full of matter. This matter is not an ethical or universal end, but it must
in a sense be universal—human nature in a particular form—or it would not excite
the horror, sympathy, and admiration it does excite. Nor, again, could it excite these
feelings if it were not composed largely of qualities on which we set a high value.

vision of a crown irresistibly bright. If he had been less determined, nay, if his conscience had been less maddening in its insistence that he had thrown the precious jewel of his soul irretrievably away, he might have paused after his first deed, might even have repented. Yet his imagination, his determination, and his conscience were things good. Hamlet's desire to do his duty is a good thing, but what opposes this desire is by no means simply evil. It is something to which a substantial contribution is made by the qualities we most admire in him. Thus the nature of tragedy, as seen in the external conflict, repeats itself on each side of this conflict, and everywhere there is a spiritual value in both the contending forces.

In showing that *Macbeth*, a tragedy as far removed as possible from the *Antigone* as understood by Hegel, is still of one nature with it, and equally answers to the account of tragedy proposed, it has been necessary to ignore the great difference between the two plays. But when once the common essence of all tragedies has been determined, their difference become the interesting subject. They could be distinguished according to the character of the collisions on which they are built, or of the main forces which move the principal agents. And it may well be that, other things being equal (as they never are), the tragedy in which the hero is, as we say, a good man, is more tragic than that in which he is, as we say, a bad one. The more spiritual value, the more tragedy in conflict and waste. The death of Hamlet or Othello is, so far, more tragic than that of Macbeth, that of Macbeth than that of Richard. Below Richard stands Iago, a figure still tragic, but unfit for the hero's part; below him persons like Regan or, in the very depth, Oswald, characters no longer (at least in the dramatic sense) tragic at all. Moral evil, that is to say, so greatly diminishes the spiritual value we ascribe to the personality that a very large amount of good of some kind is required to bring this personality up to the tragic level, the destruction of evil as such being in no degree tragic. And again, it may well be that, other things being equal, the more nearly the contending forces approach each other in goodness, the more tragic is the conflict; that the collision is, so far, more tragic in the *Antigone* than in *Macbeth,* and Hamlet's internal conflict than his struggle with outward enemies and obstacles. But it is dangerous to describe tragedy in terms that even appear to exclude *Macbeth,* or to describe *Macbeth,* even casually or by implication, in terms which imply that it portrays a conflict of mere evil with mere good.

The restatement of Hegel's main principle as to the conflict would involve a similar restatement as to the catastrophe (for we need not consider here those "tragedies" which end with a solution). As before, we must avoid any reference to ethical or universal ends, or to the work of "justice" in the catastrophe. We might then simply say that, as the tragic action portrays a self-division or intestinal conflict of spirit, so the catastrophe displays the violent annulling of this division or conflict. But this statement, which might be pretty generally accepted, would represent only half of Hegel's idea, and perhaps nothing of what is most characteristic and valuable in it. For the catastrophe (if I may put his idea in my own way) has two aspects, a negative and an affirmative, and we have ignored the latter. On the one hand it is the act of a power immeasurably superior to that of the conflicting agents, a power which is irresistible and unescapable, and which overbears and negates whatever is incompatible with it. So far, it may be called, in relation to the conflicting agents,[9] necessity or fate; and unless a catastrophe affects us in ways corresponding with this aspect it is not truly tragic. But then if this were all and this necessity were merely infinite, characterless, external force, the catastrophe would not only terrify (as it should), it would also horrify, depress, or at best provoke indignation or rebellion; and these are not tragic feelings. The catastrophe, then, must have a second and affirmative aspect, which is the source of our feelings of reconciliation, whatever form they may assume. And this will be taken into account if we describe the catastrophe as the violent self-restitution of the divided spiritual unity. The necessity which acts and negates in it, that is to say, is yet of one substance with both the agents. *It* is divided against itself in them; they are *its* conflicting forces; and in restoring its unity through negation it affirms them, so far as they are compatible with that unity. The qualification is essential, since the hero, for all his affinity with that power, is, as the living man we see before us, not so compatible. He must die, and his union with "eternal justice" (which is more than "justice") must itself be "eternal" or ideal. But the qualification does not abolish what it qualifies. This is no occasion to ask how in particular, and in what various ways in various works, we feel the effect of this affirmative aspect in the catastrophe. But it corresponds at least with that strange double impression which is produced by the hero's death. He dies, and our hearts die with him; and yet his death matters nothing to us, or we even exult. He is dead; and he has no more to do with death than the power which killed him and with which he is one.

I leave it to students of Hegel to ask whether he would have accepted the criticisms and modifications I have suggested. Naturally I think he would, as I believe they rest on truth, and am sure he had a habit of arriving at truth. But in any case their importance is trifling, compared

[9] In relation to *both* sides in the conflict (though it may not need to negate life in both). For the ultimate agent in the catastrophe is emphatically not the finite power of one side. It is beyond both, and, at any rate in relation to them, boundless.

with that of the theory which they attempt to strengthen and to which they owe their existence.

NOTE

Why did Hegel, in his lectures on Aesthetics, so treat of tragedy as to suggest the idea that the kind of tragedy which he personally preferred (let us for the sake of brevity call it "ancient") is also the most adequate embodiment of the idea of tragedy? This question can be answered, I think, only conjecturally, but some remarks on it may have an interest for readers of Hegel (they are too brief to be of use to others).

One answer might be this. Hegel did not really hold that idea. But he was lecturing, not writing a book. He thought the principle of tragedy was more clearly and readily visible in ancient works than in modern; and so, for purposes of exposition, he emphasized the ancient form. And this fact, with his personal enthusiasm for certain Greek plays, leads the reader of the *Aesthetik* to misconstrue him.

Again, we must remember the facts of Hegel's life. He seems first to have reflected on tragedy at a time when his enthusiasm for the Greeks and their "substantial" ethics was combined, not only with a contemptuous dislike for much modern "subjectivity" (this he never ceased to feel), but with a certain hostility to morality. His first view of tragedy was thus, in effect, a theory of Aeschylean and Sophoclean tragedy; and it appears in the early essay on *Naturrecht* and more fully in the *Phaenomenologie*. Perhaps, then, when he came to deal with the subject more generally, he insensibly regarded ancient form as the typical form, and tended to treat the modern rather as a modification of this type than as an alternative embodiment of the general idea of tragedy. The note in the *Rechtsphilosophie* (p. 196) perhaps favours this idea.

But, whether it is correct or no, I believe that the impression produced by the *Aesthetik* is a true one, and that Hegel did deliberately consider the ancient form the more satisfactory. It would not follow, of course, from that opinion that he thought the advantage was all on one side, or considered this or that ancient poet greater than this or that modern, or wished that modern poets had tried to write tragedies of the Greek type. Tragedy would, in his view, be in somewhat the same position as Sculpture. Renaissance sculpture, he might say, has qualities in which it is superior to Greek, and Michael Angelo may have been as great an artist as Pheidias; but all the same for certain reasons Greek sculpture is, and probably will remain, sculpture *par excellence*. So, though not to the same extent, with tragedy.

And such a view would cohere with his general view of Art. For he taught that, in a sense, Classical Art is Art *par excellence,* and that in Greece beauty held a position such as it never held before and will not hold again. To explain in a brief note how this position bears upon his treatment of modern tragedy would be impossible: but if the student of Hegel will remember in what sense and on what grounds he held it; that he describes Beauty as the *"sinnliches* Scheinen der Idee";[10] that for him the new idea that distinguished Christianity and Romantic Art from Greek religion and Classical Art is that *"unendliche* Subjektivität"[11] which implies a negative, though not merely negative, relation to sense; and that in Romantic Art this idea is not only exhibited in the religious sphere, but appears in the position given to personal honour, love, and loyalty, and indirectly in what Hegel calls "die formelle Selbstständigkeit der individuellen Besonderheiten," and in the fuller admission of common and un-beautiful reality into the realm of Beauty,—he will see how all this is connected with those characteristics of modern tragedy which Hegel regards as necessary and yet as, in part, drawbacks. This connection, which Hegel has no occasion to work out, will be apparent even from consideration of the introductory chapter on "die romantische Kunstform," *Aesthetik,* ii. 120-135.

There is one marked difference, I may add, between ancient and modern tragedy, which should be considered with reference to this subject, and which Hegel, I think, does not explicitly point out. Speaking roughly, we may say that the former includes, while the latter tends to ignore, the accepted religious ideas of the time. The ultimate reason of this difference, on Hegel's view, would be that the Olympian gods are themselves the *"sinnliches* Scheinen der Idee," and so are in the same element as Art, while this is, on the whole, not so with modern religious ideas. One result would be that Greek tragedy represents the total Greek mind more fully than modern tragedy can the total modern mind.

[10] ["Material appearance of the Idea."]
[11] ["Infinite subjectivity."]

Joseph Wood Krutch

THE TRAGIC FALLACY*

Through the legacy of their art the great ages have transmitted to us a dim image of their glorious vitality. When we turn the pages of a Sophoclean or a Shakespearean tragedy we participate faintly in the experience which created it and we sometimes presumptuously say that we "understand" the spirit of these works. But the truth is that we see them even at best and in the moments when our souls expand most nearly to their dimensions, through a glass darkly.

It is so much easier to appreciate than to create that an age too feeble to reach the heights achieved by the members of a preceding one can still see those heights towering above its impotence, and so it is that, when we perceive a Sophocles or a Shakespeare soaring in an air which we can never hope to breathe, we say that we can "appreciate" them. But what we mean is that we are just able to wonder, and we can never hope to participate in the glorious vision of human life out of which they were created—not even to the extent of those humbler persons for whom they were written; for while to us the triumphant voices come from far away and tell of a heroic world which no longer exists, to them that spoke of immediate realities and revealed the inner meaning of events amidst which they still lived.

When the life has entirely gone out of a work of art come down to us from the past, when we read it without any emotional comprehension whatsoever and can no longer even imagine why the people for whom it was intended found it absorbing and satisfying, then, of course, it has ceased to be a work of art at all and has dwindled into one of those deceptive "documents" from which we get a false sense of comprehending through the intellect things which cannot be comprehended at all except by means of a kinship of feeling. And though all works from a past age have begun in this way to fade there are some, like the great Greek or Elizabethan tragedies, which are still halfway between the work of art and the document. They no longer can have for us the immediacy which they had for those to whom they originally belonged, but they have not yet eluded us

---

* From Joseph Wood Krutch's *The Modern Temper*, Ch. Five. Copyright, 1929, by Harcourt, Brace and Company, Inc.; renewed, 1956, by Joseph Wood Krutch. Reprinted by permission of the publishers.

Joseph Wood Krutch (1893–   ), former Columbia University Professor, has written many books on literary subjects as well as on general humanistic matters, his *The Modern Temper* being one fine example of his latter interest.

entirely. We no longer live in the world which they represent, but we can half imagine it and we can measure the distance which we have moved away. We write no tragedies today, but we can still talk about the tragic spirit of which we would, perhaps, have no conception were it not for the works in question.

An age which could really "appreciate" Shakespeare or Sophocles would have something comparable to put beside them—something like them, not necessarily in form, or spirit, but at least in magnitude—some vision of life which would be, however different, equally ample and passionate. But when we move to put a modern masterpiece beside them, when we seek to compare them with, let us say, a *Ghosts* or a *Weavers,* we shrink as from the impulse to commit some folly and we feel as though we were about to superimpose Bowling Green upon the Great Prairies in order to ascertain which is the larger. The question, we see, is not primarily one of art but of the two worlds which two minds inhabited. No increased powers of expression, no greater gift for words, could have transformed Ibsen into Shakespeare. The materials out of which the latter created his works—his conception of human passions, his vision of the amplitude of human life—simply did not and could not exist for Ibsen, as they did not and could not exist for his contemporaries. God and Man and Nature had all somehow dwindled in the course of the intervening centuries, not because the realistic creed of modern art led us to seek out mean people, but because this meanness of human life was somehow thrust upon us by the operation of that same process which led to the development of realistic theories of art by which our vision could be justified.

Hence, though we still apply, sometimes, the adjective "tragic" to one or another of those modern works of literature which describe human misery and which end more sadly even than they begin, the term is a misnomer since it is obvious that the works in question have nothing in common with the classical examples of the genre and produce in the reader a sense of depression which is the exact opposite of that elation generated when the spirit of a Shakespeare rises joyously superior to the outward calamities which he recounts and celebrates the greatness of the human spirit whose travail he describes. Tragedies, in that only sense of the word which has any distinctive meaning, are no longer written in either the dramatic or any other form and the fact is not to be accounted for in any merely literary terms. It is not the result of any fashion in literature or of any deliberation to write about human nature or character under different aspects, any more than it is of either any greater sensitiveness of feeling which would make us shrink from the contemplation of the suffering of Medea or Othello or of any greater optimism which would make us more likely to see life in more cheerful terms. It is, on the contrary, the result of one of those enfeeblements of the human spirit not unlike that described in the previous chapter of this essay, and a further illustration of that gradual weakening of man's confidence in his ability to impose upon the phenomenon of life an inter- pretation acceptable to his desires which is the subject of the whole of the present discussion.

To explain that fact and to make clear how the creation of classical tragedy did consist in the successful effort to impose such a satisfactory interpretation will require, perhaps, the special section which follows, al- though the truth of the fact that it does impose such an interpretation must be evident to any one who has ever risen from the reading of *Oedipus* or *Lear* with that feeling of exultation which comes when we have been able, by rare good fortune, to enter into its spirit as completely as it is possible for us of a remoter and emotionally enfeebled age to enter it. Meanwhile one anticipatory remark may be ventured. If the plays and the novels of today deal with littler people and less mighty emotions it is not because we have become interested in commonplace souls and their unglamorous ad- ventures but because we have come, willy-nilly, to see the soul of man as commonplace and its emotions as mean.

2

Tragedy, said Aristotle, is the "imitation of noble actions," and though it is some twenty-five hundred years since the dictum was uttered there is only one respect in which we are inclined to modify it. To us "imitation" seems a rather naive word to apply to that process by which observation is turned into art, and we seek one which would define or at least imply the nature of that interposition of the personality of the artist between the object and the beholder which constitutes his function and by means of which he transmits a modified version, rather than a mere imitation, of the thing which he has contemplated.

In the search for this word the estheticians of romanticism invented the term "expression" to describe the artistic purpose to which apparent imita- tion was subservient. Psychologists, on the other hand, feeling that the artistic process was primarily one by which reality is modified in such a way as to render it more acceptable to the desires of the artist, employed various terms in the effort to describe that distortion which the wish may produce in vision. And though many of the newer critics reject both romanticism and psychology, even they insist upon the fundamental fact that in art we are concerned, not with mere imitation, but with the imposition of some form upon the material which it would not have if it were merely copied as a camera copies.

Tragedy is not, then, as Aristotle said, the *imitation* of noble actions, for, indeed, no one knows what a *noble* action is or whether or not such a thing as nobility exists in nature apart from the mind of man. Certainly the action of Achilles in dragging the dead body of Hector around the walls of Troy and under the eyes of Andromache, who had begged to be allowed to give it decent burial, is not to us a noble action, though it was such to Homer, who made it the subject of a noble passage in a noble poem. Certainly, too, the same action might conceivably be made the subject of a tragedy and the subject of a farce, depending upon the way in which it was treated; so that to say that tragedy is the *imitation* of a *noble* action is to be guilty of assuming, first, that art and photography are the same, and, second, that there may be something inherently noble in an act as distinguished from the motives which prompted it or from the point of view from which it is regarded.

And yet, nevertheless, the idea of nobility is inseparable from the idea of tragedy, which cannot exist without it. If tragedy is not the imitation or even the modified representation of noble actions it is certainly a representation of actions *considered* as noble, and herein lies its essential nature, since no man can conceive it unless he is capable of believing in the greatness and importance of man. Its action is usually, if not always, calamitous, because it is only in calamity that the human spirit has the opportunity to reveal itself triumphant over the outward universe which fails to conquer it; but this calamity in tragedy is only a means to an end and the essential thing which distinguishes real tragedy from those distressing modern works sometimes called by its name is the fact that it is in the former alone that the artist has found himself capable of considering and of making us consider that his people and his actions have that amplitude and importance which make them noble. Tragedy arises then when, as in Periclean Greece or Elizabethan England, a people fully aware of the calamities of life is nevertheless serenely confident of the greatness of man, whose mighty passions and supreme fortitude are revealed when one of these calamities overtakes him.

To those who mistakenly think of it as something gloomy or depressing, who are incapable of recognizing the elation which its celebration of human greatness inspires, and who, therefore, confuse it with things merely miserable or pathetic, it must be a paradox that the happiest, most vigorous, and most confident ages which the world has ever known—the Periclean and the Elizabethan—should be exactly those which created and which most relished the mightiest tragedies; but the paradox is, of course, resolved by the fact that tragedy is essentially an expression, not of despair, but of the triumph over despair and of confidence in the value of human life. If Shakespeare himself ever had that "dark period" which his critics and biographers have imagined for him, it was at least no darkness like that bleak and arid despair which sometimes settles over modern spirits. In the midst of it he created both the elemental grandeur of Othello and the pensive majesty of Hamlet and, holding them up to his contemporaries, he said in the words of his own Miranda, "O brave new world that hath *such* creatures in it."

All works of art which deserve their name have a happy end. This is indeed the thing which constitutes them art and through which they perform their function. Whatever the character of the events, fortunate or unfortunate, which they recount, they so mold or arrange or interpret them that we accept gladly the conclusion which they reach and would not have it otherwise. They may conduct us into the realm of pure fancy where wish and fact are identical and the world is remade exactly after the fashion of the heart's desire or they may yield some greater or less allegiance to fact; but they must always reconcile us in one way or another to the representation which they make and the distinctions between the genres are simply the distinctions between the means by which this reconciliation is effected.

Comedy laughs the minor mishaps of its characters away; drama solves all the difficulties which it allows to arise; and melodrama, separating good from evil by simple lines, distributes its rewards and punishments in accordance with the principles of a naive justice which satisfies the simple souls of its audience, which are neither philosophical enough to question its primitive ethics nor critical enough to object to the way in which its neat events violate the laws of probability. Tragedy, the greatest and the most difficult of the arts, can adopt none of these methods; and yet it must reach its own happy end in its own way. Though its conclusion must be, by its premise, outwardly calamitous, though it must speak to those who know that the good man is cut off and that the fairest things are the first to perish, yet it must leave them, as *Othello* does, content that this is so. We must be and we are glad that Juliet dies and glad that Lear is turned out into the storm.

Milton set out, he said, to justify the ways of God to man, and his phrase, if it be interpreted broadly enough, may be taken as describing the function of all art, which must, in some way or other, make the life which it seems to represent satisfactory to those who see its reflection in the magic mirror, and it must gratify or at least reconcile the desires of the beholder, not necessarily, as the naiver exponents of Freudian psychology maintain, by gratifying individual and often eccentric wishes, but at least by satisfying the universally human desire to find in the world some justice, some meaning, or, at the very least, some recognizable order. Hence it is that every real tragedy, however tremendous it may be, is an affirmation of faith in life, a declaration that even if God is not in his Heaven, then at least Man is in his world.

We accept gladly the outward defeats which it describes for the sake of the inward victories which it reveals. Juliet died, but not before she had shown how great and resplendent a thing love could be; Othello plunged the dagger into his own breast, but not before he had revealed that greatness of soul which makes his death seem unimportant. Had he died in the instant when he struck the blow, had he perished still believing that the world was as completely black as he saw it before the innocence of Desdemona was revealed to him, then, for him at least, the world would have been merely damnable, but Shakespeare kept him alive long enough to allow him to learn his error and hence to die, not in despair, but in the full acceptance of the tragic reconciliation to life. Perhaps it would be pleasanter if men could believe what the child is taught—that the good are happy and that things turn out as they should—but it is far more important to be able to believe, as Shakespeare did, that however much things in the outward world may go awry, man has, nevertheless, splendors of his own and that, in a word, Love and Honor and Glory are not words but realities.

Thus for the great ages tragedy is not an expression of despair but the means by which they saved themselves from it. It is a profession of faith, and a sort of religion; a way of looking at life by virtue of which it is robbed of its pain. The sturdy soul of the tragic author seizes upon suffering and uses it only as a means by which joy may be wrung out of existence, but it is not to be forgotten that he is enabled to do so only because of his belief in the greatness of human nature and because, though he has lost the child's faith in life, he has not lost his far more important faith in human nature. A tragic writer does not have to believe in God, but he must believe in man.

And if, then, the Tragic Spirit is in reality the product of a religious faith in which, sometimes at least, faith in the greatness of God is replaced by faith in the greatness of man, it serves, of course, to perform the function of religion, to make life tolerable for those who participate in its beneficent illusion. It purges the souls of those who might otherwise despair and it makes endurable the realization that the events of the outward world do not correspond with the desires of the heart, and thus, in its own particular way, it does what all religions do, for it gives a rationality, a meaning, and a justification to the universe. But if it has the strength it has also the weakness of all faiths, since it may—nay, it must—be ultimately lost as reality, encroaching further and further into the realm of imagination, leaves less and less room in which that imagination can build its refuge.

3

It is, indeed, only at a certain stage in the development of the realistic intelligence of a people that the tragic faith can exist. A naiver people may have, as the ancient men of the north had, a body of legends which are essentially tragic, or it may have only (and need only) its happy and child-like mythology which arrives inevitably at its happy end, and where the only ones who suffer "deserve" to do so and in which, therefore, life is represented as directly and easily acceptable. A too sophisticated society on the other hand—one which, like ours, has outgrown not merely the simple optimism of the child but also that vigorous, one might almost say adolescent, faith in the nobility of man which marks a Sophocles or a Shakespeare, has neither fairy tales to assure it that all is always right in the end nor tragedies to make it believe that it rises superior in soul to the outward calamities which befall it.

Distrusting its thought, despising its passions, realizing its impotent unimportance in the universe, it can tell itself no stories except those which make it still more acutely aware of its trivial miseries. When its heroes (sad misnomer for the pitiful creatures who people contemporary fiction) are struck down it is not, like Oedipus, by the gods that they are struck but only, like Oswald Alving, by syphilis, for they know that the gods, even if they existed, would not trouble with them, and they cannot attribute to themselves in art an importance in which they do not believe. Their so-called tragedies do not and cannot end with one of those splendid calamities which in Shakespeare seem to reverberate through the universe, because they cannot believe that the universe trembles when their love is, like Romeo's, cut off or when the place where they (small as they are) have gathered up their trivial treasure is, like Othello's sanctuary, defiled. Instead, mean misery piles on mean misery, petty misfortune follows petty misfortune, and despair becomes intolerable because it is no longer even significant or important.

Ibsen once made one of his characters say that he did not read much because he found reading "irrelevant," and the adjective was brilliantly chosen because it held implications even beyond those of which Ibsen was consciously aware. What is it that made the classics irrelevant to him and to us? Is it not just exactly those to him impossible premises which make tragedy what it is, those assumptions that the soul of man is great, that the universe (together with whatever gods may be) concerns itself with him and that he is, in a word, noble? Ibsen turned to village politics for exactly the same reason that his contemporaries and his successors have, each in his own way, sought out some aspect of the common man and his common life—because, that is to say, here was at least something small enough for him to be able to believe.

Bearing this fact in mind, let us compare a modern "tragedy" with one of the great works of a happy age, not in order to judge of their relative technical merits but in order to determine to what extent the former deserves its name by achieving a tragic solution capable of purging the soul or of reconciling the emotions to the life which it pictures. And in order to make the comparison as fruitful as possible let us choose *Hamlet* on the one hand and on the other a play like *Ghosts,* which was not only written by perhaps the most powerful as well as the most typical of modern writers but which is, in addition, the one of his works which seems most nearly to escape that triviality which cannot be entirely escaped by any one who feels, as all contemporary minds do, that man is relatively trivial.

In *Hamlet* a prince ("in understanding, how like a god!") has thrust upon him from the unseen world a duty to redress a wrong which concerns not merely him, his mother, and his uncle, but the moral order of the universe. Erasing all trivial fond records from his mind, abandoning at once both his studies and his romance because it has been his good fortune to be called upon to take part in an action of cosmic importance, he plunges (at first) not into action but into thought, weighing the claims which are made upon him and contemplating the grandiose complexities of the universe. And when the time comes at last for him to die he dies, not as a failure, but as a success. Not only has the universe regained the balance which had been upset by what *seemed* the monstrous crime of the guilty pair ("there is nothing either good nor ill but thinking makes it so"), but in the process by which that readjustment is made a mighty mind has been given the opportunity, first to contemplate the magnificent scheme of which it is a part, and then to demonstrate the greatness of its spirit by playing a rôle in the grand style which it called for. We do not need to despair in *such* a world if it has *such* creatures in it.

Turn now to *Ghosts*—look upon this picture and upon that. A young man has inherited syphilis from his father. Struck by a to him mysterious malady he returns to his northern village, learns the hopeless truth about himself, and persuades his mother to poison him. The incidents prove, perhaps, that pastors should not endeavor to keep a husband and wife together unless they know what they are doing. But what a world is this in which a great writer can deduce nothing more than that from his greatest work and how are we to be purged or reconciled when we see it acted? Not only is the failure utter, but it is trivial and meaningless as well.

Yet the journey from Elsinore to Skien is precisely the journey which the human spirit has made, exchanging in the process princes for invalids and gods for disease. We say, as Ibsen would say, that the problems of Oswald Alving are more "relevant" to our life than the problems of Hamlet, that the play in which he appears is more "real" than the other more glamorous one, but it is exactly because we find it so that we are condemned. We can believe in Oswald but we cannot believe in Hamlet, and a light has gone out in the universe. Shakespeare justifies the ways of God to man, but in Ibsen there is no such happy end and with him tragedy, so called, has become merely an expression of our despair at finding that such justification is no longer possible.

Modern critics have sometimes been puzzled to account for the fact that the concern of ancient tragedy is almost exclusively with kings and courts. They have been tempted to accuse even Aristotle of a certain naiveté in assuming (as he seems to assume) that the "nobility" of which he speaks as necessary to a tragedy implies a nobility of rank as well as of soul, and they have sometimes regretted that Shakespeare did not devote himself more than he did to the serious consideration of those common woes of the common man which subsequent writers have exploited with increasing pertinacity. Yet the tendency to lay the scene of a tragedy at the court of a king is not the result of any arbitrary convention but of the fact that the tragic writers believed easily in greatness just as we believe easily in meanness. To Shakespeare, robes and crowns and jewels are the garments most appropriate to man because they are the fitting outward manifestation of his inward majesty, but to us they seem absurd because the man who bears them has, in our estimation, so pitifully shrunk. We do not write about kings because we do not believe that any man is worthy to be one and we do not write about courts because hovels seem to us to be dwellings more appropriate to the creatures who inhabit them. Any modern attempt to dress characters in robes ends only by making us aware of a comic incongruity and any modern attempt to furnish them with a language resplendent like Shakespeare's ends only in bombast.

True tragedy capable of performing its function and of purging the soul by reconciling man to his woes can exist only by virtue of a certain pathetic fallacy far more inclusive than that to which the name is commonly given. The romantics, feeble descendants of the tragic writers to whom they are linked by their effort to see life and nature in grandiose terms, loved to imagine that the sea or the sky had a way of according itself with their moods, of storming when they stormed and smiling when they smiled. But the tragic spirit sustains itself by an assumption much more far-reaching and no more justified. Man as it sees him lives in a world which he may not dominate but which is always aware of him. Occupying the exact center of a universe which would have no meaning except for him and being so little below the angels that, if he believes in God, he has no hesitation in imagining Him formed as he is formed and crowned with a crown like that which he or one of his fellows wears, he assumes that each of his acts reverberates through the universe. His passions are important to him because he believes them important throughout all time and all space; the very fact that he can sin (no modern can) means that this universe is watching his acts; and though he may perish, a God leans out from infinity to strike him down. And it is exactly because an Ibsen cannot think of man in any such terms as these that his persons have so shrunk and that his "tragedy" has lost that power which real tragedy always has of making that infinitely ambitious creature called man content to accept his misery if only he can be made to feel great enough and important enough. An Oswald is not a Hamlet chiefly because he has lost that tie with the natural and supernatural world which the latter had. No ghost will leave the other world to warn or encourage him, there is no virtue and no vice which he can possibly have which can be really important, and when he dies neither his death nor the manner of it will be, outside the circle of two or three people as unnecessary as himself, any more important than that of a rat behind the arras.

Perhaps we may dub the illusion upon which the tragic spirit is nourished the Tragic, as opposed to the Pathetic, Fallacy, but fallacy though it is, upon its existence depends not merely the writing of tragedy but the existence of that religious feeling of which tragedy is an expression and by means of which a people aware of the dissonances of life manages nevertheless to hear them as harmony. Without it neither man nor his passions can seem great enough or important enough to justify the sufferings which they entail, and literature, expressing the mood of a people, begins to despair where once it had exulted. Like the belief in love and like most of the other mighty illusions by means of which human life has been given a value, the Tragic Fallacy depends ultimately upon the assumption which man so readily makes that something outside his own being, some "spirit not himself"— be it God, Nature, or that still vaguer thing called Moral Order—joins him in the emphasis which he places upon this or that and confirms him in his feeling that his passions and his opinions are important. When his instinctive faith in that correspondence between the outer and the inner world fades, his grasp upon the faith that sustained him fades also, and Love or Tragedy or what not ceases to be the reality which it was because he is never strong enough in his own insignificant self to stand alone in a universe which snubs him with its indifference.

In both the modern and the ancient worlds tragedy was dead long before writers were aware of the fact. Seneca wrote his frigid melodramas under the impression that he was following in the footsteps of Sophocles, and Dryden probably thought that his *All for Love* was an improvement upon Shakespeare, but in time we awoke to the fact that no amount of rhetorical bombast could conceal the fact that grandeur was not to be counterfeited when the belief in its possibility was dead, and turning from the hero to the common man, we inaugurated the era of realism. For us no choice remains except that between mere rhetoric and the frank consideration of our fellow men, who may be the highest of the anthropoids but who are certainly too far below the angels to imagine either that these angels can concern themselves with them or that they can catch any glimpse of even the soles of angelic feet. We can no longer tell tales of the fall of noble men because we do not believe that noble men exist. The best that we can achieve is pathos and the most that we can do is to feel sorry for ourselves. Man has put off his royal robes and it is only in sceptered pomp that tragedy can come sweeping by.

4

Nietzsche was the last of the great philosophers to attempt a tragic justification of life. His central and famous dogma—"Life is good *because* it is painful"—sums up in a few words the desperate and almost meaningless paradox to which he was driven in his effort to reduce to rational terms the far more imaginative conception which is everywhere present but everywhere unanalyzed in a Sophocles or a Shakespeare and by means of which they rise triumphant over the manifold miseries of life. But the very fact that Nietzsche could not even attempt to state in any except intellectual terms an attitude which is primarily unintellectual and to which, indeed, intellectual analysis is inevitably fatal, is proof of the distance which he had been carried (by the rationalizing tendencies of the human mind) from the possibility of the tragic solution which he sought; and the confused, half-insane violence of his work will reveal, by the contrast which it affords with the serenity of the tragic writers whom he admired, how great was his failure.

Fundamentally this failure was, moreover, conditioned by exactly the same thing which has conditioned the failure of all modern attempts to achieve what he attempted—by the fact, that is to say, that tragedy must have a hero if it is not to be merely an accusation against, instead of a justification of, the world in which it occurs. Tragedy is, as Aristotle said, an imitation of noble actions, and Nietzsche, for all his enthusiasm for the Greek tragic writers, was palsied by the universally modern incapacity to conceive man as noble. Out of this dilemma, out of his need to find a hero who could give to life as he saw it the only possible justification, was born the idea of the Superman, but the Superman is, after all, only a hypothetical being, destined to become what man actually was in the eyes of the great tragic writers—a creature (as Hamlet said) "how infinite in capacities, in understanding how like a god." Thus Nietzsche lived half in the past through his literary enthusiasms and half in the future through his grandiose dreams, but for all his professed determination to justify existence he was no more able than the rest of us to find the present acceptable. Life, he said in effect, is not a Tragedy now but perhaps it will be when the Apeman has been transformed into a hero (the *Übermensch*), and trying to find that sufficient, he went mad.

He failed, as all moderns must fail when they attempt, like him, to embrace the tragic spirit as a religious faith, because the resurgence of that faith is not an intellectual but a vital phenomenon, something not achieved by taking thought but born, on the contrary, out of an instinctive confidence in life which is nearer to the animal's unquestioning allegiance to the scheme of nature than it is to that critical intelligence characteristic of a fully developed humanism. And like other faiths it is not to be recaptured merely by reaching an intellectual conviction that it would be desirable to do so.

Modern psychology has discovered (or at least strongly emphasized) the fact that under certain conditions desire produces belief, and having discovered also that the more primitive a given mentality the more completely are its opinions determined by its wishes, modern psychology has concluded that the best mind is that which most resists the tendency to believe a thing simply because it would be pleasant or advantageous to do so. But justified as this conclusion may be from the intellectual point of view, it fails to take into account the fact that in a universe as badly adapted as this one to human as distinguished from animal needs this ability to will a belief may bestow an enormous vital advantage as it did, for instance, in the case at present under discussion where it made possible for Shakespeare the compensations of a tragic faith completely inaccessible to Nietzsche. Pure intelligence, incapable of being influenced by desire and therefore also incapable of choosing one opinion rather than another simply because the one chosen is the more fruitful or beneficent, is doubtless a relatively perfect instrument for the pursuit of truth, but the question (likely, it would seem, to be answered in the negative) is simply whether or not the spirit of man can endure the literal and inhuman truth.

Certain ages and simple people have conceived of the action which passes upon the stage of the universe as of something in the nature of a Divine Comedy, as something, that is to say, which will reach its end with the words "and they lived happily ever after." Others, less naive and therefore more aware of those maladjustments whose reality, at least so far as outward events are concerned, they could not escape, have imposed upon it another artistic form and called it a Divine Tragedy, accepting its catastrophe as we accept the catastrophe of an *Othello*, because of its grandeur. But a Tragedy, Divine or otherwise, must, it may again be repeated, have a hero, and from the universe as we see it both the Glory of God and the Glory of Man have departed. Our cosmos may be farcical or it may be pathetic but it has not the dignity of tragedy and we cannot accept it as such.

Yet our need for the consolations of tragedy has not passed with the passing of our ability to conceive it. Indeed, the dissonances which it was tragedy's function to resolve grow more insistent instead of diminishing. Our passions, our disappointments, and our sufferings remain important to us though important to nothing else and they thrust themselves upon us with an urgency which makes it impossible for us to dismiss them as the mere trivialities which, so our intellects tell us, they are. And yet, in the absence of tragic faith or the possibility of achieving it, we have no way in which we may succeed in giving them the dignity which would not only render them tolerable but transform them as they were transformed by the great ages into joys. The death of tragedy is, like the death of love, one of those emotional fatalities as the result of which the human as distinguished from the natural world grows more and more a desert.

Poetry, said Santayana in his famous phrase, is "religion which is no longer believed," but it depends, nevertheless, upon its power to revive in us a sort of temporary or provisional credence and the nearer it can come to producing an illusion of belief the greater is its power as poetry. Once the Tragic Spirit was a living faith and out of it tragedies were written. Today these great expressions of a great faith have declined, not merely into poetry, but into a kind of poetry whose premises are so far from any we can really accept that we can only partially and dimly grasp its meaning.

We read but we do not write tragedies. The tragic solution of the problem of existence, the reconciliation to life by means of the tragic spirit is, that is to say, now only a fiction surviving in art. When that art itself has become, as it probably will, completely meaningless, when we have ceased not only to write but to *read* tragic works, then it will be lost and in all real senses forgotten, since the devolution from Religion to Art to Document will be complete.

SELECTED BIBLIOGRAPHY

1. Arthur Schopenhauer, *The World as Will and Idea*, Part III, section 51. Tragedy as mere existence itself because of the inevitable presence of suffering in it.
2. W. B. Yeats, "The Tragic Theatre," in *Essays*, Macmillan and Company, 1924; reprinted in M. Schorer, *et al.*, *Criticism*. Tragedy as passionate lyricism.
3. Francis Ferguson, *The Idea of a Theater*, esp. "Introduction" and Ch. I, Princeton University Press, 1949. Tragedy as myth and ritual. (Available as Anchor paperback).
4. DeWitt Parker, *The Analysis of Art*, Ch. IV, Yale University Press, 1926. A good example of the treatment of 'Art and Pain' from a voluntarist point of view.

V

The Problem of Response to Art

Introduction

Since Immanuel Kant, the problem of aesthetic response or the aesthetic experience, as it is sometimes called, has been uppermost in philosophical discussions of art. Indeed, because of the historical fact that the term "aesthetic" was revitalized by Kant's predecessor, A. G. Baumgarten, and defined in terms of a certain kind of experience, it almost became a synonym for response to art or beauty. Until recently, to talk about the aesthetic was to talk about the qualities of the experience in our response to the beautiful.

The problem of response to art can be raised quite independently of its eighteenth-century setting. The problem is this: Given that there are works of art in the world, what sort of response do we, as spectators, readers or listeners, have to them? It is this question that philosophers have discussed since Plato.

Now, it must be realized that there are two formulations of the problem, and, although most theorists have not adequately distinguished between them, they must be separated. One can ask: "How *do* we respond to works of art?"; or one can ask: "How *ought* we to respond to works of art?" There is all the difference in the world between these, for one is a descriptive, the other a normative question.

It seems obvious that the normative is primary and that the descriptive is relevant only as a negative condition of what is possible. This is in keeping with the maxim in ethics that "*Ought* implies *can*" but not vice-versa. In this Part, no attempt is made to solve these two questions, or even to choose between them. Instead, five important views on response to art are presented, in which the descriptive-normative aspects of the problem are fused. It is simply an historical fact that every major theory of aesthetic response has blended these two different questions.

The readings begin with Leo Tolstoy's version of response as emotional communion with the work of art. Included are two selections, rarely reprinted, in which Tolstoy reveals some of the moral implications of his theory for the criticism and evaluation of art, and especially of music.

Tolstoy is followed by Vernon Lee (Violet Paget), in her clear statement of empathy. The third theory is the Freudian one of response as sublimation. Here it is represented by a selection from Sigmund Freud's *Civilization and Its Discontents* (rather than from other works, since this selection deals with response better than his other, more famous papers on aesthetics) and a fine survey of Freud's whole work in aesthetics by a devoted follower and student of his, Richard Sterba. Hedonism is represented by George Santayana's discussion of response as the objectification of pleasure. The selections end with the relevant portions of the modern classic of Edward Bullough on the contemplative theory. These five, perhaps, cover the major views on the problem of aesthetic response.

Leo Tolstoy

EMOTIONALISM*

In order to define art correctly it is necessary first of all to cease to consider it as a means to pleasure, and to consider it as one of the conditions of human life. Viewing it in this way we cannot fail to observe that art is one of the means of intercourse between man and man.

Every work of art causes the receiver to enter into a certain kind of relationship both with him who produced or is producing the art, and with all those who, simultaneously, previously, or subsequently, receive the same artistic impression.

Speech transmitting the thoughts and experiences of men serves as a means of union among them, and art serves a similar purpose. The peculiarity of this latter means of intercourse, distinguishing it from intercourse by means of words, consists in this, that whereas by words a man transmits his thoughts to another, by art he transmits his feelings.

* From Leo Tolstoy's *What Is Art?*, trans., Aylmer Maude, pp. 120–126; Ch. XV; pp. 221–224; p. 249. Copyright, 1930, by the Oxford University Press. Reprinted by permission of the Oxford University Press.

Leo Tolstoy (1828–1910), world-famous Russian novelist, was an essayist as well and wrote much on social, religious and aesthetic matters, of which *What Is Art?* is a summative example.

The activity of art is based on the fact that a man receiving through his sense of hearing or sight another man's expression of feeling, is capable of experiencing the emotion which moved the man who expressed it. To take the simplest example: one man laughs, and another who hears becomes merry, or a man weeps, and another who hears feels sorrow. A man is excited or irritated, and another man seeing him is brought to a similar state of mind. By his movements or by the sounds of his voice a man expresses courage and determination or sadness and calmness, and this state of mind passes on to others. A man suffers, manifesting his sufferings by groans and spasms, and this suffering transmits itself to other people; a man expresses his feelings of admiration, devotion, fear, respect, or love, to certain objects, persons, or phenomena, and others are infected by the same feelings of admiration, devotion, fear, respect, or love, to the same objects, persons, or phenomena.

And it is on this capacity of man to receive another man's expression of feeling and to experience those feelings himself, that the activity of art is based.

If a man infects another or others directly, immediately, by his appearance or by the sounds he gives vent to at the very time he experiences the feeling; if he causes another man to yawn when he himself cannot help yawning, or to laugh or cry when he himself is obliged to laugh or cry, or to suffer when he himself is suffering—that does not amount to art.

Art begins when one person with the object of joining another or others to himself in one and the same feeling, expresses that feeling by certain external indications. To take the simplest example: a boy having experienced, let us say, fear on encountering a wolf, relates that encounter, and in order to evoke in others the feeling he has experienced, describes himself, his condition before the encounter, the surroundings, the wood, his own lightheartedness, and then the wolf's appearance, its movements, the distance between himself and the wolf, and so forth. All this, if only the boy when telling the story again experiences the feelings he had lived through, and infects the hearers and compels them to feel what he had experienced—is art. Even if the boy had not seen a wolf but had frequently been afraid of one, and if wishing to evoke in others the fear he had felt, he invented an encounter with a wolf and recounted it so as to make his hearers share the feelings he experienced when he feared the wolf, that also would be art. And just in the same way it is art if a man, having experienced either the fear of suffering or the attraction of enjoyment (whether in reality or in imagination), expresses these feelings on canvas or in marble so that others are infected by them. And it is also art if a man feels, or imagines to himself, feelings of delight, gladness, sorrow, despair, courage, or despondency, and the transition from one to another of these feelings, and expresses them by sounds so that the hearers are infected by them and experience them as they were experienced by the composer.

The feelings with which the artist infects others may be most various— very strong or very weak, very important or very insignificant, very bad or very good: feelings of love of one's country, self-devotion and submission to fate or to God expressed in a drama, raptures of lovers described in a novel, feelings of voluptuousness expressed in a picture, courage expressed in a triumphal march, merriment evoked by a dance, humor evoked by a funny story, the feeling of quietness transmitted by an evening landscape or by a lullaby, or the feeling of admiration evoked by a beautiful arabesque— it is all art.

If only the spectators or auditors are infected by the feelings which the author has felt, it is art.

To evoke in oneself a feeling one has once experienced and having evoked it in oneself then by means of movements, lines, colors, sounds, or forms expressed in words, so to transmit that feeling that others experience the same feeling—this is the activity of art.

Art is a human activity consisting in this, that one man consciously by means of certain external signs, hands on to others feelings he has lived through, and that others are infected by these feelings and also experience them.

Art is not, as the metaphysicians say, the manifestation of some mysterious Idea of beauty or God; it is not, as the aesthetic physiologists say, a game in which man lets off his excess of stored-up energy; it is not the expression of man's emotions by external signs; it is not the production of pleasing objects; and, above all, it is not pleasure; but it is a means of union among men joining them together in the same feelings, and indispensable for the life and progress towards well-being of individuals and of humanity.

As every man, thanks to man's capacity to express thoughts by words, may know all that has been done for him in the realms of thought by all humanity before his day, and can in the present, thanks to this capacity to understand the thoughts of others, become a sharer in their activity and also himself hand on to his contemporaries and descendants the thoughts he has assimilated from others as well as those that have arisen in himself; so, thanks to man's capacity to be infected with the feelings of others by means of art, all that is being lived through by his contemporaries is accessible to him, as well as the feelings experienced by men thousands of years ago, and he has also the possibility of transmitting his own feelings to others.

If people lacked the capacity to receive the thoughts conceived by men who preceded them and to pass on to others their own thoughts, men would be like wild beasts, or like Kasper Hauser.[1]

And if men lacked this other capacity of being infected by art, people might be almost more savage still, and above all more separated from, and more hostile to, one another.

And therefore the activity of art is a most important one, as important as the activity of speech itself and as generally diffused.

As speech does not act on us only in sermons, orations, or books, but in all those remarks by which we interchange thoughts and experiences with one another, so also art in the wide sense of the word permeates our whole life, but it is only to some of its manifestations that we apply the term in the limited sense of the word.

We are accustomed to understand art to be only what we hear and see in theaters, concerts, and exhibitions; together with buildings, statues, poems, and novels. . . . But all this is but the smallest part of the art by which we communicate with one another in life. All human life is filled with works of art of every kind—from cradle-song, jest, mimicry, the ornamentation of houses, dress, and utensils, to church services, buildings, monuments, and triumphal processions. It is all artistic activity. So that by art, in the limited sense of the word, we do not mean all human activity transmitting feelings but only that part which we for some reason select from it and to which we attach special importance.

This special importance has always been given by men to that part of this activity which transmits feelings flowing from their religious perception, and this small part they have specifically called art, attaching to it the full meaning of the word.

That was how men of old—Socrates, Plato, and Aristotle—looked on art. Thus did the Hebrew prophets and the ancient Christians regard art. Thus it was, and still is, understood by the Mohammedans, and thus it still is understood by religious folk among our own peasantry.

Some teachers of mankind—such as Plato in his *Republic,* and people like the primitive Christians, the strict Momammedans, and the Buddhists—have gone so far as to repudiate all art.

People viewing art in this way (in contradiction to the prevalent view

---

[1] "The foundling of Nuremberg," found in the marketplace of that town on 23rd May 1828, apparently some sixteen years old. He spoke little and was almost totally ignorant even of common objects. He subsequently explained that he had been brought up in confinement underground and visited by only one man, whom he saw but seldom.

of to-day which regards any art as good if only it affords pleasure) held and hold that art (as contrasted with speech, which need not be listened to) is so highly dangerous in its power to infect people against their wills, that mankind will lose far less by banishing all art than by tolerating each and every art.

Evidently such people were wrong in repudiating all art, for they denied what cannot be denied—one of the indispensable means of communication without which mankind could not exist. But not less wrong are the people of civilized European society of our class and day in favoring any art if it but serves beauty, that is, gives people pleasure.

Formerly people feared lest among works of art there might chance to be some causing corruption, and they prohibited art altogether. Now they only fear lest they should be deprived of any enjoyment art can afford, and they patronize any art. And I think the last error is much grosser than the first and that its consequences are far more harmful.

·   ·   ·

Art in our society has become so perverted that not only has bad art come to be considered good, but even the very perception of what art really is has been lost. In order to be able to speak about the art of our society it is, therefore, first of all necessary to distinguish art from counterfeit art.

There is one indubitable sign distinguishing real art from its counterfeit—namely, the infectiousness of art. If a man without exercising effort and without altering his standpoint, on reading, hearing, or seeing another man's work experiences a mental condition which unites him with that man and with others who are also affected by that work, then the object evoking that condition is a work of art. And however poetic, realistic, striking, or interesting, a work may be, it is not a work of art if it does not evoke that feeling (quite distinct from all other feelings) of joy and of spiritual union with another (the author) and with others (those who are also infected by it).

It is true that this indication is an *internal* one and that there are people who, having forgotten what the action of real art is, expect something else from art (in our society the great majority are in this state), and that therefore such people may mistake for this aesthetic feeling the feeling of diversion and a certain excitement which they receive from counterfeits of art. But though it is impossible to undeceive these people, just as it may be impossible to convince a man suffering from colour-blindness that green is not red, yet for all that, this indication remains perfectly definite to those whose feeling for art is neither perverted nor atrophied, and it clearly distinguishes the feeling produced by art from all other feelings.

The chief peculiarity of this feeling is that the recipient of a truly artistic impression is so united to the artist that he feels as if the work were his own and not some one else's—as if what it expresses were just what he had long been wishing to express. A real work of art destroys in the consciousness of the recpient the separation between himself and the artist, and not that alone, but also between himself and all whose minds receive this work of art. In this freeing of our personality from its separation and isolation, in this uniting of it with others, lies the chief characteristic and the great attractive force of art .

If a man is infected by the author's condition of soul, if he feels this emotion and this union with others, then the object which has effected this is art; but if there be no such infection, if there be not this union with the author and with others who are moved by the same work—then it is not art. And not only is infection a sure sign of art, but the degree of infectiousness is also the sole measure of excellence in art.

The stronger the infection the better is the art, as art, speaking of it now apart from its subject-matter—that is, not considering the value of the feelings it transmits.

And the degree of the infectiousness of art depends on three conditions:—

(1) On the greater or lesser individuality of the feeling transmitted;
(2) on the greater or lesser clearness with which the feeling is transmitted;
(3) on the sincerity of the artist, that is, on the greater or lesser force with which the artist himself feels the emotion he transmits.

The more individual the feeling transmitted the more strongly does it act on the recipient; the more individual the state of soul into which he is transferred the more pleasure does the recipient obtain and therefore the more readily and strongly does he join in it.

Clearness of expression assists infection because the recipient who mingles in consciousness with the author is the better satisfied the more clearly that feeling is transmitted which, as it seems to him, he has long known and felt and for which he has only now found expression.

But most of all is the degree of infectiousness of art increased by the degree of sincerity in the artist. As soon as the spectator, hearer, or reader, feels that the artist is infected by his own production and writes, sings, or plays, for himself, and not merely to act on others, this mental condition of the artist infects the recipient; and, on the contrary, as soon as the spectator, reader, or hearer, feels that the author is not writing, singing, or playing, for his own satisfaction—does not himself feel what he wishes to express, but is doing it for him, the recipient—resistance immediately springs up, and the most individual and the newest feelings and the cleverest technique not only fail to produce any infection but actually repel.

I have mentioned three conditions of contagion in art, but they may all be summed up into one, the last, sincerity; that is, that the artist should be impelled by an inner need to express his feeling. That condition includes the first; for if the artist is sincere he will express the feeling as he experienced it. And as each man is different from every one else, his feeling will be individual for every one else; and the more individual it is—the more the artist has drawn it from the depths of his nature—the more sympathetic and sincere will it be. And this same sincerity will impel the artist to find clear expression for the feeling which he wishes to transmit.

Therefore this third condition—sincerity—is the most important of the three. It is always complied with in peasant art, and this explains why such art always acts so powerfully; but it is a condition almost entirely absent from our upper-class art, which is continually produced by artists actuated by personal aims of covetousness or vanity.

Such are the three conditions which divide art from its counterfeits, and which also decide the quality of every work of art considered apart from its subject-matter.

The absence of any one of these conditions excludes a work from the category of art and relegates it to that of art's counterfeits. If the work does not transmit the artist's peculiarity of feeling and is therefore not individual, if it is unintelligibly expressed, or if it has not proceeded from the author's inner need for expression—it is not a work of art. If all these conditions are present even in the smallest degree, then the work even if a weak one is yet a work of art.

The presence in various degrees of these three conditions: individuality, clearness, and sincerity, decides the merit of a work of art as art, apart from subject-matter. All works of art take order of merit according to the degree in which they fulfil the first, the second, and the third, of these conditions. In one the individuality of the feeling transmitted may predominate; in another, clearness of expression; in a third, sincerity; while a fourth may have sincerity and individuality but be deficient in clearness; a fifth, individuality and clearness, but less sincerity; and so forth, in all possible degrees and combinations.

Thus is art divided from what is not art, and thus is the quality of art, as art, decided, independently of its subject-matter, that is to say, apart from whether the feelings it transmits are good or bad.

But how are we to define good and bad art with reference to its content or subject-matter?

·   ·   ·

A few days ago I was returning home from a walk feeling depressed, as sometimes happens. On nearing the house I heard the loud singing of a large choir of peasant women. They were welcoming my daughter, celebrating her return home after her marriage. In this singing, with its cries and clanging of scythes, such a definite feeling of joy, cheerfulness, and energy, was expressed, that without noticing how it infected me I continued my way towards the house in a better mood and reached home smiling and quite in good spirits. That same evening a visitor, an admirable musician, famed for his execution of classical music and particularly of Beethoven, played us Beethoven's sonata, Opus 101. For the benefit of those who might otherwise attribute my judgment of that sonata of Beethoven to non-comprehension of it, I should mention that whatever other people understand of that sonata and of other productions of Beethoven's later period, I, being very susceptible to music, understand equally. For a long time I used to attune myself to delight in those shapeless improvizations which form the subject-matter of the works of Beethoven's later period, but I had only to consider the question of art seriously, and to compare the impression I received from Beethoven's later works, with those pleasant, clear, and strong, musical impressions which are transmitted, for instance, by the melodies of Bach (his arias), Haydn, Mozart, Chopin (when his melodies are not overloaded with complications and ornamentation), of Beethoven himself in his earlier period, and above all, with the impressions produced by folk-songs,— Italian, Norwegian, or Russian,—by the Hungarian *csárdás,* and other such simple, clear, and powerful music, for the obscure, almost unhealthy, excitement from Beethoven's later pieces, which I had artificially evoked in myself, to be immediately destroyed.

On the completion of the performance (though it was noticeable that every one had become dull) those present warmly praised Beethoven's profound production in the accepted manner, and did not forget to add that formerly they had not been able to understand that last period of his, but that they now saw he was really then at his very best. And when I ventured to compare the impression made on me by the singing of the peasant women —an impression which had been shared by all who heard it—with the effect of this sonata, the admirers of Beethoven only smiled contemptuously, not considering it necessary to reply to such strange remarks.

But for all that, the song of the peasant women was real art transmitting a definite and strong feeling, while the 101st sonata of Beethoven was only an unsuccessful attempt at art containing no definite feeling and therefore not infectious.

For my work on art I have this winter read diligently, though with great effort, the celebrated novels and stories praised by all Europe, written by Zola, Bourget, Huysmans, and Kipling. At the same time I chanced on a story in a child's magazine, by a quite unknown writer, which told of the Easter preparations in a poor widow's family. The story tells how the mother managed with difficulty to obtain some wheat-flour, which she poured on the table ready to knead. She then went out to procure some yeast, telling the children not to leave the hut and to take care of the flour. When the mother had gone, some other children ran shouting near the window calling those in the hut to come to play. The children forgot their mother's warning, ran into the street, and were soon engrossed in the game. The mother on her return with the yeast finds a hen on the table throwing the last of the flour to her chickens, who were busily picking it out of the dust of the earthen floor. The mother, in despair, scolds the children, who cry bitterly. And the mother begins to feel pity for them—but the white flour has all gone. So to mend matters she decides to make the Easter cake with sifted rye-flour, brushing it over with white of egg and surrounding it with eggs. "Rye-bread we bake is as good as a cake," says the mother, using a rhyming proverb to console the children for not having an Easter cake of white flour, and the children, quickly passing from despair to rapture, repeat the proverb and await the Easter cake more merrily even than before.

Well! the reading of the novels and stories by Zola, Bourget, Huysmans, Kipling, and others, handling the most harrowing subjects, did not touch me for one moment, and I was provoked with the authors all the while as one is provoked with a man who considers you so naïve that he does not even conceal the trick by which he intends to take you in. From the first lines one sees the intention with which the book is written, the details all become superfluous, and one feels dull. Above all, one knows that the author had no other feeling all the time than a desire to write a story or a novel, and so one receives no artistic impression. On the other hand I could not tear myself away from the unknown author's tale of the children and the chickens, because I was at once infected by the feeling the author had evidently experienced, re-evoked in himself, and transmitted.

.   .   .

Beethoven's *Ninth Symphony* is considered a great work of art. To verify its claim to be such I must first ask myself whether this work transmits the highest religious feeling? I reply in the negative, since music in itself cannot transmit those feelings; and therefore I ask myself next: Since this work does not belong to the highest kind of religious art, has it the other characteristic of the good art of our time—the quality of uniting all men in one common feeling—does it rank as Christian universal art? And again I have no option but to reply in the negative; for not only do I not see how the feelings transmitted by this work could unite people not specially trained to submit themselves to its complex hypnotism, but I am unable to imagine to myself a crowd of normal people who could understand anything of this long, confused, and artificial production, except short snatches which are lost in a sea of what is incomprehensible. And therefore, whether I like it or not, I am compelled to conclude that this work belongs to the rank of bad art. It is curious to note in this connection, that attached to the end of this very symphony is a poem of Schiller's which (though somewhat obscurely) expresses this very thought, namely, that feeling (Schiller speaks only of the feeling of gladness) unites people and evokes love in them. But though this poem is sung at the end of the symphony, the music does not accord with the thought expressed in the verses; for the music is exclusive and does not unite all men, but unites only a few, dividing them off from the rest of mankind.

Vernon Lee

EMPATHY*

The mountain rises. What do we mean when we employ this form of words? Some mountains, we are told, have originated in an *upheaval.* But even if this particular mountain did, we never saw it and geologists are still disputing about HOW and WHETHER. So the *rising* we are talking about is evidently not that probable or improbable *upheaval.* On the other hand all geologists tell us that every mountain is undergoing a steady *lowering* through its particles being weathered away and washed down; and our knowledge of landslips and avalanches shows us that the mountain, so far from rising, is *descending.* Of course we all know that, objects the Reader,

---

* From Vernon Lee's *The Beautiful*, Ch. IX. Copyright, 1913, by the Cambridge University Press. Reprinted by permission of the Cambridge University Press.

Vernon Lee, pen-name of Violet Paget, (1856–1935), British psychologist, formulated the theory of empathy independently of her German contemporaries, Theodor Lipps among them, who were also working out the theory of empathy.

and of course nobody imagines that the rock and the earth of the mountain is rising, or that the mountain is getting up or growing taller! All we mean is that the mountain *looks* as if it were rising.

The mountain *looks!* Surely here is a case of putting the cart before the horse. No; we cannot explain the mountain *rising* by the mountain *looking,* for the only *looking* in the business is *our* looking *at* the mountain. And if the Reader objects again that these are all *figures of speech,* I shall answer that *Empathy* is what explains why we employ figures of speech at all, and occasionally employ them, as in the case of this rising mountain, when we know perfectly well that the figure we have chosen expresses the exact reverse of the objective truth. Very well; then, (says the Reader) we will avoid all figures of speech and say merely: when we look at the mountain *we somehow or other think of the action of rising.* Is that sufficiently literal and indisputable?

So literal and indisputable a statement of the case, I answer, that it explains, when we come to examine it, why we should have a thought of rising when we look at the mountain, since we cannot look at the mountain, nor at a tree, a tower or anything of which we similarly say that it *rises,* without lifting our glance, raising our eye and probably raising our head and neck, all of which raising and lifting unites into a general awareness of something *rising.* The rising of which we are aware is going on in us. But, as the Reader will remember also, when we are engrossed by something outside ourselves, as we are engrossed in looking at the shape (for we can *look* at only the shape, not the *substance*) of that mountain we cease thinking about ourselves, and cease thinking about ourselves exactly in proportion as we are thinking of the mountain's shape. What becomes therefore of our awareness of raising or lifting or *rising?* What can become of it (so long as it continues to be there!) except that it coalesces with the shape we are looking at; in short that the *rising* continuing to be thought, but no longer to be thought of with reference to ourselves (since we aren't thinking of ourselves), is thought of in reference to what we *are* thinking about, namely, the mountain, or rather the mountain's shape, which is, so to speak, responsible for any thought of rising, since it obliges us to lift, raise or rise ourselves in order to take stock of it. It is a case exactly analogous to our transferring the measuring done by our eye to the line of which we say that it *extends* from A to B, when in reality the only *extending* has been the extending of our glance. It is a case of what I have called the tendency to merge the *activities* of the perceiving subject with the qualities of the perceived object. Indeed if I insisted so much upon this tendency of our mind, I did so largely because of its being at the bottom of the phenomenon of *Empathy,* as we have just seen it exemplified in the *mountain which rises.*

If this is Empathy, says the Reader (relieved and reassured), am I to understand that Empathy is nothing beyond *attributing what goes on in us when we look at a shape to the shape itself?*

I am sorry that the matter is by no means so simple! If what we attributed to each single shape was only the precise action which we happen to be accomplishing in the process of looking at it, Empathy would indeed be a simple business, but it would also be a comparatively poor one. No. The *rising* of the mountain is an idea started by the awareness of our own lifting or raising of our eyes, head or neck, and it is an idea containing the awareness of that lifting or raising. But it is far more than the idea merely of that lifting or raising which we are doing at this particular present moment and in connection with this particular mountain. That present and particular raising and lifting is merely the nucleus to which gravitates our remembrance of all similar acts of raising, or *rising* which we have ever accomplished or seen accomplished, *raising* or *rising* not only of our eyes and head, but of every other part of our body, and of every part of every other body which we ever perceived to be rising. And not merely the thought of past *rising* but the thought also of future rising. All these risings, done by ourselves or watched in others, actually experienced or merely imagined, have long since united together in our mind, constituting a sort of composite photograph whence all differences are eliminated and wherein all similarities are fused and intensified: the general idea of *rising,* not "I rise, rose, will rise, it rises, has risen or will rise" but merely *rising as* such, *rising* as it is expressed not in any particular tense or person of the verb *to rise,* but in that verb's infinitive. It is this universally applicable notion of rising, which is started in our mind by the awareness of the particular present acts of raising or rising involved in our looking at that mountain, and it is this general idea of rising, *i.e.,* of *upward movement,* which gets transferred to the mountain along with our own particular present activity of raising some part of us, and which thickens and enriches and marks that poor little thought of a definite raising with the interest, the emotional fullness gathered and stored up in its long manifold existence. In other words: what we are transferring (owing to that tendency to merge the activities of the perceiving subject with the qualities of the perceived object) from ourselves to the looked at shape of the mountain, is not merely the thought of the rising which is really being done by us at that moment, but the thought and emotion, the *idea of rising as such* which had been accumulating in our mind long before we ever came into the presence of that particular mountain. And it is this complex mental process, by which we (all unsuspectingly) invest that inert mountain, that bodiless shape, with the stored up and averaged and essential modes of our activity—it is this process whereby we make the mountain *raise itself,* which constitutes what, accepting Professor Titchener's translation of the German word *Einfühlung*, I have called Empathy.

The German word *Einfühlung*, "feeling into"—derived from a *verb to feel oneself into something* ("sich in Etwas einfühlen") was in current use even before Lotze and Vischer applied it to esthetics, and some years before Lipps (1897) and Wundt (1903) adopted it into psychological terminology; and as it is now consecrated, and no better occurs to me, I have had to adopt it, although the literal connotations of the German word have surrounded its central meaning (as I have just defined it) with several mischievous misinterpretations. Against two of these I think it worth while to warn the Reader, especially as, while so doing, I can, in showing what it is not, make it even clearer what Empathy really is. The first of these two main misinterpretations is based upon the reflexive form of the German verb *"sich einfühlen"* (to feel *oneself* into) and it defines, or rather does not define, Empathy as a metaphysical and quasi-mythological *projection of the ego* into the object or shape under observation; a notion incompatible with the fact that Empathy, being only another of those various mergings of the activities of the perceiving subject with the qualities of the perceived object wherewith we have already dealt, depends upon a comparative or momentary abeyance of all thought of an ego; if we became aware that it is *we* who are thinking the rising, we who are *feeling* the rising, we should not think or feel that the mountain did the rising. The other (and as we shall later see) more justifiable misinterpretation of the word Empathy is based on its analogy with *sympathy*, and turns it into a kind of sympathetic, or as it has been called, *inner, i.e.,* merely *felt, mimicry* of, for instance, the mountain's *rising*. Such mimicry, not only *inner* and *felt,* but outwardly manifold, does undoubtedly often result from very lively *empathic* imagination. But as it is the mimicking, inner or outer, of movements and actions which, like the *rising* of the mountain, take place only in our imagination, it presupposes such previous animation of the inanimate, and cannot therefore be taken either as constituting or explaining Empathy itself.

Such as I have defined and exemplified it in our Rising Mountain, Empathy is, together with mere Sensation, probably the chief factor of preference, that is of an alternative of satisfaction and dissatisfaction, in esthetic contemplation, the muscular adjustments and the measuring, comparing and coördinating activities by which Empathy is started, being indeed occasionally difficult and distressing, but giving in themselves little more than a negative satisfaction, at the most that of difficulty overcome and suspense relieved. But although nowhere so fostered as in the contemplation of shapes, Empathy exists or tends to exist throughout our mental life. It is, indeed, one of our simpler, though far from absolutely elementary, psychological processes, entering into what is called imagination, sympathy, and also into that inference from our own inner experience which has shaped all our conceptions of an outer world, and giving to the intermittent and heterogeneous sensations received from without the framework of our constant and highly unified inner experience, that is to say, of our own activities and aims. Empathy can be traced in all modes of speech and thought, particularly in the universal attribution of *doing* and *having* and *tending* where all we can really assert is successive and varied *being*. Science has indeed explained away the anthropomorphic implications of *Force* and *Energy, Attraction* and *Repulsion;* and philosophy had reduced *Cause* and *Effect* from implying intention and effort to meaning mere constant succession. But Empathy still helps us to many valuable analogies; and it is possible that without its constantly checked but constantly renewed action, human thought would be without logical cogency, as it certainly would be without poetical charm. Indeed if Empathy is so recent a discovery, this may be due to its being part and parcel of our thinking; so that we are surprised to learn its existence, as Molière's good man was to hear that he talked prose.

Sigmund Freud

SUBLIMATION*

Life as we find it is too hard for us; it entails too much pain, too many disappointments, impossible tasks. We cannot do without palliative remedies. We cannot dispense with auxiliary constructions, as Theodor Fontane said. There are perhaps three of these means: powerful diversions of interest, which lead us to care little for our misery; substitutive gratifications, which lessen it; and intoxicating substances, which make us insensitive to it. Something of this kind is indispensable.[1] Voltaire is aiming at a diversion of in-

* From Sigmund Freud's *Civilization and its Discontents,* trans., Joan Riviere, pp. 25, 33–35, 38–39. Copyright, 1930, by The Hogarth Press, Ltd. Reprinted by permission of The Hogarth Press, Ltd.

Sigmund Freud (1856–1939), Austrian psychologist, inventor of psychoanalysis, brilliant and lucid writer on many different topics, wrote some essays on aesthetic matters (surveyed in the following essay by Richard Sterba). The selection from *Civilization and its Discontents,* rarely reprinted, reveals better than other selections Freud's views on the nature of aesthetic response.

[1] Wilhelm Busch, in *Die fromme Helene,* says the same thing on a lower level: "The man who has cares has brandy too."

terest when he brings his *Candide* to a close with the advice that people should cultivate their gardens; scientific work is another deflection of the same kind. The substitute gratifications, such as art offers, are illusions in contrast to reality, but none the less satisfying to the mind on that account, thanks to the place which phantasy has reserved for herself in mental life. The intoxicating substances affect our body, alter its chemical processes. . . .

Another method of guarding against pain is by using the libido–displacements that our mental equipment allows of, by which it gains so greatly in flexibility. The task is then one of transferring the instinctual aims into such directions that they cannot be frustrated by the outer world. Sublimation of the instincts lends an aid in this. Its success is greatest when a man knows how to heighten sufficiently his capacity for obtaining pleasure from mental and intellectual work. Fate has little power against him then. This kind of satisfaction, such as the artist's joy in creation, in embodying his phantasies, or the scientist's in solving problems or discovering truth, has a special quality which we shall certainly one day be able to define metapsychologically. Until then we can only say metaphorically it seems to us "higher and finer", but compared with that of gratifying gross primitive instincts its intensity is tempered and diffused; it does not overwhelm us physically. The weak point of this method, however, is that it is not generally applicable. It presupposes special gifts and dispositions which are not very commonly found in a sufficient degree. And even to these few it does not secure complete protection against suffering; it gives no invulnerable armour against the arrows of fate, and it usually fails when a man's own body becomes a source of suffering to him.

This behaviour reveals clearly enough its aim—that of making oneself independent of the external world, by looking for happiness in the inner things of the mind; in the next method the same features are even more marked. The connection with reality is looser still; satisfaction is obtained through illusions, which are recognized as such, without the discrepancy between them and reality being allowed to interfere with the pleasure they give. These illusions are derived from the life of phantasy which, at the time when the sense of reality developed, was expressly exempted from the demands of the reality-test and set apart for the purpose of fulfilling wishes which would be very hard to realize. At the head of these phantasy–pleasures stands the enjoyment of works of art which through the agency of the artist is opened to those who cannot themselves create.[2] Those who are sensitive to the influence of art do not know how to rate it high enough as

[2] Cf. "Formulations regarding the Two Principles in Mental Functioning," (1911), *Collected Papers*, vol. iv; and *Introductory Lectures on Psycho-Analysis* (1915–17), London, 1922, chapter xxiii.

a source of happiness and consolation in life. Yet art affects us but as a mild narcotic and can provide no more than a temporary refuge for us from the hardships of life; its influence is not strong enough to make us forget real misery. . . .

We may here go on to consider the interesting case in which happiness in life is sought first and foremost in the enjoyment of beauty, wherever it is to be found by our sense and our judgement, the beauty of human forms and movements, of natural objects, of landscapes, of artistic and even scientific creations. As a goal in life this aesthetic attitude offers little protection against the menace of suffering, but it is able to compensate for a great deal. The enjoyment of beauty produces a particular, mildly intoxicating kind of sensation. There is no very evident use in beauty; the necessity of it for cultural purposes is not apparent, and yet civilization could not do without it. The science of aesthetics investigates the conditions in which things are regarded as beautiful; it can give no explanation of the nature or origin of beauty; as usual, its lack of results is concealed under a flood of resounding and meaningless words. Unfortunately, psycho–analysis, too, has less to say about beauty than about most things. Its derivation from the realms of sexual sensation is all that seems certain; the love of beauty is a perfect example of a feeling with an inhibited aim. "Beauty" and "attraction" are first of all the attributes of a sexual object.

Richard Sterba

THE PROBLEM OF ART IN FREUD'S WRITINGS*

No aspect of the human mind and its activities has been left untouched by Sigmund Freud; and even if only once the searchlight of his genius has been thrown in passing, its powerful beam has always been directed upon the most essential points of the field in question. Depth and enlightenment are to be found in every sentence.

The ensuing pages are a work of compilation such as falls to a fol-

* From Richard Sterba's *"The Problem of Art in Freud's Writings,"* originally published in *The Psychoanalytic Quarterly,* Vol. IX, No. 2, April, 1940, and revised especially for inclusion in this anthology by the author. Published by permission of the author.

Richard Sterba (1898–   ), Vienna-trained psychoanalyst, is a practicing psychoanalyst in Detroit, Michigan, and author of technical papers on psychoanalysis as well as on aesthetics, including a work on Beethoven, *Beethoven's Nephew.*

lower and part contemporary of Freud. A full and complete presentation of psychoanalytic observations on art and artists is not to be found as such in Freud's works. In examining his papers from the standpoint of the enlightenment they contain regarding the problems of art and the artist, one encounters two sources which stand in a complemental relationship to each other. One source is a number of different papers on the theory of the neuroses, and in introductory presentations of psychoanalysis in which are to be found scattered remarks and observations about art and artists. The disclosures, the investigations and parallels which to a certain extent are only marginal remarks in these papers devoted to other themes are, as far as the theoretical problem of the psychology of art is concerned, of more value and profit than those deriving from the other, direct sources of information, papers in which artists and works of art are submitted to analysis. Among these are: Delusion and Dream based on Jensen's Gradiva, Leonardo da Vinci: A Psychosexual Study of an Infantile Reminiscence, The Moses of Michelangelo, A Childhood Recollection from Dichtung and Wahrheit. The essential general value of these papers lies not so much in their wealth of disclosure concerning the psychological problems of art; nor, indeed, is it their original aim to shed light on such problems. The goal of these papers is very much more to demonstrate that the range of validity of psychoanalysis extends far beyond the field of dreams and neurosis, and to demonstrate that our highest cultural activities and accomplishments also have their roots deeply implanted in the unconscious whence they draw their dynamic force. To read these papers is both fascinating and profitable because the general accessibility of the subject of art makes it much easier to follow the author's processes of thinking and investigation. One learns also from these papers in a particularly effective way the characteristics of the technique of psychoanalysis; how psychoanalysis is able to draw the most profoundly convincing and decisive conclusions from what Freud calls the "refuse," by which he means details which are in general laid aside and neglected. The above-mentioned complemental relationship between the two sources of information consists then in the theoretical enlightenment about art and the artist to be found in papers devoted to the psychoanalytic theory of neurosis, while in those papers devoted to an examination of specific objects of art and artists we are given insight into a more general aspect of analytic theory and method.

In Freud's paper, Das Interesse an der Psychoanalyse,[1] there is a paragraph entitled, Das Kunstwissenschaftliche Interesse; there is another more detailed contribution to the psychological problem of the work of art in *The*

---

[1] "The Claims of Psycho-Analysis to Scientific Interest," *Standard Edition*, 13, 165.

Introductory Lectures on Psychoanalysis at the end of the twenty-third lecture, entitled, The Paths of Symptom Formation. A presentation of Freud's contribution to the psychology of art should begin with a resumé of these two sources.

The practice of art is an activity whose aim is to assuage unappeased wishes. This aim is achieved not only from the standpoint of the creator but also from that of the person enjoying the creation. At the basis of artistic creation we find the same instinctual forces which are effective as components of intrapsychic conflicts—those same conflicts which drive the individual into neurosis and compel society to build up its great institutions, religions and other group productions. The work of art is therefore the product of psychic forces which are in opposition to each other, such as desire and inner prohibition. It represents a reconciliation between these conflicting forces and has therefore the character of a compromise, as have also those psychopathological formations—errors, dreams and neurotic symptoms—which are well understood. The fundamental dynamic force at the root of a work of art is an unfulfilled wish of the artist; just as in dreams and fantasies, the work of art represents this wish as fulfilled.

Psychoanalysis has taught us to recognize the enormous importance of the gratification which the individual obtains through fantasies and daydreams. Everyone has daydreams and the ego of the normal adult admits this kind of satisfaction to some extent. In daydreams one imagines desires and wishes, mostly of an erotic and egotistic nature, as fulfilled. The enjoyment of the gratification of the imaginary fulfilment is the motivating force for our phantasy activity. In certain cases, and under certain conditions where there is a marked increase of instinctual tension or an intense frustration in real life, these fantasies are enormously extended. In the wish content of fantasies, however, there is always some fraction of long-forgotten wishes from childhood; if the ability of the individual to obtain gratification in the world of reality is not very great and he is thus not capable of enduring the high tension of his instinctual needs, there is the danger of regression to early childhood wishes and of these being in a large measure reawakened, which is the preliminary step towards neurosis. It depends therefore on psycho–economic conditions, that is to say on the quantities of libidinal energy, whether an individual develops a neurosis or not. Should the dammed–up instinctual energies become overwhelmingly powerful and should the individual continue to be incapable of attaining gratification, these energies will turn and stream backwards along the course of the libido development to those early stages at which they were once able to obtain full satisfaction. Analysis calls these outstanding points in the course of development of the libido, fixations. Objects and erotogenic zones which at one time in early childhood had brought about intense psychosexual gratification, are loaded anew with psychic cathexis. But from early childhood the psychic organization of the individual has undergone such a transformation through the establishment of cultural barriers such as morals, disgust, shame, that conscious gratification in those early regions of pleasure experience is later on impossible. To the external frustration, after the regression of the libido, is added also an inner frustration and this inner frustration necessitates the exclusion from consciousness of the offending psychic impulses which are excluded from reality, and the representations and ideas belonging to them, are obliged after their repression to follow other paths of discharge than those impulses which are freely admitted to consciousness. If they become overwhelmingly powerful they are able in spite of the repression to break through into consciousness and to obtain satisfaction in the form of substitute gratifications and actions. But these are regarded by the conscious personality as foreign bodies not belonging to the ego, and their existence is painful to the individual. We call these substitute formations and actions, neurotic symptoms.

It will be apparent from what we have said that the psychic condition of the intense daydreamer is labile; for such an individual there is the danger that with an increase of instinctual demands the libido will regress to infantile positions, a process which the ego is not able to tolerate. The inevitable result is then repression, followed by symptom formation. The psychic condition in which the individual cannot discharge his libidinal energy through satisfaction with real objects, but gains, or tries to gain gratification through fantasy, is called after C. G. Jung, "introversion." The introverted individual stands between the normal and the neurotic.

The artist is an introvert. Since he is unable to satisfy his overpowering instinctual needs in the world of reality, he is obliged to turn away from the real world to the realm of fantasy thus taking the way which leads to neurosis. But it is here that the creative process sets in, enabling him through discharge of instinctual energy and the effect of the work of art on the outside world to save himself from neurosis and to regain contact with reality. He is able through the creation of a work of art to obtain sufficient gratification of his intense childhood wishes which he represents as fulfilled in his creation. Through this work of art the artist obtains a far greater gratification than through the hallucinatory representations in fantasy or daydreams because the work of art, although modelled from fantasy, is formed of a material corresponding to the real outside world. His particular method of representation, possible to the artist on account of his talent, enables him in a certain measure to find a way back from fantasy to reality, obtaining in this roundabout way a means of gratifying actual wishes and of achieving success for which, in a direct way, his forces would never have been adequate. For the artist therefore the work of art signifies on the one hand, deliverance from neurosis through the instinctual gratification which it brings him and, on the other hand, the possibility of real success which would have been denied him had he not found the device, represented by the work of art, for satisfying his instinctual wishes. Both gratification of instinctual wishes by the work of art and the ensuing success in the real world make it possible for the artist to escape from neurosis because the dynamic result is a considerable decrease of tension in the psyche.

Artistic production is directly connected with daydreaming and fantasy. We have already mentioned that the daydream represents not only the satisfaction of actual wishes but also of early childhood wishes whose existence the individual is prohibited to remember, since their fulfillment would be in contradiction to the norms which have in the meantime been established in his personality. But these unfulfilled wishes which have become unconscious have still retained their dynamic force and a continuous expenditure of energy is required to hold them in repression, while they on the other hand, take advantage of every opportunity to force their way through to consciousness and to motor expression. They succeed particularly well in cases where a wish from the ego, that is, a wish admitted by the conscious personality but refused by reality, is still active in the psychic apparatus. The infantile wishes then combine with this actual wish and supply with psychic energy the fantasy built out of the actual wish, modifying the fantasy in such a way that they can obtain satisfaction at the same time as the actual wish. A thorough psychoanalytic examination therefore discloses in the fantasy admitted by the ego, the fulfillment of old, repressed childhood wishes. Just as a dream allies itself with unresolved experiences of the day preceding the dream and analysis recognizes that in the hallucinatory wish fulfillment of the dream picture a forbidden wish of earliest childhood has allied itself with an actual experience, achieving gratification at the same time, so we find also that in the daydream an actual and an infantile wish obtain their common satisfaction through the fantasy. The satisfaction of the infantile wish occurs unconsciously and it requires an analysis of the dream, as of the daydream, to prove the presence of the infantile wish in the manifest picture.

If the work of art springs from a daydream, we must expect that in it too, besides the actual causative material, there are also infantile unconscious wishes which will be represented therein as fulfilled. Analysis maintains that the dynamic effect of the work of art, the satisfaction which it brings not only to the artist but also to the spectator, is produced through the fulfillment of the repressed infantile wishes; that the "latent" part, as Freud calls it, of the pleasure of art is in the opinion of psychoanalysis far greater than the manifest and aesthetic part. This opinion gave analysis the task of proving the presence of infantile wishes in the work of art, and it has fulfilled this task. In The Interpretation of Dreams, Freud demonstrated that the profound emotional effect of Sophocles' Tragedy of Oedipus is caused by the specific content of the drama, which brings about the fulfillment of an unconscious wish common to all mankind, but which represents also the carrying out of the punishment which every individual has feared as a consequence of this very wish and, in the hidden depths of the unconscious, still does. In his Interpretation of Dreams Freud has shown too that this same latent content is expressed in Shakespeare's Hamlet.

The disclosure of the fact that unfulfilled wishes, originating in the unconscious, are satisfied in the work of art, and that it is possible through analysis of the work of art to discover these; that, furthermore, the enjoyment of the work of art derives principally from the satisfaction of these infantile wishes, is Freud's most important contribution to the psychology of the work of art.

Since repressed infantile wishes succeed in obtaining satisfaction through the work of art, it must be possible to find connections between the experiences the artist has had during his life, especially the impressions of early childhood, and his artistic creations. These connections are actually to be found not only in the subject matter but also in the artist's specific method of creation.

As a classic example of an analytical discovery of the connections between creation and infantile experience we may take Freud's famous paper on Leonardo da Vinci. In this contribution, Freud proceeds from a single childhood memory communicated by Leonardo, and attempts to explain the picture of St. Anna, the Virgin Mary, and the Christ child, an unconscious puzzle picture. In general, Freud uses poetry as a paradigmatic basis for his investigations in the field of the psychology of art because, of all the material employed to form the work of art, poetry stands nearest to the dream and the fantasy, those all-important objects of psychological research. It may be also that the art of poetry lay nearest to Freud's own creative expression.

Since the work of art represents the fulfilment of intense unconscious infantile wishes, the artist's own ego must necessarily be as much at the center of the work of art, as the dreamers and daydreamers ego are at the center of their productions. The elaboration however which the daydream has to undergo if it is to be transformed into a work of art, about which we shall have more to say later, must very often be abolished by dissolving displacements, removing distortions and condensations, sometimes by combining two personages in order to recognize as the chief character, the "hero" in the work of art, the creative artist himself. But in the hallucinatory fulfilment of infantile wishes lies also the source of the pleasure of enjoyment of the work of art, that is to say, the secret of its effect on others, since these infantile wishes are common to all human beings. They are the same wishes from which our dreams originate, the same from which myths—those "secular dreams of mankind"—are formed, the same wishes which mankind combats by means of its great institutions, the most important of which are religion and the moral laws. Banned by culture, suppressed and repudiated by education, these wishes are repressed by the ego and kept back from consciousness. But to a great extent they retain their psychic energy and try unceasingly to force their way through the consciousness. Under certain conditions consciousness actually does admit their fulfilment as in the dream, the fantasy and the work of art. The dynamic effect of the work of art upon those who enjoy it consists in the fact that through the imaginative participation in the artist's infantile fantasy, the wishes of the person enjoying the work of art are also satisfied, since such wishes are common to all of us. Through this social participation in the act of wish fulfilment, the work of art differs from the dream and the fantasy. Dream and fantasy are, even as the work of art, wish fulfilments of a hallucinatory character, but the gratification which dreams and fantasies bring about serves only for the individual producing them and if communicated leaves others indifferent, or has the effect of repelling them. "The essential 'ars poetica' lies in the technique by which our feeling of repulsion is overcome, and this has certainly to do with those barriers erected between every individual and all others."[2] With this statement which can be extended over every kind of artistic production, the problem of the work of art has to be considered as one of group psychology. The possibility offered by the work of art of an identification with the hallucinatory wish fulfilment—on the basis of kindred wishes—one can even say, the invitation of the work of art to this identification, must be considered as the essential feature of the work of art.

The next subject of investigation will therefore be the technique used by the artist to overcome the refusal of others to participate in his own individual fantasies. Freud points out three technical methods by means of which the

[2] Freud: "The Relation of the Poet to Day-Dreaming," *Coll. Papers* IV, p. 183.

artist can make his daydreams enjoyable to others. 1) By the transformation of the fantasy; 2) By the elaboration of its content in such a way as to represent the fantasy; and 3) By the effect of aesthetic principles in this elaboration.

The original daydream before being transformed into the work of art has to be stripped of all that is egotistical and egocentric. For this purpose, everything personal must be removed from the daydream; all that could be considered repulsive in the wishes represented by the work of art has to be tempered in order completely to conceal its origin in forbidden sources. This transformation of the daydream may be compared to the distortion that occurs in dreams. In dream representation also, all that is repulsive is tempered and made unrecognizable by disguise, so that it can get past the censorship of the superego and enter the consciousness of the dreamer.

The discovery of the original fantasy through the undoing of the distortion and the discovery of the unconscious wishes at the basis of the work of art are possible because of the technical knowledge which analysis acquired during the investigation of dreams and other psychological formations. Thus analysis makes possible the recognition of the latent content of the work of art. The distortion of the original fantasy and its basic infantile wishes is the result of the critical influence of the superego, not only of the artist, but also of society. This social superego is much severer and more inexorable in its demands than the superego of the individual, the former admitting only what others are permitted to know, the latter paying no attention to others who are unable to discover its intentions. The distortions of the work of art must therefore, on account of the social superego, be a great deal more extensive than in the case of the daydream. It will be apparent after what we have said that the work of art has to be considered the result of a psychic compromise, since it mediates between the demands of the unconscious wishes and the demands of the social conscience.

The second means of abolishing the barriers between one's own and other people's egos, is the artist's mysterious faculty of being able to form a certain material so that the fantasy expressed therein appears as a new kind of reality—an image of reality. Such images of reality are highly valued by mankind for reasons which will be explained later. The esteem earned by the work of art for representing a new kind of reality makes it possible for the fantasy at the origin of the creation to be sanctioned and used as a source of pleasure.

This imitation of reality which plays such an important part in the formation of the material, does not take place only because of the necessity for submission to the demands of the reality principle in order to succeed as it were in bribing those who enjoy the work of art. The imitation of reality in itself represents a primitive kind of mastery of reality which is made possible by an exchange of psychic for actual reality. The technique of such mastery is magic, it is based on, "mistaking an ideal connection for a real one" (Frazer). The foundation of this magical technique resides in the pleasure principle; it originates in a very early phase of psychic development at which the individual still looks upon himself as omnipotent because wishes are experienced at this period as if their fulfilment in reality were achieved by the mere act of wishing. We call this the stage of "omnipotence of thought." The magic creation of a pseudo reality, in which not the laws of the outside world but conscious and unconscious wishes are the determining factors, signifies a regression to this phase of the omnipotence of thought. The early childhood tendencies of this period of omnipotence of thought are preserved in all of us and the pseudo reality of the work of art brings them a profound satisfaction.

If one makes a comparison between those parts of the work of art formed under the laws of reality and those formed under the pleasure principle, one will find that the influence of the latter is markedly the greater. The original fantasy, particularly in its unconscious aspects, is formed according to the pleasure principle. The formation of the material as an image of reality takes place under the influence of the reality principle, but it is this very creation of a pseudo reality with its magic significance which is able to bring satisfaction to psychic tendencies that, being extremely primitive, are so entirely dominated by the pleasure principle that they are normally held back from consciousness. The mutual permeation of the fields of domination of the pleasure and reality principles led Freud to call art a kind of reconciliation between the two principles in mental functioning.

The same magic tendencies which are found at the basis of the work of art, are found at the basis of children's play. And like the child at play, the artist also creates a world of fantasy in the likeness of reality which he takes in all seriousness and loads with enormous quantities of affective energy. Those who enjoy the work of art can permit themselves an extensive identification with the represented work because the alternating influence of their belief in the reality of the work of art and their consciousness that it is only play affords them this possibility. The release of quantities of affective energy through the work of art is brought about through this fluctuating mixture of delusion and admission that "it is only play" which creates an atmosphere enabling various cathexes to escape to some extent the control of the censor, just as in dreams our conscience consoles us when we say to oursevles: "it is only a dream." Language expresses the parallel between the play of artists and that of children in the use of the word "play" to denote theatrical performance and musical activities.

As the third and last means of abolishing the barriers between the ego of the artist and the egos of other people, Freud specifies the aesthetic features of the work of art. During the formation of the material, the artist follows certain laws of beauty, whose investigation belongs to the field of aesthetics. These aesthetic features in the work of art are particularly suited to incite those who enjoy it, to identification, and it is to a great extent these aesthetic qualities through which the work of art becomes a social phenomenon. The deeper effect of the aesthetic qualities is more comprehensible through the principle of aesthetic assistance or enhancement, first described by the German philosopher, G. Th. Fechner.[3] Freud, in his famous contribution, Wit and Its Relation to the Unconscious, explains in detail this principle and its share in the effect of wit and jokes. He calls it the "forepleasure principle" and shows that a process giving rise to permitted pleasure is also able to release other sources of pleasure which have been until this time repressed owing to their forbidden nature if they are linked up with the first process. In wit these combined processes bring about a far deeper pleasure than the apparently innocent technical wit formation can give by itself. The technique of wit, the use of puns, strange and funny combinations and the like, seduce us to the enjoyment of sadistic or obscene tendencies, whose expression would repel us were it not combined with the enjoyment of the skilful technical formation of the joke. Freud calls the pleasure of the technical side of wit the forepleasure through which the deeper and forbidden pleasure, forbidden because of its aggressive or obscene nature, is released. The aesthetic side of the work of art has a similar forepleasure effect; it seduces the individual into the enjoyment of forbidden instinctual wish gratifications without his even becoming conscious of the latent sources of his pleasure. But at the same time the effect of the aesthetic side of the work of art is considerably overestimated, by our conscious mind. It is valued as if the entire quantity of pleasure caused by the work of art were brought about by the aesthetic features, while the real sources of pleasure remain for the most part unconscious. The amount of pleasure radiating from these unconscious sources is automatically ascribed to the processes which bring about pleasure consciously, that is, to the aesthetic features of the work of art. The result of this is the overestimation of the aesthetic side. Exactly the same thing occurs in the case of the joke: the clever construction of the latter is overestimated and is

---

[3] Cf. his *Vorschule der Aesthetik*, 1897.

regarded as the main source of the pleasure effect. Actually the gratification of unconscious tendencies, either obscene or aggressive, is released through the forepleasure which arises from the technical construction of the joke.

With the description of the effect of the mechanism of forepleasure in the work of art discovered by Freud, we come to the end of our subject. Freud's findings in the field of the psychology of art are, as we have seen, principally concerned with the psychodynamics of the art form, with the conditions, possibilities and mechanisms achieving these dynamic results and with the mechanisms which make the artistic creations a social phenomenon. The wealth of contributions based on Freud's findings which have been made by others is in itself both tribute and witness to the manifold discoveries and ways that the genius of this great thinker has opened up in the field of the psychology of art.

George Santayana

PLEASURE*

THE DIFFERENTIA OF ESTHETIC PLEASURE NOT ITS DISINTERESTEDNESS

The distinction between pleasure and the sense of beauty has sometimes been said to consist in the unselfishness of esthetic satisfaction. In other pleasures, it is said, we gratify our senses and passion; in the contemplation of beauty we are raised above ourselves, the passions are silenced and we are happy in the recognition of a good that we do not seek to possess. The painter does not look at a spring of water with the eyes of a thirsty man, nor at a beautiful woman with those of a satyr. The difference lies, it is urged, in the impersonality of the enjoyment. But this distinction is one of intensity and delicacy, not of nature, and it seems satisfactory only to the least esthetic minds.[1]

* From George Santayana's *The Sense of Beauty*, pp. 37–52. Copyright, 1896, 1936, by Charles Scribner's Sons. Reprinted from *The Sense of Beauty* by George Santayana by permission of Charles Scribner's Sons and Constable and Company, Ltd.

George Santayana (1863–1952), poet, critic, philosopher and essayist, wrote, as his first of many books, this work on aesthetics, which has become one of the more important contemporary books on the subject.

[1] Schopenhauer, indeed, who makes much of it, was a good critic, but his psychology suffered much from the pessimistic generalities of his system. It concerned him to show that the will was bad, and, as he felt beauty to be a good if not a holy thing, he hastened to convince himself that it came from the suppression of the will. But even in his system this suppression is only relative. The desire of individual objects, indeed,

In the second place, the supposed disinterestedness of esthetic delights is not truly fundamental. Appreciation of a picture is not identical with the desire to buy it, but it is, or ought to be, closely related and preliminary to that desire. The beauties of nature and of the plastic arts are not consumed by being enjoyed; they retain all the efficacy to impress a second beholder. But this circumstance is accidental, and those esthetic objects which depend upon change and are exhausted in time, as are all performances, are things the enjoyment of which is an object of rivalry and is coveted as much as any other pleasure. And even plastic beauties can often not be enjoyed except by a few, on account of the necessity of travel or other difficulties of access, and then this esthetic enjoyment is as selfishly pursued as the rest.

The truth which the theory is trying to state seems rather to be that when we seek esthetic pleasures we have no further pleasure in mind; that we do not mix up the satisfactions of vanity and proprietorship with the delight of contemplation. This is true, but it is true at bottom of all pursuits and enjoyments. Every real pleasure is in one sense disinterested. It is not sought with ulterior motives, and what fills the mind is no calculation, but the image of an object or event, suffused with emotion. A sophisticated consciousness may often take the idea of self as the touchstone of its inclinations; but this self, for the gratification and aggrandizement of which a man may live, is itself only a complex of aims and memories, which once had their direct objects, in which he had taken a spontaneous and unselfish interest. The gratifications which, merged together, make the selfishness are each of them ingenuous, and no more selfish than the most altruistic, impersonal emotion. The content of selfishness is a mass of unselfishness. There is no reference to the nominal essence called oneself either in one's appetites or in one's natural affections; yet a man absorbed in his meat and drink, in his houses and lands, in his children and dogs, is called selfish because these interests, although natural and instinctive in him, are not shared by others. The unselfish man is he whose nature has a more universal direction, whose interests are more widely diffused.

But as impersonal thoughts are such only in their object, not in their subject or agent; since all thoughts are the thoughts of somebody: so also unselfish interests have to be somebody's interests. If we were not inter-

---

is absent in the perception of beauty, but there is still present that initial love of the general type and principles of things which is the first illusion of the absolute, and drives it on to the fatal experiment of creation. So that, apart from Schopenhauer's mythology, we have even in him the recognition that beauty gives satisfaction to some dim and underlying demand of our nature, just as particular objects give more special and momentary pleasures to our individualized wills. His psychology was, however, far too vague and general to undertake an analysis of those mysterious feelings.

ested in beauty, if it were of no concern to our happiness whether things were beautiful or ugly, we should manifest not the maximum, but the total absence of esthetic faculty. The disinterestedness of this pleasure is, therefore, that of all primitive and intuitive satisfactions, which are in no way conditioned by a reference to an artificial general concept, like that of the self, all the potency of which must itself be derived from the independent energy of its component elements. I care about myself because "myself" is a name for the things I have at heart. To set up the verbal figment of personality and make it an object of concern apart from the interests which were its content and substance, turns the moralist into a pedant, and ethics into a superstition. The self which is the object of *amour propre* is an idol of the tribe, and needs to be disintegrated into the primitive objective interests that underlie it before the cultus of it can be justified by reason.

THE DIFFERENTIA OF ESTHETIC PLEASURE NOT ITS UNIVERSALITY

The supposed disinterestedness of our love of beauty passes into another characteristic of it often regarded as essential—its universality. The pleasures of the senses have, it is said, no dogmatism in them; that anything gives me pleasure involves no assertion about its capacity to give pleasure to another. But when I judge a thing to be beautiful, my judgment means that the thing is beautiful in itself, or (what is the same thing more critically expressed) that it should seem so to everybody. The claim to universality is, according to this doctrine, the essence of the esthetic; what makes the perception of beauty a judgment rather than a sensation. All esthetic precepts would be impossible, and all criticism arbitrary and subjective, unless we admit a paradoxical universality in our judgment, the philosophical implications of which we may then go on to develop. But we are fortunately not required to enter the labyrinth into which this method leads; there is a much simpler and clearer way of studying such questions, which is to challenge and analyze the assertion before us and seek its basis in human nature. Before this is done, we should run the risk of expanding a natural misconception or inaccuracy of thought into an inveterate and pernicious prejudice by making it the center of an elaborate construction.

That the claim of universality is such a natural inaccuracy will not be hard to show. There is notoriously no great agreement upon esthetic matters; and such agreement as there is, is based upon similarity of origin, nature, and circumstance among men, a similarity which, where it exists, tends to bring about identity in all judgments and feelings. It is unmeaning to say that what is beautiful to one man *ought* to be beautiful to another. If their senses are the same, their associations and dispositions similar, then the same thing will certainly be beautiful to both. If their natures are different, the form which to one will be entrancing will be to another even invisible, because his classifications and discriminations in perception will be different, and he may see a hideous detached fragment or a shapeless aggregate of things, in what to another is a perfect whole—so entirely are the unities of objects unities of function and use. It is absurd to say that what is invisible to a given being *ought* to seem beautiful to him. Evidently this obligation of recognizing the same qualities is conditioned by the possession of the same faculties. But no two men have exactly the same faculties, nor can things have for any two exactly the same values.

What is loosely expressed by saying that any one ought to see this or that beauty is that he would see it if his disposition, training, or attention were what our ideal demands for him; and our ideal of what any one should be has complex but discoverable sources. We take, for instance, a certain pleasure in having our own judgments supported by those of others; we are intolerant, if not of the existence of a nature different from our own, at least of its expression in words and judgments. We are confirmed or made happy in our doubtful opinions by seeing them accepted universally. We are unable to find the basis of our taste in our own experience and therefore refuse to look for it there. If we were sure of our ground, we should be willing to acquiesce in the naturally different feelings and ways of others, as a man who is conscious of speaking his language with the accent of the capital confesses its arbitrariness with gaiety, and is pleased and interested in the variations of it he observes in provincials; but the provincial is always zealous to show that he has reason and ancient authority to justify his oddities. So people who have no sensations, and do not know why they judge, are always trying to show that they judge by universal reason.

Thus the frailty and superficiality of our own judgments cannot brook contradiction. We abhor another man's doubt when we cannot tell him why we ourselves believe. Our ideal of other men tends therefore to include the agreement of their judgments with our own; and although we might acknowledge the fatuity of this demand in regard to natures very different from the human, we may be unreasonable enough to require that all races should admire the same style of architecture, and all ages the same poets.

The great actual unity of human taste within the range of conventional history helps the pretension. But in principle it is untenable. Nothing

has less to do with the real merit of a work of imagination than the capacity
of all men to appreciate it; the true test is the degree and kind of satisfaction
it can give to him who appreciates it most. The symphony would lose
nothing if half mankind had always been deaf, as nine-tenths of them actually
are to the intricacies of its harmonies; but it would have lost much if no
Beethoven had existed. And more: incapacity to appreciate certain types
of beauty may be the condition *sine qua non* for the appreciation of another
kind; the greatest capacity both for enjoyment and creation is highly
specialized and exclusive, and hence the greatest ages of art have often
been strangely intolerant.

The invectives of one school against another, perverse as they are
philosophically, are artistically often signs of health, because they indicate
a vital appreciation of certain kinds of beauty, a love of them that has grown
into a jealous passion. The architects that have pieced out the imperfections
of ancient buildings with their own thoughts, like Charles V. when he
raised his massive palace beside the Alhambra, may be condemned from a
certain point of view. They marred much by their interference; but they
showed a splendid confidence in their own intuitions, a proud assertion of
their own taste, which is the greatest evidence of esthetic sincerity. On
the contrary, our own gropings, eclecticism, and archaeology are the symptoms of impotence. If we were less learned and less just, we might be more
efficient. If our appreciation were less general, it might be more real, and
if we trained our imagination into exclusiveness, it might attain to character.

THE DIFFERENTIA OF ESTHETIC PLEASURE: ITS OBJECTIFICATION

There is, however, something more in the claim to universality in esthetic
judgments than the desire to generalize our own opinions. There is the expression of a curious but well-known psychological phenomenon, viz, the
transformation of an element of sensation into the quality of a thing. If
we say that other men should see the beauties we see, it is because we think
those beauties *are in the object,* like its color, proportion, or size. Our
judgment appears to us merely the perception and discovery of an external
existence, of the real excellence that is without. But this notion is radically
absurd and contradictory. Beauty, as we have seen, is a value; it cannot
be conceived as an independent existence which affects our senses and
which we consequently perceive. It exists in perception, and cannot exist
otherwise. A beauty not perceived is a pleasure not felt, and a contradiction.
But modern philosophy has taught us to say the same thing of every

element of the perceived world; all are sensations; and their grouping into objects imagined to be permanent and external is the work of certain habits of our intelligence. We should be incapable of surveying or retaining the diffused experiences of life, unless we organized and classified them, and out of the chaos of impressions framed the world of conventional and recognizable objects.

How this is done is explained by the current theories of perception. External objects usually affect various senses at once, the impressions of which are thereby associated. Repeated experiences of one object are also associated on account of their similarity; hence a double tendency to merge and unify into a single percept, to which a name is attached, the group of those memories and reactions which in fact had one external thing for their cause. But this percept, once formed, is clearly different from those particular experiences out of which it grew. It is permanent, they are variable. They are but partial views and glimpses of it. The constituted notion therefore comes to be the reality, and the materials of it merely the appearance. The distinction between substance and quality, reality and appearance, matter and mind, has no other origin.

The objects thus conceived and distinguished from our ideas of them, are at first compacted of all the impressions, feelings, and memories, which offer themselves for association and fall within the vortex of the amalgamating imagination. Every sensation we get from a thing is originally treated as one of its qualities. Experiment, however, and the practical need of a simpler conception of the structure of objects lead us gradually to reduce the qualities of the object to a minimum, and to regard most perceptions as an effect of those few qualities upon us. These few primary qualities, like extension which we persist in treating as independently real and as the quality of a substance, are those which suffice to explain the order of our experiences. All the rest, like color, are relegated to the subjective sphere, as merely effects upon our minds, and apparent or secondary qualities of the object.

But this distinction has only a practical justification. Convenience and economy of thought alone determine what combination of our sensations we shall continue to objectify and treat as the cause of the rest. The right and tendency to be objective is equal in all, since they are all prior to the artifice of thought by which we separate the concept from its materials, the thing from our experiences.

The qualities which we now conceive to belong to real objects are for the most part images of sight and touch. One of the first classes of effects to be treated as secondary were naturally pleasures and pains, since it could commonly conduce very little to intelligent and successful action to conceive our pleasures and pains as resident in objects. But emotions are essentially capable of objectification, as well as impressions of sense; and one may well believe that a primitive and inexperienced consciousness would rather people the world with ghosts of its own terrors and passions than with projections of those luminous and mathematical concepts which as yet it could hardly have formed.

This animistic and mythological habit of thought still holds its own at the confines of knowledge, where mechanical explanations are not found. In ourselves, where nearness makes observation difficult, in the intricate chaos of animal and human life, we still appeal to the efficacy of will and ideas, as also in the remote night of cosmic and religious problems. But in all the intermediate realm of vulgar day, where mechanical science has made progress, the inclusion of emotional or passionate elements in the concept of the reality would be now an extravagance. Here our idea of things is composed exclusively of perceptual elements, of the ideas of form and of motion.

The beauty of objects, however, forms an exception to this rule. Beauty is an emotional element, a pleasure of ours, which nevertheless we regard as a quality of things. But we are now prepared to understand the nature of this exception. It is the survival of a tendency originally universal to make every effect of a thing upon us a constituent of its conceived nature. The scientific idea of a thing is a great abstraction from the mass of perceptions and reactions which that thing produces; the esthetic idea is less abstract, since it retains the emotional reaction, the pleasure of the perception, as an integral part of the conceived thing.

Nor is it hard to find the ground of this survival in the sense of beauty of an objectification of feeling elsewhere extinct. Most of the pleasures which objects cause are easily distinguished and separated from the perception of the object: the object has to be applied to a particular organ, like the palate, or swallowed like wine, or used and operated upon in some way before the pleasure arises. The cohesion is therefore slight between the pleasure and the other associated elements of sense; the pleasure is separated in time from the perception, or it is localized in a different organ, and consequently is at once recognized as an effect and not as a quality of the object. But when the process of perception itself is pleasant, as it may easily be, when the intellectual operation, by which the elements of sense are associated and projected, and the concept of the form and substance of the thing produced, is naturally delightful, then we have a pleasure intimately bound up in the thing, inseparable from its character and constitution, the seat of which in us is the same as the seat of the perception. We naturally fail, under these circumstances, to separate the pleasure from the other objectified feelings. It becomes, like them, a quality of the object, which we distinguish from pleasures not so incorporated in the perception of things, by giving it the name of beauty.

THE DEFINITION OF BEAUTY

We have now reached our definition of beauty, which, in the terms of our successive analysis and narrowing of the conception, is value positive, intrinsic, and objectified. Or, in less technical language, Beauty is pleasure regarded as the quality of a thing.

This definition is intended to sum up a variety of distinctions and identifications which should perhaps be here more explicitly set down. Beauty is a value, that is, it is not a perception of a matter of fact or of a relation: it is an emotion, an affection of our volitional and appreciative nature. An object cannot be beautiful if it can give pleasure to nobody: a beauty to which all men were forever indifferent is a contradiction in terms.

In the second place, this value is positive, it is the sense of the presence of something good, or (in the case of ugliness) of its absence. It is never the perception of a positive evil, it is never a negative value. That we are endowed with the sense of beauty is a pure gain which brings no evil with it. When the ugly ceases to be amusing or merely uninteresting and becomes disgusting, it becomes indeed a positive evil: but a moral and practical, not an esthetic one. In esthetics that saying is true—often so disingenuous in ethics—that evil is nothing but the absence of good: for even the tedium and vulgarity of an existence without beauty is not itself ugly so much as lamentable and degrading. The absence of esthetic goods is a moral evil: the esthetic evil is merely relative, and means less of esthetic good than was expected at the place and time. No form in itself gives pain, although some forms give pain by causing a shock of surprise even when they are really beautiful: as if a mother found a fine bull pup in her child's cradle, when her pain would not be esthetic in its nature.

Further, this pleasure must not be in the consequence of the utility of the object or event, but in its immediate perception; in other words, beauty is an ultimate good, something that gives satisfaction to a natural function, to some fundamental need or capacity of our minds. Beauty is therefore a positive value that is intrinsic; it is a pleasure. These two circumstances sufficiently separate the sphere of esthetics from that of ethics. Moral values are generally negative, and always remote. Morality has to do with the avoidance of evil and the pursuit of good: esthetics only with enjoyment.

Finally, the pleasures of sense are distinguished from the perception of beauty, as sensation in general is distinguished from perception; by the objectification of the elements and their appearance as qualities rather of things than of consciousness. The passage from sensation to perception is gradual, and the path may be sometimes retraced: so it is with beauty and the pleasures of sensation. There is no sharp line between them, but it depends upon the degree of objectivity my feeling has attained at the moment whether I say "It pleases me," or "It is beautiful." If I am self-conscious and critical, I shall probably use one phrase; if I am impulsive and susceptible, the other. The more remote, interwoven, and inextricable the pleasure is, the more objective it will appear; and the union of two pleasures often makes one beauty. In Shakespeare's LIVth sonnet are these words:

> O how much more doth beauty beauteous seem
> By that sweet ornament which truth doth give!
> The rose looks fair, but fairer we it deem
> For that sweet odor which doth in it live.
> The canker-blooms have full as deep a dye
> As the perfumèd tincture of the roses,
> Hang on such thorns, and play as wantonly
> When summer's breath their maskèd buds discloses.
> But, for their beauty only is their show,
> They live unwooed and unrespected fade;
> Die to themselves. Sweet roses do not so:
> Of their sweet deaths are sweetest odors made.

One added ornament, we see, turns the deep dye, which was but show and mere sensation before, into an element of beauty and reality; and as truth is here the coöperation of perceptions, so beauty is the coöperation of pleasures. If color, form, and motion are hardly beautiful without the sweetness of the odor, how much more necessary would they be for the sweetness itself to become a beauty! If we had the perfume in a flask, no one would think of calling it beautiful: it would give us too detached and controllable a sensation. There would be no object in which it could be easily incorporated. But let it float from the garden, and it will add another sensuous charm to objects simultaneously recognized, and help to make them beautiful. Thus beauty is constituted by the objectification of pleasure. It is pleasure objectified.

Edward Bullough

'PSYCHICAL DISTANCE' AS A FACTOR IN ART AND AN AESTHETIC PRINCIPLE*

1

The conception of "Distance" suggests, in connection with Art, certain trains of thought by no means devoid of interest or of speculative importance. Perhaps the most obvious suggestion is that of *actual spatial* distance, *i.e.*, the distance of a work of Art from the spectator, or that of *represented spatial* distance, *i.e.*, the distance represented within the work. Less obvious, more metaphorical, is the meaning of *temporal* distance. The first was noticed already by Aristotle in his *Poetics;* the second has played a great part in the history of painting in the form of perspective; the distinction between these two kinds of distance assumes special importance theoretically in the differentiation between sculpture in the round, and relief-sculpture. Temporal distance, remoteness from us in point of time, though often a cause of misconceptions, has been declared to be a factor of considerable weight in our appreciation.

It is not, however, in any of these meanings that "Distance" is put forward here, though it will be clear in the course of this essay that the above mentioned kinds of distance are rather special forms of the conception of Distance as advocated here, and derive whatever *aesthetic* qualities they may possess from Distance in its general connotation. This general connotation is "Psychical Distance."

A short illustration will explain what is meant by "Psychical Distance." Imagine a fog at sea: for most people it is an experience of acute unpleasantness. Apart from the physical annoyance and remoter forms of discomfort such as delays, it is apt to produce feelings of peculiar anxiety, fears of invisible dangers, strains of watching and listening for distance and unlocalized signals. The listless movements of the ship and her warning calls soon tell upon the nerves of the passengers; and that special, expectant, tacit anxiety and nervousness, always associated with this experience, make a fog the

* From Edward Bullough's " 'Psychical Distance' as a Factor in Art and an Aesthetic Principle," *British Journal of Psychology*, V, 1912, pp. 87–98. Reprinted by permission of the *British Journal of Psychology*.

Edward Bullough (1880–1934) was Professor of Italian Literature at Cambridge University and wrote, among other things, a number of important essays on aesthetic problems.

dreaded terror of the sea (all the more terrifying because of its very silence and gentleness) for the expert seafarer no less than for the ignorant landsman.

Nevertheless, a fog at sea can be a source of intense relish and enjoyment. Abstract from the experience of the sea fog, for the moment, its danger and practical unpleasantness, just as every one in the enjoyment of a mountain-climb disregards its physical labor and its danger (though, it is not denied, that these may incidentally enter into the enjoyment and enhance it); direct the attention to the features "objectively" constituting the phenomenon—the veil surrounding you with an opaqueness as of transparent milk, blurring the outline of things and distorting their shapes into weird grotesqueness; observe the carrying-power of the air, producing the impression as if you could touch some far-off siren by merely putting out your hand and letting it lose itself behind that white wall; note the curious creamy smoothness of the water, hypocritically denying as it were any suggestion of danger; and, above all, the strange solitude and remoteness from the world, as it can be found only on the highest mountain tops; and the experience may acquire, in its uncanny mingling of repose and terror, a flavor of such concentrated poignancy and delight as to contrast sharply with the blind and distempered anxiety of its other aspects. This contrast, often emerging with startling suddenness, is like a momentary switching on of some new current, or the passing ray of a brighter light, illuminating the outlook upon perhaps the most ordinary and familiar objects—an impression which we experience sometimes in instants of direst extremity, when our practical interest snaps like a wire from sheer over-tension, and we watch the consummation of some impending catastrophe with the marveling unconcern of a mere spectator.

It is a difference of outlook, due—if such a metaphor is permissible—to the insertion of Distance. This Distance appears to lie between our own self and its affections, using the latter term in its broadest sense as anything which affects our being, bodily or spiritually, e.g., as sensation, perception, emotional state or idea. Usually, though not always, it amounts to the same thing to say that the Distance lies between our own self and such objects as are the sources or vehicles of such affections.

Thus, in the fog, the transformation by Distance is produced in the first instance by putting the phenomenon, so to speak, out of gear with our practical, actual self; by allowing it to stand outside the context of our personal needs and ends—in short, by looking at it "objectively," as it has often been called, by permitting only such reactions on our part as emphasize the "objective" features of the experience, and by interpreting even our "subjective" affections not as modes of *our* being rather as characteristics of the phenomenon.

The working of Distance is, accordingly, not simple, but highly complex. It has a *negative*, inhibitory aspect—the cutting-out of the practical sides of things and of our practical attitude to them—and a *positive* side—the elaboration of the experience on the new basis created by the inhibitory action of Distance.

2. Consequently, this distanced view of things is not, and cannot be, our normal outlook. As a rule, experiences constantly turn the same side towards us, namely, that which has the strongest practical force of appeal. We are not ordinarily aware of those aspects of things which do not touch us immediately and practically, nor are we generally conscious of impressions apart from our own self which is impressed. The sudden view of things from their reverse, usually unnoticed, side, comes upon us as a revelation, and such revelations are precisely those of Art. In this most general sense, Distance is a factor in all Art.

3. It is, for this very reason, also an aesthetic principle. The aesthetic contemplation and the aesthetic outlook have often been described as "objective." We speak of "objective" artists as Shakespeare or Velasquez, of "objective" works or art forms as Homer's *Iliad* or the drama. It is a term constantly occurring in discussions and criticisms, though its sense, if pressed at all, becomes very questionable. For certain forms of Art, such as lyrical poetry, are said to be "subjective"; Shelley, for example, would usually be considered a "subjective" writer. On the other hand, no work of Art can be genuinely "objective" in the sense in which this term might be applied to a work on history or to a scientific treatise; nor can it be "subjective" in the ordinary acceptance of that term, as a personal feeling, a direct statement of a wish or belief, or a cry of passion is subjective. "Objectivity" and "subjectivity" are a pair of opposites which in their mutual exclusiveness when applied to Art soon lead to confusion.

Nor are they the only pair of opposites. Art has with equal vigor been declared alternately "idealistic" and "realistic," "sensual" and "spiritual," "individualistic" and "typical." Between the defense of either terms of such antitheses most aesthetic theories have vacillated. It is one of the contentions of this essay that such opposites find their synthesis in the more fundamental conception of Distance.

Distance further provides the much needed criterion of the beautiful as distinct from the merely agreeable.

Again, it marks one of the most important steps in the process of artistic creation and serves as a distinguishing feature of what is commonly so loosely described as the "artistic temperament."

Finally, it may claim to be considered as one of the essential characteristics of the "aesthetic consciousness"—if I may describe by this term that special mental attitude towards, and outlook upon, experience, which finds its most pregnant expression in the various forms of Art.

2

Distance, as I said before, is obtained by separating the object and its appeal from one's own self, by putting it out of gear with practical needs and ends. Thereby the "contemplation" of the object becomes alone possible. But it does not mean that the relation between the self and the object is broken to the extent of becoming "impersonal." Of the alternatives "personal" and "impersonal" the latter surely comes nearer to the truth; but here, as elsewhere, we meet the difficulty of having to express certain facts in terms coined for entirely different uses. To do so usually results in paradoxes, which are nowhere more inevitable than in discussions upon Art. "Personal" and "impersonal," "subjective" and "objective" are such terms, devised for purposes other than aesthetic speculation, and becoming loose and ambiguous as soon as applied outside the sphere of their special meanings. In giving preference therefore to the term "impersonal" to describe the relation between the spectator and a work of Art, it is to be noticed that it is not impersonal in the sense in which we speak of the "impersonal" character of Science, for instance. In order to obtain "objectively valid" results, the scientist excludes the "personal factor," *i.e.*, his personal wishes as to the validity of his results, his predilection for any particular system to be proved or disproved by his research. It goes without saying that all experiments and investigations are undertaken out of a personal interest in the science, for the ultimate support of a definite assumption, and involve personal hopes of success; but this does not affect the "dispassionate" attitude of the investigator, under pain of being accused of "manufacturing his evidence."

1. Distance does not imply an impersonal, purely intellectually interested relation of such a kind. On the contrary, it describes a *personal* relation, often highly emotionally colored, but of a *peculiar character*. Its peculiarity lies in that the personal character of the relation has been, so to speak, filtered. It has been cleared of the practical, concrete nature of its appeal, without, however, thereby losing its original constitution. One of the best-known examples is to be found in our attitude towards the events and characters of the drama: they appeal to us like persons and incidents of normal experience, except that that side of their appeal, which would usually affect us in a directly personal manner, is held in abeyance. This difference, so well known as to be almost trivial, is generally explained by reference to

the knowledge that the characters and situations are "unreal," imaginary. . . .
But, as a matter of fact, the "assumption" upon which the imaginative emotional reaction is based is not necessarily the condition, but often the consequence, of Distance; that is to say, the converse of the reason usually stated
would then be true: viz., that Distance, by changing our relation to the characters, renders them seemingly fictitious, not that the fictitiousness of the
characters alters our feelings toward them. It is, of course, to be granted
that the actual and admitted unreality of the dramatic action reënforces the
effect of Distance. But surely the proverbial unsophisticated yokel whose
chivalrous interference in the play on behalf of the hapless heroine can
only be prevented by impressing upon him that "they are only pretending,"
is not the ideal type of theatrical audience. The proof of the seeming paradox
that it is Distance which primarily gives to dramatic action the appearance
of unreality and not *vice versa*, is the observation that the same filtration of
our sentiments and the same seeming "unreality" of *actual* men and things
occur, when at times, by a sudden change of inward perspective, we are
overcome by the feeling that "all the world's a stage."

2. This personal but "distanced" relation (as I will venture to call this
nameless character of our view) directs attention to a strange fact which
appears to be one of the fundamental paradoxes of Art: it is what I propose
to call "the antinomy of Distance."

It will be readily admitted that a work of Art has the more chance of
appealing to us the better it finds us prepared for its particular kind of appeal. Indeed, without some degree of predisposition on our part, it must
necessarily remain incomprehensible, and to that extent unappreciated. The
success and intensity of its appeal would seem, therefore, to stand in direct
proportion to the completeness with which it corresponds with our intellectual and emotional peculiarities and the idiosyncrasies of our experience.
The absence of such a concordance between the characters of a work and
of the spectator is, of course, the most general explanation for differences of
"tastes."

At the same time, such a principle of concordance requires a qualification, which leads at once to the antinomy of Distance.

Suppose a man who believes that he has cause to be jealous about his
wife, witnesses a performance of *Othello*. He will the more perfectly appreciate the situation, conduct and character of Othello, the more exactly
the feelings and experiences of Othello coincide with his own—at least he
ought to on the above principle of concordance. In point of fact, he will
probably do anything but appreciate the play. In reality, the concordance
will merely render him acutely conscious of his own jealousy; by a sudden

reversal of perspective he will no longer see Othello apparently betrayed by Desdemona, but himself in an analogous situation with his own wife. This reversal of perspective is the consequence of the loss of Distance.

If this be taken as a typical case, it follows that the qualification required is that the coincidence should be as complete as is compatible with maintaining Distance. The jealous spectator of *Othello* will indeed appreciate and enter into the play the more keenly, the greater the resemblance with his own experience—*provided* that he succeeds in keeping the Distance between the action of the play and his personal feelings: a very difficult performance in the circumstances. It is on account of the same difficulty that the expert and the professional critic make a bad audience, since their expertness and critical professionalism are *practical* activities, involving their concrete personality and constantly endangering their Distance. [It is, by the way, one of the reasons why Criticism is an art, for it requires the constant interchange from the practical to the distanced attitude and *vice versa,* which is characteristic of artists.]

The same qualification applies to the artist. He will prove artistically most effective in the formulation of an intensely *personal* experience, but he can formulate it artistically only on condition of a detachment from the experience *qua personal.* Hence the statement of so many artists that artistic formulation was to them a kind of catharsis, a means of ridding themselves of feelings and ideas the acuteness of which they felt almost as a kind of obsession. Hence, on the other hand, the failure of the average man to convey to others at all adequately the impression of an overwhelming joy or sorrow. His personal implication in the event renders it impossible for him to formulate and present it in such a way as to make others, like himself, feel all the meaning and fullness which it possesses for him.

What is therefore, both in appreciation and production, most desirable is the *utmost decrease of Distance without its disappearance.*

3. Closely related, in fact a presupposition to the "antinomy," is the *variability of Distance.* Herein especially lies the advantage of Distance compared with such terms as "objectivity" and "detachment." Neither of them implies a *personal* relation—indeed both actually preclude it; and the mere inflexibility and exclusiveness of their opposites render their application generally meaningless.

Distance, on the contrary, admits naturally of degrees, and differs not only according to the nature of the *object,* which may impose a greater or smaller degree of Distance, but varies also according to the *individual's capacity* for maintaining a greater or lesser degree. And here one may remark that not only do *persons differ from each other* in their habitual measure of Distance, but that the *same individual differs* in his ability to maintain it in the face of different objects and of different arts.

There exist, therefore, two different sets of conditions affecting the degree of Distance in any given case: those offered by the object and those realized by the subject. In their interplay they afford one of the most extensive explanations for varieties of aesthetic experience, since loss of Distance, whether due to the one or the other, means loss of aesthetic appreciation.

In short, Distance may be said to be *variable both according to the distancing-power of the individual, and according to the character of the object.*

There are two ways of losing Distance: either to "under-distance" or to "over-distance." "Under-distancing" is the commonest failing of the *subject,* an excess of Distance is a frequent failing of Art, especially in the past. Historically it looks almost as if Art had attempted to meet the deficiency of Distance on the part of the subject and had overshot the mark in this endeavor. It will be seen later that this is actually true, for it appears that over-distanced Art is specially designed for a class of appreciation which has difficulty to rise spontaneously to any degree of Distance. The consequence of a loss of Distance through one or other cause is familiar: the verdict in the case of under-distancing is that the work is "crudely naturalistic," "harrowing," "repulsive in its realism." An excess of Distance produces the impression of improbability, artificiality, emptiness or absurdity.

The individual tends, as I just stated, to under-distance rather than to lose Distance by over-distancing. *Theoretically* there is no limit to the decrease of Distance. In theory, therefore, not only the usual subjects of Art, but even the most personal affections, whether ideas, percepts, or emotions, can be sufficiently distanced to be aesthetically appreciable. Especially artists are gifted in this direction to a remarkable extent. The average individual, on the contrary, very rapidly reaches his limit of decreasing Distance, his "Distance-limit," *i.e.,* that point at which Distance is lost and appreciation either disappears or changes its character.

In the *practice,* therefore, of the average person, a limit does exist which marks the minimum at which his appreciation can maintain itself in the aesthetic field, and this average minimum lies considerable higher than the Distance-limit of the artist. It is practically impossible to fix this average limit, in the absence of data, and on account of the wide fluctuations from person to person to which this limit is subject. But it is safe to infer that, in art practice, explicit references to organic affections, to the material existence of the body, especially to sexual matters, lies normally below the Distance-limit, and can be touched upon by Art only with special precautions. Allusions to social institutions of any degree of personal importance—in particular, allusions implying any doubt as to their validity—the questioning of some generally recognized ethical sanctions, references to topical subjects occupying public attention at the moment, and such like, are all dangerously near the average limit and may at any time fall below it, arousing, instead of aesthetic appreciation, concrete hostility or mere amusement.

This difference in the Distance-limit between artists and the public has been the source of much misunderstanding and injustice. Many an artist has seen his work condemned, and himself ostracized for the sake of so-called "immoralities" which to him were *bona fide* aesthetic objects. His power of distancing, nay, the necessity of distancing feelings, sensations, situations which for the average person are too intimately bound up with his concrete existence to be regarded in that light, have often quite unjustly earned for him accusations of cynicism, sensualism, morbidness or frivolity. The same misconception has arisen over many "problem plays" and "problem novels" in which the public have persisted in seeing nothing but a supposed "problem" of the moment, whereas the author may have been—and often has demonstrably been—able to distance the subject-matter sufficiently to rise above its practical problematic import and to regard it simply as a dramatically and humanly interesting situation.

The variability of Distance in respect to Art, disregarding for the moment the subjective complication, appears both as a general feature in Art, and in the differences between the special arts.

It has been an old problem why the "arts of the eye and of the ear" should have reached the practically exclusive predominance over arts of other senses. Attempts to raise "culinary art" to the level of a Fine Art have failed in spite of all propaganda, as completely as the creation of scent or liquor "symphonies." There is little doubt that, apart from other excellent reasons of a partly psycho-physical, partly technical nature, the actual, *spatial distance* separating objects of sight and hearing from the subject has contributed strongly to the development of this monopoly. In a similar manner *temporal remoteness* produces Distance, and objects removed from us in point of time are *ipso facto* distanced to an extent which was impossible for their contemporaries. Many pictures, plays and poems had, as a matter of fact, rather an expository or illustrative significance—as for instance much ecclesiastical Art—or the force of a direct practical appeal—as the invectives of many satires or comedies—which seem to us nowadays irreconcilable with their aesthetic claims. Such works have consequently profited greatly by lapse of time and have reached the level of Art only with the help of temporal distance, while others, on the contrary, often for the same reason have suffered a loss of Distance, through *over*-distancing.

Special mention must be made of a group of artistic conceptions which present excessive Distance in their form of appeal rather than in their actual presentation—a point illustrating the necessity of distinguishing between distancing an object and distancing the appeal of which it is the source. I mean here what is often rather loosely termed "idealistic Art," that is, Art springing from abstract conceptions, expressing allegorical meanings, or illustrating general truths. Generalizations and abstractions suffer under this disadvantage that they have too much general applicability to invite a personal interest in them, and too little individual concreteness to prevent them applying to us in all their force. They appeal to everybody and therefore to none. An axiom of Euclid belongs to nobody, just because it compels every one's assent; general conceptions like Patriotism, Friendship, Love, Hope, Life, Death, concern as much Dick, Tom and Harry as myself, and I, therefore, either feel unable to get into any kind of personal relation to them, or, if I do so, they become at once, emphatically and concretely, *my* Patriotism, *my* Friendship, *my* Love, *my* Hope, *my* Life and Death. By mere force of generalization, a general truth or a universal ideal is so far distanced from myself that I fail to realize it concretely at all, or, when I do so, I can realize it only as part of my *practical actual being, i.e.,* it falls below the Distance-limit altogether. "Idealistic Art" suffers consequently under the peculiar difficulty that its excess of Distance turns generally into an *under*-distanced appeal—all the more easily, as it is the usual failing of the subject to *under*-rather than to *over*-distance.

The different special arts show at the present time very marked variations in the degree of Distance which they usually impose or require for their appreciation. Unfortunately here again the absence of data makes itself felt and indicates the necessity of conducting observations, possibly experiments, so as to place these suggestions upon a securer basis. In one single art, viz., the *theater,* a small amount of information is available, from an unexpected source, namely the proceedings of the censorship committee,[1] which on closer examination might be made to yield evidence of interest to the psychologist. In fact, the whole censorship problem, as far as it does not turn upon purely economic questions, may be said to hinge upon Distance; if every member of the public could be trusted to keep it, there would be no sense whatever in the existence of a censor of plays. There is, of course, no doubt that, speaking generally, theatrical performances *eo ipso* run a special

[1] Report from the Joint Select Committee of the House of Lords and the House of Commons on the Stage Plays (Censorship), 1909.

risk of a loss of Distance owing to the material presentment[2] of its subject-matter. The physical presence of living human beings as vehicles of dramatic art is a difficulty which no art has to face in the same way. A similar, in many ways even greater, risk confronts *dancing:* though attracting perhaps a less widely spread human interest, its animal spirits are frequently quite unrelieved by any glimmer of spirituality and consequently form a proportionately stronger lure to under-distancing. In the higher forms of dancing technical execution of the most wearing kind makes up a great deal for its intrinsic tendency towards a loss of Distance, and as a popular performance, at least in southern Europe, it has retained much of its ancient artistic glamour, producing a peculiarly subtle balancing of Distance between the pure delight of bodily movement and high technical accomplishment. In passing, it is interesting to observe (as bearing upon the development of Distance), that this art, once as much a fine art as music and considered by the Greeks as a particularly valuable educational exercise, should—except in sporadic cases—have fallen so low from the pedestal it once occupied. Next to the theater and dancing stands *sculpture.* Though not using a *living* bodily medium, yet the human form in its full spatial materiality constitutes a similar threat to Distance. Our northern habits of dress and ignorance of the human body have enormously increased the difficulty of distancing Sculpture, in part through the gross misconceptions to which it is exposed, in part owing to a complete lack of standards of bodily perfection, and an inability to realize the distinction between sculptural form and bodily shape, which is the only but fundamental point distinguishing a statue from a cast taken from life. In *painting* it is apparently the form of its presentment and the usual reduction in scale which would explain why this art can venture to approach more closely than sculpture to the normal Distance-limit. . . . *Music* and *architecture* have a curious position. These two most abstract of all arts show a remarkable fluctuation in their Distances. Certain kinds of music, especially "pure" music, or "classical" or "heavy" music, appear for many people over-distanced; light, "catchy" tunes, on the contrary, easily reach that degree of decreasing Distance below which they cease to be Art and become a pure amusement. In spite of its strange abstractness which to many philosophers has made it comparable to architecture and mathematics, music possesses a sensuous, frequently sensual character: the undoubted physiological and muscular stimulus of its melodies and harmonies, no less than its rhythmic aspects, would seem to account for the occasional disappearance of Distance. To this might be added its

---

[2] I shall use the term "presentment" to denote the manner of presenting, in distinction to "presentation" as that which is presented.

strong tendency, especially in unmusical people, to stimulate trains of thought quite disconnected with itself, following channels of subjective inclinations— day-dreams of a more or less directly personal character. *Architecture* requires almost uniformly a very great Distance; that is to say, the majority of persons derive no aesthetic appreciation from architecture as such, apart from the incidental impression of its decorative features and its associations. The causes are numerous, but prominent among them are the confusion of building with architecture and the predominance of utilitarian purposes, which overshadow the architectural claims upon the attention.

SELECTED BIBLIOGRAPHY

I. Emotionalism:
1. Yrjö Hirn, *The Origins of Art*, The Macmillan Company, 1900. A modern version of the doctrine of Catharsis.
2. Eugene Véron, *Aesthetics*, Chapman & Hall, 1879. A classic in the emotionalist tradition.

II. Empathy:
1. Herbert Langfeld, *The Aesthetic Attitude*, Harcourt, Brace & Howe, 1920. A good summary in English of predominantly German developments, especially by Theodor Lipps, the great exponent of empathy.

III. Sublimation:
1. Lionel Trilling, "Art and Neurosis," *The Liberal Imagination*, The Viking Press, 1950. An excellent evaluation of Freud's contribution to aesthetics and criticism. (Available as Anchor paperback.)
2. Ernest Kris, *Psychoanalytic Exploration in Art*, esp. Ch. I, International Universities Press, 1952. A fine discussion of psychoanalysis and art.
3. Hanns Sachs, *The Creative Unconscious*, Sci-Art Publishers, 1942. An original version of Freud, concentrating on "the community of daydreams" as the basis of art and its enjoyment.

IV. Pleasure:
1. Henry Rutgers Marshall, *Pain, Pleasure, and Aesthetics*, Macmillan Company, 1894. One of the classics in aesthetic hedonism.

V. Contemplation:
1. Clive Bell, *Art*, Chatto & Windus, 1914. A justification of the contemplative approach to art.
2. Roger Fry, "Some Questions in Esthetics," *Transformations*, Chatto & Windus, 1926. Fry's version of contemplation as response to relations in art. (Available as Anchor paperback.)
3. Immanuel Kant, *Critique of Judgment*. The whole of Part One is the most famous statement of aesthetic response as a form of contemplation.

VI

Criticism

Introduction

Criticism is studied talk of art. Sometimes it indulges in general theoretical questions, such as "what is art?," sometimes in questions of poetics, such as "what is metaphor?," but, if it is criticism, it always says something about some particular work of art or some collection of works.

There are numerous problems here. When the critic discusses works of art, does he merely report on them and, if so, are his utterances verifiable, true or false? Or, does he do more than report or describe when he interprets and judges works of art? And if he does do more than report, is this something more also verifiable and hence true or false? Should the critic go beyond the description of art? If he does, according to what criteria shall he interpret and judge?

These are only some of the basic problems of criticism. In this part, there are two essays on criticism, one by a leading practicing critic and the other by a philosopher. Richard Blackmur's essay is a thorough statement of what criticism can do, actually does, and cannot do. Margaret Macdonald's is a probing analysis of the kinds of procedures, arguments and utterances critics as a matter of logical fact do engage in. Both add up to an incisive introduction to the philosophy of criticism.

Richard P. Blackmur

A CRITIC'S JOB OF WORK*

1

Criticism, I take it, is the formal discourse of an amateur. When there
is enough love and enough knowledge represented in the discourse it is
a self-sufficient but by no means an isolated art. It witnesses constantly in
its own life its interdependence with the other arts. It lays out the terms
and parallels of appreciation from the outside in order to convict itself
of internal intimacy; it names and arranges what it knows and loves, and
searches endlessly with every fresh impulse or impression for better names
and more orderly arrangements. It is only in this sense that poetry (or
some other art) is a criticism of life; poetry names and arranges, and
thus arrests and transfixes its subject in a form which has a life of its own
forever separate but springing from the life which confronts it. Poetry
is life at the remove of form and meaning; not life lived but life framed and
identified. So the criticism of poetry is bound to be occupied at once with
the terms and modes by which the remove was made and with the relation between—in the ambiguous stock phrase—content and form; which is
to say with the establishment and appreciation of human or moral value.
It will be the underlying effort of this essay to indicate approaches to
criticism wherein these two problems—of form and value—will appear
inextricable but not confused—like the stones in an arch or the timbers
in a building.

These approaches—these we wish to eulogize—are not the only ones,
nor the only good ones, nor are they complete. No approach opens on
anything except from its own point of view and in terms of its own prepossessions. Let us set against each other for a time the facts of various
approaches to see whether there is a residue, not of fact but of principle.

The approaches to—or the escapes from—the central work of criticism
are as various as the heresies of the Christian church, and like them testify

* From Richard P. Blackmur's "A Critic's Job of Work," in *Language as Gesture*.
Copyright, 1935, by Richard P. Blackmur. Reprinted from *Language as Gesture* by
Richard P. Blackmur by permission of Harcourt, Brace and Company, Inc. and by
George Allen & Unwin Ltd.

Richard P. Blackmur (1904–   ), one of America's leading literary critics, at present
Professor of English at Princeton University, has written a number of fine collections of
criticism as well as certain essays on the nature of criticism of which the present
selection is one example.

to occasional needs, fanatic emphasis, special interest, or intellectual pride, all flowing from and even the worst of them enlightening the same body of insight. Every critic like every theologian and every philosopher is a casuist in spite of himself. To escape or surmount the discontinuity of knowledge, each resorts to a particular heresy and makes it predominant and even omnivorous.[1]

For most minds, once doctrine is sighted and is held to be the completion of insight, the doctrinal mode of thinking seems the only one possible. When doctrine totters it seems it can fall only into the gulf of bewilderment; few minds risk the fall; most seize the remnants and swear the edifice remains, when doctrine becomes intolerable dogma.[2] All fall notwithstanding; for as knowledge itself is a fall from the paradise of undifferentiated sensation, so equally every formula of knowledge must fall the moment too much weight is laid upon it—the moment it becomes omnivorous and pretends to be omnipotent—the moment, in short, it is taken literally. Literal knowledge is dead knowledge; and the worst bewilderment—which is always only comparative—is better than death. Yet no form, no formula, of knowledge ought to be surrendered merely because it runs the risk in bad or desperate hands of being used literally; and similarly, in our own thinking, whether it is carried to the point of formal discourse or not, we cannot only afford, we ought scrupulously to risk the use of any concept that seems propitious or helpful in getting over gaps. Only the use should be consciously provisional, speculative, and dramatic. The end-virtue of humility comes only after a long train of humiliations; and the chief labor of humbling is the constant, resourceful restoration of ignorance.

The classic contemporary example of use and misuse is attached to the name of Freud. Freud himself has constantly emphasized the provisional, dramatic character of his speculations: they are employed as imaginative illumination, to be relied on no more and no less than the sailor relies upon his buoys and beacons.[3] But the impetus of Freud was so great that a school of literalists arose with all the mad consequence of schism and heresy and fundamentalism which have no more honorable place in the scientific than the artistic imagination. Elsewhere, from one point of view,

---

[1] The rashest heresy of our day and climate is that exemplified by T. S. Eliot when he postulates an orthodoxy which exists whether anyone knows it or not.

[2] Baudelaire's sonnet *Le Gouffre* dramatizes this sentiment at once as he saw it surmounted in Pascal and as it occurred insurmountably in himself.

[3] Santayana's essay "A Long Way Round to Nirvana" (in *Some Turns of Thought in Modern Philosophy*) illustrates the poetic-philosophic character of Freud's insight into death by setting up its analogue in Indian philosophy; and by his comparison only adds to the stimulus of Freud.

Caesarism in Rome and Berlin is only the literalist conception of the need for a positive state. So, too, the economic insights of Marxism, merely by being taken literally in their own field, are held to affect the subject and value of the arts, where actually they offer only a limited field of interest and enliven an irrelevant purpose. It is an amusing exercise—as it refreshes the terms of bewilderment and provides a common clue to the secrets of all the modes of thinking—to restore the insights of Freud and Fascism and Marxism to the terms of the Church; when the sexual drama in Freud becomes the drama of original sin, and the politics of Hitler and Lenin becomes the politics of the City of God in the sense that theology provides both the sanctions of economics and the values of culture. Controversy is in terms absolutely held, when the problems argued are falsely conceived because necessarily abstracted from "real" experience. The vital or fatal nexus is in interest and emotion and is established when the terms can be represented dramatically, almost, as it were for their own sakes alone and with only a pious or ritualistic regard for the doctrines in which they are clothed. The simple, and fatal, example is in the glory men attach to war; the vital, but precarious example, is in the intermittent conception of free institutions and the persistent reformulation of the myth of reason. Then the doctrines do not matter, since they are taken only for what they are worth (whatever rhetorical pretensions to the contrary) as guides and props, as aids to navigation. What does matter is the experience, the life represented and the value discovered, and both dramatized or enacted under the banner of doctrine. All banners are wrong-headed, but they make rallying points, free the impulse to cry out, and give meaning to the cry itself simply by making it seem appropriate.

It is on some analogue or parallel to these remarks alone that we understand and use the thought and art of those whose doctrines differ from our own. We either discount, absorb, or dominate the doctrine for the sake of the life that goes with it, for the sake of what is *formed* in the progressive act of thinking. When we do more—when we refine or elaborate the abstracted notion of form—we play a different game, which has merit of its own like chess, but which applied to the world we live in produces false dilemmas like solipsism and infant damnation. There is, taking solipsism for example, a fundamental distinction. Because of the logical doctrine prepared to support it, technical philosophers employ years[4] to get around the impasse in which it leaves them; whereas men of poetic imagination merely use it for the dramatic insight it con-

---

[4] Santayana found it necessary to resort to his only sustained labour of dialectic, *Scepticism and Animal Faith*, which, though a beautiful monument of intellectual play, is ultimately valuable for its *incidental* moral wisdom.

tains—as Eliot uses it in the last section of the *Wasteland;* or as, say, every-one uses the residual mythology of the Greek religion—which its priests nevertheless used as literal sanctions for blood and power.

Fortunately, there exist archetypes of unindoctrinated thinking. Let us incline our minds like reflectors to catch the light of the early Plato and the whole Montaigne. Is not the inexhaustible stimulus and fertility of the Dialogues and the Essays due as much as anything to the absence of positive doctrine? Is it not that the early Plato always holds conflicting ideas in shifting balance, presenting them in contest and evolution, with victory only the last shift? Is it not that Montaigne is always making room for another idea, and implying always a third for provisional, adjudicating irony? Are not the forms of both men themselves ironic, betraying in its most intimate recesses the duplicity of every thought, pointing it out, so to speak, in the act of self-incrimination, and showing it not paled on a pin but in the buff life? . . . Such an approach, such an attempt at vivid questing, borrowed and no doubt adulterated by our own needs, is the only rational approach to the multiplication of doctrine and arrogant tech-nologies which fills out the body of critical thinking. Anything else is a succumbing, not an approach; and it is surely the commonest of ironies to observe a man altogether out of his depth do his cause fatal harm merely because, having once succumbed to an idea, he thinks it necessary to stick to it. Thought is a beacon not a life-raft, and to confuse the functions is tragic. The tragic character of thought—as any perspective will show—is that it takes a rigid mould too soon; chooses destiny like a Calvinist, in infancy, instead of waiting slowly for old age, and hence for the most part works against the world, good sense, and its own object: as anyone may see by taking a perspective of any given idea of democracy, of justice, or the nature of the creative act.

Imaginative scepticism and dramatic irony—the modes of Montaigne and Plato—keep the mind athletic and the spirit on the stretch. Hence the juvenescence of the *Tempest,* and hence, too, perhaps, the air almost of precocity in *Back to Methuselah.* Hence, at any rate, the sustaining power of such varied works as *The Brothers Karamazoff, Cousine Bette,* and *The Magic Mountain.* Dante, whom the faithful might take to the contrary, is yet "the chief imagination of Christendom"; he took his doc-trine once and for all from the Church and from St. Thomas and used it as a foil (in the painter's sense) to give recessiveness, background, and contrast. Virgil and Aristotle, Beatrice and Bertrans de Born, have in their way as much importance as St. Thomas and the Church. It was this security of reference that made Dante so much more a free spirit than were, say, Swift and Laurence Sterne. Dante had a habit (not a theory) of imagination which enabled him to dramatize with equal ardour and effect what his doctrine blessed, what it assailed, and what, at heart, it was indifferent to. Doctrine was the seed and structure of vision, and for his poems (at least to us) never more. The Divine Comedy no less than the Dialogues and the Essays is a true Speculum Mentis.

With lesser thinkers and lesser artists—and in the defective works of the greater—we have in reading, in criticizing, to supply the scepticism and the irony, or, as may be, the imagination and the drama, to the degree, which cannot be complete since then we should have had no prompts, that they are lacking. We have to rub the looking-glass clear. With Hamlet, for example, we have to struggle and guess to bring the motive out of obscurity: a struggle which, aiming at the wrong end, the psychoanalysts have darkened with counsel. With Shelley we have to flesh out the Platonic Ideas, as with Blake we have to cut away, since it cannot be dramatized, all the excrescence of doctrine. With Baudelaire we have sometimes to struggle with and sometimes to suppress the problem of belief, working out the irony implicit in either attitude. Similarly, with a writer like Pascal, in order to get the most out of him, in order to compose an artistic judgment, we must consider such an idea as that of the necessity of the wager, not solemnly as Pascal took it, but as a dramatized possibility, a savage, but provisional irony; and we need to show that the scepticisms of Montaigne and Pascal are not at all the same thing—that where one produced serenity the other produced excruciation.

Again, speaking of André Gide, we should remind ourselves not that he has been the apologist of homosexuality, not that he has become a communist, but that he is par excellence the French puritan chastened by the wisdom of the body, and that he has thus an acutely scrupulous ethical sensibility. It is by acknowledging the sensibility that we feel the impact of the apologetics and the political conversion. Another necessity in the apprehension of Gide might be put as the recognition of similarity in difference of the precocious small boys in Dostoieffsky and Gide, e.g. Kolya in *Karamazoff* and young George in *The Counterfeiters:* they are small, cruel engines, all naked sensibility and no scruple, demoniacally possessed, and used to keep things going. And these in turn may remind us of another writer who had a predilection for presenting the *terrible* quality of the young intelligence: of Henry James, of the children in *The Turn of the Screw,* of Maisie, and all the rest, all beautifully efficient agents of dramatic judgment and action, in that they take all things seriously for themselves, with the least prejudice of preparation, candidly, with an intelligence life has not yet violated.

Such feats of agility and attention as these remarks illustrate seem a poem and the poem as there is between words used about a painting and the painting. The gap is absolute. Yet I do not mean to suggest that Santayana's essay—that any philosophical criticism—is beside the point. It is true that the essay may be taken as a venture in philosophy for its own sake but it is also true that it reveals a body of facts about an ulterior purpose in Lucretius' poem—doubtless the very purpose Lucretius himself would have chosen to see enhanced. If we return to the poem it will be warmer as the facts come alive in verse. The re-conversion comes naturally in this instance in that, through idioms differently construed but equally imaginative, philosophy and poetry both buttress and express moral value. The one enacts or represents in the flesh what the other reduces to principle or raises to the ideal. The only precaution the critic of poetry need take is negative: that neither poetry nor philosophy can ever fully satisfy the other's purposes, though each may seem to do so if taken in an ulterior fashion. The relationship is mutual but not equivalent.

When we turn deliberately from Santayana on Lucretius to Van Wyck Brooks on Henry James, we turn from the consideration of the rational ulterior purpose of art to the consideration of the irrational underlying predicament of the artist himself, not only as it predicts his art and is reflected in it, but also, and in effect predominantly, as it represents the conditioning of nineteenth century American culture. The consideration is sociological, the method of approach that of literary psychology, and the burden obsessive. The conversion is from literary to biographical values. Art is taken not as the objectification or mirroring of social experience but as a personal expression and escape-fantasy of the artist's personal life in dramatic extension. The point for emphasis is that the cultural situation of Henry James' America stultified the expression and made every escape ineffectual—even that of Europe. This theme—the private tragedy of the unsuccessful artist—was one of Henry James' own; but James saw it as typical or universal—as a characteristic tragedy of the human spirit—illustrated, as it happened for him, against the Anglo-American background. Brooks, taking the same theme, raises it to an obsession, an omnivorous concept, under which all other themes can be subsumed. Applied to American cultural history, such obsessive thinking is suggestive in the very exaggeration of its terms, and applied to the predicament of Henry James the man it dramatically emphasizes—uses for all and more than it is worth—an obvious conflict that tormented him. As history or as biography the book is a persuasive imaginative picture, although clearly not the only one to be seen. Used as a nexus between James the man and the novels themselves, the book has only possible relevance and cannot

facile and even commonplace, and from facile points of view there is no need to take them otherwise. Taken superficially they provide escape from the whole labor of specific understanding; or, worse, they provide an easy vault from casual interpretation to an omnivorous world-view. We might take solemnly and as of universal application the two notions of demonic possession and inviolate intelligence in the children of Gide, Dostoieffsky, and James, and on that frail nexus build an unassailable theory of the sources of art, wisdom, and value; unassailable because affording only a stereotyped vision, like that of conservative capitalism, without reference in the real world. The maturity of Shakespeare and of Gertrude Stein would then be found on the same childish level.

But we need not go so far in order to draw back. The modes of Montaigne and Plato contain their own safety. Any single insight is good only at and up to a certain point of development and not beyond, which is to say that it is a provisional and tentative and highly selective approach to its field. Furthermore, no observation, no collection of observations, ever tells the whole story; there is always room for more, and at the hypothetical limit of attention and interest there will always remain, quite untouched, the thing itself. Thus the complex character—I say nothing of the value—of the remarks above reveals itself. They flow from a dramatic combination of all the skills and conventions of the thinking mind. They are commonplace only as criticism—as an end-product of function. Like walking, criticism is a pretty nearly universal art; both require a constant intricate shifting and catching of balance; neither can be questioned much in process; and few perform either really well. For either a new terrain is fatiguing and awkward, and in our day most men prefer paved walks or some form of rapid transit—some easy theory or outmastering dogma. A good critic keeps his criticism from becoming either instinctive or vicarious, and the labour of his understanding is always specific, like the art which he examines; and he knows that the sum of his best work comes only to the pedagogy of elucidation and appreciation. He observes facts and he delights in discriminations. The object remains, and should remain, itself, only made more available and seen in a clearer light. The imagination of Dante is for us only equal to what we can know of it at a given time.

Which brings us to what, as T. S. Eliot would say,[5] I have been leading up to all the time, and what has indeed been said several times by the

---

[5] . . . that when "morals cease to be a matter of tradition and orthodoxy—that is, of the habits of the community formulated, corrected, and elevated by the continuous thought and direction of the Church—and when each man is to elaborate his own, then *personality* becomes a thing of alarming importance." (*After Strange Gods.*) Thus Mr. Eliot becomes one of those viewers-with-alarm whose next step forward is the very hysteria of disorder they wish to escape. The hysteria of institutions is more dreadful than that of individuals.

way. Any rational approach is valid to literature and may be properly called critical which fastens at any point upon the work itself. The utility of a given approach depends partly upon the strength of the mind making it and partly upon the recognition of the limits appropriate to it. Limits may be of scope, degree, or relevance, and may be either plainly laid out by the critic himself, or may be determined by his readers; and it is, by our argument, the latter case that commonly falls, since an active mind tends to overestimate the scope of its tools and to take as necessary those doctrinal considerations which habit has made seem instinctive. No critic is required to limit himself to a single approach, nor is he likely to be able to do so; facts cannot be exhibited without comment, and comment involves the generality of the mind. Furthermore, a consciously complex approach like that of Kenneth Burke or T. S. Eliot, by setting up parallels of reference, affords a more flexible, more available, more stimulating standard of judgment—though of course at a greater risk of prejudice—than a single approach. What produces the evil of stultification and the malice of controversy is the confused approach, when the limits are not seen because they tend to cancel each other out, and the driving power becomes emotional.

The worse evil of fanatic falsification—of arrogant irrationality and barbarism in all its forms—arises when a body of criticism is governed by an *idée fixe*, a really exaggerated heresy, when a notion of genuine but small scope is taken literally as of universal application. This is the body of tendentious criticism where, since something is assumed proved before the evidence is in, distortion, vitiation, and absolute assertion become supreme virtues. I cannot help feeling that such writers as Maritain and Massis—no less than Nordau before them—are tendentious in this sense. But even here, in this worst order of criticism, there is a taint of legitimacy. Once we reduce, in a man like Irving Babbitt, the magnitude of application of such notions as the inner check and the higher will, which were for Babbitt paramount—that is, when we determine the limits within which he really worked—then the massive erudition and acute observation with which his work is packed become permanently available.

And there is no good to be got in objecting to and disallowing those orders of criticism which have an ulterior purpose. Ulterior is not in itself a pejorative, but only so when applied to an enemy. Since criticism is not autonomous—not a light but a process of elucidation—it cannot avoid discovering constantly within itself a purpose or purposes ulterior in the good sense. The danger is in not knowing what is ulterior and what is not, which is much the same as the cognate danger in the arts themselves.

The arts serve purposes beyond themselves; the purposes of dramatize or represent at that remove from the flux which gives and meaning and value; and to deny those purposes is like ass the function of a handsaw is to hang above a bench and that to is to belittle it. But the purposes are varied and so bound in his su the artist cannot always design for them. The critic, if that is his concern himself with those purposes or with some one among th obsess him; but he must be certain to distinguish between what is ulterior to the works he examines and what is merely irrelevant must further not assume except within the realm of his special that other purposes either do not exist or are negligible or that t may not be profitably discussed apart from ulterior purposes an amples of dramatic possibility alone.

2

Three examples of contemporary criticism primarily concern the ulterior purposes of literature should, set side by side, exhib the defects and the unchastened virtues of that approach; thoug must do so only tentatively and somewhat invidiously—with an ex tion for effect. Each work is assumed to be a representative ornan its kind, carrying within it the seeds of its own death and multipl Let us take then, with an eye sharpened by the dangers involved, yana's essay on Lucretius (in *Three Philosophical Poets*), Van Wyck *Pilgrimage of Henry James*, and Granville Hicks' *The Great Tra* Though that of the third is more obvious in our predicament, the u in the approach is equal in all three.

Santayana's essay represents a conversion or transvaluation actually poetic ordering of nature to the terms of a moral philos which, whatever its own responsibilities, is free of the special responsi of poetry. So ably and so persuasively is it composed, his picture s complete and to contain so much of what was important in Lucretius *De Rerum Natura* itself can be left behind. The philosophical natur the insight, its moral scope and defect, the influence upon it of the De critan atom, once grasped intellectually as Santayana shows us how to g them, seem a good substitute for the poem and far more available. what Santayana remembers but does not here emphasize since it beyond his immediate interest, there is no vicar for poetry on earth. Poe is idiom, a special and fresh saying, and cannot for its life be said oth wise; and there is, finally, as much difference between words used abo

be held as material. *Hamlet*, by a similar argument, could be shown to be an unsuccessful expression of Shakespeare's personality. To remain useful in the field of literary criticism, Brooks' notions ought to be kept parallel to James' novels but never allowed to merge with them. The corrective, the proof of the gap, is perhaps in the great air of freedom and sway of mastery that pervades the Prefaces James wrote to his collected edition. For James art was enough because it moulded and mirrored and valued all the life he knew. What Brooks' parallel strictures can do is to help us decide from another point of view whether to choose the values James dramatized. They cannot affect or elucidate but rather—if the gap is closed by will—obfuscate the values themselves.

In short, the order of criticism of which Brooks is a masterly exponent, and which we may call the psycho-sociological order, is primarily and in the end concerned less with the purposes, ulterior or not, of the arts than with some of the ulterior *uses* to which the arts can be appropriately put. Only what is said in the meantime, by the way—and does not depend upon the essence of argument but only accompanies it—can be applied to the arts themselves. There is nothing, it should be added, in Brooks' writings to show that he believes otherwise or would claim more; he is content with that scope and degree of value to which his method and the strength of his mind limit him; and his value is the greater and more urgent for that.

Such tacit humility, such implicit admission of contingency, are not immediate characteristics of Granville Hicks' *The Great Tradition*, though they may, so serious is his purpose, be merely virtues of which he deliberately, for the time being and in order to gain his point, deprives himself of the benefit. If that is so, however expedient his tactics may seem on the short view they will defeat him on the long. But let us examine the book on the ground of our present concern alone. Like Brooks, Hicks presents an interpretation of American literature since the Civil War, dealing with the whole body rather than single figures. Like Brooks he has a touchstone in an obsessive idea, but where we may say that Brooks *uses* his idea—as we think for more than it is worth—we must say that Hicks is victimized by his idea to the point where the travail of judgment is suspended and becomes the mere reiteration of a formula. He judges literature as it expressed or failed to express the economic conflict of classes sharpened by the industrial revolution, and he judges individual writers as they used or did not use an ideology resembling the Marxist analysis as prime clue to the clear representation of social drama. Thus Howells comes off better than Henry James, and Frank Norris better than Mark Twain, and, in our own day, Dos Passos is stuck on a thin eminence that must alarm him.

Controversy is not here a profitable exercise, but it may be said for the sake of the record that although every period of history presents a class struggle, some far more acute than our own, the themes of great art have seldom lent themselves to propaganda for an economic insight, finding, as it happened, religious, moral, or psychological—that is to say, interpretative—insights more appropriate impulses. If *Piers Plowman* dealt with the class struggle, *The Canterbury Tales* did not, and Hicks would be hard put, if he looked sharp, to make out a better case of social implication in Dostoieffsky than in Henry James.

What vitiates *The Great Tradition* is its tendentiousness. Nothing could be more exciting, nothing more vital, than a book by Hicks which discovered and examined the facts of a literature whose major theme hung on an honest, dramatic view of the class struggle—and there is indeed such a literature now emerging from the depression. And on the other hand it would be worth while to have Hicks sharpen his teeth on all the fraudulent or pseudo art which actually slanders the terms of the class and every other struggle.

The book with which he presents us performs a very different operation. There is an initial hortatory assumption that American literature ought to represent the class struggle from a Marxist view point, and that it ought thus to be the spur and guide to political action. Proceeding, the point is either proved or the literature dismissed and its authors slandered. Hicks is not disengaging for emphasis and contemporary need an ulterior purpose; he is not writing criticism at all; he is writing a fanatic's history and a casuist's polemic, with the probable result—which is what was meant by suggesting above that he had misconceived his tactics—that he will convert no one who retains the least love of literature or the least knowledge of the themes which engage the most of life. It should be emphasized that there is no more quarrel with Hicks' economic insight as such than there was with the insights of Santayana and Van Wyck Brooks. The quarrel is deeper. While it is true and good that the arts may be used to illustrate social propaganda—though it is not a great use—you can no more use an economic insight as your chief critical tool than you can make much out of the Mass by submitting the doctrine of transubstantiation to chemical analysis.

These three writers have one great formal fact in common, which they illustrate as differently as may be. They are concerned with the separable content of literature, with what may be said without consideration of its specific setting and apparition in a form; which is why, perhaps, all three leave literature so soon behind. The quantity of what can be said directly about the content alone of a given work of art is seldom great, but the least saying may be the innervation of an infinite intellectual structure, which however valuable in itself, has for the most part only an asserted relation with the works from which it springs. The sense of continuous relationship, of sustained contact, with the works nominally in hand is rare and when found uncommonly exhilarating; it is the fine object of criticism: as it seems to put us in direct possession of the principles whereby the works move without injuring or disintegrating the body of the works themselves. This sense of intimacy by inner contact cannot arise from methods of approach which hinge on seized separable content. We have constantly—if our interest is really in literature—to prod ourselves back, to remind ourselves that there was a poem, a play, or a novel of some initial and we hope terminal concern, or we have to falsify facts and set up fictions[6] to the effect that no matter what we are saying we are really talking about art after all. The question must often be whether the prodding and reminding is worth the labor, whether we might not better assign the works that require it to a different category than that of criticism.

3

Similar strictures and identical precautions are necessary in thinking of other, quite different approaches to criticism, where if there are no ulterior purposes to allow for there are other no less limiting features—there are certainly such, for example, for me in thinking of my own. The ulterior motive, or the limiting feature, which ever it is, is a variable constant. One does not always know what it is, nor what nor how much work it does; but one always knows it is there—for strength or weakness. It may be only the strength of emphasis—which is necessarily distortion; or it may be the worse strength of a simplifying formula, which skeletonizes and transforms what we want to recognize in the flesh. It may be only the weakness of what is unfinished, undeveloped, or unseen—the weakness that follows on emphasis; or it may be the weakness that shows when pertinent things are deliberately dismissed or ignored, which is the cor-

---

[6] Such a fiction, if not consciously so contrived, is the fiction of the organic continuity of all literature as expounded by T. S. Eliot in his essay, "Tradition and the Individual Talent." The locus is famous and represents that each new work of art slightly alters the relationships among the whole order of existing works. The notion has truth, but it is a mathematical truth and has little relevance to the arts. Used as Eliot uses it, it is an experimental conceit and pushes the mind forward. Taken seriously it is bad constitutional law, in the sense that it would provoke numberless artificial and insoluble problems.

responding weakness of the mind strong in formula. No mind can avoid
distortion and formula altogether, nor would wish to; but most minds rush
to the defense of qualities they think cannot be avoided, and that, in itself,
is an ulterior motive, a limiting feature of the mind that rushes. I say
nothing of one's personal prepossessions, of the damage of one's private
experience, of the malice and false tolerance they inculcate into judgment. I know that my own essays suffer variously, but I cannot bring myself to specify the indulgences I would ask; mostly, I hope, that general indulgence which consists in the task of bringing my distortions and emphases
and opinions into balance with other distortions, other emphases, and
better opinions.

But rather than myself, let us examine briefly, because of their differences from each other and from the three critics already handled, the
modes of approach to the act of criticism and habits of critical work of I.
A. Richards, Kenneth Burke, and S. Foster Damon. It is to characterize
them and to judge the *character* of their work—its typical scope and value
—that we want to examine them. With the objective validity of their varying theories we are not much here concerned. Objective standards of
criticism, as we hope them to exist at all, must have an existence anterior
and superior to the practice of particular critics. The personal element
in a given critic—what he happens to know and happens to be able to
understand—is strong or obstinate enough to reach into his aesthetic theories; and as most critics do not have the coherence of philosophers it
seems doubtful if any outsider could ever reach the same conclusions as
the critic did by adopting his aesthetics. Aesthetics sometimes seems only
as implicit in the practice of criticism as the atomic physics is present in sunlight when you feel it.

But some critics deliberately expand the theoretic phase of every
practical problem. There is a tendency to urge the scientific principle and
the statistical method, and in doing so to bring in the whole assorted world
of thought. That Mr. Richards, who is an admirable critic and whose love
and knowledge of poetry are incontestable, is a victim of the expansiveness
of his mind in these directions, is what characterizes, and reduces, the
scope of his work as literary criticism. It is possible that he ought not to
be called a literary critic at all. If we list the titles of his books we are in
a quandary: *The Foundations of Aesthetics, The Meaning of Meaning* (these
with C. K. Ogden), *The Principles of Literary Criticism, Science and Poetry,
Practical Criticism, Mencius on the Mind,* and *Coleridge on Imagination.*
The apparatus is so vast, so labyrinthine, so inclusive—and the amount of
actual literary criticism is so small that it seems almost a by-product in-

stead of the central target. The slightest volume, physically, *Science and Poetry*, contains proportionally the most literary criticism, and contains, curiously, his one obvious failure in appreciation—since amply redressed,— his misjudgment of the nature of Yeats' poetry. His work is for the most part *about* a department of the mind which includes the pedagogy of sensibility and the practice of literary criticism. The matters he investigates are the problems of belief, of meaning, of communication, of the nature of controversy, and of poetic language as the supreme mode of imagi- nation. The discussion of these problems is made to focus for the most part on poetry because poetry provides the only great monuments of imagination available to verbal imagination. His bottom contention might I think be put as this: that words have a synergical power, in the realms of feeling, emotion, and value, to create a reality, or the sense of it, not contained in the words separately; and that the power and the reality as experienced in great poetry make the chief source of meaning and value for the life we live. This contention I share; except that I should wish to put on the same level, as sources of meaning and value, modes of imagination that have no medium in words—though words may call on them—and are not susceptible of verbal reformulation: the modes of great acting, archi- tecture, music, and painting. Thus I can assent to Mr. Richards' positive statement of the task of criticism, because I can add to it positive tasks in analogous fields: "To recall that poetry is the supreme use of language, man's chief co-ordinating instrument, in the service of the most integral purposes of life; and to explore, with thoroughness, the intricacies of the modes of languages as working modes of the mind." But I want this criticism, engaged in this task, constantly to be confronted with examples of poetry, and I want it so for the very practical purpose of assisting in pretty im- mediate appreciation of the use, meaning, and value of the language in that particular poetry. I want it to assist in doing for me what it actually assists Mr. Richards in doing, whatever that is, when he is reading poetry for its own sake.

Mr. Richards wants it to do that, too, but he wants it to do a great deal else first. Before it gets to actual poetry (from which it is said to spring) he wants literary criticism to become something else and much more: he wants it to become, indeed, the master department of the mind. As we become aware of the scope of poetry, we see, according to Mr. Richards, that "the study of the modes of language becomes, as it at- tempts to be thorough, the most fundamental and extensive of all inquiries. It is no preliminary or preparation for other profounder studies. . . . The very formation of the objects which these studies propose to examine takes place through the processes (of which imagination and fancy are modes) by which the words they use acquire their meanings. Criticism is the science of these meanings. . . . Critics in the future must have a theoretical equipment which has not been felt to be necessary in the past. . . . But the critical equipment will not be *primarily* philosophical. It will be rather a command *of the methods of general linguistic analysis*."[7] I think we may take it that *Mencius on the Mind* is an example of the kind of excursion on which Mr. Richards would lead us. It is an excursion into multiple definition, and it is a good one if that is where you want to go and are in no hurry to come back: you learn the enormous variety and complexity of the operations possible in the process of verbally describing and defining brief passages of imaginative language and the equal variety and complexity of the result; you learn the practical impossibility of verbally ascertaining what an author means—and you hear nothing of the other ways of apprehending meaning at all. The instance is in the translation of Mencius, because Mr. Richards happens to be interested in Mencius, and because it is easy to see the difficulties of translating Chinese; but the principles and method of application would work as well on passages from Milton or Rudyard Kipling. The real point of Mr. Richards' book is the impossibility of understanding, short of a lifetime's analysis and compensation, the mechanism of meaning in even a small body of work. There is no question of the exemplary value and stimulus of Mr. Richards' work; but there is no question either that few would care to emulate him for any purpose of literary criticism. In the first place it would take too long, and in the second he does not answer the questions literary criticism would put. The literal adoption of Mr. Richards' approach to literary criticism would stultify the very power it was aimed to enhance—the power of imaginative apprehension, of imaginative coordination of varied and separate elements. Mr. Richards' work is something to be aware of, but deep awareness is the limit of use. It is notable that in his admirable incidental criticism of such poets as Eliot, Lawrence, Yeats, and Hopkins, Mr. Richards does not himself find it necessary to be more than aware of his own doctrines of linguistic analysis. As philosophy from Descartes to Bradley transformed itself into a study of the modes of knowing, Mr. Richards would transform literary criticism into the science of linguistics. Epistemology is a great subject, and so is linguistics; but they come neither in first nor final places; the one is only a fragment of wisdom and the other only a fraction of the means of understanding. Literary criticism is not a science—though it may be the object of one; and to try to make it one is to turn it upside

[7] All quoted material is from the last four pages of *Coleridge on Imagination*.

down. Right side up, Mr. Richards' contribution shrinks in weight and dominion but remains intact and preserves its importance. We may conclude that it was the newness of his view that led him to exaggerate it, and we ought to add the probability that had he not exaggerated it we should never have seen either that it was new or valuable at all.

From another point of view than that of literary criticism, and as a contribution to a psychological theory of knowledge, Mr. Richards' work is not heretical, but is integral and integrating, and especially when it incorporates poetry into its procedure; but from our point of view the heresy is profound—and is far more distorting than the heresies of Santayana, Brooks, and Hicks, which carry with them obviously the impetus for their correction. Because it is possible to apply scientific methods to the language of poetry, and because scientific methods engross their subject matter, Mr. Richards places the whole burden of criticism in the application of a scientific approach, and asserts it to be an implement for the judgment of poetry. Actually, it can handle only the language and its words and cannot touch—except by assertion—the imaginative product of the words which is poetry: which is the object revealed or elucidated by criticism. Criticism must be concerned, first and last—whatever comes between—with the poem as it is read and as what it represents is felt. As no amount of physics and physiology can explain the *feeling* of things seen as green or even certify their existence, so no amount of linguistic analysis can explain the *feeling* or existence of a poem. Yet the physics in the one case and the linguistics in the other may be useful both to the poet and the reader. It may be useful, for example, in extracting the facts of meaning from a poem, to show that, whether the poet was aware of it or not, the semantic history of a word was so and so; but only if the semantics can be resolved into the ambiguities and precisions created by the poem. Similarly with any branch of linguistics; and similarly with the applications of psychology —Mr. Richards' other emphasis. No statistical description can either explain or demean a poem unless the description is translated back to the imaginative apprehension or feeling which must have taken place without it. The light of science is parallel or in the background where feeling or meaning is concerned. The Oedipus complex does not explain *Oedipus Rex;* not that Mr. Richards would think it did. Otherwise he could not believe that "poetry is the supreme use of language" and more, could not convey in his comments on T. S. Eliot's *Ash Wednesday* the actuality of his belief that poetry is the supreme use.

It is the interest and fascination of Mr. Richards' work in reference to different levels of sensibility, including the poetic, that has given him both a wide and a penetrating influence. No literary critic can escape his influence; an influence that stimulates the mind as much as anything by showing the sheer excitement as well as the profundity of the problems of language—many of which he has himself made genuine problems, at least for readers of poetry: an influence, obviously, worth deliberately incorporating by reducing it to one's own size and needs. In T. S. Eliot the influence is conspicuous if slight. Mr. Kenneth Burke is considerably indebted, partly directly to Mr. Richards, partly to the influences which acted upon Mr. Richards (as Bentham's theory of Fictions) and partly to the frame of mind which helped mould them both. But Mr. Burke is clearly a different person—and different from anyone writing today; and the virtues, the defects, and the élan of his criticism are his own.

Some years ago, when Mr. Burke was an animating influence on the staff of *The Dial*, Miss Marianne Moore published a poem in that magazine called "Picking and Choosing" which contained the following lines.

> and Burke is a
> psychologist—of acute and racoon-
> like curiosity. *Summa diligentia;*
> to the humbug, whose name is so very amusing—very young
> and ve-
> ry rushed, Caesar crossed the Alps on the 'top of a
> *diligence.*' We are not daft about the meaning but this
> familiarity
> with wrong meanings puzzles one.

In the index of Miss Moore's *Observations,* we find under Burke that the reference is to Edmund, but it is really to Kenneth just the same. There is no acuter curiosity than Mr. Burke's engaged in associating the meanings, right and wrong, of the business of literature with the business of life and vice versa. No one has a greater awareness—not even Mr. Richards—of the important part wrong meanings play in establishing the consistency of right ones. The writer of whom he reminds us, for the buoyancy and sheer remarkableness of his speculations, is Charles Santiago Saunders Peirce; one is enlivened by them without any *necessary* reference to their truth; hence they have truth for their own purposes, that is, for their own uses. Into what these purposes or uses are it is our present business to inquire.

As Mr. Richards in fact uses literature as a springboard or source for a scientific method of a philosophy of value, Mr. Burke uses literature, not only as a springboard but also as a resort or home, for a philosophy or psychology of moral possibility. Literature is the hold-all and the persuasive form for the patterns of possibility. In literature we see unique possibilities enacted, actualized, and in the moral and psychological philosophies we see the types of possibility generalized, see their abstracted, convertible forms. In some literature, and in some aspects of most literature of either great magnitude or great possibility, we see, so to speak, the enactment or dramatic representation of the type or patterns. Thus Mr. Burke can make a thrilling intellectual pursuit of the subintelligent writing of Erskine Caldwell: where he shows that Caldwell gains a great effect of humanity by putting in *none himself*, appealing to the reader's common stock: i.e., what is called for so desperately by the pattern of the story must needs be generously supplied. Exactly as thrilling is his demonstration of the great emotional role of the outsider as played in the supremely intelligent works of Thomas Mann and André Gide. His common illustrations of the pervasive spread of symbolic pattern are drawn from Shakespeare and from the type of the popular or pulp press. I think that on the whole his method could be applied with equal fruitfulness either to Shakespeare, Dashiell Hammet, or Marie Corelli; as indeed he does apply it with equal force both to the field of anarchic private morals and to the outline of a secular conversion to Communism—as in, respectively, *Toward a Better Life* and *Permanence and Change*.

The real harvest that we barn from Mr. Burke's writings is his presentation of the types of ways the mind works in the written word. He is more interested in the psychological means of the meaning, and how it might mean (and often really does) something else, than in the meaning itself. Like Mr. Richards, but for another purpose, he is engaged largely in the meaning of meaning, and is therefore much bound up with considerations of language, but on the plane of emotional and intellectual patterns rather than on the emotional plane; which is why his essays deal with literature (or other writings) as it dramatizes or unfolds character (a character is a pattern of emotions and notions) rather than with lyric or meditative poetry which is Mr. Richards' field. So we find language containing felt character as well as felt coordination. The representation of character, and of aspiration and symbol, must always be rhetorical; and therefore we find that for Mr. Burke the rightly rhetorical is the profoundly hortatory. Thus literature may be seen as an inexhaustible reservoir of moral or character philosophies in action.

It is the technique of such philosophies that Mr. Burke explores, as he pursues it through curiosities of development and conversion and duplicity; it is the technique of the notions that may be put into or taken out of literature, but it is only a part of the technique of literature itself. The final reference is to the psychological and moral possibilities of the mind, and these certainly do not exhaust the technique or the reality of literature. The reality in literature is an object of contemplation and of feeling, like the reality of a picture or a cathedral, not a route of speculation. If we remember this and make the appropriate reductions here as elsewhere, Mr. Burke's essays become as pertinent to literary criticism as they are to the general ethical play of the mind. Otherwise they become too much a methodology for its own sake on the one hand, and too much a philosophy at one remove on the other. A man writes as he can; but those who use his writings have the further responsibility of redefining their scope, an operation (of which Mr. Burke is a master) which alone uses them to the full.

It is in relation to these examples which I have so unjustly held up of the philosophical, the sociological or historical, the tendentious, the semasiological, and the psychological approaches to criticism that I wish to examine an example of what composes, after all, the great bulk of serious writings about literature: a work of literary scholarship. Upon scholarship all other forms of literary criticism depend, so long as they are criticism, in much the same way that architecture depends on engineering. The great editors of the last century—men such as Dyce and Skeat and Gifford and Furness—performed work as valuable to the use of literature, and with far less complement of harm, as men like Hazlitt and Arnold and Pater. Scholarship, being bent on the collection, arrangement, and scrutiny of facts, has the positive advantage over other forms of criticism that it is a cooperative labor, and may be completed and corrected by subsequent scholars; and it has the negative advantage that it is not bound to investigate the mysteries of meaning or to connect literature with other departments of life—it has only to furnish the factual materials for such investigations and connections. It is not surprising to find that the great scholars are sometimes good critics, though usually in restricted fields; and it is a fact, on the other hand, that the great critics are themselves either good scholars or know how to take great advantage of scholarship. Perhaps we may put it that for the most part dead critics remain alive in us to the extent that they form part of our scholarship. It is Dr. Johnson's statements of fact that we preserve of him as a critic; his opinions have long since become a part of that imaginative structure, his personality. A last fact about scholarship is this, that so far as its conclusions are sound they are subject to use and digestion not debate by those outside the fold. And of bad scholarship as of bad criticism we have only to find means to minimize what we cannot destroy.

It is difficult to find an example of scholarship pure and simple, of high character, which can be made to seem relevant to the discussion in hand. What I want is to bring into the discussion the omnipresence of scholarship as a background and its immediate and necessary availability to every other mode of approach. What I want is almost anonymous. Failing that, I choose S. Foster Damon's *William Blake* (as I might have taken J. L. Lowe's *Road to Xanadu*) which, because of its special subject matter, brings its scholarship a little nearer the terms of discussion than a Shakespeare commentary would have done. The scholar's major problem with Blake happened to be one which many scholars could not handle, some refused to see, and some fumbled. A great part of Blake's meaning is not open to ordinarily well-instructed readers, but must be brought out by the detailed solution of something very like an enormous and enormously complicated acrostic puzzle. Not only earnest scrutiny of the poems as printed, but also a study of Blake's reading, a reconstruction of habits of thought, and an industrious piecing together into a consistent key of thousands of clues throughout the work, were necessary before many even of the simplest appearing poems could be explained. It is one thing to explain a mystical poet, like Crashaw, who was attached to a recognized church, and difficult enough; but it is a far more difficult thing to explain a mystical poet like Blake, who was so much an eclectic in his sources that his mystery as well as his apprehension of it was practically his own. All Mr. Damon had to go on besides the texts, and the small body of previous scholarship that was pertinent, were the general outlines of insight to which all mystics apparently adhere. The only explanation would be in the facts of what Blake meant to mean when he habitually said one thing in order to hide and enhance another; and in order to be convincing—poetry being what it is—the facts adduced had to be self-evident. It is not a question here whether the mystery enlightened was worth it. The result for emphasis is that Mr. Damon made Blake exactly what he seemed least to be, perhaps the most intellectually consistent of the greater poets in English. Since the chief weapons used are the extended facts of scholarship, the picture Mr. Damon produced cannot be destroyed even though later and other scholarship modifies, re-arranges, or adds to it with different or other facts. The only suspicion that might attach is that the picture is too consistent and that the facts are made to tell too much, and direct, but instructed, apprehension not enough.

My point about Mr. Damon's work is typical and double. First, that the same sort of work, the adduction of ultimately self-evident facts, can be done and must be done in other kinds of poetry than Blake's. Blake is merely an extreme and obvious example of an unusually difficult poet who hid his facts on purpose. The work must be done to the appropriate degree of digging out the facts in all orders of poetry—and especially perhaps in contemporary poetry, where we tend to let the work go either because it seems too easy or because it seems supererogatory. Self-evident facts are paradoxically the hardest to come by; they are not evident till they are seen; yet the meaning of a poem—the part of it which is intellectually formulable—must invariably depend on this order of facts, the facts about the meanings of the elements aside from their final meaning in combination. The rest of the poem, what it is, what it shows, its final value as a created emotion, its meanings, if you like, *as* a poem, cannot in the more serious orders of poetry develop itself to the full without this factual or intellectual meaning to show the way. The other point is already made, and has been made before in this essay, but it may still be emphasized. Although the scholarly account is indispensable it does not tell the whole story. It is only the basis and perhaps ultimately the residue of all the other stories. But it must be seen to first.

My own approach, such as it is, and if it can be named, does not tell the whole story either; the reader is conscientiously left with the poem with the real work yet to do; and I wish to advance it—as indeed I have been advancing it *seriatim*—only in connection with the reduced and compensated approaches I have laid out; and I expect, too, that if my approach is used at all it will require its own reduction as well as its compensations. Which is why this essay has taken its present form, preferring for once, in the realm of theory and apologetics, the implicit to the explicit statement. It is, I suppose, an approach to literary criticism—to the discourse of an amateur— primarily through the technique, in the widest sense of that word, of the examples handled; technique on the plane of words and even of linguistics in Mr. Richards' sense, but also technique on the plane of intellectual and emotional patterns in Mr. Burke's sense, and technique, too, in that there is a technique of securing and arranging and representing a fundamental view of life. The advantage of the technical approach is I think double. It readily admits other approaches and is anxious to be complemented by them. Furthermore, in a sense, it is able to incorporate the technical aspect, which always exists, of what is secured by other approaches—as I have argued elsewhere that so unpromising a matter as T. S. Eliot's religious convictions may be profitably considered as a dominant element in his technique of revealing the actual. The second advantage of the technical approach is a consequence of the first; it treats of nothing in literature except in its capacity of reduction to literary fact, which is where it resembles scholarship, only passing beyond it in that its facts are usually further into the heart of the literature than the facts of most scholarship. Aristotle, curiously, is here the type and master; as the *Poetics* is nothing but a collection and explanation of the facts of Greek poetry, it is the factual aspect that is invariably produced. The rest of the labor is in the effort to find understandable terms to fit the composition of the facts. After all, it is only the facts about a poem, a play, a novel, that can be reduced to tractable form, talked about, and examined; the rest is the product of the facts, from the technical point of view, and not a product but the thing itself from its own point of view. The rest, whatever it is, can only be known, not talked about.

But facts are not simple or easy to come at; not all the facts will appear to one mind, and the same facts appear differently in the light of different minds. No attention is undivided, no single approach sufficient, no predilection guaranteed, when facts or what their arrangements create are in question. In short, for the arts, *mere* technical scrutiny of any order, is not enough without the direct apprehension—which may come first or last—to which all scrutinies that show facts contribute.

It may be that there are principles that cover both the direct apprehension and the labor of providing modes for the understanding of the expressive arts. If so, they are Socratic and found within, and subject to the fundamental scepticism as in Montaigne. There must be seeds, let us say— seeds, germs, beginning forms upon which I can rely and to which I resort. When I use a word, an image, a notion, there must be in its small nodular apparent form, as in the peas I am testing on my desk, at least prophetically, the whole future growth, the whole harvested life; and not rhetorically nor in a formula, but stubbornly, pervasively, heart-hidden, materially, in both the anterior and the eventual prospect as well as in the small handled form of the nub. What is it, what are they, these seeds of understanding? And if I know, are they logical? Do they take the processional form of the words I use? Or do they take a form like that of the silver backing a glass, a dark that enholds all brightness? Is every metaphor—and the assertion of understanding is our great metaphor—mixed by the necessity of its intention? What is the mixture of a word, an image, a notion?

The mixture, if I may start a hare so late, the mixture, even in the fresh use of an old word, is made in the pre-conscious, and is by hypothesis unascertainable. But let us not use hypotheses, let us not desire to ascertain. By intuition we adventure in the pre-conscious; and there, where the adventure is, there is no need or suspicion of certainty or meaning; there is the living, expanding, *prescient* substance without the tags and handles of conscious form. Art is the looking-glass of the pre-conscious, and when it is deepest seems to participate in it sensibly. Or, better, for purposes of criticism, our sensibility resumes the division of the senses and faculties at the same time that it preens itself into conscious form. Criticism may have as an object the establishment and evaluation (comparison and analysis) of the modes of making the pre-conscious *consciously* available.

But this emphasis upon the pre-conscious need not be insisted on; once recognized it may be tacitly assumed, and the effort of the mind will be, as it were, restored to its own plane—only a little sensitive to the tap-roots below. On its own plane—that is the plane where almost everything is taken for granted in order to assume adequate implementation in handling what is taken for granted by others; where because you can list the items of your bewilderment and can move from one to another you assert that the achievement of motion is the experience of order;—where, therefore, you must adopt always an attitude of provisional scepticism; where, imperatively, you must scrutinize until you have revealed, if it is there, the inscrutable divination, or, if it is not, the void of personal ambition; where, finally, you must stop short only when you have, with all the facts you can muster, indicated, surrounded, detached, somehow found the way demonstrably to get at, in pretty conscious terms which others may use, the substance of your chosen case.

Margaret Macdonald

SOME DISTINCTIVE FEATURES OF ARGUMENTS USED IN CRITICISM OF THE ARTS*

[The original of this paper was the last of three in a Symposium in which the other two symposiasts were Mr. A. H. Hannay and Mr. John Holloway. The first part, therefore, contained references to their contributions. It has been impossible to delete these without completely destroying the original paper but they have been made as far as possible self-explanatory and footnote references added for those who wish to consult the original papers. I apologize to my fellow symposiasts. Part 2 has been expanded and partly re-written. I have not fundamentally altered the original doctrine but only tried to make clearer what I was trying to express in 1949. I no longer agree with all the views expressed in the paper. But I think it illustrates certain complexities in our use of the terms 'work of art' and 'æsthetically good' which are worth considering.—M.M.]

I

In his Preface Wordsworth says that he would not wish it to be supposed that he entertained the foolish hope of *reasoning* the reader into an approbation of the Lyrical Ballads. Certainly, it does seem queer to suppose that anyone could be *argued* into admiring *Persuasion* or condemning *The Stag at Eve*. This seems as absurd as to imagine that one could love and hate by argument. Yet the Preface increased the size of the volume by more than a score of pages. Whether or not this was argument, Wordsworth evidently did not regard it as a complete waste of time.

Works of art are esoteric objects.[1] That they hang on walls, together with cobwebs; stand on shelves, with aspidistras and cacti; are heard as are the noises of birds and trains, disguises their complexity. For they are not simple objects of sense perception. This may be less misleadingly expressed by saying that we do not use the term 'work of art' as simply equivalent to any terms describing physical objects and events. Those who listen to a concert, walk round a gallery, read a poem may have roughly similar sense perceptions, but some get a great deal more than others from what is perceived and judge it differently. What is this 'something more', how is it

* From Margaret Macdonald's "Some Distinctive Features of Arguments Used in Criticism of the Arts," *Proceedings of the Aristotelian Society*, Supplementary Volume XXIII. Reprinted by permission of the Aristotelian Society.

Margaret Macdonald (1903–1956), Editor of *Analysis*, frequent contributor to philosophical journals, wrote a number of provocative essays on aesthetic matters.

[1] Cf. also John Holloway, "What are the distinctive features of arguments used in criticism of the arts?" (*Proc. Aris. Soc. Supp.* vol. XXIII, p. 173).

acquired, and by what criterion is the subsequent judgment of value deemed to be right or wrong?

Wordsworth obviously thought that the Ballads might misfire and be received with indifference, amazement or contempt. He tried to forestall this reaction by some account of the poems and their production which should show that such a judgment would be hasty and ill-considered, if not wrong. He was writing as a critic and not as a poet. For critics attempt a certain kind of explanation of works of art with the object of establishing correct judgments of their artistic merit.

This kind of explanation of works of art may be distinguished from two others; those of scholarship and history. Scholarship establishes, *e.g.*, the original text of a literary, and the correct score of a musical, work. The scholar may, perhaps, without derogation, be compared to the expert picture cleaner. Both enable us to become acquainted with an original something instead of a begrimed and inaccurate substitute. The historian provides dates and other biographical and social information. We know as the result of these what was produced and why by a particular artist at a certain date. We still do not know its artistic value, *i.e.*, whether and why it is a good specimen of its kind. To fill this gap is the task of the critic. The aesthetic problem is to elucidate what he does and how he does it. It is natural to assume that if disputation about art is not mere futile wrangling there must be some standards of appeal by which dispute may be terminated. Such standards are provided in logic by the principles of deductive inference; in science by scientific method and verifiable fact. These apply also in scholarship and history. The propositions of scholars and historians are about verifiable facts and are established by, or by something very like, the normal procedures of scientific method and logical argument. The question is whether there are comparable criteria in art criticism. No one seriously thinks that all judgments about art are of equal value. That critical procedures are admitted to differ from those of the establishment of facts is perhaps shown by the circumstance that Fleet Street employs political, sporting and scientific 'correspondents'; but literary, music, art, and dramatic 'critics'. Correspondents report facts; critics are evidently expected to perform a different task.

Some aesthetic philosophers, however, do seem to want to establish a criterion of agreement about critical conclusions in some procedures of reasoning and verification similar to those of deductive and inductive inference. Mr. A. H. Hannay, for example, has said,[2] 'behind individual criticisms of a work of art there always lies some general theory whether it is implicit or explicit'. I am puzzled about this use of 'theory'. It seems to

---

[2] A. H. Hannay, *loc. cit.*, p. 166.

assume that from observation of a selection of works of art, critics formulate hypotheses about a standard which all artists ought to achieve and by which their works may be judged. Further observation reveals contrary instances and the hypothesis is then superseded by an alternative. This is the familiar scientific procedure. But what sort of observation is relevant and what con-stitutes contrary instances, in art? Was Wordsworth establishing a contrary instance to the theory that all good poetry is written in a certain style? If so, it would seem, one must reject Milton and Pope in favor of Wordsworth and Coleridge as one rejects Newton in favor of Einstein. Or, perhaps, one should re-interpret the Augustan poets as 'limiting cases' of romanticism as Newton's theory may be re-interpreted as a limiting case of the more general theory of relativity. But this is surely wrong. Whatever the value of generali-zation in science, in art it invariably leads to sheer distortion. The scientist discovers new facts which refute the old theory or to which it must be adapted. Mr. Hannay seems to apply this procedure to Reynolds and the 'grand style'. He 'would question the validity of the reasons given by Reynolds for disparaging the Venetians',[3] presumably by showing that Vene-tian painting is good though it does not conform to Reynolds' criterion. It thus constitutes a contrary instance. He would reinforce his contention by showing Reynolds various causes why his opinion might be mere prejudice. But he does not indicate about precisely what Reynolds can be proved to be mistaken and prejudiced. The Aristotelian physicists who refused to look down Galileo's telescope rejected the new facts which would refute their theories. Since what is seen through telescopes is relevant to the truth of astronomical theories, they must be condemned as prejudiced. But what new facts about the Venetians has Mr. Hannay discovered which Reynolds refused to admit? Roger Fry observes:

> Reynolds was so entirely at home in Venetian art; he felt its appeal so in-tensely, even basing upon it his own most magnificent designs and learning from it the secret of his rich and transparent colouring; that in the endeavour not to rate beyond its worth a style of which he was himself a master, he actually decried it more than justice required.[4]

It may be agreed that he did, but not, I suggest, from ignorance or prejudice. I doubt whether anyone could enlighten Reynolds on Venetian art. Yet he judged it inferior because not in the manner of Michael Angelo and Raphael. The Venetians were merely 'ornamental'. Mr. Hannay's dis-agreement with Reynolds seems to resolve itself into one not about facts

---

[3] *Loc. cit.*, p. 166.
[4] Reynolds, *Discourses*, ed. Roger Fry, 1905. Introduction to 4th Discourse.

or logic but nomenclature. This may not be trifling, but is quite different from disagreement about theory.

I think, however, that the view which Mr. Hannay wishes to oppose to that of Reynolds is that judgments of artistic merit are immediate responses to certain emotional states conveyed by artists in their work which we know from experience and can reproduce imaginatively in evaluating the work. Works of art are not judged by general rules as Reynolds supposed. To understand and check up on Reynolds' criticisms of Rigaud, for example, one must look at his portraits and 'try to repeat the imaginative process of the artist'.[5] The vulgarity of a piece of furniture is 'a process that we can observe and repeat in ourselves'.[6] We can recognize the laborious effort of George Eliot in producing the characters of *Daniel Deronda*. About these agreement is possible by something like an empirical test.

It would be foreign to the theme of this paper to discuss the thesis that works of art express emotional states. But it would be interesting to know by what criterion Mr. Hannay or anyone else could determine whether or not he had correctly reproduced the emotional state of any artist. What seems to me wrong in such a suggestion is that critical discussion conducts a factual investigation into the mental processes either of an artist or the members of his audience. For this seems to make criticism just another exercise in empirical, including perhaps clinical, psychology. Do we really care whether a portrait painter feels genuine sentiment for his sitters? I don't believe we do or that it affects our judgment of his work. There is, however, no doubt that some critics do take this view. Certain critics of Shakespeare, for example, describe themselves as trying to discover 'what Shakespeare really meant'; 'what was in his mind'; 'what he was trying to express', etc. The temptation to say this is very understandable since such information might provide an objective standard of interpretation, if not of evaluation. For the problem of agreement about the interpretation of a work is often as acute as that about its merit. If one could know the state of mind in which a work was produced one could surely interpret it correctly. But this is an illusion. For a work of art is not a state of mind or the effect of such a state plus technical ability to handle a medium. However skilfully Shakespeare later described his mental state when writing *King Lear* this would not be the play he wrote. Nor are description and play the same thing in different words. This is obvious. One is about Shakespeare and the other about Lear and his daughters. Still less do we evaluate our own states of mind in judging a work of art or make them the criterion of its artistic

---

[5] *Loc. cit.*, p. 167.
[6] *Ibid.*, p. 169.

merit. The critic's task is not to write his own or the artist's biography but to explain and evaluate a work of art.

Mr. John Holloway in his discussion of this subject[7] denies that criticism is a process of inferring a value judgment from the interpretation of a work of art. It is rather a technique to direct observation rightly, call attention to significant features, stimulate and develop aesthetic sensibility towards particular works. Critics do not formulate general standards and apply these mechanically to all, or to classes of, works of art. For every work of art is unique and in the last resort, perhaps, can be judged by no standards but its own. But, though unique, a work of art does not occur in isolation, but as part of bodies of similar works and within an artistic tradition. Throughout the history of an art there have accumulated a number of rules, prescriptions, prohibitions, called 'canons of the art'. A wise critic relates his spontaneous judgments to the wisdom distilled in these formulae though neither artist nor critic regards them as absolute norms. Indeed, their very existence may prove a challenge to defy or go beyond them. ('The Blue Boy' was Gainsborough's answer to one of Reynolds' strictures about color.) Critical canons are more like rules of etiquette than morals and very unlike scientific laws or logical principles. They may be infringed and do not form a closed system. Nevertheless, they are of use in setting artistic problems and connecting critical judgments within a framework which discourages crankiness and partiality. The final standard, however, is the direct response to a work of art; the judgment of personal taste, and this may contravene all canons.

I should not quarrel with this as an account of much critical procedure. Mr. Holloway does not, however, examine its logical structure or estimate its value as a method of obtaining reliable judgments about works of art. He does not, for example, say whether the judgment of aesthetic value is an expression of certain feelings about the work or is of some other form. He observes that[8] 'The value judgment finds its proof, directly, in the object; but what validates it can be seen only by a sensitive observer whose attention is properly directed'. What is drawn attention to, however, does not, strictly, *prove* the value judgment, since this is not an inferred conclusion. But Mr. Holloway does not discuss whether the procedure is, alternatively, that of persuading to acceptance of the value judgment, or of some other type. I am also puzzled by this feature 'in the object' which can be seen only by a specially qualified observer. It is plain that a person who is tone deaf cannot appreciate Bach; that a blind man is bereft of the en-

[7] *Loc. cit.*, p. 175.
[8] *Loc. cit.*, p. 175.

joyment of pictures. Perhaps only great stupidity or very narrow experience prevents the enjoyment of literary works. But Mr. Holloway is not concerned with these unfortunates. He assumes that criticism is addressed to those normally endowed with senses and understanding. He observes that critical, unlike ethical, discussion is designed to modify the sensibility of others. But what sort of endowment is this which talking can modify? What is its relation to features in an object of which we seem to be aware only by sense perception and understanding, *e.g.* colors, shapes, language and musical notation? Discussion does not improve eyesight and hearing, though it may assist understanding by giving new information or fresh ways of dealing with old information. But it is not quite clear what information is being given by the critic and how. Some philosophers have, of course, held that Taste is a special kind of sensation or flair possessed at least by some people. But how is this recognized apart from appreciating works of art? An affirmative answer to this might explain some of the disturbing differences in judgments about works of art. If some people are born philistines their views about art could be safely ignored. Like those of a blind man about pictures, they could only parrot those of the better endowed. Unfortunately, there seems no means of identifying these empty vessels. A rich experience of art, combined with critical reflection will generally improve aesthetic judgment. But this bears no resemblance to the sense in which a prolonged and discriminating experience of foods and drinks may literally modify an epicure's palate so that he can distinguish savors blurred or inaccessible to cruder tastes. It is, however, much less clear what kind of improvement occurs in aesthetic judgment.

Finally, this point is connected with the fallibility of all artistic canons. About a judgment in accordance with accepted canons there will generally be agreement among critics. But since canons have an 'open character' they will sometimes be contravened by a work of art or a critical judgment. The question then arises of what distinguishes a justified from an unjustified contravention. Mr. Holloway does not discuss this but he would probably agree that the decision is not simply one of personal preference. If only, however, it were a breach in favour of a feature discriminated by a special or more carefully trained sense its independence of mere whim or folly would be assured.

2

The logical type of value judgments affects the question whether critical discussion is argument to prove true and false propositions. I shall assume it to be generally agreed that value judgments are not simply descriptions of physical or psychological fact. For the statement that an object has certain physical qualities or an observer certain states is not an evaluation. 'This is good' does not *say* either. 'This has certain observable qualities' or 'I admire this'. Nor shall I recapitulate the arguments against the view that judgments of æsthetic value assert the presence in an object of the non-natural quality 'æsthetic goodness' or 'beauty'. Moreover, while those who affirm value judgments take favourable or unfavourable attitudes to what is evaluated, value judgments seem to do more than express personal attitudes. They are 'objective' at least to the extent that those who agree or disagree with them do so without necessarily referring to any private feeling or sentiment. 'I admit that Raphael is a great painter but I do not like his work; it does not move me'. Such a statement is not self-contradictory, and very often true. If so, it is hard to believe that 'Raphael is a good painter' expresses a favourable attitude which the speaker denies. To suppose that he is expressing the attitude of no one in particular (if, indeed, this makes sense) is to remove the chief charm of the theory. 'This is good' is ostensibly similar to 'This is red'. If 'good' does not name a simple quality like 'red' then the sole alternative, it has been supposed, is that it names a simple feeling in the assertor. But 'This is good' also has the form of the impersonal verdict 'He is guilty' with which it may perhaps be more profitably compared. For a verdict does not describe the accused nor express the feelings of judge and jury. It affirms a decision reached by a definite procedure but unlike that of relating evidence to conclusion in deductive and inductive inference.[9] This is a situation which extends far beyond law courts, to show rings, examiners' meetings, selection boards. All these estimate qualifications and indicate a decision by certain signs, a prize, diploma, appointment. It is this activity, far more than those of logicians and scientists, which resembles the critic's. For he, too, adjudicates; he affirms merit or demerit. By calling a work 'good' he places the hall mark on an artistic performance. But he does not describe it or himself. So that to affirm a work good is more like bestowing a medal than naming any feature of it or of the states of its creators and audience. Verdicts and awards are not true or false. They may be reversed but not disproved. But they can be justified and unjustified. Both the verdict and the competence of the judges may be contested. The opposition protests that the verdict was wrong or unjust; not that it was false or invalid.

If this account is accepted then it follows that critical discussion cannot

[9] Cf. also J. Wisdom, 'Gods', *Logic and Language*, p. 187, and M. Macdonald, 'Natural Rights', *Proc. Aris. Soc.*, 1946–47, esp. pp. 242–50.

establish value judgments by deductive and inductive inference. They are neither deduced nor confirmed by empirical evidence. So no one, as Wordsworth said, can be *argued* into a favourable verdict on the Lyrical Ballads. Does it follow that such a verdict can be obtained only by graft, sales talk, wheedling or whatever other device will influence a capricious fancy? No, for though these may obtain, they do not *justify,* a decision. The word 'judge' does not properly apply to those, like the Duchess in *Alice in Wonderland,* who indulge a liking for cutting off heads. Nor to those, more amiable, like the Dodo, who give prizes to everyone. Even a bad judge makes some pretence of observing a procedure other than mere caprice. So, too, a critic is worthy of the name only if he distributes verdicts with discrimination. But discrimination about what, and what sort of procedure justifies a value judgment about art? What sort of considerations are invoked, and how, to justify a critical verdict?

I have said that we ordinarily distinguish a work of art from a physical object. That we use these terms differently. 'That', exclaims A triumphantly, pointing to his newly acquired canvas, 'is a great picture'! 'I should not call it a picture', retorts B, 'but only a pot of paint flung in the face of a gullible public'![10] It seems clear that both have located the same physical object but that not both have located a work of art. Nor will it be of much use to tell B to look more closely and carefully when he will find the work of art hidden in the paint, like the monkey in the branches of a child's puzzle. He may look as hard as you please, but he will not succeed, for in *that* sense there is nothing more to find. It is not perceptual tricks which distinguish a painted canvas from a work of art. Remember Reynolds and the Venetians. What B lacks is not observation but that which A must supply as a critic to support his judgment, instruction, and interpretation. The distinction between physical object and work of art is even more complicated for the non-plastic arts. Even if one *can* locate 'Cremorne Lights' on the wall of a certain room in the National Gallery, where can one locate Shakespeare's plays or Beethoven's symphonies? I have an object on my bookshelf, of the same type as the shelf, a copy of Shakespeare's Works; I have the score and a set of records of a Beethoven symphony. So have thousands of others, and they have the same works. When I talk of these works I do not refer only to my particular copies. But by 'Cremorne Lights' I mean the original by Whistler in the National Gallery of which anything resembling it is a mere copy and *not* the same work. The type/token distinction applies to literary and musical but not to works of the plastic arts. I do not propose to discuss this further except to say that it shows that while a work of the pastic arts

[10] Cf. Ruskin *v.* Whistler.

cannot, logically, be in more than one place at one time, this is not true of literary and musical works. Hence it is much more plausible to suppose that in painting and sculpture one refers simply to a physical object when talking of a work of art. But this is not true of any works of art. Because it is not, certain idealist æsthetic philosophers, *e.g.* Croce[11] and Collingwood,[12] have held that a work of art is a mental image, an imaginary or 'ideal' object for which its physical expression in words, paint, stone, sounds, etc., is a mere vehicle, a stimulus to the reproduction of the 'real' work in an observer's mind. For Alexander[13] the work of art is a material thing magically endowed with mysterious life by the artist and so turned into an illusion, though a beautiful illusion. For Sartre, too, the work of art is 'something unreal' for which the artist constructs a material analogue in the external world.[14] There is obviously a very strong temptation to treat the work of art as a mysterious entity, somewhat like a genie in its physical bottle. But if a work of art is not a physical object, it does not follow that it is a mental state or ghost. These do not exhaust the possibilities for not all discourse which uses substantival words and phrases need be 'about' objects. If one wished to be metaphysically paradoxical one might say that a work of art is not an object of any sort but only, as it were, a manner of speaking, though this, of course, is also highly misleading if taken seriously. But æsthetic, like all other philosophical problems, are those of how words are used rather than of what kinds of objects exist.

The problem of how 'work of art' is used, which I confess I cannot satisfactorily solve and may even be wrong in considering a problem, does at present seem to me connected with the question of how value judgments in art are justified and hence with that of critical interpretation. 'Work of art' is a cultural, not an everyday term. Like 'electron' its use is learned by a more sophisticated process than that of 'table'. Someone may object that this is only because 'work of art' is a general term and these should be avoided in philosophy. Everyone knows the difference between a poem, a play, a picture, a statue, a symphony. These are 'works of art' so why so much fuss? I can only say that even in particular cases there sometimes seems to be difficulty about what is being discussed and evaluated in art.

I shall introduce my difficulties by referring to some points in Mrs. Helen Knight's discussion of 'The Use of "Good" in Æsthetic Judgments'.

[11] *Æsthetic*, trans. D. Ainslie. London, Macmillan, 1922.
[12] *Principles of Art*. Oxford University Press, 1938.
[13] Cf. *Beauty and other Forms of Value*. London, Macmillan, 1933; also Paul Ziff on 'Art and the "Object of Art" ', *Mind*, 1951.
[14] *The Psychology of Imagination*, trans. New York, Philosophical Library, 1948. Conclusion, Section 2, "The Work of Art".

Mrs. Knight compares the use of 'good' in *'Persuasion* is a good novel', 'Cézanne's "Green Jar" is a good picture' with its use in such judgments as ' "Serena" is a good Persian cat', ' "Lady Jane" is a good arum lily', 'Joan is a good knitter,' etc. The similarity in all such uses in the existence of a set of criteria-qualities for good novels, good Persian cats, good knitters, etc., which, when indicated, justify the use of 'good' for each type of performance. Works of art may be good for many such 'reasons'. There are many different criteria of merit recognized by critics. They form an indefinite and increasing family. Their exemplification can, however, be recognized in particular works of art which may be judged accordingly.

Mrs. Knight's interesting account does not quite satisfy me, for two reasons. (1) Two Persian cats, two tennis players, two roses, two knitters, may tie for first place. There may be 'nothing to choose between them'. They exemplify the agreed criteria-characters to an indistinguishable degree. But I am not sure that it makes sense to say that *Emma* and *Persuasion* might compete for the same place; that two works, even by the same artist, might excel by exhibiting certain meritorious characters in a way which makes them qualitatively indistinguishable. There could be twin prize cats, but it seems to me logically impossible that there should be twin masterpieces in art. Works of art are unique. Their performance cannot be repeated even by the artist. In this they seem to differ from certain other performances in which what is produced, though numerically different, may be qualitatively exactly similar. This is not a mysterious natural fact, but simply a characteristic of the way in which we talk about works of art. No doubt the borrower from a circulating library who just wants a 'good' novel for the week-end will accept any standard work. But then he is not interested in art. For those who are, though *The Portrait of a Lady* has much in common with *The Wings of the Dove* and both are good novels, it would seem absurd to list their characteristics and suppose them to add up to the same sum. One would not be content to lose either so long as the other were retained. They are not simply substitutable for each other. This would be admitted by any competent critic. (2) My second objection to Mrs. Knight's account is that it seems to assume that a work of art is an object rather like a cake, whose meritorious features may be picked out, like plums, and exhibited. The model suggested to me is of a combination of ingredients which it is the business of the critic to exhibit to justify his approval of the work. There is, *e.g.*, one object, the play of *Hamlet,* whose features can be revealed once and for all by expert interpretation and the result evaluated. Mrs. Knight gives an example of this in the description of its characters by which she would support a favourable verdict on Cézanne's 'Green Jar'.

If this is the correct story, it is strange that the task of interpreting and evaluating a work of art seems to be never completed. In art, the dead are never finally buried. The re-interpreting and revaluating of established, and the resurrecting of forgotten, works is a favourite activity of critics. One need only think of the procession of critics of Shakespeare. Yet many of them from Johnson to the latest name may still be read with profit. Is it because the features of Shakespeare's plays are so inexhaustible that no one critic can ever finally list them as adequate grounds for value judgments? Or is it because the plays are not simple objects whose features can be presented for listing? To suppose that they are is, again, to be misled by the methods of science. Scientists observe and explain the behaviour of objects. Whether bodies are observed to fall by X in Italy in the sixteenth century or by Y in London in the twentieth does not affect the result, unless new facts are relevant. I have suggested that new facts in this sense about works of art are discovered only by scholars and historians whose methods are scientific. There are few such facts about Shakespeare's plays known to-day which were unknown to Dr. Johnson, though later interpretations of the plays and perhaps their evaluation have differed. It is often said that a great artist is reinterpreted in every age and no doubt by some of these interpretations he would be much astonished. Yet even the apparently bizarre interpretations are often illuminating. It seems to follow that interpretation is partly subjective invention, but about this there could be endless argument of the sort that would hardly be necessary about the description of a chair or horse, except perhaps in extreme borderline cases. Certainly, the critic claims to be interpreting the work, not supplying his own fancies. But the work is what it is interpreted to be, though some interpretations may be rejected. There seems to be no work apart from *some* interpretation.

This critical function may be illustrated by another form of interpretation. The presentation of the character of 'Hamlet' by actors from Richard Burbage to John Gielgud is of 'the same character'. Each actor impersonates 'Hamlet' and speaks the lines given in any text of the play. Yet the effect of each interpretation may be very different but, apart from presentation through someone, what is *the* character 'Hamlet'? Does each actor find something in 'Hamlet' missed by the rest or is it not rather that the character is a construction from this series of interpretations upon a text and evaluated by means of its members? Music and its executants are another example of interpretations which seem to constitute a work of art. A musical work is composed for performance but each performance while playing the notes of the same score varies, often widely, from any other. A great conductor, with a responsive orchestra, may give an entirely fresh meaning to a hackneyed composition. Yet, again, the composition does not exist as a *musical* work apart from some performance. It is a construction from such performances. Nor need such performances be actual. In reading *Hamlet* or following a score one imagines a performance, gives a certain interpretation to the words and notes even though this may be a very poor relation of that given by a great actor or executant. The point is that there is no object which is 'the real' play or sonata which exists independently of any interpretation. If it be said that there is such an object, *viz.* the play or sonata as it existed in the minds of Shakespeare or Mozart, then the reply must surely be that if this is so we must remain not only ignorant of, but literally *without* these works, since we cannot restore the dead. I do not think we are condemned to such a pessimistic conclusion. Nor does this view conflict with the statement that a work of art is unique. For the fact that there could not be another play of exactly the same merit as *Hamlet* is not incompatible with its construction from many interpretations. This is an attempt to explain what is meant when we say that there is such a play, or any work of art.

I suggest that the task of the critic resembles those of the actor and executant rather than those of the scientist and logician. Another fruitful comparison might be with that of a good Counsel. The Counsel, too, has the 'facts' but from them he 'creates' his client's case. So the critics must present what is not obvious to casual or uninstructed inspection, *viz.* a work of art. Of course, he is not to be identified with an actor, executant or Counsel. He differs from these in one very important respect, in being also a judge of what he presents. That a critic is 'creative' is not very revolutionary doctrine and most great critics have been great showmen of their subjects. Such were Ruskin on Turner, Clive Bell and Roger Fry on Cézanne and the Post-Impressionists, Coleridge on Shakespeare and, finally, Wordsworth on the Lyrical Ballads. Should we have the works we value, without these and other advocates? But to a lesser degree we are all critics in relation to art. Some construction must precede serious judgment.

To judge a work of art, therefore, is to give a verdict on something to which the judge has contributed and this also 'justifies' the verdict. It is an odd sort of justification, perhaps more like that by which we try to 'justify' our affections and antipathies. For a work of art appeals to more than the intellect. People often develop for their favourite works an almost personal relationship for which 'reasons' seem irrelevant. This should not be exaggerated, but is an element in the attitude to art which makes an account of

'proving' a value judgment by the listing of criteria- characters seem in-
appropriately mechanical. Not in that way, one protests, is conviction induced.

But if each interpretation is individual how is one to explain the fact
that different ages or even different persons in any age evaluate the 'same'
work of art? One might suggest that 'same' here is used analogously to its
use in 'same function' and *Hamlet* is a function of which individual interpretations are valeus as '*x* is a man' is a function of which individual men are
values. Of course, they are not exactly similar for *Hamlet* is not a universal
or set of universals of which its interpretations are instances as 'Man' is a
universal of which individual men are instances. My reading of *Hamlet* is
not an 'instance' of *Hamlet* though it is one of a vast number of more or
less similar performances without which, I suggest, it would make no sense
to speak of the play. The idea of a 'work of art-in-itself' which can never
conceivably by experienced is as mythical as a 'material object-in-itself'
which can never conceivably be perceived. But neither are its interpretations
connected in the construction of a work of art as sense data are connected
in the construction of a physical object on the phenomenalist thesis. If the
work of art is such a construction as I have suggested, it is unique and not
to be identified with any others with which it may be compared. The history
of the arts, of criticism and evaluation, does seem to show that 'work of
art' is not used for simple, identifiable objects which can be indicated
like a pebble on a beach or a book on a shelf, but rather for something
like a set of variations on a basic theme.

I wonder whether æsthetic philosophers do not make too much fuss
about 'sameness' and 'objectivity' in art. Art is different from morals. It may
be important that for Shakespeare as for us stealing a purse is theft, and
wrong; wrong, perhaps, for all rational beings who acknowledge private property. I am much less sure that the play which Shakespeare's audience enjoyed
as *Hamlet* is identical with that enjoyed now. Not only in matters such as
text, which scholarship can rectify, but as a work of art. Since our circumstances and background are utterly different from those of the first
Elizabethans, such an identity seems most unlikely. A simple, but important,
difference is that the work would have *sounded* very different in Elizabethan
English. As different as Bach's music would sound on the instruments for
which it was originally composed. If we and our ancestors could change
places each might loathe the other's version and we might wrangle inter-
minably about which was the 'real' work. The answer is, surely, *both* and
that there are and will continue to be innumerable members of the family.
This may also be part of the answer to our differences with Reynolds about

the Venetians. The problem becomes one of choosing an emphasis: same work but *different versions*; different versions but the *same work*. Either alternative is valid.

So, to affirm that a work of art is good or bad is to command or condemn, but not describe. To justify such a verdict is not to give general criteria as 'reasons' but to 'convey' the work as a pianist might 'show' the value of a sonata by playing it. Critical talk about a work is, as it were, a construction of it by someone at a particular time, in a certain social context. Thus criticism does not, and cannot, have the impersonal character and strict rules, applicable independently of time and place, appropriate to science and mathematics. A mathematician who claimed to have squared the circle, a scientist who announced a law for which he could give no empirical evidence, would be justly ridiculed. But to attempt to legislate for art is to invite successful infringement of any law, as the 'Unities' showed. Criticism is, therefore, I suggest, an indefinite set of devices for 'presenting' not 'proving' the merits of works of art. It has none of the stability of logical truth, scientific method, legal and moral law. It varies with time, place and audience, while not being completely subject to these limitations. For it is certainly possible to appreciate the work of artists and critics of other ages and cultures. But the differences are as important as any common characters and must be equally respected. It is mythical to suppose that one can distil some 'eternal essences' which are works of art and some uniform method of their appraisal from the vast and complex system of relationships between artists and their audiences throughout the history of art. Art is creation, not discovery. Criticism and appraisal, too, are more like creation than like demonstration and proof.

Does it follow from this that all judgments about art are of equal value, which I began by denying? I do not think so. But they are not measured by correspondence with the qualities of some mythical object, the 'real work of art' independent of all interpretation. Instead, they are generally appraised in relation to qualities of the critic. The judgments of a skilful, sympathetic, widely experienced critic are better than those of one without these, and other appropriate qualities. But 'better' and 'worse' judgments are probably all that can be achieved in this field. No critic, even the best, is infallible and sometimes we may be well advised to trust our own judgment rather than that of any expert.